WRITING AND
AUTHORITY
IN EARLY CHINA

SUNY Series in Chinese Philosophy and Culture
David L. Hall and Roger T. Ames, editors

WRITING AND AUTHORITY IN EARLY CHINA

Mark Edward Lewis

State University of New York Press

Published by
State University of New York Press, Albany

© *1999 State University of New York*

All rights reserved

Printed in the United States of America

*For information, address the State University of New York Press,
State University Plaza, Albany, NY 12246*

Production by Dana Foote
Marketing by Patrick Durocher

Library of Congress Cataloging-in-Publication Data

Lewis, Mark Edward, 1954–
Writing and authority in early China   /   Mark Edward Lewis.
p. cm. — (Suny series in Chinese philosophy and culture)
Includes bibliographical references and index.
ISBN 0–7914–4113–X (alk. paper).
ISBN 0–7914–4114–8 (pbk. : alk. paper)
1. Chinese literature—To 221 B.C.—History and
criticism—Theory, etc.   2. Chinese literature—political aspects.
I. Title.   II. Series.
PL2280.L48   1999
895.1'09001—dc21
98–43852
CIP
10   9   8   7   6   5   4   3   2   1

CONTENTS

ACKNOWLEDGMENTS

My greatest debt is to all the scholars whose research has been incorporated into my own. Their names are listed in the notes and bibliography. I would also like to thank my graduate students and several members of the Needham Research Institute who read all the chapters of the book as they were produced, and offered many valuable suggestions: K. E. Brashier, Roel Sterckx, Andreas Janousch, John Moffet, T. J. Hinrichs, and Elizabeth Hsu. Peter Kornicki prevented numerous errors. Above all I would like to thank my wife, Kristin Ingrid Fryklund, for her work in the preparation of the manuscript. An award from the British Academy made possible an additional term of leave during the writing of this book.

INTRODUCTION

POWERS OF WRITING

This book is about the uses of writing to command assent and obedience in early China. It does not deal explicitly with the opposition between the written and the oral, nor does it attempt to assess the changing forms or degree of literacy. Instead it examines the types of writing employed in state and society to generate and exercise power. It situates writing within the forms of control, examining the role that it played in the formation of diverse groups who claimed the right to instruct and to command. The title pairs "writing" with "authority" because the latter word is commonly applied in the political, intellectual, and religious realms, and the powers of written graphs in early China lie in the intersection of these areas. The book deals primarily with the Warring States period, that is, the centuries leading up to the creation of the first unified empires, but it concludes with a discussion of the reasons for and consequences of the establishment of an official state canon roughly one century after political unification.

Most studies of writing focus on the questions of orality and literacy noted above, rather than its roles in the generation of authority. In this introduction I will sketch at least six such roles noted in Western studies: (1) the use of writing as a technique of state power, primarily in the form of administrative and legal documents; (2) the creation of groups through the shared experience of reading a common body of materials; (3) the transcending of time and space; (4) the invention within texts of figures of authority, often the implicit author, who both speak to the readers and offer models for social roles; (5) the use of written graphs to create or preserve "artificial" or "technical" languages whose mastery distinguishes elements within a society; and (6) the treatment of written graphs as magical or sacred objects containing hidden meanings and powers. All these roles figured also in Warring States China.

The best-known aspect of the authority of writing is its use by the state. Bureaucratic administration relies on the use of written documents. Population records, fiscal accounts, inventories, regulations both for officials and populace, and written communications are its nerves and sinews. Moreover, the priority of "office" over "person" in the Weberian definition of bureaucratic authority depends on writing to create a body of information and technique independent of any individual who employs it and which consequently can be transferred to each new holder of an office. Closely linked are the written codes and case records that define the legal sphere and impose its authority.[1]

Writing also served to form groups through shared education and reading experiences. This use of writing has figured primarily in discussions of nationalism. In his study of the creation of nations as "imagined communities," Benedict Anderson gives pride of place to the emergence and dissemination of new "print-languages." These languages, employed in such genres as the newspaper article or the novel, gave fixed form to standardized national dialects. They were comprehensible in written form to large numbers of people within a delimited geographic area whose spoken tongues were not necessarily mutually comprehensible. At the same time, the establishment of a standard dialect created a hierarchy of spoken versions based on their proximity to the written standard. Ernest Gellner similarly places mass education and the written dissemination of a standard, national language at the center of his theory of nationalism.[2] These scholars also note that a particular "script-language" was essential to many premodern dynastic states, and that mastery of such a script was a hallmark of the privileged clerisy.

Writing also formed groups through its role in the constitution of a "public" sphere. This was notable in certain city-states of classical Greece where the display of written law codes, open to inspection by all citizens and hedged with curses on any who damaged or altered them, was the clearest sign of the *isonomia*, "equality in the law," that defined the *polis*. This publication of the laws marked their removal from the control of the king or despot, and it also both granted great powers and placed considerable restraints on the scribes responsible for their creation and maintenance.[3]

The power of writing to outlast the moment of its inscription, and thereby to cross great distances without alteration, also granted authority to its users. The clearest form of power generated by the temporal range of writing was its ability to survive the death of its "speaker" and thereby make him or her "immortal." Examples of such voices from beyond the tomb include funerary inscriptions, such as those in archaic Greece in which statues spoke in their own voices or the persona of the deceased. Similarly, Orphic writings placed in the tomb granted their bearer life after death, and the work of an author lived on as a form of immortality.[4] Writing also conquered time as a veridical record supplanting a past known only through memory or inspiration.[5] The power of writing to deliver words across great distances likewise gave an aura of magic to the commands of a remote figure. This theme figures prominently in Greek accounts of tyrants and Eastern monarchs.[6] Moreover, writing often serves as an "international" language whose mastery imparts power in part because of its geographic range.[7]

Writing likewise mastered time and space by depicting them on delimited surfaces, thus enabling people to envisage and manipulate the limitless. Written depictions of time include calendars, genealogies, and chronological tables, while those of space include maps or written accounts of regions, the world, or the universe. The use of such written forms to define the structures of space and time has been central to political and intellectual authority since ancient times and has continued into the modern world.[8]

The fourth role of writing in generating authority derives from the reader's tendency to discover a "person" or "speaker" within the text. These become models to be emulated or a voice that commands the reader's assent. Thus the invocation of the muses at the beginning of early Greek texts claimed inspired status for the author or presented his words as spoken by the gods.[9] Other writings are presented as transcriptions of the words of a master, a figure known to the world only through the voice created for him within the texts. A prominent example in the West is Socrates, who left no written works behind and is known only through the conflicting accounts of Plato, Xenophon, and Aristophanes.[10] Other examples are Buddha, Confucius, and Christ, all of whom not only became fountainheads of new teachings but also defined new social roles for their heirs: enlightened one, master, or saint.

A fifth aspect of the power of writing derives from the distinction between written languages and spoken ones. The differences could be little more than a larger vocabulary and longer, more elaborate sentences. They might include a distinct literary grammar, as in French. At their greatest the literary language is a distinct tongue, such as Latin or Sanskrit. But the difference always exists, and only the educated in any society employ its written forms. Consequently all written languages are a form of expertise, and those who master them gain new abilities or powers. The shared experience of education also sets apart those proficient in the written language as a distinct and self-conscious group. Certain people acquire further technical vocabularies imparting mastery of law, medicine, or other disciplines. Writing can also lead to skills involving structured knowledge that is not linguistic, as in mathematical or musical notation.[11]

Finally, writing is known by all to be significant, but its significance is known only to the few. As bearers of secret meanings, texts or written graphs can become magical or religious objects that inspire reverence or fear. The connection between the silence or secrecy of writing and its authority takes several forms. First, masters of writing can appear to the illiterate as magicians. This attitude appears in the story told by Lévi-Strauss in *Tristes tropiques*, in which the chief of the Nambikwara witnesses the anthropologist writing, and begins to make wavy lines on paper that he pretends to read. He thereby seeks to borrow for himself the magic and prestige of the outside world.[12] Second, the secret messages of writing could be conflated with celestial signs. In some cases, the gods might even communicate with men through writing.[13] Links between divinity and hidden meanings of writing also figure in theology or any tradition based on a corpus of venerated texts. Belief in the infinite meanings of such writings leads their devotees to attribute to them hidden depths that allow for ever new interpretations.[14]

All these forms—administrative documents, projection of language across time and space, the invention of new models of authority in the voices generated in texts, the formation of new groups who claim authority through mastery of languages and lore preserved in their documents, the reading of ever new meanings into writings that were declared sacred—were fundamental to the transformation of authority in the Warring States period. However, the culminating role of writing in the period, and the key to its importance in imperial China, was the creation of parallel realities within texts that claimed to depict the entire world. Such worlds created in writing provided models for the unprecedented enterprise of founding a world empire, and they underwrote the claims of authority of those who composed, sponsored, or interpreted them. One version of these texts ultimately became the first state canon of imperial China, and in this capacity it served to perpetuate the dream and the reality of the imperial system across the centuries.

WRITING AND THE FORMATION OF
THE CHINESE EMPIRE

Writing permeates our images of China. An urban scene distinguished by column upon column of graphs, visual arts defined by the brush and graphic line of the calligrapher-painter, a political order controlled by a mandarinate selected for textual mastery, a religious practice relying on written documents to communicate with the spirits: at every level of life script holds sway. Explanations of this pervasive role of writing give pride of place to the supposedly bureaucratic nature of the Chinese state, to religious practice as an imagined projection of the earthly government, and to the centrality of calligraphy for the scholar-official.

I will argue in this book that the ultimate importance of writing to the Chinese empire and imperial civilization did not derive from its administrative role. Rather the Chinese empire, including its artistic and religious versions, was based on an imaginary realm created within texts. These texts, couched in an artificial language above the local world of spoken dialects, created a model of society against which actual institutions were measured. More important, they provided the basis of an educational program that embedded the vision of empire within the upper reaches of local communities. A shared commitment to these texts thus created the links between the imperial system and localities, links far more numerous and penetrating than those provided by a bureaucratic administration dwarfed by the realm it was supposed to govern. The implanting of the imperial vision in local society in the form of the written language and its texts also provided the mechanism by which the institution of the empire survived the collapse of each of its incarnations. It was the intellectual commitment of local elites to the text-based dream of empire, and their economic dependence on its reality, that both secured the longevity of the imperial system and led to the omnipresence of the written graph in Chinese culture.

This book deals with the emergence of this textual double of the polity, a double incarnated in the parallel figures of the sage and the ruler, and the way in which it became tied to the state structure. Chapter 1 examines uses of writing in state administration, and shows how from the beginning even these practical uses of writing were enmeshed in the realm of the imaginary, specifically in religious beliefs and practices. In the archaic states of the Shang and Western Zhou writing served for communication with the spirit realm that defined both the ruling dynasty and the nobility, and generated the power of both. As the state redefined itself through the incorporation of the rural hinterland, the nobility was gradually eliminated and the role of writing in divination became less central to the definition of the polity. Other religious uses of writing—such as blood covenants—were adapted to control the actions of the common people and of the officials who regulated them. Written legal codes, population registers, statistical accounts of grain, records of legal cases or administrative decisions, formal annual reports, and related written forms became the primary means of holding the state together and carrying the ruler's writ to the distant reaches of his realm. Several of these new administrative forms—as well as inscribed coinage or metals—also figured in depictions of the realm of the spirits and communications with the dead. Techniques adapted from or imagined in terms of spirit possession and trance were used to form a theory of the preternatural powers of the ruler to read the actions of his officials and flexibly respond to them. Thus the new forms of written administration were grounded in religious practice, and the spirit world was also re-imagined in light of new practices.

Chapter 2 introduces uses of writing to create groups outside the ambit of the state. Such groups were composed primarily of members of the old nobility who lost their position through the destruction of states and the emergence of new administrative forms. The most significant of these new groups were formed by master-disciple traditions that relied on writing both to transmit doctrine or information and to establish group loyalties. The earliest of these were anthologies of sayings of philosophical masters compiled by generations of disciples. Such texts first appeared in the late fifth century B.C. as supposed transcriptions of the master's words. Internal evidence of shifting usage and doctrinal contradictions shows that several of the works evolved over long periods of time. The masters were invented and certified as wise men in this progressive rewriting by disciples, while the disciples in turn received authority from the prestige that they generated for their master. Each element—master, disciple, and text—was dependent on the other two, and together they generated a distinctive type of group. As members of these traditions were distinct from those in state service and offered projects of political reform, their relation to contemporary political practice was generally one of opposition and criticism.

Over time the importance of direct teacher-disciple contact declined, and texts became the primary means of communicating doctrine. This is reflected in the fact that after the middle of the fourth century B.C. most texts ceased to be compilations of quotations but rather took the form of essays, speeches, or dialogues by fictional or historical characters, and dialogues with monarchs. Texts from this period, notably the *Zhuangzi* and to a lesser extent the *Mozi*, can also be divided into several distinct layers in which the later sections incorporate ideas from numerous traditions. This clearly shows that intellectual commitments were no longer defined by loyalty to the doctrine of a single teacher. Such interchanges between traditions continued, and by the late Warring States period all texts were characterized by a highly syncretic nature.

In addition to the philosophical traditions devoted to government and morality, other text-based traditions dealt with such technical disciplines as astrology, divination, calendars, medicine, and the military arts. The philosophical traditions distinguished themselves from their rivals by claiming to represent a flexible wisdom that encompassed technical arts and made them useful to society. As such they assimilated their role to that of rulers or administrators, which reinforced the tensions between the traditions and the state. While the technical traditions sold their services to officials or wealthy families, the philosophical ones relied on money from teaching, service as ritual experts, or patronage. As such they often depended on social elements distinct from the emerging states—such as village communities and surviving smaller states—or cadres of the leading states acting in an unofficial capacity, such as the enfeoffed noble administrators of the third century B.C. By the late Warring States period the possibility of patronage had begun to pull the philosophical traditions more closely into the state sphere, but the existence of competing states and of rival factions and nobles within states still preserved a substantial degree of scholarly independence.

Chapter 3 deals with another form of writing that emerged from the archaic state but developed among the scholars: accounts of the past. The past, which had previously consisted of genealogy and chronicle, was reworked to provide an empirical ground for the critiques of the schoolmen and their claims to possess a higher wisdom. The embodiments of this wisdom were the ancient sage kings: the Shang and Zhou founders, as well as mythical kings adapted from tales of clan origins or other early divinities. The sages represented a world in which political authority and philosophical wisdom had been united, and they thus embodied the aspirations of the philosophers to the status of ruler or adviser. Accounts of the sages took several forms. First, speeches attributed to the founders of the Zhou, originally composed for performance in ancestral rituals or for use in factional debates at court, were preserved and employed to articulate theories of government. These were supplemented with new narratives or speeches attributed to the earlier rulers of the Xia, Shang, and high antiquity. In addition, all the texts produced by the schoolmen cited named or unnamed sages as the origins of their own doctrines. Certain proto-Daoist texts went even further, and traced their social and political programs back to principles revealed in accounts of the world's origin.

In addition to grounding their philosophies in tales of cosmic origins or the invention of human society by sages, certain philosophical traditions adapted more recent history to their purposes. On the one hand, in the case of legalist writers, such as Han Fei and his followers, these consisted primarily of tales of skillful or blundering decisions by political figures that demonstrated principles of statecraft. The Confucian or *ru* tradition, on the other hand, employed chronicles to derive lessons from history. The *Zuo zhuan* presented narratives of political events, punctuated both by speeches attributed to participants and judgments assigned to Confucius or an unnamed "gentleman." These speeches and judgments assessed the conduct of actors in terms of the dictates of ritual and thereby justified their success or failure. They often took the form of prophecies that were invariably fulfilled. The *Gongyang* commentary, however, explained the *Spring and Autumn Annals* as a coded set of judgments in which Confucius, the presumptive author, assumed the role of king and allotted rewards and punishments. It developed a theory of a text-based kingship that originated in the absence of a true king, paralleled the real world as a critique, and ultimately became the basis of legislation when a true sage ruled once again, that is, with the rise of the Han dynasty.

Chapter 4 discusses verse, another form of writing that served to criticize the state through its textual doubling. This took two primary forms. First, the old Zhou odes, some of which had served to criticize factions at court and to conduct diplomacy in the Eastern Zhou, were brought into the realm of philosophy. Certain texts, notably the *Xunzi*, treated the poems as coded expressions of the sages' principles of statecraft. More important, the collective body of *Odes* was read as a depiction of the rise and fall of the Zhou, generating a model of history that celebrated the Zhou founders but condemned their successors and, by implication, the Eastern Zhou. The *Mao* preface also developed a theory of reading the poems in which the virtue of the early kings survived in their influence on the historians who remembered them. Thus true kingship was preserved not in contemporary rulers but in texts.

The second major form of Warring States verse derived from southern musical traditions. In the *Zhuangzi*, such verse was employed to suggest epiphanies and other experiences not amenable to conventional language. Other southern verse is preserved in the *Chu ci*, in which literary versions of spirit travel and ritual confrontations with deities were employed to express both human emotions and political critique. Ultimately compiled as an anthology of the works of Qu Yuan and his imitators, these poems fashioned a rhetoric devoted to the theme of unrecognized virtue. They provided a language for the assertion of private worth in the face of political failure, and the anthology served as the ultimate model for the idea of private authorship. However, the ease with which the rhetoric of the "Li sao" (離騷), the central poem of the *Chu ci* anthology, was adapted to form a triumphal account of a Daoist adept attaining perfection ("Yuan you" 遠遊) or a Han emperor gaining universal lordship ("Da ren fu" 大人賦) shows that this particular language of self-justification worked by claiming lordship for the poet.

Chapter 5 deals with tales in which figures credited with the invention of writing and the production or preservation of the early texts likewise appear as the king or his double. Many Warring States accounts of history divided the past into three periods: a high antiquity of individual sage rulers, a middle antiquity of historical dynasties—Shang, Zhou, and Xia—and the recent antiquity of the Eastern Zhou. These three periods were mapped onto the history of writing through the theory that the *Yi jing*, whose trigrams were treated as the origins of writing, had been successively composed by Fu Xi, the Duke of Zhou, and Confucius. Fu Xi invented symbols from the observation of natural signs, and also acted as a deity of procreation who coupled with the female creation spirit Nü Wa. In these two roles he was the mythic embodiment of the creation of the material world and the world of written graphs as parallel realms each endowed with its own fecundity and dynamism. He was also the first of the sage kings, and represents a world where mastery of signs and political lordship were united. The Duke of Zhou, by contrast, was credited with the creation or transmission of many Zhou texts—developer of the *Yi*, author of early speeches in the *Shang shu*, the rituals of Zhou, and several *Odes*—but was never a king. Instead he doubled the king in a range of roles—brother, minister, and regent. In the final age, the time of Confucius, monarchy and textual authority were completely separated. In the elaborate mythology of Confucius summarized in his *Shi ji* biography, the final literary sage was unable to carry out his political policies in the world. Instead he assumed the role of king and the heritage of the Duke of Zhou in the texts he authored or edited, and thus transmitted the kingly Way to future times. There his literary kingship was validated when he was offered sacrifices by later scholars who took him as their textual ancestor.

Chapter 6 analyzes how the *Yi jing*, embodiment of the doubling of kingship and textual mastery, was employed to develop a theory of the natural foundations of visual signs and writing. The *Yi jing* was originally a manual for divination; we find the first evidence for its adoption by the philosophical traditions in anecdotes in the *Zuo zhuan* and *Guo yu*. These use the *Yi* as a supplement to analyses and prophecies based primarily on the moral assessment of character and conduct. However, the later commentarial sections of the text, most notably the "Great Tradition," developed a theory in which the trigrams and hexagrams were visual signs invented by the sages to epitomize the patterns underlying all natural processes. These signs used lines to depict the mathematical combination of all possible alternations of *yin* and *yang*, and thus allowed a visual reproduction in proto-graphs of all possible processes or dynamic tendencies. Some commentaries linked the lines to the world by identifying each constituent of the trigrams with natural forces, so that the trigrams depicted their interactions. Others treated the relations of the individual lines in the hexagram as schematic representations of processes. All these theories linking the origins of writing to natural regularities used the same term that was applied to astral phenomena, *xiang* 象, thus equating observation of the Heavens and reading of the lines as two modes of decoding the world. The same term was also central to the rubrics employed in the first systematic taxonomy of written graphs, thereby linking trigrams, astral phenomena, and graphs as variants of a common system of signification.

The commentaries also developed a natural philosophy of writing through the explanation of the hexagrams in terms of numbers. The earliest hexagrams recovered in tombs were composed of numbers, and the lines with which they were depicted in later texts were still assigned numerical equivalents. The commentaries developed theories in which the *Yi* text, and by extension writing, developed through the numerical process of repeated division, and the organization of the text was explained through numerical correspondences with the structure of the world. Similarly, the casting of a hexagram depended on numerical operations that were supposed to recapitulate fundamental natural processes. Thus the *Yi* text provided the origins of writing and of the numerical correspondences through which scholars analyzed the world. It served as the foundation for such number-based elements of statecraft as the calendar, the pitchpipes, units of weight, units of volume, and units of measure. The manipulation of stalks to generate numbers as a guide to action also figured in early military texts, and in the *liu bo* board game. In this way the *Yi* was declared to be the foundational text for all possible depictions of reality through signs.

Chapter 7 deals with the manner in which the depiction of the entire world in writing became central to the scholars of the late Warring States and the first empires. The rejection of disputation and the ideal equation of the sage with the ruler led to a common mode of argument in which each philosophical tradition claimed to represent the all-encompassing wisdom of the early sages, while their rivals clung to some fragment thereof. These arguments were linked with a historical model in which the appearance of competing philosophical traditions resulted from the political fragmentation of the Zhou state. The intellectual unification that each school claimed for itself was then linked to an anticipated return of political unity under a new sage. In the same period different traditions began to declare central works, chapters, or passages to be *jing* 經 "canons/classics," a term that included the notions of "division," "structure," "regulation," and "constancy." These texts that embodied a constant truth or provided a structure for the world were paired with commentarial, explanatory sections or works. The latter gave specific examples of general principles or explications of cryptic, lapidary maxims. The pairings of "canon" and "commentary" translated the philosophical school's hierarchical couplet of "whole" and "part" into the textual realm. This posited the existence of constant or encompassing texts at the pinnacle of a hierarchy of writings.

The dream of an overarching wisdom that would unite the competing traditions also inspired several leading political figures who began to take a more active role in directing the work of the scholars whom they patronized. First Lü Buwei, chief minister of Qin, and later Liu An, King of Huainan and uncle of the Han emperor Wu, gathered scholars from all traditions and had them compose large, synthetic works that claimed to re-unite the parts of the original unity and thereby retrieve the vanished, encompassing wisdom of the sages. Both these texts employed complex temporal schemata, based on the calendar and on the Daoist cosmogonic model, to reconcile competing traditions in a larger whole.

The reign of Emperor Wu also witnessed the first efforts by individual scholars to adapt the forms of writing developed in the Warring States to compose all-encompassing works. Sima Qian expanded the model of the commentaries to the *Spring and Autumn Annals* to compose a universal history tracing the origins of imperial unity back to the introduction of rule through force by the Yellow Emperor. Shortly before the writing of Sima Qian's opus, Sima Xiangru had adapted the rhapsody verse form developed in the late Warring States and early Han to compose a set of poems and essays encompassing the entire world.

The final great encyclopedic work of the Western Han was the catalog of the imperial library, which gave written form to the transformation of the textual field brought about by Emperor Wu's establishment of a state canon. The catalog is structured on the principle that the complete body of texts constitutes a double of the state, with the canon corresponding to the ruler and the other categories to his officials. It also adopted the historic model in which the primal unity of the sages—imperfectly preserved in the corpus of the canon—had fragmented with the political order and could now, with the reappearance of sage rule under the Han, be restored in the form of the imperial library. Not yet an accomplished reality, the catalog accepted this program as its ideal.

Chapter 8 deals with the establishment of the canon. This was the culmination of the dream of a constant, encompassing text that would reunify polity and library, king and sage. The establishment of the canon and the Grand Academy by Emperor Wu, and the use of Academy scholars as a source for recruiting officials were the result of the personal history of the ruler and the situation that confronted him. The triumph of the canon in the intellectual and political realms, however, resulted from fundamental changes in the nature of the Chinese polity and social order. The suppression of the feudatories brought an end to the possibility of the large-scale warfare that had been the raison d'être of the Warring States, and led to the gradual abandonment of universal military service that had defined the polity. Associated with this was a new form of elite in which powerful families combined imperial service, large-scale landownership, and trade. As bureaucratic control retracted with the abandonment of compulsory military service and of restrictions on ownership of land, the influence of the state in local communities depended increasingly on the loyalty of this new elite. That loyalty in turn was secured through the promise of office, the income from which was essential to preserve family wealth from the decline imposed by partible inheritance. Since office was ideally attained through study, the canon and its associated texts became the key written links between the court and local society, more important even than administrative documents.

But the final triumph of the textual realm over the administrative reality did not take place until the fall of the Han. In the late Han the court had been dominated by eunuchs and imperial affines. Opposition took the form of networks of local families bound together through ties of teacher and disciple. They were committed, with more or less sincerity, to textual studies that defined them and constituted their claim to authority. Thus when the reality of imperial power collapsed, it survived as a dream, or rather as a mass of signs, in the parallel realm formed by the canon and its associated texts. Only by recreating the order articulated in these literary works could the great families secure the honored status and the income from office that were essential to their continuity. Having been disseminated from the old philosophical traditions to the new elite through the agency of the state, the textual dream at last swallowed up the political reality. Dynasties with their administrative codes and population registers came and went, but the Chinese empire survived them all in the form of a set of texts carried forward by locally based families who would re-establish a new dynasty in the rubble of the old.

CHAPTER ONE

WRITING THE STATE

The so-called bureaucratic polity in China emerged from a theocratic state organized around the ancestral cult, in which writing had served to communicate with the dead and political documents had provided the content for such communications. The political uses of writing that re-created the state during the Warring States period (ca. 481–221) entailed the adaptation of these earlier religious uses. The earliest stages of the transition involved the use of religiously potent forms of writing to lend authority to institutional innovations. Even in the developed bureaucracy the palpable religious origins of many practices, the overlap of the forms of cult and administration, and the incorporation of new state practices into the imagined realm of the dead blurred any separation between politics and religion. Instead the world of the spirits became the first imaginary double of the emerging state, a doubling marked by their shared use of written forms.

The most important modification in the shift to an administrative polity was the extension of writing to new elements of the population. The attributes of the Zhou nobility that had been inscribed on their commemorative bronzes were transferred to the common people in the administrative documents of the new state. This widening range of inscription into the state order altered the social meaning of being recorded from a sign of power to one of subjection. Thus in the sphere of writing the new state was created through the extension and reworking of the elements that had defined the old, and the redefinition of what had been noble as what was common and base.[1]

The extension of the state and its writings to new elements of the population also introduced new content in the politico-religious complex that defined authority. Most important was the use of elements of religious practice from outside the Zhou state sphere to sanction authority. In this period religion provided the most influential images and languages of power, and political innovations often relied on these to be understood and respected. Thus the radical differences between Warring States kings and their ministers, on the one hand, and the old dukes and their hereditary nobles, on the other, were often marked by the emergence in writing of ideas and practices that had passed unnoticed, because unrecorded, in the Zhou state.

This chapter will analyze the origins and forms of this doubling of the state and religious spheres, concentrating on the role of writing as the common medium of both. It will examine the manner in which the written forms of authority in the new state derived first from the ritual practices that had created political authority in the Shang and Zhou states and then were supplemented by appeals to religious authority from outside the old state sphere. Starting with a brief sketch of the roles of writing in the archaic Shang and Zhou states, it will examine how these evolved into the characteristic texts employed in local government, at the court, and in the definition of the ruler himself. It will show at each stage how supposedly bureaucratic administration was based on an adaptation of religious ritual. In the final section it will examine how this pairing of administration and religion was written into the ideal model of a state in the *Zhou li*, one of the first texts that attempted to produce a model of the entire world.

THE ARCHAIC BACKGROUND

Devoted to communication with spirits, signs carved on ox scapulae and tortoise shells or cast into bronze vessels generated power in the Shang and Zhou states for kings and nobles who derived their ascendancy from privileged access to gods and ghosts. Moreover, their use in divination and sacrificial communication with the spirits charged graphic forms with a numinous power that affected even their use in nonreligious practices. This emergence of writing in the archaic state at the nexus of religious practice and political authority influenced the forms it took and the roles it played in the formation of later, territorial states in the Warring States period.

While isolated marks appear on neolithic pots, the earliest use of linked graphs in a written language is the oracle inscriptions of the Shang dynasty.[2] Divination by cracking bones through the application of fire was widespread across north Asia, but the decisive Shang innovation was to carve inscriptions into the bone after the application of fire had produced cracks. These inscriptions invariably record the topic of the divination, more rarely "prognostications" that assigned a meaning, and very infrequently a "verification" stating that something actually happened. The purpose of making these inscriptions is not clear. Some scholars think that they were purely archival in nature, while others argue they were necessary to make the ritual efficacious.[3] While the latter position is more persuasive, there is in either case a clear genetic relationship between the sets of cracks that signaled the attitudes of the spirits, and the patterns of lines in which the Shang people recorded, and perhaps sought to magically bring about, the meaning read into those cracks. The Shang diviners apparently made an oral "charge," the spirits indicated their responses through producing patterns of cracks, and these were then translated into the human world in the form of sets of lines inscribed beside the original cracks. This transformation of the lines that signaled the reaction of the spirits into lines that recorded and verified their significance for men produced the first systematic writings in China.

Not only was the making of cracks and assigning them meaning through inscription fundamental to the cultic practices of the Shang, but those practices were in turn the bases of political power. All modern scholars agree that the Shang state was a "Bronze Age theocracy," in which the state was inseparable from the king and the royal lineage, and these in turn drew their power from ancestral cult. The most detailed and persuasive study of the Shang state argues that it was a nested hierarchy of cults, in which the Shang had extended their power through the absorption into their own cultic complex of the local gods and ancestral deities of tribes or statelets. Moreover, the diviners whose names are preserved on many inscriptions may well have included chieftains from these statelets that had been absorbed by the Shang.[4] Thus in its earliest known forms writing in the civilizations of the Yellow River valley was, through its role in religious cult, fundamental to political power.

Some scholars speculate that these earliest script forms had been developed for use in daily activities, but that the evidence of this has vanished with the perishable materials to which such writings were committed. In fact, the early graph forms are clearly tied in form and significance to divination through the reading of lines, the brief formulae of the early inscriptions are a radically simplified form of a natural language, and the development of graphs can be directly traced to their role in religious cult.[5] Whatever other roles writing played in Shang times, it was in the inscription of the religious activities of the rulers that the graphs found their definitive import, and it was their dual function as link to the spirits and emblem of royal power that first placed them at the center of Chinese civilization.

Shang divinatory records provide evidence for the development of another key element in the written expression of political power, the calendar. The Shang counted time in a sixty-day cycle divided into six ten-day units, and inscriptions regularly indicate the day on which a divination took place. Months were noted as astronomical phenomena and increasingly used to locate inscriptions in time, but they did not correlate with the sixty-day cycles and hence they figure as events to be noted, rather than as recurring units in terms of which time was organized. In earlier periods the Shang regularly divined about which day sacrifices to ancestors were to be performed, but during the reign of Zu Jia they established a fixed, ritual calendar in which specified ancestors received sacrifice on fixed days, with the posthumous name of the ancestor indicating the day. This ritual cycle lengthened as the number of ancestors increased, and by the late Shang it came close to coinciding with a solar year. At this time, inscriptions also sometimes included the number of ritual cycles that had passed during the reign of a ruler, as a means of distinguishing different days with the same name in terms of the sixty-day cycle.[6] The crucial feature of this calendar was that it was based on liturgy. Cycles were fixed by cultic practices and linked to astronomical cycles only after the fact. The ritual character of the calendar and its ties to the political order continued to be a feature of Warring States and imperial societies.

The Zhou rulers ceased to inscribe shells or scapulae, and consequently preserved no divinatory records. However, as inscriptions cast in bronzes writing continued to link nobles to the spirit world and thereby generate political authority. The Shang had inscribed a few bronze vessels, and bronze inscriptions are as ancient a form of writing as oracle bones. Nevertheless, the number of such objects increased dramatically under the Zhou, and some inscriptions became quite long. These vessels were ritual implements placed in the lineage temples of the nobility and used to make offerings to ancestors. Consequently, it seems that the intended recipients of the inscribed messages were the ancestral spirits.[7] A minimal inscription proclaimed the casting and dedication of the vessel, while others added closing "auspicious words" that described the favorable response of the ancestors and the use of the vessel through the generations. These latter elements are identified in commentaries to the "Li yun" chapter of the *Li ji* as the message delivered from the spirits to their descendants, and would have been pronounced by an invocator in the ancestral temple.[8] Finally, some inscriptions narrated the achievement that had led to the casting of the vessel—usually some service done for the king—and the consequent ceremony of investiture involving the receiving of a title, land, attached population, regalia, and perhaps metal for the casting of the commemorative vessel. Thus a long inscription described the achievements of the donor and his ancestors; identified lands, titles, offices, and honors received; proclaimed the casting of the vessel; and finished with "auspicious words" that transformed it into a ritual message to and from the ancestors. Such vessels were charters for the powers and privileges of the Zhou nobility. They were sanctioned ultimately through communication to ancestral spirits who in turn were charged with preserving the prosperity of their noble descendants.

The form of polity depicted in such inscriptions, in which authority was based on the power of genealogically graded ancestral spirits, had at least two important consequences for later developments. First, since the authority of the spirits and their relations to the living were based on their place within the kin order, this world had a highly formal character in which the powers of spirits and the forms of cult they received were determined by their genealogical position or rank. Thus genealogy provided a flow chart of power in the spirit world. Moreover, since the relation of the dead to the living changed with each death and succession, over time individual spirits moved through a set of positions in Heaven, and the spirits' capacities changed as they became more remote. In short, the structure of the ancestral cult established the precedent of a graded hierarchy in which position took priority over personal character and each named individual moved through a series of roles. Thus the Shang-Zhou ancestral cults, which determined the structure of both state and kin groupings, anticipated several of the basic principles attributed to bureaucracy in the later state.

Second, the predominance of political ancestors in religion and the close relation of the kinship system to the state meant that the archaic polity already tended to transpose political structures directly into the world of the spirits. Shang and Zhou gods were organized according to the principles that defined the ruling social group, and the passage of time entailed a steady transfer from the world of men to the world beyond. As a result, the power of the spirits followed the same principles and had the same structures as political power in the human world, and the spirits were themselves transpositions of those who had been living rulers or ministers. Thus the principle observed by Jean Levi for imperial China, that gods were transformations of dead men, was both an organizing rule of the archaic state and the ultimate origin of what is often called the bureaucratization of the Chinese spirit world.[9]

The characters cast in bronze, however, were not the sole form of writing used by the Zhou. Sources mention record keepers (*zuo ce* 作冊) and scribes (*shi* 史) who wrote on perishable bamboo or wood, and, as Lothar von Falkenhausen has argued, the longer bronze inscriptions probably drew on these documents. Wood and bamboo documents were stored in archives for use by the living, while elements of them were reported to the ancestors through inscriptions inside sacrificial vessels.

Such administrative documents on perishable materials were another mode of written power, but they were still inextricably linked to cult. First, the power of rulers ultimately derived from that of ancestral spirits, and consequently those texts transmitted to and from the spirits remained the highest and definitive forms of writing. More important, as first demonstrated by Shirakawa Shizuka, the scribes had begun as religious specialists. The graph which identified this office probably depicted a ritual in which inscribed strips of wood were presented to the spirits in a basket-container. Such writings were used to make binding pledges to spirits in exchange for their support.[10] Thus even political and literary writings on perishable materials were drawn into the cultic complex.

In addition to administrative documents produced in the Zhou state, the few surviving literary works of the period also were tied to religious cults and political power. The earliest recorded songs were hymns sung collectively in the temple, and many of the later poems describe rituals in the temple or celebrate agricultural success as demonstrations of the ancestral blessings. The other main body of preserved Zhou literature records speeches attributed to kings and ministers. These were likewise inseparable from ancestral cult, for they were the words of the ancestors, and it is possible that they were recited in a cultic context. They will both be discussed in later chapters.

The Spring and Autumn and Warring States periods witnessed a proliferation in the political uses of writing, but these new practices did not constitute a radical break with those of the Zhou. The major institutional developments were derived from and dependent on the Zhou rituals, and the uses of writing in government were adapted from its earlier cultic roles. In the subsequent sections of this chapter I will first demonstrate the links of Warring States administrative documents to

Zhou ritual inscriptions, and then show how these continued links resulted in an administrative system that blurred into ritual practice, and a religious realm that operated through administrative documents.

For purposes of exposition I will organize the presentation around three administrative loci with their characteristic forms of writing: (1) the courts (*ting* 庭) of the local officials, (2) the court (*chao* 朝 or 庭) of the ruler, and (3) the person of the ruler. In each of these three theaters power was created and exercised through distinctive modes of writing and graphic emblems. The characteristic modes in the local courts were the written legal codes, population registers, and maps; those at the central court the patterned exchanges of inscribed seals or tallies and written reports; and those in the person of the ruler the standardization of correct language and writing through sagely actions.

LAWS AND REGISTERS

The Warring States were created through the extension of tax and service obligations to lower elements in society and to rural hinterlands. Consequently, their key loci were the courts of local officials responsible for the direct administration of the peasantry. The functioning of such offices far away from the capital depended on writing. First, they required written laws and regulations stipulating obligations of individuals, penalties for crimes, procedures for keeping accounts, and so forth. Writing was also needed to transmit orders to subordinates and information to superiors. Again, the extraction of taxes and services required accurate population registers. In short, the administration of large territorial states depended on the capacity of writing to communicate accurately over great distances, organize and tabulate masses of data, and preserve information across time.

In standard treatments of the Warring States period, the new written legal codes were opposed to the old Zhou order. This idea, largely derived from the interschool polemics of the late Warring States, is presented in the guise of a debate between "law" (*fa* 法) and "ritual" (*li* 禮). The former distinguishes bureaucratic rule through codes and documents, as articulated in the texts of what are commonly called legalist writers. By contrast, accounts of ritual as a form of governance, based on an idealized Zhou model, figure largely in writings of the Confucians. This schema identifies "law" as a form of bureaucratic rationality representing a sharp break with earlier political systems. However, the discovery of actual materials employed in late Warring States and Qin administration, along with the rereading of received texts in the light of these discoveries, reveal a different picture of the emergence and the role of written, legal codes in the period. Far from being tools of rational administration or of brutal realpolitik, the Warring States administrative codes remained embedded within the religious and ritual practices of the society from which they emerged.

The most important of these discoveries are the finds of covenant (*meng* 盟) texts at Houma, Wenxian, and Qinyang. Stories in the *Zuo zhuan*, set in the seventh through the fifth centuries B.C., depict Zhou aristocrats ritually invoking powerful spirits with blood sacrifices and calling on them to enforce the terms of oaths. These covenants, sanctified through smearing the lips of the participants with the blood, were used to form alliances between states or lineages. They also dictated the rules to be observed by all who joined into such leagues. Later texts identified these covenants with oaths known as "bonds" (*yue* 約) that were the bases of legal codes in the state and regulations in the army.[11]

The covenant texts discovered in excavations augment these written accounts, for they have revealed a transitional stage between the interlineage covenants of the Spring and Autumn aristocracy and the law-based polities of the late Warring States. In this transition we can see how the use of writing in the religious rituals of the old Zhou elite played a fundamental role in the emergence of codified law.

These covenants, which date from the end of the Spring and Autumn period, were elements in the internecine wars of the period and formed the primary mode of state expansion. The sacrificial oath ceremonies were organized by the head of the Zhao lineage, one of the militarized local clans fighting for power in Jin. The participants were lesser members of the elite who dwelt in secondary (or tertiary) towns of the emerging Zhao realm. The participants pledged loyalty to the master of the covenant, that is, the Zhao chief, swore to defend his ancestral temple, and foreswore any contact with or attempts to restore clans that had been expelled from the state in the recent civil war. The covenant texts provided detailed lists of the names of those who were thus exiled and anathematized. In other texts individuals pledged (*zhi* 質) themselves to the lord. After the pledges, the texts invoked the gods who were to enforce the oath, and finally they stipulated the punishment that was to befall the participant and his kin should he violate the oath.[12] The texts were buried in the sacrificial pits at the end of the rite, presumably to communicate them to ancestral spirits who dwelt beneath the earth.

The texts furnish evidence on several points essential to our understanding of the role of writing in the emerging territorial states. First, the range of the oaths reveals the downward extension of state power through the application of an established religio-political ritual to new purposes and the widening of the circle of participants. As Gosei Tadako has shown, early landholdings of individual lineages were fragmented, and the creation of a unified polity required the incorporation of the territories of independent groups. The ritual of covenant performed the dual function of binding unrelated groups together in the emerging states, and expelling other elements from the new body politic.[13] Those who accepted the oaths imposed by the Zhao clan were bound by rules of conduct rendered potent through the invocation of spirits by blood sacrifice. Thus the creators of the territorial states adapted the primary political ritual of the Spring and Autumn aristocracy, a ritual based on written texts, to their own ends.

Second, while the major actors in the rites were still the lineages, named individuals swore the oaths and served as targets of the bans. As Guo Moruo noted, the covenants took the form of a large number of tablets where the name of the participant was altered in otherwise identical oath formulae, rather than a single text listing all the names.[14] Such oaths from and bans on individuals and their immediate kin reveal the origins of the direct control of the individual and the household that defined political power in the Warring States and early empires.[15] We will return to the creation of the "administrative individual" in the discussion of the uses of naming. These oaths also mark the beginnings of the collective family responsibility that became a basic principle of Warring States law.

Shiga Shūzō, one of the few scholars to examine the evolution of law in pre-Qin China, identifies the most important features of archaic law as oath, covenant, curse, and mutilating punishments. Oaths were oral performances to create solidarity among large groups of subordinates, usually warriors about to enter battle. Covenants invoked spirits in writing to establish ties between figures not linked by relationships of kinship or political subordination. Both rituals also served to denounce wrongdoers and expel them from the community of mutual obligation. Such exile was a form of death sentence in a world where security depended on the threat of vengeance by the victim's kin. Mutilating punishments similarly expelled the criminal from the human community.[16] However, covenants were not merely a feature of primitive law based on inclusion in or expulsion from the group. Using writing to impose rules on those who remained within the community, they also formed one basis for the more elaborate written codes that developed in the Warring States.

The aforementioned inscriptions on bronze vessels were a second ritually potent form of writing that influenced the development of administrative law. Several late Western Zhou and Spring and Autumn period bronzes bear inscriptions commemorating decisions made in legal cases. These most commonly dealt with disputes over land, but some recorded corporal punishments, such as the condemnation of a cowherd to be whipped and tattooed recorded on an *yi* 匜 vessel discovered in the cache at Dongjia cun.[17] The *Zuo zhuan* records that in the sixth century B.C. bronze vessels were used for the consecration of law codes in the states of Zheng (B.C. 536) and Jin (B.C. 513).[18] Thus the inscriptions on the sacred vessels used to fix power and privilege under the Zhou were adopted to perform the same function for the written, codified powers of the emergent territorial states.

This sacralization of written law in the covenants and bronzes did not vanish with the development of more elaborate codes written on bamboo or wooden strips, for these continued to be tied to religious rites and assimilated to ritual structures. First, ceremonial oaths were employed in the Warring States to establish regulations in the army and in civil society. These oaths, sometimes still accompanied by blood sacrifice, were identified with legal codes in the philosophical texts of the period. Histories narrate several occasions in the Qin-Han interregnum and early Han when such ceremonies were used to consecrate laws. Moreover, the usage of the period shifted emphasis to the *text* of the oath as the binding force, insisting on the fundamental power of sanctified *writing*. Finally, the law-creating oaths of the Warring States were linked in terminology and symbolism to certain rituals of popular magic used to create bonds, usually sexual, between two people or between people and spirits.[19]

However, the links of Warring States legal codes to the earlier covenants and bronzes entails more than the filling of old cultic vessels with new wine. In fact, the social and political role of the codes in the new state order also derived from the roles of the earlier sacralizing texts. Substantial samples of Warring States law have been discovered in tombs at Yunmeng and Baoshan precisely because such texts were buried in tombs, that is, they played a role in funerary ritual. It is unclear whether the documents were buried because they were powerful, sacred texts that would protect the deceased in the afterlife, or whether they were simply another element in the general program of equipping the tomb with all the materials needed to continue the deceased's mode of living in the world beyond. In either case, in the still overlapping realms of funerary cult and political authority they played a role homologous to that of the Zhou bronzes. They were texts that the deceased was entitled to hold through the gift of the ruler, and they served as signs and implements of the holder's power over his subordinates. Texts that both bound and empowered, they were carried into the afterlife to preserve the status of the deceased. The legal texts of Yunmeng and Baoshan thus inherited the role of the documents cast on Zhou funerary bronzes, except that, like the covenant texts, they shifted the emphasis from the lineage to the individual.

The legal texts were also successors of the Jin covenants. First, like the latter they were ultimately buried in the earth and thus transferred to the spirit realm. More important, they played a literally pivotal role in the creation of the state. They served to control those political actors who were tied directly to the ruler and who transmitted royal policies. The actors in the covenants had been the leading members of local clans, so those who participated in the sacrificial rites and left their names on the buried texts were the heads of locally powerful sublineages within the Zhao sphere. The ritual bound these lineage chiefs to the ruler of the emerging state, and through the chief it bound the lesser members of the lineage. Thus the ritual had extended the range of the state in two stages. First, it had incorporated the local worthies who actually came into the presence of the Zhao chief and swore loyalty to his person and lineage. Second, through the agency of those who swore the oaths, the power of the Zhao chief was indirectly transmitted to those under the sway of the local worthies.

In the same way, the legal texts at Yunmeng and Baoshan are devoted primarily to the control of local officials, and the common people appear in a secondary role. Like the earlier bronzes and covenants, the law codes of the Warring States were ritual texts bestowed on the agents of the state, who were bound to the ruler through the receipt of these inscribed objects. The physical bestowal of the written statutes and associated documents at or in the wake of the ceremony of appointment was central to the law's function, and this ritualization of the code was carried forward in its role in burial. The emerging territorial state was thus both created and maintained through the physical transfer of writings to its agents, and the contents of these text then imposed the writ of the state on the populace.

The focus of the Yunmeng legal documents on controlling the officials is demonstrated by their contents.[20] The first and longest section in the groupings used by the modern editors, the "Eighteen Statutes," deals almost entirely with rules for official conduct, guidelines for keeping accounts, and procedures for the inspection of officials. The second section, the "Rules for Checking," is concerned entirely with the maintenance of official stores and the records thereof. The content of the third section, "Miscellaneous Statutes," is closely related to that of the first two. The fourth section, "Answers to Questions Concerning Qin Statutes," defines terms and stipulates procedures so that officials interpret and execute items of the code in the manner intended by the court. The fifth section, "The Models for Sealing and Investigating," instructs officials in the proper conduct of investigations and interrogations so as to secure accurate results and transmit them to the court. Thus as evidenced by the Qin documents of the late Warring States period, the legal codes focused on the rigorous control of local officials. It is also noteworthy that the procedures stipulated in the code entailed keeping detailed *written* records.

This emphasis on the control of officials reappears in the text "On the Way of Being an Official (*wei li zhi dao* 爲吏之道)" found in the same tomb.[21] The official is charged to obey his superiors, to limit his own wants and desires, and to build roads so that directives from the center can be transmitted rapidly and without modification. It praises loyalty, absence of bias, deference, and openness to the actual facts of cases as the highest of virtues. It attacks personal desires, acting on one's own initiative, resisting superiors, and concentrating on private business as the worst of faults. In short, it proclaims the new ideal of the official as a responsive conduit who transmits the facts of his locality to the court and the decisions of the court to the countryside without interposing his own will or ideas. Like the sacred writings of the Zhou and the Qin legal documents, it both stipulates and physically embodies the obedience owed by political agents to the ruler.

If the bases of Warring States law in Zhou religious ritual are clearest in the organization and uses of the texts, the contents also are permeated by the ritual practices of the period. This is shown best not in specific items, such as the statute that adopts the ritual program of the "Monthly Ordinances" as law, or the legal incorporation of family relations, but rather in underlying principles.[22] Two of these which can be traced back to Zhou rituals are the modeling of punishment as a form of *do ut des* reciprocity and the fundamental place granted to titles and names. I will discuss each of these in turn.

As Donald Harper has demonstrated in several unpublished papers, divination materials found with the legal texts in the Baoshan tomb reveal a system of curing/exorcism through sacrifice which follows the Shang pattern.[23] The doctor/

diviner divines to ascertain the identity of the spirit causing the disease, its relation to the patient, and the type and number of sacrifices necessary to assuage it. The ritual is a mechanical form of exchange with no moral dimension. A similar process of identification of the spirit culprit and mechanical ritual expulsion or appeasement informs the "Demonography" found in the Yunmeng tomb. This text's title 詰 *jie* functions in the legal documents as a technical term meaning "interrogation" but also refers to the commanding of spirits through the use of written spells, for in Zhou documents this term meant "to obligate oneself to the spirits by means of a written document."[24] Thus a term for the use of writing in relations with the spirits was applied to the Warring States legal practice of making written records of testimony by witnesses. Indeed there is a close connection between religious and legal language throughout the texts from Yunmeng.[25]

Texts on exorcism and demon control share with the legal documents not only their role as apotropaic or status-granting objects in burial and their common vocabulary, but also a mode of practice. In both spheres order is maintained through the identification of malefactors and the application of graded responses sufficient to counteract the threat imposed or damage inflicted. Indeed, the links between the Yunmeng legal documents and the mantic materials are even closer, for a guide to thief catching appears in the "Book of Days" (*ri shu* 日書), a manual indicating which days were favorable or unfavorable for certain activities. The guide provides descriptions of the physical appearance of the thief based on the day on which the crime occurred. Other strips deal with appropriate days to take up a post and indicate the consequences of holding audiences at various times of the day. Since these mantic texts were buried together with the legal materials, it is likely that the deceased official or his subordinates employed them in their administrative activities. As Robin Yates has noted, the administrative and mantic texts must be studied together in order to avoid serious misconceptions.[26]

The links of legal practices to the magical universe of the accompanying tomb texts are also revealed in the scales of punishments. The texts exhibit no sense of an absolute immorality in an act that merits a specific punishment, nor do they operate on the legalist principle of imposing severe punishments in order to intimidate potential criminals. Instead, the legal texts suggest a model in which a criminal act entails a form of obligation that must be redeemed through the performance of certain acts or the paying of certain objects. Actors of different statuses have different means for paying off the obligation created through violation of the codes. Consequently, the status of the actor along with the nature of the crime enters into the calculation of the appropriate punishment. Thus the assignment of legal punishments operates according to the same *do ut des* principle of exchange based on identity and status that underlies the Baoshan divinations for the treatment of demon-produced ailments.

In contrast to the standard presentations of the "law versus ritual" debate derived from the philosophical texts, in which law is imposed on all without consideration of rank, while in ritual "punishments do not reach up to the high officials," the Qin code and the Baoshan materials both include officials and tailor punishments to the status of the accused. The primary distinctions invoked in the code are those between officials and commoners, and those pertaining to the ranks of nobility gained through military service. However, underlying these distinctions is the broader principle that the form of punishment was determined by the relation of the culprit to the ruler. This relationship was marked by the receipt of certain items that entered into the reciprocal exchanges built into the penal codes. Consequently legal punishments functioned within a broader framework created by the ritual bestowals of the ruler that produced specified relations, statuses, and obligations.

The clearest example of this is the titles of rank. These ranks were received as gifts from the ruler in exchange for service, and they were the chief reward obtainable by the common people. Holders of titles could surrender them for a reduction of punishment.[27] Prior reward thus established a closer relation to the ruler. This in turn meant that an identical later crime would be punished less severely, or more precisely, that the title could be returned to the ruler in exchange for a reduction of the normal penalty. In short, the principle of reducing punishments in respect of status that was held to characterize ritual theory was worked out in a highly elaborated form in the Qin legal order.

A second example was the treatment of officials. The Qin code tends to punish violations by officials with fines, usually expressed as a certain number of suits of armor.[28] Thus individuals even closer to the ruler, who already received some protection as holders of higher ranks of nobility, enjoyed the added privilege of redeeming misconduct with forced contributions of material to the army. Most scholars assume that this was a financial penalty, since the suits would presumably have been purchased. Hence the Qin code hints that not only could those who received titles from the ruler use them to redeem their crimes, but also those who received cash in the form of salary could return it to him in order to escape servitude. However, this principle is not absolute, for individuals without office accused of cash-related crimes and lapses in the performance of military duties also pay fines of armor.[29] People with neither rank nor office could redeem their crimes only through providing labor for a fixed term or as state slaves.[30] Once again, the punishment imposed reflected the ties of the individual to the ruler, for labor service was the primary obligation of the peasant.

The one major element of the penal statutes not linked to this scheme of status-based reciprocity was the use of mutilating punishments. As noted above, these were features of archaic law. They dated back at least to the Shang and Zhou and represented traditional, or even archaic, elements in Warring States law. However, even these archaic punishments were partially incorporated into the system of status-based reciprocity, for graded degrees of mutilation were adapted to the position and privileges of the criminal. A whole range of mutilations, from the shaving of beards and hair, through tattooing and cutting off of the nose or foot, to castration or death, was used in order to make minute distinctions in the scale of punishments and balance them against past rewards.[31]

The system of punishments in the Qin code shared underlying ideas and practices with the divinatory and exorcistic practices of the period, in which one had to first identify the hostile agent and then determine the appropriate response in terms of his identity and status. The homology was not absolute, for the spirit "culprit" might be a petty criminal to be punished or expelled, or a major power to be assuaged. In the latter case, it was the human who was cast in the role of malefactor seeking redemption vis-à-vis a spirit authority. Thus in the religious *jie* the mortal could alternatively obligate himself or the god through the power of written words. The punishments also incorporated the minute, mathematical gradations that had characterized sacrificial reponses to threatening behavior since the Shang. Finally, they were steeped in ritualistic notions of status as defined by differential relations to the ruler created through a hierarchy of gifts. Warring States law thus served to instantiate a ritually designated social hierarchy as well as to impose obedience through the force of sanctions.[32]

The hierarchy created through the system of ranks was itself an extension and modification of earlier ritual practices commemorated in inscriptions. The Zhou state had featured a variety of titles held by rulers of states and their leading ministers, and these titles had been theoretically received from the king. The distribution of titles by the king to the populace was a universalization of a ritual practice linked to writing that had defined the old nobility. Indeed, many of the titles in the Qin hierarchy had been titles of nobility in earlier centuries, or were created through modification of old titles.[33]

The practice of regulation through the awarding of titles points to another feature of Warring States documentary administration derived from earlier ritual practices: the granting of family names. Our current understanding of Shang and Zhou naming practices suggests that the patronym (*xing* 姓) first appeared under the Zhou as a function of the division of the single royal ancestral cult into a multitude of noble lineages and sublineages. The Zhou aristocracy was divided into a small number of patronyms distinguished by a taboo on intermarriage, and a larger number of "clan names" (*shi* 氏) usually derived from names of fiefs or official titles. The establishment of cults to the founders of the feudal states and the lineages of hereditary officials was followed by the royal granting of family names to all those tracing descent from a common ancestor. Both patronym and clan name were granted in the enfeoffment process and were hence a noble privilege, while commoners had no family names.[34]

There is no direct evidence of the extension of this privilege to the masses. However, as service obligations were extended, governments began to register peasants by name, perhaps as early as the eighth century B.C., and certainly by the sixth.[35] To register tens of thousands of households solely on the basis of personal names would have been impossible, so it is a reasonable hypothesis that the granting or recognition of surnames took place in association with the process of registration. While no government registers have survived, other remains provide evidence of the appearance of family names among the common people during the Warring States period. Inscriptions on pottery found in excavations at the capital of the state of Qi often include the names of craftsmen. Inscriptions on pots produced in government shops include the personal name of the craftsman, his political unit, and the location of the shop. Those from the hands of private craftsmen recorded personal name, town, and quarter. Thus at first there is no evidence of family names, but place of residence was used instead. However, where craftsmen were organized on kin lines and produced certain vessel types over several generations, in some cases the name of the founding ancestor came to identify the workshop and was adopted as a clan name. In addition, pre-Qin seals contain thousands of examples of individuals with both personal and family names.[36] Thus it was in the early Warring States that the phrase "hundred surnames" (*bai xing* 百姓) ceased to refer to the nobility and came to mean "the common people." Just as the incorporation of the common people into state administration entailed the granting of ritual titles, it also included the ritual gift and subsequent inscription of a family name based on the model of the old Zhou nobility. This practice was fundamental not only to registration but to the execution of law, for the "Models for Sealing and Investigations" from the Yunmeng legal documents states explicitly that any testimony begins with the name, status (i.e., rank), and legal residence of the witness, and the cases from Baoshan provide numerous examples of this practice.[37]

However, while the inscription of the common people into the territorial state involved granting them attributes that had previously defined the nobility, the meaning of these attributes changed within the new order. Just as the process of universalizing military service had transformed an insignia of nobility into a token of servitude, so the universalizing of naming, titling, and registration meant that these ceased to be attributes of authority. When the Zhou nobility had received titles and surnames from the king, they had inscribed these in reports to their ancestors who granted them claims to power and status not wholly dependent on the king. By contrast, the names and titles of the Warring State peasant, although signaling status as a legally free member of the political order, were inscribed on registers whose ultimate recipient was the ruler of the state. Thus to be inscribed marked subjection. The intermediate status once held by nobles, through being written into ancestral cult, instead belonged to officials, through their possession of the population registers in which the names and residences of the common people were recorded.

Consequently population registers, and the maps associated with them, came to be metonyms for authority and the hallmark of the ruler.[38] Indeed these written depictions of population and territory came to magically embody the objects that they represented. When Jing Ke attempted to assassinate the First Emperor, he used as a pretext a mission to surrender territory to Qin through the formal presentation of the relevant population registers and maps.[39]

While no registers have survived, references in Warring States texts suggest the nature of their contents. One passage in the *Zuo zhuan*, a fourth-century B.C. text, describes a census held in the state of Chu in 548 B.C. It listed quantities of armor and offensive weapons; details of arable land, mountains, and forests; designations of areas for special treatment or taxation at concessionary rates (such as hilly land or poor soil); amounts of land damaged by stagnant water; dues for wagons and carriages; and a register of horses. A passage in the *Guanzi*, tentatively datable to the late Warring States or early Han, speaks of registers that record numbers of households and the amount of arable land. A record of the compilation of a household register in Qin in 375 B.C. preserved in a Han source links this act to the establishment of units of joint responsibility for crimes. Finally, a recently discovered text entitled "Wei tian lü 爲田律," or "Statute for forming arable plots," dated to 309 B.C. decrees statutory measurements for plots of land, rules for setting field boundaries and channels, and instructions for the upkeep of bridges.[40]

While the registration of names was derived from earlier Zhou ritual, by the late Warring States period it had become an element of religious practice and depictions of the spirit world. The clearest evidence is a story found in a third-century B.C. Qin tomb at Fangmatan. In this story a man committed suicide to avoid the disgrace of an unjust execution. Documents addressed to the "Master of Life Spans *si ming* 司命" led to his body being dug up by a white dog at the command of a scribe (*shi* 史) of the god and gradually restored to life.[41] This shows that people in the late Warring States already believed in an underworld bureaucracy that kept registers, and that communication with the spirit world took the form of written documents patterned on those of terrestrial governments. It is also significant that the underworld administration is invoked to correct a death resulting from failings of earthly legal procedure. "Spirit registrars" controlling the human life span also figure in anecdotes preserved in the *Mozi* and the *Guo yu*, as well as accounts in the early Han *Huainanzi*. The Chu silk manuscript likewise contains evidence of a bureaucratic pantheon in the Warring States.[42]

A final element of Warring States local administration derived from religious practice involving the use of writing is the interrogation procedure described in the Yunmeng legal documents.[43] As noted above, the term for this procedure derived from older practices using writing to make pledges to spirits. The official is instructed to accurately record the words of each witness. Even if he knows that the witness is lying, he should wait until the statement is completed. Then the official should challenge any weak points and contradictions, and again record the explanations offered by the witness. Each time the official must repeat the process of notation and challenge. Finally, when the witness cannot provide further explanations, persists in changing his account, and refuses to confess, then the official should have him beaten. However, the use of the bastinado must be included in the final report.

In this procedure the official repeatedly allows the witness to state his case and try to prove that it corresponds to the material facts. He remains silent but keeps an exact account of the witness's words and then matches the accounts for internal consistency and their relation to material evidence. This derives from the earlier process of invoking spirits as judges of the veracity of oaths and pledges, and it also corresponds to the procedures described in various texts, notably the *Han Feizi*, under the rubric of "forms and names (*xing ming* 形名)." This was a ritual that was used to impose the control of the monarch on his ministers. Here we find it, however, being applied at the lower levels of administration. The local official stands in the position of the ruler and the witness in the position of the official. The witness must name himself and give an account of his actions that will be transformed into writing, while the official sits silently and measures everything against his knowledge of the facts. Both the local official and the ruler stand in the position of the divinity in the religious oath or pledge. This model of administration through a hierarchical series of staged personal encounters was fundamental to Warring States government. It was also a version of the formalized confrontations of superior and inferior that formed the Confucian theory of ritualized order, a theory that itself developed from the staged encounter of man and spirit in the performance of divination and sacrifice.

REPORTS, TALLIES, AND SEALS

The preceding section demonstrated how the uses of writing in local administration during the Warring States period—law codes, hierarchies of rank, registration of names—all derived from Zhou ritual procedures and evolved in association with religious practices of the Warring States period. The central court was in turn marked by the staged confrontations of the ruler with his courtiers, in which the exchange of writings played a fundamental role. This section will examine the ceremonial and religious elements underlying the use of writing in these "techniques (*shu* 術)" by which the ruler sought to control his ministers and compel them to serve his interests. Like the practices described earlier, these techniques had roots in Zhou ritual and religion.

In contrast to local administration, for which we possess working documents that stipulate conduct, evidence for the central courts comes primarily from narrative or philosophical sources. The single major exception is the legal materials discovered in a tomb, dated to 316 B.C., near Baoshan in what was then the state of Chu. These documents reveal the level of government above the local administrator. The man buried in the tomb had been chief legal officer to the king of Chu. Whereas the Yunmeng materials consist primarily of rules for official conduct, the Baoshan texts record large numbers of cases transmitted from local officials to the central court for adjudication. These include instances of failure to register population, denunciations by one official of the high handed behavior of another, and remarks by higher officials on a variety of criminal cases. The documents record the plaintiffs and defendants, the officials who first examined the case, and those to whom reports were sent. In one case a note on the back of a strip commands dispatch to yet another official. A few strips reveal details of legal practice. The case on strips 131–39 shows that both parties could summon large numbers of witnesses (one side called two hundred and eleven) and that these were all obliged to swear blood oaths with appended curses (*meng zu* 盟詛) before giving testimony. The case is also of interest in that the king himself became involved.[44] Both parties also give testimony in a story in the *Zuo zhuan*, but in this account the accuser and the defendant were obliged to prepare their own written accounts and bring them to the court session.[45] Apart from detailed data on Chu titles, procedures, and the nature of social conflicts, these texts provide a sense of the abundance of documents employed in Warring States administration, and the great care that was taken to account for their movements.

The absence of other detailed accounts of procedures at the central court reflects the fact that the actions of the ruler were not susceptible to detailed prescription, and that the effectiveness of many of these procedures depended on their being kept secret. Nevertheless, from references in stories and philosophical accounts we can reconstruct elements of contemporary practice, and link these both to earlier Zhou rituals and analogous procedures from the religious realm.

Confrontations of rulers and ministers appear often in Warring States writings, but they are written from two perspectives. Since most philosophical works, and many of the anecdotes, were written by and for aspiring scholars, these accounts depict the ruler as a passive sounding-board for the arguments and rhetoric of some thinker. *Mencius, Xunzi*, and the *Book of Lord Shang* all contain scenes in which the eponymous philosopher addresses a ruler, and texts such as the *Zhanguo ce* and the *Yanzi chun qiu* consist almost entirely of meetings between diplomats or ministers and rulers. However, such texts reveal more of the ideas and self-images of Warring States scholars than of administrative practice. For such information one must turn to passages which deal with ruler-minister relations from the perspective of the ruler, that is, following the lines of authority within the court.

The first meeting between ruler and minister was the ceremony of appointment. The new official prostrated himself before the ruler and received a title and seal of office. Seals were inscribed with the name of the office and were used to validate official commands through the reproduction of characters in clay. Thus they were embodiments of the power of writing, for the impression of the characters on the sealing made the text an object of obedience. They were worn at the official's waist as an insignia of power, but it was a power that was visibly removable. The surrender of seals of office figures often in the biographies of the period.[46]

Parallel to the granting of seals to a civil official was the bestowal of half a tiger tally on a general. A general could mobilize his troops and set out on an expedition only if he received the ruler's half of the tally. These objects, cast in the form of tigers to invoke ferocity, were inscribed with texts that stipulated the conditions and limits of the general's power, such as his right to mobilize up to fifty men on his own authority. Tallies also permitted entry and exit at border passes and in the inner chambers of the ruler. Like other elements in the new modes of written administrations, the use of tallies had its religious correlate, for the ancient sages were said to "match tallies" with the spirits as a sign of attaining world rule. In a related context, the tally was also the standard metaphor for the potency (*de* 德) of the perfected man.[47] In addition to bestowing the tally that empowered the commander to mobilize his troops, the despatching of an expedition also involved a ceremonial meeting of ruler and general in which the former bestowed the axes of command, symbolic of the powers of life and death.[48]

A more regular ritual involved the use of other tallies to control local officials. This entailed using contracts (*juan* 卷) in the annual statistical assessment of officials' performances. Patterned on, or offering the pattern for, contracts used in land purchase agreements and other transactions, such contracts consisted of budget projections written on a single sheet of silk, which was torn in half. One half was kept by the ruler and one by the local official. Each year the official was obliged to come to court, a variant of the Zhou system in which vassals had attended the court of the ruler, and to present a statistical report on stocks in public granaries, registered population, land opened to cultivation, tax and labor services collected, and the state of public security. In addition to the annual reports, a "great inspection" was held every third year. Through matching the figures reported by officials with their projections, the ruler could assess the performance of the individual official.[49] Such tallies or contracts were also used for recording and validating legal testimony.[50] These procedures fit closely with Han Fei's account of the practice of "form and name," which will be discussed below.

In addition to seals and tallies, the ruler bestowed other forms of inscribed objects on his ministers in order to bind them to him. The most important was coinage. Early coins were usually reduced replicas of utilitarian objects, such as spades and knives, with a brief inscription. The choice of spades and knives was probably not arbitrary, for they symbolized the two bases of state power, agriculture and warfare. Inscriptions on Warring States coins included characters used as marks in the casting process, place names, and the value of the coin. While the coins were supposed to contain the amounts of metal inscribed on their surfaces, they relied on the power of writing to convert them from simple pieces of metal or replicas of tools into standardized measures of value.

Evidence of the state's interest in coins comes from the "Statutes on Currency" in the Yunmeng legal documents. These specify the rates at which coins are exchanged for one another or for bolts of cloth also employed as a medium of exchange. They also insist that officials and merchants must not make distinctions between fine and bad pieces of money.[51] This indicates that the states attempted to fix the value of money at its inscribed level as opposed to the physical properties of the object. Coinage thus ultimately depended on the authority of the ruler to guarantee the exchange of coins for goods at fixed rates. Like the law codes and registers, coins were a universalizing, inscribed authority intended to bring all values and human ties within a single sphere defined by the state. And just as the legal codes and hierarchies of ranks allowed mathematical measurement of links between crime and punishment, coinage allowed similar precision in fixing commensurability of value between goods.[52] Salaries were measured in grain, and perhaps paid partially in that form, but there is evidence of gifts from the ruler of metal and coin, and it is likely that coin also figured in the payment of salaries.[53]

The shift from gifts of land to more fluid items such as cash in part reflects changes in the economy, but one should not exaggerate the role of currency in this period. As Anna Seidel has noted, coinage in the early periods was used primarily within the sphere of government. Coins and precious metal served above all as a means of paying capitation taxes and as a store of value. More important, coins also began to figure in grave offerings, where precious metals were buried in tombs to be carried into the next world, just as gold and silver inlay became a major feature of bronze vessels. Just as the inscription on the coin turned common metal into a defined value, sometimes the tomb contained common metals or clay that were simply labeled as gold.[54] Thus writing created or standardized value.

The use of coinage is also related to other religious practices of the period. During the Warring States it was increasingly common to fill tombs with objects of daily life or imitations, often in reduced size, of such objects. The most notable examples are the puppets (in the south) or miniature clay figures (in the north) that apparently acted as servants or companions in the tomb. This magical ability of reduced copies to act as the original characterized the use of money in the period. It is noteworthy that replicas of money were often buried along with actual currency, which was itself only replicas. In the Han this practice led to the placement of "money trees" in some graves.[55]

As noted above, the practice of submitting written reports was closely linked to a theory of administrative control, "*xing ming*," "forms and names [or 'words']." The fundamental role of names and naming appeared in the discussion of Warring States local government, along with its roots in Zhou ceremonies of bestowing names. However, most accounts of "forms and names" situate it within the broader context of the idea of "rectification of names *zheng ming* 正名."[56] The idea of names as a means of rule appears for the first time in the *Lun yu*. In reply to a question of what policy he would advocate for the state of Wei, Confucius stated that he would begin by rectifying names. He elaborated that if names were not correct then words would not correspond to the world, affairs would not be regulated, rites and music would not flourish, punishments would be incorrect, and the people would not know how to behave. This list appears to be sequential, so the correct use of names is the foundation of the system of rites which in turn makes possible the adequacy of punishments. Other passages linked to this doctrine are Confucius' statement that the ruler must be made a ruler, the subject a subject, the father a father, and the son a son; his exclamation about a ritual vessel that does not match its name; a discussion of the different terms by which the ruler's wife will be named depending on the speaker; and the argument over whether the term "upright (*zhi* 直)" should be applied to those who reported the crimes of kin, or to those who kept them hidden.[57] Thus the earliest *theory* of authority through naming emerged in the context of rites—with the nomenclature applied to kin and ritual vessels held to be fundamental. However, even at this stage it was already concerned with the application of correct naming in the realm of law and punishments.

The concern with names developed in three forms within the Confucian tradition. First, the chapter on the rectification of names in the *Xunzi* articulated a more sophisticated form of the theory of ruling through naming, in response to the philosophical challenge of the later Mohists and philosophers of language. Second, as will be discussed in chapter 3, the *Gongyang zhuan* 公羊傳 read the *Spring and Autumn Annals* as a coded text in which such factors as the choice of titles or the mention of a name indicated judgments that were equated with the rewards and punishments bestowed by a ruler. In this hermeneutic theory the text was the blueprint for an imaginary kingdom of Lu, and Confucius ruled as "uncrowned king" through the application of names. Since condemnations were generally held to indicate that actions were "contrary to ritual (*fei li* 非禮)," this text still identified "rectification of names" with ritual correctness, and insisted that rites were the basis of the state. The third form in which "rectification of names" developed within Confucianism was the detailed discussion of terms of kinship in the ritual classics—most notably the "Sang fu (喪服)" chapter of *Yi li* and the "Tan gong (檀弓)" chapter of *Li ji* and their Han commentaries. These texts not only provided rubrics for the different forms of kin ties, but also specified types of obligation and taboo, for example, which forms of marriage constituted incest, and explained the social consequences of the failure to observe these strictures.

While Confucian writers developed theories of ritual nomenclature as the basis of social order, a parallel discourse applied such ideas to administration and law. The evidence regarding the earliest phases of this development is relatively late, but it still dates from the Warring States period. The first figure who links theories of nomenclature and law is Deng Xi (鄧析). In the *Lü shi chun qiu* 呂氏春秋 he is described as a clever sophist who taught people how to win legal cases through the manipulation of language. The *Zuo zhuan* 左傳 states that he drafted a legal code on bamboo strips and was executed in 501 B.C. A book attributed to Deng Xi is listed in the bibliographic chapter of the *Han shu* 漢書 as the first text of the "school of names." Surviving fragments indicate that his followers combined elements of rhetoric and dialectic with a concern for legal administration. A second celebrated sophist, Hui Shi (惠施), was also reputed to have drafted a law code, and he figures prominently in the chapters on naming in the *Lü shi chun qiu*.[58] These stories suggest that systematic discussion of naming developed in association with the drafting of legal codes, and that the idea of rule through law was linked with a political version of the hitherto ritually defined "rectification of names."

Probably the earliest reference to the term *xing ming* asserts that those who expound this doctrine "all say that a white horse is not a horse," that is, were followers of sophists such as Hui Shi, Gongsun Long, and Deng Xi.[59] This supports the argument that *xing ming* in its orgins was closely linked to arguments about language as related to law and administration. It is possible that 形名 *xing ming* originally had the sense of the homophonous 刑名 "punishments and names," and that it referred to drafting laws and imposing standardized legal terms.[60] Certainly correct use of terms was important in law. As noted earlier, a section of the Yunmeng legal documents gave standard definitions. However, the full-blown form of the theory in the writings attributed to Han Fei puts punishments in a secondary position, and deals instead with the technique of controlling ministers through written language.

Before examining accounts of *xing ming* in the *Han Feizi*, one should note two anecdotes in the text that link, in an unfavorable light, sophists and the development of law. Ni Yue defended the paradox that "a white horse is not a horse" at the Jixia academy in Qi. He defeated everyone in debate, but when he rode a white horse through a customs post (*guan* 關) he was compelled to pay the tax on horses. The law code and administrative regulations here appear as the ultimate arbiters of language, refuting the philosopher's specious manipulation of words.[61]

The second anecdote deals with techniques for controlling ministers. When Zi Zhi was chief minister of Yan, he pretended to have seen a white horse dash past the gate. His subordinates all said that they had seen nothing, save for one who ran out through the gate after the supposed horse, and on his return claimed to have seen the animal. Through this stratagem Zi Zhi identified a flatterer among his entourage.[62] In this ironic tribute to the argument of Gongsun Long, Han Fei presents a white horse which is indeed not a horse, but merely an empty word set as a trap. As Jean Levi has pointed out, this story also anticipates the account in *Shi ji* of how Zhao Gao established his control of the Qin court by identifying a deer as a horse, and executing those who dared to contradict him.[63] However, these uses of names do not exemplify the central role attributed to them in the *Han Feizi*.

The text discusses *xing ming* in several passages. The ruler is advised to hold himself quiet and allow the ministers to name themselves, that is, to give an account of the administrative tasks that they will accomplish. As Makeham has persuasively shown, the word *ming* in this context does not mean simply "title," as some scholars have suggested, but has the broader sense of "language, speech, declaration, or claim."[64] These "names" were originally oral, but since they were to serve as a standard for judgment in the future, they must have been set in writing. Only thus could the ruler match claims against results obtained. This written aspect of the procedure is indicated by the use of the metaphor of the "tally" or "contract/bond" (*yao* 要 = *yue* 約) to describe the process.[65] If the two halves of the tally, the claim and performance, matched then the official was rewarded; if not, he was punished. In other passages the application of "forms and names" figures as one step in a process. The ruler must first listen to the views and reports of all his ministers, next obtain programs of performance, then match programs against results, and finally bestow rewards and punishments.[66] This theory corresponds to the use of contracts and annual verifications described in accounts of administrative practice.

Just as control through written law paralleled procedures for commanding spirits, so the theory of rule through correct naming had religious parallels. The ability to name unusual phenomena was in some texts an aspect of sagehood, and it was the first step to controlling or expelling dangerous spirits. The latter remained protean and threatening so long as they were not bound by a name. Thus Confucius, putative creator of the theory of government by the rectification of names, was also a master of naming in the realm of the spirits. The only hint of this in the *Lun yu*, where Confucius is said to avoid talk about spirits and prodigies, is the passage in which he counsels the study of the Zhou *Odes* as a means of learning the names of birds, beasts, grasses, and trees.[67] Since many animals and plants cited in texts of the period had religious or magical significance, this passage probably is not simply speaking of a knowledge of zoology or botany. However, the earliest portrayal of Confucius as a master of occult names appears in the *Guo yu*, where he identifies a strange creature found by a man digging a well, and then lists the names of the prodigies associated with wood, stone, water, and earth. In another passage he identifies by name the source of a giant bone uncovered by a landslide at Kuaiji.[68] In the *Zuo zhuan*, Zi Chan cures the illness of the Duke of Jin by identifying the strange creature that appeared to him in a dream.[69] Identifying and naming prodigies in order to properly respond to them or prevent them doing harm is likewise a central function of the aforementioned "Demonography" from Yunmeng.

The *Zuo zhuan* assigns a similar role to the ancient sage Yu. According to this text, Yu cast images of all harmful demons on bronze tripods so that people who entered the mountains or waters could identify these spirits and thereby avoid harm.[70] It does not refer to Yu naming the demons, but some of them are named, and the same names appear in Confucius' list of prodigies, the list of demons expelled in the Han exorcism, the list of demons in Wang Mengshou's nightmare poem, and in related sources. Moreover, the images cast on the tripod are called *xiang* 象, and as shall be discussed in chapter 6 this term was fundamental to Warring States theories of the origin and significance of written characters. It is also significant that the tripods that provided mastery over spirits were the Nine Tripods that embodied world sovereignty.

The tradition of Yu as the sage who ruled through his ability to name spirits is also developed in the *Shan hai jing*. This work lists magical creatures, both auspicious and malevolent, and identifies the effect they have if seen or eaten. It locates the creatures, describes their appearance, and names them. The conclusion of the earliest section of the book states that it was compiled by Yu as part of his task of recreating the world after the flood, once again linking the naming of spirits with world sovereignty.[71] If the *Shan hai jing* included illustrations, as the text itself sometimes suggests, then its links to the story of Yu's tripods would be even closer.

These traditions of the sage as one who gains power over all creatures by naming them are not limited to accounts of controlling evil demons. The listing of the names of rare animals, plants, and minerals is a major feature of the Han rhapsody. In the rhapsodies on imperial hunting parks and capitals this was certainly a literary ritual of power. As Donald Harper has argued, the idea of commanding men and spirits through the spellbinding power of naming was central to the rhapsody genre.[72] When Sima Xiangru presents the emperor with a hunting park transformed into an entire world through the magic of words, he enacts the idea of ruling through naming. The rhapsody as an example of attaining mastery through written language will be further discussed in chapter 7.

WRITING AND THE KING

At the center of the above forms of writing was the monarch. People entered the political realm as servants of the ruler, status was defined in relation to him, and writings were authoritative through their connection to him. Laws, seals, tallies, and coins came from the ruler, while registers, maps, legal cases, reports, and claims returned to him. However, although the ruler was the font of *authority* in writings, he was not their *author*. Instead he was cast in the role of listener or reader. He held himself attentive at the center and responded to what was presented to him, whether in the writings of his officials or in the signs offered by the world. In the new forms of generating power through writing the ruler occupied the position of the spirits and ancestors in the archaic state, a receiver of written communications and bestower of blessings. This section reverses the process followed thus far, starting at the center and gradually working outward. First it examines the ruler's role in *xing ming* and the rectification of names, then his links to law codes, and finally the role of writing in the ruler's progresses through his realm.

The preceding section treated the *Han Feizi*'s theory of *xing ming* and associated administrative techniques as practical procedures of government that developed in association with traditions of word magic. In fact, the theory of "forms and names" was based on religious beliefs and rituals reworked in the form of cosmological theories. In the *Han Feizi* the ruler's ability to control subordinates through bestowing names and assignments hinges upon his self-identification with the cosmic Way and consequent transformation into a near divinity. Thus the chapter "Zhu dao (主道)" states:

> The Way is the beginning of all things and the guiding principle of judgments. So the wise ruler holds to the beginning in order to know the origin of all things, and regulates guiding principles in order to know the cause of failure and success. Empty and in repose he waits for the course of nature to enforce itself so that all names will be defined of themselves and all affairs settled by themselves. Empty, he knows the essence of fullness; reposed, he corrects all motion. Who utters a word creates himself a name; who undertakes an affair creates himself a form. Compare forms and names and see if they are identical. Then the ruler will find nothing to worry about as everything reverts to its reality.[73]

The chapter concludes that if the ruler holds himself still and responds to his ministers' initiatives, he will distinguish the maladroit from the skillful without making a conscious selection, and recognize good fortune or calamity without calculation. His rewards will appear spontaneously like a timely rain, and his punishments like a bolt of lightning.

The same interplay between "form and name," sagely intelligence, and cosmic origins/principles pervades the silk manuscript from Mawangdui identified as the *Huangdi si jing*. The very first section "The Model of the Way (*dao fa* 道法)" discusses the formation of things out of primeval blackness (*ming ming* 冥冥) and asserts that these things can be known only through "emptiness and nonpossession." As soon as the most minute beginnings take shape, then there must be form and name. When form and name are established, then black and white are distinguished.[74] The later chapter "Assessing Basic Points (*lun yue* 論約)" makes a similar argument:

> In observing the world one who holds to the Way must closely examine the origin of things, and ascertain their forms and names. When the forms and names are settled, opposition and obedience will be assigned their positions; death and life will be divided; survival, perishing, rising, and falling will have their places. Then one checks it against [參, also a key technical term in *Han Feizi*'s theory of 'form and name'] the constant way of Heaven and Earth, and one can settle wherein lie calamity or good fortune, life or death, rising or falling.[75]

Other passages discuss the links between name and reality (*shi* 實), and name and achievement (*gong* 功). They employ the same model of a sagely intellect that penetrates into the origins/principles of all things and so can unfailingly guide the state.[76] The last of the four texts, the "Origin of the Way (*dao yuan* 道原)," describes the emergence of the universe from primal chaos. This account is closely linked to those in the chapters on the "Origin of the Way" in the *Wenzi* (文子) and the *Huainanzi* (淮南子). Unlike the other two texts, the Mawangdui account pairs "form and name." These do not exist in the primal chaos, but emerge with the formation of things. The common people do not recognize them, and they are perceived only by the sage who rules through the bestowing of names.[77]

While appeals to cosmic pattern and sagely percipience as the basis of administration through "forms and names" are not immediately based in religious ritual, there is evidence that they derive from reworkings of religious practices of the period. Specifically, they originate in meditation or trance procedures which are mentioned in proto-Daoist works and which provide the basis of the psycho-physiological theories which from at least the third century B.C. "embraced both self-cultivation and politics into one coherent system based upon a cosmology of the Tao."[78]

Studies of these theories have concentrated on the four chapters of the *Guanzi* describing meditative practices or "inner cultivation": "The Techniques of the

Heart/Mind (*xin shu* 心術)" (in two chapters), "The Purification of the Heart/Mind (*bai xin* 白心)," and "Inward Training (*nei ye* 內業)." "Inward Training" is the earliest, probably dating to the fourth century B.C., and consequently it is the most valuable for revealing the religious roots of the Daoist cosmopsychological synthesis. Accounts in the *Guo yu* state that people of the Warring States period employed "spirit intermediaries (*wu* 巫)," illuminated beings who could hear and see the spirits (*shen* 神) and into whom the latter would descend.[79] "Inward Training" is ultimately based on the experiences of such people, but it places them within the model of a world formed of quintessential energy (*jing* 精 or *jing qi* 精氣).

> In all cases the essence of things
> Is that which forms life.
> Below it gives birth to the Five Grains,
> Above it forms the arrayed stars.
> Flowing between heaven and earth,
> We call it ghosts and spirits (*gui shen* 鬼神).
> Who stores it in the breast
> We call the sage.[80]

Here spirit possession is re-imagined as a process of guiding the quintessential cosmic energies into the heart/mind of the devotee. Indeed, at one point the text speaks explicitly of a spirit that enters and departs from the practitioner.

> There is a spirit which naturally is found within one's person.
> Now it goes, now it comes.
> None can conceive of it.
> Lose it, inevitably there is disorder.
> Obtain it, inevitably there is order.
> If reverently you clear its dwelling place,
> The quintessential will spontaneously come.[81]

The method of drawing in these spirits or energies depended on the control of passions and emotional disturbances through measured breathing and meditative procedures. "In the anxious or sad, pleased or angry, the Way has nowhere to settle." Once the heart was fixed, then the senses all became acute and the limbs firm. The ingested energy vitalized the body and spirit, and it allowed true understanding. Having achieved such a state, one could govern the entire world.

> If one grasps the One and does not lose it,
> One can be lord of the ten thousand things.
> The gentleman employs these things,
> Is not employed by them.
> If one obtains the pattern of the One,

The regulation of the heart/mind will be found within it.
Regulated words will issue from the mouth,
Regulated tasks will be imposed on the people,
Then the whole world will be regulated.
. . .
If you concentrate your energy and become like a spirit,
The ten thousand things will be completely at your disposal.[82]

The two chapters on the "Techniques of the Heart/Mind" are valuable because they are based on "Inward Training," but whereas the latter is largely in verse and devoted to techniques of meditation and inner cultivation, the former adds substantial prose passages that emphasize and develop the applications of inner cultivation to government. In short, the shift from the earlier chapter to its later commentaries presents a clear-cut, textual example of the manner in which religious practices were adapted to the practice of government. This same pattern, as Roth notes, figures in the structure of the *Zhuangzi*, where the early chapters deal with "individual transformation through inner cultivation," while the later ones develop these ideas in a cosmological and, above all, political direction.[83]

The close ties in these texts between meditative procedures, spirit possession, and the emergent theory of the sagely mind also figure in the roughly contemporary early chapters of the *Zhuangzi*. "Discourse on Evening Things Out," tells how Ziqi of Nanguo put himself into a trance through controlled breathing and thus made his body "like withered wood" and his mind "like dead ashes." As A. C. Graham has argued, there is a close connection between this account of trance or possession and the stories of cooks, carpenters, swimmers, boatmen, and insect catchers who perfect their arts through total concentration and spontaneity. These images provide the model for the Daoist sage who differs from them only in that he devotes his concentrated energies not to a single task, but rather to all events. "The utmost man uses the heart like a mirror; he does not escort things as they go nor welcome them as they come; he responds and does not store."[84]

This image of the sage's mind as a mirror or water (which figures elsewhere in the *Zhuangzi*) and the insistence on the ruler's total detachment and spontaneous response also figure in the *Xunzi*. The chapter "Dispelling Obsession" focuses attention on the mind of the ruler, and it follows the ideas outlined above. It presents the metaphors of the mirror and water, emphasizes emptiness and stillness, and repeats strictures on neither welcoming nor clinging. It differs from the Daoist works in appeals to the classics and insistence on the early sage kings as the ultimate model, but the ideal of the mind and the techniques of its cultivation derive directly from the earlier texts, or from a common pool in the religious practices of the period.[85] The *Xunzi* likewise repeatedly refers to *shen ming* (神明), the "spirit illumination" of the sages perception, which is another adaptation of religious beliefs into a theory of government.[86] Although not yet appealing to techniques of stillness or metaphors of spontaneous reflection, the ideal of the sage flexibly responding to the needs of the moment already figures in the earlier Confucian works *Lun yu* and *Mencius*.[87] As in its discussion of the "rectification of names," the *Xunzi* simply availed itself of contemporary developments in other schools to elaborate more sophisticated models of themes already present in the Confucian tradition.

The links between these texts and the accounts of the cosmic and psychological underpinnings of administration through "names and forms" in the *Han Feizi* and the *Jing fa* are clear. All speak of a sagely intellect which through stillness and concentration identifies itself with the origins or principles of all things and thereby controls them through appropriate response and correct naming. Since this model of the mind derives from practices of trance used by religious specialists of the period, it offers a clear example of the religious underpinnings of the re-invention of rulership during the Warring States period. Holding himself still and free from attachment, the ruler was able in the court to match proposals of ministers against their actions, and in the cosmos to spontaneously apply appropriate names to all things. The culmination of this model of rulership was thus the ability to read the world.

In the context of local administration the ruler was the giver of laws. In this capacity he again received a new attribute fashioned through the re-imagining of religious rites as internal powers based on the mastery of cosmic patterns. Specifically, the ruler was regarded as a great diviner who could read the changes in the world and adapt his government to cope with them.[88]

Divination, as noted above, had been a foundation of royal authority in the Shang state, and it preceded major state actions under the Zhou. The development of administrative forms of government during the Warring States did not eliminate the old model of ruler as diviner. Instead the ability to perceive the patterns underlying the flux of circumstance and to select appropriate actions to meet them was identified as the hallmark of leadership. This talent figures in all the roles defining the Warring States—general, diplomat-rhetorician, and reforming minister—but it was above all the mark of the ruler.

The idea of the ruler as master of change had two primary forms. Texts later identified as legalist insisted on the necessity of obeying existing laws while defending the innovations that created the Warring States. They did this through a model of history in which the evolution of society demanded periodic institutional innovations. The man who could perceive the need for such innovations and find their proper form was the sage-ruler. "Hence," as the *Shang jun shu* argued, "the wise invent the standards by which the foolish are curbed; the worthy reform the rites by which the inadequate are constrained." Likewise the *Han Feizi* states, "Those who praise the way of Yao, Shun, Tang, and Yu to the present age will certainly be laughed at by the new sages. The sage does not assign truth to high antiquity, nor take as law any constant proprieties. He assesses the affairs of the age and prepares himself in response to them." Or as summarized in the *Lü shi chun qiu*, "Those who do not dare discuss the laws are the masses. Those who defend the laws to the death are the officials. Those who change the laws in response to the times are the rulers."[89] While the ruler was the author of the legal codes, they were not expressions of his arbitrary will. The sage wrote only in response to the conditions of the age. In this way, the actions of the ruler as legislator paralleled those in *xing ming* or in the cosmic "rectification of names." He observed what presented itself and responded accordingly.

Parallel to the idea of the sage as the master of innovation in the sphere of law, Confucian scholars developed a model of history based on successive sagely innovations in the realm of rites. Beginning with statements in the *Lun yu*, such as the argument that rites were secondary expressions of underlying principles and hence should be changed to meet circumstances, a range of Confucian thinkers from the redactors of the *Zuo zhuan*, through Xun Kuang, on to Shusun Tong and Fu Sheng in the Qin academy progressively developed the idea that rites required regular change, and that making such changes was the role of the sage-ruler. The *Gongyang* tradition's assertion that the institutions of Confucius' imaginary kingdom of Lu were a prophecy of the Han state also derived from this idea.[90] The ruler again acted as legislator, but rather than adapting the laws he worked his reforms through the medium of the rites out of which law emerged.

As we have seen above in the discussion of the *Han Fei*'s theory of *xing ming*, the Daoist tradition also emphasized the sages's ability to change and his refusal to cling to the established state of affairs. As Isabelle Robinet has demonstrated, no fewer than three chapters of the *Huainanzi*, the early Han *summa* of proto-Daoism, developed the idea that mastery of change defined the sage.[91]

The calendrical ritual texts that appeared at the end of the Warring States and in the early Han also defined the ruler through his ability and obligation to regularly modify laws, rituals, and policies. In these texts the ruler proceeded through the year reading the signs of imminent change in the actions of animals and plants, and adapted his own conduct accordingly. He modified his diet, changed his music, altered his physical appearance, and even transformed his moral character in response to the signs offered by nature. Practicing compassion in the spring, but killing without mercy in the autumn and winter, the sage ruler was the earthly embodiment of the seasonal changes that defined the way of Heaven in the world. Advocacy of altering policies in accord with natural signs and seasonal patterns also appears in chapters of the *Guanzi* and is an organizing principle of the *Huangdi si jing*.[92]

Even those who rejected the theory of ruler as master of change could not escape from it. In a series of stone inscriptions erected to proclaim his achievements, the First Emperor declared that his dynasty and its institutions were fixed for all time. However, the same inscriptions declare that his accomplishments and the empire he had founded were without historical precedent. Thus even while announcing his personal ambition to put an end to the process of history, he embraced the theory that the sage ruler was the figure who met the demands of a new age through the imposition of change.[93]

In addition to the adaptation of trance/meditation and divination, a final element of religious ritual that fed into the Warring States invention of rulership was the sacred procession. The Shang state was defined, as David Keightley has shown, through the marches of the king across the landscape in ceremonial hunts and military campaigns. He "showed the flag to his allies," intimidated his enemies, and engaged in sacrifices at the sacred sites through which he passed, renewing his ties to the land and creating his own spiritual authority through the feeding of the spirits. Each stage of his progress was marked in the divinatory record.[94] The early Zhou kings also engaged in regular campaigns and processions. Warring States texts preserved traditions of the Duke of Zhou, as well as the sages Yao and Shun, making sacred progresses or campaigns through their realms, and such processions figured in the political theory of the period.[95] Royal progresses also became a major element, wherein writing played a central role, in the re-imagining of royal power in the Warring States.

Warring States rulers traveled to the sacred sites of their realms, but the only detailed account left to us is that of the ritual processions of the First Emperor of Qin.[96] In addition to visiting the sacred sites of his new empire and offering sacrifice, the victorious ruler erected inscribed stelae on the major mountains that he visited. In these inscriptions he proclaimed his achievements and celebrated the new realm of peace and order that he was instituting in the world. While these texts were a form of propaganda, their placement on mountain peaks suggests that they were also intended to communicate his messages to the spirits. The culminating act of his ritual progresses, the *feng* sacrifice at Mount Tai, involved placing on the peak of the mountain a sealed chest with a written message to the gods.[97]

Parallel to the practice of ritual processions with accompanying inscriptions, a model of spirit travel from the shamanistic cults of the period was adapted to political discourse. The best-known example is the use of the language of spirit-travel to speak of politics in the "Li sao."[98] This poem will be discussed in chapter 4, so here it is sufficient to note the application to the political sphere of religious images centered around the theme of spirit travel. The same topos was subsequently adapted by an unknown author to describe a triumphant ascent to immortality, and by Sima Xiangru in "Rhapsody on the Great Man." In this last poem spirit travel became the ultimate form of imperial progress, a ritual of conquest that marked the emperor's ascent to universal authority and immortality.[99]

Spirit travel also figured as a topos in the myths of the sage kings. The most famous of these was the journey of the Yellow Emperor with his retinue of divinities to the summit of Mt. Tai for the performance of pure *jiao* music.[100] While this mythical journey was based on the invocation of spirit retinues in rituals for the protection of processions by the dead as well as the living, it also provided a literary model for the actual travels of the emperor, as well as the spirit travels which would be the expected culmination of certain rites.[101] The case of spirit travel is not strictly parallel to those of trance or divination, in that it was primarily a way of restaging, reimagining, and rewriting actual rituals rather than inventing a sagely intelligence capable of reading the hidden order of the world. Nevertheless, all these transformations of religious practices into models or tokens of the ruler's daimonic powers were part of the process of creating a ruler whose divine attributes could match his exalted place as the center and embodiment of the new state order. Whereas local and central administration were largely created through reworking and rewriting the ritual bases of the old Zhou order by means of a rationalizing cosmology, the re-invention of rulership drew on the contemporary religious realm and what is sometimes described as shamanism to provide images of cosmic power.

A final contrast between the transformation of lower levels of government and that of the ruler is their differential relation to writing and texts. As noted earlier, the reworking of local administration and royal court can be traced through documents created to control officials, while the ruler figures as implied author (law codes) or reader (registers, reports, audits, and legal cases). As a result, the study of the re-invention of the ruler has relied on texts from outside the state sphere, specifically from the philosophic traditions who adapted their own visions of philosophical mastery to develop new theories of political authority through sagehood. The philosophical traditions and their relation to the state are the subject of chapter 2, and the interplay between ruler and philosophical master forms the core of this book.

THE OFFICES OF ZHOU

The derivation of bureaucratic administration and its documentary substrate from religious rituals and their sacred writings found theoretical elaboration in a Warring States text, the *Zhou guan* or "Office(r)s of Zhou."[102] The *Zhou guan* is a list of offices with descriptions of their tasks that offers a model of a world-state based on principles of cosmology. Scholarship has focused on questions of its dating and its reliability as an account of actual institutions, but ignored its value as evidence of the mental universe of the men who created the administrative, territorial state in China.[103] It shows how the apparatus of the Warring States bureaucracy could be portrayed as a formal structure based on cosmology and numerology, a structure systematically calqued onto the cultic practices and ritual theories of the period. The fact that the work later became known as the *Zhou li* "Rituals of Zhou," and was ranked as one of the three ritual classics by Zheng Xuan in the Eastern Han demonstrates how closely administration and ritual intertwined in the text, and in the world that produced it.

Despite its reputation as a ritual text, a Confucian classic, and a collection of implausible offices, the *Zhou guan* is closely linked to the major legal and administrative reforms of the Warring States period.[104] First, the administration is described in terms of *fa* 法 "standard/law." "Ritual" appears as a subelement of law.

Thus the account of the "da zai 大宰," the chief minister, begins with the six major divisions of the administration, followed immediately by the "eight laws" that control the officials. The text stipulates that the chief minister must display his laws to the common people on a tower of the palace gate at the beginning of the year. This stipulation is repeated for each of the six departments. Land use is to be controlled by law, as are sacrifices, funerals, divination, and all ritual performances. The identification of demons, reminiscent of the "Demonography," was to be done according to the law. In addition to insisting that government is defined by laws, that officials are controlled by laws, and that such laws are to be written and publicly displayed, the text also devotes one of the six government bureaus to penal law.[105]

Not only did the *Zhou guan* insist on law as the defining feature of the state, but it used theories of punishment closely tied to legalist theories. Thus the text insists that the population and officials alike must be controlled through punishments, and occasionally rewards. Even those officials charged with education are to rely on punishment. The *Zhou guan* even adopts the administrative policy, associated with Shang Yang of Qin, of forming the population into units of five and ten who are held mutually liable for crimes and share in rewards. These units are linked to form larger units, which in turn make up larger units, and so on in the pattern so common in administrative theory.[106] Not only does the text adopt many of the legal practices of Shang Yang, but it also advocates such elements of Qin government as the creation of a regular grid for the allotment of fields, reliance on labor services, enslavement as a punishment with redemption for those who held titles, and universal military service with rewards of land and titles.[107] By contrast, it says little about the interpersonal relationships central to Confucian thought.[108]

In addition to emphasizing law and punishment, the *Zhou guan* also devotes attention to the other techniques of written administration that emerged during the Warring States. There are numerous discussions of registers of population and property, and scattered references to maps. Sometimes officials charged with the preparation of maps also handled registers, and those in charge of registers also dealt with legal cases.[109] Annual assessments of performance leading to promotion or demotion, along with major assessments every third year, are mentioned under several offices.[110] The importance of written documents is stressed, with repeated references both to archives in which they are stored, and to regular public presentations.[111] Thus the *Zhou guan* incorporates all the administrative procedures that defined the Warring States polity, and grants pride of place to the political uses of writing.

However, while the *Zhou guan* embraces Warring States administration, it makes it part of a structure that goes beyond the bounds of a conventional bureaucratic polity. This difference can be demonstrated in two ways. First, the *Zhou guan*'s government operates on the principle that every office has a double function: administrative and religious. The authors of the text may not have recognized this distinction, but we must move through our own categories to reach an understanding of the alien world that produced such a work. Second, the officers are organized to function as a symbolic reproduction of the structure and work-ings of the cosmos. In this way the text offers one of the earliest and most elaborate versions of the idea, central to Chinese civilization, that the world is fundamen-tally congruent with a bureaucratic order.[112] I will examine each of these features in turn.

The practice of pairing administrative roles with those of cult can be dem-onstrated by an examination of the first and highest officer, the chief of the "Officers of Heaven," the *da zai*. After listing "laws," "principles," "levers," and other means of controlling his officials, the text goes on to describe the role of this chief minister in the sacrifices to the five directional gods (*di* 帝), those to other major gods, and those to royal ancestors; tells what he is to do in major funerals; and finally sum-marizes how he should lead his officials in any major state ceremonial. The refer-ence to the sacrifices to the five *di*, which recur under many offices, are particularly significant, because this was the most important cult in Qin. Thus accounts of cults reinforce the impression that the text was greatly influenced by Qin.[113]

The doubling of administrative tasks with those in religious rites is followed in the case of the *xiao zai* 小宰 and most of the major officials.[114] Lesser offices also doubled their routine tasks with roles in religious ritual. Officials charged with running the king's kitchen and preparing his food also provided food for sacrificial offerings and handled the laying out of sacrificial vessels at funerals. Likewise those responsible for cultivating the royal fields provided grain for daily consumption and for all ritual performances.[115] Officials in charge of ice, mats, tapestries, and fur-lined cloaks provided parallel services for use in the palace and in major reli-gious ceremonies.[116] Thus the royal household also acted as a machine to provide the necessary materials and skills for all ritual performances.

Since the king was a high priest, it is not surprising that his personal staff and servants should be drawn into religious activities. However, the officials of the second department, the "Officers of the Earth" charged with education, likewise performed religious rites parallel to their administrative tasks. The *zhou zhang* 州長 "district chiefs" were to play a leading role in the sacrifices to the god of the soil in their jurisdiction. They also directed local archery ceremonials used to select those who would officiate at the suburban altar sacrifice. Finally they presided over all major sacrifices and funerals in their territories.[117] Another official in this department had the dual responsibility of marking the frontiers of the state and the limits of the sacred area around an altar. His subordinates were charged with the planting of trees at the altar, the preparation and binding of the victims, and the songs and dances that accompanied a sacrifice. Also in this category were the drummers, who relayed orders and provided rhythm for collective action in the army and in field labor, but who also accompanied each major sacrifice on a dif-ferent type of drum.[118] Thus education, which as noted above was routinely based on law and punishments, also relied on the power of religious ritual to control men's actions.

The third department of government, that of the "Officers of Spring," needs no discussion in this context, since it was devoted to religious rituals to the celestial spirits, the ancestors of men, and the chthonic powers of the earth. Officials included those who prepared animal victims, those who readied implements and garments for sacrifices, guardians of tombs and the ancestral temple, musicians and dancers who accompanied rituals, diviners with tortoise shells and yarrow stalks, interpreters of dreams, invocators who chanted sacred formulae, spirit intermediaries, and astrologer/astronomers.

Even military officials in the "Offices of Summer" played roles in the state cults. Seasonal hunts commanded by the highest military official, the *da si ma* 大司馬, served not only to train troops but also to provide wild animals offered up in some rituals. Military rituals were accompanied by ceremonial oaths, divinations, and the ceremonial dedication of war drums with blood. The account of the duties of the chief military officer ends with a description of his role in major state sacrifices and funerals.[119] Lesser officials likewise performed dual functions. The *liang ren* 量人 "Measurer," who made maps and records of cities, markets, roads, and fortresses for use on campaigns, also regulated the size of offerings in sacrifices and ritual banquets, and controlled the use of ritual vessels for funerary offerings. Officials in this department were in charge of obtaining animals for sacrifice. The official who assembled sons of leading families into military units also directed their participation in sacrifices, funerals, and assemblies. The *fang xiang shi* 方相士 "Exorcist," who used weapons to expel baleful influences in the new year season and at funerals, was an official in this department.[120]

If the inseparability of liturgy and government is manifest in accounts of individual offices, it is even clearer in the structure of the entire work. The text is arranged according to principles of numerology and ritual calendrics that emerged to prominence in the late Warring States period. The composition of the *Zhou li* was thus a ritual act that conjured into existence a graphic image of the state as cosmic mandala. I will sketch here the origins and significance of such a project.

While official titles figure prominently in the writings of the archaic state, schematic lists were rare. Probably the earliest example is the "Li zheng 立政" chapter of the *Shang shu* 尚書. This text, purporting to be the instructions of the Duke of Zhou to the young King Cheng on the establishment of good government, includes several lists of official titles.[121] Another work that described Zhou administration and official titles was the "Wang du ji 王度記," supposedly composed in the fourth century B.C., incorporated in the Han dynasty *Da Dai li ji* 大戴禮記, but now surviving only in fragments.[122] Discussions of Zhou institutions in the *Mencius* list no offices, but they name the five official ranks (*jue* 爵). This list includes the king as the first rank rather than placing him above the hierarchy of titles.[123] The "Wang zhi 王制" chapter of the *Xunzi* contains a ranked list of the official titles in the administration of the true king. This list includes sixteen offices listed in ascending order of importance and, like the *Mencius*, it includes the king himself as an officer.[124]

Listing the king as an official or a rank is significant, because by the early Han this practice had ceased. The "Wang zhi" chapter of the *Liji*, according to a Han source composed under the Emperor Wen (文, r. B.C. 180–57), quotes from the *Mencius*'s account of Zhou institutions. However, when it lists the five ranks of nobility it states that the king "institutes" (*zhi* 制) these titles, but does not include the sovereign himself among them.[125] This shift indicates the elevation of the status of the ruler at the end of the Warring States and the early empire. As will be discussed below, the practice of separating the ruler from the officials figures prominently in the *Zhou guan*.

Thus there was a small body of early works that offered lists of Zhou officials as a model for rulers, but these had little relation to the *Zhou guan* in scale or organization. The roots of this change lie in the late Warring States development of cosmological models for government as part of the larger trend to explain the structure and operation of the world through systematic correlative thought.[126]

Perhaps the earliest evidence of this development is a story in the *Zuo zhuan*. A visitor to the court of Lu was asked to explain the tradition that his ancestors, officials for the sage king Shao Hao 少皞, had held titles named for birds. He replied that each of the five *di*, here referring to the sage kings of antiquity, had ruled according to the natural sign that had announced his rise, fixed his calendar (*ji* 紀) by that sign, and given his officials titles based on it. Thus the officials of the Yellow Emperor had cloud titles, those of the Fiery Emperor fire titles, those of Gonggong (共工) water titles, those of Da Hao (大皞) dragon titles, and those of Shao Hao, whose ascension was signaled by the appearance of the phoenix, bird titles. The visitor then listed the bird names held by the clans of officials, and explained the task performed by each of them. Finally he observed that since the time of Zhuan Xu (顓頊) men could no longer set calendars from the "distant," here referring to celestial powers, and instead did so from the "near by," that is, the affairs of men.[127]

There are many themes running through this story. The reference to Zhuan Xu and the loss of the "distant" links the story to the myth of the separation of the world of men from that of the spirits.[128] Vandermeersch argues that the dragons, birds, and natural forces were transformations of the insignia of the corporations of officers under the Shang, insignia that constituted much of the decor of Shang bronzes. The story would thus reflect the shift from archaic religion based on magical powers to the formalizing schemata of Warring States calendrists and ritualists. On firmer ground, he notes that the account is related to emerging Five Phases theory, as indicated by the number of rulers, the attribution to each of a natural correlate, and the presence of two of the five phases. He less plausibly equates dragon with metal (scales = armor), phoenix with wood (signs of spring and rebirth), and clouds with earth (mountains and jade as the source of clouds).[129] The story places a list of Zhou titles in the context of a process of change based on the Five Phases, and sets the whole account against the backdrop of the birth of sacrificial ritual through the withdrawal of the gods. It thus functions as a parable of the shift from religious authority to administrative government through the agency of rites and cosmology, with a central emphasis placed on the role of writing and calendars (*ji* 紀).

A less archaic version of the mapping of administration onto cosmology appears in the chapter "The Five Phases" in the *Guanzi*. The section on government begins with an account of how the Yellow Emperor obtained six worthy ministers identified with Heaven, Earth, and the four directions. It then gives a calendar of government in which the year is divided into five periods of seventy-two days, each period dominated by a different phase and administered by a different official. As in the calendars of government cited earlier, the ruler and his officials were to pattern their conduct on the annual cycle.[130]

The correspondances between this chapter and the *Zhou guan* are striking, although their relationship is uncertain. Both speak of six high officials, and both divide space and time into five units with a government department assigned to each unit. The correspondances of the directions with the seasons are the same, and they are both identical to those in the *Lü shi chun qiu*.[131] The *Zhou guan* is distinctive in making the sixth official head of an overarching department charged with supervising the rest. The key point here, however, is the evidence that the rise of correlative cosmology in the late Warring States led to new models of governance based on imitation of natural patterns. This was already noted in the politicoritual calendars, as well as the *Huangdi si jing*. The *Zhou guan* reworked the old practice of listing Zhou officials in the light of this new theory of government, and thereby provided a model of the state that incorporated current cosmological theory, state cults, and administrative practice. The pairing of ritual functions with administrative practice, as well as the organization of the state in terms of the calendar, both emerged from this context.

A feature of the text derived from its incorporation of the cosmological reworking of archaic state and religion was the importance of numerology. Each department is prefaced with a list of offices and the number of people who served in them. The numbers five and six recurred as organizing principles in the texts cited above, and they were incorporated into the *Zhou guan*. In addition to the six departments that formed the overarching structure, each department also was fitted to a numerical pattern. Thus the Department of Heaven lists 360 officers, corresponding to the number of days of the year. Since this department was intended to control the other five, which formed a full year, this number created an arithmetic concordance between the department's function and its natural correlate, a concordance that presumably brought the administration into line with Heaven and secured its successful operation. There are 62 offices in the Department of Heaven, 77 in Earth, 68 in Spring, 69 in Summer, and 66 in Autumn. (Winter was early lost and replaced with a work on types of manufacture.) Nemoto Makoto has demonstrated that if one counts offices of immediate subordinates (for example, the *xiao zai* and *zai fu* 宰夫 in relation to the *da zai*) and the various local administrators, then each department has exactly sixty offices. They would thus each correspond to the sixty-day cycle that was the base of the Chinese calendar, and together would form a single year in number as well as in name.[132] Thus the profusion of titles is not only an attempt to create a government responsible for all aspects of the world, but also a function of the perceived necessity of achieving meaningful correlations between the state and the cosmic forces from which it was to draw its powers.

This insistence on the state as a replica or image of the cosmos is significant. As noted earlier, the belief that the world of the spirits was a replica of that of men had been implicit in archaic ancestral cult and had developed over the course of the Warring States. Similarly, funerary practice was increasingly organized on the principle of making the tomb a replica of the conditions that a person had enjoyed in life. This idea of replication and doubling underpins the increasing importance granted to writing, for the culmination of the authority of writing in the Warring States was texts that sought to record the entire cosmos. The *Zhou li* is an early example of such a text created as a model of the world. Chapter 7 will be devoted to the dream of capturing the world in writing that came to dominate the intellectual realm in the third and second centuries B.C.

A final feature worthy of note is that the king does not appear as an officer within the text. Like the percipient ruler in the *Han Feizi*'s "form and name," the king in the *Zhou guan* remains hidden, formless, and inactive behind the visible, formed, and active figures of the officials. While he does not figure as an officer, he is dispersed throughout the text, standing behind each of the specific offices. Thus the entire work begins with the statement:

> The king establishes the state. He distinguishes the regions/directions and corrects the positions/statuses. He gives form to the capital and makes boundary lines through the fields. He sets up offices and divides responsibilities, and thereby provides a standard for the people.

This formula recurs at the beginning of each new department. Moreover, the introduction to the duties of each department head includes the formula that he "assists" (*zuo* 佐) the king in the particular area of his responsibilities, and the entries on many lesser offices also describe their duties in terms of the king's needs.[133] Thus the *Zhou guan* recapitulates the pattern observed in administrative documents in which the common people are inscribed in registers and laws; the officials are inscribed in laws and seals, and inscribe themselves in reports; but the ruler remains outside the body of writings as the ultimate recipient and the highest reader.

CONCLUSION

By the late Warring States period the state order was maintained by a set of written administrative procedures derived from the ritual uses of writing in the archaic state and in contemporary religion. The law codes and registers of local administration derived from the covenants, enfeoffment ceremonies, and inscribed ceremonial bronzes of the Zhou. The seals, tallies, and coins distributed by the ruler to his servants derived from distributions of regalia that had constituted the Zhou nobility. Regular presentation of accounts at the central court was patterned on the obligation of nobles to ceremonially visit the king. The ruler's control of his officials through the checking of accounts was expounded in terms of theories of mental powers derived from trance experiences in contemporary religious practice. The re-invention of rulership through the ideal of the sage borrowed a set of images, theories, and practices from the religious uses of trance, divination, and spirit travel. The travels of the monarch were also inscribed at sites of communications with the spirits. All these new forms of power ultimately depended on the image of the ruler as the supreme reader of natural processes and social action. He was the bestower of appropriate names, the chief practitioner of the highest forms of spirit travel as celebrated in verse, and the man who communicated with the gods through inscribed messages. At the same time, the afterlife was imagined as a parallel administrative order working through written documentation. In this conclusion I will briefly examine the mechanism for this change.

Under the Shang and Western Zhou, state power and the ruling elite had been defined through a set of ritual practices organized primarily around the ancestral cult. In both these states the authority of the living was underpinned by their privileged access to the spiritual powers of dead kin that was maintained through the use of writing. Relations between living and dead were based on ties preserved in the sacrificial cult, so membership in the ruling elite and the rankings of its individuals and lineages were determined by differential roles within a hierarchy of sacrificial cults. In the Zhou state these cults were organized in a segmented hierarchy determined by the position of the founder of the line with relation to the Zhou king. Writing played an essential role in communicating with the spirits. It was also fundamental to the two primary modes of ordering the cultic service, genealogy and the calendar.

As noted earlier, this resulted in a polity defined by formal kin structures in which the individual's status and role shifted with each generational shift. This established the bureaucratic principles that status was fixed by role rather than person, and that such roles were regularly modified. In addition, the authority of spirits followed the pattern set by living rulers, since the spirits were primarily former rulers and their wives transposed into the spirit realm. Thus in the Shang and Western Zhou states the spirit world was a replica of the structures of the human state, into which the actual participants in the latter were transposed at the times of their deaths. As Lothar von Falkenhausen has noted, the predominance in burials of weapons of war and implements of sacrifice—the tools necessary for the two "great services" that defined the Zhou elite—shows that the burial ritual was intended to transfer the ritually and politically significant aspects of the individual to the next world.[134] With the state and spirit world established as mirror images, each new extension of the Zhou state to wider reaches of society entailed a similar extension of the spirit realm. This was facilitated by the fact that the political order was expanded through modifications and extensions of cultic practices.

The extended use of covenants brought a new range of the population into the purview of the gods and spirits invoked to enforce them, even as it sanctified new uses of writing to impose order and obligations. Since matching copies of the covenants were despatched to the gods and preserved in state archives, the covenants entailed a parallel bureaucratization of the human state and the realm of the spirits. This led to the politicization of the commoners' ancestral cult. In the same process, the casting of laws on bronzes assimilated emerging legal codes to the status of communications with the spirits. Somewhat later, the receipt of legal codes and official documents along with an appointment played the same role as the earlier casting of bronzes to record the receipt of privileges, and these codes and documents became appurtenances of burial that established the status of the deceased in the next life. In this way the expanding spirit world was increasingly filled with subjects and the written oaths that bound them to obedience, as well as officers and the documents that empowered them to command. The early imperial practice of offering cult to dead officials was a direct outgrowth of such practices.[135] The granting of surnames and titles to registered individuals who gave military service probably also entailed an extension of ancestral cult to the lower reaches of the population. This process is reflected in the inclusion of prayers for those who died in battle in a fourth-century B.C. hemerological manuscript discovered at Jiudian, Hubei, as well as the song of the spirits of dead warriors in the "Guo shang" poem of the *Chu ci*.[136] Thus the underworld came to include not merely those who participated in covenants and received legal charges, but those who were the objects of registration. This is the state of belief in the third century B.C., as reflected in the document from the Fangmatan grave wherein an underworld bureaucracy kept its own records and responded to written petitions.

This process of the transformation of a politicized spirit world defined by genealogy to a politicized spirit world defined by office is clearly indicated by the belief, for which the earliest records are in the *Zuo zhuan*, that offices had a genealogy. Based ultimately on the hereditary offices of the Zhou state, this idea appeared above in the story of offices named for clouds, fire, water, dragons, and birds that also served as the names of the clans that held them. Another passage explaining the disappearance of dragons from the world relates that spirit beings formerly had officials who controlled them. As long as the officials devoted themselves to their tasks, the spirit creatures came, but when the posts were neglected they vanished. This is a variant of the myth of the separation of men and spirits. Among these officials were five who were responsible for the Five Phases and the spirit creatures who embodied them. These divine offices were passed down within family lines that maintained sacrifices to the first holder of each office. This tradition of treating divinity as an office that was passed from father to son was carried forward in the calendrical chapters of the *Lü shi chun qiu* and related literature.[137] Nor were such offices restricted to spirits, for Sima Qian traces his own family's tradition of serving as astrologers back to the mythic Chong and Li who were charged with the task of administering the affairs of Heaven and Earth after their separation.[138]

These variations on the myth of the separation of the world of men and spirits are linked also, as we have seen above, to the shift from the Shang's calendar of sacrifices to potent spirits to the calendar of a ritual cycle derived from the Five Phases. This new form of calendar provided the structure for the parallel ritual corporation and administrative state of the *Zhou guan*, as well as the texts that articulated the calendrical model of monarchy at the end of the Warring States. Thus the two organizing principles of the Shang cult—genealogy and calendar—were both reworked into formal patterns of ritual that underlay the invention of the administrative state. But like the imaginary state in the *Zhou guan*, the Warring States polity and that of imperial China remained as much religious institutions as administrative organs.

While the invention of bureaucracy was achieved primarily through the re-working of the cultic practices of the Zhou, a process that turned the kin-based Zhou spirit world into a parallel spirit bureaucracy, another set of cultic practices was invoked to create a new model of leadership. Encompassing the Five Phases in the *Zhou Guan*, or successively embodying all of them in the calendrical models, the ruler provided the principle of unity and change that drew together the disparate functions of the officials. This new power of the monarch, and the parallel claims of his scholar advisers, were justified through developing the trances and spirit travels of the shamans of early China into a rationalized vision of a sagely mind that could wield the principles of the cosmos to insure order in the world. This development was a correlate of the shift from formalized kin structures to formal-ized ranks as the organizing principle of the state, for the shift from the former to the latter voided claims to rule through kin ties to the spirits, and shifted them to claims of expertise. The only expertise that justified world mastery was command of the comprehensive, cosmic Dao, so the ruler merged with the sage to create a new figure that infused the polity with meaning. Just as the process of creating the Warring State from the Zhou order entailed parallel earthly administration and celestial bureaucracy, so the emergence of a ruler-centered state entailed the conflation of the person of the ruler with the power that guided the natural world. Both these processes depended on the power of writing to generate parallel realms that provided a model for human affairs.

However, this vision of the sage-ruler was not articulated in the writings generated by the state, nor in the great imaginary state of the *Zhou guan*. Insight into this phenomenon was obtained from such works as the *Han Feizi*, the *Huangdi si jing*, and the *Guanzi*. These writings belong to another form of authoritative text generated in the Warring States period, those produced by the scholarly traditions writing in the name of "the masters," and the vision of the sage-ruler was insepa-rably enmeshed in that of the master. It is to these that we now turn our attention.

Chapter Two
WRITING THE MASTERS

Outside the state sphere another form of social organization based on writing developed, the scholarly tradition or "school." Based on ties of loyalty distinct from those to the ruler, they remained separate from the state structure. However, they were never free of its influence, but interacted in forms ranging from patronage, through mimicry, to indifference, and even opposition. Like the state they relied on writings to project their influence across space and to transmit it over time. Again like the state, they used it to form new kinds of links, new social roles, and new patterns of fictive attributes, that is, attributes generated in the activities of writing and reading, that created authority within the tradition. Ultimately the forms of authority created in the writings of the schools, the authority attributed to the masters in the textual traditions, were drawn back into the political sphere and, as shown in chapter 1, they helped to define and alter the modes of state authority.

The schools, like the territorial state, emerged from the breakdown of the earlier society wherein status was determined by position within a nested hierarchy of ancestral cults. As nobles lost their positions through defeat in internecine wars, new elements of the population were drawn into the state sphere through the extension of military service and the range of covenants. However, many people displaced by the shifting political order could not obtain, or did not desire to obtain, political office. Some of them formed private associations to maintain themselves or improve their conditions outside the ambit of the ruler and his agents. The most notable of these were the "wandering bravoes (*you xia* 游侠)." These men bound themselves together in armed bands through oaths supported by an ethic of the inviolability of one's word, the virtue of vengeance, and the willingness to die in order to keep faith.[1] Similar in form to the associations of bravoes, and paired with them in the *Han Feizi*, were the scholarly associations.[2]

While associations of scholars resembled those of the bravoes in form, they were distinct in their ethic and in their modes of forming groups. The bravoes depended on personal ties defined by oaths and moral debts owed for recognition or assistance, but the schoolmen were bound by loyalties to a common master as embodied in writings collected under his name. Thus the master in the school stood in the same relation to his disciples as the ruler, or more accurately the dynasty, to the populace. Likewise writings associated with the master played a role similar to that of the law codes or decrees promulgated by the state, for they stipulated a social program or mode of behavior, subordinated the disciple to the master in the act of receiving them, and granted the disciple a form of authority through his participation in the wisdom expounded in the text. The scholarly texts were also like the writings generated by the state through the fact that *authorship* was a sign not of *authority* but of subordination, while the master was in life the reader or responder and in death the topic or theme.

Once invented in the texts dedicated to him, the master became a ground on which his followers inscribed their theories. This creation of masters in texts meant that actual teachers were transformed over time, and that ancient or imaginary figures served as eponymous masters in the same manner as historical founders of traditions. Consequently, the texts that bore the masters' names became more important than the men themselves. The process of preserving, elaborating, or inventing the master in the act of writing his canon also led to the creation of certain characteristics that defined the master as a type. Most notable was the insistence on veiled meanings or hidden dimensions in his discourse that were unfolded over time or applied variably to new situations. This in turn encouraged the development of new modes of reading based on the assumption of such hidden or unfolding meanings in texts.

This chapter focuses on the role of texts within the schools and the manner in which the use of texts generated authority both within the scholarly traditions and in society at large. It will examine first the social nature of the schools, their relation to the state, and their economic underpinnings; second, the patterns of text generation within the schools; third, the characteristics of the master produced by these textual practices; fourth, the developing theories of reading that emerged from the types and uses of writings generated by the schools; and finally the appearance of authorship as a social role.

SCHOLARLY TEXTS

Texts composed in this period, as recent discoveries in tombs have reminded us, did not take the form of "books." The most common physical medium for texts was the bamboo or wooden strip, while some were written on silk. The former were bound together with cords, but the number of strips joined in a bundle was limited, and over time the cords rotted away to leave the strips prey to disorder.[3] The situation was thus not unlike that in the West before the invention of the codex, when a single work might require a large number of scrolls that had no physical links, and hence easily became separated or confused. Writings transmitted in such media have a fluidity and openness that sharply contrasts with the fixity and clear limits to which we have grown accustomed. A chapter or even a subsection was an independent unit. New units could be added, old ones removed, or the order re-arranged without doing physical violence to the work.[4] As Erik

Maeder has described it, Warring States texts worked like a loose-leaf binder into which one inserted essays or notes by different hands, and added, removed, or re-arranged the material to suit the evolving interests of the compiler. Longer units of text were fixed more permanently, but more expensively, by transcription onto sheets of silk. Far from being a problem, as it appears to modern scholars, this means of transmitting texts facilitated forming intellectual lineages, defining group loyalties, and adapting traditions to changing circumstances.[5]

Given the physical characteristics of writings, texts were invariably social creations passing through numerous hands. The notion of authorship was weak or absent. By contrast, the role of reader or transmitter involved a more active role than that assigned to someone who picks up a modern book. To create any text involved a group of people gathered together, often in a teaching situation, and to preserve or expand it across time required that this initial situation be constantly repeated. Should any text cease to be cared for and transmitted by such a group, it could survive only as a bundle of strips that would fall into disorder and perish. Thus the group preserved the text, and the text likewise preserved the group, for common loyalty to an ancestral master embodied in the text was the only link that created a group larger than those assembled in a room, and preserved this group longer than the lifespan of a single teacher. The master played the role of the apical ancestor in the later Chinese lineage, and the text functioned as both gene-alogy and "family instruction." Because the groups who produced and transmitted these texts were organized around the relationship of master and disciple, they are often described as "schools." The term carries many inappropriate associations, and a phrase such as "textual tradition" would be more accurate. However, I will continue to use the word "school" as shorthand for these groups defined by loyalty to a common master and "his" text.

The school of the Warring States period was not a single and constant en-tity. The schools emerged at different times and in different places. Consequently each took on a distinct character due to shifting relations with other schools and the states. Moreover, evidence is very scarce, so it is difficult to analyze the tradi-tions in any but the broadest terms. Finally, as texts became more numerous and available in the late Warring States period, commitment to a master or group was increasingly replaced by attachment to texts that combined the doctrines of nu-merous traditions. Consequently, I will simply sketch the major features of the schools as a form of social organization and a mode of authority, particularly as these were linked to the production of texts.

As a working definition, the essential elements of a school were a master and his followers. It was from the former that the tradition took its name. When inter-school polemics developed in the fourth century B.C., participants were identified by the names of their masters, for example, Yang Zhu and Mo Di.[6] Later enumer-ations of schools were enumerations of masters. When the writings of the schools became a bibliographic category they were described alternatively as the *zhu jia* (諸家) "various schools" or *zhu zi* (諸子) "various masters."[7] To be a school meant to have a master, and to be a master meant to have a school. One became a master by serving as eponym or focus of the writings of a school. Learning in solitude may have existed, but the generation and transmission of texts was a collective activity. The *Xunzi* insists on the need to receive a text from a teacher, accompanied by his oral explanations, in order to understand it.[8]

The earliest known group formed on the basis of teaching was that of Confucius (traditionally 551–479 B.C.) and his disciples. This is also the only scholarly tradition that has left any substantial record of its academic practices, in the form of the *Lun yu* and the *Zuo zhuan*. The former is a compilation by generations of followers, which includes words attributed to the master, discussions of what he said, and observations by leading disciples. Because some of these sayings are given a setting or a dialogue form, they suggest the nature of the associations formed and activities pursued. For want of records from other schools, these must serve as evidence of more general practices, although they reflect only the early phases of scholarly activity. Since the text was compiled over several centuries, the practices that constituted the school underwent changes that are now masked by their conflation in a single source.[9] Most scholars concur that passages with information on background and setting, or longer dialogues, are later developments. The *Zuo zhuan* makes statements about the life of Confucius and some of his disciples, and certain discussions echo the teaching scenes from the *Lun yu*. However, these were written down more than a century after the lives of the figures with whom they deal, and they can only be used with caution. Nevertheless, a few general observations can be made.

First, we are clearly not speaking of a school in any formal sense. Where we obtain glimpses of the people who surround Confucius, they are grown men. Some of them held posts with the powerful Ji family that shared in the government of Lu. One disciple held a fief.[10] The pronouncements and discussions deal primarily with ethics or government. The group thus appears to have emerged as a discussion society that became a school only through the dominating presence of a single master around whom the others gathered and to whose opinions they generally deferred. Some passages indicate personal closeness and emotional involvement between the disciples and Confucius. The *Mencius* says that the disciples mourned Confucius for the three-year period prescribed for a father, and one disciple doubled this. Although this is a late account, it suggests the direction in which schools evolved, and there are references in the *Lun yu* to sacrifices on Confucius' behalf.[11]

Second, the accepted early strata contain few references to any sort of texts, but later strata indicate the study of certain writings, notably the *Odes* and the *Documents*, and debates over points of ritual practice. This probably reflects a shift in the concerns of the school. E. Bruce Brooks has also noted that meetings outside or in the homes of disciples in earlier chapters tend to shift toward meetings in Confucius' house, and that this dwelling grows more splendid in the telling over time.[12] This, like Confucius' interventions in politics and the higher status of his interlocutors in the later strata, reflects the attempt of later generations to create a more glorious career for the founder.

It is also important to note, however, that whereas other schools are named for their master, those we call "Confucians" are usually identified as *ru* (儒). This word indicated a social category comprised of teachers and masters of ritual.[13] In a list of schools in the *Zhuangzi* dating from the end of the Warring States period the *ru* are characterized as "gentry of Zou and Lu" and "teachers" who explain the *Odes* and *Documents*, and they appear outside the list of the "Hundred Schools."[14] This indicates that the Confucian text-based schools differed from other traditions in that they were part of a broader social grouping of men who did not invariably devote themselves to the transmission of texts. However, the background presence of groups of *ru* not organized around texts does not alter the pivotal role of transmitted writings such as the *Lun yu* in the development of the *ru* philosophers.

As for the *Lun yu*, the most important single feature is that the "enunciatory scene" portrayed in the text, which may or may not correspond to the actual "communication situation" in which the recorded phrases were produced, is one in which the author is a recorder of words attributed to an authoritative figure, either Confucius or a leading disciple.[15] As a consequence "authorship" and "authority" are separated, and the writer casts himself in the role of a secretary transcribing the speech of another. The communication situation that this mode of enunciation mimics is the act of teaching in which the master, whose words are quoted, addresses an implicit audience of one or more students. As narrative settings are added, this implicit audience can be specified as a disciple, disciples, or a political figure. Other passages assume dialogue form in which a question is asked and answered, and sometimes a longer exchange takes place. However, the writer always remains in the background and speaks only to name the participants and, sometimes, the place.

This format, which characterizes not only the *Lun yu* but other early texts such as the *Mozi*, the *Sunzi*, and the *Mencius*, had a significant impact on the emergence and later development of writing in China. In the case of the *Lun yu* this textual strategy may at first have directly reflected a historical reality of disciples seeking to preserve what they remembered of an inspiring teacher. However, in the later strata, written by men who had never known the master, the perpetuation of this form cannot be explained as a reproduction of any lived, historical reality. Moreover, when the *Mencius* and the *Mozi* begin to produce longer and more elaborate discourses resembling essays, they are still textually enunciated as addresses by the master to an audience of presumed disciples, or a dialogue with a named interlocutor recorded by a silent disciple/witness. No early texts explain the significance of this insistence on simulating the teaching scene in the enunciation of the text, probably because this procedure was taken for granted and would have lost its raison d'être had anyone acknowledged it. However, an explanation is suggested by the nature of the texts and their social role.

Texts were written as collections of quotations because they derived their authority from the supposed wisdom of the master. The master in turn derived his authority from the presence of disciples.[16] A simple exposition in essay form would have been the ungrounded assertions of an isolated individual. What made the words worth listening to was the fact of their having been heeded by others, and that fact was proven only in the re-enunciation of the teaching scene. The authority of the master, in turn, was essential to that of the disciples. To the extent that they could claim to be transmitters of the wisdom of a great sage or teacher, they could present themselves in turn as teachers, or seek patronage from wealthy individuals. Thus the text, the master, and the disciples were inextricably bound together. Without the text there was no master and no disciples (beyond the lives of the individuals involved); without the master there was no authoritative text or transmitters of the text; without the disciples the text was not written or transmitted, and the master vanished together with his teachings.

Another consequence of this mode of producing texts was that the master was invented, or written as a character, in the text dedicated to him. This does not mean that some teachings were not enunciated by a historical Confucius or an actual Mencius, but such figures have left no writings of their own. All that we know of them was set down by disciples and disciples' disciples, so that we know them only as the figures who speak in the texts. They pronounce the words that the disciples attribute to them, and the latter had their own interests and programs that have left clear traces in the text.

The *Lun yu* preserves evidence of factional splits. First, passages celebrate different disciples as being the most perceptive. *Analects* 3.8 depicts a conversation in which Zixia asks about a particular ode, the master makes a cryptic reply, and the disciple poses a further question that shows he has grasped the master's meaning. The story concludes with Confucius saying that Zixia is someone fit to discuss the *Odes*. *Analects* 1.15 presents a similar story, except it is Zigong who proves himself to be perceptive. These stories, as Steven Van Zoeren has noted, reveal the *Lun yu* evolving over time as a text in which disciples not only preserve or elaborate the words of the master, but stake out claims for their unique percipience or closeness to their teacher, which enables them to act in turn as teachers.[17] Another feature of the *Lun yu* reflecting internal divisions is the fact that different disciples pose a question on the same topic and receive different answers. This is conventionally interpreted as the master's tailoring of his teachings to the needs and capacities of the questioners, but it just as likely to indicate variable traditions preserved by different lines of disciples. The increasing interest in ritual and ancient texts evinced in later chapters was also probably a factional development, with new chapters reflecting the interests of certain subtraditions.

Since the text evolved over time and reflects divisions, it is likely that different collections of quotations would have been preserved by different lines of transmission. The *Han Feizi* speaks of eight factions of *ru* in the late Warring States, and it is possible that all of them had their own versions of what would become the *Lun yu* under the Han.[18] Three versions of the text existed in the early Han, although the differences do not seem to have been great.[19] The forthcoming publication of the version discovered in a tomb at Dingxian will provide evidence regarding the degree of variation. In addition, quotations attributed to Confucius figure in the *Xunzi*, the *Mencius*, and the *Li ji*, all of which continue to seek authority in the voice of the founding master. Even some tales of Confucius in the *Zhuangzi* are related to anecdotes at the end of the *Lun yu* wherein Confucius encounters madmen or hermits who offer him advice or challenge, by example, his commitment to the world.[20] Thus by the late Warring States period many people offered different versions of Confucius' words and deeds.

While asserting their own positions, the disciples who figure in the *Lun yu* did not write texts in their own right, but expressed their thoughts through the voice of the master, or in a document assembled under his aegis. The shared master remained the common point of the school, although factions developed within it. Even those like Mencius and Xun Kuang, who formed independent textual traditions, remained loyal to Confucius through their proclamations of his exalted status.

Another text in which were inscribed the factional divisions of those proclaiming loyalty to a common master was the *Mozi*. Scholars have long recognized that the highly corrupted sections dealing with logic and military affairs were composed much later than the other chapters.[21] On the basis of linguistic analysis, Stephen Durrant has demonstrated that the dialogue chapters were written later than the chapters enunciated by Master Mo.[22] Most significant for studying the social character of the text was A. C. Graham's demonstration that the inclusion of three essays under each title reflected the division of the Mohist school, mentioned in the *Han Feizi*, into three factions. Each faction produced its own essay on the principles of Master Mo's teachings, with significant variations in the positions articulated.[23] These factional essays in turn were combined in a single text by later editors.

Erik Maeder developed Graham's analysis by going beneath the level of individual "chapters" (*pian* 篇) to try to locate smaller units which might be the *ce* (冊), bound sets of bamboo slips out of which a chapter was composed.[24] He identified recurring smaller units of text that were employed in different chapters, suggesting that the essays in the form studied by Graham were themselves "the product of a long evolution" involving work on pre-existing written materials. In some cases the same passage recurs in each of the three versions of the essay, suggesting an early date of composition. In another case two passages are parallel, except that one attributes the speech to the sage kings and the other to Master Mo. As Maeder argues, this suggests the existence of an original text containing only a quotation particle *yue* 曰, which two different traditions adapted in different directions. These and more detailed arguments indicate the sorts of written materials that the schoolmen of the Warring States had at their disposal, their manner of working on them, the constraints under which they operated, and the degree of freedom which they had for creative compilation and adaptation of pre-existing materials. It also suggests the primacy of written materials in the scholarly activities of the period.[25]

The literary *ru* and the Mohists are the only two schools that have left evidence of organized teacher-disciple transmission. Indeed, late Warring States texts such as the *Han Feizi* and the *Lü shi chun qiu* treat them as the only traditions that formed scholarly associations, as opposed to participating in literary traditions defined through texts.[26] Some later textual traditions, notably military texts such as the *Wuzi* and the *Sun Bin*, continued to be written as the recorded words of a master. However, as new traditions developed in the fourth century B.C., the enunciatory strategy of texts began to change. Texts from this time onward contained four primary elements: essays, anecdotes, aphorisms, and dialogues, often with rulers. All of these are third-person discourse in which an unspecified author develops ideas or tells stories. Before considering the significance of this shift, or rather the emergence of new forms, I will examine some of the major examples of texts from this period.

Of texts later classified as Daoist, the most studied is the *Zhuangzi*.[27] Most scholars attribute the seven "Inner Chapters" to the late fourth century B.C. The "Outer" and "Miscellaneous" chapters were written during the late Warring States and perhaps the early Han, covering one and a half or two centuries. Western scholars generally believe that the whole was put together in the early Han, perhaps under the sponsorship of Liu An, the King of Huainan who was patron of the early Daoist compendium, the *Huainanzi*.[28] Liu Xiaogan argues that since thirty passages from fourteen different chapters of the *Zhuangzi* are quoted in the *Lü shi chun qiu* and the *Han Feizi*, the *Zhuangzi* in something like its present form was completed by the 240s B.C.[29] There is general agreement that there was no organized school, in the manner of the *ru* or the Mohists, after the death of Zhuang Zhou. He had *followers* who obtained copies of writings attributed to him that were elaborated or modified to form the "Outer" and "Miscellaneous" chapters.[30] Finally, there is agreement that the Outer Chapters represent several traditions. Graham, developing the analysis of Guan Feng, divides these chapters into five sections: School of Chuang Tzu, Fragments, Primitivist, Syncretist, and Yangist. Liu, generally supported by Munro, divides them into a "transmitter faction (*shu Zhuang pai* 述莊派)" roughly equivalent to Graham's "School of Chuang Tzu," a "Huang-Lao faction (黃老派)" comparable to Graham's "Syncretists," and an "anarchist faction (*wu jun pai* 無君派)" that includes both Graham's "Primitivist" and "Yangist" traditions. Liu insists that all these factions should be regarded as followers of Zhuang Zhou, while Graham sees the "Primitivist" and "Yangist" chapters deriving from related but independent traditions, such as the "School of the Tillers (*nong jia* 農家)."

The *Zhuangzi* thus in some ways resembles the texts discussed above. A collective work adapted and expanded over more than a century, it carries markings of internal divisions. However, it is also different in some ways. First, the text is not written as a transcript of the words of the master. Although some modern scholars treat Zhuang Zhou as the author of the Inner Chapters, the compilers of the text did not share this opinion, for the Inner Chapters contain three stories of Zhuang Zhou narrated in the third person. Moreover, the Inner Chapters are simply collections of "fables, anecdotes, stories, dialogues, and debates." Even Graham admits that they are the products of later selection and editing.[31] Thus the major difference between this text and those discussed above is that it is treated as a written work with no convention of the text as transcription. This probably reflects its later origins.

The second great proto-Daoist text, the *Laozi* or *Dao de jing*, is less tractable to analysis because of its brevity and the fact that it consists of nothing but brief aphorisms. Thus it is difficult to find signs of the social character of its production within the text. Its dating also remains controversial. Most Western scholars, following the line of argument initiated in the pages of *Gu shi bian* 古史辨, agree on a date of between 350 and 250 B.C. Reports of finds of copies of the *Dao de jing* in two fourth-century B.C. tombs suggest that the date should be moved toward the earlier part of the suggested period, but no conclusions can be drawn until these are published. Recently several Chinese scholars have revived the traditional theory based on the *Shi ji* that it was written by an older contemporary of Confucius. However, they have presented no convincing arguments refuting the evidence that it uses terms and ideas that appear in texts only after the middle of the Warring States period.[32]

In spite of the difficulties, Michael LaFargue has attempted to make sense of the *Laozi* through a model of its origins within the world which we know from other Warring States texts, particularly the *Mencius*. He argues that the text was constructed from oral sayings employed for teaching by a school committed to a dual program of personal self-cultivation through meditation and reform of political practice through the systematic undermining or reversal of contemporary values. On the basis of this model he is able to explain not only the sense of individual aphorisms, but also the principles underlying their grouping in chapters. Moreover, through internal evidence and evidence from contemporary texts he distinguishes aphorisms from added commentary. He even distinguishes aphorisms intended for use in debates with other schools or appeals to rulers from those employed to train more advanced pupils.[33] Although the argument is circular, it provides the clearest reading of the *Dao de jing* yet attained, and it fits well with what we know of the textual and intellectual practices in the period.

Like the *Zhuangzi*, the *Dao de jing* is written entirely in the third person, with no implicit teaching scene. Indeed, a master to whom it could be attributed had to be invented after the fact. With an otherwise unknown author invented as a ground for the text, and its use of the title *jing* (經 "canon" or "classic"), this work marks an emerging trend that will be discussed in chapter 7. The decision to compose a text entirely of aphorisms, like that of the writers of the *Zhuangzi* to intermix parable,

poetry, and anecdote with brief philosophic arguments, may reflect a rejection on
the part of the authors of the formal, reasoned prose that was developed by the
Mohists and dominated third-century texts.

The third century is characterized by the emergence of the essay and dialogue
forms. The *Xunzi*, the *Shang Jun shu*, and the *Han Feizi* (parts of which are almost
certainly second century) all contain extensive pieces of sustained argument written in the third person with no convention of quotation. Another important development is the staging of dialogues between rulers and masters. Such set pieces
already figured in the *Mencius*, but they were interspersed among dialogues with
disciples and speeches attributed to the master.[34] From the third century on there
emerged works composed of dialogues with rulers, such as the texts compiled into
the *Zhan guo ce* or the related materials from Mawangdui, the *Yanzi chun qiu*, the *Tai
gong liu tao*, and the chapters of the *Guanzi* depicting dialogues between Guan Zhong
and Lord Huan of Qi. Although primarily composed of essays, the *Shang Jun shu*
begins with a debate staged in the presence of the lord of Qin, and the *Han Feizi*
begins with a memorial to the king of Qin and a debate between Han Fei and Li Si
in the form of writings addressed to the monarch. The received text of the *Wei
Liaozi* also begins with a single exchange between the ruler and Wei Liao, although
it is possible that this was a late addition to attach the text to a celebrated name.[35]
In the *Xunzi* the chapter "Debate on Warfare" consists of a debate staged before
the King of Zhao, and the chapter "The Effectiveness of the *Ru*" contains one
section in which Xun Kuang lectures the king of Qin on the value of *ru* to the state.
Finally, the later chapters of the *Mozi* also contain dialogues between Master Mo
and rulers of states.

These shifts in the enunciatory form taken by the philosophical texts of the
Warring States indicate several changes. First, they suggest that with the emergence
of traditions that did not form strong associations, the teaching scene became
secondary to the textual transmission. The multiplication of schools also led to
interschool polemics, which encouraged the development of forms of argument.
These appeared as early as the Mohist assault on the *ru* (see next section) and
developed into sophist and later Mohist discussions of language and proofs.[36] In a
world of competing traditions, the authority of individual masters took second
place to the persuasive power of arguments, and tight teacher-disciple bonds were
replaced by more open, text-based groupings. The emphasis on discussions with
rulers or debates in their presence indicates the increasing importance of the state
to the scholarly traditions (see next section). Finally, as will be discussed in chapter
7, participants in the interschool polemics of the third century, struck by the increasing divisions in the intellectual realm, asserted authority through claims to
possess an encompassing wisdom of which all the other schools grasped only one
element. This encompassing wisdom took the form of encyclopedic works (in the
original sense of "comprehensive cycle of learning") claiming to contain all necessary knowledge, or of fundamental texts claiming to reveal the hidden, constant
truths running through all changes.[37] As such works took pride of place in the

intellectual world of the late Warring States, writings of individual masters were reduced to a secondary position. Thus the appearance of the master as an author, an isolated and individual voice whose disciples were excluded from the scene of his text, was a function of, or a step toward, his disappearance as the fundamental textual authority. In Chinese philosophy "authorship" emerged in the space vacated by the shift of authority to the "classic."

SCHOLARLY TRADITIONS AND THE STATE

Through much of imperial Chinese history scholarly activities were primarily a route to office holding, and the highest ambition of the intellectual was state service. Because social and political order were central to most Warring States philosophies, the later situation has often been read back into this period. To do so, however, is a serious error, a form of intellectual short-circuit that prevents full understanding of the relations of scholarship to political authority, both in the Warring States and in later, imperial China. The truth is that although the schools and the state ultimately converged, in the earliest stages of their history they were distinct and often opposed. The divergence in attitudes and values formulated at this time was never entirely effaced, and the role of scholars in later Chinese history was fundamentally shaped by the fact of this initial opposition.

Forming associations outside the state sphere at a time when the state resisted such associations, the philosophical schools formulated theories of political order and ideal kingship on the basis of the values and practices cultivated within their own circles. These theories, claiming authority through the complex of master/disciple/text, challenged the state order, which the schoolmen accepted only to the extent that it conformed to their models. Even as the schools were drawn into the state sphere through changing patterns of patronage, and even as they increasingly wrote for kings and included kings within their teaching scene, their claims to direct the conduct of kings remained an assertion of ultimate authority. The master became a double of the king, and the relation of the one to the other was marked by a degree of tension and opposition. The question of careers in state service for participants in the text-based philosophical traditions will be discussed in the next section. This section will examine attitudes of the schools to the political order in which they emerged, or which emerged together with them, and demonstrate this tension between textual tradition and administrative polity.

One of the few works that examines the sociology of scholarly associations and highlights their rejection of the state is Robert Eno's *The Confucian Creation of Heaven*. This book is devoted to the activities and concerns of the nontextual *ru*, and it contains both serious weaknesses and important insights. Eno argues that the *ru* were communities of men pursuing sagehood through self-cultivation in isolation from the state, and who developed prescriptive social programs based on the cultivation of ritual, music, and personal virtue. Political action was possible, but only after self-cultivation and only in the state of a virtuous ruler.[38] While he makes part stand for whole and downplays the significance of the text formations around the figures of Confucius, Mencius, and Xun Kuang, his approach is a healthy corrective to the modern scholarly consensus that interprets the *ru* entirely through their writings and philosophy. His model explains the ambiguous status of the Confucian school in the lists of masters. It is also valuable for emphasizing the ambitions of the *ru* outside the realm of politics.

In fact, a systematic study of references to government service in the *Lun yu* and the *Mencius* demonstrates that even those *ru* who composed texts espoused attitudes similar to those sketched by Eno. The *Lun yu* repeatedly emphasizes that one should worry only about developing one's own worth without concern for recognition by others, including recognition by the ruler. Confucius himself, although expressing a desire to serve in the proper circumstances, is depicted only declining offices or resigning from them.[39] Other passages state that simply being a filial son is equivalent to being in government, that office can only be properly obtained through benevolence, that the master was pleased when a disciple declined to take office, that disciples who were capable of holding office were not benevolent, that one should refuse service in a bad state and leave it, that abdicating office was the highest virtue, that holding office in the absence of the Way was shameful, that an appointment would ruin a man, and that one could not work in a government alongside petty men.[40] Confucius rejected discussion of law, administration, or military strategy, while insisting on the possibility of rule through ritual and example, even by nonofficials.[41] The few passages that endorse government service treat it as a secondary extension of moral cultivation, or as an act of desperation by the aging Confucius.[42]

These do not constitute a rejection of state service as such, but they make it conditional on the ruler's commitment to the Confucian school's program. The Confucian scholar demanded total acceptance of his Way or withdrew from service, and this Way entailed a rejection of the major institutions of the Warring States polity. The Confucian school developed an imaginary counterstate based on distinct principles and practices, and demanded that a ruler adopt this alternate model as the condition of their accepting appointment.

The advocacy of transforming the state and refusal to serve in those adhering to conventional Warring States practice runs throughout the *Mencius*. Repeatedly rulers ask Mencius for advice on administration, and he responds each time with a blanket call for "benevolent" government and following "the Way of Yao and Shun." The specifics of this policy are sketchy, but suggestions include the abolition of all taxes in the markets and at the frontiers, a drastic reduction or abolition of land taxes, the restoration of the "well-field" system and the consequent abolition of private property in land, the end of mutual responsibility for crimes, a restoration or preservation of hereditary office, and a refusal to inflict punishments. The radical nature of these policies is indicated by the fact that Mencius acknowledges himself to be the only man in Qi advocating such a program.[43]

The text also denounces discussion of military affairs as criminal, and dismisses the use of force with the simple formula that the benevolent ruler will have no match because everyone will support him.[44] Citing the sages of antiquity, he argues that territory is not necessary for security or conquest. He further refuses to discuss, or savagely denounces, both the hegemons who dominated the seventh and sixth centuries B.C., and the architects of the systems of alliances that defined his own political world.[45] In short, he calls for the total abolition of the reforms of the preceding centuries, and the restoration of the world of antiquity as he imagines it to have been. When the ruler of Deng complains about being a small state trapped between large ones, Mencius actually suggests that he should imitate the ancestral Zhou kings by taking his people and moving elsewhere. Acknowledging that this might not be possible, he advises the king to cultivate his virtue and await destruction.[46]

Besides advocating the abolition of the political present, the *Mencius* carries forward the *Lun yu*'s refusal to serve an unworthy prince. This takes the form of strictures against compromising moral principle for the sake of office, and the comparison of such behavior to illicit sexual union; lists of failings by the ruler that justify resignation; and repeated citations of the examples of Bo Yi—who would not serve in a state where any bad people lived—and Confucius—who was more accommodating but would still not serve an unworthy ruler. The text praises Shun, who would have abandoned the empire to help his father; describes the trials and humiliations of holding office; denounces someone who used his learning to secure a post; proclaims that one should never take office for money unless starving, and then only a low position; insists that the honors bestowed by Heaven (moral virtues) are more important than those bestowed by men (office); presents a hierarchy of servants/ministers, with those of the ruler at the bottom and those of Heaven at the top; and explicitly excludes political authority from a list of the things in which a gentleman delights. It condemns as criminals all those who fill the ruler's coffers or expand his territory, that is, all officials of the Warring States who performed their duties.[47]

Going a step beyond the *Lun yu*, the *Mencius* stipulates that the worthy scholar-official should be nobler than the king and should, in practice, demand his obedience. It argues that the minister should be the king's teacher and that as such he cannot be summoned into the royal presence. Instead, the king must go to the teacher/minister and treat him with the highest respect. Moreover, the text states that if the ruler will not listen to remonstrances then the minister should retire, which means that he will serve as minister only so long as the king obeys his dictates. This conflation of the role of scholar and king, or substitution of the former for the latter, became a fundamental theme in late Warring States Confucianism. It finds expression in Mencius' speculation that he might be the one chosen by Heaven to restore the world more than seven hundred years after the establishment of the Zhou.[48] As Benjamin Schwartz has noted, much of Mencius' writing is informed by an almost religious sense of his own vocation as world savior at a time of epochal transition.[49] This probably accounts for his refusal to brook any compromise with the world as it existed.

While the *Xunzi* is more interested in the political realities of its day than the *Mencius*, and more sympathetic to the innovations of the preceding centuries, it carries forward the position of the earlier *ru*. The text upholds the ideal of a king who governs through ritual principles and virtue as *the* model for all rulers. Later essays grudgingly accept the practices of the Spring and Autumn hegemons when no true king exists, but they condemn recent developments. The *Xunzi* maintains that the scholar's virtue is more important than title or salary, and that consequently office should be held only under a ruler who is virtuous in Confucian terms. The true "ministers of the altars of the grain and soil," argues one passage, are those who remonstrate, quarrel, and oppose the ruler, unless the ruler is a sage. Indeed, it states that the true scholar should not respond to a ruler who does not pose the correct questions. It condemns the rulers of its day as treacherous thieves and violent pillagers, the officials as greedy and grasping, and the leading political figures as "sham ministers." Again, it argues that the great *ru* are greater than the "feudal lords"—regarding the ruler's claims to the royal title as usurpation—and that Confucius was greater than any ruler of the period and surpassed all the states. In what is probably an early essay, the *Xunzi* denounces rulers who devote themselves to the accumulation of wealth and the building up of strong armies, that is, those activities that defined the Warring States polity. In several places it adopts the Mencian policies of abolishing taxes on markets and goods in transit, drastically cutting agricultural taxes, and opening up forests and wastelands for use. Finally, one passage insists that the present world is marked by the separation of scholars and rulers.

> The rulers who desire this [good government and its fruits] are packed shoulder to shoulder, and no generation is without scholars who could establish it. So why for a thousand years have they [rulers and scholars] not come together? It is because rulers are not unbiased and public-spirited [*gong* 公], and ministers are not loyal. Rulers expel the worthy [*ru* scholars] and are biased in their appointments. Ministers fight for office and are jealous of the worthy. This is why they do not come together.[50]

The reality of these denunciations of current practice, refusals to serve, and claims of regal authority in the role of teacher/adviser are confirmed by the adversaries of the *ru*, specifically the textual traditions devoted to administrative reforms. Both the *Shang Jun shu* and the *Han Feizi* denounce the scholars of their day who apply the models of the ancient sages to the present, use received Zhou documents such as the *Odes* and *Documents* to criticize current practices and cast doubts on the law, set up their "private teaching (*si xue* 私學)" or "private righteousness (*si yi* 私義)" against public regulations, treat refusal to serve as a form of moral heroism, and try to master the prince through remonstrances. These actions, notes the *Han Feizi*, transform the relation of minister to ruler into that of teacher to disciple:

> Forcibly remonstrating in order to master their prince, if their words are heeded and affairs carried out, then it is like the relation of teacher to disciple.

In response to the claims of the *ru*, these theoreticians of administration insist that the law should be the only authoritative text within the frontiers, and the officials the only teachers.[51] Thus the oppositional stance of the *ru* and their claim to authority over the ruler were clear to their contemporaries.

Another challenge to state authority by the text-based *ru* traditions is the mobility of the school. In the Warring States period rulers tried to fix the common people in place through registration, while the declining numbers of local courts due to conquest meant that physical mobility became a hallmark of authority. We have already seen this in the use of processions and spirit travels.[52] The Confucius of the *Lun yu*, at first restricted to the state of Lu, later made visits to Qi as an observer and to Wei in order to arrange music. In some of these travels he was accompanied by disciples. In one anecdote he declines office in a foreign state. This pattern becomes even more prominent in the *Mencius*, wherein the eponymous master travels widely and converses with kings in Wei and Qi, and lesser lords in other states.[53] In moving freely from state to state, the schoolmen arrogated to themselves a status above that of ordinary commoners, at the same time that they refused the authority of any particular state.

The second school to appear in the records, or the first if we treat the *ru* as a social category, is the Mohist. Its canon provides few details of the interaction of masters and disciples, but several features can be deduced. First, much of the Mohist philosophy is an explicit rejection of Confucian doctrine. The denunciation of music and elaborate funeral rites, the advocacy of concern for all (in contrast to the family-oriented ethics of the Confucians), the doctrine of "conforming upward" which makes the state the source of morality, the insistence on the "elevation of worth" (in contrast to the *Mencius*, which still sometimes advocated hereditary officials), the insistence on the active role of ghosts in the world and the denial of a fate determined by Heaven, all contradict central teachings of the Confucian school. This shows how schools defined themselves through systematic opposition to other positions constituted in the intellectual field of the period. Once the first teaching had emerged, it was no longer sufficient to simply assert one's own wisdom in order to attract students or patrons. One also had to demonstrate how it was superior to others who claimed to be masters of truth. Thus the Mohist school marks the beginning of interschool polemics in the period, and in order to dispute more effectively it also became the first to elaborate principles of argument.[54]

The differences in Mohist philosophy also led to a distinctive relation to the states and those who entered their service. Denouncing emphasis on family ties, elaborate rituals, and music, they rejected the underpinnings of the old Zhou elite and those who maintained intellectual or emotional ties to its world. By contrast, the principles of promoting through talent, conforming to superiors, and treating all equally without regard to family ties were essential to emerging state practice. The Mohists' devotion to military activities and imposition of a military discipline on their organization also led to closer links with the states of the period.

This military bent of the Mohist school appears in an anecdote portraying Mo Di as a craftsman and military technician. Hearing that Gongshu Pan has invented a scaling ladder with which Chu will attack the capital of Song, Master Mo proceeds to Chu, demonstrates that his machines can counter everything that his rival's could manage, and argues that it will do no good to kill him because he already has 300 disciples operating engines of defense on the walls of Song.[55] Here Master Mo's disciples act as a military unit who uphold his doctrine of defensive war in the service of small states.

Other anecdotes depict the Mohists as a disciplined community, or rather three communities, for by the late Warring States they had split into factions denouncing one another as heretics. Members were dispatched on missions by their chief, they were obliged to contribute funds to the organization, and any disobedience could lead to expulsion. In one anecdote a bereaved father of a Mohist disciple killed in battle upbraided the master. This indicates that military action was one aspect of Mohist education. Indeed, the last two chapters (卷 *juan*) of the Mohist canon are devoted to the technology and methods of organization used in defending besieged cities.[56]

The links of the Mohist school with military discipline and the practice of warfare also figure in other sources. These provide further information about the organization of the school and the nature of ties between master and disciple. One anecdote in the *Lü shi chun qiu* tells how the Mohist master Meng Sheng received a tally from the prince of Yangcheng and swore an oath (*yue* 約) that on the matching of the tally he would obey any orders. When Yangcheng was attacked by the state of Chu, Meng Sheng resolved to die in order to fulfill his oath. A disciple urged him not to die in a doomed cause and thereby endanger the survival of the Mohist school. Meng Sheng replied that he was both friend and servant of the prince of Yangcheng. Betrayal of his oath would mean that disciplined armies, true friends, and loyal servants would no longer be found among the Mohists. Death was the only means to perpetuate the "duty/righteousness of the Mohists (*Mo zhe zhi yi* 墨者之義)" and thus preserve the school. In the ensuing battle Meng Sheng died along with one hundred and eighty of his followers. By the end of the Warring States period the Mohist school was identified with warfare, so in one early Han text this is set in parallel opposition to the Confucian school's dedication to virtue and the Way.[57]

Liang Qichao recognized that the Mohist insistence on loyalty to the death for the sake of one's word and one's friends was closely linked to the ethic of the "wandering bravoes" described earlier. Moreover, as Masubuchi Tatsuo has pointed out, this ethic shared by the Mohists and the bravoes is part of the increasing emphasis on interpersonal ties created by oaths.[58] The linkage of violence, loyalty, and discipline figures in another anecdote about the Mohist school preserved in the *Lü shi chun qiu*. The only son of a Mohist master living in Qin committed murder, but the king of Qin offered to spare the boy out of respect for the scholar's great age and his lack of other progeny. In exchange for this favor the king demanded obedience. The master replied that according to Mohist law (*Mo zhe zhi fa* 墨者之法) whoever killed someone was put to death, and whoever injured someone was punished. Insisting that he was obliged to follow this law, he had his son executed. Since the laws were based on "bonds," this story is linked to the preceding one, and reveals another facet of the organization of the Mohist school.[59] In adopting their own code of laws, the Mohist organization assumed a statelike character, particularly notable when combined with their military capacities. While more closely tied to the states than were the *ru*, they still insisted on maintaining their independence from royal authority, and gave precedence to their own laws over the will of the ruler.

The *ru* and the Mohists were the only traditions that formed disciplined associations and hence were recognized as schools in Warring States writings. The other so-called schools were textual traditions formed around writings attributed to a particular master. Some of these traditions had affinities or common roots that led to their being drawn together as bibliographic categories under the Han, and these affinities included common attitudes toward the state. One such cluster of textual traditions was formed by the texts that were linked to the practice of meditative self-cultivation that ultimately emerged as Daoism.[60] While the *ru* would in theory have accepted state service if the ruler adopted their program, and the Mohists sought service as military men organized into their own units, the meditation-based schools initially rejected all service and devoted themselves to self-cultivation. The predecessors of these schools were the followers of Yang Zhu, who advocated "keeping one's nature intact, protecting one's genuineness, and not letting the body be tied to things."[61] While these maxims do not imply an attitude toward the state, a chapter in the *Lü shi chun qiu* linked to Yangist thought is devoted to stories of men who rejected world rulership in order to preserve their natures. It was doubtless this rejection of even the most honored form of public service that provoked Mencius' remark that Yang Zhu would not pluck out one hair on his body to benefit the world.[62]

Prominent among the texts dealing with self-cultivation through meditation was the *Zhuangzi*. It is notable for espousing in its earlier sections a radical rejection of public service. The "Inner Chapters" include denunciations of those who serve a prince, tales of worthies who rejected the rule of the empire as beneath them, and an account of a perfected man so wondrous that "the dust from his body could be moulded into a Yao or Shun." One of the "Inner Chapters" is devoted entirely to tales of individuals who through self-cultivation acquired the power to influence others without taking office, or who through cultivating uselessness escaped the unwanted attentions of the government. Another chapter tells of sages whose powers transcend those of kings, or who scorned worldly kingship as a form of bullying or drudgery.[63] All these anecdotes proclaim a rejection of government and state service.

Later chapters develop these themes and present additional strictures against participation in government. One, clearly in the Yangist tradition, is devoted to stories of men who refuse to accept the rule of the empire. Other passages argue that holding office is a form of servile fawning scorned by sages, that those who take office are destroyed by it, and that living in poverty is better than living at court. Stories portray Zhuang Zhou comparing taking office to being a sacrificial ox or tortoise, because one surrenders one's life for short-lived glory. In other anecdotes he compares serving the king to acting as a physician who earns his pay by licking piles, or to eating a half-rotten rat. In conversation with Confucius, Lao Dan argues that the sage-kings were responsible for plunging the world into confusion, and that Confucius was lucky to find no ruler to employ him. The idea attributed to Lao Dan, that the state is responsible for the sufferings of the world, is developed in the four chapters Graham has labeled "primitivist." The chapters devoted to the "Great Man (大人 *da ren*)" likewise argue that the sage-kings, mythic creators of the state and prototypes of the Warring States monarchs, were nothing compared to the sage who understands the vastness and total indifference of the universe.[64]

The other major text that became identified as Daoist in the Han was the *Dao de jing*. This work contains passages that echo or anticipate the "primitivist" chapters of the *Zhuangzi* by asserting the existence of a primitive paradise of autarchic villages ruined by the sage-kings' introduction of moral virtues and productive technologies. The *Dao de jing* does not denounce the current fact of monarchy, and many of the later passages of the text are devoted to advice for the ruler, but it insists that political authority be based in meditative self-cultivation and sagely understanding. In this way and through calls for the inversion of conventional values, the *Dao de jing* still participates in the oppositional stance that we have thus far observed as characteristic of the relations of the schools to the state.[65]

Another cluster of schools was formed by the textual traditions that produced the military treatises. In contrast with the *ru*, Mohist, and proto-Taoist schools, military thinkers were firmly tied to the state. They had no body of doctrine or practice to be cultivated outside the state sphere, and consequently no base for opposition and no claim to superiority to the rulers of the day. Nevertheless, the military treatises articulated a form of limited independence and opposition within the overarching authority of the state. They claimed that due to his need to respond immediately to shifting circumstances, the commander in the field could not be subject to the ruler. The commander took up his office through the ruler's appointment, and he submitted himself to the ruler on his return, but for the duration of the campaign he was to be lord in his own domain with the power of life and death over his men.[66] Thus as in the cases of the other traditions, the schoolmen's claim to expertise contained within it an assertion of some degree of independence from the dictates of the state.

Even closer to the state were the traditions of the theorists of administration, whose texts would be classified as "legalist" under the Han. These works, of which the only surviving examples are the *Shang Jun shu* and the *Han Feizi*, articulated and defended at length the new patterns of landholding, taxation, military service, and population registration. They also espoused a powerful monarchy, and elaborated theories for controlling bureaucratic administrations. Nevertheless, even in the act of creating theoretical underpinnings for the Warring States polity, they created a distance between themselves and the actually existing order that led to a form of opposition.

First, as noted in chapter 1, the Qin punishments revealed in the Yunmeng documents rejected the absolute indifference to the status of the accused advocated in the legalist texts. As is often the case, philosophic consistency entailed a rejection of actual practice. The Warring States preserved versions of traditional practices, such as fiefs for high officials, and enfeoffed lords dominated many courts. The execution of Lord Shang, leading reformer in fourth-century Qin, demonstrates the scale of resistance to the full legalist program. Even in the early third century the Qin court was dominated by Wu Rang and a clique of newly created nobles who treated conquered territory as a source of personal income. Calls for a regime based on invariant laws and manipulative "techniques" was in its way as much a rejection of current practice as appeals for the restoration of feudalism.

Finally, the very act of writing texts constituted a challenge to the Warring States polity. This dilemma is articulated in a passage in the *Han Feizi* which, true to its own logic but perhaps not entirely conscious of its own implications, states:

> Now the people within the border all speak of social order. As for those who collect the methods of Lord Shang and Guan Zhong [i.e., legalist writings], every household has them, but the state grows poorer. [This is because] those who speak of agriculture are numerous, but those who grasp a plow are few. . . . If they cultivate literary studies and practice fine speech, then without the toil of agriculture they have the fruit of wealth. Without the danger of warfare they have the honor of noble rank. Who would not act thus? Therefore the state of the discerning ruler has no documents or writing on bamboo strips but takes the law as its teaching. They have no words of the former kings, but take the officials to be their teachers.[67]

Similar passages calling for the state to establish its administrative documents as the unique teaching and its officials as the only teachers appear elsewhere in late Warring States texts.[68] In a state where all wealth and honor were to come through agriculture and warfare, the schoolman and his texts, even those devoted to administration or the army, had no place and indeed constituted a positive menace.

The text speaks of the *Shang Jun shu* and the *Guanzi*, but it stands condemned by its own charges. Only administrative documents could be allowed in the properly governed state. The writings of the schoolmen were by definition subversive.

The above text could serve as an explanation for the permanent and inevitable opposition between the masters and the state. However, it is not complete. When the policy espoused in this passage was put into practice by Qin Shihuang, who banned the private ownership of the texts of the "hundred schools" and stipulated that only officials could serve as teachers, an explicit exception was made for technical writings devoted to subjects such as medicine, divination, agriculture, and forestry.[69] This indicates a division in the Warring States intellectual field between writings of the philosophical masters and texts devoted to techniques for mastering the natural world. This distinction must be briefly examined in order to fully understand the relation of the philosophical schools to the state.

Experts on nature in the Warring States included astrologers, diviners, physicians, almanac makers, and experts on agriculture and forestry. Anecdotes in early texts tell of such individuals serving the nobility, but their writings had been lost. Evidence that they had textual traditions like those of the philosophers came only from biographies in the *Shi ji* and the titles of vanished texts in the *Han shu* bibliographic monograph.[70] However, excavations since the 1970s have revealed manuscripts on divination, astrology, hemerology (auspicious and inauspicious days), demonology, and medicine. These date from the fourth to the mid-second century B.C. The frequency and geographic range of these finds indicate their importance as well as their acceptance among the Warring States elite.[71]

Thus it was not teacher-disciple or text-based transmissions as such that challenged the state, but something distinctive to the philosophical masters. That "something" was indicated in Li Si's memorial calling for the suppression of the schools, as well as analogous passages in the legalist texts. It consisted of the systematic criticism of present policy. This criticism was based on the masters' claims to a wisdom that gave them the right to be monarchs or to command them. In contrast with the experts on nature, who provided technical services to assist administration, the philosophical masters offered comprehensive doctrines and practices useful only at the level of the monarch. The schoolmen challenged the state by claiming to possess truths and methods that defined monarchy.

This idea will be developed further in the next section, so here I will sketch the form of these claims. Chapter 1 demonstrated how proto-Daoist meditative techniques and theories of sagely perception of cosmic patterns were adopted by the legalists to underpin both techniques for controlling officials and the practice of establishing legal codes. It also showed how proto-Daoist texts argued that kingship depended on wisdom derived from meditation and philosophical contemplation. Actual kings were treated as destroyers of the natural order, and only hidden sages or kings acting as sages could achieve peace. The *ru* insisted on a government based on the virtues and the rituals of which they were the masters. They held up as models of kingship the ancient sages whose practices and texts they alone still understood. They made serving the king conditional on his adoption of their models and policies. In the case of the *Mencius*, they even dreamed of reshaping the world as monarchs in all but name, and the role of de facto monarch was attributed by the *Mencius* to Confucius as author of the *Spring and Autumnn Annals*.[72] Thus all the masters claimed to be the unique holders of the secrets of kingship, and as such they claimed the ability to define the monarch and dictate his policies. From the perspective of the ruler, such claims would inevitably appear as a challenge or a threat.

The exception is the writings of the military authors who claimed not authority over the monarch but independence from him within their realm of expertise. They thus resembled the experts on nature, with their technical expertise, more than the philosophers, with their claims to dictate the forms and practices of supreme authority. It is probably for this reason that the military texts do not figure in the lists of masters that began to appear in the interschool polemics of the third and second centuries B.C. The identification of the military arts as a technical skill rather than as the kingly Way grew more pronounced as texts on warfare became more specialized in nature, or were devoted to the application of *yin/yang* or "Five Phases" thought derived from the mantic traditions.[73] For this reason, like the medical and astronomical/hemerological/divinatory traditions, they were listed as a separate category in the first Han bibliography, and compiled by a specialist rather than by Liu Xiang himself.[74]

SOCIAL AND ECONOMIC BASES OF THE TRADITIONS

Having defined schools through their commitment to a common master and the transmission of a textual tradition, and noted their enduring tension with the state, we must examine the bases of their independence and ability to survive over time, that is, their economic and social foundations.

Some modern scholars have argued that since state administration required the skillful and efficient handling of documents, and since the schoolmen were trained in using texts, the schools and schoolmen provided state service for their income. A standard formulation of this thesis appears in Hsu Cho-yun's *Ancient China in Transition*.[75] Hsu states that the schools emerged "to meet the demand for training the new administrative experts and strategists," and that Confucius was the first to found such a school. According to Hsu, the students acquired a "liberal education" and moral training that made them "highly appreciated by rulers who had reason to be uneasy about unethically ambitious students." Thus Confucius "opened up a new and lasting path by which any low-born but able young man could gain high office by his own competence."

Almost every proposition in this argument is wrong. The schools were not created to train administrators for the state. As we saw above they were all ideologically in opposition to the state as it was then constituted. Their educational programs were devoted to skills that were of no use for administrators—the *Odes* and the *Documents*, ritual, music, meditation, linguistic paradoxes, rules of argument, principles by which a king should control his ministers, and so on. Whereas successful officials such as Li Kui, Shen Buhai, Shang Yang, Wu Qi, and others attracted followers, or at least men who wrote under their names, none of the leading scholars from the text-based traditions gained a significant office. Certain individuals, such as Shang Yang, Fan Sui, Cai Ze, and Li Si studied in their youth and then acceded directly to high office through attracting the attention of a ruler. Doubtless other students were inspired by their example to hope that philosophical training might lead to a position as adviser. However, these were obviously exceptional cases distinct from the careers of most schoolmen. It is noteworthy that they obtained position through gaining the ear of the *ruler* and becoming chief advisers, the very position assumed in the teachings of the masters. This has nothing to do with the recruitment of administrators, who rose through the ranks of service or were appointed by lower officials.[76]

The tombs at Yunmeng, Baoshan, and Fangmatan provide us with the first real evidence of the literary culture of administrators in the period, and the evidence is striking. The tombs contain administrative documents and texts from the occult traditions used in government, but the writings of the schoolmen do not figure in their collections. An argument from silence is weak, and there is no reason to think that no administrator had any knowledge of the texts of the philosophical schools. Nevertheless, on the basis of the evidence currently available, one must conclude that the schoolmen and their texts were, at best, peripheral to those who were charged with the daily running of the state. The "Bian nian ji 編年記" from Yunmeng sketches the career of a local official, and it shows him rising through military service followed by a local appointment.[77]

Finally, one cannot disprove that rulers were eager to recruit *ru* because of their moral character, but the world of the courts portrayed in the texts of the period does not place a high value on conspicuous moral posturing. Certainly the *Han Feizi* criticizes employing men who are devoted to the preservation and display of their moral purity.[78]

In assuming a direct connection between literary studies and state service, based on that found in later imperial China, this argument not only ignores the entire body of received Warring States texts and those found in tombs, it also produces a radically impoverished model of the links between writing and authority that existed in the period. As we have already seen in part and shall see even more in subsequent pages, the links were less direct than those suggested by Hsu, and they involved many more aspects of the civilization of the period. Certain features of later Chinese political and religious practice can be understood only by explaining how the schools actually became sources of authority.

If scholarship was not primarily a road to office, then its economic bases lay elsewhere. However, to understand the social role of the philosophical schools, their economic foundations, and the links between the two, it is necessary to situate them within the broader intellectual field of the Warring States period.[79] Several social roles involved the mastery of texts. The means of obtaining a livelihood, the identity of customers or patrons, the type of texts employed, and their use all depended on which role one assumed. Moreover, the roles did not evolve independently, but by a process of exclusion or opposition in which each form of literary activity was defined by the alternative activities that it rejected. One example of this process was the manner in which disciples of Confucius or Mencius defined themselves as those who would not serve rulers pursuing conventional policies, and denounced as enemies those who did so. This opposition, however, is but one case in a larger field of oppositional stances by which the literary field of the Warring States was established and through which participants defined themselves and claimed authority.

The foundational role of all literary activities was the teacher, and teaching was one way for a textually trained person to earn a living. Already in the *Lun yu* Confucius says that he allowed poor men to study with him as long as they offered a token gift.[80] This indicates that a gift/payment was necessary and that richer men might pay a considerable amount. Other texts refer to receiving gifts and payment, and to teaching as a road to success. The *Xunzi* states that if a disciple becomes successful and rich he should remember his teacher. The *Han Feizi*, for its part, says that calculating from the selfish, material interests of the boorish, petty man, the best career would be to undertake textual studies and become an eminent teacher. The *Zhuangzi* describes the elaborate clothing, the ornate chariots, and the fine horses that Zi Gong earned through teaching.[81] These refer to teachers at a high level. They presuppose lower levels where humble teachers instructed children in basic literacy. Although it is possible that such education was entirely the responsibility of parents or clan, it is more likely that there were tutors in wealthy families and perhaps even village school masters. Such schools are mentioned in the *Mencius*.[82]

Another role available to the literate was to acquire training in a technical field—medicine, astronomy/hemerology, divination—and sell one's expertise in the market or seek service with a lord. Such individuals are mentioned in the received texts, and more have appeared in the technical and occult literature discovered in tombs. Thus the medical treatise assigned the title "Shi wen 十問" found at Mawangdui depicts the physician Wen Zhi 文摯 in an audience with King Wei of Qi 齊威王 (r. 357–320), founder of the Jixia "academy" (see p. 77). At the beginning of his presentation, Wen Zhi mentions that his medical knowledge fills three hundred fascicles, indicating the important role that writing played in such disciplines.[83] Chapter 105 of *Shiji* also tells of two physicians, one from the Warring States period and one from the early Han, who treated both commoners and members of the nobility. The Warring States physician Bian Que 扁鵲 based his treatments on a magic text revealed to him by a divine being. Although Yamada Keiji has shown that Bian Que was created through the conflation of the traditions of several early physicians, including Wen Zhi, his story still preserves evidence of earning a living as a doctor in the period.[84]

The Baoshan inscriptions provide evidence of men working as professional diviners. The inscriptions contain records of divination both by tortoise shell and by yarrow stalk. Not only are the diviners listed by name, but the shells and the stalks that they employ also receive titles. The strips give divinatory records for the last years of the life of the deceased, and they deal largely with finding a cure for his ailment. The pattern of divination followed that of the Shang oracle inscriptions: a subject was presented and judged to be auspicious or inauspicious, and this was followed by a second divination to determine if the sacrificial offerings had been accepted. The same topic could be divined several times using both methods.[85] Thus in the final years of his life the occupant of the tomb employed a staff of diviners in an attempt to protect his health. Other divinations deal with his career prospects, so it is possible that such diviners had been employed throughout his professional life.

Further evidence of professional, text-based diviners appears in the chapter entitled "Yao 要" ('Summa') in the *Yi jing* manuscript found at Mawangdui. This chapter contains a justification or apologia attributed to Confucius for the use of the text. He states that he seeks only the virtue in the text, and in life he engages in virtuous conduct, benevolence, and righteousness without seeking blessings. In this way he contrasts himself with the astrologers and shamans (*shi wu* 史巫) who follow the same path, that is, also use the *Yi jing*, but seek a different destination, presumably utilitarian guidance in decision making and personal profit through divining for others.[86] The passage demonstrates not only the existence of professional diviners employing the *Yi jing*, but it also shows the schoolmen trying to separate themselves from those who employ texts as a source of technical lore to be used for profit. The *Mozi* likewise contains an anecdote which ridicules a practitioner of hemerology.[87] Just as the schools defined themselves through opposition to those who studied to obtain official posts, they distinguished themselves from those who sold technical expertise.

Another way that men used texts to support themselves, which was closer to the training of the text-based *ru*, was by providing ritual expertise for those performing ceremonies. Such services, like those of the diviners cited above, could have been sold to great families, the courts of lesser states, or the households of newly enfeoffed nobles. The *Xunzi* describes with contempt these "vulgar *ru*" who wore bizarre costumes, insisted on following the kings of antiquity, and sought to live off the generosity of those whom they duped with their talk of the ancient ways. The *Mozi* also denounces *ru* who "sell" ritual expertise, although it makes no attempt to distinguish "vulgar" *ru* from a higher variety.[88] The *Mencius*, *Zuo zhuan*, and the *Xunzi* assert that following established practices is not true ritual, which is defined by underlying principles of social order that the sage must constantly adapt to the changing needs of his own time.[89] As suggested by the *Xunzi*'s denunciation of vulgar *ru*, this was probably an attempt to distinguish true scholars from those who sold knowledge of established practices to earn a living. This would parallel the "Yao" passage that distinguished Confucius from conventional diviners.

Other men obtained positions at the royal courts by ritual expertise. Our knowledge of state ritual in the Warring States period comes almost entirely from the *Shi ji* "Monograph on the Feng and Shan Sacrifices." The section devoted to the pre-Han period deals largely with Qin, since the records of the other states had been destroyed, and they focus on the activities of Qin Shihuang.[90] He adopted the "Five Phases" model of history and established his court under the sign of the phase "water."[91] He also, as discussed in chapter 1, made progresses through his realm, offered sacrifices at sacred mountains, and commemorated these acts with inscriptions praising his achievements. He also sacrificed to the Eight Spirits, offerings that had been instituted shortly after the Zhou conquest.

For the sake of establishing this ritual program he consulted scholars from Lu and Qi, both followers of the *ru* tradition and adepts of immortality. In addition, he kept a large number of "broadly learned scholars (*bo shi* 博士)" at his court to advise him on ritual matters. From accounts of their later careers, we know that many of them were devoted to the Zhou classics and the *ru* tradition.[92] This reliance on text-based scholars for advice on ritual matters was probably the single greatest avenue for *ru* scholars to employment in state service. Certainly at the beginning of the Han the desire to exalt the ruler through court rituals led to the introduction of scholars into government. However, the men who introduced the *ru* tradition into Han government met fierce criticism from those who insisted that the true gentleman should avoid service until a dynasty had accumulated merit for a century.[93] Thus *ru* strictures against serving a ruler who was not a sage continued to have influence well into the Han.

A final source of income for scholars was patronage. This was distinguished from office-holding in that it entailed no administrative work but was carried out simply for the prestige of the patron, or because of his commitment to some element of a scholar's program. Evidence for this activity is scarce, but the little that exists suggests that it became prominent in the mid-fourth century B.C. The *Mencius* refers to the master's receipt of substantial gifts from rulers, and one passage asserts that he had several hundred followers who lived off princely generosity.[94] In the same period that Mencius visited King Hui of Liang (梁惠王), the astronomer Shi Shen (石申) was also active there, and presumably received support from the same king.[95] A decade later King Wei of Qi began to grant titles, salaries, and the right to wear distinctive costumes to scholars solely so that they might assemble, compose or transmit essays, and participate in court debates. These men carried out their activities outside the Ji gate of Qi's capital Linzi (臨淄) and hence came to be called the "men of broad learning beneath the Ji gate (稷下 *Ji xia*)." The nature of this patronage is not clear, and modern scholars' practice of referring to a "Jixia Academy" is certainly incorrect. The practice is a minor variation on that

of gaining power and prestige through attracting free-floating elements of the population to one's court. Nevertheless, it marks a gradual shift in the relations of the
schools to the states, because some rulers began to act as patrons of scholarship
out of the apparent conviction that support of cultural pursuits was a proper function of the prince, or a means of increasing his prestige.

That this development took place in the decades following the middle of the
fourth century B.C. may not be accidental. It was at this time that some rulers, led
by the aforementioned Hui of Liang in 344 and followed by Wei of Qi a decade
later, began to claim for themselves the title of king. By 323 the rulers of all the
major states had adopted the title.[96] The decision of leading rulers at this time to
act as patrons of literary culture might well be linked to their assumption of the
new title. Having declared themselves to be kings, rulers demonstrated their new
status through ritual innovations and acting as patron of authors, much as Augustus
Caesar did to lend a civilized patina to his seizure of power.

One should not, however, interpret this development as the beginning of an
alliance between states and scholarly traditions. There are two reasons. First, as
noted above, offering patronage to scholars was part of a broader tendency for
rulers to enhance their prestige by attracting people to their courts. This derives
from the fact that the territorial states were created through the ability of rising
monarchs to surround themselves with free-floating elements of the population
who were dependent on them and did their bidding. The ability to "obtain (*de* 得)"
men became a key demonstration of the ruler's "virtue (*de* 德)," and the exchange
of service for recognition defined the political realm.[97] In time this led to rulers
attempting to lure hermits or recluses to their courts; the tribute system of imperial
China emerged from the same ideas. In the Warring States period, the men attracted
to courts by royal bounty included not only scholars but also "wandering bravoes,"
trainers in using weapons, masters of occult arts, assassins, strategic advisers, and
entertainers. The Prince of Mengchang was famous for collecting 3,000 such retainers, many of them "refugees who were accused of some crime." One anecdote
shows that his retainers included a thief who disguised himself as a dog and a man
who could imitate the call of a rooster.[98] Hence scholars receiving patronage were
in decidedly mixed company.

The second reason is that patronage of scholars was not a state preserve.
When Xun Kuang left the Jixia scholars, he was given a minor post by Huang Xie
(黃歇), Prince of Chunshen.[99] This is significant, for Huang Xie was one of the
"Four Princes" who were celebrated for their dedication to assembling large numbers of retainers.[100] Scholars figured among these, but they were not the most
numerous or esteemed. As in the case of rulers, to whom the Four Princes were
related and with whom they shared common values and interests, the most important thing was the ability to attract adherents. The *Shi ji* states that when Lü Buwei
(呂不韋), chief minister of Qin from 250–38 B.C., began to assemble the retainers
who composed the *Lü shi chun qiu*, he was inspired by his jealousy of the Four
Princes. As the dominant state, Qin could not allow itself to be surpassed in any

field.[101] The need of Qin to attract scholars indicates that the practice of sponsoring literary studies had spread from Wei and Qi to other states and become an attribute of authority. The fact that the Four Princes, members of royal lineages and high officials but not themselves of royal rank, were the primary targets of jealousy indicates that royal courts may well have been surpassed in this field by the great officers in their fiefs.

On the basis of the above examples, we can draw a map of the divisions in the literary field of Warring States China. An advanced level of literacy could lead to at least four careers: (1) state service, (2) teaching or acting as a ritual specialist for a powerful family or local community, (3) technical expertise in some field of protoscience or occult studies, and (4) participation in one or more of the philosophical textual traditions.[102] In terms of income, those who opted for the first path drew sustenance from the state, and those who chose the second lived off the local communities or clan(s). These two alternatives marked the fixed poles at either end of the social scale. Those who opted for careers in the third and fourth categories were mobile figures who oscillated between the two poles. The lesser technical experts or literary scholars converged with the village diviner or schoolteacher. The most eminent provided services at royal courts, while those at intermediate levels found service with a leading minister and holder of a fief, a local official, or an eminent local family.

The schoolmen claimed superiority over those in state service through their condemnation of venal interests and contemporary institutions. For the literary *ru*, superiority was marked by the refusal to serve and the cultivation of rites and virtues, for the Mohists by a distinctive lifestyle in disciplined units, and for the proto-Daoists by the cultivation of meditative practices and philosophical perceptiveness. They asserted superiority over village schoolmasters and ritual experts, where they acknowledged their existence, through denunciations of the latter's pettiness (*xiao* 小), close association with vulgar yokels (*su* 俗, *bi* 鄙), and their conservatism.[103] Geographically and socially mobile, active in higher social circles, but not serving rulers who rejected their programs, the schoolmen and technical specialists, both with textual traditions, enacted the positions they articulated in their writings and thereby set themselves apart from mere officials or petty instructors and ritualists.

The division between technical specialists and philosophical schoolmen was not so clearly marked, and its terms not entirely clear. The *Mencius* praises the skill of astronomers, and its doctrine of *qi* as the ground of links between man and the cosmos had unacknowledged links to the traditions of the technical experts.[104] Moreover, the philosophical schools often borrowed terms—such as "Five Phases"—and images—such as the metaphor of the body as a bellows—from the mantic or medical traditions.[105] In the passage from "Yao" cited above, the schoolmen recognized their common ground with the diviners, while trying also to distinguish themselves as those who worked for the common good rather than profit. Criticisms within the *ru* tradition of appeals to ghosts and spirits, reliance on sacrifice to obtain good fortune, and physiognomy would also serve to distinguish them from many of the technical disciplines. The *Han Feizi* also contains passages denouncing occult skills as unnecessary where proper procedures are in place, and as means of duping the people.[106]

The most important argument for the superiority of the philosophical schools, however, was the idea that expertise within a delimited field was inferior to an encompassing, adaptive intelligence that combined and regulated particular skills in the service of a higher good. This is a crucial point. First, it demonstrates once again how the philosophical schools claimed a status approaching that of royalty, for bringing together and regulating were the functions of a king. Second, it leads directly to the dichotomy of universal/encompassing versus partial/delimited that dominated the interschool polemics of the third and second centuries B.C.[107] This will be developed at length in chapter 7. I will discuss here the question of universal wisdom as opposed to limited technique because of its importance in defining the philosophical schools within the intellectual field of the period, and its links to their claims to highest authority.

The definition of the gentleman by his flexible, encompassing intelligence in contrast to skill at performing specific tasks appears throughout the *Lun yu* in passages disparaging the man who acts as a *qi* (器), a vessel or utensil suitable only for use by others. One passage states that the gentleman does not act as a vessel. Another mocks a disciple for being a mere vessel, and then consoles him by noting that he is at least a precious one. A third contrasts the gentleman, who in employing others treats them simply as vessels/utensils (with the implicit sense of "according to their capacities"), while the petty man demands everything (*bei* 備 "complete") from them.[108] These indicate that human *qi* are used for specific tasks, and that the gentleman treats others as such but should not himself be so treated.

In addition to these injunctions against being employed for specific tasks, the *Lun yu* also calls into question the value of particular skills. A villager remarks on the breadth (*bo* 博, the adjective that would describe the Qin and Han court erudites) of Confucius' learning, but notes that he has consequently not achieved a reputation. When he hears of this, Confucius mockingly asks whether he should specialize in charioteering or in archery, and opts for the former. The preference for broad cultivation over particular skills is clear. In another story a high official marvels at the variety of Confucius' talents. The latter explains that he was of humble birth and consequently acquired many skills, but that a true gentleman should not be like this. The next passage again depicts Confucius apologizing for his knowledge of many arts because of never having been tried in a position of responsibility. When a disciple asks how to grow crops, Confucius replies that for such a question he is not as good as an old farmer. After the disciple departs, Confucius sneers at him for his pettiness in thinking about farming, when he should be worrying about rituals. Finally, two late passages attributed to Zi Xia argue that the minor arts have their value and that the craftsmen perfect their skills by staying in their workshops, but that the gentleman must avoid such arts for fear of becoming bogged down in detail. He instead cultivates the Way through literary or philo-sophic learning.[109]

The privileging of general intelligence over particular skills continues in later *ru* writings. In an encounter with a follower of the "School of the Tillers," who advocated that all men should engage in agriculture, Mencius argues for the divi-sion of labor. In this argument the farmers and the craftsmen produce products and exchange them, while the ruler supervises from on high. After the famous formulation of the division between the great men who work with their minds and the petty men who work with their muscles, the *Mencius* goes on to recount the creation of civilization by the sage-kings. This identifies the maintenance of an encompassing culture as the task of the ruler, while leaving agriculture and crafts to the common people.[110] The *Xunzi* devotes an entire chapter, "Jie bi 解蔽," to the argument that men are blinded by focusing on a limited aspect of reality and that only the sage can free himself from such partiality. The same text also argues that the gentleman or the ruler cannot possibly know as much as the farmer, crafts-man, or merchant in their particular fields, but that through mastery of the Way they can give each subject his proper role and harmonize their actions.[111]

This argument was later applied to the political realm in the Han founder's explanation of why he had defeated his rivals. Lacking the strategic skills of Zhang Liang, the organizational abilities of Xiao He, and the military genius of Han Xin, he had triumphed through his ability to use other people's skills, and consequently he had conquered.[112] Whether or not Gaozu actually made such an argument is irrelevant, for it indicates that by the first century of Han rule the opposition of generalist intellect versus specific skills, with the assumption that the former con-trolled the latter, had become a standard formula in the political as well as the scholastic sphere.

The Mohists, with their interest in technology and military skills, do not deride the technical arts, but their theory of government through "elevation of the worthy" assumes that those with skills will be employed as officials by the ruler. The ruler's employment of officials is compared to his employing a tailor to make his clothing or a butcher to prepare his meat. The ruler, on the other hand, has no specific skills or tasks, but allocates and coordinates the activities of his officials. The same schema is repeated in the *Han Feizi*, which employs the Daoist rhetoric of emptiness and inactivity to describe the ruler, while assigning specific tasks and duties to the officials.[113] The *Zhuangzi* likewise argues that "techniques (*ji* 技)" are definitive of an inferior status or servitude.[114] The entire bureaucratic model of government, in which tasks are performed by *guan* 官 (both "official" and "bodily organ"), is based on the idea that techniques and expertise—metaphorically identi-fied with the limbs, sense organs, teeth, or claws—are subordinated to the encom-passing mind of the ruler.[115]

The contrast between general intelligence and limited skills primarily justifies the distinction between those who rule and the common people, or between the ruler and his officials. However, it also entails a hierarchical distinction between the philosophical traditions and those devoted to expertise in the natural world or the occult arts. The former assimilated themselves to the condition of the ruler through claims to possess a body of doctrine and practice essential to any true monarch. These claimed to be the foundations of any human society, like the ritual teachings of the *ru*, or to enable flexible and appropriate responses to changing circumstances, like the mental cultivation of the proto-Daoists. As universal methods, the wisdom of these textual traditions shared in the prestige of ruler over ruled, mind over body, or supervisor over workers. In contrast, the arts of the doctors, diviners, astrologists, and exorcists, although also textually based, were restricted to technical applications and entailed serving a superior. Thus the distinguishing feature of the philosophical traditions in the intellectual field, the terms in which they claimed the highest rank among the wielders of texts, grew directly out of their claims to command the state through their wisdom.

The ability of the philosophical traditions to maintain a degree of independence vis-à-vis the state indicates at least three features of the political order in the age of the Warring States. First, was the fact of division. The existence of multiple states allowed competition for the prestige of cultural sponsorship, and this competition permitted scholars to hold themselves apart from any individual court. Thus, both Mencius and Xun Kuang departed Qi when they were dissatisfied, and Mencius made a comfortable living moving from court to court.

Second, for most of the period there was no attempt to impose a state orthodoxy, probably because the schoolmen and their writings were initially of little value or interest to those active in political life. The rise of patronage as a prestige activity in the second half of the Warring States, along with the emergence of textual traditions devoted to political practices, increased ties between states and schoolmen. Interschool polemics in the third century led to calls by the scholars themselves for the suppression of rival doctrines. These developments culminated in Qin's attempt to suppress private writings and absorb scholarship into the state realm. Thus schoolmen increasingly were drawn into the state sphere, but only at the end of the Warring States period did any state try to eliminate autonomous literary traditions and bring claims to textual authority under government control.

The third feature of Warring States politics indicated by the history of the textual traditions was the survival of significant groups that did not function according to the legalist model of a single, all-encompassing state order. The best documented are the powerful, enfeoffed ministers exemplified by the Four Princes. These men, generally relatives of the ruling house, dominated several state courts, and with wealth drawn from their fiefs they maintained private households with thousands of personal retainers. While as office holders they were usually members of the state order, they were also rivals to royal authority, and the latent tensions between the titular ruler and these ministers sometimes burst into open conflict. Thus in the early third century the Marquis of Wurang in Qin used the army's victories to expand his own fiefs and those of his faction at court, until he was finally toppled in the name of royal centralism. The Prince of Mengchang was chief minister of Qi, but was forced to flee when accused of planning a coup. The Prince of Xinling illegally mobilized the army of Wei with a stolen tally in order to rescue relatives by marriage besieged in the Zhao capital of Handan. Such powerful figures devoted to acting as patrons provided an economic base to groups who defied the state order, particularly the bravoes and the schoolmen.

Other sources of patronage outside the state order have left no written traces, being too far removed from the social sphere of our texts. The most important of these would have been powerful local families or village communities. Most patronage at this level would probably have gone to local ritualists, schoolteachers, and experts in the protosciences or occult arts, although the noble houses of lesser states that survived into the third century, as well as members of secondary royal lineages, could have supported more literary activities. The *Shang jun shu* asserts that in a state where officials are recruited through literary expertise, the powerful families will all abandon agriculture and devote themselves to the study of the *Odes* and *Documents*.[116]

This support at lower levels would have benefited only the *ru* traditions, and perhaps certain proto-Daoists. The Mohists relied on their military skills, which were of interest only to courts, and the teachings of the legalist, diplomatic, and military traditions all depended on the survival of a system in which states competed for wealth and power. As noted above, the *ru* and the technical experts, in contrast to other wielders of texts, enjoyed a bipolar social character—able to move between the courts and local society, between public service and private retirement. This is one reason why these intellectual traditions survived and flourished after the unification under Qin rendered obsolete the doctrines and skills of Warring States courtiers and generals.

THE MASTER AS MODEL

As noted earlier, the master began to figure as the author of his own text only in the fourth century B.C. In the earliest philosophical writings he appeared as a figure whose words were addressed to followers or political figures, and recorded by an implied scribe. The texts were produced by those who shared a common master, and reproduced within themselves the factional splits or debates among these followers. As object rather than subject of writing, and as an object offering a ground for disputed narratives, the master acquired distinctive characteristics that had a formative impact on later Chinese writing practices. In order to accommodate the multiple agents speaking through him over the centuries, the master appeared not as a consistent philosophic voice speaking in the form of binding universals, but rather as a set of individual propositions whose underlying principles, or lack thereof, had to be deduced by the reader. This focus on underlying motives also made the ultimate object of inquiry the master, rather than any philosophical doctrine he pronounced.

This situation resulted in several reading strategies that underpin much of later Chinese theories of writing. Most important, the master tends to appear as a figure of veiled meanings and hidden depths, someone who expresses himself indirectly and whose meaning adapts constantly to circumstances.[117] For these attributes the classic instance is Confucius, but the traits attributed to this first and most influential of the masters appear in the other textual traditions as well. Even when masters became authors in the fourth century, the tradition of attributing authority to veiled utterances and to indirection continued to affect the manner in which their texts were read, the use of quotations, and above all to the reduction of the masters and their texts to a secondary rank by new types of writing that more fully developed the masters' own attributes.

The first characteristic of the master evinced by Confucius was suspicion of language. The entire structure of the *Lun yu* problematizes language, since it is devoted to presenting and explaining what "the master said." This is an issue because the sayings are not transparent; they do not explain their own meanings. This problem in part reflects the enunciatory practice in which the master figured as an object for transcription by others. His words were observable facts, but they were fixed and could not elaborate or explain themselves, as an author might. Thus the disciples collected and added to the words, and then worked at them in order to derive some sense. If language could serve as an unproblematic vehicle of meaning, and if the communication of a meaning was all that language was intended to achieve, then the whole project of the *Lun yu* would have been pointless.

The problem of language is not only built into the structure of the book, but also articulated by the master. This takes several forms. Confucius condemns those who are skillful in the use of words, glib, or plausible. Such men are a danger to the state and must be kept at a distance. Even the *Odes* with their inherited prestige are of no value unless put into action. One passage acknowledges the necessity of eloquence in the world of his day, but treats this as evidence of the degeneracy of the age. A decision by one disciple to take office leads Confucius to inveigh against "glib flatterers." By contrast, he insists on several occasions that the true gentleman is sparing in his words, speaks only hesitantly, and seeks only to get his point across without adornment.

> That in ancient times words were not emitted was because people would have been ashamed that they themselves would not come up to them.

> The true gentleman desires to be halting in speech but rapid in acts.

At one point Confucius declares that he shall, like Heaven, renounce speech altogether.[118]

Here language, as in most Warring States philosophical texts, is used to establish and maintain social ties. The suspicion of language does not concern the capacity of words to describe the world or enunciate truth, but rather the worry that words will not correspond to actions, and hence that trust (*xin* 信) will not be established. Admonitions to be careful and sparing in words speak in terms of making words match with actions. Other remarks insist on the importance of maintaining trust in one's words, and some argue that trust is the foundation of the social order, more important to the state than even grain or weapons. As a correlate to the supreme value of deeds, the text asserts the possibility of ruling without commands, through the sheer force of example.[119] The "rectification of names" discussed in chapter 1 is an extension of this concern for the reliability of language in maintaining social ties.

If maintaining trust was one of the major reasons for worrying over the inadequacy of language, a second motive was pedagogic. The more the master spoke, the less the disciples would think. By speaking little and indirectly, the master used his words as a spur to activity on the student's part. Thus the text insists that students should be able "if given one corner to recognize the other three" or "if given one to realize ten." This point appears in Confucius' summary of the *Shi jing* in the single phrase: "Thoughts without straying [*si wu xie* 思無邪]." While most scholars worry about how to understand the phrase, the perceived desirability and possibility of communicating so much (three hundred poems) in so few words (three) is also central to the project of the *Lun yu*. Elsewhere the master states that he can only teach students who are desperate to understand. The finest student was the one who never spoke, because he understood the master's sense without questions. Some anecdotes show the master giving a clue and the disciple recognizing his meaning and developing it further. Other stories tell how the master refuses to answer questions from those dissatisfied with his initial propositions, or gives replies that add no information. In still others he rebuffs questions, and after the questioner has departed explains his own actions to suggest a lesson to the others. Finally, there are anecdotes that depict the disciples deducing lessons from the hints they obtain.[120]

This pedagogy is presented as Confucius' personal method, but it also reflects the nature of the text. Given a mass of quotations collected after the master's death, the disciples were responsible for making sense of individual statements and the links between them. So while the text perhaps mirrors Confucius' teaching, this teaching is also an expression of the text's form. The insistence that the master only gave one step and demanded the rest from the disciples implied that their reinterpretations or extensions of the master's words were implicitly there from the beginning. The master's reticence as built into the organization of the *Lun yu* established a ground where creative work could be carried out in the guise of following authority. This pattern was repeated in other texts.

A final feature of the *Lun yu*, closely related to the suspicion of language and the minimalist pedagogy, was the insistence on teaching through particulars. When asked about government or rites, the master never responds with a definition or a formal discussion. Instead he offers specific maxims or rules, and when asked the same question by another individual he gives an entirely different reply. One chapter presents in succession five scenes where a disciple asks about being filial, and in each case the master replies with specific observations—always comply with rites, do not cause parents worry, just feeding parents is not enough, be careful about the expression on your face—but does not extract any general principles.[121] Questions about government elicit such replies as "sufficient food, sufficient arms, the people's trust," or "have the prince be a prince and the subject a subject" or "encourage the people to work hard by setting an example" or "follow the calendar of Xia, ride in the carriage of Yin, and wear the ceremonial cap of Zhou."[122] The all-important opposition between the "gentleman" and the "petty person" is never defined, but simply adumbrated by a series of oppositions: the gentleman agrees without echoing, the petty person echoes without agreement; the gentleman is at ease without being arrogant, the petty person is arrogant without being at ease; the gentleman is easy to serve but difficult to please, the petty person is difficult to serve but easy to please.[123] Teaching through particulars also figures in the practice of collecting quotations that amount to little more than lists.[124]

The absence of definition and generalization in the responses of Confucius has several consequences. First, all knowledge derives from particular cases and is never separated from them. Second, no response is to be taken as adequate or complete. Each presents an element of the topic under discussion, and according to later commentarial theory that element was selected on the basis of the situation at hand and the character of the interlocutor.[125] In theory the observations on benevolence or good government could be extended to infinity, with the sole guarantor of the constant adequacy of the responses being the wisdom or skill of the master. Consequently, the lesson for the disciples is not *any* of the particular responses, but the mind that can make them, the "thread" that runs through them.[126] Thus a third consequence of the absence of generalization is that each proposition within its context (or within the text) is read as a pointer to something beyond itself. No matter how direct it seems, it is to be regarded as an indirect indicator of some additional meaning; no matter how shallow it appears, it must have hidden depths. This is the "subtle" or "hidden" speech (*wei yan* 微言) that became Confucius' virtue in later accounts.[127] It also explains why most Western readers find the text to be a collection of simple, moral platitudes, while the disciples and later commentators find in it profound meanings that no amount of explication can fully elucidate.[128]

Thus the hermeneutic of the *Lun yu*, which is closely tied to the enunciatory structure of the text, shaped the Chinese understanding of the sage intellect and the authoritative text. A suspicion of the ultimate reliability of language and the possibility of fixed definitions, a denial of absolute and unchanging truths or rules, the location of meaning and authority within the endlessly adaptable wisdom of the sage mind, the preference for locating truth within particular propositions that suggested broader truths, the tendency to privilege the indirect over the explicit, all these traits appeared within the writing and reading of the *Lun yu* and became central to later notions of wisdom. One form of this complex of ideas was the model of the endlessly adaptive mind of the sage ruler described in chapter 1, but it also figured in other textual traditions of Warring States philosophy.

The most direct inheritor of this model of the master was the *Mencius*. While the orations attributed to Mencius scarcely bespeak a suspicion of language, the theme of the danger of words and argumentation runs throughout the text. It states that empty words are ill-omened, and that misfortune will befall those who use them to obscure the worthy. The point of language was efficacy, and words were not as efficacious as music. Being a poor speaker was not a problem, because the gentleman disliked those who spoke too much, and Confucius and King Wen had been men of few words. Inappropriate speech was identified with voyeurism or illicit sexual union. The gentleman spoke only of the near at hand, but gave it far-reaching meaning.[129] All these remarks develop themes from the *Lun yu*, and the figure of Confucius is explicitly cited as an authority.

Responding to fourth-century developments, the *Mencius* applies the suspicion of words to the rival schools that had emerged, the traditions of Yang Zhu and the Mohists. The latter in particular were noted for developing models of argument and standards of proof, and they became major targets for the *Mencius* and later masters. Mencius asserts that his knowledge of words consists entirely of an ability to recognize those that are flattering, immoderate, heretical, or evasive and how they can blind, destroy, or lead astray. Such words harm government and public business, and if a sage were to return he would agree.[130] This denunciation is certainly aimed at the philosophical disputants of his day.

That the targets of his attack are the rival schools is also indicated by the reference to the reappearance of sages. The text contains four other passages that invoke the sages as counterexamples to the disputatious, fourth-century schoolmen, and two of these invoke a model of the periodic recurrence of sages. These both use parallelism to equate the emergence of disputing philosophical schools with the intrusion of birds and beasts into the world of men at the time of the flood. By implication the return of the sage (Mencius?) will lead to the expulsion of the Yangist/Mohist beasts. One passage even uses the words cited in the paragraph above to describe the evil language of the Yangists and Mohists, and the same phrases to narrate the process by which they harm government.[131] In conclusion Mencius denies the charge that he is fond of disputation, which is the product of an age of decline, but insists that he must protect the world from the doctrines of Yang and Mo, doctrines that will first let animals devour men and ultimately lead to men devouring men.

It is noteworthy that the *Mencius* does not engage the schools of Yang and Mo in a dispute, which would be to accept the behavior he condemns. Instead he presents the Way of the sages as an alternative to dispute, or rather he presents dispute as a result of the decline of the sagely Way and the breakdown of civilization. In this model of history he casts Confucius and himself as the defenders of the sagely tradition against the onslaught of animals and barbarians.[132] This attitude figures in the two instances where he has exchanges with individual Mohists.

In one he confounds the Mohist Yi Zhi not by refuting his arguments but by show-ing that Yi Zhi's own behavior and attitudes are inconsistent with those positions. The second exchange again consists not of a refutation of the Mohist's argument, but a suggestion that it would have untoward social consequences. Even his ex-change of analogies on human nature with Gaozi is scarcely a philosophic debate, for nothing is demonstrated or proven. Instead it aims, as noted by Wang Fuzhi, simply to confound heterodox opinions and to induce people to think.[133] Situating himself above the fray, Mencius awaits the return of order and the reabsorption of the Yangists and Mohists into the truth of the *ru*. To debate with them is "like chasing stray pigs."[134]

The *Mencius* also follows the *Lun yu* in its theory of pedagogy. In a passage that lists the five types of education, it identifies the highest form as teaching that acts like timely rain, that is, it helps the student develop with no active interven-tion, the second completes his virtue, the third perfects his talent, the fourth replies to questions, and the fifth leaves an example that may be *indirectly* emulated.[135] Thus verbal instruction is the second lowest form of teaching, and the lowest involv-ing direct contact between teacher and disciple. The theme of emulation appears in several places, most importantly in discussions of the lingering influence of Confucius and the time span over which the impact of a great man is felt.[136] The text also insists that teaching can be done through not speaking, arguing that the *ru* do not speak of the hegemons. Mencius notes that refusing to teach someone can also be a form of teaching.[137]

As in the *Lun yu*, teaching is generally done through invoking particulars. One notable example is that just as measurable quantities in Chinese are often expressed by a compound of the adjectives describing the two limits ("long-short"), so in the *Mencius* abstractions are presented through parallel invocations of the two extremes. A passage on the essential identity of all sages juxtaposes Shun and King Wen. The former comes from the "barbarians" of the east, the latter from the west; the former is ancient, the latter a thousand years more recent. After placing the two sages on these axes of geographic and temporal separation, the passage concludes that when they came to rule in the center, they matched like the two halves of a tally. Separated in time and space, they met in the condition of sagehood.[138]

Other examples of this pattern not only define abstractions through the jux-taposition of specific cases, but also articulate the model of sagehood as constant adaptation. The question of taking state service is discussed by citing historical figures: Bo Yi, who would not serve in a state with a bad ruler; Liu Xia Hui or Yi Yin, who would serve under any ruler; and Confucius—or the "gentleman"—who would adjust his decision to meet different circumstances.[139] Rather than offering an abstraction on the propriety of taking office, the text defines a continuum by noting the two historical extremes, and then celebrates Confucius for finding the "middle way" responding to time and circumstance. A similar continuum invokes the followers of Yang Zhu as the extreme of selfishness, those of Mozi as the extreme of selflessness (because of their doctrine of "universal love") and places Confucius or Mencius in the middle. However, as one passage argues, clinging to the middle is no better than adhering to one extreme, because it still singles out one position at the expense of a hundred.[140] No fixed rule can be given, because the sage must flexibly adapt to what is proper. Rules and demonstrations are the province of the rival schools that mark the destruction of the Way of the sage in the world.

Although speech is suspect, writing comes to the fore in the *Mencius*. Apart from the frequent use of quotations from earlier works as authorities, to be analyzed in chapters 3 and 4, it also argues that one can encounter the ancients as friends through the medium of their writings. The *Mencius* also offers the first theory on the reading of poetry.[141] These uses of quotation and a theory of reading indicate the increasing importance of written documents in the educational practices of the day.

Appealing to anterior texts, notably the *Shi*, the *Shu*, and sayings of Confucius, marks a major development among the schools. Whereas the ultimate authority of the *Lun yu* lay in the text itself or in the person of the master, the master's authority in the *Mencius* is derivative. Disciples textually established Confucius as a master by assembling bundles of quotations. The disciples of Mencius do the same, but they quote him quoting other sources, thereby marking a prior stage of authority that he establishes in the act of quotation just as the disciples establish him. The pattern of authority through quotation is doubled by the historical model of sages who return periodically, for the works quoted are those attributed to Confucius and the Zhou founders, the two most recent incarnations of sagehood and the immediate models for Mencius' aspiration to be a world-redeeming master of wisdom. This deferral of authority to higher texts anticipates the development in which the master became an author just as the emergence of higher texts placed the philosophical traditions in a secondary, derivative position.[142]

Also drawing on the figure of Confucius was the *Zhuangzi*. This text is distinctive in the minor role given to its eponymous master. Confucius and his disciples, in contrast, appear in more than forty stories. The depiction of the *ru* sage takes three forms. First, when Confucius is portrayed talking with his disciples he instructs them in Daoist philosophy and often praises hidden sages. On two occasions he notes that he has learned from the student, echoing remarks in the *Lun yu* where he expresses a willingness to learn from others. Several of the anecdotes, such as his encounter with the madman Jieyu and with an old farmer, are longer versions of stories that appear in the *Lun yu*. Second, when he talks with one of the Daoist masters, most notably Lao Dan, or with those who have cultivated unusual skills, then he appears in the role of student. Only when discussed by others in the third person does he become a target of criticism as a pedant devoted to ancient writings and false sages. Even in one third-person discussion he is praised in extravagant terms by Zhuang Zhou.[143]

These stories of Confucius invoke an established master to lend authority to the teachings of Zhuang Zhou and the "hidden sage." Confucius thus acts as a barker for Zhuang Zhou's Daoist freak show. However, what is crucial for the *Zhuangzi* is not the presence of Confucius, but the absence of any single master. Most of the text depicts variations of the teaching situation in which one figure poses questions and another answers, but the figures of authority change constantly. Apart from Zhuang Zhou and Confucius, teachers in the text include Lao Dan; the Yellow Emperor; Master Lie; Prince Mou of Wei; the Robber Zhi; Xu You; unknown sages; hermits, fishermen, butchers, and insect catchers; men whose legs have been chopped off; and finally figures who are nothing more than emblematic names such as "Do-Nothing-Say-Nothing," "Wild-and-Witless," or "Great Ignorance." Due to the multiplicity of teachers, the same figure appears sometimes as teacher and sometimes as student. This is true not only of Confucius, but also the Yellow Emperor, Master Lie, and even Zhuang Zhou himself in the dream dialogue where a skull instructs him on the folly of valuing life more than death.[144]

The reason for this multiplicity of teachers is explained at the beginning of chapter 20 "Imputed Words (*yu yan* 寓言)." In "imputed words" one "makes use of an outside standpoint to expound" because "a father cannot act as a go-between for his son, as his praising a son is not as good as one who is not the father." If statements are presented in a single voice, then whoever agrees will take it to be correct, and whoever disagrees will regard it as false, that is, it will enter the realm of interschool debate.[145] The enunciatory strategy of imputing words to multiple authorities avoids the weakness of a single author. By placing itself in multiple standpoints and proving the case from each of them, the argument acquires persuasive force and, in theory, escapes from the limits of an individual viewpoint. Two other linguistic devices are discussed in this passage—"repeated words [or 'weighty words']," that is, quotations from authorities, and "spillover words," that is, words that spontaneously come forth like wine from a goblet that tips when full but rights itself when empty. These likewise generate authority through distinguishing themselves from the ordinary utterances of reflective consciousness. The centrality of these enunciatory devices to the compilers of the book is shown by the fact that they are repeated and elaborated in the final chapter's account of Zhuang Zhou's place in intellectual history.[146]

In addition to being a literary strategy, the use of multiple authorities reflects an epistemological commitment. Chapter 6 of the *Zhuangzi* is entitled "The Great Ancestral Teacher (*da zong shi* 大宗師)." The section from which the title derives celebrates the Way as the highest teacher:

> My teacher! My teacher! (S)He grinds ['blends'] the myriad things but does not work at righteousness. His/her blessings reach down through the centuries, but (s)he does not work at benevolence. Longer lived than high antiquity, (s)he is not old. (S)He covers Heaven and supports Earth. (S)He carves all forms, but does not work at skill.

The syncretist compilers of the text also re-used this passage in a later chapter where the speech is attributed to Zhuang Zhou.[147] Thus underlying the appeal to multiple human authorities was the claim that the ultimate teacher, the ancestral teacher to whom all these figures traced their wisdom, was the universal Way. This same argument probably underpins the decision of the compilers of the *Dao dejing* to eschew any reference to a master whatsoever, but rather to enunciate the text as eternal truth based on direct visions of the Way.[148]

Another innovation in the *Zhuangzi* is its assertion of authority by dramatizing the vastness of its doctrine within the enunciatory scene. This is achieved by concluding a speech with a description of the recipient as dazed, overwhelmed, and unable to speak.[149] Rhetorically this mode of argument through invoking an overwhelming totality was the inverse of that of the rhetoricians, who are always characterized as making minute distinctions and splitting hairs. It is a cosmic variant of the philosophical traditions' claims to authority through a comprehensive understanding. It is also the direct predecessor of the conclusions of debates in the great Han rhapsodies.

While the *Zhuangzi* is distinctive in its textual enunciation and enactment of authority, it nevertheless carries forward the major themes we have seen in the *ru* textual tradition. The suspicion of language is carried to unparalleled lengths.[150] The three literary devices cited above all attempt to escape the unreliability of language. Closely associated with suspicion of language is the denunciation of the rhetoricians. Hui Shi, the famous expounder of paradoxes, is a frequent foil for Zhuang Zhou's barbs, to the extent that one passage portrays the latter mourning the death of his adversary. Attacks on "disputers" appear throughout the text.[151] The *Zhuangzi* agrees with the *Mencius* in denouncing the argumentative schools epitomized under the names "Yang and Mo." Unlike the *Mencius*, however, the *Zhuangzi* includes the *ru* as a sectarian school linked with the Mohists (in this it anticipates the *Han Feizi*), and also once identifies Hui Shi as head of a school.[152] Distinct from the *ru* in its enunciatory strategies and in its claims to an authority grounded in the cosmic Way, the *Zhuangzi* shares with them a hostility to disputation and a commitment to an ideal of sagehood that was temporally prior to the rival textual traditions, and which remains above the fray.

The *Mencius's* reliance on textual authority developed further in the *Xunzi*. This text, assembled by Liu Xiang at the end of the Western Han, consists of three types of materials: essays (or fragments thereof), compilations of received materials, and traditions preserved by disciples in the form of dialogues in which the master participates. The ideal of the teacher and modes of teaching in the text largely follow those of the *Mencius*, but there are several developments. First, the mode of enunciation is dominated by the third-person essay, suggesting a further suppression of the teaching scene and the dominance of texts as the model form of instruction. This tendency is also marked by the increasing frequency of quotation and the elaboration of longer lists of authoritative early texts, now taking the form of the five classics accepted by Han *ru*. Another development related to the increasing prevalence of writing is longer lists of rival schools or masters against which the Way of the sages was to be defended, combined with substantial borrowings from several enemy textual traditions.[153] Finally, the text argues for giving precedence to the later kings, particularly the Zhou founders, rather than the early sages because sufficient *written records* of the former survive.[154]

Despite these extensions and elaborations, the *Xunzi* preserves the model of an ancient sagely Way based on flexible adaptation, a Way antithetical to disputations based on fixed definitions and rules of argument. The Way is preserved through an educational program based on classic texts and rituals that generate an authority capable of suppressing the new realm of debate and disputation. This authority converged with the new vision of kingship sketched in the last section of chapter 1.

While the teaching scene is not depicted in the *Xunzi*, the text emphasizes education and the role of the teacher. The first two chapters of Liu Xiang's arrangement of the text are devoted to education and self-cultivation. The text insists on the importance of teachers, specifies that the aim of learning is to make one's mind identical with the teacher's, argues that the teacher and the model/law (*fa* 法) are the basis of social order, and asserts that for an individual to become a sage or a state to flourish both depend on teachers. It also lists the primary techniques of teaching: (1) being majestic and instilling fear, (2) being white-haired and inspiring trust, (3) making no errors in recitation and explanation, (4) recognizing the most minute or subtle when making judgments.[155]

The *Xunzi* carries forward the *ru* suspicion of glibness and loquacity. Thus one section on "sincerity/single-mindedness (誠 *cheng*)," perhaps based on a similar passage in the *Lun yu*, notes that Heaven, Earth, and the four seasons do not speak, but men recognize their nature. This is because their sincerity produces a constant regularity. Likewise, the gentleman of supreme virtue teaches while remaining silent, forms intimate links without bestowing gifts, and awes without growing angry.[156] The Son of Heaven is able to speak, but he makes proclamations only through his officials. Like Heaven he is trusted without speaking.[157]

> If he speaks much, then it is always patterned and categorized. Throughout the day he discusses the reasons for things. In speaking of a thousand acts or ten thousand transformations, his controlling category [*tong lei* 統類] remains single. This is the sage's wisdom. If he speaks little, then it is direct and succinct. His judgments follow a model, as if drawn with an inked cord. This is the scholar-gentleman's wisdom. His words are flattering and his actions perverse. What he recommends, he often regrets. This is the petty man's wisdom. Quick, forthcoming, facile, and glib but without categories; of diverse abilities and vast but useless; hair-splitting, rapid, and thoroughly analytic but with no urgency; caring not for right or wrong, not assessing the crooked or straight; devoted to cheating and vanquishing others [in debate]. This is the menial's wisdom.[158]

Here the sage may speak because of his unique mastery of the guiding categories that underlie language. This is the image of the sage of the Mawangdui *Jing fa*, the Confucius of the *Guo yu*, or the Yu of the *Shang hai jing*, those who have the almost magical power to accurately name all things. The scholar, by contrast, is defined by few words. The lowest category, the philosopher of language and paradox, is characterized by volubility, rapidity of speech, and the relentless analysis of words. He represents the triumph of language for its own sake, detached from the concerns of human society.

The *Xunzi* takes these adepts of disputation and their manipulations of language as one of its primary targets. Chapter 18, "Rectifying Judgments (*zheng lun* 正論)" is devoted to the refutation of propositions attributed to "vulgar men of the world who engage in persuasions."[159] Likewise the chapter "Rectifying Names," while adopting much of the terminology of the theoreticians of language, calls for the suppression of disputation through a restoration of the sagely Way in which names were fixed by the percipient monarch.[160] Other passages attacking disputation are scattered through the text. Most of these are simply denunciations, but the chapter on rituals specifically sets the sages against the rhetoricians by asserting that the kind of intelligence involved in paradoxes and logical disputations is out of its depth when confronted with the principles underlying rituals.[161]

The later chapters in the *Xunzi* draw together the above arguments into a model of the relation between education, the Way of the sages, and royal authority. First, sagehood is the end of education, and the sage is both the standard and the goal for anyone engaged in study.[162] Second, there is one constant Way of the sage, which links together all the methods by which wise rulers have brought order to the world.[163] Third, it describes the sage-king, or any true ruler, as a teacher. Related to this are passages cited earlier that link the teacher to the model/law.[164] While earlier *ru* texts charged teachers with the defence of the Way of the sages against the challenge of disputers, the *Xunzi* conflates the teacher with the monarch in the figure of the sage-king. Consequently, attacks on the theoreticians of language turn into calls for active royal intervention to restore order to the intellectual realm, and denunciations of the multitude of intellectual traditions invoke the king and the sage as twin authorities to restore a vanished unity.

The placing of an idealized monarch in the site previously occupied by the master parallels other developments in the history of the schools. Texts increasingly featured an enunciatory scene based on dialogues with monarchs, the hierarchy of texts elevated state-sponsored compendia (see chapter 7) or texts claiming to preserve the teachings of early kings or ministers, and patronage by the state or leading officials became important as a means of making a livelihood from scholarship. The idealization of the king as a teacher, an idea mythically presented in the tradition that ancient sage rulers created the arts and technologies of civilization, was yet another expression of the increasing shift of the schools into the state sphere. Yet even in the *Xunzi* the king's status as teacher was conditional on his being sagelike, and in this incomplete identity of sage and king in the world of the Warring States the schools continued to maintain a degree of independent existence and an oppositional stance.

This is visible even in the legalist writings. As noted earlier, the *Shang Jun shu* and the *Han Feizi* argued that the laws of the state should serve as the only instructional texts and officials as the sole teachers. This argument carried the position of the *Xunzi* one step further by denying the authoritative example of past sages. Indeed, a couple of passages in the *Xunzi* take the law or the regulations of the king as one leg of instruction, thus nearly joining with the theoreticians of the absolute state, but the *ru* text still pairs the law with the texts inherited from the earlier sages.[165] However, even the central legalist text, the *Han Feizi*, does not make the law the sole authoritative text. Law controlled local officials and commoners, but it did not direct the ruler and his courtiers. Moreover, since law had to be periodically adapted to changing circumstances, it could not be the highest teaching. This role belonged to the principles that directed the periodic legal reforms. One textual foundation for such principles was the *Han Feizi* itself, which directed the ruler in making his state powerful. However, by the end of the Warring States period the individual master as author had lost most of his authority, which now resided in more universalist texts. As discussed in chapter 1, accounts of the techniques by which the ruler controlled his officials, most notably "name and form," employed a Daoist vocabulary and images. This commitment to some version of Daoist thought as the ultimate guide for the ruler was formalized by the inclusion in the *Han Feizi* of a two-chapter commentary on the *Dao de jing*. In this way Han Fei or his immediate followers availed themselves of the pattern of writing that emerged in the third century B.C. in which authors grounded their authority in a fundamental "classic (*jing* 經)" to which they offered commentary.[166] Thus even here the appeal to the king was paired with that to the sage, the authority of law with that of a sacred text rendered potent by its presentation of all-encompassing principles. The sage had become the textual double of the king, and the text the replica of the world-state.

CONCLUSION

The scholarly tradition or school was a new form of social organization that developed in the Warring States through the same principle of voluntary association that created leagues of bravoes and the courts. Formed by the association of disciples with a master, they were perpetuated across time and space through the production of texts. The master, disciples, and text formed an interlocking complex in which none could exist without the other. The master was defined as such through his ability to attract disciples but could only preserve his status beyond death through being inscribed in their writings. The disciples, in turn, obtained authority as teachers in their own right through the prestige of their master and his doctrine, both of which depended on writing for their preservation and dissemination. The texts, composed of bundles of bamboo or wooden strips, survived only through active transmission and study, and they remained intellectually alive through the constant addition and adaptation of material made possible by their open format. This openness and their evolution over time allowed the texts of the philosophical traditions to become fields in which the factional tensions or splits within a tradition were inscribed, and basic doctrines were adapted to new circumstances.

Within the format of the text described above, the notion of authorship was weak. The writers of the early texts would seldom, and the editors and transmitters never, have been the master himself. Consequently, the master was always to some degree an invention of the text. This made possible the later development of traditions in which the master was entirely fictional, or an ancient historical figure who had no relation to the formation of the text. Authority was imputed to a voice, which in the early texts was actually written into the "enunciatory scene." Writing was treated as a form of transcription, like that performed by the mythical historians of the right and the left who recorded every word and deed of the king. Thus from the very beginning authority appeared in the guise of quotation, with the quoted words rendered authoritative by the implicit presence of disciples as audience and scribes.

Over the course of the Warring States period the enunciatory scene gradually suppressed the act of teaching and shifted toward third-person essays or dialogues between scholar/general/persuader and king. This change in the form of textual enunciation reflects the rising importance of the texts themselves as the means of forming increasingly open intellectual traditions. However, authority was still often located in quotation, now incorporating earlier texts into later ones, and in collective writing and transmission, in the form of state-sponsored encyclopedia, classics attributed to ancient or hidden sages, and the increasingly influential literary remains of the Zhou. These developments will be treated in subsequent chapters, and here it is sufficient to note that the shift toward writing in the third-person voice of the master was linked to a relative decline in the authority of the philosophical traditions vis-à-vis other forms of writing.

Social groups preserved across time with the aid of writing, philosophical traditions were independent of the state. Since the masters preserved or invented within the texts offered doctrines for creating and maintaining social order, doctrines distinct from actual practices, the initial relation of the schoolmen to the state was one of opposition. This was intensified by the gathering of scholars in groups that had no sanctioned place in the state order. Different traditions formed different relations to the polity: the *ru* advocating service only in states that accepted their doctrines, the Mohists serving states as independent units or as individuals still pledged to support Mohist law, the textual tradition of Zhuang Zhou denouncing state service outright, the military men serving the state but claiming autonomy in their own realm, and the legalists sketching the unconditional imposition of certain features of Warring States administration. However, to have abandoned the principle of formal separation and opposition would have meant the end of the tradition and the disappearance of its doctrine. This fact is clearest in the writings of theorists of law and administration, who denounced the spread of textual traditions that challenged the state and called for the laws to serve as the only licit teaching, but thereby condemned their own activities.

This long-term oppositional stance was made possible through the availability of economic alternatives to state service. To the extent that our sources provide any evidence, there were at least four major avenues of gaining a livelihood from literacy. First, there was state service. Evidence from the few excavated tombs of officials that included texts suggests that these men devoted their studies to administrative documents and mantic materials employed in their work. Such men rose through military service or experience in the low levels of local administration and had no links to the textual traditions. A second form of livelihood was as a low-level schoolteacher or ritual expert. Such men were the nontextual *ru*. They are almost invisible in the written record, but were denounced by their text-based colleagues and can virtually be assumed as a social necessity. A third career was to acquire text-based expertise in some technical discipline such as astrology, hemerology, medicine, divination, or exorcism. Accounts of such men appear in the received sources, and tomb texts have provided significant new materials pertaining to them and their activities. Finally, and in all likelihood smallest in number, were the schoolmen devoted to a philosophical tradition. Such men earned their living through teaching and ritual instruction at a higher level, or in exceptional circumstances through gaining the ear of a ruler. Over the course of the Warring States period patronage of such figures by royal courts, high officials, enfeoffed lords, or locally powerful families also became more common.

The intellectual field of the Warring States period was constituted by these different career patterns and their associated intellectual commitments. The philosophical traditions constituted only one element. In their writings they consciously distinguished themselves from the other groups and careers, denouncing state service or the use of technical texts for mercenary purposes as unworthy of a scholar, and similarly accusing their lower-level, nontextual equivalents of greed and petty-minded conservatism. They also distinguished themselves as exponents of a generalist, regulatory intelligence comparable to that of the monarch, in contrast to the particular, technical skills of other text-based traditions. In many ways less socially important than their three rivals, they nevertheless acquired significance because of their insistence on aiming their writings at the conduct and character of the ruler. As the Zhou monarchy and its nobility faded, and emerging rulers claimed royal titles of which the significance was not clear, new definitions of or models for authority became necessary. The philosophical traditions were the only groups developing theories in this field. Consequently they played the role of Shelley's "unacknowledged legislators" or Diderot's *encyclopédistes* who secretly controlled society through their power to make definitions. And just like those associated with Shelley and Diderot, their immediate, actual influence was as small as their ambitions were overweening.

Separated from actual power, the schoolmen derived models of authority from the master as he was created in their texts. This had several consequences. First, generated within texts as a transcription open to addition and modification, the early masters were veiled figures who left room for interpretation and elaboration. Since multiple traditions emerged from a single master, contradictory statements were traced to the same source, requiring reconciliation. This established commentary as a fundamental mode of reading at the beginning of the Chinese intellectual tradition.

Second, given the development of doctrine *within* a tradition, the inevitable silence of the master on new problems, and the consequent need for adaptation over time, the social nature of the schools encouraged a suspicion of language and of the possibility of formulating absolute, eternal truths. The exceptions to this, as A. C. Graham has argued, were the Mohists and the associated philosophers of language. However, this development was rejected by the other textual traditions, who treated disputation as a destructive activity reflecting the decline of the sagely Way. Masters of textual traditions thus were not philosophers, but rather sages who presented an alternative to philosophy, an encompassing truth whose victory over disputation was necessary to the survival of civilization.

This rejection of interschool rivalries as a dangerous aberration, along with closer ties to the state based on patronage, led to a tendency to identify the authority of the master/sage with that of the king. This idea was mythically embodied in the ancient sages, who were both rulers and repositories of wisdom. It was articulated as doctrine in such third-century works as the *Xunzi*, the later sections of the *Zhuangzi*, and in the *Shang Jun shu* and *Han Feizi*. Another mode of asserting this identity was the re-interpretation of the Zhou heritage as testimony to the most recent period, and the only one documented, when sagely and royal authorities had not yet parted. Thus the parallel between sage and king, school and state, was developed in new modes of writing about the past.

Chapter Three
WRITING THE PAST

Writing about the past is inevitably tied to present concerns. In narrations of origins people sanction present practice, imagine lost paradises that highlight current failings, or posit eras of primitive savagery from which humanity has been redeemed by recent innovations. Moreover, models of the past maintain associations through the creation of an apical ancestor or a founding moment which members of the group accept as the beginning of their history. Lineages, states, intellectual traditions, and artistic schools all define themselves through establishing a shared origin and a genealogy. Finally, the past provides exemplars who define the virtues and vices by which a society judges itself and others. In the choice of its heroes, a group establishes models for the conduct of its members. Writing is not essential to any of these functions, but where it exists it is employed in the tasks of establishing groups, defining social ideals, and declaring models for emulation. Moreover, people's relation to the past is inevitably altered when it is defined by written documents that are granted authority as objective records.

In the Warring States period the past was generated in a variety of texts and employed by a range of groups for their own purposes. The Zhou odes were used by some authors as historical records. The more explicitly historical documents inherited from the Zhou state were preserved under the rubric of *shu* 書 "writings" or "documents." Most prominent were those assembled in the Han under the rubric of *Shang shu* 尚書, but others are now included in the work known as the *Zhou shu* 周書 or the *Yi Zhou shu* 逸周書.[1] In the dozen or so core documents of the *Shang shu* members of the Zhou nobility had used speeches attributed to the Zhou founders to enunciate or debate the principles underlying their state. It is unlikely that the texts were actually written by the figures in whose voices they are spoken, and they were probably written long after the fact to commemorate earlier triumphs and articulate principles, as is indicated by discrepancies, discussed in Chapter 5, between the texts and early Western Zhou bronzes. In any case, these core writings, usually known as *gao* 誥, are together with the bronze inscriptions and the odes our primary evidence regarding early Zhou depictions of the past and the uses to which the past was put.

As the monarchy crumbled and new states emerged, many of the issues that had been central to the Zhou became peripheral, and new modes of writing the past were developed to articulate new institutions and beliefs. Certain writings accumulated around the received Zhou documents. This involved the development of new categories of "document," such as the *shi* 誓 "oaths" supposedly presenting addresses given by commanders prior to major engagements, or the *mo* 謨 "plan" or "counsel" attributed to leading officials.[2] It also entailed a widening of chronological scope to include both documents from periods later than those presumed in the core documents, and ones that claimed to derive from earlier dynasties and sages. The latter established a model of written history that transcended the dynasty, and thereby provided a ground for political and intellectual authority that was prior and hence superior to those of the ruling house. Such a ground was essential to the oppositional stance and the claims to independent authority of the Warring States' philosophical traditions. The importance of these new documents is indicated by the fact that throughout the Warring States period the core texts, with the sole exception of the "Kang gao" 康誥, almost never figure in citations, while the more recent ones constantly recur.

In addition to new genres of speeches and the extension of their chronological range, the late documents of the *Shang shu* developed new themes. Some, such as the "Lü xing" 呂刑, gave sage origins to institutional developments of the Warring States. Others, notably the "Yao dian" 堯典 and the "Yu gong" 禹貢 demonstrated the tendency in the middle and late Warring States period to compose texts that depicted the entire world, placing them under the aegis of ancient sages.

In addition to composing new documents that lent the prestige of antiquity to discussions of current issues, and to quoting these compositions as authorities in their textual traditions, Warring States schoolmen also incorporated history directly into their own writing. The *Mencius* contains narratives of the deeds of the early sages that provide both a critique of Warring States practice and models for reform. The *Xunzi*, by contrast, largely rejects traditions of the early sages and focuses on precedents provided by the Zhou kings. Both these texts, as well as parts of the *Mozi*, invoked the past as a means of criticizing and reforming the present. Such late Warring States compositions as the *Han Feizi* and the *Lü shi chun qiu*, works that closely identified themselves with or were sponsored by contemporary political actors, sought the lessons of the past in more recent history, which provided models of correct and incorrect practices. However, these texts also invoked earlier sages as models for their own policies.

Warring States writers also reworked Zhou chronicles and political speeches into new forms of historical texts. The earliest of these were the works that became the *Zuo zhuan* and the *Guo yu*. The latter is a set of speeches and debates attributed to historical figures and arranged by state of origin. Like some of the documents of the *Shang shu*, but at greater length and with more sophisticated arguments, this text sets "philosophy and rhetoric in a historical setting" and uses speeches attributed to historical actors to enunciate principles.[3] The former also contains speeches and debates, but these are appended to a court chronicle of events in the state of Lu. They are accompanied by extensive narratives and by judgments placed in the mouth of Confucius or an unnamed "gentleman." It works the entire textual program of the *ru*—the *Documents*, the *Odes*, the *Yi* (*Changes*), and the *Li* (*Rites*)—into an historical narrative that elaborates and certifies the value of each of these literary forms.

Another form of writing the past that appeared in the late Warring States was the *Gongyang* commentary to the *Spring and Autumn Annals*. This work assumed that the chronicle had been transmitted by Confucius after being reworked into a set of coded judgments in which seemingly straightforward historical narrative concealed praise or condemnation for the figures involved. This theory, first suggested in the *Mencius*, read an account of the past as the form *par excellence* for the articulation of political philosophy. In its commentaries it also developed an elaborate theory of the relation of "writing" (*wen* 文) to "reality" (*shi* 實) and the manner in which true kingship could reside in the former. This theory of Confucius' textual kingship in an imaginary kingdom created within the chronicle itself provides one of the clearest and most striking demonstrations of the forms of textually based authority in the Warring States period, an authority which in this case hinged on the ability to properly narrate the past.

THE PAST IN SPEECHES

The *Shang shu* came to be regarded as the earliest historical work in China. It is a diverse text, mixing documents that may be the earliest surviving examples of East Asian literature with fourth-century A.D. forgeries. Even the twenty-eight genuine New Text documents range in date from the middle or late Western Zhou to the mid–Warring States period. Their contents also cover a wide range of topics, reflecting the evolving concerns of the authors over the centuries during which they were composed. Despite the difficulties of dating many of the documents, and of understanding their precise import, one can trace the outlines of the evolution of the text. This evolution offers insights into the changing construction of the past associated with political and scholastic developments in the Eastern Zhou period.

Most scholars agree that the earliest documents in the work are the five labeled *gao* and some of the half dozen texts closely linked with them.[4] These are all associated with the first part of the reign of King Cheng (r. 1042/35–1006 B.C.) when effective power supposedly lay in the hands of the regent, the Duke of Zhou. They take the form of "announcements" or speeches by leading political actors, and their content consists "primarily of political argumentation" and the articulation of the principles underlying Zhou power.[5] The issues dealt with include the role of Heaven in political affairs, the principles of succession, the relation of the deceased ruler to his heir, the uses of divination and sacrifice, the balance between king and ministers, the role of punishments, the establishment of a capital, and other problems related to securing Zhou dynastic power. Scholars dispute whether the works are contemporary transcripts of political speeches, or later re-creations to commemorate major events or to use in factional struggles, but most accept that these are Western Zhou compositions and indicate central concerns of the political actors of the period.

The possibility that the documents are related to actual proclamations is strengthened by evidence from bronze inscriptions describing the process of their own composition. In these accounts the recipient of the honors recorded in the bronzes comes into the presence of the king where the decree of the bestowal is read and written down in a second copy by the scribe (*shi* 史). At the end of the ceremony one copy was kept by the recipient and one by the king. At least one inscription cites word for word a passage from a presentation made six years earlier. This indicates the existence of royal archives. Detailed accounts of transcription are rare, but mention of scribes (*shi* 史 or *zuo ce* 作冊) are much more common, as is the application of the adjective "inscribed [on bamboo strips *ce* 冊]" in such phrases as "inscribed commands" (*ce ling* 冊令). A cache of 103 bronzes discovered in 1976 at Zhuangbai 莊白, near Fufeng 扶風 in Shaanxi shows a high degree of intertextuality. One 106-character inscription is composed of text that appears on two earlier bronzes, one from an earlier generation. This shows the existence of written documents in lineage archives that were transcribed onto bronzes. If such archives preserved the texts of routine bestowals, it is not unlikely that they also stored those of major proclamations by leading political figures.[6]

With the eclipse of the Zhou house, however, many of the old issues ceased to be of importance. The Zhou continued to rule in name, however, and the documents dealing with the bases of their power still enjoyed prestige in some circles. For this reason certain individuals composed additional documents devoted to questions of more immediate concern. Notable among these were the texts purporting to depict the oaths proclaimed by commanders prior to the battles that established the Xia, Shang, and Zhou dynasties, as well as two historical cases from the Spring and Autumn period. The latter two would be contemporary documents, while the other three are clearly projections into the past of Eastern Zhou practices.[7] The emphasis on the battle as the basis of dynastic power, and the rewards and punishments distributed by the ruler, probably indicate the increasing importance of warfare and the ritual presentation of booty in the self-definition of the Spring and Autumn elite.

The composition of documents treating the Xia and Shang conquests as equivalent to that by the Zhou also indicates the emergence of a model of history defined by regular dynastic transitions. The idea of dynastic succession as a recurring event emphasizes the transcience of royal power. It was already present in the earlier documents, which treat the shifting of the mandate from Shang to Zhou, but with these new documents a unique achievement of the Zhou founders became just one in a series. This new attitude toward the dynasty indicates a recognition of the waning power of Zhou and the possibility of its downfall.

Even later are a small number of New Text documents whose contents, language, and placement in the canon indicate origins in the Warring States or even the Qin. The most important of these are the "Yao dian" 堯典, the "Gao Yao mo"

皋陶謨, the "Yu gong" 禹貢, and the "Hong fan" 洪範. The first three are attributed to the sages of high antiquity and, together with one of the oath texts, they constitute the entirety of surviving New Text documents attributed to predynastic rulers. The "Hong fan" offers a comprehensive model of government supposedly presented to King Wu of the Zhou by a virtuous noble of the Shang. It is a variation on the Warring States *topos* of the retired or hidden man of virtue who is sought out by the ruler and presents him with lessons in the Way of government.[8]

These documents have several distinctive features. First, several are presented explicitly as written texts. The character 典 "dian" in the title of the "Yao dian" is often associated with texts in the Warring States period, and the document begins with a lengthy third-person narrative before turning into a dialogue between Yao and some of his officials. The "Yu gong" for its part, consists entirely of third-person narrative with no passages of quotation. Thus the shift toward third-person narrative previously noted in the philosophical texts appears even in the *Shang shu*, a work generally identified as a collection of speeches.

Another innovation is the prominence of numerical categorization in several documents. The "Yu gong" in its first part divides China into nine sections on the model of the magic square, and it presents major geographic features grouped under such numerological rubrics as the "Nine Rivers," the "Nine Wastes," or the "Four Peaks." Its final section presents a model of China as five concentric zones defined by their increasing distance from the ruler and the consequent decline in their level of civilization. The numbers nine and five both figured prominently in the numerological speculations of the late Warring States and Han, particularly the latter, which attained a predominant position in the theory of the "Five Phases." The theory of statecraft in the "Hong fan" is articulated largely in terms of numbered lists: the nine divisions of the "Great Plan," the five phases, the five personal matters, the eight objects of government, the five dividers of time, the three virtues, and the five sources of happiness. The "Gao Yao mo" relies on numerical categories such as the nine branches of kin, nine virtues, five duties, five forms of generous conduct, five ceremonial robes, five ornaments [of the robes], and five punishments. The "Yao dian" uses fewer such lists, but its discussion of calendrical measurements exhibits the Warring States belief in numbers as a form of control.[9]

This constant use of enumeration indicates a final significant feature of these documents, their claims to be comprehensive accounts of the world. The recourse to numbered lists so prominent in this period was an expression of the ambition to attain an all-inclusive wisdom that brought the whole world within the purview of intellect, without collapsing under the weight of endless details. Numbers had the dual virtue of suggesting completeness—the five flavors or five notes standing for all possible flavors or notes—while presenting the subject in a manageable form. Larger categories that escaped ready enumeration could be named and thus brought under control through use of such numbers as *bai* 百 "hundred," where the category was theoretically countable, or *wan* 萬 "ten thousand, myriad," where it was finite but beyond counting. Finally, enumeration allowed the fixing of equivalences that drew diverse phenomena into comprehensive schemata through the simple fact of being numbered.

The "Yao dian," which derives from early Chinese mythology relating to the course of the sun, is an example of the use of numbers for schematic purposes. It deals with the sage king Yao's delimitation of the world and invention of the calendar as a model for statecraft.[10] His defining time and space, and incorporating both into the human realm, is achieved through the play of variations on the number "four." He assigns a separate astronomer—figures derived from the old sun god—to each of the four directions. These figures thus form a mandala spatially encompassing the world. Each astronomer-god and his direction are also identified with one of the four seasons and with the solstice or equinox that defines that season. Finally each astronomer-god/direction/season/solstice-equinox is linked to the changes of birds and beasts, and the associated alterations in human conduct, that mark that season. In this way the text provides an enumerated schema of the world calqued onto the cycle of the solar year, thereby offering a comprehensive space-time chart and a model for human conduct. This textual schema anticipates or derives from the calendrical model of government that informs the *Lü shi chun qiu* and its derivatives. Although compact, it aims at the comprehensive depiction of the world's structure that became the textual ideal in the late Warring States.

The "Yu gong" uses recurring groups of nine to furnish a schematic map in which the arrangement of mountains and rivers is numerically linked to a grid structure that defined the known world. This grid, in turn, was proven to be significant through its identification with the magic square that had come to the fore in Warring States models of intelligible structures.[11] The number nine is also important, because it indicated completeness, a sense which underlay its use in the title of song cycles in the *Chu ci*.[12] The final section shifts the model of the world from the square based on "nine" lesser squares to the circle based on "five" concentric rings. This is probably a late addition to the text, reflecting the rise of the number five at the end of the Warring States to a dominant position among the magic numbers. It also shows the open character of texts sketched in chapter 2. However, both sections share a common aspiration toward the generation of a comprehensive model made intelligible through the power of enumeration.

The "Hong fan" and "Gao Yao mo" likewise employ enumerated lists in order to combine completeness with intelligibility, but they organize the world not in terms of time and space but rather human attributes and activities. The "Hong fan" or "Great Plan" begins with an account of the revelation of its "nine divisions" to Yu, the same sage who instituted the nine-square division of the world in the "Yu gong." After enumerating the nine divisions, the text announces each division by its number and then lists its contents. At the center of the structure, in slot number five, appears the "sovereign ultimate" or "royal standard" (*huang ji* 皇極). This section, the longest in the document, textually and numerologically defines the position of the single monarch in whom all numerical categories converge and from whom order and civilization proceed. As Michael Nylan has argued, the royal power that this section articulates is the central meaning of the text.[13] This is shown by its numerical position and by the fact of being the sole category that exists as a unity, surrounded by rubrics that are invariably plural.

The history of the composition of the *Shang shu* can thus be summarized as a gradual transition from the realm of the state to that of the schools. The concern of the earliest documents with the nature of the dynasty and related political questions suggests that they were composed by or intended for political actors devoted to the Zhou. The second layer includes texts patterned on political speech or writing, but the history they suggest is one of a succession of dynasties. Their audience seems to have been ambitious nobles of the Spring and Autumn period, whose aspirations had begun to look beyond the Zhou. In the final layer political questions largely disappear, or rather they are translated into schematizing moral and cosmological theory. The appeal to models organized around numbers and numerical correspondences is a feature of late Warring States philosophical writings. The fact that they appear as organizing principles in late *Shang shu* documents indicates that the collection had become the property of schoolmen. The past had become a realm in which schoolmen discovered the sagely origins of their own concerns and practices, and history the ground on which the schoolmen asserted their independence from the state order. This independence is ultimately justified by the transitory character of royal power, and by the fact that the sagely model underpinning all successive dynasties survives in the body of texts preserved and generated by the schools, which consequently became the permanent ground of an ephemeral worldly authority.

The schoolmen's cooptation of the literary remains of the Zhou state, and their use of these remains and their derivatives to establish their own position, can also be traced through the shifting patterns of quotations of the *Shu*. In the *Lun yu*, three passages explicitly cite the *Shu*, and three others include phrases cited in other texts—the *Mozi* and the *Zuo zhuan*—as quotations from the *Shu*.[14] No titles are cited. Although Yao, Shun, Yu, the Xia and the Shang are invoked, one passage states that Confucius cannot prove anything about the rituals of Shang and Xia because of the absence of documentation. Another depicts Confucius declaring loyalty to Zhou because it could examine all of the three dynasties.[15] The absence of written records for periods prior to the Zhou, and the consequent taking of Zhou as a model, indicate a *Shang shu* limited to chapters claiming to date from the Zhou. It is also possible that an active commitment to the Zhou heritage and the Zhou state led to the rejection of the supposedly earlier chapters as unreliable.

In the next generation of textual traditions the situation changes. First, the frequency of citations increases dramatically. The *Mencius* cites the *Shang shu* twenty-five times. Nine cases cite titles, and seven titles are mentioned. The *Mozi* cites thirty-five passages, fourteen with titles, and includes the titles of ten documents. The *Zuo zhuan* cites fifty-four passages, fifteen with titles, and includes the names of nine documents. This text is distinctive in citing texts by the name of the dynasty with which they were identified. The *Guo yu* cites only fourteen passages, providing the document titles for nine of them.[16] This rise in the frequency of quotations suggests the increasing importance of textual authority within the schools.

Also significant is the dynastic distribution of the chapters cited. Whereas the *Lun yu* asserted the absence of reliable records prior to the Zhou, texts appearing in the fourth century frequently cite documents attributed to earlier periods. Of the twenty-five passages cited in the *Mencius*, six are attributed to the era of Yao and Shun, one to the Xia, ten to the Shang, and eight to the Zhou. Out of thirty-five quotations in the *Mozi*, nine are attributed to the Xia, eight to the Shang, and the rest to the Zhou. Of fifty-four quotations in the *Zuo zhuan*, one is attributed to the time of Yao, fifteen to the Xia, nine to the Shang, and two are not chronologically located. The remaining twenty-seven, or one half, are Zhou. Of fourteen in the *Guo yu*, three are Xia, three Shang, two not located, and the rest Zhou. Thus pre-Zhou texts, denied in the *Lun yu*, represent more than half of the corpus of citations from the *Shang shu* in fourth-century texts.

Several factors contribute to this development. First, the passage of time led to an increase in the number of supposedly early chapters composed and thus available for citation. Second, the decline of the Zhou house and rise of ambitious territorial rulers claiming the title of king brought to the fore the theme of dynastic decline and transition. This theme was read into the past through increasing emphasis on repeated transfers of sovereignty. Appeal to the transfer of power from one dynasty to another is particularly important in the *Mencius*, with its explicit defense of the overthrow of wicked monarchs and its belief in the imminent arrival of a new sage. The *Mencius*'s appeals to pre-Zhou history also indicate the rejection of contemporary political practice described in chapter 2, a rejection couched in references to the Way of Yao and Shun.

Other fourth-century texts are also marked by appeals to fictive pre-Zhou documents, but the pattern is different from that of the *Mencius*. Most notable is the absence of references to documents from the era of Yao and Shun. Whereas these emblems of rule through virtue are quoted frequently in the *Mencius*, they are absent from the *Mozi* and *Guo yu* and appear only once in the *Zuo zhuan*. These texts are distinguished by the predominance among the fictive pre-Zhou documents of attributions to the Xia. An examination of chapter titles cited in the *Mozi* indicates many documents associated with the Xia that did not survive into the Han. The presence in the Mohist canon of many Xia chapters probably reflects the adoption of Yu as the patron sage of this textual tradition. The *Zuo zhuan*, in contrast, is marked by the number of titles of Zhou documents cited. A comparison of the titles cited in the *Zuo zhuan* and those in the Han New Text *Shang shu* indicates that the latter had largely taken shape by the last decades of the fourth century.

On the basis of differential patterns of citations, Matsumoto Masaaki argues that by the late fourth century there existed at least two and probably three distinct *Shang shu*, a *ru* version exemplified by the citations in the *Mencius*, a Mohist version, and a historian's version indicated by the citations in the *Zuo zhuan* and the *Guo yu*.[17] Given the intellectual positions adopted in the last two texts, they would represent an alternative version of the *ru* tradition. Whether or not one accepts this particular taxonomy, the variations in citations, particularly those between the Mohists and the others, suggest that by the fourth century the *Shang shu* had in fact become the property of the schoolmen. As such it was modified through the composition of new documents applied to the specific programs of each tradition. The changing patterns of citation indicate, as did the changes in content discussed above, the shift of the *Shu* from the world of political actors to that of schoolmen and their textual traditions.

This transformation of political proclamations into tools of scholastic argumentation, with the intellectual commitments of the authors fixing different collections of documents to be cited as authorities, continued into the late Warring States and early Han period. The clearest split was between the *ru* and the non-*ru*. Among the latter, as represented by the *Han Feizi* and the *Lü shi chun qiu*, documents quoted or adapted in arguments are primarily pre-Zhou, dealing with the ancient sages. The Zhou kings appear primarily as the last figures on lists of dynastic founders. The former, as represented by the *Xunzi* and the *Li ji*, cite primarily the Zhou documents, and with one exception the non-Zhou citations derive from the Shang. Quotations in the *Xunzi*, apart from one dated to the Shang, are all attributed to the Zhou. The divergence between the *Xunzi* and the *Li ji*, marked by the substantial inclusion of Shang documents in the latter, suggests divisions, perhaps regional differences, within the *ru* tradition. Another notable feature is that three quarters of the passages quoted in the *Xunzi* appear in the Han New Text *Shang shu*, indicating the probable derivation of the latter from the former.[18] The pattern of citations indicates a basic intellectual divide of the period. The *ru* upheld a re-interpreted Zhou as the model of kingship. Sources tied more closely to the state sphere espoused a model in which the primary lesson of the past was the fact of change.

There were, however, common features to middle and late Warring States uses of the *Shang shu* that suggest important aspects of the writing of the past shared by rival textual traditions in the period. First, citations were drawn largely from documents more recent in date of composition, although often more ancient in their supposed origins. Of the seven or eight documents that represent the probable core of the anthology, only the "Kang gao" is quoted more than once or twice in the Warring States period. Other than this, the documents quoted more than ten times are the "Tai shi" 太誓, the "Hong fan," the "Lü xing," and the "Yao dian." Even when earlier documents like the "Kang gao" are cited, the passages quoted are linguistically close to the language of the Warring States texts and hence more comprehensible.[19] This suggests that by the Warring States period the written language had changed so much that even scholars found it difficult to understand ancient texts. This impression is confirmed by the "Yao" commentary to the *Yi jing* discovered at Mawangdui. One passage in this text justifying the use of the *Yi* states that the *Shang shu* has "many obstructions" [*duo e* 多闕], that is, passages that cannot be understood.[20] The past was accessible only in writings composed long after the events they presumed to narrate. The earlier chapters were preserved, perhaps out of veneration for their obvious antiquity, but they were not employed by Warring States scholars in their active reconstruction of history.

In addition to being linguistically bound to their own textual products or those of their immediate predecessors, the past written by the scholars was defined by their own concerns. Documents cited in the Warring States could be divided into two categories: those concerned with government practice, especially the uses of punishment, and those devoted to schematic world models. In the first category the most important were the "Kang gao," "Lü xing," and the "Hong fan," while the latter included the "Hong fan," the "Yao dian," and the "Yu gong." If the Warring States "Tai shi" was similar to the Han version that has come down to us, then it too was about the use of punishments in the broad sense, since it demonstrates the last Shang king's wanton cruelty in his use of physical torture and military force, and contrasts this with the justified, punitive warfare of King Wu.

In summary, the supposed proclamations of the political actors of the Western Zhou were initially preserved by the Zhou nobility out of reverence for their dynastic founders and as articulations of the principles and practices that defined the state. As new forms of ritual speech, the prebattle oath and ritual of enfeoffment, became central to the Zhou nobility, and as the decline of the dynasty led to revived interest in historical precedents for dynastic transition, new documents were produced articulating these concerns. The latest documents of the anthology include comprehensive schemata of the world and of government. These rely on numbered rubrics, and are themselves sometimes organized in numerical structures. Several of them also contain substantial third-person narratives preceding and framing the pronouncements of the political actors depicted in the text. The "Yu gong" consists entirely of narration. These documents indicate the shift of textual production from political actors to scholars committed to philosophical programs. The changing pattern of quotations in the philosophical traditions indicates a similar process. At the beginning the *Lun yu* insists on the Zhou documents as the sole reliable ones. In the next stage interest shifts toward nominally pre-Zhou texts, the works of Yao and Shun in the case of the *Mencius*, and the Xia in the cases of the *Mozi* and the *Zuo zhuan*. At the end of the period differential patterns of quotation indicate a split between the *ru*, drawing on the Zhou in the case of the *Xunzi* or the Shang and Zhou in the case of the *Li ji*, and the statist traditions, which cite largely pre-Zhou documents. All traditions, however, privileged the quotation of texts that were composed relatively late, and which offered theories of punishment or schematic models of the world. In this way the *Shang shu* anthology, when treated as a totality and a source of quotation, presents a palimpsest of the changing uses of the past that accompanied the decline of the Zhou nobility and the rise of the scholarly textual traditions.

THE PAST IN POLITICAL PHILOSOPHY

Depictions of the past by the philosophical traditions were not confined to the composition and citation of speeches attributed to sages and ministers. The masters themselves, or the disciples who framed their words, narrated and interpreted past events. Like the documents, the writings of the textual traditions created an image of the past that sanctioned the authority of the schools and provided sagely precedents for their philosophical concerns or social programs. The sanction provided by the past took a variety of forms. As we have already seen, in the middle chapters of the *Shang shu*, the past demonstrated the transient nature of individual dynasties, and thereby relegated political power to a secondary level. The higher level attributed to Heaven or the lingering influence of earlier sages existed in the form of the scholastic textual traditions or earlier Zhou works preserved by the schoolmen. In this way the past as embodied in their texts provided the schoolmen with a foundation for their claims of independence vis-à-vis the state. It also provided a sanction for their programs based on the presumed wisdom and authority of early sages and dynastic founders. Furthermore, the written past underpinned theories of change and the mastery thereof that constituted an essential element of the ideal of political and philosophical sagehood (see chapter 1). Finally, the past provided the ground for an artificial language that existed exclusively in texts and served as a privileged medium for intellectual traditions and ultimately for the imperial state.

Most of these themes already appear in the *Lun yu*, although not yet in fully developed form. The replacement of one dynasty by another is not mentioned, but the sequence of dynasties appears in discussions of the evolution of rituals.[21] One passage states that although the master can discuss the rites of the Xia and the Shang, the successor states created to preserve their sacrifices provide no written evidence for study. Another states that the Zhou had an overview of the two earlier dynasties, and consequently was "fully patterned" or "splendid in cultural attainments" (*yu yu* 郁郁). In a third the disciple Zai Wo tells Duke Ai of Lu about the different trees planted at the altar of the soil by each of the three dynasties. A later chapter argues that each dynasty inherited the rites of its predecessor and made modifications, but there is a constant thread running through them. Another states that one should adopt the calendar of the Xia, the carriage of the Shang, and the ceremonial cap of the Zhou. A final passage asserts that the three dynasties held to the straight path by using the people as their "standard (*shi* 試)."[22]

In all these passages the Three Dynasties appear not as demonstrations of political impermanence, nor as exemplary models, but rather as proofs of the constant adaptation of rites, and as resources to be drawn on. Zhou is privileged by its position as the culmination, but the practices of Xia and Shang can both be adapted where they prove valuable. Confucius' response to Zai Wo suggests a desire to avoid taking any past practice as definitive. Instead, as suggested by the remark about the people as a constant standard and by the belief in a continuity underlying changes in specific practices, authority is located in human nature as recognized by the sage.

While the *Lun yu* rejects past practice as an absolute authority, it invokes the past as a foundation for claims to truth and virtue. First, Confucius describes himself as a man who "loves antiquity," and antiquity is asserted as a standard for criticizing current practice. In an early chapter Confucius cites the *Odes* to prove that the Ji lineage has no right to perform a certain sacrifice. Other passages take the old Zhou court music as a standard to condemn more recent songs; assert that the men of antiquity were exemplary in being disinclined to speak; state that due to his love of antiquity Confucius transmits without creating—as opposed to those who "create without knowing;" condemn the "filiality of the present" as inferior; contrast men of antiquity who studied to improve themselves with men of the present day who study to impress others; note approvingly that all the men of antiquity observed the three-year mourning period; contrast ancient times when the Zhou still "had the Way" with the decline of more recent days; and argue that even in their faults the men of antiquity were superior to those of the present.[23] While rejecting any specific dynastic precedent as authoritative, the authors of the *Lun yu* espouse the belief in an undefined antiquity that possessed the true Way, an idealized state existing virtually out of time against which the present is judged and found wanting.

To the extent that this antiquity has any specific content, it lies in the sages, or in the less exalted roles of worthy minister and true gentleman. The most frequently cited ancient exemplar was the Duke of Zhou, with whom the Confucius of the *Lun yu* strongly identifies as the embodiment of the virtuous minister, creator of the Zhou order, and founder of Confucius' home state of Lu. Also frequently cited are the brothers Bo Yi and Shu Qi, who along with Liu Xiahui embody the ideal of knowing when to take up service and when to withdraw, or in some passages an excessive virtue that contrasts with Confucius' ideal of the "middle way." The *Lun yu* also cites the ancient sages Yao, Shun, and Yu. The former two serve as general exemplars of sagehood, while Shun also figures once as the model of the king who rules through non-action. Yu appears twice, once in association with Hou Ji, and in both cases he is identified as a model for abstemiousness and the willingness to toil. The Zhou kings scarcely appear in the text. King Wen is cited once in a passage that puns on his name. King Wu appears only in a quotation from the *Shang shu*, and with his father Wen in an attribution of Confucius' wisdom to the lingering influence of the Zhou founders.[24] In this appeal to individual sages rather than to specific doctrines or rules the *Lun yu* uses the past to ground not any teachings, but rather the figure of the master himself. The authority of the text derives from that of the master, and he in turn is historically sanctioned through the image of earlier sages.

The *Lun yu* also discusses more recent political figures from the Spring and Autumn period. Most prominent among these is the minister of Qi, Guan Zhong. Other political actors assessed include the hegemons Duke Huan of Qi and Duke

Wen of Jin, as well as the reforming minister Zi Chan of Zheng. Whereas the sages are cited as a form of sanction, with little discussion of their conduct, those closer to the time of Confucius are the objects of detailed critiques leading to the bestowal of praise or blame. Guan Zhong is condemned in the earliest chapters for his ritual violations, but in later chapters Confucius defends him by arguing that he rescued Zhou culture from destruction by barbarians. His master Duke Huan is also praised, while Duke Wen of Jin is condemned.[25] Here the past is employed not as a ground of authority but as an arena in which the sage exercises his moral acumen. These passages are closely related to those in which Confucius judges the character of his own disciples, and they anticipate his role as putative author of the *Chun qiu*, where he codes judgments in his choice of words.

One passage in the *Lun yu* also uses the past as the locus of an ancient language that distinguishes scholars from ordinary men. It states that Confucius used the "refined language" (*ya yan* 雅言) for the *Odes*, the *Documents*, and the *Rites*.[26] Here a privileged body of texts is set apart by the distinctive character of its language which defines scholars as an elite group granted authority through their linguistic ties to past sages. Two other passages make the related claim that cults, both ancestral and those to nature deities, are at least in part made sacred through their ancient origins.[27]

While recent scholarship emphasizes its logical methods of argument, the Mohist canon routinely, indeed obsessively, inscribes its social program in an imagined antiquity and appeals to the authority of past writings. This reliance on the past takes several forms. First, all the items of the Mohist program—elevation of the worthy, identification with superiors, rejection of aggressive warfare, reliance on the will of Heaven, frugality, rejection of fate, critique of music and elaborate funerals—are attributed to "the ancient sages" or the "sages of the three dynasties." The sages often appear in lists—Yao, Shun, Yu, Tang, King Wen, and King Wu—as an undifferentiated mass representing a common ideal. Against this list of ancient sages are set the "violent" (*bao* 暴) kings of antiquity—Jie, Zhou, You, and Li—who are blamed for all positions contrary to Mohist teachings. Thus they were the first to espouse belief in fate, thereby denying responsibility for their downfalls, and the first to deny the existence of spirits and thus to fail to offer sacrifice. Appeals to antiquity decline in the later "dialogue" chapters and do not figure in those on logic, but they remained central to the Mohist program as defined in its canon.[28]

The evil kings of antiquity are not, however, the primary targets of criticism. Like the *Lun yu*, the Mohist canon uses its imagined past to criticize the practices and beliefs of its own day, but it denounces *ru* doctrines as well as existing political institutions. Against the normative value of the "ancient" (*gu* 古) the "modern" (*jin* 今) is an object of criticism. At the end of many chapters modern rulers are enjoined to adopt as their models the old sage kings or the Mohist social program, which is their theoretical equivalent. Apart from a few passages in praise of the hegemons, accounts of Eastern Zhou history oppose a positive "ancient" to a negative "modern." They focus on the prevalence of warfare and corrupting luxury in recent times.[29]

The Mohist tradition makes the appeal to antiquity an epistemological principle. The chapters "Against Fate" note the need for "standards" (*yi* 儀) by which to judge arguments. They posit the existence of three such standards, called either "gnomons" (*biao* 表) or "models" (*fa* 法). The first of these (the "root" *ben* 本) is "the affairs of the ancient sage kings" (*gu zhe sheng wang zhi shi* 古者聖王之事). Using this standard of proof, the *Mozi* demonstrates that fate does not exist by noting that the same conditions that led Jie and Zhou to lose their kingdoms allowed Tang and King Wu to establish theirs. Hence it is human will and morality rather than Heaven or circumstance that determine the course of events.[30] Just as the sages provided a model for correct political action, they also offered a ground of proof.

The Mohist authors assume that their opponents also appeal to the sages as a form of proof. They depict hypothetical adversaries who argue that the sages practiced warfare, insisted that fate controlled the course of events, or withdrew from the world to live a spartan existence and cultivate themselves in solitude. The sages are here established as a field of disputation, and the Mohists offer arguments to show that their opponents have misunderstood the sages' actions. They do this by making distinctions, for example, between aggressive warfare and the punishment of evil, or by showing the greater benefit resulting from the Mohist reading of the sages' deeds.[31]

Ancient history is more than one of three standards of proof, for in the middle chapter on fate the sage kings provide two out of the three. The second standard ("origin" *yuan* 原), which is elsewhere described as the "content [or 'nature' *qing* 情] of the eyes and ears of the common people" *bai xing er mu zhi shi* 百姓耳目之實, that is, what all people see and hear, in this passage is described as "proving it by means of the writings of the earlier kings" *zheng yi xian wang zhi shu* 徵以先王之書.[32] When hypothetical adversaries elsewhere challenge the validity of appeals to the perceptions of the common people, which are prone to error, the Mohists appeal to the pronouncements of the sages, which are unquestionably accurate and have the added authority of being in writing.[33]

Not only is the second standard supplanted or underwritten by appeal to precedent, but the third standard, "utility" (*yong* 用), hinges on appeal to the "affairs of the ancient kings." All the chapters against fate prove that belief in a power controlling human destiny is not useful by arguing that it was espoused by "fraudulent" people and "violent" kings in antiquity. This led them to ignore their duties and to behave wantonly, in the assurance that their actions had no impact on their destiny. In contrast, the sages denied the existence of fate, worked diligently at their tasks, and took charge of their own fates.[34] Thus the standard of utility was also inseparable from models provided by the sages and villains of antiquity.

These appeals to the historical sages were part of a broader reliance on accounts of the early kings to prove that Mohist doctrine could be put into practice in the real world. At several points the text defends itself against the charge that the ideals it espouses—the elevation of the worthy, identification with one's superior, and universal love—were simply the "words of Master Mo" with no application in the political sphere. The defense takes the form of citing the texts of the sages—the *Odes* and the *Documents*—to demonstrate that the Mohist political program had actually been used by the sages in governing.[35] In this manner the example of the sages served not only as model and proof, but also as a certification of the applicability of what would otherwise have been dismissed as the textual fantasy of a philosophical tradition.

The example of the sage kings depended on writing for its existence, and the *Mozi* is unique among Warring States texts in the attention devoted to writing. It repeatedly cites supposedly early documents from the *Shi* and the *Shu*, discusses the importance of writing in the society of its day, and develops a theory of why certain texts were written down by the sages. In these observations, the *Mozi* articulates the first theory of the use of writing as a form of authoritative language and a means of maintaining order. Based on the theory of the sagely origins of certain poems and historical documents, these discussions of writing translate the principle of the authority of the sage kings into a doctrine of the authority of their writings, and by extension provide a mythohistorical charter for the Mohist textual project.

The Mohist theory of writing has several aspects. First, the canon repeatedly appeals to the authority of the "writings [or 'words' or 'laws'] of the previous [or 'sage'] kings." Such phrases usually introduce quotations from the Mohist version of the *Shang shu* or the Zhou odes.[36] To quote from the *Documents* and *Odes* is common in other texts of the same period, but the insistence that these are writings of the ancient kings establishes a theory of writing as a mode of language made powerful through its ability to preserve the teachings of great men across time.

In addition to insisting on the *written* character of the works it cites, the Mohists dwell on the activity of the sages as writers. In a formula that appears in several essays, they note that the sages "write [their teachings] on bamboo and silk, carve them on metal and stone, and engrave them on platters and basins."[37] This formula first occurs after a hypothetical interlocutor has argued that extending benevolence and duty to all men would be as impossible as "taking Mt. Tai under one's arm and crossing over the great rivers." Master Mo replies that no one had ever carried Mt. Tai across a river, but that universal love was practiced by the sages. He knew this to be so because they had caused their practices to be written, carved, and inscribed, and thus allowed later generations to know of them. The writings of the sages were the remains of a vanished world surviving only in texts, and they criticized Warring States practices. Through the incorporation of these remains, the Mohist textual tradition became an alternative model of monarchy that claimed a pedigree and efficacy superior to the states of its own day.

The other appearances of the formula on writing, carving, and inscribing follow a similar pattern. First a doctrine of the Mohists is presented, then it is asserted that the sages practiced it, and it concludes that the sages set down this practice in writing to transmit it to later generations. The text sometimes rhetorically asks why this was done, and replies that it was in order that the descendants of the sages might understand the doctrine in question. Finally, it presents a quotation from some supposedly early text as proof. The one major variation occurs in the chapter on ghosts. After stating that the sages wrote down the doctrine of the existence of ghosts on bamboo and silk in order to instruct their descendants, it states that they were afraid that these texts might rot or be eaten by insects, so they had them carved on metal and stone and inscribed on vessels in order to emphasize their importance. In order to make certain that their descendants respectfully learned this doctrine, they also filled up sheets of silk and rolls of bamboo with discussions of the existence of ghosts. This passage thus elaborates one of the earliest versions of the idea of preserving true doctrines through inscription in durable materials, and also insists on the increasing abundance of writing and its deliberate use to combat error.

The pedagogic role of writing figures in several other passages in the *Mozi.* First, the passage on writing, carving, and inscribing in the chapter "Against Fate" insists that the evil kings of antiquity had argued, in order to explain their own downfalls, that fate determined the course of human events. This teaching had spread to the "unworthy" people of antiquity, so the sages had written texts denying the existence of fate in order to combat the spread of popular error. Those who espoused the idea of the nonexistence of spirits are said to be in opposition to the *writings* of the sages, where the text thus comes to stand for the sages themselves in their role as political and intellectual authorities.[38]

The chapter on funerals notes that those who endorse lavish ceremonies claim to be following the Way of the sages. After refuting this with quotes from sagely law and accounts of the funerals of the sages, the text argues that the use of lavish funerals was the practice of the evil kings. It then posits an interlocutor who asks how a doctrine contrary to the sages came to be practiced by all the princes in the "middle states." Master Mo replies that it is purely a matter of "familiarity" (*xi* 習) and "custom" (*su* 俗), and he then shows how custom among other peoples also justifies the murder of firstborn sons, cannibalism, and the abandonment of widows.[39] Here the writings of the sages, which provide principles valid across time and space, are set against unwritten custom that expresses local character and the genius of place. In this way the opposition of "writing" versus "custom" becomes a variant on the argument for the superiority of the comprehensive over the partial. This theme will re-appear in chapter 7 as a central element in the theory of the canonical text.

A final variant in the Mohist theory of writing as a form of rule is passages that refer to the sages promulgating their writings as laws (*xian* 憲 or *fa* 法), codes of punishments (*xing* 刑), and oaths (*shi* 誓). They are said to have distributed writings in these three forms—roughly corresponding to the later documents in the *Shang shu*—to their people in order to teach them that fate does not exist.

Other passages refer to the sages issuing texts as a means of instructing the peasantry. These and related statements insist on the abundance of texts in the world and trace this fact back to the activities of the sages.[40]

The role of writing as a means of control also appears in a negative context. One chapter describes rulers who recorded their military conquests in chronicles. As a result, their descendants knew them only as conquerors and assumed that slaughter and destruction were proper for a ruler.[41] This passage employs the formula of "writing, carving, and inscribing" commonly applied to the writings of the sages. This creates an exact parallel between proper writings that lead men in the path of truth, and deviant writings that transmit criminal models to descendants in the form of inscriptions on bronzes or the royal chronicles kept by each of the Warring States. These arguments also assume that people knew their ancestors only through writings, which are the sole means by which the past transmits its influence, for good or for ill, into the present.

While writing in Mohist theory serves primarily to preserve past examples and guide conduct, it also plays several subordinate roles. First, it provides empirical data about the world. The primary proof for the existence of ghosts is stories drawn from state chronicles. The conclusions of all but one story include the formula, "At that time all those who were present saw it, and all those who were far away heard of it. It is written in the *Annals* of X [state]."[42] The fact of inscription demonstrates the truth of an account. It is granted a weight equal to that of direct perception.

A final role of writing in the *Mozi* is its use in rituals and communication with spirits. In order to settle a long-standing legal dispute between two nobles, the king of Qi had each party write down his account of the case. A goat was sacrificed and each party swore an oath that was consecrated by smearing the blood of the animal on their lips. Then each of the parties read his inscribed testimony, and when the guilty party spoke the corpse of the goat sprang up and butted him.[43] This ceremony is linked to the blood covenants employed in the political realm of the period, as well as the legal practice of requiring written testimony guaranteed by oaths. In each of these cases the text had to be inscribed in order to be effective.

Another ritual use of writing was the composition of eulogies (*hao* 耗) for the dead. The ruler of Lu was so pleased with a eulogy written for a favorite concubine that he appointed the author to an office. This act was criticized by Master Mo because the purpose of a eulogy was to narrate the will/ambitions (*zhi* 志) of the deceased, an act which scarcely qualified one to serve as an administrator.[44] The story suggests a link in Mohist thought between the ritual uses of writing in funerals and the role of verse, which was defined through its ability to testify to *zhi* 志 (see chapter 4). It also indicates that literary attainments were a path to officeholding in the period, but one not universally approved.

The *Mencius* shared major features with the Mohist essays in its use of the past, but it also had distinctive traits. As noted in chapter 2, it proposed an idealized antiquity as an alternative to the institutions of its day, and as will be discussed in chapter 4 it used the Zhou *Odes* as historical sources to demonstrate the reality and efficacy of the practices of the sages. It also cited, as shown in the first section of this chapter, the *Shang shu*, where the pre-Zhou sages and Zhou kings appeared with equal frequency. In the text virtually every aspect of Warring States institutions is denounced, and the practice of one or more of the sages presented as a model of how dynasties should be founded, relations between rulers and ministers conducted, land distributed, taxes levied, interstate relations maintained, wars and punishments carried out, royal processions performed, and hunting parks organized.[45] It condemns the hegemons and leading Eastern Zhou ministers as at best inferior imitations and at worst as criminals.[46] In this manner the sages figure as models of kingship to be emulated by contemporary rulers.

The sages were models not only for rulers but for all men. In the *Mencius* sages are cited as models of proper human sexual relations, of the proper treatment of teachers by students, as the standards for correct funerals, as archetypes for the ability to learn from errors, as definitive of the virtues that distinguish men from beasts, as patterns for the practice of filial piety, as examples of the forms of friendship between superior and subordinate, as demonstrations of how virtue is acquired by study, and as exemplars of adaptation to circumstances.[47] This double role of the sages as both model kings and moral exemplars reflects the *ru* theory of the grounding of statecraft in personal morality, as well as the schoolmen's common practice of identifying kingship with the virtues cultivated in the scholastic setting.

The scholastic grounding of the sages divided the *Mencius* from the *Mozi*. Whereas the latter discovered in antiquity sages who denied the entire *ru* program, the former included Confucius and his leading disciples among the exemplary figures of the past.[48] Moreover, the Way of the earlier sages described in the *Mencius* negated the Mohist program, as when it states that the benevolence of Yao and Shun did not extend to all men, but was particularly strong for their kin.[49] With the emergence of interschool debates the same exemplary figures of the past who had embodied the critique of current political practice were used to assert the truth of one's own doctrine and the errors of one's rivals.

Dramatic examples of the use of past sages to condemn intellectual adversaries appear in the *Mencius*'s two accounts of Yu's taming of the flood. The first targets the "School of the Tillers," a minor intellectual tradition advocating that all men without exception should grow their own food.[50] After demonstrating the advantages of the division of labor and asserting a fundamental division between rulers who work with their minds and subjects who toil with their muscles, Mencius narrates the creation of human civilization by the ancient sages. Yao was confronted with a world in which the flood had eliminated all distinctions and boundaries. Wild plants grew everywhere while grains did not ripen, and animals lived among men. Yao appointed Shun to deal with the problem, and the latter in turn charged Yu to restore the waters to their channels and Yi to use fire to expel the birds and beasts. After this Hou Ji taught the people agriculture, while Xie instructed them in the hierarchic divisions that defined human relations. Thus the role of the king and his ministers is to maintain the arts that define human society, so they have no time for agricultural toil. In conclusion he states that his interlocutor is a "southern barbarian," as shown by the fact that he "denies the Way of the Former Kings" (*fei xian wang zhi dao* 非先王之道).[51]

The second flood narrative is part of a longer account of human history elicited by the accusation that Mencius is fond of disputation. Denying such a proclivity, he insists that he argues only because he has no alternative. He traces the course of history as a series of crises in which society collapses, only to be rescued by sagely intervention. The first such crisis was the flood, described in terms similar to the first account. The second follows the disappearance of the sages, when violent kings arose, destroyed the dwellings of the people, introduced "heterodox theories," and the animals returned. In response the Duke of Zhou assisted King Wu to destroy the Shang, expel the animals, and restore the world.

When the sagely Way declined again in the Eastern Zhou, ministers killed their princes and sons their fathers. In response Confucius composed the *Spring and Autumn Annals*. In this he played the role of the Son of Heaven, but no new sage king arose. Consequently the world continued to disintegrate, and the sayings of Yang Zhu and Mo Di filled the empire. The selfishness advocated by the former and the undiscriminating love advocated by the latter both destroyed human ties, reduced men to the level of animals, and "led beasts to devour men." If the teachings of the heterodox schools were not blocked, then not only would animals devour men, but men would soon devour one another. Mencius concludes that he must engage in disputation in order to save the sagely Way from the attacks of Yang and Mo, and thereby protect men from the return of the wild beasts expelled by the earlier sages.[52]

This account employs the past to paint the current intellectual struggle in the most lurid colors imaginable. First it identifies the work of the sages as the rescue of humanity from an original brutish state marked by the absence of moral and physical boundaries between people and animals. It locates the second decline in the era of the evil kings of antiquity. The reign of Shang Zhou is marked not only by the resurgence of the animals, but also the first appearance of heterodox theories. In assigning the origins of false doctrines to Jie and Zhou, the *Mencius* concurs with the *Mozi*. However, in the next stage this convergence ends. Instead the Mohists and Yangists are treated as the rebirth of the heterodox theories of the late Shang, and they are identified not only as harbingers of the renewed assault of man-eating beasts, but the sources of a moral collapse that will end in general cannibalism. Thus the history of the flood, itself a rationalized version of an earlier myth, is here rewritten as a narrative archetype for the interschool polemics that emerged in the fourth century B.C.

The *Mencius* also describes earlier historical writings. It states that the *Spring and Autumn Annals* appeared when the *Odes* ceased to be written. This indicates both the perceived role of the *Odes* as morally charged history and the function of the *Annals* as a form of judgment and suasion. The same passage states that the end of the *Odes* was a result of the disappearance of the "kingly traces" (*wang ji* 王 迹).[53] Confucius' composition of the *Annals* was his "royal" response to the fear inspired by the moral collapse of his age, and the text itself similarly produced "fear" in the rebellious ministers and murderous sons who were its targets.[54] These passages agree that the writing of history was a political task properly pursued by the Son of Heaven and his servants. It was a form of judgment, a literary punishment that restored order through inspiring fear. This Mencian theory of the writing of verse and history anticipates the Mao preface (see chapter 4), where poetry was a matter of celebration or censure whose ultimate subject was always the king. It also anticipates, as discussed in the final section of this chapter, the theory of writing history in the *Gongyang Commentary* to the *Annals*.

Another aspect of the *Mencius*'s theory of writing history is suggested in its final reference to the *Annals*.

> In the *Annals* there are no righteous wars, although one might be a bit better than another. Expeditions are superiors punishing subordinates, but equal states do not attack one another.[55]

The *Mencius* here attributes its own rejection of warfare to the *Spring and Autumn Annals* and hence to Confucius. However, the statement is incorrect, as Dong Zhongshu admitted in his commentary to the *Annals*, even as he tried to defend the *Mencius*.[56] The writing of its own rejection of warfare into earlier histories also leads to the statement "it would be better to have no *Shang shu* at all than to completely believe the *Shang shu*. I accept only two or three strips of the 'Completion of War' (*wu cheng* 武成)."[57] The target of this censorship is the statement in the document, of which the original was lost and only a fourth-century A.D. forgery survives, that so much blood was shed at King Wu's defeat of the Shang that "currents carried [wooden] staves." These passages demonstrate that the authors of the *Mencius* were sufficiently committed to realizing their own theories in the past that the written record had, if necessary, to be altered or destroyed. History was a story in which one discovered moral truths and passed judgment on others, so inconvenient facts or rival narratives had no place in a correctly written past. These passages also echo the *Mencius*'s doctrine on the reading of odes, which insisted that one should not let the surface meaning of words interfere with one's perception of the author's moral intent.[58]

The *Xunzi* developed the vision of the past as the field in which one discovered the confirmation of one's own moral program and the refutation of rival schools.[59] It placed more emphasis on teacher-disciple relations than any other Warring States text, and it treated the past as an extension of the classroom. The "Exhortation to Learning" proclaims that one could not know the meaning of learning without the "inherited words of the First Kings." Learning begins with the recitation of the "classics" (*jing* 經), that is, the textual corpus inherited from the Zhou. It starts with the *Shang shu* and *Odes*, the study of which creates a scholar, and culminates in the texts of *Rituals*, the study of which results in sagehood. A second list, perhaps an interpolation, includes *Rituals*, *Music*, *Odes*, the *Shang shu*, and the *Annals*, and it states that all of Heaven and Earth are complete in these texts. For the first time a body of writing defined the civilized heritage and the path to sagehood. However, as the *Xunzi* notes at several points, these texts can be approached only with the aid of a teacher or, as a second-best alternative, a knowledge of ritual. Without the one or the other the study of the *Odes* and the *Shang shu* will result in nothing but jumbled facts and rote glosses, and leave the student a boorish, untutored *ru*. Here learning and sagehood lie in texts that reveal the truths of past ages, but they can only be approached through the knowledge of a living master.[60]

The importance of the master entails that the sages and evil kings of antiquity were the result of either successful or failed education. The "Exhortation to Learning" and later chapters assert that Jie, Zhou, and the Robber Zhi were insufficiently learned to recognize the principles of humanity and moral obligation. By contrast, Yao and Yu became sages through self-cultivation, and those who cultivated their own character could be the equals of the ancient sages. The sages and evil kings are not actors in narratives of a distant past, but exemplars of education's consequences. This leads to the assertion that the past exists in the present and that one can know the practices of the ancient sages through studying the Later Kings, or even examining a true gentleman or teacher.[61] The doctrine of the potential sagehood of all men, which became a fundamental principle in late imperial China, appears here as a sanction for the power of the teacher. It asserts not the equality of men—an empty potentiality unrealizable in the world—but the power of instruction.

Despite the identity of past and present in underlying principles, the *Xunzi* remained committed to the *ru* position that the institutions and political figures of the past were exemplary. The rituals created by the ancient sages are the basis of any possible civilization, and the Duke of Zhou and King Wen define the ideal types of minister and ruler. More recent political figures, by contrast, are inferior. The Zhou rulers are uniquely valuable models, because they alone have left a sufficient textual record to be of use.[62] In the late Warring States period values survived only in the texts preserved by the *ru* tradition and the teachers who understood them. The only other group that had preserved traces of the former kings was households of hereditary officials. For generations they had saved the laws, measures, maps, and registers of earlier kings, not daring to add or subtract. However, they preserved traditions without understanding their meaning.[63]

An exemplary past surviving only within the textual traditions of the *ru* also figures in the *Xunzi*'s demonstrations that the Way of the sages completely rejects the doctrines of non-*ru* intellectual currents. Having established Confucius' sagehood and the fundamental identity of sagehood across time, the *Xunzi* describes all intellectual alternatives to its own tradition as assaults on civilization.

One passage parallels the sages who have no position of power (*shi* 勢)—Confucius and Zi Gong—and those who do—Shun and Yu. The former allow no rival thinkers into their presence, while the latter first silence and then morally transform them. Intellectual sagehood repels non-*ru* textual traditions, while political sagehood brings them to a halt. The parallel of the sage and the king is cast in the guise of twin modes of censorship. The next passage states that the sages are the model for all mental work, and that all theories not in accord with the "significance of rituals" (*li yi* 禮義) created by the sages are villainous (*jian* 姦) and to be suppressed.[64]

Elsewhere the *ru* are described as those who pattern themselves on the sage kings, while rival textual traditions, most notably the Mohists, are shown to be enemies of the sages. A discussion of the Duke of Zhou concludes that only a sage could have done what he did, and then describes his achievements as those of a "great *ru*." The Mohists, by contrast, with their condemnation of music produce anarchy and with their call for frugality generate poverty. Their Way is antithetical to that of the ancient sages, and brings disorder.[65] The identification of non-*ru* traditions as the negation of the sages is elaborated in the chapter "Dispelling Obsession." Here the sagely Way is defined by a comprehensive wisdom, while ordinary men are blinded by their obsession with one, limited aspect of the "Great Principle(s)" (*da li* 大理). As examples of those who are blind, it begins with evil rulers, follows with their evil ministers, and concludes with the non-*ru* schools. In contrast, Confucius is free from partiality and obsession, and his teachings are "equal to that of the ancient kings." The text is particularly scathing in its attack on the theoreticians of disputation, who are described as criminals.[66] Such doctrines have arisen only because the sage kings have perished and contemporary gentlemen lack the power to control them. Should a true king rise again, they would be suppressed.[67]

So essential to the schools was the model of authority provided by the ancient sages that even the legalist advocates of institutional reforms claimed them as their models. This is noteworthy because these texts sometimes denied that the past could provide a model for present actions. The *Shang Jun shu* begins with a debate in which the eponymous master defends his program of governmental reform by insisting on the need for new policies to meet new circumstances. Received practices are dismissed as mere "custom" (*xi* 習 or *su* 俗). By contrast, past sages were all reformers. "The Three Dynasties, using different rituals, were [all] kings; the Five Hegemons, using different laws, were [all] hegemons."[68] Even this call for reform is justified by the sagely precedent of earlier changes, and appeals to the past run throughout the text.

The appeal to the authority of earlier sages takes several forms. The authors argue that their policies were employed by unnamed "former kings" (*xian wang* 先王) or "sages" (*sheng ren* 聖人). Sometimes this is applied to specific ideas, such as the basing of the state on agriculture and warfare or the patterns of land measurement. Sometimes it figures as a general imprimatur for the authors' programs.[69]

The authors cite specific ancient rulers as exemplary, and the figures named are the same as those in texts of other schools: Shen Nong, Yao, Shun, Yu, Tang, King Wen, and the Duke of Zhou.[70] Elsewhere they echo the first chapter by arguing that the actions of the sages prove the necessity of regular reform, or treat the diverse policies of earlier sages as options from which current rulers could select those suitable to their own times.[71] Finally, one passage takes "long ago" (*xi* 昔) as exemplary, while the characters *jin* 今 ("now") or *shi* 世 ("in this generation") routinely introduce discussions of errors and incorrect practices.[72]

While the *Shang Jun shu* resembles *ru* and Mohist texts in treating sages as exemplary and in the figures it calls sages, it is distinct in two ways. First, the invocation of the sages to prove the necessity of reform moves away from the use of an idealized past as a permanent standard. However, this move is inconsistent, and many passages take the former kings as authoritative models for specific policies. Second, some passages cite recent history as a source of historical lessons. One example of this is the pairing of the "Five Hegemons" with the "Three Kings" as exemplars of the ruler. However, with this single exception all the lessons drawn from recent history are negative.[73]

The other great legalist text, the *Han Feizi*, also sometimes insists that changing circumstances require new policies, and one chapter uses this argument to deny the applicability of the model of the ancient sages to the present. Another chapter denounces Yao, Shun, Tang, and Wu as regicides and enemies of filial piety, although it also cites the Three Kings as exemplary rulers. More frequent are chapters that accept the sages as great rulers and moral exemplars, but insist that they operated according to the same principles as lesser rulers who followed them. This is done by placing the sages in lists of worthy rulers or officials that include figures from the Eastern Zhou period.[74] The primary targets of criticism are not the sages themselves, but scholars who blindly follow certain textual traditions regarding the earlier kings, and the need for written evidence is stressed.[75] Thus the criticisms in the *Han Feizi* are not different in kind from those in the *Mozi*, which denounces the *ru* for misunderstanding the meaning of the sages, or the *Xunzi*, which denounces those who adhere to ancient ways and slavishly follow the letter of the *Odes* and the *Documents*.

The most common attitude toward the sages in the *Han Feizi* is little different from that of earlier philosophical texts. It treats them as exemplars who created the policies advocated by the authors of the text. Passages assert that the former kings ruled by means of "laws and methods" and handed down these techniques to the present day. Others state that the sages Yao and Shun ruled through rewards and punishments. The commentary on the *Dao de jing* in the *Han Feizi* gives a standard list of sages—the Yellow Emperor, Yao, Shun, Yu, Tang, and King Wu—and asserts that they all ruled by means of the Way, while the evil Jie and Zhou ignored the Way and thus perished. Such sage ministers as Hou Ji, Gao Yao, Yi Yin, Tai Gong Wang, the Duke of Zhou, and Guan Zhong are also held up as models. Another passage speaks of writings handed down by the sages which are still followed by all who desire order. Another notes that Yao and Shun have no territory in the Warring States world, but their Way still prevails.[76]

The *Han Feizi* also shares in the rhetorical pattern noted above where "ancient" (*gu* 古) is invoked as the standard of excellence against the failures of current practice marked by the characters 今 *jin* ("now") or 世 *shi* ("this generation"). Apart from the "former kings," the epithet *gu* 古 is applied to "those who are skilled in preserving [their states]," "those who are skilled in using people," "those who achieved merit and fame," and "those who preserve intact the great principles." "Traditions" (*zhuan* 傳), "sayings" (*yan* 諺), and even ordinary "people" (*ren* 人) all become authoritative when prefaced by the character *gu* 古. By contrast, the character *jin* 今 ("now") routinely signals an object of criticism.[77]

As in the *Shang Jun shu*, the *Han Feizi*'s insistence that the policies of the distant past are anachronistic is marked only by increased reliance on examples drawn from recent history. This practice, represented by only a handful of passages in the *Shang Jun shu*, dominates the *Han Feizi*, where whole chapters are filled with examples from the Spring and Autumn and Warring States periods. However, it is noteworthy that, as in the *Shang Jun shu*, the vast majority of examples from recent history are negative lessons revealing errors to be avoided.[78] Thus even as recent centuries became part of the usable past, they continued to figure in a model of history in which the immediate past was a time of error and decay.

Modern scholars have noted contradictions between different passages or chapters in the *Han Feizi*, and these have generally been explained through appeals to multiple authorship. One set of positions is held to represent the historical Han Fei, and chapters or arguments that do not fit are dismissed as the work of late followers. Such arguments are always circular, because they assume a model of the author, and then demonstrate its truth through the exclusion of all contradictory evidence. However, even if we accept the extreme hypothesis that only the two chapters denying the authority of the sages are the work of the historical Han Fei, and all the rest the work of followers, this does not affect the conclusion that belief in an authoritative past dominates the text. That followers of a hypothetical master who rejected the past would themselves still embrace the authority of antiquity indicates how powerful were the forces that enthroned ancient times. Nor were these forces a simple conservatism, for the immediate past was rejected by all philosophical schools in the name of exemplary ancient times. Among the Warring States philosophers, appeals to the past were a form of calling for change.

The forces that impelled Warring States thinkers to appeal to the past can best be understood by an analysis of those who unsuccessfully tried to deny its authority. The contradictory mix of, on the one hand, theoretical assertions of the necessity of change and occasional attacks on the ancient sages with, on the other, an overwhelming tendency to treat the distant past as authoritative and criticize present practice defined the position of the legalist thinkers. The first position was forced on them by their situation in the intellectual field of Warring States schools.

They were obliged to distinguish themselves from established traditions such as the *ru* and the Mohists, who had always appealed to ancient sages as a means of criticizing the present. To attack these earlier traditions and defend calls for institutional reforms they had to deny the authority of precedent. However, in the absence of models of superior institutions from a distant past, they had no means to establish the validity of their critique of present practices and their program of innovations. François Jullien has argued that without a transcendental dimension, Chinese scholars had no firm ground for a critique of the established order.[79] In fact, the ground for critique was established in the Warring States period through a historical leapfrogging into an imagined antiquity that had the twin virtues of being sufficiently distant from received practices to allow for a critique, and sufficiently lacking in documentation that one could assign to it whatever practices one desired. Since the existence of the schools required an oppositional stance toward the state, all the philosophical traditions were obliged to endorse the ultimate authority of the past, even if interschool debates and intellectual programs forced them to make gestures toward a rejection of antiquity. It is this dilemma, rather than simple multiple authorship, that produces the internal contradictions in the *Shang Jun shu* and *Han Feizi*.

Having discovered the basis of their independence and the efficacy of their teachings in an antiquity where kings were endowed with the attributes of their masters, the intellectual traditions each found in this textual past the sanction for their own doctrines and the condemnation of those of their rivals. By the late Warring States period the critique of political institutions was paired with denunciations of competing schools. These often called for or prophesied the coming of a true king who would silence the clamor of rival doctrines and establish the all-encompassing sagely Way which the schoolmen agreed had once held sway. These calls were linked with ever closer ties between scholarly activity and political power, and they jibed closely with the projects of the intellectual advocates of centralized, state power. They thus anticipated the absorption of the intellectual traditions into a state orthodoxy in the early empire.

THE PAST IN COSMOGONY

The past, however, was not merely a space where the schools grounded their claims to independent authority, but also a realm where they fashioned their own image. The sages cited by all the schools were mythic embodiments of the identity of philosopher and king, and their actions were based on the programs and practices cultivated within the schools. Thus the past in which the philosophers grounded their authority was a world shaped and controlled by images of themselves. Ruling through intellect and moral worth, the sages were the inventors of the techniques and moral patterns necessary to a human existence as defined by the schools. Thus the past in which state and school had been united was mythically articulated in accounts of the creation of order, first natural and then human, out of undifferentiated chaos.

This argument was developed in its most extreme form in the proto-Daoist texts. While the other traditions inscribed their doctrines in a political past defined by sage rulers, the proto-Daoists wrote accounts of the beginnings of the world. These sketches of cosmic origins were ultimately derived from visions achieved in trance or meditation, in which the devotee stripped away wordly diversions to discover the underlying source of things. This individual experience was rewritten as a historical narrative that stripped away the technical innovations and moral principles of the later sages to discover the origin of things in the undifferentiated chaos that existed before the beginnings of time. While the *ru*, the Mohists, and the legalists traced their programs back to the sages, the proto-Daoists sought their roots in even earlier times, grounding their program in the guiding principles of prehuman nature.

The earliest text to base its teachings on a vision of cosmic origins was probably the *Dao de jing*. Numerous aphorisms employ such characters as *shi* 始 "beginning," *mu* 母 "mother," or *zong* 宗 "ancestor." The devotee is urged to "return" (*fan* 反) to these origins in order to gain understanding and power. Things are explained by that which produces (*sheng* 生) them. The work begins with the lines on the "Way" and "names," followed immediately by an account of the origins of Heaven and Earth, the "mother" of the myriad objects, and the means by which the devotee may observe (*guan* 觀) these hidden beginnings.[80] Another passage states, "Knowing the ancient origins is called the guiding thread of the Way." Yet another asserts, "Returning is the movement of the Way," and traces the world back to its origins in nothingness.[81]

The trope of a return to origins figures in at least three contexts. First, it refers to a psychological state of the devotee that must be cultivated, probably through meditation. Typical of these passages are appeals to "learn to be unlearned; go back to the place that the ordinary masses have passed," or "guard the feminine . . . return to being an infant . . . return to being an uncarved block."[82] These urge the practitioner to strip away the refinements of education and return to his undifferentiated, fertile origins.

Second, some passages refer to an original doctrine from which the aphorisms of the school are derived. Like the psychological passages, those on doctrine invoke images of human generation, in this case the image of the "ancestor" or "father." One states, "What others taught I also teach . . . I will make it the father of my teaching." A similar idea figures in the statement, "The words have an ancestor, and the practice a master."[83] The "father" or "ancestor" probably refers to a trance state, so that these passages on the beginnings of doctrine point back to the sayings about the psychic origins of true perceptions.

A final set of passages, and those most relevant to the present topic, refers to the origins of the cosmos from undifferentiated chaos. This theme figured in the opening passage cited above, and subsequent aphorisms refer to "the gate of the primal female, which is known as the root of Heaven and Earth," or exclaim, "Profound! It seems to be the ancestor of the myriad things . . . I do not know whose son it is. It seems to be prior to God-on-High."[84] Other passages describe the origins of the world.

> There was something formed in chaos, born prior to Heaven and Earth. Isolated! Still! Independent and unchanging, endlessly revolving, one can take it to be the world's mother. I do not know its name, but one might style it the "Way."

Other references to "the world's mother" state that through knowledge of the mother one can also know the child. One cosmogonic account describes the formation of the world as an arithmetic progression: "The Way produced the One, the One produced the Two, the Two produced the Three, and the Three produced the myriad things."[85] In these passages the Way at the center of Daoist teachings becomes the origin of all things. Through knowledge of this origin the devotee gains power over the world.

Calls to reverse the process of education elsewhere expand from the individual to the collectivity by denouncing the work of the sages. The opening of the second part of the text argues that benevolence, duty, and rites appeared only when the Way was lost. These moral inventions of the sages are described as "the beginning of disorder" and "the origins of stupidity." The technological creations of the sages are also rejected. An aphorism near the end of the text calls for the abandonment of vessels, boats, carriages, and weapons. Even writing is to be given up, so that people would return to keeping records with knotted cords.[86] The *Dao de jing*'s call for returning to the Way is thus a variant of the general scholarly practice of grounding authority in accounts of origins. It trumps the other schools by appealing not to the origins of civilization but to the emergence of the physical world, and then denouncing the origins appealed to by others as a falling away from nature.

Grounding in cosmic origins developed into a topos of writing on the "origins of the Way" (*dao yuan* 道原) or "the original Way" (*yuan dao* 原道). Such texts purport to ground intellectual programs in the inherent principles of the universe. These principles are revealed through accounts of the primal chaos, the moment when it first divided into Heaven and Earth, and the manner in which the sage or perfected man achieved mastery through his insights into the time of origins. Hitherto the earliest known example of sustained writing on this theme was the opening chapter of the early Western Han *Huainanzi*, entitled "Yuan dao." The opening chapter of the received version of the *Wenzi* (文子) is entitled *Dao yuan* and contains many passages that also figure in the *Huainanzi* chapter. Passages from the *Huainanzi* chapter also appear in chapters 3 and 4 of the *Wenzi*, and passages from the *Wenzi* chapter appear in chapters 9 and 12 of the *Huainanzi*.[87] The order in the two texts differs, and the *Huainanzi* chapter is much longer.

Modern scholars had achieved a consensus that the *Wenzi* version was adapted from the *Huainanzi*, although some believed in an earlier proto-*Wenzi*.[88] However, the discovery in an early Western Han tomb of a large number of strips containing lines from the *Wenzi* has called this consensus into question. Several Chinese scholars now argue that substantial portions of the received *Wenzi* antedate the *Huainanzi*, and that it was the latter that borrowed from the former.[89] The fragmentary state of the tomb text and the damage it suffered in a fire hinders conclusions, but both texts must now be treated as usable primary sources for the late Warring States and early Han periods.

A third version of the same topos, shorter than the other two, was discovered in the early Western Han tomb at Mawangdui.[90] This text is probably the immediate ancestor of the other versions, and its briefer scope clarifies the structure of the argument. It consists of two parts. The first is a description of primeval chaos and the attributes of the cosmic Way. The account of chaos is full of watery metaphors and terms for stillness and void. The discussion of the Way tells how it gives all things their attributes, and then celebrates its immutable and lofty character. The second half tells how the sage's knowledge of cosmic origins and the Way gives him the power to rule. It begins, "Only the sage can examine the formless and hear the soundless. Knowing the substance of the void . . . he penetrates the essence of Heaven and Earth." On the basis of this knowledge of the extreme limits and pivots, the sage causes "the whole world to submit, without likes or dislikes." The passage concludes with a vision of the sage as the master of time: "Observing highest antiquity, he completely knows the why; seeking out the not yet, he obtains the wherefore."

The chapters from the *Huainanzi* and the *Wenzi* both contain sections resembling the first half of the Mawangdui text, but they are more elaborate. Their accounts of the Way's giving all things their attributes contain longer lists, which include celestial bodies and mythic animals.[91] The *Wenzi* is organized as a series of questions, posed by Master Wen in the received text or King Ping of Chu in the bamboo strips, and answers, given by Master Lao in the received text and Master Wen in the strips. The *Huainanzi* adds references to ancient sages, discussions of alien peoples, materials from the medical traditions, and a passage on the "Great Man" (*da zhangfu* 大丈夫) who is escorted by divinities through the Heavens, in the manner of poems in the *Chu ci*, or the "Rhapsody on the Great Man" (*da ren fu* 大人賦) of Sima Xiangru.[92] Both the *Wenzi* and the *Huainanzi* add long passages on water as the image of the Way.[93]

The *Wenzi* and *Huainanzi* also tell how the sage rules the world through his understanding of the Way and cosmic origins, but these points are scattered throughout the chapters. They include materials on the sage's cultivation of his self and his physical energies as the basis of his authority. This concern with preserving life and the consequent incorporation of medical thought is also reflected in the fact that both the *Wenzi* and the *Huainanzi* contain chapters devoted to the energies of the human body that begin with accounts of the primal chaos.[94] These discussions are similar to those in the Yangist chapters of the *Zhuangzi* and seem to owe more to this tradition than their Mawangdui prototype. The *Huainanzi* also contains passages that echo the Primitivist chapters of the *Zhuangzi* in arguing that the sage rejects the technological innovations by which man ravages nature in a misconceived pursuit of his own ends.[95]

Appeals to an authority inscribed in accounts of cosmic origins also appear in other writings. The "Sixteen Classics" (*shiliu jing* 十六經) discovered at Mawangdui contain dialogues between the Yellow Emperor and his officials in which a speaker traces the principles of statecraft back to the emergence of the cosmos from primal chaos. Thus in the section "Observations" (*guan* 觀) the Yellow Emperor gives a long account of the primal chaos, the division into *yin* and *yang*, and the subsequent emergence of four seasons. From this he develops a theory of government based on the imitation of natural principle. In four other sections either the Yellow Emperor or one of his ministers describes the origins of the cosmos and uses this account to ground a theory of government.[96]

The non-Daoist schools also developed a discourse of origins devoted to the creation of human society. Here the sage kings figured not as prototypes of political programs but as inventors of the technologies and virtues that separated men from animal nature. This is also a form of cosmogony, in that it depicts the emergence of an ordered realm from a chaos without distinctions.[97] In this mythology the schools used the sages to perform three functions: division, unification, and self-identification. In the first, each tradition claimed for itself the status of defenders of what was essential to humanity, and condemned its rivals as enemies of civilization. In the second role, the genealogy of sages that emerged in the period allowed for a change from a rhetoric of opposition to one of inclusion. By arranging the sages in a chronological sequence, the actions of specific culture heroes could be explained as functions of a particular time, and the programs of the associated schools could be explained as a lesser truth that found its true meaning as part of the whole. Finally, the figure of the sage king, in which political and intellectual authority were united in a single figure, provided the mythic prototype for philosophers who invoked their supposed wisdom as the basis for serving as advisers to kings.

The sages as culture heroes figured in polemics as the patrons of specific intellectual traditions. This is clearest in the case of a figure such as Shen Nong, who was virtually the invention of one school and the embodiment of their program.[98] As depicted in the *Mencius*, the political program incarnated in Shen Nong rejected other philosophical traditions, whose followers did not engage in agriculture. Perhaps because this school denounced even the existence of nonlaboring intellectual traditions, it disappeared as an independent movement and survived only as an element of archaizing, agrarian romanticism in other teachings.

The *ru* mythologically traced their doctrines to Yao and Shun, who ruled through virtue and ritual, sought out worthy ministers in whom they entrusted their government, and yielded their throne to the most worthy.[99] Their role in interschool polemics was shown above, in Mencius' uses of the story of the taming of the flood and the separation of men from beasts. Their story was used in the dispute with the "School of the Tillers" to demonstrate that the labor of kings took the form of preserving civilization, work which excused them from toiling in the fields and which they exchanged for taxes. Thus the myth of Yao and Shun—and Mencius places Yu's work under the aegis of Yao—refutes that of Shen Nong. The *Mencius*'s second use of the flood story justifies a call to suppress philosophical disputation. Here it is the dialecticians who stand condemned by fundamental principles revealed in the account of origins. In another passage the same sages are invoked to demonstrate the folly of the Mohist doctrine of universal love.[100]

The Mohists contested this vision of the past with their own origin myths. First, they rejected the Confucians' claim to be the intellectual descendants of Yao, Shun, Yu, Tang, and the Zhou founders. They traced their origins to the same figures, and then appealed to the test of utility in order to prove the truth of their version.[101] In addition, they introduced two myths of sage innovations that sanctioned the Mohist project as essential to civilization. First, they told how men had originally lived in a linguistic chaos in which each person used words to mean what he or she wanted. This resulted in a bedlam of unresolved disputation that undercut the possibility of human community and reduced men to the level of animals. Consequently the wisest men were established as the Son of Heaven, the Three Dukes, feudal lords, and village chieftains. These fixed standards for right and wrong, thus creating common moral meanings and judgments.[102] The sages' work here served as the mythic prototype for the fixed definitions advocated by the Mohist school. As in the *Mencius*, the existence of rival schools was equated with the breakdown of the separation between men and animals, and the Mohist program recapitulated the creation of society.

A second account of the sages used their invention of tools, the separation of men from beasts, and the liberation of men from dwelling in caves to justify the Mohist principle of frugality. The invention of cooked food, clothing, weapons, carriages, boats, and dwellings was equated with the institution by the sages of sumptuary regulations for their proper use. The introduction of the objects was conflated with proclaiming rules for their use. In this way the sage kings' technical activities merged with their role as law givers, and the Mohist principle of frugality became inseparable from the human realm.[103]

The projection of interschool polemics into antiquity also underlies the *Shang Jun shu*'s account of the origins of civilization. In this version the only groupings of people in antiquity were based on kinship, so the world was divided into warring clans. People tried to resolve this situation by "elevating the worthy," but competition for eminence among the worthy soon plunged the world back into chaos. Consequently the sages used force to impose hierarchical divisions, and only then was order achieved.[104] In this account the original chaos is marked by men's devotion to kin, a central virtue in the *ru* tradition. The unsuccessful attempt to create an ordered society relies on "elevation of the worthy," central to the Mohist tradition. Once again the mythic chaos at the beginning of time is imagined in the form of rival traditions, and the sagely innovations that separated men from beasts are equated with the text's own program.

The *Han Feizi* also employs accounts of the work of the sages to underpin its arguments. The relevant passages deal not with particular innovations, but rather the fact of change itself. The theme of the sages appears three times. First the text argues that each sage introduces innovations to meet the needs of his time, and that consequently the specific innovations have no authority as models. Second it argues that the simplicity of life in antiquity and the willingness then to yield office was made possible by a small population and a low level of economic development. A third use of the theme of evolution links different modes of rule to different levels of economic and social development.[105] The point in all three cases is that sagehood lies not in copying the work of past sages, but in imitating their ability to innovate for the sake of the collective good. Once again sagely wisdom is identified with the teachings of the text that offers it, and that which is opposed to the sage—in this case the adoption of the virtues and policies of ancient rulers as permanent models—are the teachings of the rival schools, specifically the *ru* and the Mohists.

The accounts of the cosmogonic role of sages in ending chaos by dividing people from the beasts thus served in interschool polemics. Each textual tradition identified its teachings with the essentials of civilization, and denounced rivals as later versions of a primitive bestiality. However, accounts of the sages also functioned as a unifying discourse common to the schools, because a standard list of sages—including Shen Nong, the Yellow Emperor, Yao, Shun, Yu, Tang, and the Zhou founders—figured in all philosophical texts by the middle of the Warring States period. While different schools or thinkers invoked different sages in their arguments, they increasingly employed a common list. Even the Daoist *Huainanzi* invoked most of the ancient sage kings as exemplary figures. This list of sages, systematized as a political genealogy, provided the structure for the pre-Zhou section of Sima Qian's comprehensive account of history from the beginnings to his own day. In the process of locating sanctions for their individual programs in antiquity, the schools as a collectivity composed a common past for the educated class of the late Warring States.

This past centered on the figure of the sage king, which provided a model for those claiming authority on the basis of intellect and virtue. Perhaps originally gods or high ancestors of major clans, these ancient cultural heroes were rewritten within the textual traditions as historical figures. They established an ideal of the ultimate identity of political and intellectual authority. The articulation of the new ideal of ruler in terms of the skills cultivated within the schools, and the concomitant assimilation of the philosophical master to the status of monarch, found expression in textual accounts of the origins of civilization and the invention of government. This same process was applied to more recent history through the use of political chronicles as a mode of expounding intellectual doctrines, and ultimately as a means of articulating a theory of a kingship created through the writing of texts.

THE PAST IN CHRONICLE

Chronicles were another form of writing that had originated in the state sphere. They were lists, compiled by astrologers/historians (*shi* 史) responsible for maintenance of calendars, of major events related to the court that sponsored their composition. Warring States sources indicate that each state kept its own records, so the keeping of a chronicle was an attribute of political authority.[106] Inversely, the conquest of a state left its chronicle at the mercy of the victor, and the chronicles of almost all of the states were destroyed. The exceptions have survived only because they were buried in tombs and subsequently rediscovered, or because they were adopted by a scholarly tradition as a means of teaching. The major case of the former is the *Bamboo Annals* (*Zhu shu ji nian* 竹書紀年), and the only known case of the latter is the chronicle of the state of Lu, the so-called *Spring and Autumn Annals*.

The *Spring and Autumn Annals* was transmitted by groups closely related to the *ru*. In order to turn the chronicle into a vehicle for the exposition of doctrine, they added extensive commentaries. The only examples that can be assigned to the Warring States period are the *Zuo zhuan* (左傳) and the *Gongyang zhuan* (公羊傳), both of which later became classics in the state-sponsored Confucian canon. The pattern of quotation in the *Zuo zhuan* is different, however, from that in other *ru* texts, and the work diverges in other ways from the *ru* philosophical tradition.[107] Modern scholars have hypothesized that the authors were either court historians, or related in some manner to court-based intellectual circles.[108] Thus the history of these texts follows the same pattern as that of the *Shang shu*, in which works generated in political circles were adopted and developed by the *ru* tradition as a means of elaborating their own vision of the world.

Adapted for the exposition of doctrine, chronicles provided examples of good and bad conduct and their consequences. *Ru* writings on the Spring and Autumn period emphasized conduct contrary to the dictates of ritual and duty, so the historian acted as critic and judge. The *Zuo zhuan* contains two parables on this theme. In the first story, Cui Shu assassinated Lord Zhuang of Qi.

> The Grand Historian wrote, "Cui Shu assassinated his prince." Cui Shu killed the historian. Two of his younger brothers followed him in recording it, and they were both killed. Another younger brother wrote it, and he was finally released. The Historian of the South heard that the whole family of the Grand Historian had been killed, so he went there with his bamboo strips. When he heard that it had already been recorded, he departed.[109]

The historians act as heros who defy the usurper in order to preserve moral order through the power of inscription. Writing here is an arena of authoritative judicial or moral judgment.

The second story emphasizes not the courage of the historians, but the need to make astute judgments in assigning responsibility and adjusting the record.

Zhao Xuan killed Lord Ling in the Peach Garden. Xuanzi [Zhao Dun], not yet having crossed the frontier, returned. The Grand Historian wrote, "Zhao Dun assassinated his prince." He displayed it to the assembled court. Xuanzi said, "It is not so." [The historian] replied, "You were a full official. When you fled you did not cross the frontier, and when you returned you did not punish the criminal. If you are not guilty, then who is?"[110]

In response to this renewed accusation Zhao Dun admitted his guilt, and both he and the historian are praised by Confucius. The historian's account is not literally true, but he explains how his record reflects the actual moral responsibility for the deed. This practice of diverging from the facts in order to record a true judgment, and then explaining the divergence through an appended commentary, was basic to the *Gongyang Commentary*. The story also insists on the public role of writing achieved through its display.

While these purport to be the deeds of actual historians, the values they depict reflect less those of court-based scribes—who were primarily servants of the powerful—than those of scholars who used the chronicles to further philosophical programs. The oppositional stance of these historians, their heroism, and their concern for making moral distinctions tell us more about the self-image of the authors of the *Zuo zhuan* and *Gongyang zhuan* than they do about those who produced actual state chronicles.

Recounting historical events to elucidate moral or political theories did not originate with the late Warring States adaptation of chronicles. Several chapters of the *Shang shu* begin with the announcement of an event, which they use as the pretext for delivering an address on principles of government. Among the core chapters the "Kang gao," "Shao gao," and "Luo gao" all begin with narratives of the building of the new capital and associated ritual performances. These brief accounts introduce extensive speeches or dialogues in which political actors expound aspects of government.[111] "Duo shi" and "Duo fang" set the scene with narratives composed of a single sentence.[112] Later chapters, such as the oaths before battles or Pan Geng's speeches, are also introduced by brief narratives.[113] The *Guo yu* also announces an event to set the scene and provide the topic for lengthy dialogues or speeches.

While these works attach speeches to historical events, they are simply collections of speeches arranged by their editors in rough chronological order or by state. More elaborate methods of linking the exposition of principles to the narration of events were developed in the commentaries to the *Spring and Autumn Annals*. The *ru* scholars or historians who composed these works were convinced that what seemed to be a simple record of events contained teachings of fundamental importance on the nature of the state and social order. The first evidence of this belief is the *Mencius*'s remarks on Confucius' composition of the *Annals*, which state that he adopted the form (*wen* 文) of the historians to the affairs of the Son of Heaven and the hegemons. By the end of the Warring States period the two traditions cited above sought to extract lessons from the record of events between 722 and 468 B.C. These works mark the first attempts to use extended accounts of past events arranged by year and season to demonstrate basic principles of statecraft and ethics. In contrast to the mythology of the sages, which dealt with origins and precedents, chronicles offered models of evolution over time, demonstrations of cause and effect, confirmations of philosophical teachings by showing them at work in the world, and examples of the relations of writing to political authority. They were the written form par excellence of accounts of the past.

Studies of the *Zuo zhuan* have been dominated by the question of its dating, to the detriment of considering the nature of the text.[114] Its purpose was to validate *ru* teachings, both texts and the doctrines they contain, through writing them into a narrative of the past. This takes the form of the repeated quotation of works— the *Documents*, the *Odes*, the *Yi* (*Changes*), and the *Li* (*Rituals*)—the dramatization of people's employment of these texts, and the demonstration that the teachings contained in the texts define the course of history. It is a complete curriculum presented as history, a narrative dramatizing the incipient Confucian textual canon as the Ariadne's thread through the labyrinth of the recent past.

Like the philosophical traditions, the author or authors of the *Zuo zhuan* used the past to interpret and sanction the present, and in this way they too were communicating a particular philosophy. However, rather than formulating arguments that were validated or given substance by the incorporation of historical references, they narrated historical events from which they developed philosophical truths. These truths were articulated in three forms. First, the narrative itself indicated truths of human nature and society by demonstrating the consequences of certain actions. Second, participants or witnesses written into the narrative gave extended speeches not unlike those in the *Shang shu* or the *Guo yu*. Third, some stories concluded with a comment attributed to either Confucius or an unnamed gentleman, both of whom appear to be authoritative guises in which the author presented his judgments. In the speeches of participants and concluding comments, the texts that would later make up the Confucian canon are routinely cited to lend textual authority to the truths derived from the course of events.

The ideas presented in the *Zuo zhuan* are diverse, and even partial treatments of them have filled monographs.[115] Here I will focus on the way in which the authors presented doctrine through writing about the past, and how this presentation depended on references to other texts. Specifically, I will focus on the *Zuo zhuan*'s demonstration of the essential role of "ritual" (*li* 禮) in defining and maintaining human society. This is not only because this theme is in many ways the organizing principle of the text, but also because I discuss in subsequent chapters the *Zuo zhuan*'s incorporation of the other major writings of the *ru* canon.

Because of ritual's dual nature in the *ru* writings, where it was both the major form of communicating with spirits and the sole method of forming human society, the topos of ritual in the *Zuo zhuan* once again marks the formulation of new visions of political power through the adaptation of elements from the religious sphere. Just as appeals to the sages transformed old religious practice into a mythic fusion of the school and the state, so the interpretation of chronicled events in terms of the role of ritual inscribed both religious and textual practices of the *ru* schoolmen into the foundations of the political order.

The centrality of ritual in the *Zuo zhuan* was noted as early as the Han dynasty.[116] More recently Li Zongtong has given a statistical formulation of this importance. The anonymous third-person narrator refers to particular actions being "ritual" sixty-seven times, and he describes them as "violations of ritual" (*fei li* 非禮) thirty-two times. Figures in the narrative refer to actions as "ritual" six times, and "violations" sixteen times. The "gentleman" refers to "ritual" or "violations" six times. In addition Confucius twice discusses actions in terms of *li*. Therefore one hundred and twenty-nine actions in the *Zuo zhuan* are assessed in terms of ritual.[117] In addition, the concept is implicit in many passages that do not employ the character *li* 禮. [118]

The frequency of occurrence of the character *li* 禮 and passages where it is implicit only hints at the importance of the concept to the text, because actual ritual performances are much more frequent. The *Zuo zhuan* contains six hundred and thirty-seven references to blood covenants, and it also employs an elaborate vocabulary pertaining to different forms of interstate assemblies. It recounts hundreds of military campaigns, which were framed by and enacted according to a carefully prescribed set of rituals.[119] The *Zuo zhuan* also mentions many sacrifices to major divinities, the stages and degrees of funerary rituals, and the whole range of family rituals such as betrothal, marriage, and capping. Rituals of sociability, including rules for staging banquets, drinking wine, and performing music and song are also both narrated and discussed.[120] In this way the ritual texts of the *ru* school are dramatized in narrations of the past.

In addition, many stories revolve around ritual issues. The first story in the *Zuo zhuan*, for example, deals with the relations between elder and younger brothers, the question of changing the succession, the practice of enfeoffment, strictures on the height of city walls allowed for each level of nobility, filiality, and oaths. The narrative would be unintelligible without recourse to the ritual dictates preserved in texts of the period.[121] Other stories deal with replacing an heir apparent, settling the hierarchy of rulers at an interstate assembly, or the number of sacrificial offerings appropriate to an occasion.[122] Given the range and detail of ritual prescriptions for the Zhou nobility, there is scarcely a story in the work that can be read without knowledge of the rituals that inform the actions of the participants and the readings intended by the authors.

However, the authors did not rely on their readers to recognize all the issues and to make correct assessments, so they provided judgments in their own voices, those of participants in the narrative, or that of Confucius or the gentleman. These took several forms. At the highest level of abstraction, some offered definitions of *li*. When asked what is meant by ritual, Zi Da Shu begins by quoting Zi Chan, "Ritual is the constant principle of Heaven, the duties of Earth, and the conduct of men." After a long discussion in which the attributes of ritual are analyzed in terms of numerical categories he concludes, "Ritual is the guiding cord of superior and subordinate, the warp and weft of Heaven and Earth, the means by which people are born."[123] Ritual is here defined as the underlying principle of order in the cosmos and the basis of life.

The idea of ritual as the foundation of life appears repeatedly. Having witnessed a ritual faux pas by the Jin emissary Xi Qi during a ceremony of welcome, Meng Xianzi predicts Xi Qi's imminent death.

> Ritual is the trunk of the self, and respect is its foundation. Master Xi has no foundation. Moreover, being the hereditary minister of the earlier rulers, he has received the charge [*ming* 命] to request an army [from Lu]. When he is protecting the altars of grain and soil he is lax and abandons the charge from his prince. What could he do but perish?

Other passages identify ritual as the "trunk" of the self, the key to self preservation, that without which one cannot stand, and essential to survival.[124]

Between its role as guiding principle of the cosmos and key to individual survival, *li* also brought order to the state. In an early passage the gentleman stated, "Ritual regulates the state, fixes the altars of grain and soil, places the people in order, and benefits one's descendants." In criticizing the giving of an unusual name, a Jin official formulated a version of the "rectification of names." "By names one fixes duties, by duties one produces rituals, by rituals one gives form to government, and by government one corrects the people."[125] A passage that appears twice invokes the image of "trunk," but it states that *li* is the trunk of the state rather than the self. It concludes that without *li* superiors and subordinates are benighted, and the generations of the state cannot be prolonged.[126] Another one states that ritual as the means of guiding a state is "coeval with Heaven and Earth." It then lists all the relationships that create states and families, and it asserts that these are all "ritual."[127] A final set of passages on ritual and the state discusses the distinction between the rules of ritual performances (*yi* 儀) and the underlying principles defining ritual (*li* 禮). "Ritual is the means by which one preserves a state, puts into practice the government's commands, and does not lose the [support of] the people."[128]

A final theme is ritual's relation to Heaven. The clearest expression of this appears in a speech by Ji Wenzi of Lu, who argues that Qi's invasion of Lu will lead to disaster for the invader.

> How can the Lord of Qi escape [disaster]? He himself has no rites, and he attacks those who do. He says, "Why do you practice rituals?" Rituals are the means of obeying Heaven; they are the Way of Heaven. If one goes contrary to Heaven and further attacks others, it is difficult to avoid disaster. . . . Having seized his own state through rebellion, even if he performed rituals in order to keep it, I still fear he could not bring it off. Repeatedly violating ritual, he will not survive.[129]

Here the dictates of ritual are equated with those of an anthropomorphized Heaven that punishes violations. This belief in rituals that are almost magically potent, however, is qualified by the assertion that even their performance cannot counteract the consequences of immoral conduct.

In addition to general definitions of ritual, the authors and figures in the narrative indicate specific features of ritual as a form of action. First, ritual was a means of maintaining hierarchical distinctions, as defined in the "lineage law" (*zong fa* 宗法) of the period. Thus when the rulers of Xue and Teng arrived in Lu at the same time, Xue claimed precedence on the basis of having been enfeoffed as early as the Xia, while Teng claimed precedence on the basis of having the same surname as the Zhou king. The latter argument is accepted.[130] In a related case, the rulers of Guo and Jin attended the court of the Zhou king at the same time, and the king gave them identical gifts despite their difference in status. The authors criticize this as a violation of ritual. Another passage stipulates rules for the status of the individual charged to receive a bride, a status that varied depending on the bride's position in sequence of birth and the importance of the state to which she was going.[131] A case much discussed in later imperial literature involved a decision by Xiafu Fu Ji to give the spirit tablet of Lord Xi of Lu priority over that of his predecessor, Lord Min. The gentleman insists that this is wrong, for even a sage can never be given precedence over his father.[132] These cases show that ritual was central to the *Zuo zhuan* because it defined the proper form of human relations.

A second element emphasized in the text is the importance of "yielding" (*rang* 讓). The most prominent case was a changing of the command of the Jin armies in 560 b.c. In each case the man first named yielded the post to someone he deemed superior, and as a result "the people of Jin were harmonious and the feudal lords at peace." This narrative on the efficacy of yielding is followed immediately by a speech in the voice of the gentleman.

> Yielding is the ruling principle of ritual. . . . In ages of social order, the gentleman honors the capable and yields to those beneath him, while the petty man toils in agriculture to serve his superior. Thereby superior and subordinate have rituals, and slanderers are demoted and expelled. This is due to not quarreling, and it is called "exemplary virtue." When it grows disordered, the gentleman boasts of his merits to set himself above the petty man, while the petty men vaunt their arts and thereby take advantage of the gentlemen. Thereby superior and subordinate lack ritual, so chaos and cruelty arise together. This is due to quarreling over who is best, and it is called "benighted virtue." The ruin of states and families inevitably arises from this.[133]

Once again ritual is identified with the principles that maintain human associations, but here those principles are equated with a spirit of yielding that eschews competition for supremacy.[134]

The centrality of ritual for the authors is reflected in the emphasis placed on its role in warfare. The text records numerous details about the rites which began a campaign and brought it to a close, as well as those which were conducted on the march and on the field of battle. In addition, the authors stress that success in battle often depended on a meticulous observance of the spirit of rituals. In the first story in the *Zuo zhuan*, Lord Zhuang of Zheng yields to demands from his younger brother out of duty to his mother, who favors the younger child. He cites duty to parents, assures his officials that the brother's hubris will lead to failure, and predicts his own victory. This prophecy is fulfilled, and the gentleman praises Lord Zhuang for his filiality. Another early battle account that concludes with praise from the gentleman tells how the state of Song refused to attend the king's court, and how Zheng invaded Song to restore proper ritual behavior.[135]

Lord Zhuang's prediction of his victory on the basis of the conduct of the two adversaries indicates another means by which the *Zuo zhuan* uses historical narrative to expound its philosophical positions. Throughout the text figures in the stories, and sometimes Confucius, predict the fate of persons or states on the basis of whether or not their actions conform to ritual. These prophecies complement the judgments pronounced after events have taken place. Examples abound, and they play a fundamental role in communicating the authors' vision of the world.[136]

These prophecies play at least three major roles. First, like the post facto judgments they show the reader how the flow of events reflects the workings of cosmic principles and the moral rules derived therefrom. Second, they allow the authors to specify those principles and rules, and thereby write a philosophical program into their account of the past. Third, the perceptive, moral individuals who pronounce the prophecies provide a historical sanction for the text's authors. These speakers in the text, of whom the highest example is Confucius himself, stand above the action and reveal the ineluctable moral laws of history by their ability to foretell the course of events. They not only speak for the authors, but also provide a model for the philosophical and political use of writing historical narrative.

The prophecies in the text are too numerous to be dealt with here, so I will merely present a few examples to indicate their use. As already noted, prophecies are prominent in military campaigns. The major campaigns of the period culminate long narratives in which the relative moral worth and ritual propriety of the combatants are established. On the basis of these, observers often forecast the victor some years before a battle takes place. Signs of the relative moral/ritual standing of the opposing sides are traced up to the field of battle itself, accompanied by prophecies and omens that announce the victor.

The first great campaign presented as the outcome of years of accumulated ritual action is the battle between Qin and Jin at Han.[137] The moral/ritual origins of this campaign lay in the fact that the lord of Jin, Yiwu, had in his youth been an exile in Qin, and had become ruler with Qin's aid. In exchange he had promised to give Qin certain cities, but then reneged on his promise. When famine struck

Jin, Yiwu received grain from Qin, but when the situation was reversed he declined to return the assistance. Thus the ruler of Jin had systematically violated basic rules of ritual obligation and reciprocity. The first prophecy of Jin's defeat is recorded four years before the battle, when the ghost of Shen Sheng, whose forced suicide had allowed Yiwu to become ruler, appeared to his former charioteer.

> The heir-apparent [Shen Sheng] had him mount and drive. He told him, "Yiwu has violated ritual, so I will obtain my request from God-on-High. He will give Jin to Qin, and Qin will make sacrifices to me." [The charioteer] replied, "I have heard that spirits do not enjoy sacrifices from non-kin, and the people do not sacrifice to those not of their clan. Will not your sacrifices be cut off? Moreover, what crime did the people commit? You will punish improperly and lose your sacrifices, so I beg you to re-consider." "You are right. I will make a new request. In seven days a shaman at the west edge of Xincheng will have a vision of me." [The charioteer] agreed, and [Shen Sheng] vanished. On the appointed day he went, and [the voice of Shen Sheng] told him, "God-on-High has allowed me to punish the miscreant. The defeat will take place at Han."[138]

This story of prophecy, rich in information about religious beliefs of the period, is atypical in being made by a ghost and naming the exact place of battle. Nevertheless, it follows the classic pattern of basing the prediction on violations of ritual and treating the results as a judgment from Heaven.

One year before the battle the collapse of a hill led to another prediction of Jin's imminent disaster by a man whose name indicates that he was a diviner. This is followed in the text by the debate over whether Jin should send grain to Qin. In this debate Qing Zheng argues that refusing to give the grain means abandoning reciprocity and thus being without allies, taking advantage of another's disasters and thus lacking benevolence, being greedy and thus attracting misfortune, and provoking a neighbor and thereby failing in duty. Abandoning all virtues and losing the support of his own people, Yiwu cannot preserve his state.[139]

Thus the years preceding the campaign witness a series of prophecies of Jin's approaching defeat. Some of these treat the defeat as a divine punishment, others as the consequence of losing support in the world of men, but they agree in tracing the disaster to the moral and ritual failings of one side and the proper action of the other. This parallel explanation by means of both divine intervention and human action continues in the account of the campaign itself. Yarrow divinations predict the outcome, indicating Heaven guiding events. At the same time the authors show Yiwu rejecting remonstrances, and conclude that disaster resulted from his actions and not those of Heaven.[140] This use of parallel explanations reflects the dual nature of ritual, which was both communication with spirits and a mode of maintaining human relationships. Failure in ritual led to rejection both by Heaven and by men, and speakers could appeal to either explanation. Accounts of ritual failings and consequent prophecies precede other major battles in the *Zuo zhuan*.[141]

Prophecies figure not only in accounts of battles but in tales of the fate of states. A notable example is recorded under the year 539 B.C. In a lengthy passage Yan Ying of Qi and Shu Xiang of Jin both predict the end of their ruling lines due to the breakdown of proper ritual hierarchies between ruler and minister.[142] Several passages depict Confucius prophesying the end of a state for ritual failings, or the rise of a new ruling house because of the virtue of its current leader.[143] By attributing prophecies to Confucius and such eminent political figures as Yan Ying and Shu Xiang, the text signals the importance of the activity and identifies the ability to make predictions through moral analysis as a hallmark of the sage.

Just as ritual is the trunk of both state and individual, so prophecies based on ritual actions apply to the fate of both states and individuals. Moreover, these prophecies evince the same doubling of religious belief and sociological analysis as the predictions of the outcome of battles. The prophecy of Xi Qi's death cited above was based on his laxity in the execution of the *ming* (命 "charge, appointment") from his lord. The prediction of the death of the lord of Cheng is based on the same error ("disrespect" *bu jing* 不敬) in a ritual context (receiving the meat at a sacrifice). It also invokes *ming*, in a different but related sense.

> I have heard that people are born through the balance of Heaven and Earth. This is called *ming* ["appointed life span"]. Therefore we have models for action, ritual duty, and awesome deportment in order to fix this *ming*. The capable nourish it and thereby obtain blessings; the incompetent destroy it and thereby obtain calamity. Therefore the gentleman is diligent in ritual, while the petty man uses up his physical strength. As for being diligent in ritual, nothing is as important as being supremely respectful; as for using up one's strength, nothing is as important as simple sincerity. Respect lies in nourishing the spirits; sincerity lies in keeping one's occupation. The great services of the state are sacrifice and warfare. In the sacrifices one takes the meat from the sacrifices in the ancestral temple, and in warfare one receives the meat from the sacrifices at the *she* altar. These are the great ceremonies of the spirits. Now the lord of Cheng is lax and abandons his *ming*. He will not return [from the campaign]![144]

Here the term *ming* refers both to the appointed life span received from Heaven and one's position in the world. The lord of Cheng abandons his *ming* through laxness in performing the rituals incumbent on his position, the same crime as Xi Qi, but since he is a ruler his *ming* is received from Heaven and inseparable from his life span. This theme is stressed in the passage, because the nobles' duty of making sacrifice parallels the commoners' duty of keeping their inherited occupations. Ritual is here the means by which one both obeys Heaven and keeps faith with one's ruler. Consequently the prophecy of death can be given both a religious and a sociological reading, like the prophecies in the accounts of battles.

Other stories do not refer explicitly to *ming* but invoke related terms from the protoscientific reworkings of religious belief. The *ming* from Heaven was physically transmitted through energies (*qi* 氣) received, and some accounts of ritual errors are explained in terms of loss of *qi*.

> Viscount Shan met Han Xuanzi at Qi. His gaze was downcast and his speech slow. Shu Xiang said, "Viscount Shan is soon to die! Court audiences have their fixed positions and interstate assemblies their banners [to mark locations]. Robes have their collar-joins and belts their knots. Words in audiences and assemblies must be heard in all the fixed positions, in order to make clear the sequence of service. The gaze does not go outside the belt-knot and collar-join, to control facial expression. One uses words to charge (*ming* 命) them, and facial expression to make it clear to them. Any error leads to omissions. Now Viscount Shan is the senior of the king's officials, and he announces the charges of affairs at assemblies. However, his gaze does not rise above the belt, and his words go no further than a pace. Thus his expression is not controlled, and his words are not clear. If one's expression is not controlled, they will not be respectful; if one's words are not clear, they will not obey. He no longer has the protecting energies/breath [*shou qi* 守氣]."[145]

Other stories attribute ritual errors to the individuals in question having lost their *po* or *hunpo* (魂魄), generally translated by "soul."[146] To have "lost one's *hunpo*" meant madness, and it led to death. Once again the fact that ritual error led to death could be interpreted both as a natural account in which one had lost the mental capacity for a human existence, or a religious one in which the failure was the cause or sign of a break with Heaven. Thus one speaker who observes a ritual error states:

> Using ritual to observe [*guan* 觀, a term with divinatory overtones] them, the two princes will both die. Ritual is the embodiment [*ti* 體] of life or death, survival or perishing. In moving left or right, turning round, advancing or retreating, looking down or up, we select between them [life and death]. In court audiences, sacrifices, funerals, or military campaigns we observe them.[147]

This is the program to which the *Zuo zhuan* devotes much of its account of the past.

The second Warring States articulation of a philosophical program through the exposition of a chronicle was the *Gongyang zhuan*. Its dating is debated, but the best studies conclude that it was written down in its present form under the Qin or the early Western Han. The current text, however, is almost certainly based on earlier written or oral traditions.[148] Unlike the *Zuo zhuan*, a narrative incorporating the textual resources of the *ru* tradition, the *Gongyang zhuan* is a commentary devoted to explaining the text of the *Chun qiu*. It deals primarily with the meaning and usage of particular terms, and how the choice of words indicates moral approbation or blame. In some cases the commentary adds details to the story to explain and justify the judgments of the chronicle's author. It also includes a handful of dramatic narratives, all the more striking for their appearance in the midst of a dry catechism.

The structure of the *Gongyang* has several important implications for the uses of writing about the past. First, by adopting the commentarial mode it emphasizes the importance of writing. The *text* of the *Chun qiu* is treated as authoritative, if not sacred, and its meaning is assigned to the choice of words rather than the events they recount. In the *Zuo zhuan*, lessons derived from the textual canon are written into the events, the speeches of figures in the narrative, and the judgments of Confucius or the authors. In the *Gongyang*, by contrast, the lessons are read entirely at the level of the author, who was identified with Confucius during the Warring States period. Thus the *Gongyang* used the implicit judgments of the sage to charge historical events with moral or political meanings.[149] The text is not about past events in themselves, but rather about the moral judgments of the sage inscribed in the telling of the events. Thus when asked why Confucius wrote the *Chun qiu*, Sima Qian quotes Dong Zhongshu:

> When the Way of Zhou declined and was abandoned, Confucius was chief magistrate in Lu. The feudal lords did him harm, and their officials blocked his path. Confucius knew that his words would not be employed and his way not put into practice. He judged the rights and wrongs of 242 years to create a standard for the world. He criticized the Son of Heaven, demoted the feudal lords, and punished the high officials, all in order to complete the tasks of the king. The Master said, "Rather than to record it in empty words, it is more trenchant and clear to reveal it in the conduct of affairs."[150]

Linking the *Chun qiu* to Confucius' supposed role as a judge is significant. Law, together with religion and government, is one of the spheres of activity in which language most frequently plays a performative role. The declarations of the judge, like those of the official or the priest, produce social realities. His pronouncement of guilt creates the fact of guilt in a way not possible for ordinary people. Thus when the *Chun qiu* assigns guilt or innocence, or grants or withholds a certain status, it plays the role of judge. The parables from the *Zuo zhuan* cited above likewise assigned to historians the role of judges who fixed the guilt for the crime of murder. One of them, moreover, praised the historian for not sticking to the literal facts of the case but seeking out the underlying responsibility. The metaphor of the historian as judge is commonplace in the West, but the stories in the *Zuo zhuan* and the commentary of the *Gongyang* treat this figure of speech as a literal reality. As will be shown in chapter 6, Confucius' role as a judge and his imposition of punishments was central to the myth that had developed around him by the early Han.

This assigning of significance to events through the person of the author is also indicated by treating him as the center of time and space. The chronicle, according to the *Gongyang*, is divided into "Three Epochs" (*san shi* 三世) depending on how the author obtained his knowledge of events. The most recent epoch is that which the author personally witnessed, preceded by that which he heard from direct witnesses, and the earliest that which he knew only from transmitted testimony, that is, from writing. For each epoch the author uses different principles in recording dates, titles, and names.[151] The *Gongyang* also treats the author's home state of Lu as "inside" (*nei* 內), while the other states were "outside."[152] The practices of recording events vary depending on their temporal and geographic relation to the person of the author.

The *Gongyang* does not yet speak of an imaginary kingdom of Lu that within the text has inherited the Mandate from Zhou and is ruled by Confucius as a "king without attributes" (*su wang* 素王).[153] Nor does it suggest, as Han authors did, that the text prophesied Han institutions.[154] However, the *Mencius* already stated that in writing the *Chun qiu* Confucius performed the "tasks of the Son of Heaven," and that the *Chun qiu* was written when the "traces of the kings" had vanished. Combined with the doctrine that Lu was to be treated as "inner" and all else as "outer," this comes very close to proclaiming the kingship of the author. In fact the *Gongyang* does develop a theory of its own textual kingship. Insisting on the matchless power of the true king, the *Gongyang* denies the status of monarch to the impotent Zhou sovereigns. It asserts that there is "no king above," and that consequently actions illicit under a genuine monarch could "in reality" or "as an expedient" be performed. In contrast with the king-less reality of the period it narrates, the *Gongyang* asserts a monarchy that belongs to the realm of "pattern/writing" (*wen* 文) or the "constant/classic" (*jing* 經). Identifying political order with the person of the monarch and denying the existence of such a figure in its own time, the text of the *Gongyang* finds the principles of monarchy in the *Chun qiu* and its author.[155]

The centrality of the monarch is proclaimed in the opening passage of the *Gongyang*.

> First [*yuan* 元] year. Spring. The King's first month. Why does it say, "first year?" Because this is the first year of the prince [Lord Yin of Lu]. Why "spring?" Because it is the beginnning of the year. To whom does "king" refer? It refers to King Wen [founder of the Zhou]. Why does it first say "king" and then say "first month?" It is the king's first month. Why does it speak of the "king's first month?" Because it is the Grand Unity [*da yi tong* 大一統].[156]

This discussion of origins links the beginning of the lord's reign to the beginning of the year. The link exists through the king's calendar, so these two in turn are traced back to the origins of the dynasty. The Eastern Han commentator He Xiu reads the initial character *yuan* as referring to the *yuan qi* 元氣, the primal energies from which the world emerged. Whether or not the authors of the *Gongyang* intended to trace the play of origins back to the Daoist *urzeit*, they clearly placed the work under the aegis of a unified kingdom.

The theme of the single, unique monarch and the united kingdom is reiterated throughout the text. First, the king is given special attributes, such as a unique verb to describe his death, and the privilege of sacrificing to Heaven and the most sacred peaks.[157] Second, the *Gongyang* appeals to his unique qualities to explain the methods of recording an event. These include such statements as "there is nothing outside the king," "the king has no equal," "it is not permissible to attack the Son of Heaven," and "it is not permissible to summon the Son of Heaven."[158] When a minister of the king is said to "come" to Lu, the commentary asks why it does not refer to him being "sent." It replies that he was fleeing, but to refer to "fleeing" would imply that he had escaped the king, and "there is nothing outside the king." Another example explains that Confucius refers to the queen elect as *wang hou* 王后, when it is the practice to call an unmarried woman outside her state "maiden" *nü* 女. As the wife of the Zhou king, there is no "outside" of her state.

Since the king is absolute monarch, the nobility are reduced to the level of bureaucratic officials. All hereditary offices below the level of lord of a state are repeatedly denounced as violations of ritual.[159] The text also insists that feudal lords and their ministers did not "initiate action" (*sui shi* 遂事) nor act on their own accord (*zhuan* 專), but only on the orders of the king.[160] The Zhou king and his nobility are thus rewritten in the image of the Warring States polity.

Although the *Gongyang* proclaimed the supremacy of the Son of Heaven, it did not attribute this exalted role to the Eastern Zhou monarchs. Instead the ideal king was a standard in terms of which the decaying Zhou order is condemned. The actual Zhou kings are criticized for ritual failings. Several are condemned for requesting aid from powerful nobles. In doing so they fail "to carry on the institutions and preserve the laws of King Wen," and lose the right to be called kings.[161] In one case the text refers to the king "departing" his state, an impossibility in a world where there is nothing outside the king. The commentator explains that the king is said to depart because he could not properly serve his mother, and hence was not a king.[162] By contrast, Duke Huan of Qi plays the role of a king by repelling the barbarians and preserving states, so he is described in terms appropriate to a king.[163]

The clearest rejection of the Zhou monarchy is a group of passages explaining the *Chun qiu* in terms of the contrast between "ideal pattern/text" (*wen* 文) and "reality" (*shi* 實). When Lord Huan restores two states destroyed by barbarians, the text refers to "armies" without naming their lord. The *Gongyang* explains that as a feudal lord Huan did not have the right to restore states, an act which was tantamount to enfeoffment. "Reality" approved, but the "pattern/text" does not. These diverged because

> above there was no Son of Heaven and below no lords of the Four Quarters. The feudal lords destroyed one another. If one was able to save them through force, then it was proper to save them.

This same formula recurs five times, and other invocations of the *wen/shi* dichotomy imply the absence of a Son of Heaven.[164] The *Gongyang* thus denies the status of king to the reigning monarchs and embraces the hegemony as a necessary expedient.[165] True monarchy existed only in the text (*wen* 文).

Expedient improvisation in an imperfect world is embraced through a second dichotomy, that of "constant norm/classic" (*jing* 經) and "expedient assessment" (*quan* 權).[166] These explain the *Chun qiu*'s respect for Ji Zhong, chief minister of Zheng who deposed his lord in collaboration with the state of Song.

> What is worthy in Ji Zhong? He can be regarded as understanding "expedient assessment." In what way? . . . Lord Zhuang died. After his burial Ji Zhong went to inspect Liu. The road went through Song. The men of Song seized him and said, "Expel Hu [the heir] for us and set up Tu." If Ji Zhong did not obey them, then his prince would certainly die and his state certainly perish. If he obeyed them, then the prince would live instead of dying, and the state would survive instead of perishing. If he could draw out the process, then Tu could be expelled and Hu restored. If this were not possible it would be a great loss, but there would still be a state of Zheng. Ji Zhong was certainly one of the men of antiquity who could make calculations of expedience.

> What is "expedient assessment?" It is that which is contrary to "constant norms" (*jing* 經) but has some good. Expedient assessment can only be applied in matters of life and death. The practice of expedient assessment possesses its own Way. You must degrade or damage yourself in practicing it, but not harm others in doing so. To kill others in order save your own life, or cause other [states] to perish to preserve your own is not the action of a gentleman.[167]

Just as in the absence of a true king the demands of reality may supersede the patterns of an ideal culture, so where the survival of a superior or a state is at stake the results of utilitarian calculation may take precedence over the dictates of eternal norms. Although no other passage speaks explicitly of *quan* and *jing* several argue that ministers can act on their own initiative or disobey a ruler to "preserve the state altars."[168]

These explanations in terms of *wen/shi* or *jing/quan* place the act of writing at the center of the *Gongyang*'s political theory. The character *wen* 文 at the broadest level refers to any meaningful pattern, but its more limited sense is "writing" or "written character." *Jing* meant a "constant norm," but by the late Warring States period it also referred to the highest written works, or those sections in a text held to be of enduring truth or worthy of elucidation. Thus both dichotomies posited an ideal linked with written texts, and then set that textually based standard against the realities and compromises of a decadent age. The identification of the ideal with the text is not simply based on the uses of the terms *wen* and *jing*, but is a presupposition of the *Gongyang*. It treats the king as the embodiment of political order, but insists that in the period recounted in the *Chun qiu* "there is no Son of Heaven above." The ideal king survives only in the prescripts of the text and the judgments that it delivers. If Confucius as author of the *Gongyang* is not yet the "king without attributes," it is because the *Chun qiu* itself acts as king.

However, the kingship of the text is confined to the realm of *wen* and *jing*, that is, the classic itself, whereas the world of reality is incorporated in the commentary. Thus the split between "pattern/text" and "reality" that informs the judgments of the *Gongyang* is recapitulated in the structure of the work. The chronicle names people and recounts events according to the eternal principles that define the true king, but the facts of the real world, which often contradict the version presented in the classic, are preserved in the commentary. The two planes exist in a balance of mutual support and mutual repulsion. The classic refuses to divulge negative information out of respect for the worthy, or hides positive information in order to condemn the wicked, but the commentary then divulges both in order to explain the workings of the classic's judgments. Thus the upper layer continually suppresses what the lower reveals, while the lower exposes what the upper seeks to hide. Nevertheless, without the revelations provided by the commentary the moral judgments of the classic would vanish; the commentary must reveal that Lord Xiang of Qi destroyed the state of Ji in order to explain how the classic suppressed this information to praise his act as just revenge.[169] Similarly, without the moral judgments and ideal kingship preserved in the classic, the "reality" of the commentary would degenerate into a chaos of savagery, random violence, and utilitarian calculations. Locked in a dual structure in which each level both refutes the other and depends on it for meaning, the classic and the commentary form a seamless, textual totality that offers kingship in a kingless world, and the realities of power and expediency in a realm of pure pattern.

CONCLUSION

History as a genre did not exist in the pre-imperial period, and writings about the past were dispersed in many textual forms associated with different groups and purposes. The earliest known records of the past were genealogies preserved in the ancestral cult, and perhaps chronicles of events pertaining to rulers. Bronzes used in sacrifices to ancestors were inscribed with historical records adapted from state archives. These records celebrated achievements and honors received, reported them to ancestors, and thereby sought to secure the blessing of future prosperity. At some point the Zhou began to produce speeches in which the founders of the dynasty propounded principles of government and offered counsel to their descendants. These may have been performed in association with ancestral rites, or written to articulate factional disputes at court. With the decline of the monarchy these texts lost their political role, but they were preserved by scholastic traditions that concerned themselves with theories of government. These same traditions also composed new documents in the voice of ancient rulers, or narrated their deeds. Some of these adapted myths to provide ancient charters for contemporary practice. Others were attributed to more recent rulers, and adopted Eastern Zhou forms of discourse, such as the prebattle oath or ceremony of infeudation.

Even as schoolmen preserved or created documents of early rulers, they filled their aphorisms and essays with references to the past, both distant and recent. The former dealt largely with the deeds of the sage kings, mythic rulers of antiquity who combined supreme political and intellectual authority. These sages were probably adapted from ancient gods or clan founders, so once again the schoolmen used elements of politicoreligious authority from the archaic state. Certain scholarly traditions espoused particular sages as their founders or patrons, but standard lists of sages soon took shape. The sole exception was certain currents within the proto-Daoist tradition, which denied any positive role to the conventional sages, and instead proclaimed an ideal of anonymous "perfected men" who had eschewed service and remained hidden from the world. Incarnating an ideal of an age in which philosophers had been rulers, and lending the sanction of proven efficacy to doctrines in opposition to current practice, the sages embodied a past that served as the ground par excellence for claims of scholastic autonomy and criticisms of Warring States institutions. Consequently all scholastic traditions made routine appeal to sages as models.

The sages provided charter myths for the political programs of the schools, but some proto-Daoist traditions sought deeper foundations for their doctrines in the principles of the cosmic Way. Such claims were often cast in the guise of accounts of cosmogony, which described the appearance of ordered existence out of a primal chaos. The basic principles manifest in this moment of origin were held to underpin all natural processes, and the insights provided by these cosmogonies enabled the adept to attain mastery over the world. Such beliefs provided the Daoistic underpinnings to the *Han Feizi's* theory of "form and name," as well as related administrative practices. Other intellectual traditions also appealed to a mythology of origins from chaos, but they defined this as the age in which men were not distinguished from animals. In this context they celebrated the technical inventions and moral innovations of the sage kings that had made possible the separation of a human realm from the state of savagery. Each school then identified the key element of this separation with the fundamental tenets of their own social program, and condemned their rivals as savage beasts who threatened the very possibility of a human existence.

Writing about the past in the Warring States period also took the form of chronicles of political events with appended commentaries. These writings also originated in the state sphere and then shifted to the scholastic realm. The chronicles had been a defining aspect of the ruler, but as the states disappeared their chronicles were lost, and only those preserved in tombs or maintained by the *ru* intellectual traditions survived into the imperial period. The major surviving examples of the latter are the *Zuo zhuan* and the *Gongyang* commentary to the annals of Lu state.

Both these texts use historical chronicles to expound political theories, and both define these theories through the dictates of ritual. However, they articulate their ritual-based theories in different ways. The *Zuo zhuan* works the full panoply of *ru* textual learning into extensive narratives that demonstrate moral lessons.

The narrative is interspersed with participants' speeches that expound lessons on the proper conduct of a public life. These speeches invoke earlier texts associated with the *ru* educational program. In addition to the disquisitions of figures within the narratives, the latter are interspersed with judgments on individuals or states placed in the voice of an anonymous third-person author, Confucius, or an unnamed gentleman. This use of speeches to perform analysis and expound lessons is a common feature of early history writing, and it figures prominently in the works of Herodotus and Thucydides. Notable among the speeches are those in which narrated figures or Confucius prophesy the fate of individuals and states depending on whether or not their actions conform to ritual principles. These prophecies are invariably fulfilled, and they furnish the most dramatic means by which the authors proved the efficacy of their texts and teachings, as well as certified their own credentials as masters of wisdom.

The *Gongyang* commentary, by contrast, has few extended narratives of events and no speeches. Moral lessons are derived from analysis of the wording employed in the brief entries of the chronicle, and also of the words used by the commentary itself.[170] The *Gongyang* makes the ideal of royal power and political unity central to its theory of the state. It elaborates the proper relations of the feudal lords and officials to the king, and the significance of the disappearance of royal power. Given its identification of political order and morality with the king, and its insistence that there was no king, the *Gongyang* implies that texts, above all the *Chun qiu*, were the sole locus of kingship and political authority in the Eastern Zhou. This theory of textual kingship is both presupposed in its teachings and structurally enacted in the interplay between classic and commentary. The idea of the kingship of texts in a work that depended for its meaning on decoding the presumed intent of the author also led to the idea that Confucius had ruled as an authorial "king without attributes" in a kingdom defined by the texts that he created. This apotheosis of text and author at the end of the Warring States period marks the emergence of the paradigm that underpinned the establishment of a canon of authoritative sacred texts, and the near deification of those credited with their production.

Chapter Four
WRITING THE SELF

Another type of authoritative text that developed in the Warring States period was verse. In imperial China poetry was the form for expression of the self and the mode of writing most closely identified with an individual, authorial voice. Although the roots of this development can be traced back to the pre-imperial period, the writing of verse in early periods, like that of philosophy and history, was collective in nature. Emerging in cult practices and court entertainments, verse was generated and transmitted within small social groups that thereby gave form to their shared communal code of values. Although an isolated self figured in some Zhou lyrics, it was an anonymous self still nested in and giving expression to "the ceremonies and the habits of feeling of small, closed communities."[1] As the communities broke up, verse was transposed into larger, written works by other groups who read them in a new manner for new purposes. Poetry was incorporated into written narratives, philosophical discourse, and finally anthologies. Once again the editor and anthologist played the role of author, and authority was derived from the collective or traditional nature of the work. Only at the very end of the Warring States period, in the context of forming one such anthology, did readers begin to treat poems as the public expressions of the private experience of named individuals, and the idea of authoritative *self*-expression detached itself from writing understood as public and collective. Thus in the history of putting verse into texts in pre-imperial China one can trace first the emergence of new groups organized around writing, and then the invention of the social role of author.

Verse writings of the Warring States can be divided into three major categories. First, a limited body of songs from the Zhou period was preserved, and perhaps supplemented through later imitations. These were ultimately collected in the canonical *Shi jing*. Second, verse was incorporated into the texts of philosophical traditions to make their writing more memorable and persuasive. Some works, such as the *Dao de jing* and the *Huangdi si jing*, contained substantial verse passages. Others, such as the *Zhuangzi* and the *Xunzi* interspersed numerous poetic passages among the prose. The *Xunzi* also included two chapters of verse. Third, verse forms derived from songs employed in shamanic rituals were employed to compose literary poetry as a form of protest or persuasion. These, along with derivative Han pieces, were collected in the *Chu ci*. In all these forms the reading and writing of verse became an essential element to claims of intellectual authority in the Warring States period.

The poems preserved in the *Shi jing* were sung in the temples and courts of the Zhou state to accompany banquets, religious rituals, hunts, and other activities of the Zhou nobility. Some scholars have sought to derive a substantial number of these odes, particularly those known as "Guo feng" (國風 "Airs of the States"), from popular folk songs, but the current consensus holds that the songs in the *Shi jing* were produced for nobles at court.[2] Whatever folk elements may have inspired certain pieces, they were reworked by court musicians into a Zhou version of pastoral verse.[3] The origins of the odes lie beyond the range of this study, but of crucial importance for Warring States poetry was the appearance among later examples of a poetry of isolation, criticism, and resentment. These are the ultimate roots of the later theory and practice of poetry as an expression of individual feelings and aspirations.

The transition between the ancient Zhou odes and the written poetry of the Warring States period took place in the courts of the Spring and Autumn period. At this time the odes were still performed with music at banquets or in temple rituals, so they were preserved by hereditary musicians. However, they served an important supplementary role as a form of refined speech employed primarily in diplomatic missions or other exchanges between people from different states. Fragments of odes or individual stanzas were recited in order to certify the speaker as a cultivated nobleman, to establish emotional bonds between him and his listeners, and to move the audience through the force of images in the verse. In this context the ability to employ verse distinguished the educated man of noble breeding, much as quoting Greek and Latin did in early modern Europe, and it lent authority to conventional speech.

This practice, known as "presenting odes" (*fu shi* 賦詩), had several consequences. First, the sense of the quoted fragments did not appeal to any original sense of the verse, but instead depended on "breaking apart the stanza to extract a meaning" (*duan zhang qu yi* 斷章取義). This established a precedent for assigning to poems meanings not visible in their surface reading, and thus made them apt objects for commentary. Second, since it often served to establish links between a ruler and an exiled noble, it was part of the general shift toward artificially created bonds in the political order. Moreover, it underpinned Warring States tales of kindred spirits or true friends who recognized one another in music (*zhi yin* 知音). Finally, it transferred knowledge of poetry from the hereditary experts to noble generalists, and detached the lyrics from musical accompaniment. This opened the way for verse to become a written art.

As the lesser courts and associated nobility vanished, the practice of verse quotation was preserved in scholarly traditions, notably those of the *ru* and the Mohists. In this context their nature shifted from oral performance to written text. Within the *ru* tradition, the presentation of verse as a form of testimony to one's character became part of the educational program, leading to literary versions of the practice of diplomatic quotation collected in the *Zuo zhuan*. As texts became central to the curriculum, quotation of verse became an aspect of argument. Even as the *ru* reinforced their arguments through quotation of Zhou odes, such proto-Daoist works as the *Zhuangzi*, the *Dao de jing*, and the *Huangdi si jing* incorporated substantial elements of verse into their collections of aphorisms and essays. This shows that the authority of verse was not dependent on claims to a Zhou origin, but also stemmed from the emotional power of imagery, the affective capacity of parallelism and rhyme, and the ability to suggest truths beyond the literal.

Although the *ru* of the first half of the Warring States period had developed a theory of poetry as individual expression in the context of explaining the Zhou odes, there is no evidence of the writing of verse by named individuals. However, the theory ultimately bore fruit in practice, and toward the end of the period the poetry of protest and resentment re-appeared in the poetic chapters of the *Xunzi* and in the writings attributed to Qu Yuan. These writings, originally a set of independent poems united by shared images and recurring themes of abandonment and despair, were brought together by attribution to a presumed common author. A set of conventional poetic gestures was read as the expression of a distinctive temperament that became the privileged ground of interpretation. In the creation of this anthology and the act of reading or rereading its poems in the light of one another, the men of the early Han created the foundation for the lyric vision of poetry as the expression of self.[4]

While these poems provided the ultimate foundation for the later theory of the lyric (*shi* 詩) as a record of personal experience, they took as their theme the poet's relations with the ruler. Just as the ruler was the silent origin and focus of administrative documents, and the master the topic of his disciples' writings, so the king was the mute inspiration of personal testimony in verse. Poetry, which had been used to establish ties between nobles and rulers in the Spring and Autumn period now served above all to record their rupture.

The canonical readings of the Zhou odes ultimately fixed in the Mao commentary similarly paired the anthology as form and the king as theme. This Western Han commentary assigns meaning to the poems by identifying the ruler under whom they were produced, and demonstrating how the poem expresses the moral character of his reign. This idea, already anticipated in anecdotes in the *Zuo zhuan*, makes the king the ultimate ground of poetic interpretation.[5] Thus the pattern of adopting an idealized monarch as the standard of judgment that we noted in the writings of the philosophical schools appears also in the Warring States conventions of reading verse. And the appearance of the author as an individual voice coincides with the transfer of textual authority to the idealized monarch and his all-inclusive wisdom.

COMPOSING THE ODES

Verse in ancient China originated in the context of rituals. Several elements of this will be discussed in this chapter, but the links are expressed in the etymology of the word "ode" (*shi* 詩). As Chow Tse-tsung has shown, the character began as the combination of the graphs for hand and foot, indicating the gestures, songs, and dances that accompanied a sacrifice. As music and words came to the fore, the character was marked by the addition of significs for mouth (*kou* 口) and ultimately for speech (*yan* 言).[6]

The first step in the collective creation of the individual voice dates back to the early Zhou. As Edward Shaughnessy has demonstrated, the earliest songs in the *Shi jing* anthology appear to be lyrics of liturgical hymns sung and danced collectively by those in attendance at the temple during the performance of ancestral rites. The entire cultic association sings in a collective first person that marks the communal nature of the action. In hymns depicting rituals from later strata of the text, however, a single poet describes the actions of an individual celebrant and the responses of a congregation.[7] Shaughnessy links this development to the "ritual revolution" of the tenth century B.C. suggested by Jessica Rawson. This changed rites from private matters celebrated collectively by a small group of people into large-scale spectacles performed by specialists and witnessed by an audience.[8] For the history of written texts, however, the key fact is the appearance of an individual narrator standing outside the action, although it is still an anonymous voice presenting an idealized account of the community's norms and actions.

The early hymns consisting of collective addresses to the spirits and praises to the ancestor appear in the "Zhou song" 周頌 section of the anthology. Three of the poems in this section can be identified with stanzas from the "Wu" 武, a major song-and-dance ritual that re-enacted the conquest of the Shang.[9] The poems are brief, unornamented, and consist of eulogistic accounts of the achievements of the Kings Wen and Wu. Another set of three poems from the same section can be identified with those performed at the installation of the Zhou kings.[10] In this case two of the odes are in the first-person, indicating the words to be recited by the king at the installation, and they are all brief and unadorned. Other poems in the section are longer and more complex, but pronouns indicate collective chanting by the assembled participants, or the king directly addressing his ancestors. In the case of the ode "Yong 雝" the text indicates an alternation between the congregation, who refer to the ancestral spirits in the third person, and the king, who addresses them.[11]

In contrast with these ritual libretti, the poems on rites in the "Da ya" 大雅 ("Greater Elegantia") are more elaborate, employ such poetic devices as "evocation" (*xing* 興) and "comparison" (*bi* 比), and consist of third-person narratives describing the elements of the ritual and the performances of ritual actors. The stanzas of the ode "Han lu" 旱麓 (Mao 239) alternate between praising the sacrificer and describing the items employed in the ritual. The ode "Xing wei" 行葦 (Mao 246) describes the audience of "brethren" sitting together on their mats, the foods laid out for the ancestors, the musical performances, the archery ritual, and the actions of the "impersonator" (*shi* 尸) who presides over the ritual. First-person references have vanished, although some passages still address the ancestors in the

second person.[12] This distinction could be explained as a chronological development or as a division in function, in which the "Song" section recorded liturgies
employed in rites, while the "Ya" recorded events in the name of collective memory.[13]
In any case, the use of the third-person narrative in the latter section implies an
observing author.

The emergence of an implied author out of the ritual context is followed by
the appearance of an alienated individual in the poems of resentment or complaint contained in both the "Great" and "Little Elegantia" (*xiao ya* 小雅).[14] The
complaints against rapacious officials and laments over the duration of military
service are well-known and set a pattern for later poetry of protest against government malfeasance.[15] However, more significant for the emergence of the individual
poetic voice are the plaints against the unreliability of language, the prevalence of
slander, the treachery of Heaven, and the inversion of proper order. These songs
establish themes that would dominate verse at the end of the Warring States period,
as exemplified in the poems attributed to Qu Yuan and Xun Kuang. Consequently
certain Han writers regard anger and dissatisfaction as the defining characteristics
of the "Little Elegantia."[16]

Many odes in the "Little Elegantia" deal with the dishonesty of men and the
unreliability of language. We have seen the latter as a topic of the philosophers,
but in the Zhou odes of resentment the primary target was the dishonesty of men
who slandered the poet to his superiors. Sometimes the poems attack "rumor"
(*e yan* 訛言), sometimes "slander" (*chan yan* 讒言 or *zan yan* 譖言), sometimes
"clever speech/glibness" (*qiao yan* 巧言), and once even "thievish speech" (*dao yan*
盜言), but they share the same target and recurring motifs. All speak of a vanished
social unity, the destructive villainy of cliques—who seemingly dominate the court—
and the failure of the ruler to separate flattery and slander from truth. They dwell
on separation from the ruler and on the righteousness of the poet's own speech
compared to the evil of others. Each poem is a claim to rectitude that marks its
creator as a speaker of truth.

The song "Mian shui" 沔水 (Mao #182), one of the briefest and simplest on
the theme, begins with images of great waters flowing into the sea "as though
going to a court," and flocks of birds flying together. These announce the ideal of
unity in the state. After variants of the initial images, it proclaims the poet's sorrow
over the deviance of certain men. It then decries the spread of rumors which no
one prohibits, and contrasts his friends with the slanderers. Other poems state that
unchecked slanders cause calamities; that they destroy trust; that the spread of
rumors blurs the difference between good and bad; that the voices of the innocent
are drowned out in the clamor of slanderers; that good men are rendered speechless while glib phrases flow like rivers; that evil speech destroys the wisdom of the
ancestors; that slanderers are as numerous as the stars, bully the common people,
and should be thrown to the wolves; that they swarm like flies, stop at nothing, and
throw the state into turmoil; that the divisions produced by slander reduce men
beneath the level of the deer living peaceably in herds; that women's slander destroys

states; and that the recitation of verses is no longer heeded.[17] The ode "Qiao yan" 巧言 (Mao #198) is devoted entirely to horrors produced by glib deceivers, which include disasters befalling the innocent and the undermining of covenants.[18]

The prevalence of slanderers and the ruler's failure to suppress them have several consequences. First, the king's tolerance of slander and flattery means that honest speech becomes a form of treason, and is either silenced or punished. As a consequence, the poet and any kindred spirits are cut off from the court. This results in a sense of total isolation that prefigures the emergence of poetry as the standard genre for the voice of individual subjectivity. In these poems, however, the *topos* of isolation appears as a blight. Several times the poem will employ the formula "I alone am X [worried, suffering, etc.]; all others are Y [at their ease, well nourished, etc.]."[19] This hyperbolic formulation anticipates the *Li sao*'s rhetoric of total solitude. However, the number of such poems and their preservation across centuries indicate that they had become a conventional form of rhetoric for a significant group within the elite.

Closely related to the theme of the triumph of slander and the isolation of the just is the motif of "the world turned upside down." Poems state that slanderers and wicked men are employed or rewarded by the ruler, while men of virtue and honest speech are punished or exiled. Others cite inversions of social order, such as women taking control of the outer court, or the prince calculating like a peddlar. The idea is also expressed in physical images, such as the leveling of mountains, the raising up of valleys, or the humbling of Heaven. Finally, some passages mark the *topos* of inversion through use of the characters 覆 (*fu* "invert") or 反 (*fan* "reverse"). They sometimes function as verbs, but most frequently as adverbs indicating "contrary to what is normal or proper." One line refers to virtue being 顛 覆 (*dian fu* "turned upside down"). In one ode this image takes on apocalyptic overtones, with the sun and the moon eclipsed, mountains collapsing, rivers escaping their banks, valleys becoming hills, and cliffs becoming valleys.[20] This theme also became prominent in the *Li sao* and the poems of scholarly lament derived from it.

The vision of the collapse of social order and the inversion of all values leads several poems to call into question the justice of Heaven. Some speak of Heaven sending down calamities on the people, but justify this as a warning to a ruler who "pays no heed to Heaven." The calamities do not descend from Heaven but arise from men.[21] Other poems go further and speak of Heaven's injustice and cruelty. Some proclaim the end of the Zhou order, the collapse of civilization, and the onset of universal slaughter. The ode "Sang rou" denounces Heaven as pitiless. It states that even animals have no peace, human society is afflicted with natural calamities, Heaven no longer nourishes, and corrupt officials rule through slander and violence.[22]

Several odes also declare the bankruptcy of divination and sacrifice, the religious rituals that had underpinned the Zhou state. Particularly graphic is the ode "Yun han" 雲漢 (Mao #258), which evokes a major drought. It begins with the king asking what crime the people have committed that they are thus punished.

No spirit will act, none will accept his sacrifices, his jade tablets have all been used up, but no one hears his plea. With a refrain that insistently returns to the horrors of the drought, the balance of the ode lists the rituals performed in turn to each of the spirit powers: Heaven, the royal ancestors, the myriad divinities. No reply is forthcoming, no solace given, and the only spirit that appears is the drought demon. Like several other odes, the "Yun han" invokes natural calamities to proclaim the imminent end of the Zhou mandate.[23]

However, this questioning of Heaven in some songs does not indicate a theological revolution or an intellectual rupture. Several poems still proclaim Heaven as the progenitor of the people, an agent of virtue, and a defender of the Zhou house.[24] Moreover, the same ode may cite both the indifference of Heaven and the failings of government as an explanation for disaster. What the odes indicate is the presence of a space in the intellectual field, perhaps newly opened, wherein it was possible to question the virtue of Heaven or its active response to human actions, and to proclaim personal innocence—or even superiority—in the face of failure or suffering. These developments would play a major role in later Chinese writing.

In the face of suffering and the possibility of a Heaven indifferent to questions of virtue or guilt, several of the odes employ formulae articulating a sense of radical insecurity and the need for constant vigilance. Some employ metaphors, several of which passed into common usage in later China, of acting as though walking on thin ice, standing at the edge of an abyss, or looking down a precipice. Others focus on the dangers of particular activities, most notably speech. They insist that the virtuous do not dare to speak, or must be cautious in speech.[25] Still others echo chapters of the *Shang shu*, which warn of the loss of the mandate and call for vigilance, but the themes of anxiety and dread are developed to a much higher degree.

Another aspect of the emergence of the individual poetic voice is the appearance of odes where the author names himself, or speaks of having written the ode but gives no name. While earlier poems sometimes indicated an implicit authorial voice through use of pronouns, these are the earliest surviving literary works in Chinese civilization credited to an author, excluding bronze inscriptions intended for communication with the spirits. There are four odes where the author names himself at the end, and three others where he concludes by stating the reasons for which he has written the poem without indicating his own identity.

Of the four poems by named authors, two are claimed by Yin Jifu 尹吉甫, a high official in the court of King Xuan 宣 (r. 827/25–782 B.C.).[26] Both poems— "Song gao" 崧高 (Mao #259) and "Zheng min" 烝民 (Mao #260)—celebrate the glories of the Zhou revival under this monarch. At the end of the songs, after claiming their authorship and asserting their quality, Yin Jifu states that they were presented to colleagues whom they praised.[27] The other two authored odes—"Jie nan shan" and "Shan bo"—are claimed by figures who are otherwise unknown. One has the title *si ren* 寺人, an office which was little more than a personal servant at court. The poems are classic examples of the odes of discontent discussed above. They denounce both slanderers and the ruler's failure to check them, and they include references to the cruelty of Heaven. One song concludes by stating that it was written to "thoroughly present the accusations [i.e., slanders]" in the realm in the hope that the king will reform. The other calls on "all the princes" to respectfully listen to his denunciation of the slanderers.[28]

The three songs that end with an assertion of authorship but offer no name are also highly critical in nature. One seems to target a particular individual, and it concludes by saying it was written to fully present his dishonesty. A second, in which the author styles himself "the gentleman," says that it proclaims his sorrow. The third ode, a savage portrayal of the cruelty of Heaven and the ruler, denounces the officials as bandits and men of violence. Even should they deny this, the author concludes, I have written this song.[29]

The announcement of authorship is perhaps related to the perception of breakdown and isolation, but Yin Jifu's adoption of the practice argues against this. It more certainly indicates the improved status of song composition. The practice of denouncing slanderers in verse suggests that it was conventionally viewed as an efficacious form of speech suited to assertions of personal virtue. This use of verse to assert character and to make authoritative moral pronouncements became central to Warring States poetic practice.

A final element significant for later developments is the connection between these plaints of the poet's righteous isolation and odes on the theme of the abandoned woman. As Shirakawa Shizuka has shown, there are close links in vocabulary, images, and formulae between odes praising a nobleman in his political or ritual functions, and songs in the voice of a woman praising her beloved.[30] This overlap between the political and amatory realms also figures in odes dealing with social breakdown and isolation. The best example is the ode "Xiao bian." Shirakawa identifies this as the plaint of an abandoned woman, on the basis of its use of lines that appear in other poems on this theme, as well as one reference to an implement linked with widows.[31] However, the Mao commentary explains it as a denunciation of King You 幽, and several modern scholars accept it as a political ode.[32] It features denunciations of slanderers, the formula "Others are all X, I alone am Y," a remark on the injustice of Heaven, and the complaint that the poet is isolated. In short, it employs the same repertoire as the poems of political resentment. Moreover, it employs phrases identical to those that appear in political odes, such as calling on someone not to break an oath, or lamenting that the poet was born under an unlucky star.[33] Whether the ode is a woman's plaint borrowing from the rhetoric of political resentment, a political jeremiad drawing on formulae and images from songs of the sorrows of women, or part of a general body of tropes of isolation, the overlap is indisputable.

The shared rhetoric in the "Elegantia" of political and amatory praise, and political and amatory despair, is significant, because once again it sets the pattern for developments in Warring States verse. The Mao commentary routinely gives a political reading to amatory odes, and the *Li sao* intermixes sexual and political *imagery*. This practice had already begun in the later strata of the Zhou odes.

The reasons for the emergence of slander and isolation as poetic themes in the late Zhou is unclear, particularly since their dating is uncertain. Nevertheless, the poems almost certainly reflect the decline of royal power and the breakdown of the institutions that defined the archaic Zhou state. They indicate struggles at court, with elements of the elite losing power but still sufficiently influential that their songs of resentment were put into circulation. These songs also adapted traditional themes, such as the fragility of Heaven's mandate. The political breakdown further cast doubt on the religious cults that had defined the structure of the state. Some at the top, like Yin Jifu, asserted that the old order was intact and Heaven still defended the king. Some saw the world in decay, but put the blame on human malfeasance. Others gave full voice to a sense of social breakdown, of inverted hierarchies and values, of a world where the old gods no longer appeared and the old rituals no longer worked. It was these last that set the pattern for the poetic compositions of the Warring States. Separated from the cultic practices in which it had emerged, the individual voice served not as social converse but as a sign of disaster and disintegration. Resentment and isolation were its themes, for only when cast out of society did the voice write its justification in verse.

SPEAKING THROUGH THE ODES

The mechanism for the transmission of the odes is no better known than the date of their composition. The shift from a ritual liturgy to a narrated account, and the associated transition from collective rites to a performance witnessed by an audience, indicate the emergence of specialists in the presentation of the odes and their music. These appear in Warring States texts as "music masters" (*shi* 師).[34] The *Zhou li* tells how the chief music master taught the odes, and a *Zuo zhuan* anecdote shows the role of court musicians in preserving them. In this story, set in 544 B.C. but appearing in a late fourth-century text, Ji Zha visits Lu to listen to the traditional Zhou music still performed there.[35] The list of odes performed accords with the received text of the *Shi jing*, although the order of states in the "Guo feng" is different. Together with an account in the *Lun yu* of the dispersal of the music masters, this anecdote suggests that the odes were preserved by musical specialists in the courts, although many were lost. The state of Lu preserved the largest number, according to the Confucian tradition that originated there.

These accounts suggest that the music masters preserved earlier odes and offered instruction in their performance, but there is also evidence of the composition of new songs. The clearest is the denunciation, repeated in many Confucian texts, of the music of the states of Zheng 鄭 and Wei 衛. This music, as has been confirmed by the set of bells excavated in the tomb of Marquis Yi of Zeng (buried

433 B.C.), introduced half tones which made it sound debased to those trained in the classical tradition.[36] When this began is not clear, but it had taken place by the fifth century B.C. It was sufficiently controversial that passages from the late strata of the *Lun yu* and from the *Li ji* still denounce it as an innovation.[37] This assault on innovations in music in recent centuries indicates that new compositions were still emerging, but they were not accepted for study and transmission by many ritual specialists. The paucity of surviving lyrics from this period is probably due to this rejection of innovations by what became the dominant literary tradition.

While music masters preserved the odes and their music down to the time of Confucius, poetic allusions were also used by nobles to grace polite speech in the courts and to assist in persuasions. More than thirty examples of this practice of "presenting odes" (*fu shi* 賦詩) figure in the *Zuo zhuan*. The most common use was to praise as a form of greeting, but they were also employed in diplomatic negotiations. Presentation of poetry served to issue warnings, make recommendations, and petition for assistance. In all these forms it served to alter the resolve of the recipient and impel him to act in the fashion desired.[38]

Before analyzing the use of poetic presentation in these stories, I will first examine their historicity. The *Zuo zhuan* is probably a late fourth-century text, but it narrates events dating from 723 to 469 B.C. While the dating of major events may be based on earlier chronicles, the anecdotes and speeches are almost certainly later literary compositions that may or may not have a historical kernel in earlier written accounts or oral traditions. However, there is evidence in the *Lun yu* of using poetry in diplomatic missions. One passage questions whether the odes are of any use if a man can recite all three hundred of them but when sent on a diplomatic mission he cannot use them in conversation.[39] Although this passage might not be earlier than the *Zuo zhuan*, it is significant because rather than asserting or dramatizing the practice, it takes it as a given to prove the point that learning is only of value if applied. As unintentional testimony, it is good evidence that verses were actually used in exchanges at court. In light of this, a statement that without the odes one lacks the means to speak also probably refers to the use of citations to make speech graceful and effective.[40] Thus the practice of presenting odes appears to have been a historical reality.

The first major example of the exchange of odes, and the one routinely analyzed by scholars, is that between Chonger, the future Duke Wen of Jin, and the Duke of Qin. Having been forced to flee his state, Chonger had met with a hostile reception elsewhere. On arrival in Qin he was invited to a feast of welcome. He first recited an ode, identified in the text only by its name. The duke replied by reciting another ode, also identified only by name. In response to instruction from an adviser, Chonger descended the dais and bowed. The Duke of Qin then rose to decline the bow.[41]

The surface story thus consists of two recitations of odes, a bow, and an acknowledgment. As later events reveal, and as an informed reader would have realized from the names of the odes, what had taken place was a request by Chonger for aid to return to his state, an agreement from the Duke of Qin to provide such aid, and a bow because the help is preferred in the name of "setting aright the king's land." This can be deduced from the content of the odes. The first stanza of the ode recited by Chonger reads as follows:

> Replete the rushing waters
> Going to the court of their ancestor the sea.
> Rapid the flying hawk
> Now flying, now halting.
> Alas my brothers,
> My countrymen, and all my friends,
> None deigns to think of the disorders of the land,
> But which of them lacks father and mother?[42]

The opening lines flattered the Duke of Qin, to whom the people of the world flow like rivers to the sea. Chonger casts himself in the role of a tributary current, and also appears as the poor hawk that now flies, now rests, but finds no permanent resting place. The balance of the stanza refers to the difficulties that had driven Chonger from Jin, where disorder had arisen between brothers. The duke replied:

> The sixth month is unquiet,
> The war chariots all arrayed.
> The teams of four stallions are strapping and strong,
> Carrying their regular armament.
> The Xianyuan are in full blaze,
> So we make urgent haste.
> The king sets out to battle,
> To put right the king's land.[43]

This is a straightforward response which, except for the reference to the sixth month and the Xianyuan, could have been composed for the occasion rather than quoted from an existing body of verse.

We have no contemporary explanation for preferring the use of verse presentations rather than a prose appeal. Steven Van Zoeren grounds his explanation in the famous formulation that "Odes express the intent" (*shi yan zhi* 詩言志). This is a scholastic idea that may well be read into the practice by the fourth-century B.C. authors of the *Zuo zhuan*, but cannot explain the earlier, historical practice. With no contemporary accounts, we must rely on what we know of using poetry in later China and other societies.

First, men of the Warring States and early imperial periods argued that poetry was a uniquely powerful mode of speech because of its ability to stimulate and guide emotions. With its musical rhythms and graphic images, poetic language stirred people to action in a way that intellectual persuasion could never manage.

Several anecdotes in the *Zuo zhuan* contrast the weakness of reasoned persuasion with the power of verse.[44] The scholastic theories of poetry likewise emphasized its relation to music, with its emotional resonances, and on the power of moral judgments couched in proper words.

However, if the use of *poetry* were the key, then a composition tailored to the occasion would have been more appropriate. The essential feature of the poems in the *Zuo zhuan* anecdotes is that they are *citations*, drawn from a stock of verse shared by the educated men of the period. The citation of known verse performed several functions. First, it certified the speaker as an educated man and a member of a cultured nobility, much as did the ability to throw Greek and Latin tags into writing and conversation in early modern Europe. Second, it claimed kinship of spirit in the assumption that the listener would recognize the ode and understand its import. Third, since the ode was applied to a situation other than that which had inspired it, the meaning imparted to it in the scene of presentation often differed from a presumptive original meaning. In fact, the practice of "breaking apart the stanza to extract a meaning" is presented by one speaker in the *Zuo zhuan* as fundamental to "presenting odes."[45] While this practice often distresses modern scholars—but not postmodern ones—who privilege original meanings and an author's intent, the men of the Spring and Autumn and early Warring States period perhaps valued the ability to make the poem say something other than what had originally been intended. To repeat a poem was a simple-minded enterprise, but to actively adapt it to new circumstances required skill and perception. This use of the odes in the Spring and Autumn courts may have set a pattern for the Confucian ideal of adapting teaching—including the meaning given to key terms—to the circumstances and the interlocutor. It also anticipates the later philosophical and commentarial assumption that the *Odes* contain hidden meanings.

Poetic citation may also have played another role in the society of the period. Diplomatic exchanges were the major venue for these performances, and their use in such settings implied a limited body of odes shared by the nobles of the Eastern Zhou ecumene. As the links provided by kinship and loyalty to the Zhou house weakened, new institutions and practices were developed to maintain interstate ties. Notable among these were regular interstate missions or assemblies to formalize links through the exchange of gifts or through written covenants.[46] States also maintained shared cultural traits, such as types of bronze bells and the makeup of ritual orchestras, while asserting independence through introducing local variations.[47]

Part of the inheritance that defined the late Spring and Autumn ecumene was the shared body of verse used as a *lingua franca* for polite exchanges and coded negotiations between members of different states. The *Lun yu* account of the dispersal of the music masters among the states indicates the same phenomenon.[48] As the Zhou vanished as a political reality, it transmuted into literary and cultural remains that provided the common ground on which the emerging states could meet. While laws, chronicles, and administrative documents were confined to single states, and the philosophical texts defined specific traditions, the literary remains of the Zhou formed the only body of writings shared by all Eastern Zhou states. Since authority was associated with mobility and geographic range, the omnipresence of the odes gave them great prestige, and made the ability to cite them definitive of cultural power.

A final source of authority for cited verse was its ties to religion. The first section of this chapter discussed links of the Zhou odes to the inscribed bronzes and chanted liturgies of the ancestral cult. Other odes were related to rituals of purification and to seasonal festivals.[49] Moreover, as Zhou Cezong has argued, the "six principles of poetry 六義," described in the *Zhou li* are all related to its uses in early shamanism.[50] Just as the states borrowed authoritative linguistic forms from the realm of religion, so the trans-state texts that defined the Eastern Zhou ecumene invoked the authority of sacred language.

The power that odes derived from their rhythms and images, their role as a hallmark of cultured nobility, their geographic range, and their ties to religious song are hypothetical, because we have no texts from the period. In the Spring and Autumn period the odes were primarily used in oral performance, although probably preserved in writing.[51] The transformation into writing of the practice of diplomatic citation is part of the larger intellectual project of the *Zuo zhuan* of demonstrating the efficacy of the *ru* textual heritage through its incorporation in narrative (see chapter 3). This marks the next step in the evolution of the authority of verse in the Warring States period.

The most important consequence of the incorporation of verses into texts is that the narratives in which they were inserted fixed the manner in which they were to be read. Just as the emissaries coded their exchanges in fragments of verses, where the meaning of the verse was derived from the situation of the speaker, so the author(s) of the *Zuo zhuan* delivered their messages in the form of historical narratives, where the significance of the verse was not simply the message delivered by the speaker, but what the message and the ability to deliver it revealed about the participants. In short, the incorporation of poetry into a larger narrative changed its role from communication between speaker and recipient into a *sign* about the speaker or recipient, a sign intended for the implicit reader. This use of verse as a sign or token assumed a theory about the social uses and powers of poetry.

Within the *Zuo zhuan* narrative, the meaning of the story of Chonger and the Duke of Qin lies in what it shows about these two figures, and what it reveals about the power of presenting the odes. As for the first, their ability to communicate and to recognize virtue through apt citation shows their high moral and intellectual character. As for the second, Chonger becomes ruler and ultimately hegemon through his ability to wield the power of the odes. The diplomatic practice of presentation is here incorporated into a scholastic program of assessing moral character and advocating textual study.

Other anecdotes reveal aspects of this scholastic program. First, several stories mark the persuasive power of presented verse by having a speaker first offer a

reasoned persuasion, which is met with polite refusal. Only after this initial failure
does he resort to the odes, by means of which he overcomes the resistance of his
interlocutor. Mu Shu, a figure celebrated in the *Zuo zhuan* for his skill in using the
odes, tried to persuade the state of Jin to protect Lu from its larger neighbor, Qi.
He described the piteous state of Lu and its longing for rescue. However, he was
told that the Jin ruler was preparing a major sacrifice, and the people had not yet
rested from an earlier expedition, so nothing could be done. He sought out two
leading Jin courtiers, and recited odes to them. To the first he recited an ode
criticizing an official whose dereliction inflicted suffering on the people, leading
his interlocutor to apologize for his earlier failure and pledge support. To the second
he presented an ode which invoked the dolorous calls of wild geese as an image for
the sufferings of a people at war. His interlocutor likewise was moved to pledge his
support to Lu.[52] Other stories similarly portray the persuasive powers of verse after
the failures of exposition and argument.[53]

   Some anecdotes depict the success of poetry through accumulation of force.
In one the ruler of Zheng and one of his ministers ask the Duke of Lu to intercede
with the Duke of Jin on their behalf. The request is accompanied by a chanting of
the poem "Hong yan" 鴻鴈 (Mao #181), the same poem cited in the previous
paragraph for its evocation of the mournful call of the wild goose. A Lu official
politely declines, and chants a poem on the sorrows of men too long away from
home in the service of their lord. The minister of Zheng reiterates the appeal,
increasing its plangency through citing a poem composed in the voice of a woman
married into a distant land, where the speaker ends by describing herself as empty-
handed and with no one to whom she can turn. Overwhelmed by this ode, the Lu
minister chants lines on the preparation of chariots for departure, and the unspoken
agreement is sealed by mutual bowing.[54]

   As François Jullien has noted, in all these stories the role of the verse is to
affect the sentiments of the listener, to shake his resolve, and to stir him to action.
Information is not communicated, nor is any real argument made. Moreover, the
same odes are used in different anecdotes, to the extent that in some cases there
emerges a mechanical coding in which particular sentiments are evoked by specific
odes.[55] Detached from their original sense, the odes function through their decontextualized emotional applicability. Rather than the meaning, it is the power of the
verse, and the bond it establishes between the speaker and his audience, that are
crucial. The latter is emphasized through the *exchange* of odes, creating a link between the two parties and highlighting the breeding that made this link possible.
The privileging of verse over prose argument, in Spring and Autumn practice,
indicates the importance of songs in the education of the nobility. Within the *Zuo
zhuan* text it demonstrates the importance of studying classical verse, and attacks
the theoreticians of disputation and their science of argument. The importance
granted to the performance of songs in the *Zuo zhuan* also distinguishes this work
from other *ru* texts. This may be linked to the tradition that the putative author of
the text, Zuo Qiuming, was blind, since court musicians were usually blind.[56]

In addition to the suprarational, almost magical character of the odes' suasive force, the *Zuo zhuan* anecdotes indicate other features of the social and scholarly uses of verse. First, the failure to recognize a poem and the inability to reply are not merely proofs of boorishness, but also presages of disaster. The story of Qing Feng, who seized power in the court of Qi only to have his whole family massacred, includes two scenes in which his failures in ritual elicit criticisms in the form of chanted odes. In both cases he does not recognize the ode and makes no response. This leads to prophecies of impending disaster, which are soon fulfilled.[57] Failings in rituals, ignorance of the odes, and political disaster form a single complex.

Another anecdote makes a similar point, but it focuses on the *content* of the odes as a form of moral instruction. An emissary from the state of Song visits Lu. At a banquet someone chants an ode composed in the voice of a new bride singing the praises of her husband at ease amidst his kin. The emissary does not recognize the ode and cannot answer with another one. A Lu noble who witnesses this scene predicts the emissary's ruin, because his ignorance of the poem suggests that he cannot appreciate and will not receive the virtues and blessings enumerated in it. This might suggest that lack of knowledge of verse indicated such an absence of breeding that no real virtues were possible, or it might hint at a version of the word magic discussed by Donald Harper in the context of the rhapsody, in which the ability to chant the words in the context of a poem gave one power over the things themselves (see chapter 1).

However, in stories where both the actors in the tale and the reader of the text must look beneath surface meanings, the same action does not always have the same significance. In some anecdotes, the failure to reply is evidence of virtue. Ning Wuzi of Wei came on a mission to the court of Lu, and at the opening banquet the Duke of Lu chanted two odes. Ning Wuzi offered no thanks and chanted no odes in reply. When the duke later sent a messenger to inquire about such behavior, Ning Wuzi replied that he had assumed that the duke was merely practicing the chanting of the odes. These had been used by the Son of Heaven when rewarding nobles presenting the spoils of victory, so to reply to the odes when chanted by the duke for a visiting emissary would have been a gross violation of ritual. By not replying, and creating the ingenious fiction of a rehearsal, Ning Wuzi saved both himself and the ruler of Lu from a serious fault.[58]

Another feature of the presentation of odes, both a source of power and a weakness, was its ambiguity. The mystique of cited verse, as suasive force and as means of mutual recognition, hinged on its indirection, on the communication of a message that was not the explicit sense of the words spoken. Consequently, readers and participants in the stories both sometimes need post facto commentaries in order to understand what has taken place. As shown above, the same action could be either a gross error that prefigured disaster or a mark of percipience and virtue. The participants and the readers could not distinguish the one from the other without the addition of an explanation, which is obtained by the literary invention of a messenger who is sent to request one. Likewise the same ode, depending on its context, could serve multiple functions, or different odes might be applied to the same situation in order to reveal different aspects.[59] Finally there are cases where the ambiguity results in the reader not being certain what has taken place. In one story Ji Wuzi of Lu returns from a mission and is invited to a banquet by the ruler. He chants an ode attributing his success to the ruler's acumen, and in reply the ruler chants an ode describing a gentleman who is the glory of his state, and wishing him long life, eternal fame, and flourishing progeny. In reponse Ji Wuzi flees while saying, "I cannot bear it." Some commentators take the ode at face value and assume that Ji Wuzi's response is modesty. Others, noting that the Ji clan's power had long overshadowed that of the ruler, take the ode as a veiled criticism and an encouragement toward genuine loyalty.[60]

Finally, several anecdotes invoke the theory that the odes were a means by which people expressed character and overarching aims. This idea is summarized in the paronomastic definition "the odes articulate aims," the most influential sentence in Chinese poetic theory.[61] The character *zhi* 志 is a protean term, ranging from a narrow meaning of "target" or "aim" in a chapter of the *Shang shu*, to the meaning of "[worldly] amibitions or aims" in the *Zuo zhuan*, to "the project of a morally committed person," "the thrust of a person's being" in the major *ru* philosophical texts.[62] In the anecdotes cited above, the only applicable sense of *zhi* 志 would be "worldly ambition," since the actors are trying to secure an alliance, military assistance, or some political goal. Moral character comes into play in a negative sense, in those anecdotes where the inability to recognize or chant odes is taken as a sign of serious failings.

A few stories, however, adopt the articulation of *zhi* 志 as their organizing principle and focus on a moral conception of personality. The best known tells of the visit of Zhao Meng and Shu Xiang to Zheng. At the banquet Zhao Meng asks seven officers of Zheng to chant an ode so that he may "observe their ambitions (*guan zhi* 觀志)." The anecdote lists the titles of the odes and presents Zhao Meng's responses. Afterward he and Shu Xiang compare their observations and predict the futures of the participants. One in particular draws their wrath for having selected an ode contrasting the matings of birds with an illicit match by a corrupt ruler. This indicates his treasonous intentions and prefigures his doom.[63]

As Steven Van Zoeren has pointed out, this and related stories are patterned on, or provide a model for, two anecdotes in the *Lun yu*. In one story Confucius asks three disciples to tell him their *zhi*, and in response to a question from Zi Lu he then offers his own. No comments are made or judgments passed. In the second, the longest passage in the *Lun yu*, Confucius asks four disciples what they would do if they were employed by a ruler, and at one point he identifies these proposals as *zhi*. After each disciple has finished, Confucius offers comments, and he states which proposal he favors.[64] Here the subject is the reading of character. The disciples each offer ambitions of which they think Confucius will approve, but he sees through them and reveals the personality hidden beneath their constructed facades.

Only one disciple reveals a desire that is genuine in its lack of pretension, and Confucius chooses this one for approval.

The structure of this story and the two in the *Zuo zhuan* are identical. Both focus on the ability of the central figure to read the truth of the reciter behind the mask of his words. Confucius was created as a master through the compilation of texts in his name, but his mastery extended to an ability to read the disciples. Through their ability to observe (*guan* 觀) moral character in the presentation of verse, Zhao Meng and Master Xuan are both certified as figures of moral authority in the image of Confucius.

There are, however, three significant differences between the two texts. First, the scene in the *Lun yu* is the class rather than the court, so Confucius shares his insights with the disciples. In the *Zuo zhuan* stories the insights are presented in private discussions after the banquets have dispersed. Second, as an extension of the first point, Confucius uses his insights to guide the disciples, while the *Zuo zhuan* observers make prophecies that are not revealed to those whose fates they foretell. The role of prophecy in these stories, like that in many of the accounts of verse quotation, is identical with that in the narratives of ritual failure discussed in chapter 3. Third, the *Lun yu* account does not involve the use of verse, and indeed although the *Lun yu* offers numerous reasons for studying the odes it never links them with the articulation of *zhi*.[65] These differences collectively point to a fundamental divergence between the *Zuo zhuan*, on the one hand, and the *Lun yu* and other *ru* philosophical texts on the other. In the former the odes provide power to move men or to read them, and they certify membership within a cultural elite. They do not, in stories of quoted verse, provide moral guidance. Detached from any original sense and deriving meaning within the narrative from the uses to which they are put by the actors, these presented odes do not claim authority over ultimate goals. Together with the ambiguity that is essential to the practice of quotation, an ambiguity preserved by the refusal of the narrative to explain itself, this use of the odes as a means to personal ends leaves them ultimately open to "the moral peril of an uncontextualized poem."[66] To ground the odes securely within a morally authoritative structure required a different form of quotation.

THE ODES AS PROOF AND SANCTION

Thus far the odes have appeared as an element in the rituals and festivities of the Zhou elite, a conventional means of expressing alienation or discontent, a method of forming ties with others and persuading them to undertake a course of action, and a key to reading character and predicting destinies. Detached from their ritual context, the odes had become a means by which the isolated noble spoke authoritatively through his talent as composer or his skill at presentation. But whether as composition or citation, verse served primarily to give the individual voice power over others.

However, poetry also appeared in the writings of the period as a form of authoritative wisdom that did not express the individual, but rather imposed obligations on both speaker and audience. This practice of quoting odes within an argument as a form of proof or command became the major use of poetry among the schools.

As with most school practices, the quotation of Zhou odes as a form of compelling truth or moral authority began with the sayings attributed to Confucius. In addition to those quoted above urging the study of the odes, three passages employed quotations as a source of authority or understanding. In two anecdotes cited in chapter 2, a disciple is able to draw a lesson from a couplet, or apply a couplet to a lesson offered by the master. The third passage is the famous sentence "As for the three hundred odes, a single line can cover them: 'Thoughts not straying.'"[67] The subject is always the odes themselves. The first two draw lessons from the odes, but do this to demonstrate the usefulness of studying them, and to reveal that a particular disciple was gifted in this field of study and received special lessons from the master. The third extracts a meaning from a line of the odes, but it is held to be a summation of their wisdom, or the verse that says best what all the others say in different ways. In short, the passages employing quotation use specific examples to deliver the same message as the generalizing discussions of the uses of the odes. Arguments on other themes are not supported by quotations. Much as the *Lun yu* emphasizes the value of the Zhou odes, it never gets beyond *proclaiming* their usefulness.

In the *Mencius* this changes completely. From the beginning its authors cite Zhou odes to prove arguments. However, the odes are used primarily as historical sources. As shown in chapter 2, the *Mencius* calls on Warring States rulers to adopt the practices and institutions by which the early sages had ruled the world. The odes are cited as evidence that these institutions had actually existed, that they had created wealthy states with contented subjects, and that consequently they should be restored. The *Mencius* uses the odes, like the historical accounts discussed in chapter 3, primarily as a means of demonstrating the realism of a political program totally at odds with the practices of its own day.

For example, a Zhou ode is cited in a conversation with King Hui of Liang held in one of his parks. The poem describes the park built by King Wen. It tells how the people flocked in ever-increasing numbers to help build the park, and celebrates its contents. Mencius uses this poem to prove that the people will delight in the king's parks if he will only share them, and he thereby criticizes the vast hunting parks kept as private preserves by King Hui and other Warring States rulers.[68] King Xuan of Qi confesses to Mencius his weaknesses for heroism, money, and women. In reply to each Mencius offers a quotation from odes depicting the martial valor, devotion to accumulation, and desire for consorts of the early sages. However, the valor must be used to suppress the criminal, the accumulated wealth to assist people in need, and the desire for a mate extended to all subjects.[69] The odes are also used as sources for institutional history, as in the account of the mix of public and private lands under the "well-field system."[70] Other odes are quoted to demonstrate that one can rule the state through regulation of one's own family, that holding Heaven in awe preserves a state, that if the ruler is benevolent then people will come from all directions to submit, that the Mandate will be preserved or lost depending on the conduct of the ruler, and that the true ruler is not fond of words.[71]

Mencius' theory of reading an ode is also devoted to the question of using poetry as a historical source. Troubled about the relations of a ruler to his father, a disciple of Mencius cites the ode that says that all land under Heaven is the king's and all men his subjects. That being so, then Shun's father must have been Shun's subject. Mencius replies that this is misreading the ode, which was a plaint by officials too busy in the king's service to attend to their own affairs. In reading poetry, Mencius argues, one must not allow rhetorical ornaments (*wen* 文) to obstruct the meaning of sentences (*ci* 辭), nor the meaning of sentences to obstruct the intent of the author (*zhi* 志). One must recapture that intention through sympathetic understanding. The ode cited was a case of rhetorical hyperbole and not to be taken at face value. As another example Mencius cites the lines, "Of the remaining people of Zhou, there were none who survived." If this line were true, then the entire Zhou population had perished in the drought, which was not the case.[72] While this passage is best known as one of the earliest theories of reading poetry, it is important to note that the *Mencius* offers its hermeneutic as a screening device to separate historical truth from rhetorical flourishes. This demonstrates the importance placed on the role of poetry as evidence of historical realities.

In addition to providing written evidence of historical facts, some odes are cited as testimony in a form of proto-anthropology. A discussion of the different systems of land ownership and taxation employed by the Three Dynasties is preceded by a brief account of the activities and moral nature of peasants. As evidence the *Mencius* cites a passage from the ode "Qi yue" 七月 (Mao #154), the earliest surviving account of the seasonal activities of the common people.[73] A second example of the anthropological use of the odes is a demonstration of the "barbarian" nature of southerners at the end of the debate with the followers of the "School of the Tillers." Mencius finishes with an *ad hominem* argument in pointing out that his interlocutor had studied with Chen Liang, a man from the southern state of Chu who had come north to study the teachings of Confucius and the Duke of Zhou. Now that Chen Liang had died, his erstwhile disciple had abandoned his teacher's path and adopted the doctrine of a "southern barbarian." In conclusion he cites an ode describing the Duke of Zhou's campaigns against the southerners, thereby proving that the men of the south had always been barbarians, and that those who took them as teachers abandoned civilization.[74]

While most citations in the *Mencius* prove points of historical or cultural fact, in a half dozen cases odes are cited as moral maxims. These are almost invariably straightforward propositions, with only a single citation requiring interpretation. Thus the quoted verses instruct the reader to prepare against the rain before the clouds gather, not to bend the rules—using the images of charioteering and archery, and not to try to hold onto something hot. They also state that the evil will all perish together; the Way of Zhou is smooth as a grindstone and straight as an arrow, followed by the gentleman and passively regarded by the petty man; and that if the people hold onto their constant nature they will cherish superior virtue.[75]

Thus the odes in the *Mencius* are not treated as a distinctive form of speech, but rather as a body of writing that is authoritative through its antiquity and its role as written testimony to the deeds of the sages. Their messages are straightforward, and poetic language is regarded as a source of confusion or obscurity that must be screened out in order to reach the intent of the author, an intent which is clear, direct, and morally exemplary. This vision of the odes as a record of the past and a body of moral maxims explains why the *Mencius* stated that when the creation of odes vanished together with the traces of true kingship, the *Chun qiu* chronicle arose.[76] Both were records of the past that presented judgments to those who could read them, and the poetic character of the one was not significant to its proper use.

At approximately the same time that the *Mencius* was quoting Zhou odes as a source of historical precedents and moral maxims, the *Zuo zhuan* was doing likewise. This manner of "quoting verse" (*yin shi* 引詩) is distinguished from the previously discussed "presentation of verse" (*fu shi* 賦詩) by the mode of enunciation within the text. In the latter, the poems were cited *in the narrative* by title and sometimes stanza, but the lyrics were not written out. Moreover there was ideally an *exchange* of verses. The absence of a reply was treated as a sign of boorishness, or even criminality. Finally, although the presentation might follow a failed persuasion, or be followed by a discussion of its meaning, the verse functioned on its own and had to be deciphered by the reader through his knowledge of the odes and the actions that followed from the recitation. In the case of quoting verse, the relevant lines or phrases are almost always written out, and they are placed in the mouth of an *actor* within the narrative. In the ten instances—out of more than one hundred and fifty—where only the title or stanza number is cited, it is cited by the speaker rather than the narrator.[77] There is no exchange of verses, because they are embedded within longer speeches or monologues, and any reply takes the form of another speech. Finally, the speeches dictate how the odes are to be read, clearly fixing their sense through the argument of which they form an element.

This contrast between the two ways of incorporating verses in the narrative highlights a distinction in their use. The presentation of a verse was intended to elicit a particular action. It depended on the emotive or imagistic force of the ode and the bond created by the shared recognition of veiled meanings. The text of the ode is omitted in order to draw the reader into the play of reference and hidden meanings. In the quotation of an ode, on the other hand, the ode is cited as an authority to reinforce an argument, which might seek to elicit an action, defend a decision, or give a lesson. Hence the text of the poem is included, and the surrounding argument either explicitly or implicitly dictates the meaning of the verse quoted.

As an example of the former, in one of the earliest citations of an ode by an actor in the narrative, Guan Zhong seeks to persuade Duke Huan to rescue the state of Xing from an attack by the Di people.

The Rong and Di are wolves who cannot be satiated. "All the Xia" are kin who cannot be abandoned. Idle pleasures cannot be cherished. The *Ode* says, "How could I not want to return home? I fear this strip of writing [*jian shu* 簡書, a single bamboo strip used for urgent communications]." "Strip of writing" refers to those who suffer the same evil being concerned for one another. I request that we save Xing in order to obey this "strip of writing."[78]

The original ode (*chu che* 出車, Mao #168) presents the plaint of a soldier who longs to return home but remains in awe of the royal command. Here the message is extended to include the obligation to place the collective good above individual pleasures. The initial prose passage, composed of three parallel phrases in the original, lays out the essential argument for action, and the ode simply sanctions the call to work for the common good. By adding a gloss to the term *jian shu* he insists on the general moral import of the line, and also leads to a graceful conclusion in which the appeal for help from Xing is conflated with a written royal command, and both are subsumed under the general rubric of concern for collective dangers.

This example is an element of a persuasion that differs from a presentation only in the transcription of the verse and the moralizing argument explaining its meaning. Other instances, however, served not to stir to action but to communicate doctrine. Thus after being taken prisoner by Qin, Duke Hui of Jin laments that his father did not listen to a diviner who had predicted disaster. His attendant Han Jian replies:

The tortoise shell is image (*xiang* 象); the yarrow stalks are number (*shu* 數). When objects appear, only then are there images; when there are images only then is there increase; and when there is increase only then is there number. The harm that the previous ruler did to virtue, can numbers attain it [a pun, suggesting both that the duke's misdeeds led to disaster, which had nothing to do with divination, and that they were innumerable.]? As for this divination by the astrologer Su, what benefit would there have been in following it? The *Ode* says, "The calamities of the common people do not come down from Heaven. Assembling in joy or turning against one another in hatred derives entirely from men [十月之交, Mao #193]."[79]

Here the argument on the decisive importance of moral conduct and uselessness of divination is conducted in prose, and the quoted verse serves to sanction the prose argument.

In addition to persuading and instructing, the quotation of odes was employed as a mode of self-justification. When a man was upbraided for letting branches be mixed into the packed earth of a city wall that he was building, he argued first that to build walls when there was no war was to provide bases for internal enemies. He then cited an ode (Mao #254), "To cherish virtue makes peace; the clan members form a wall."[80] Odes were also used to justify refusal of a marriage or a post, perhaps as a polite form of speech that reduced the element of personal rejection by citing a universal principle.[81] More rarely, an ode might be cited in self-criticism, as when the ruler of Qin accepted personal responsibility for the defeat at Yao, and cited one of the odes lamenting the ruler's failure to listen to criticism or employ the worthy.[82]

The above quotations are all embedded in conversations between actors in the narrative. However, many quotations are addressed to the reader. Thus one third of the quotations of verse—forty-four out of one hundred and forty-three— appear in the sections that begin "the gentleman says (*junzi yue* 君子曰)," "Confu- cius says (*Kongzi yue* 孔子曰)," or "Zhongni (仲尼, that is, Confucius) says." These quotations usually are part of a judgment placed in the mouth of the sage. There are similar passages in which after the narration of an event or a debate, a historical figure such as Shu Xiang or Zi Si will appear, pronounce a judgment on what has occurred, and sometimes prophesy the fate of an individual, a lineage, or a state.[83] This substitution of political figures for Confucius is much like the pattern noted earlier in which Zhao Meng read the intentions of those who recited odes just as Confucius analyzed his disciples' projects.

Passages in the voice of the gentleman or Confucius are generally presumed to be the latest sections of the text, in which the redactors have explicitly inserted their own judgments. By shifting from the level of actors to sage observers they grant a higher authority to these moral judgments. The frequent use of quoted Zhou odes within these quotations of Confucius further increases their weight. It also fixes the meanings of the odes by inserting them into the judgments of an acknowledged master. The problematic aspects of the presentation of odes—that the verses were left morally ungrounded and hermeneutically open—were elimi- nated through the insertion of quotations into arguments that indicated how the verses were to be read. This fixing of the moral meaning of the odes, and their intellectual gravity as a mode of argument, is carried one step further in the pas- sages that step back from the narrative and place the odes in the mouth of the sage to announce ultimate praise or condemnation.

In addition to placing the odes in both speeches and framing pronounce- ments, the *Zuo zhuan* sometimes seeks to pin down the poems by contextualizing them historically. Whereas the *Mencius* cites the odes as sources without mention- ing their composition, the *Zuo zhuan* sometimes has speakers specify the author and the circumstances of its composition. One argument for fraternal assistance between states groups them under their respective surnames, cites verses on the excellence of ties between brothers, and concludes that the poem was recited by its author to the assembled clans at the Zhou capital when the state's unity had vanished (the reign of King Li according to the Mao commentary).[84] Other verses in the narrative are also assigned to an author, including King Wu himself, in order to fix their meanings.[85] One passage mentions no authors, but assigns one quoted verse to the time of Zhou's flourishing and a second to its decline. The practice of fixing the meaning of the odes through stipulating the time of composition and the author would become fundamental to the hermeneutic of the Zhou odes in the classic Mao commentary.

The uses of quotations within the *Zuo zhuan* narrative resemble those in the *Mencius*, serving primarily as a source of moral maxims and historical information. In the latter role the odes in the *Zuo zhuan* are used less as evidence of practices and institutions than as sources of exemplary figures for the late Zhou nobility. The *Zuo zhuan* is also distinguished by a more frequent use of figurative meanings in verse, sometimes interpreting concrete images as dealing with ethics and politics. Such figurative readings appeared in a couple of passages in the *Lun yu*, but the *Mencius* had not exploited this aspect of poetry. In the *Zuo zhuan*, however, speakers invoke verses on the difficulties of travel in damp weather as a figure for disasters caused by not assessing one's own situation, picking plants as an image for selecting talent, the relations between man and woman as a model for those between strong and weak states, care in selecting cloth or women as images for vigilance, and the shame of a host who runs out of liquor as a figure for the failings of the king.[86] Such passages extracting moral lessons through positing figuration are exceptional but, like those that read verses through situating them in history, they anticipate the developments of the next century.

In the third century B.C., the *Xunzi* developed the uses of poetic citation in a new direction. In the *Mencius* and the *Zuo zhuan* the Zhou odes had served primarily to urge, to justify, or to pass judgment. An element of the pan-Zhou cultural heritage by which the nobility of the Spring and Autumn had still defined themselves, they were adapted in the *ru* literary program as a repository of precedent and moral maxims. Espoused by those who rejected disputation in the name of sagehood, they provided a form of authoritative speech that claimed powers of persuasion above those found in definition and debate. While the *Xunzi* inherited this program, it also moved into the arena of dispute and adapted rules of definition and argument pioneered by the Mohists. In this context, the odes ceased to be an alternative to argument and instead were adapted to serve as an element within argument. The author(s) of the text employed three methods of rereading the odes in order to turn archaic verse into contemporary argument: (1) granting a figurative sense to objects cited in the ode, (2) universalizing individuals or incidents described in the poems, and (3) discovering Warring States equivalents to phenomena mentioned in the Zhou verse. A fourth type of reading, used largely in poems of praise and blame, consisted of observing the original sense of the ode.

All four types of citing verse use a common formula. Like the *Mencius* and *Zuo zhuan*, the *Xunzi* sought to fix the sense of the odes by incorporating them into another mode of writing, in this case philosophic prose. The text presents an argument, cites an ode, and then concludes with either the phrase "this is what it says" (*ci zhi wei* 此之謂), or with an explanation of how the poem says the same thing as the argument. The former is much more common, figuring in about three-quarters of the quotations.

As in the *Zuo zhuan*, reference to figuration is rare, representing about 10 percent of the cases. Typically these take an object in the poem and read it as standing for a virtue or a social type. This often entails a pun or a play on words. Thus a discussion of what types one should associate with and what types one should avoid is followed by the quotation of a passage from an ode praising the splendid appearance and deportment of some nobles. The key line describes the tight binding of their leggings, but *Xunzi* reads it as referring to the absence of carelessness in their personal "ties."[87] A similar play on words involves reading a line on the freshness of a haul of fish as referring to "timeliness" (*shi* 時, a character with both meanings). Other figurative readings include interpreting a line on receiving great and small jade regalia as indicating that people great and small were content in their places; reading a line on the crane's call rising up to Heaven as indicating the gentleman becoming known through his inner cultivation; finding in the celebration of the ornaments of the royal dwelling an image of using ritual to distinguish rank; and interpreting a woman's lament for her husband's prolonged absence on campaign as a lesson in the need for mental concentration.[88]

The vast majority of the poetic citations in the *Xunzi* refer not to objects but to human actions or sentiments. These are transformed into philosophy either through reading a universal import into their particular referent, or through finding a Warring States equivalent for them. An example of the former, which echoes the *Lun yu*'s remark that "not swerving" is the key line in the odes, appears at the end of an argument that the cultivation of moral power (*de* 德) allows the gentleman to respond appropriately to any event.

> As he drives them to the left, to the left,
> The gentleman makes it proper.
> As he drives them to the right, to the right,
> The gentleman has it.

> This says that the gentleman, by means of his sense of rightness, is able to draw inward or press outward and respond to all changes and occasions.[89]

The verse describes the mastery with which a nobleman controls his team of horses, but under this surface meaning the *Xunzi* discovers a generalized celebration of appropriate response to circumstance.

In many other passages the *Xunzi* gives universal import to an event described in a poem. An ode celebrating a Zhou conquest in the Huai River valley is three times cited to demonstrate variously that the gentleman tolerates those inferior to himself, all people submit to one who rules through ritual, and the wicked are transformed by the ruler's moral force. Elsewhere a criticism of the last Shang king certifies an account of the virtues that cause people to submit; a hymn of praise for a king's successful sacrifices sanctions a description of the ideal official; a celebration of the proper order of a ritual procession demonstrates that the ruler ranks men according to their talent; a hymn to the achievement of the Zhou kings twice proves that men rather than Heaven control the course of events; a song of return from a military campaign shows how people will flock to a benevolent ruler; an encomium to the knights (*shi* 士) who followed King Wen shows that the ruler must rely on officials; and the line that all land is the king's and all people his subjects proves that the Son of Heaven is the culmination of humanity.[90]

In addition to turning verse into philosophy by reading specific scenes as universal principles, the *Xunzi* also asserts that the topics of the ancient odes are current practices. Thus odes denouncing slanderers discussed in the first section are read on four occasions as denunciations of the "petty men" (*xiao ren* 小人) of Xun Kuang's day, or the sophists and Mohists who confounded established usage. In addition, an appeal from frontier soldiers for constant endeavor on the part of those in the capital is interpreted as a demand for hard work by students; a celebration of King Wen's submission to the will of Heaven demonstrates that one should obey one's teacher; praise for King Wen's ability to cause men from every direction to submit proves that the great *ru* will cause the whole world to obey; the maxim that kind words and deeds will be requited shows that the chaos of Xun Kuang's day was due to the wickedness of the rulers; an encomium for the ruler's ritual excellence and the blessings received proves that good administration—with a special emphasis on rewards and punishments—will create wealth; the proposition that the army and nobility are the ramparts of the state showed that a ruler is secured by having scholars in his realm; and an ode on the theme of the "world turned upside down" proved that one should not allow family status to influence rewards and punishments.[91]

These examples show how the use of poetic quotation in the *Xunzi* both inherits the earlier forms and goes beyond them. As in the *Lun yu*, *Zuo zhuan*, and *Mencius* it breaks the odes into fragments and incorporates them into itself. It thereby fixes their meaning and identifies that meaning with its own authorial voice. The major innovation of the *Xunzi* was to demonstrate that the odes were not, in the political realm, a ground for the rejection of the Warring States, and in the intellectual sphere an alternative to philosophical argument. Instead it insisted that the odes spoke directly to the present world, and as we saw above, that they sanctioned a range of Warring States practices, including legal codes and the use of warfare.[92] In addition to sanctioning significant elements of the Warring States polity, the *Xunzi*'s use of the Zhou odes made them elements of contemporary intellectual practices. Just as the *Xunzi* incorporated much of the Mohist philosophy of language while condemning its creators, so it made verse an element of philosophical argument in order to denounce those who argued. In using Zhou verse to sanction Warring States political and intellectual practices, the *Xunzi* follows the same pattern that it did in its discourse on state service, that is, it moved closer to the state realm while preserving a foundation of scholastic independence. This innovation entailed that the truths demonstrated by the *Xunzi*'s arguments had been present in the odes from the beginning, an esoteric or hidden sense revealed through Xun

Kuang's skill in reading. This idea, already adumbrated in *Lun yu* passages but only elaborated in the *Xunzi*, was an attempt to demonstrate the lasting value of a heritage that was increasingly marginal to intellectual practice. The nobles depicted presenting odes in the *Zuo zhuan* used quotation to demonstrate breeding, character, and intellectual acumen; to elicit reactions from those discerning enough to recognize the meaning of the ode within the situation of its quotation; and to form bonds based on this shared understanding. The schoolmen transposed these purposes into a new social setting, quoting the odes in their texts to establish scholarly credentials, assert adherence to the traditions of Zhou, and to claim the support of those who shared that adherence. They thereby created a textual ground in the Zhou, prior to all existing states in time and encompassing them in space, for their claims to independence from Warring States administration.

The *Xunzi*'s reading of verse was also linked to the idea that the sage was a master of change. The earlier sages were no longer in the world, but they survived in the written works of the "later kings," the kings of Zhou. This availability of written records had led Confucius to embrace the Zhou as a model, an idea defended by the *Xunzi* in the face of the Warring States tendency to trace intellectual ancestry to earlier sages.[93] Since the esoteric principles contained in the Zhou texts were unchanging, the way of the "earlier kings" and of any future sages could be known through them. However, just as the sage himself adapted to changed circumstances, so their writings presented a modified message to each age. The *Xunzi*, at least in its later chapters, accepted many of the political reforms of Qin and the verbal techniques of the logicians. However, it rejected their programs of invariant law and fixed definitions. Instead it asserted the need for the constant adaptation to changing circumstances embodied in the ideal of the sage. It created a model for such adaptation in its vision of the revitalized authority of an inherited, text-based culture, which was flexibile over time, amenable to circumstance, and of proven value.

Such a program depended on reclaiming the past through a philosophic rereading of the remains of archaic religion. This was achieved by asserting the polyvocality of certain special, marked texts. That the poetry of the odes communicated many messages other than its overt meanings was already a convention of the praxis of the later Zhou nobility, which had been incorporated into literary accounts of the feudal courts. The *Xunzi* attributed this recognized polyvocality of the odes to their sage authors. It then cited them to prove that its philosophic arguments were not merely the result of new techniques of argument, but also an extension of principles that had guided and would guide any successful state. This underlay the emergence of the commentarial mode of reading/writing, of which Xun Kuang was hailed as the founding figure.

This reference to commentary leads to one last version of reading the odes through incorporating them into a larger text: the anthology of odes with the accompanying Mao commentary and its "Great Preface."[94] Although some suggested dates for the composition of the Preface would place it beyond the chronological range of this study, I will examine it as the culmination of the history sketched above, and the fountainhead of later Chinese poetic theory.

The account of this text in the *Han shu* attributes it to a scholar at the court of Prince Xian of Hejian (r. 155–130 B.C.), a half-brother of the Emperor Wu. Bernhard Karlgren has demonstrated through internal references that the text was composed before 150 B.C., thus lending support to the received account.[95] A badly damaged version of the *Shi jing* including some lines of exegesis was excavated in a Han tomb discovered at Fuyang. The organization of the text, buried no later than 165 B.C., has features in common with the Mao odes. Some of its line variants are identical with those in the Mao version, and different from the so-called "Three Schools" versions. Other variants match the three schools and differ from the Mao text.[96] This indicates that there were more distinct transmissions than the four recorded in the Han histories, and it also lends support to the existence of the Mao version in the early decades of the Han. Further support for an early Han date can be derived from the citation and interpretation of odes in the "Wu xing" document discovered at Mawangdui. The readings of these odes echo a wide variety of sources, including the *Mencius*, the *Xunzi*, the *Han shi wai zhuan*, the *Shuo yuan*, and the Mao commentary.[97] Finally, the Fuyang find includes some badly damaged strips that appear to have been part of a general introduction to the odes, that is, an early version of a "Great Preface." Since Wang Xianqian has shown that the "Three Schools" versions also had general prefaces, it is likely that some version of the Mao "Great Preface" also existed in the middle of the second century B.C., although it may not yet have been the received version.[98] That was completed probably no later than the time of Wei Hong (first century A.D.).[99]

The "Great Preface" is a dense and difficult text that has been the subject of extensive commentaries and analysis. Within the confines of a few pages, I will simply demonstrate how it draws together some of the themes that have run through the earlier uses of the odes. Specifically, I will show how it carries further the process already noted in the *Xunzi* of identifying the individual poetic voice with the state order, but also finding the basis of the state in the authority of the poetic voice. This process exemplifies the manner in which the readings of individual poems were fixed in the process of being gathered in an anthology.

The Preface begins with a brief discussion of the first poem, to which it is in theory attached, and of the nature of the first section of the anthology, the "Airs" (*feng* 風). The balance of the text is devoted to a general consideration of the nature of poetry. For purposes of analysis I will divide the text into two parts, the first (pericopes four through six in the conventional arrangement) presents a psychological-expressive theory of verse derived from contemporary music theory, and the second (pericopes seven through eighteen) places the art of verse in its public context. This includes its role in creating social order, the relation of the poet to the state, a theory of literary history based on moral-political developments, a socio-aesthetic division of art into correct and decadent, and a theory of the structure of the anthology based on the sociopolitical locus expressed by each category of ode. The two divisions are unequal in length, and this imbalance indicates the importance of public/political as opposed to personal/psychological in the Mao commentary.

The psychological-expressive element begins with a reformulation of the phrase "odes articulate aims/ambitions." The new formulation states that "odes are that into which the aims/ambitions go." As Stephen Owen has noted, this yields a spatialized theory of poetic production in which a substance is transferred from inside to outside. It makes poetry part of a broader complex of theories of psychology as the movement of substance, in the form of the energetic substrate of matter (*qi* 氣).[100]

This definition of odes as physical dynamism allows the author to incorporate ideas about music, also a dynamic, emotional activity based on the movement of *qi* 氣. Thus the next two pericopes adapt passages on music from the *Xunzi* and the "Yue ji" chapter of the *Li ji*.[101] The first traces how the inner movement of emotions comes out in words. Words not being sufficient to release the energy, they are drawn out in sighs. Sighs, being insufficient, turn into song, and song, still being inadequate, manifests itself in dance. This portrays the emergence of verse and song as not only spontaneous but irresistible. Like the "spillover saying" in the *Zhuangzi*, the truth of verse is guaranteed by an unreflective spontaneity, and it is authoritative through its compelling, energetic origins. The next pericope observes that the sounds emitted must form a pattern (*wen* 文) in order to be musical tones, and with that the psychological-expressive section ends.

The rest of the Preface is devoted to the public, political face of verse. Three pericopes present the observational and the transformative powers of verse, echoing the *Lun yu*'s proposition that odes can serve to "observe" (*guan* 觀) and to "stimulate" (*xing* 興). The first describes how the character of the state appears in its songs; the second asserts the power of music to move Heaven, Earth, and the spirits; and the third states that the early kings used them to correct relations, transform people, and change customs.

Pericopes eleven through seventeen explain the structure of the anthology first as a history of the glory and decline of the Zhou, and then as a geographical hierarchy of verse types. They begin with a discussion of the social uses of the "Airs," the first rubric of the anthology. The ruler uses them to morally transform his subjects, while the people use them to obliquely criticize the ruler. Because the remonstrances are couched in verse there is no offence, but it provides a warning.[102] "Airs" thus allow the mutual influence of ruler and ruled through the medium of song, as in the indirect suasion of the *Zuo zhuan* anecdotes.

The next three pericopes deal with the problem of seemingly immoral verses from times of decline. The process begins with the lapsing of the kingly way, which leads to the appearance of "mutated" (*bian* 變) odes. As the next two pericopes explain, these are the responses of virtuous men, the "state historians" (*guo shi* 國 史), to the moral decadence of their times.[103] Pained by moral decline and government cruelty, they composed songs to express their feelings and to sway the rulers. These songs, sometimes attributed to a debauched individual, described violations of proper customs, but the reader was to recognize them as ironic criticism. As historians the authors remembered the old ways and were stirred to anger, but their feelings were expressed within the limits of ritual because they enjoyed the lingering moral influence of the earlier kings. Thus the minor preface to the first critical ode in the anthology notes, "having been transformed by King Wen, even though confronting a chaotic age they still loathed the absence of the rites."[104] Men's ability to express virtue in song during times of decline depended on the hidden moral power of earlier kings, a power preserved by the historians and their texts.

The next three pericopes present the three categories of the odes—airs, elegantia (*ya* 雅), and lauds (*song* 頌)—in ascending order based on their range of communication. The airs tell of a single state and remain tied to one individual (the poet). The elegantia tell of the entire empire and give shape to the customs of the four directions. Dealing with "the rise and fall of kingly government," they are in turn divided into "lesser" and "greater" on the basis of their contents. At the pinnacle are the lauds, which celebrate the highest virtue and go beyond the human realm to speak to the spirits.

Having defined verse as the spontaneous expression of deepest aims and emotions, the Great Preface then restricts these psychological manifestations to the political realm. The musical tones generated in pericope seven as the culmination of the outward surge of feeling are viewed strictly as factors in social order or decay; those who employ verse figure only as rulers, subjects, or state historians; and the verses themselves are classified according to their political range and relation to the ruling house. Poems are possible only as a manifestation of royal virtue, either of the present ruler or those in the past, and as Haun Saussy has noted the king is everywhere the theme of the poems.[105] Each minor preface begins by assigning the poem to a reign and explaining why it is either praise of royal virtue or criticism of royal vice. But even criticism of royal vice is really a praise of earlier royal virtue, since the possibility of criticism hinges on the once and future presence of a true king. As the heir of the sage kings who created civilization, the ruler is the sole source of the rituals and practices that constitute civilization.[106]

The Mao prefaces not only inscribe the ruler as the origin and theme of all verse, but they structure the anthology as a model of empire. Initially dispersed across the states, in poems which as "wind" are identified with customs and the influence of locality, the verses ascend to kingly government in the center, and culminate in the temple where they rise up to the ancestral spirits. Not only the spatial frame of empire is enacted, but its chronological dimension as well. The cycle of rise and decline is marked in the shift from true '(*zheng* 正) odes to their mutated (*bian* 變) forms, and also in the assumption that within each section, except for the lauds which are by definition all positive, the earlier verses celebrate and the later ones speak of decline. As both geographic chart of empire and chrono-logical schema of a dynasty, the odes form a unity in which each song takes its sense from its place within the whole. The anthology is thus a version of the uni-versalizing text, like the *Zhou li*, that aims to inscribe the entire empire *cum* ecumene.

The Mao commentary thus carries forward the *Xunzi*'s practice of identify-ing the meaning of the odes with the political order. However, the *zhi* of the poet has not vanished, and the opening pericopes are more than a nod in the direction of an inescapable classical tag. The psychological-expressive theory of verse figures twice in the political section of the Preface. First, it insists that the "Airs" are tied to an individual. The moral and historical lessons of the Odes, at least their first category, are mediated through the experience of a single person. The veracity of the record of that experience and the truths to which it leads depend on the dis-tinctive origins of poetry. The rooting of poetry in *zhi* also figures in the role of the state historians, for it is their emotional response to moral and political decay that drives them to write. The lingering influence of the former kings simply gives that anger form through ritual. While explaining the history, categories, and meaning of the odes in political terms and assigning their composition to a government office, the Preface still requires theories of *qi* 氣 and of emotional response to serve as a motor for the project and to guarantee its truth. This grounding of a political poetry in emotion and self-expression accounts for the fact that a theory of verse as lyric developed four centuries before the emergence of authored lyrics at the end of the Eastern Han. It also explains why the meanings of the poems are de-rived not from the individual poets but from their place within the anthology, and by extension their relation to the king.

However, the poet figures not only in appeals to individual consciousness and emotions, but also in the invocation of the lingering influence of kings. The composition of mutated verse was assigned to historians because such odes depended on a memory of times long past, which survived in the form of texts. The mutated airs and elegantia were possible only because of the prior existence of the correct ones and the lauds, which carried the transforming power of ancient rulers. The king was the hidden meaning of every ode, but these in turn were the definition of the king and the form of his presence in the world. The king informed the odes and the odes the king, but the ultimate grounding of what would other-wise become an endlessly retreating meaning was the written text. Just as the master was created in the text that derived from his teaching, so the ruler and the state were invented within the texts which drew their meaning from the political order. Inscribing the eclipse of royal virtue and the fact of dynastic collapse, the anthol-ogy of the odes became a seat of royalty that survived the transition from one house to the next, and that preserved the memory of ritual order when the reality had been lost. Based on the hidden monarchy of the odes anthology, the voice of the individual historian who composed or scholar who quoted could speak with the ruler's authority in times of decay. This is another form of the schoolmen's claim to virtual kingship.

ANTHOLOGY AND AUTHORSHIP

While the odes inherited from the Zhou played an ever larger role in the claims of the *ru* to authority, poetic writing developed new forms.[107] Most of the verses of the period have been lost, but some adaptations of work songs and religious hymns are preserved in scholarly works and in the anthology known as the *Chu ci* 楚辭. These show other aspects of the use of verse to generate authority during the Warring States period.

One of the most unusual poetic works of the period is the "Cheng xiang" 成 相 chapter of the *Xunzi*.[108] Although the title has aroused debate, modern scholars generally concur with Yu Yue that it was the name of a popular work chanty used in the state of Chu to provide rhythm for the threshing of grain or the beating of packed earth.[109] The rhythm of this chanty, a simple pattern that figures in some nursery rhymes, was used to compose verses. As the Qing commentator Hao Yixing noted, the poems summarize the political program of the *Xunzi* with a strong legalist bent that either reflects the developments of his old age or the thought of his disciples. It begins with a lament over contemporary corruption, sings of rule through ritual and law, praises the sage kings, sighs over the inability of the author and other worthy men to influence rulers, and concludes with a program for the creation of a well-ordered state. These poems eschew polyvocality and instead aim at a dramatically effective and memorable presentation of the *Xunzi*'s political philosophy. Several twentieth-century Chinese historians have argued that this is the first piece of popular literature in Chinese history, the ancestor of the *bianwen* 變文 and other verse genres that presented difficult doctrines or high literature in easily digestible form. It is unlikely that the work aimed at a popular audience, but it may have addressed rulers or officials who lacked a literary education, found the old odes opaque and tedious, but were fond of musical modes of popular origins.

There is an anecdote on this theme in the *Lü shi chun qiu*.[110] It tells how the rhetorician Hui Shi composed a law code for Wei. The king admired it and presented it to his minister who agreed, but when the king asked if the code could be put into effect, the minister demurred. When asked why, he replied,

> When lifting a heavy log, the leader initiates the chanty and the workers respond. It is not that there are not beautiful songs and lyrics, but they are not as good for lifting a log. Now [running] a state is indeed lifting a heavy log.

The argument is clear. Refined, sophisticated language, here embodied in the famous rhetorician Hui Shi, has its excellence, but ruling a state requires simplicity and clarity. The musical equivalent of the good law code is the work chanty. The *Xunzi* presented erudite quotations and elaborate riddles to schoolmen, but for the less learned it offered artless verses set to popular tunes. The difference in audience also suggests another explanation for the more explicitly legalist program offered in the "Cheng xiang" chapter.

The use of the work chanty as a model for verse was unique in the period, but other sources of nonclassical music and verse were adapted by the non-*ru* schools and by the authors of the first full-blown individual verse in Chinese history. Prominent among these alternative sources were the songs employed by religious specialists and spirit intermediaries in their ritual addresses to the gods. The links between shamanism and poetry have been most discussed in relation to the *Chu ci*. While this body of poetry is clearly a court-based, literary adaptation of cultic practices, there is no doubt that songs played a fundamental role in the so-called shamanic cults just as they did in the royal Zhou ancestral worship.[111] In addition to evidence from received literature, texts of a religious nature discovered in tombs, such as the famous Chu silk manuscripts, also contain substantial passages in verse.[112]

Given the role of song in shamanic religious practice, and the derivation of ideas and practices of proto-Daoism from these cults, it is not surprising that the major texts of this tradition made extensive use of poetry. Thus the "Nei ye" is written in verse, and the percentage of rhyming passages in the *Dao de jing* is so high that scholars have described it as a "philosophical poem."[113] The *Zhuangzi* and the Mawangdui *Jing fa* also frequently intersperse poetic passages in the midst of their essays and stories.[114] Thus the use of verse as a mode of argument and authoritative speech was a standard feature of proto-Daoist texts.

While the importance of verse in shamanic cults, ancestor worship, and the *ru* textual traditions might account for the use of verse in proto-Daoist texts, it is important to note how they employ poetry as a mode of argument. The distinction between verse and prose in early China is not strongly marked. Verse is distinguished by a more regular meter and by rhyme, but it is not absolutely certain which element was dominant and, as Noel Barnard has pointed out, if one assumes an irregular meter, then rhymes may be discovered almost everywhere.[115] Due to the absence of morphological markings of parts of speech and of punctuation in literary Chinese, even in prose intelligibility often hinges on regular metrical units and the use of parallelism. As Nakajima Chiaki has demonstrated, these features are particularly prominent in argument and rhetorical set pieces. Closely patterned on oral persuasions, such passages relied on perceptible rhythms and recurring patterns both for intelligibility and persuasive force. Sometimes this used a recurring grammatical structure marked by identical particles in a series of sentences, and sometimes it verged on verse with repetition of fixed metric blocks. In either case, speeches in the *Zuo zhuan* and persuasions in works such as the *Zhanguo ce* all routinely employed fixed rhythms and recurring formulae in the manner of verse.[116] Thus to a certain extent the use of poetry was an extension of the modes of prose argumentation.

However, poetry had distinctive uses. In his analysis of the *Dao de jing*, A. C. Graham notes that the use of juxtaposed, parallel couplets without logical connectives allows the author(s) to posit antithetical suppositions and argue from each of them, and it also "forces us to seek connections where least expected." The use of paradox and inversion that figures so prominently in the text is particularly suited to exposition in verse, where regular meter and balanced phrases dramatically highlight the play of oppositions. Poetry here uses language to overthrow language, thus fulfilling a basic premise of a text that insists on the inadequacy of words to express supreme truths. The most common rhetorical maneuver of the text, as Graham notes, is to establish a chain of oppositions and then reverse the conventional hierarchy of values: inaction being better than action, ignorance better than knowledge, female better than male, empty better than full.[117] The manipulation of such oppositions is particularly dramatic when done in verse. The use of rhyme also lends a sense of naturalness or inevitability which can appear as truth without formal argument.

Michael LaFargue, rejecting the belief that the *Dao de jing* is antilogical or mystical, offers a different explanation for the use of verse. Being an assemblage of aphorisms, the text's apparent illogic is a function of the use of hyperbole or exaggeration common to such language. It also espouses contradictory statements where each is aimed at a different target. The use of verse is explained by the fact that poetic aphorisms are both easier to remember and more striking to the listener/reader.[118]

The uses of verse discussed above also apply to the rhymed passages in the *Zhuangzi*. Many use the rhetorical strategy of establishing antithetical pairs in parallel phrases and inverting the values or expectations associated with them. Several read like versions of lines from the *Dao de jing*, often placed in the mouth of the putative author of that text, Lao Dan.[119] Also related to the *Dao de jing* are sets of aphoristic maxims that direct the reader's conduct.[120] Perhaps the most common use of verse in the *Zhuangzi* is to write about the ineffable. These include passages on the true (*zhen* 眞) man; on the highest (*zhi* 至) Way, highest man, or highest music; on the sage (in the Daoist sense); on the primal chaos; on the meditation experience; on roaming freely with the Way; or on the primitive purity before the innovations of the sage kings. Many of these passages use the binomes that became so important in the Han rhapsody, duplicated characters that employed sounds or visual images to evoke qualities of entities.[121]

In addition to speaking of what could not be put in words, verse in the *Zhuangzi* also anticipates a convention of the Han rhapsody. In the latter the loser in the poetric debate is routinely left dazed and speechless by the sheer power of his adversary's language. In the *Zhuangzi* accounts of the Way or the perfected man leave the listener similarly lost and unable to speak. In some stories verse is used to induce this speechlessness in the interlocutor, or to describe the state of a man whose capacity for words has collapsed through confrontation with an inconceivable truth. Most of these anecdotes use only a rhythmic prose, but given the importance of this trope in the development of Chinese poetry and in the practice of arguments in verse, it should be noted here.[122]

The authority created by verse in these texts differed from that obtained through quoting odes. The latter marked the speaker as a member of the community of educated men who certified their speech by using received phrases. The former marked wisdom by confounding conventional distinctions and evoking images of a higher realm through the play of paradox and evocative sounds. The latter worked through shared recognition of phrases that formed and empowered a distinct group, while the former presented itself as the creation of men who thereby set themselves apart from the rest of humanity. Proto-Daoist verse thus resembled the late Zhou odes in using individual, poetic voice to mark the breakdown of a ritual community, but it placed a positive value on what had earlier appeared as a disaster. The isolation of the individual, however, was still a conventional trope in collective works.

Verse also figures in the proto-Daoist texts in the form of series of questions. The use of sentence-final question particles would create a semblance of rhyme in any such series, to the extent that a word can be said to rhyme with itself. However, several of the question series in the *Dao de jing* and the *Zhuangzi* rhyme in the penultimate character, and hence are clearly verse.[123] These series perform several roles. First, they sometimes challenge conventional notions simply by questioning them, or in more elaborate form by posing a question and then answering it with a question in the opposite sense. This pattern is most common in the early chapters of the *Zhuangzi*, particularly "Qi wu lun." Such questions are not answered, because they are intended to call into question some proposition or action.[124]

Another type of series uses questions to communicate doctrine. Such questions can indicate what ought to be done, as when the *Dao de jing* poses six rhymed questions to give its most detailed account of procedures for meditation.[125] An extended poem concluding a discussion of the Way begins with pairs of rhymed rhetorical questions that deny the existence of opposites.[126] More commonly information or advice will be communicated in the form of replies to the questions. This can be written either in a question-response format, or as a long list of questions followed by a reply. Chapter 11 of the *Zhuangzi* describes the damaging impact of the emotions and senses through an alternation of questions and replies. The chapter "Tian yun" begins with a series of questions on the workings of Heaven and Earth, which anticipates or echoes the early passages of the "Tian wen," but unlike the latter the questions are answered. Question series in the *Zhuangzi* are sufficiently important that the account in the final chapter of Zhuang Zhou's historical importance begins with a set of rhymed questions on Heaven, Earth, life, death, and the destiny of man.[127]

One celebrated question series is Zhuang Zhou's address to the skull, which he interrogates as to the causes of its death before using it as his pillow. When the skull in a dream upbraids Zhuang Zhou for thinking life is better than death, it begins by accusing him of chattering like a rhetorician (*bian shi* 辯士).[128] This indicates that the technique of attacking one's adversary with a series of questions was part of the repertoire of the theoreticians of argument. The *Zhuangzi*'s frequent appeals to such lists was either a parody of this practice, or an attempt to use their own weapons against intellectual rivals.[129]

Another type of rhymed question in the *Zhuangzi* is the riddle. As is characteristic of riddles in the Warring States period, the verses describe an object—in
this case a man in a meditative trance—and ask what it is.[130] Riddles also figure in
other texts from the period, where they are often a mode of suasion and instruction. In one celebrated anecdote, which survives as the *locus classicus* of a saying still
in use, Wu Ju poses a riddle regarding a motionless bird, and thereby persuades
King Zhuang of Chu to take active charge of his state. In another story Confucius
uses a riddle to foretell his own death, and Zi Gong indicates that he has understood the message with appropriate expressions of despair.[131] Riddle collections
figured in the bibliographical treatise of the *Han shu*, and a passage from Liu Xiang's
catalog of the imperial library preserved in the commentary states that the purpose
of the riddle is to force the listener to think and thereby assure elucidation.[132] The
riddles' role thus combined the methods of teaching in the *Lun yu* with the expression of veiled meanings through verse to establish ties of shared comprehension.

A collection of riddles from the period appears in a chapter of the *Xunzi*
entitled "Fu" (賦).[133] This includes seven poems, of which the first five are riddles.
In each riddle a first speaker presents a series of attributes or metaphors in four-
character verse lines, and then asks what the object is. A second speaker replies
with a series of rhetorical questions in a variant of the verse line found in the "Li
sao." These questions suggest further attributes. The speaker concludes by identifying the object—ritual, wisdom, cloud, silk worm, and needle. These poems develop
several features noted earlier. First, they are written as dialogues—some between
minister and king, one between disciple and teacher, one between questioner and
shaman—and carry forward the link between conveying veiled meanings in poetry
and establishing political or scholastic ties. In this chapter the three pairs of speakers
define the three realms in which authoritative writing was produced—state, school,
and cult—but the political is given pride of place. As anecdotes indicate the use of
riddles by courtiers, their introduction into scholastic writings is similar to the
interplay between court procedures, as indicated in the *Zuo zhuan*, and teaching
practices portrayed in the *Lun yu*.

The riddles also indicate developments of polyvocality as a defining feature
of verse. This goes beyond the coding inherent in the riddle form, wherein one
evokes an object while disguising it so that only the discerning are rewarded, for
the meanings of the riddles are not exhausted by their solutions. Abstract entities—
"ritual" and "wisdom"—are evoked through tangible objects (patterned silks, the
sun and the moon, city walls), qualities (thickness, viscosity), and naturalistic binomes
(sound of flowing water, formless mass). All of these become natural or cosmic
correlates of the abstractions. Inversely, the material objects are given the attributes
of cosmic forces or political techniques. Thus "cloud" is evoked by phrases used to
describe the cosmic Way in the *Zhuangzi* and the *Huainanzi*. The author presumably intended for these echoes to be heard, which meant that the riddling poem on
clouds was not simply about the attributes of clouds—its explicit content—nor

about clouds themselves—its supposed solution, but also about the cloudlike nature of the Way. As the early nineteenth-century critic Chen Shen remarked, "To *fu* on silkworms is not to describe silkworms; to *fu* on clouds is not to describe clouds." These pieces, the first to bear the name *fu* although far removed from the great Han epideictic rhapsodies, already reveal the "wily," "shifting," and "polytropic" character which Bischoff argues characterizes the genre.[134] These features evolved out of the hermeneutic of the odes developed among the Warring States *ru*, and the use of question series to suggest the ineffable in the proto-Daoist texts.

The greatest collection of Warring States riddles is a poem in the *Chu ci* anthology, the "Heavenly Questions" (*tian wen* 天問).[135] It consists of 172 questions written in four-character verse derived from the *Shi jing*. The title employs "Heaven" in the broad sense, including not only celestial matters but also principles of nature, and the inherent moral principles of the world of men. Thus the chapter on Heaven in the *Xunzi* deals primarily with the question of whether or not Heaven intervenes in the world of men to punish the wicked and reward the just, and this question is also central to the "Heavenly Questions."[136]

The poem is closely related to riddles.[137] The author throughout employs kennings and other concealments to bar understanding to all but initiates. Like the riddles in the *Xunzi* it presents at least three levels of interpretation. First, one must understand the sense of the questions, which requires recognizing poetic references to a vast body of cosmological doctrine, protoscience, mythology, and recent history. Second, one should be able to answer the questions, at least those questions to which an answer is possible. Finally, one must be able to recognize the broader truths suggested by specific answers. In the case of the "Tian wen" this means understanding why the poem was written and what message was to be conveyed by this accumulation of riddles. The first two levels are the task of the translators and commentators. To understand the uses of verse in the Warring States only the final question needs consideration.

The first commentators attributed the poem to Qu Yuan, which meant that it was an expression of resentment for his treatment at court and his exile. This is stated in Wang Yi's introduction to the work (see note 131), and it informs his commentary. According to this theory, in posing the questions the author is challenging the belief in a moral, beneficent Heaven that actively rewards the just and punishes the wicked. The poet thus repeatedly notes cases where the wicked and their offspring flourish, or the worthy suffer misfortune. Most Chinese commentators prior to the twentieth century followed this reading of the poem.

Some twentieth-century scholars argued that the author questioned Heaven not solely out of resentment, but because he had developed a full-blown theory of agnostic or atheistic doubt. Guo Moruo read the poem as an overt challenge to the moralizing theism of the *ru* and Mohists. This reading was part of the interpretation of Qu Yuan as an early nationalist hero. You Guoen compares the questions in this poem to those posed by the Yellow Emperor in the "Su wen" 素問 and suggests that the work is written in a critical, scientific spirit. In a recent article

Stephen Field has demonstrated how knowledge of the "cosmograph" (*shi pan* 式 盤) and of astronomical theory informs the opening section of the poem, and he argues that this section of the poem is "materialistic" and "a record of proto-scientific inquiry."[138]

While it is true that the manner of the questions and their targets often suggest a critical spirit and resentment of the injustice of Heaven, it is necessary to look at the organization of the poem and its links to other works of the period to provide a satisfactory reading. A start on this has been made by Takeji Sadao, who points out that the overarching structure of the poem is a history of the world from the primal chaos down to the Warring States period. The first section asks about the emergence of Heaven and its structure; the second focuses on the myth of the flood, the creation of an ordered world, and the marvels that lie in distant regions; and the third, fourth, and fifth sections deal with the Three Dynasties. These last focus on the epochs of dynastic transfer. Takeji also argues that the details that fill in this structure reflect the author's fascination with the strange and the uncanny.[139] In short, the poem is a catalog of the marvelous arranged in chronological order and focusing on moments of change.

The fact that the poem is organized as a chronicle covering the entire history of the world shows that the "Tian wen" is yet another late Warring States attempt to create a work encompassing space and time. It also demonstrates the increasing tendency, noted in chapter 3, to understand Heaven in the perspective of history. The interest in the uncanny is important, but it is not the ultimate ground of explanation. In light of the earlier discussion of the use of question series in the proto-Daoist texts, the fascination with the extraordinary suggests a hypothesis for the meaning of the poem.

Although the "Tian wen" resembles riddles, it differs in one vital respect: it offers no answers. The *Zhuangzi* also posed series of questions with no answers, and their purpose was to deny the possibility of answers or any secure knowledge. Moreover, both Takeji and Hawkes have noted that many of the questions do not imply an answer, but rather insist on the impossibility of any response, or on the moral nihilism of any answer that explains why Heaven rewards the wicked.[140] Even those questions that might in theory be answered, as many are in the *Huai-nanzi* and other texts, are not answered here. This decision to deny any answers must be taken seriously. The repeated posing of questions that have no answer, the refusal to answer questions that do, and the questioning of Heaven's morality are all formal equivalents of the substantive focus on marvels and the miraculous, which are by definition that which defies explanation or answer. In its relentless questioning the poem presents the cosmos as a set of impenetrable riddles, the earth as an array of uncanny regions, and human history as a field of inexplicable occurrences. The ultimate theme of the poem is the manner in which the world escapes all man's feeble attempts to give an account of it.[141]

In this way the "Tian wen" echoes the use of poetry in the proto-Daoist texts and elsewhere, in which verse invokes things that lie beyond the reach of words.

The insistence on aberrant phenomena, the suffering of the good, and the flourishing of the bad also links the poem to the critical odes of the *Shi jing*, the last two poems of the *fu* chapter of the *Xunzi*, and other poems included in the *Chu ci*. Its insistence on the appearance of bizarre phenomena and the inversion of moral expectations, both of which are associated with times of political upheaval, links it to the themes of the collapse of the established ritual order and the perversion of moral hierarchy that figure so prominently in the rest of the anthology.

The best example of the poetic presentation of failed rituals to demonstrate that the times are out of joint is the "Jiu ge," which is also probably the oldest part of the *Chu ci*.[142] Its eleven poems depict attempts by spirit intermediaries to summon divinities, or by divinities to attract a lover/worshiper. Zhu Xi argued that these songs were dramatic performances involving frequent shifts of speaker and patterns of chanting and response. This theory has found general approval, and most modern scholars agree that the pieces form a suite of songs for dramatic performance that originally included music and dance.[143] The nature of that performance, however, is disputed. On the one hand, some think that these were liturgical pieces that accompanied sacrifices. For example, Fujino Iwatomo has collected evidence from the monographs on sacrifice in the Han histories and scattered references in other texts of state sacrifices to the spirits invoked. His argument is supported by Takeji Sadao and Hoshikawa Kiyotaka, who maintain that these pieces were used as liturgy in religious performances, like the *jiao* hymns in the *Han shu* monograph on sacrifices.[144] On the other hand, Wen Yiduo argued that only the first and last songs, which are in fact not numbered among the nine, resemble actual sacrificial hymns to deities. The rest are what he describes as songs to "entertain the gods," and the terrestrial audience as well. This distinction is based on the fact that only the first and last songs refer to ritual performances, while the middle ones describe spirit flights and unsuccessful erotic searches. Hawkes seems to support this second position, arguing that the songs were composed for the aesthetic satisfaction of the court, just as European courts had "masses and motets composed for them by celebrated musicians."[145]

While there is no way to decide whether the "Nine Songs" were liturgy or entertainment, the second position is more persuasive. We have two bodies of verifiable sacrificial hymns from early China—the "lauds" of the *Shi jing* and the hymns in the *Han shu* monograph on sacrifice. In both cases the songs are invariably celebratory, proclaiming the greatness of the rulers, the success of their sacrifices, and the blessings bestowed by the gods. In contrast with this, the nine inner songs of the "Jiu ge" dwell on the themes of failed rituals, separation, and melancholy. Thus in the "Lord within the Clouds" (*yun zhong jun* 雲中君) the deity hovers over the singers but then flies off, leaving them afflicted with "grievous longing." In the paired songs "The Goddess of the Xiang" (*xiang jun* 湘君) and "The Lady of the Xiang" (*xiang furen* 湘夫人) the singers search for the goddesses but fail to find them. In the paired songs "Greater Master of Fate" (*da siming* 大司命) and "Lesser (*xiao* 小) Master of Fate" the god—probably a male soloist—proclaims his glory, the singers—probably a female chorus—proclaim their yearning, but in both songs they are left grieving and in sorrow. The song "The Lord of the East" (*dong jun* 東君) is sung in the voice of the sun god. It begins with him rising in the east, leaving behind him the priestesses and their musical performance, and it closes with his descent into darkness. In "The River Earl" (*he bo* 河伯) a female soloist or chorus sings of longing for the eponymous god. The song ends with an eastward journey by the eager bride, and the final couplet describes how she is greeted by waves and escorted by fish. Since it was the custom to drown virgins in the Yellow River as brides of the god, the song ends with the singer as a victim of human sacrifice. The reading of the song "Mountain Spirit" (*shan gui* 山鬼) is disputed. Some think it is sung in the voice of the goddess seeking a lover, others that it is written in the voice of a human lover seeking the goddess. In either case it ends in separation and sorrow. The song "Hymn to the Fallen" (*guo shang* 國殤), thought by some to be an intrusion in the series, is unique in having a happy (?) ending. While those who sing the first half of the song have been left for dead on the field of battle, they have the consolation that they will be heroes among the dead.[146]

The theme of failure is at odds with earlier and later sacrificial hymns. Moreover, these songs are not about sacrifice at all. They talk of physical adornment, musical performance, and the longing for union, but no mention is made of offerings except in the first hymn—which is why Wen Yiduo sets apart it and the final song. While these songs may record a state-sponsored cult of mystical possession, they have no relation to sacrifice. Most likely the "Nine Songs" were a musical performance composed for court entertainment. In this performance instrumental and choral forces were used to explore human emotions in the guise of religious narratives derived from cults of possession and spirit travel. In the form of worshiping the gods, the poet expressed his sentiments. Although there are at best only hints of any political subtext, the repertoire of emotions, images, and topoi that will define the "Li sao" tradition are already present.[147] Thus the songs mark a transition between ritual performance and political plaint.

The "Li sao" was placed at the head of the *Chu ci* anthology in the Han and defined as the exemplary piece not only for that collection but for all scholars lamenting the failure of the world to recognize their worth, in a tradition identified by the term "sao." The poem was said to be the work of Qu Yuan, and the story of Qu Yuan from the *Shi ji* was used to explain the poem. In this story Qu Yuan was a virtuous courtier of noble descent who fell victim to slanderers at court, lost the favor of the king, wrote the "Li sao" to regain royal favor or to justify himself, and finally committed suicide. Many other works in the *Chu ci* were identified as his compositions—twenty-five out of seventy-six—and considerable scholarly effort has been expended in assigning particular works to particular stages in his career. Qu Yuan also became the emblematic figure of the unappreciated scholar and, in more recent times, the model of martyrdom for one's country. Consequently, to the present day, the figure of Qu Yuan has overshadowed the *Chu ci* anthology.[148]

Whereas earlier works were largely anonymous or collective, and named authors were nothing more than names, with Qu Yuan and the "Li sao" the question of authorship became fundamental to the reading of the poem. The text was bound to the narrative of a presumptive author's life and understood as a record of his experiences, so no reading of the poem could escape reference to the poet. Qu Yuan is also the first author to be identified for an individual, poetic voice, and as such he became the archetype for later Chinese poets.

The ties of the poet to the poem, however, emerged quite late. Qu Yuan was first mentioned in the poems "Divination" (*bu ju* 卜居) and "The Fisherman" (*yu fu* 漁父), probably composed long after his death. They present him as a man of virtue in a corrupt world who preserves his purity by withdrawal and death, but there is no mention of any literary compositions.[149] The first link between the story of Qu Yuan and the "Li sao" appears in the "Lament for Qu Yuan" (*ai Qu Yuan* 哀屈原) by the early Han poet Jia Yi. This poem does not mention the "Li sao," but it echoes its style and cites it in the opening of its final section.[150] Even this oblique reference appears a century after Qu Yuan's death, and the earliest identification of Qu Yuan as the author of the "Li Sao" is found in a fragment of the commentary composed by Liu An, the King of Huainan, for presentation to the Emperor Wu in the 130s B.C. This presentation was probably the occasion for the earliest anthology of verse attributed to Qu Yuan. The story of his life and writings was subsequently established in its standard form in the *Shi ji*.[151] Nothing in the poem indicates Qu Yuan's composition, and Gopal Sukhu has developed a reading of the "Li sao" without reference to his story.[152]

The appearance of the proto-*Chu ci* under the name of Qu Yuan was a crucial step in the invention of authorship in the late Warring States or early Han. A set of themes and images, probably defined by generic conventions, was redefined as the expression of an individual's response to his experiences. The mutual echoes and resonances of the poems that appeared when they were read together were explained by reference to a single author, and ultimately each poem was linked to a specific stage in the writer's life. The author was thus effectively invented out of the anthology, just as Confucius was created within the collected sayings of the *Lun yu*. However Qu Yuan, the figure of isolation, had no disciples and was thus credited with personally composing the poems.

Deferring the question of why the poem became attached to the story of Qu Yuan, I will first examine features that link it to the developments in the use of verse sketched above. First, the voice in the poem insists on its individuality and isolation. This carries forward the argument that verse was a means of writing the self, and it jibes with the character assigned to Qu Yuan in the earliest references. The insistence on isolation takes several forms. First, the first-person pronouns appear incessantly. Second, the poem insists on the isolation of the poet through the repeated use of the adverb 獨 *du* "alone, only" or related characters.[153]

The isolation of the poet is also marked through his insistence that he lives in a bad age when the requital of the wicked and the just had been abandoned or inverted.[154] This theme of the world turned upside down figured in some of the late Zhou odes, but here it is repeated so frequently as to verge on obsession. The corruption of the age and isolation of the poet are also marked by laments that none can recognize his worth or understand his feelings (*zhi ji* 知己 or *cha qing* 察情).[155] The recognition of oneself by others, either the ruler or the true friend, was crucial in Warring States political theory and the role of verse. In the "Li sao" the absence of such recognition became the message of the poem.

The theme of the poet's isolation is also signaled in the attitude to the passage of time evinced in the work. Later Chinese verse dwelt at length on the dread of the passage of time, as signaled by cyclic changes of nature. In contrast to the human life cycle, spring always returned. This attitude, in which the poet sees himself as cut off from the world around him, appears for the first time in the "Li sao." No sooner has the poet announced his worth than he proclaims the hurried passage of the seasons, the fading of natural beauty, and his fear that the beauty of the "Fair One" will soon perish, too. The passage of time, the onset of decay, and the poet's vain attempts to block them both return again and again throughout the poem.[156]

This dread of individual decline echoes the poet's attitude to the movement of public time, for both signal a falling away from an earlier plenitude. The superiority of earlier times is indicated not only negatively through denunciations of the present, but also by direct appeal to the authority of the past. This conservatism of the speaker is marked in the opening lines, where he proclaims an exalted ancestry traced back to a god. Not only is his ancestry offered as sanction for his authoritative voice, but his self-presentation is modeled on those employed in invocations (*zhu ci* 祝辭) addressed to deities in certain forms of religious petitions. These religious echoes are seconded by claims to auspicious times of birth, or rather descent into the world.[157] Having announced himself as an inheritor of the past, the speaker repeatedly states that he takes the ancient sages as his model. He cites past worthies as guides to conduct, and ancient villains as warnings.[158] Assertions of the speaker's isolation in corrupt times note that he alone holds to the models of antiquity. At the center of the poem he even presents his case to the ancient sage Shun.[159] Following the pattern of the philosophers and writers of history, the poet claims authority in the name of the ancient sages.

This appeal to the long-dead Shun to act as his judge highlights the temporal and geographic mobility of the poem. A similar temporal displacement marking the speaker's commitment to the past appears in his search for a bride. Having been repulsed from the gates of Heaven, the poet resolves to seek in the world below.[160] The women that he seeks are Fu Fei, Jian Di, and the two daughters of Lord Yu. All lived in earlier ages. The first was the wife of the god of the Yellow River, and the second had been impregnated by Di Ku and became the ancestress of the Shang. In short, even in his search for a wife the speaker links himself to the past, casting himself in the role of an ancient worthy or a god.

The poet thus claims authority for his oppositional stance by reference to an ancient virtue that he alone retains. Although at odds with the men of his time, he claims justification through appeals to a past defined by the texts that his references assume. There are several rhetorical strategies to these appeals. First, his insistence that he is devoted to the model of the ancient sages anticipates the Mao preface's statement that some individuals can poetically articulate the way of virtue even in a dark age through the lingering moral influence of the sages. Just as the memory of the earlier sages preserved in their verse allowed the "state historians" to write "mutated odes" that preserved virtue by criticizing vice, so the speaker in the "Li sao" sings his own virtue through the sagely precedents elaborated within the poem.

Another mode of claiming authority is the identification of the speaker as a being of spiritual power. This is signaled in his "cognomen" (*zi* 字), Ling Jun 靈均, for as several scholars have noted, the character *ling* 靈 in the state of Chu was a synonym for *wu* 巫 "spirit intermediary" and figured in the names of spirits or "shamans."[161] The role indicated by the name is demonstrated in the text, for Ling Jun performs numerous ritual or magical actions, soars through the cosmos, perhaps in a shamanic vision, and experiences an "epiphany" in his confrontation with the shaman Xian and a host of spirits. Moreover, Ling Jun declares shamans Peng and Xian to be his models and at the end of the poem he resolves to go to the dwelling place of these magical beings.[162]

While the appeal to religious rituals lends authority to the text and the shaman poet, it is no more efficacious in the world of the poem than appeals to the ancient sages. Just as late odes linked the Zhou decline with the failure of sacrifice, so the "Li sao" laments the bankruptcy of established rituals. Ling Jun goes through the whole repertoire of religious and secular rituals to secure the support of the ruler or a place in the world, but they all end in failure. First he gathers plants and binds them into garlands, invoking the picking and binding of plants as part of early marriage ritual or in sexual magic, as well as the offering of flowers to spirits.[163] Another mode of securing a mate, matchmaking, is attempted through the agency of birds—often used as messengers from spirits—but these attempts likewise end in failure.[164]

The poem also features accounts of Ling Jun's spirit journeys, or his travels in visions, to the edges of the earth and to Heaven. These accounts are derived from spirit travels or visions used by shamans to secure power and locate spirits. The description of the first journey also lists spirit companions derived from the *zu* (祖) travel sacrifice and the myths of the Yellow Emperor.[165] These journeys likewise gain Ling Jun nothing. As in the case of the rites of mating, the magical ritual also has its conventional correlate, the journey with the Fair One that Ling Jun proposes to undertake near the beginning of the poem. But this proposal to lead the Fair One in the "tracks of the kings of old" founders under the assaults of the slanderers.[166]

Another pair of failed rituals is two attempts to communicate with spirits. The first is a divination performed by Ling Fen, another shaman marked by the name Ling. In the second divination Wu Xian descends, accompanied by a cloud of spirits. Ling Jun witnesses his spirit radiance, makes an offering of peppered rice balls, and receives auspicious words from the mouth of the god. Both the divination and epiphany deliver a message of success if he will but seek more widely, and this advice sends Ling Jun on the second voyage.[167] In spite of the auspicious prophecies, this journey is no more fruitful than the first.

Other failed performances that could be described as rituals are the formal addresses. The first takes place within the poem, when Ling Jun makes a plaint to Shun. The word employed to describe his action is *chen ci* 陳辭, a technical term in the period. In the *Zuo zhuan* and the *Guo yu* this phrase applies to formal presentations at court, usually dealing with international relations, in which a noble attempts to secure an action from his audience. These speeches are prose, but some involve the quotation of verse and many of them are marked by fixed rhythms and recurring rhetorical patterns.[168] The poem thus assimilates Ling Jun's petition to a staged, formal discourse of diplomacy in which verse played a major role. Closely related to such formal presentations is the "Li sao" itself, an extended performance in verse intended to secure from the reader what the speaker had failed to obtain from the other characters in the poem, and the poet from the men of his day.

Unlike the rituals within the poem, the "Li sao" itself was a successful performance that in its later history attracted the attention of many who recognized its imputed author as a man of virtue and a kindred spirit. It is at this point that the figure of Qu Yuan re-appears, for if a poem is understood as testimony to individual character, then an author is required in order that the poem can be read. The Mao preface assigned meaning to the monarch and composition to an office, but such a hermeneutic could not apply to the "Li sao," which declared the failure of its "author" to find a post and announced his withdrawal from the world. Given its contents, the "Li sao" could provide a charter myth for a role that we saw emerging in previous chapters, the named author, but the author of the text had to first be given a name and a history. The Qu Yuan of the "Li sao" was a set of attitudes, recurring images, and rhetorical tropes, but the story of the rejected man of virtue and martyr gave these a time, a place, and a human core to which (whom?) readers could attribute the stances and gestures in the text, and with which they could identify. This identification was articulated in the Han poems written in the style of "Qu Yuan" that were appended to the proto-*Chu ci* to form the present anthology.

The linking of the text to Qu Yuan also inserted the poem into a narrative structure and thereby performed the same function as assigning the Zhou odes to the reigns of different monarchs. If the odes were liable to diverse uses and dangerous readings, the dreamlike allegories of the "Li sao" were infinitely more so. Anyone who has struggled with this difficult text knows the sense of relief that can be experienced by collapsing it into the tale of Qu Yuan. Moreover, the extravagant flights of language, the appeals to cults and religious practices that were increasingly rejected by literati, and the dangerous solipsism of a text that asserted the virtues of its speaker against the judgment of the world could, by assigning the poem to a biography, all be brought into the intellectual universe of the Mao commentary to the odes. Similarly the dangerous shamanic cults could be domesticated.

Once assigned to Qu Yuan and read as the prototype of the virtuous individual voice in a corrupt world, the poem and those gathered around it took on a new social role and constituted new groups, distinct from its role in the program of literary glorification of Chu pursued by Liu An. In this context the existence of the text as *written* artefact able to move freely across time and space comes to the fore. Chapter 1 traced the forms of writing that constituted the state, chapter 2 those that formed the intellectual schools, but each of these was still bound in face-to-face physical exchanges in which the text remained linked to oral performance. The *Chuci* also constituted its own group, but it was a group no longer restricted by the demands of shared physical presence. The "Li sao" and the related poems brought together all Han scholars who felt themselves insufficiently appreciated or ignored by the ruler, as evidenced by the poem of Jia Yi, the biography in the *Shiji*, and the swelling body of Han rhapsodies of scholarly grievance. Read as a written testament in which Qu Yuan at last found the kindred spirits he had sought by entrusting his work to later ages, the text became a common resource and a *lingua franca* to all Han literati.

The reference to "testament" evokes a final aspect of the links between the myth of Qu Yuan and the invention of authorship, the association of writing with death. The earliest accounts of Qu Yuan mentioned only his suicide, followed later by the attribution of poems. The fact that the earliest verse read as the self-expression of a named author was attributed to a suicide may be accidental, but there is evidence, both in the myth of Qu Yuan and in other texts, of significant links of authorship and death in early China.

The links between authorship and death in the myth of Qu Yuan derive from the use of suicide as a demonstration of integrity in isolation. The Han poem "Ai shi ming" cites Qu Yuan as one of several past worthies who died to preserve their virtue. The account of Qu Yuan is followed immediately by the line, "He would not change when faced with bodily destruction, for loyalty and faith admit no alteration." This insistence on Qu Yuan's devotion to the death echoes the self-description of the *persona* in the "Li sao" who insists on his total devotion to moral cultivation and on the fact that he seeks only the good of the state with no concern for personal safety.[169] Isolated integrity, the ground of individual authorship, and the position of those who saw their plight in that of Qu Yuan, was ultimately sanctioned by the willingness to die.

Death is more generally linked to authorship in the conventional notion that "establishing words" (*li yan* 立言) was one of the three paths to survival beyond the tomb. This idea, in its first formulation in the *Zuo zhuan* or as developed by Cao Pi in the *Dian lun*, could refer to preserving the memory of a successful career in written records or literature. More influential was the belief, tied to the figure of Qu Yuan, that failure in life could be reversed through a literary appeal to later ages.[170] One of the classic articulations of this was Sima Qian's letter to Ren An, wherein he argued that he had decided against suicide because his death would gain significance only if he first completed the literary *opus* that would make him known to later ages. In the classic phrase that "death can be as light as a feather or as weighty as Mt. Tai" he tied authorship to death. As author of the earliest source that clearly attributes multiple compositions and an ultimate suicide to Qu Yuan, Sima Qian's remarks were closely linked to the pattern defined by the former.[171]

The linkage of death and authorship figures not only in Sima Qian's justification of his own work, but also in his accounts of other literary figures. In the biography of Sima Xiangru a pair of anecdotes dealing with death frame the writer's relations with Emperor Wu. When Emperor Wu read the rhapsody on the hunting park of the King of Liang, he wished that he had lived at the same time as the author. Here the ruler assumed that authorship was an attribute of the dead. At the end of the chapter Sima Xiangru composed an essay and poem on the *feng* and *shan* sacrifices that he left in his home. After his death the emperor sent a messenger to collect any remaining works, and the messenger was given this single text that had been addressed in advance to the emperor. In this way Sima Xiangru used a literary composition to speak to Emperor Wu from beyond the grave. This action in turn relates to the subject of the composition, for Sima Xiangru describes the *feng* and *shan* sacrifices as the supreme imperial ritual in which the placement of an inscription on Mt. Tai allows the ruler to transcend death through writing a "seventh classic."[172] As will be discussed in chapter 5, Sima Qian also links authorship with death in his biography of Confucius.

Authorship, death, funerary cult, and poetry are also drawn together in an Eastern Han funerary stele.

> When the *ya* and *song* hymns arose, the ancestral temple became solemn. When the *Zhong yong* arose, the *zu* and *zong* ancestors [lacuna]. When Confucius died his disciples bound together the *Lun yu*, and the poem "Si gan" illuminated the reign of King Xuan. A posthumous title serves as the banner for virtue, and an inscription engraves merit. Therefore Heng Fang's disciples and former clerks [lacuna], quarried the excellent stone, erected the numinous stele, and engraved his abundant accomplishments, storing them away for the future. The stele's lyric says . . .[173]

Here the composition of a funerary stele, a poetic genre recognized by the Chinese but largely ignored in the West, is prefaced with general remarks that link the writing and compilation of literary works with funerary cult, individual death, and the end of a reign. Literature began in the songs of funerary cult, and it culminated (for the writer) in the composition of poetry on the dead. The compilation of a work or anthology marked the end of a life or reign, but at the same time perpetuated them in later ages. Closely related to this idea was the later Chinese practice of collecting a deceased author's work into an anthology (*ji* 集), a practice often performed by offspring or close friends and linked to funerary rites. The

Chuci was not strictly homologous with later authorial anthologies, for it included works modeled on those of Qu Yuan as well as those attributed to him. However, in making the author the focus of the collection and his prior death a defining feature, the anthology provided the ultimate model for the bibliographic category of *ji*, which became the category for verse and self-expression.

CONCLUSION

The earliest surviving verse in our sources was tied to religious cult and consisted of collectively chanted liturgy. Linked to later changes in rituals, an individual voice appeared as witness and narrator of the actions of others. As the Zhou order began to disintegrate, struggles between noble factions became a theme of verse. Metaphors or images developed in ritual hymns and songs of abandoned women were adapted to the condemnation of rival groups. These poems also developed new themes, such as "the world turned upside down" and the failure of rituals. Throughout these changes, however, individual gestures in verse were enacted in collectively transmitted, recurring themes and formulaic lines that remained part of a conventional rhetoric shared by a group.

With the fall of the Zhou monarchy, or perhaps earlier, the surviving Zhou odes detached from their ritual contexts, although the latter were preserved in more conservative states such as Lu. As a world of competing states emerged, the Zhou odes became a common heritage for the nobility of the entire cultural ecumene. This heritage was used by nobles to distinguish themselves from less educated groups and to conduct negotiations in which the shared recognition of quoted verses, and the ability to give them multiple meanings, became essential to success. With the nobility's decline the knowledge of these practices, and modified forms of the practices themselves, were preserved by schoolmen as modes of education. From the use of verse in education, the citation of the odes passed into philosophic texts. Here they were increasingly cited as a form of authority based on their putative sagely origins, and on the polyvocality which allowed those who cited them to claim constant principles while adapting their social programs to a changing world. The Mao preface and commentary, and probably the other commentarial traditions that have not survived, developed a theory of verse as a mode of self-expression made uniquely powerful and veridical through its links to emotions and its origins among the ancient sage kings. On the basis of this hermeneutic, the odes were collected into a grand historical schema in which the commentators traced the rise and fall of the Zhou, and by extension the principles of human history. Although the reading of the poems was based on a theory of self-expression, the authors remained anonymous, their work was regarded as an expression of the lingering virtue of the sages, and each poem was assigned meaning through its supposed time of composition and its place within the collection.

Parallel to the emergence of the authority of the odes in the *ru* textual traditions, verses were written into both religious texts such as the Chu silk manuscript and proto-Daoist texts including the *Dao de jing*, the *Zhuangzi*, and the *Huangdi si jing*. Poetry was used in these texts to give dramatic formulation to the play of opposites and paradoxes that were used to topple conventional wisdom; to embed truths in parallelism, rhythm, and rhyme without claiming rational proof; and to evoke topics—the primal unity, the cosmic Way, the perfected man—beyond the powers of conventional speech.

Finally, in the state of Chu certain writers adapted ritual music and verse into dramatic presentations on the theme of human passion and confrontation with divinity. These suites were in turn employed as a source of topoi and images for the writing of personal lament and political criticism. Gathered into an anthology on the basis of shared themes and lines, these poems were attributed to an author whose personal experiences and distinctive voice became the privileged ground for their interpretation. Tied to the story of Qu Yuan by the early Han and read in the light of that story, the poems became a model for the use of writing to testify to individual virtue, and to redeem failure in life through appeal to like-minded people of later times. The authorial Qu Yuan invented by Han readers redefined the Chinese intellectual universe by providing a sanction for the personal voice, defining the composition of verse as a mode of sociability between like-minded individuals, and providing a model for the later, author-based anthology. It thereby created the intellectual space for the proliferation of literary works attached to named individuals, and for the ultimate emergence of lyric verse. These developments, in turn, furthered the emergence of a pan-imperial literate class made possible by a shared knowledge of a body of literary texts that belonged neither to the state nor the school. These texts became a source of authority for all those who lacked power and position, but who still insisted on the value of their own words and writings by claiming the role of author.

Chapter Five
THE POLITICAL HISTORY
OF WRITING

The grounding of textual authority in accounts of the past depended on appeals to sages who were mythic embodiments of the identity of scholar and king. Certain sages were intimately associated with the theme of writing, and when placed in sequence they formed a schematic history of the evolution of the relationship between textuality and kingship. This history can be divided into three phases: a phase of origins in which the ruler was the pure master of visual signs, a middle period in which government and texts existed as parallel realms united in a single figure, and a final stage in which political power and textual authority were separated into spheres of pure power and empty written form. This model also pointed toward a fourth phase in which kingship and sagehood would be re-united in a text-based empire of virtue.

This three-stage model is not my invention, for many early Chinese texts divided the past into three periods. The *Mencius*'s discussion of the sages cited in chapter 3 posited three ages in each of which a sage rescued mankind from chaos: the high antiquity of Shun and Yu, a middle period marked by the Duke of Zhou, and recent times that had been textually pacified by Confucius, but still awaited a sage to bring an end to the doctrines of Yang and Mo. The *Xunzi* adopted the sequence of early kings (high antiquity), later kings (Zhou), and recent times, as did the early Han *Xin yu*. The legalist texts distinguished between a high antiquity ruled through virtue, a middle period controlled by the worthy or wise, and a recent period of government by written law with rewards and punishments.[1] The *Yi jing* also passed through three stages of authorship. This classic was identified as the origin of writing, so the three authors of the *Yi*—Fu Xi, the Duke of Zhou, and Confucius—embody the history of the relations between textual mastery and kingship.[2]

In these schemata, high antiquity was a prepolitical age, when the state had yet to be established. In its earliest period, from Fu Xi to Shen Nong, there was no use of force, and the rulers had been heroes of a pure culture untainted by recourse to violence or compulsion. The textual equivalent of this protokingship was the absence of writing, with the role later played by script divided between the trigrams, which revealed natural patterns for the innovations of the sages, and knotted cords, which kept simple records. Both of these were attributed to Fu Xi, and he became the mythological progenitor of both writing and of the kingly way. He was linked to the goddess Nü Wa as a primal couple that created humanity and embodied *yin* and *yang*. This pairing of the invention of written signs with the act of physical procreation mythically demonstrated that written graphs formed a dynamic, parallel dimension sharing attributes of the physical world.

Middle antiquity was defined by the introduction of the dynastic state and, in the sphere of writing, the multiplication of texts. The textual heritage of the Zhou was read as the written remains of the kings and their historians. As the Zhou dynasty faded from the political stage it was replaced by a purely textual entity defined by these early texts—the *Documents*, the *Odes*, the *Rites*, the *Music*, and ultimately the *Changes*. These works that defined the textual Zhou in the Warring States came to be identified with the Duke of Zhou. This development began in the early chapters of the *Shang shu*, where the Duke figured as author or speaker, and in which his role as regent sanctioned claims to rule through virtue rather than heredity. He gradually became the patron sage of textual authority in middle antiquity, figuring as both the hero of Confucius and the putative author of the textual heritage of the high Zhou. Regent and kinsman of three kings, he occupied a position intermediate between high antiquity, where the sage was king, and the Warring States, where intellectual traditions stood in opposition to the state.

The realm of pure textuality as a political reality outside the state was embodied in Confucius. As we saw in chapter 2, Confucius had emerged in the *Lun yu* as a teacher who defined the role of master. However, even within the *Lun yu* he had already taken on a political coloring. Anecdotes in later chapters show him in conversation with high nobles or rulers, playing the role of potential adviser that would become the staple of later philosophical writers. In one story Confucius fell ill, and the disciples decided to act as "ministers" (*chen* 臣) at his funeral, thus turning their scholarly relation into a political one.[3] Zi Gong describes the extraordinary things that Confucius could achieve as head of a state or lineage, and the *Mencius* also attributes discussions on this theme to Confucius' disciples.[4] This imagined rulership of Confucius develops in two directions. First, in the *Gongyang* it became the "king without attributes" and the theory of the kingship of writing. In other traditions the potential became reality, in an imaginary political career that ended in failure. This second path culminated in Sima Qian's chapter on Confucius, where the master served as model administrator and judge, rose to the highest office in the state, was expelled through the machinations of foreign enemies and internal rivals, traveled with a group of disciples who engaged in political relations with several states, endured assaults and sieges in the search for a ruler to employ him, turned to writing and editing only when all prospect of action in the world has disappeared, and ultimately became founder of a textual dynasty and recipient of cult as the ancestor of all scholars. Here literary work was a sign of desperation and failure. However, through their ability to survive across time and command men in the distant future, the texts achieved the power that their editor/author never held.

The process of creating authoritative writing began in a world without graphic signs, where kingship emerged through the ability to read the text of the world. When elaborate texts on the forms of government developed, then textuality became an attribute of kingship, symbolized by the Duke of Zhou who was regent and double of the king, and master in the realm of texts. In the end of the process the two realms separated, with a textual kingship or kingship of texts set in opposition to the rule of calculation and force. The sage was no longer king in his own life, but through the power of writing he was master of the past that he recorded and the future to which he spoke.

THE MYTHOLOGY OF FU XI

As the first of the sages Fu Xi was the creator of kingship and progenitor of human technology, a role that he fulfilled through his invention of the trigrams and, by extension, writing. Among the sagely inventions that created human civilization as understood in the Warring States, writing held pride of place. It was not one technology among others, but rather the ultimate form of those capacities that made possible all the sagely inventions and institutions. This is marked by the fact that writing was not a single, codified system of graphic communication but a hierarchical series of visual sign networks. It was thus invented not once, but several times. Derived from the milfoil divination that revealed the order of the cosmos through the play of broken and unbroken lines, writing emerged in a process leading from the first appearance of meaningful divisions within chaos to the codified graphic forms of the first dictionaries and the stone classics. Consequently accounts in Warring States and early imperial texts of the origins of writing were absorbed into tales of the emergence of the *Yijing* (易經 "Classic of Changes").

The most important account of Fu Xi, the origin of the hexagrams, and the beginning of writing occurs in the "Great Tradition," an extended essay on the cosmological significance of the *Yijing*.

> When Bao [Fu] Xi ruled the world in ancient times, he looked up to examine the images [*guan xiang* 觀象] in Heaven, and down to examine the models [*fa* 法] on Earth. He examined the markings [*wen* 文, "patterns"] of the birds and the beasts, and their suitability to the terrain. Near at hand he took it from himself, and at a distance from objects. Thereupon he first created the eight trigrams in order to communicate with the powers of spirit intelligence, and in order to categorize the natures of the myriad objects. He invented knotting cords [to keep records] and made nets and snares for hunting and fishing. He probably took [the idea for] this from the hexagram *li* [#30].

> When Bao Xi died, Shen Nong arose. He carved wood to make a plow, bent wood to make a plowshare, and taught the world the benefits of plowing. He probably

took this from *yi* [#42]. At mid-day he made a market, summoned the world's people, and gathered the world's goods. They exchanged and then withdrew, each obtaining his portion. He probably took this from *shi he* [#21].

When Shen Nong died, the Yellow Emperor, Yao, and Shun arose. They thoroughly mastered changes and thereby caused the people to not grow weary. . . . The Yellow Emperor, Yao, and Shun hung down their robes and the world was in order. They probably took this from *qian* and *kun* [#1, 2]. They scraped out wood to make boats and carved wood to make oars in order to get across the impassable. They caused the distant to come in order to benefit the world. They probably took this from *huan* [#59]. They tamed oxen and hitched teams of horses to pull heavy loads and bring people from far away, and thereby they benefited the world. They probably took this from *sui* [#17]. They doubled gates and struck alarm clappers in order to await violent outsiders. They probably took this from *yu* [#16]. They split wood to make pestles, and hollowed out the earth to make mortars. The myriad people were saved through the benefits of mortar and pestle. They probably took this from *xiao guo* [#62]. They strung wood to make bows and shaved wood to make arrows. The world was terrified through the sharpness of bows and arrows. They probably took this from *kui* [#38].

In high antiquity people lived in caves and in the wilds. In later generations the sages exchanged these for palaces and houses. They put the ridgepole above and the eaves below to guard against the wind and rain. They probably took this from *da zhuang* [#34]. In ancient burials they thickly covered them in firewood, and buried them in the wilds. They raised no mounds and planted no trees. The period of mourning had no fixed duration [literally "number" *shu* 數]. In later generations the sages exchanged this for inner and outer coffins. They probably took this from *da guo* [#28]. In high antiquity they knotted cords and thereby created order. In later generations the sages exchanged this for documents and contracts. Thereby the officals were controlled and the people supervised. They probably took this from *guai* [#43].[5]

This is the most complete account of the creation of civilization through sagely innovations. Fu Xi is not only the first of the sages, but also an encompassing figure whose discovery of the trigrams contains the work of all the sages.[6] He alone directly contemplated natural patterns, whereas all later inventions—including his own—were inspired by the hexagrams created in the primal revelation. The fact that this first invention includes all the others is also marked by the play of complementary pairs used to indicate totality—Heaven and earth, near and far, birds and beasts—and the culminating categorization of all existent objects. This primal discovery, the root of civilization, is ultimately identified as the beginning of writing.

This identification is marked both internally and externally. Within the account writing is distinguished in two ways. First, it is the final invention, forming a pendant to the initial revelation. More important, writing in the form of government documents (*shu* 書) and contracts is the only invention that supplants not a natural practice but rather an earlier invention. Specifically, it replaces and carries on the work of the knotted cords invented by Fu Xi. This clearly marks writing as the culmination of Fu Xi's invention of the trigrams. Moreover, in doing so it articulates a developmental relation built into the structure of the text itself. The *Yi jing* is, as François Jullien has noted, perhaps the strangest text ever produced, because of the manner in which it is composed.[7] It begins not with words but rather with a series of six lines, and it inventories all the sets of such lines made possible by the alternation of solid and broken lines. Graphic characters are appended to these line sets to explain their meanings and their uses, but the "Great Tradition" states that the graphs explaining the hexagrams are themselves derived from the line sets. These sets, or rather the trigrams from which the hexagrams were supposedly formed, constitute in Warring States thought the first form in which meaning was generated by lines. As I will discuss below, the earliest hexagrams were not composed of lines but numbers, but numbers were likewise composed of lines and were forms of graphs. Thus the structure of the text—moving from hexagrams to written characters—recapitulates the historical invention or discovery of writing. All later forms of graphic communication in China, and indeed the very possibility of discerning meaning from signs, derived from Fu Xi's primal markings.

In addition to this internal evidence from the *Yi jing* itself, several passages indicate that scholars regarded the invention of the trigrams as the ultimate origin of written characters. First, in the apocryphal literature the trigrams are described as "old script" (*gu wen* 古文) characters. Thus, for example, the trigram *qian* composed of three unbroken lines is described as the old character for "Heaven" (*tian* 天).[8] Second, the history of the evolution of the Han script in the postface to Xu Shen's dictionary *Shuo wen jie zi* (說文解字) begins with a direct quotation of Fu Xi's discovery of the trigrams through the contemplation of Heaven, Earth, and the markings of animals. Since it is concerned only with writing, this account then leaps directly to the invention of written script, which it attributes to a minister of the Yellow Emperor named Cang Jie. It also presents a modified quotation of the account in the "Great Tradition" of the uses of graphs and their inspiration by the hexagram *guai*.[9] Here the invention of writing is traced directly to the trigrams. Third, the most detailed account of Cang Jie's invention of graphs is simply an expanded version of the account of Fu Xi's discovery of the trigrams.[10] The early Jin dynasty *Di wang shi ji* attributes the invention of writing directly to Fu Xi, and makes it contemporary with the discovery of the trigrams. The same position is adopted in the fourth-century A.D. *Shi yi ji*.[11] Thus Cang Jie is a minor double of Fu Xi, of interest in that he is a minister rather than a ruler. Eponym for Qin's unified script, he was the mythic prototype for officials fixing standard forms of written characters, but his work was dependent on the primal invention of Fu Xi.

Closely related to Fu Xi's discovery of the trigrams was his receiving the "[Yellow] River Chart" (*he tu* 河圖). This was a document or chart presented to sage rulers by a divine creature that rose out of the Yellow River. Like the trigrams the River Chart was composed of written signs that revealed the secret patterns of Heaven to its recipient. It thus prefigured the attainment of the Mandate of Heaven and the establishment of a new dynasty.[12] By the Han dynasty, the River Chart was routinely paired with the "Luo [River] Writing" (*luo shu* 洛書), a magic talisman of similar origins and significance that probably derived from the proto-Daoist scholarly traditions.[13] At the end of the Warring States period the River Chart was cited in the "Great Tradition" in close association with the trigrams.

> Therefore the *Yi* has the Supreme Ultimate [*tai ji* 太極, i.e., the primal unity]. This produces the Two Standards [*liang yi* 兩儀, i.e., *yin* and *yang*, the broken and unbroken lines of the *Yi*]. The Two Standards produce the Four Images [*si xiang* 四象, the four possible pairs of broken and unbroken lines]. The Four Images produce the Eight Trigrams. The Eight Trigrams fix the auspicious and inauspicious. The auspicious and inauspicious produce the Great Enterprise [*da ye* 大業, i.e., the establishment of a royal dynasty].

> Of images and models, nothing is greater than Heaven and Earth. Of transformations and comprehensiveness, nothing is greater than the four seasons. Of suspended images and clear illumination, nothing is greater than the sun and moon. Of exalted loftiness, nothing is greater than wealth and nobility. In completing things and putting them to use, establishing them as implements to be of benefit to the world, nothing is greater than the sage. In probing the profound, searching the unknown, fishing the deeps, and summoning the distant, all in order to settle the world's fate and complete the world's labors, nothing is greater than the milfoil and the tortoise shell.

> Heaven produces the numinous objects, and the sage takes them as his model. Heaven and Earth transform, and the sage imitates them. Heaven hangs down its images to reveal fate, and the sage takes them as his pattern. The Yellow River produces its chart and the Luo River its writing, and the sage takes them as his model. The *Yi* has the Four Images in order to reveal. It appends words to them [the images and trigrams] in order to announce. It fixes them as auspicious or inauspicious in order to decide.[14]

The opening section adapts the *Dao de jing*'s account of cosmogony through division to describe the emergence of the *Yi* as a text, and it proclaims this text as the foundation of royal power.[15] The second applies the structure of the text to the physical cosmos, and places the sage with his mastery of divination in the position of the king. The third enumerates the cosmic signs that serve as models for the sage, including the magical charts and text revealed by the rivers. These lead directly to the images in the *Yi* text, and the written words that explain their meaning. Thus the physical cosmos and the *Yi jing* form two parallel series of signs, each of which reveals the truth of the other, and both culminate in the written text that announces meanings and settles fates.

While the "Great Tradition" links Fu Xi's trigrams with the signs revealed on the River Chart and the Luo Writing, it is only in Han texts that the identity of the two revelations is asserted.[16] Moreover, an account of Cang Jie states that one of the natural sources from which he derived characters was the markings on the back of a tortoise, there is an Eastern Han terracotta tortoise with the Eight Trigrams carved on its back, and the Luo Writing is often described as appearing on the back of a tortoise.[17] Thus by the Eastern Han the conflation of the accounts of the revelation of the trigrams and those of the magical writings was complete. These Han accounts merge three traditions already closely linked in the Warring States period: the idea that Fu Xi discovered the trigrams through contemplating patterns in nature, the idea that nature itself revealed written signs to sages about to assume power, and the idea that both the signs discovered in nature and those which nature spontaneously presented were the ancestors of written characters that people used.

Closely related to accounts of Fu Xi as the discoverer of the trigrams, recipient of the River Chart or Luo Writing, and ultimate ancestor of writing are traditions that he was the inventor of numbers. Since Chinese numbers are depicted through their own written graphs, Fu Xi's invention of writing already includes numbers. Moreover, the *Zuo zhuan* states that tortoise shell divination was associated with "image," while divination by the yarrow stalk was done through "number" (*shu* 數).[18] As progenitor of yarrow divination, Fu Xi was also the patron sage of numbers. The *Shi ben* contains a reference to an otherwise unknown inventor of divination through number, and this figure can probably be identified with Fu Xi.[19] The *Zhou bi suan jing* and the *Jiu zhang suan shu*, the two earliest surviving treatises on mathematics, both trace the art of calculation back to Fu Xi. The former also argues that numbers are ultimately derived from the carpenter's square, which is an iconographic feature of Fu Xi in Han art.[20]

Fu Xi's role in the origin of writing is also marked by the fact that the trigrams were closely linked to the magic square. From at least the Han dynasty the eight trigrams were arranged in a circle to form a cosmic mandala, as on the back of the terracotta tortoise cited in note 17. There were two standard orders of trigrams, the Former Heaven order attributed to Fu Xi and the Later Heaven order attributed to King Wen.[21] As discussed in one of the later chapters of the *Yi jing*, the Later Heaven order of the trigrams could be mapped onto the eight directions and thus used to trace the annual cycle generated by the shifting of the prevailing winds.[22] Moreover, this same pattern was traced out in the annual cycle of the movements of the Son of Heaven through the "Hall of Light" (*ming tang* 明堂),

which also formed a magic square. One passage in a chapter of the Han dynasty *Da dai li ji* assigns the numbers one to nine to each of the nine rooms that make up the "Hall of Light," and these numbers form the simplest type of magic square, that is, a grid of nine boxes in which adding any three consecutive numbers results in a sum of fifteen.[23] According to an apocryphal Han work attributed to Fu Xi, the magic square traced by the Son of Heaven in his travels through the Hall of Light paralleled a celestial magic square mapped out by the god Taiyi as he moved through the nine rooms of his celestial palace.[24] Thus the underlying identity of spatial structure and temporal process, and the natural foundations of monarchy therein, were reproduced both in the numerical pattern of the magic square and the symbolic array of the trigrams.[25] The discoverer of these patterns was Fu Xi.

Taken in isolation, Fu Xi was the first of the sages and the initiator of man's emergence from his animal state. The discoverer of the trigrams and the numerical underpinnings of reality, he was the father of writing and the ultimate inspiration of the civilizing process. The earliest recorded mythic role of Fu Xi was as the inventor of the calendar. The cosmogonic myth in the fourth-century B.C. Chu silk manuscript relates that prior to the existence of the sun and moon Bao [Fu] Xi and his wife engendered four sons, the seasons, who measured the year by pacing it out with their feet.[26] This not only indicates Fu Xi's role as the first regulator of time, but also anticipates his link and that of his later wife, Nü Wa, to the sun and the moon in Han art.

The pairing of Fu Xi with the goddess Nü Wa as a primal couple that created both the natural world and the human race is not attested prior to the Han dynasty.[27] However, it grows directly out of myths and intellectual concerns of the Warring States period, so the mythology of Nü Wa sheds further light on the Chinese understanding of writing and its relation to the physical world. Nü Wa was associated with the process of creation. The "Tian wen" asks, "Nü Wa had a body, but who fashioned it?"[28] In isolation the sense of the question would not be certain, but given later texts' accounts of Nü Wa's physical creation of the human race, it is certain that the author of the "Tian wen" knew such stories, and posed the question of who had created *her*. The early Western Han *Huainanzi* contains a cryptic sentence that refers to Nü Wa's physical creation of humanity through her power to work transformations, specifically the transformations undergone by a fetus. This indicates the early existence of accounts such as those inplied by the "Tian wen."[29] To explain the origins of social divisions the late Eastern Han *Fengsu tongyi* tells of Nü Wa's creation of the human race. In this story Nü Wa at first fashions men entirely from yellow earth. Because the process takes too much time she later resorts to dipping cords in mud to form human creatures. The rich and noble descend from the creatures formed of yellow earth, while the cord and mud hybrids are the ancestors of the commoners.[30] While the text is relatively late, the tradition of Nü Wa as creator of mankind clearly existed by the late Warring States period.

Nü Wa also figures as creator of the physical world in one version of the account of the restoration of the world after the flood.

> But he [the Yellow Emperor] did not yet equal the Way of Fu Xi. In ancient times the four extremities [of the Earth] had been cast off and the nine provinces [the inhabited world] torn apart. Heaven did not completely cover [the Earth] and the earth did not completely support [Heaven]. Blazing and scorching, the fires were not extinguished. Rushing and overflowing, the waters did not rest. Savage beasts devoured the innocent people, while birds of prey seized the old and the weak. Thereupon Nü Wa smelted the five-colored minerals in order to patch the azure Heaven. She cut off the legs of the tortoise in order to fix in place the four extremities. She killed the black dragon in order to save Ji Province [modern Hebei and Shanxi provinces, here a metonym for the world]. She collected the ashes of reeds in order to halt the rampant waters.[31]

The passage then describes the rule of Fu Xi, in which all men did what they chose and dangerous animals never revealed their teeth and claws.[32] Here Nü Wa, apparently an agent of Fu Xi, does the primary work of both physically restoring the world and of bringing an end to the flood.

These passages are the only Han textual sources that explicitly link Fu Xi and Nü Wa. However, the passage immediately following tells of two spirits who emerge within the primal chaos and engender the divisions between *yin* and *yang*. The two deities are not named, and the Eastern Han commentator describes them only as the "spirits of *yin* and *yang*." In Han tomb art Fu Xi and Nü Wa are constantly paired, and appear to have played their most important role as the spirits who embodied *yin* and *yang*. The closeness of these two passages may indicate that the linking of Fu Xi and Nü Wa, and their identification with *yin* and *yang*, began by the early Western Han.[33]

In most accounts the taming of the flood is credited to Yu, to whom Nü Wa is linked in several accounts. Both the late Warring States *Shi ben* and the third-century A.D. *Di wang shi ji* identify Nü Wa as Yu's wife.[34] Since Nü Wa figured primarily as the wife of Fu Xi, it is possible that the latter was either a mythic transformation of Yu, or an alternative local version of the flood queller.

The link between Fu Xi and Yu is marked also by the fact that both of them appear to have been originally snake or dragon spirits. Indeed, all the leading actors in the flood saga—Gun, Yu, Gong Gong, and Nü Wa—have names indicating aquatic origins as snakes, fish, or related creatures, and they are described as having the bodies of snakes or being transformations of dragons. Even in more humanized versions they are often assisted by dragons.[35] Fu Xi's name is written with a variety of characters indicating a phonetic cluster associated with "wriggling," "twisting," or "curving." Moreover, in Han art both he and Nü Wa are regularly depicted with human heads and the bodies of snakes that sometimes coil round one another in a depiction of intimate union. Han apocryphal literature states that he had the form of a dragon.[36]

Fu Xi's dragon form indicates important mythic attributes. Many of the achievements of Fu Xi and Nü Wa are directly linked to the characteristics of the dragon in early Chinese thought. First, the movements of the dragon made it a link between Heaven and Earth. Through its association with water it could either hide in the depths of rivers or oceans or soar up on the clouds. This ability to move between Earth and Heaven enabled dragons to act as chariot steeds for those who set out on spirit journeys. Moreover, dragons linking Heaven to Earth appear in stories of the origins of certain sacred sites and in Han art.[37] This role of linking Heaven to Earth also figures in the depictions of Fu Xi and Nü Wa.

First, in Han tombs their elongated, serpent bodies stretch from the bottom of the register to the top, and in later depictions this vertical ascent becomes even clearer. In Sichuan sarcophagi they play the iconographic role of the dragons on the Mawangdui banners who physically link the earthly realm to that of Heaven. This idea is reinforced through the regular inclusion of two other iconographic traits. Fu Xi and Nü Wa are often depicted with the sun and the moon, and they are shown holding a carpenter's square (Fu Xi) and a drawing compass (Nü Wa). The former are metonyms for Heaven and the celestial equivalents of *yin* and *yang*. The latter suggests the linking of square Earth to the round Heaven.[38] Most scholars agree that the role of the intertwined Fu Xi and Nü Wa was to depict the interaction of *yin* and *yang* that underlies cosmic order and thereby secure an auspicious environment for the denizen of the tomb.

The carpenter's square wielded by Fu Xi in Han art and associated with him in some texts stands not only for the square earth, but also for the trigrams and the hexagrams that he invented. One passage in the Han apocryphal literature states that Fu Xi lived when all was chaotic and undivided, and that he used the carpenter's square to divide it and create the trigrams. The "Great Tradition" of the *Yi* states that the trigrams are square while the yarrow are round, thus making *Yi* divination a replica of the universe.[39] The idea that the carpenter's square was fundamental to world creation through its ability to generate lines may also underlie the myths of Chui, an alternative inventor of the square who is routinely cited in Daoist writings as an image of the destructive power of the craftsman's skills.[40] Through this association with the carpenter's square, the tales of Fu Xi's invention of the trigrams parallel the pattern of cosmic generation or maintenance depicted in the Han tomb representations of Fu Xi and Nü Wa.

The role of Fu Xi as a link between Heaven and Earth figures also in the texts of the period.

> Fu Xi's power united above and below. Heaven responded with the patterned markings of birds and beasts, while Earth responded with the River Chart and the Luo Writing. He then imitated (*xiang* 象) these and made the *Yi*.[41]

Here Fu Xi's invention of the trigrams results from his ability to link Heaven and Earth. This ability is identified with the "Great Tradition's" description of him "looking up" and "looking down." Passages in the apocryphal literature also argue that the *Yi* is the "Way of Heaven and Earth," and that the hexagrams serve to "unite" (*tong* 統) Heaven and Earth. With the bottom trigram corresponding to Earth and the top to Heaven, the hexagram forms the image (*xiang*) of the universe. In other passages rulers such as King Wen are said to "establish the hexagrams to unite Heaven and Earth, and they thereby secure their power."[42]

A second feature of the dragon was its association with clouds and rain, and by extension with fertility. This is particularly noteworthy in tales of spirit progenitors of sages or dynastic founders, who were often sired by dragons. In several accounts the dragon not only impregnates the woman but also delivers a magic chart (*tu* 圖, like the River Chart) that prophesies the rise of the sage about to be conceived.[43] In one story, dragon semen stored in a box during the Xia dynasty spontaneously generated its own offspring in the shape of a black tortoise. This tortoise impregnated the mother of Bao Si, the concubine who brought about the fall of the Western Zhou.[44] The belief that dragons impregnated women spread into less exalted circles, for later popular literature contains many stories of village women being inseminated while washing clothes at the river bank and later giving birth to dragon children.[45]

Dragons and snakes were also linked to the theme of childbirth through the figure of the *wu* (巫), the spirit intermediary or shaman. The *Shan hai jing* tells of *wu* who carry snakes in their hands as they climb up and down mountains, of rainmakers who wield snakes, of *wu* who give elixirs of immortality to snake-bodied beings, and of mountains named *wu* inhabited by snakes.[46] Depictions of figures corresponding to these accounts have been found in Warring States tombs.[47] Since *wu* played an important role in securing childbirth, their link with snakes may well be connected to the latter's role as guarantors of fertility.[48]

The links of *wu*, dragons, and fertility are also revealed in a set of definitions in the *Shuo wen*. The character 壬 *ren* is glossed

> *Ren* is the position of the northern quadrant. It is the ultimate of *yin* and facilitates birth. Therefore the *Yi* says, "Dragons fight in the field [top line of the hexagram *kun*, hence the ultimate *yin*]." "Fight" means to "join" [i.e., "to couple"]. It imitates the form of a pregnant [*huai ren* 懷妊] person. Following on *hai* [in the sequence of Earthly Branches], the character *ren* thereby causes the child [子 *zi*, "child," but also the Branch following *hai*] to be born. *Ren* has the same meaning as *wu* "spirit intermediary."[49]

This character that refers to pregnancy and birth is glossed as a synonym of *wu*, and its relation to birth is explained through reference to dragons in the primal *yin* hexagram. The character 工 *gong* ("skill, craftsman"), which is explained as the image of a person with a compass and carpenter's square, is also said to have "the same meaning as *wu*." It is likewise the phonetic of 仜 *gong*, which is defined as "a large belly."[50] Thus pregnancy and the skill of the spirit intermediary are again closely linked.

Just as the dragon was an embodiment of fertility, so the *Yi* hexagrams generate (*sheng* 生) the world. One apocryphal text states that the *Yi* generates Heaven and Earth, and that the primal hexagrams *qian* and *kun* are the "ancestors of the myriad objects" (*wan wu zhi zu zong* 萬物之祖宗). Another says that in creating the Four Images (*si xiang* 四象, the four possible pairs of broken and unbroken lines), Fu Xi "opened the gate of generation" (*fa sheng men* 發生門). Others explain that the three lines of the hexagrams correspond to the life process of all objects— beginning, flourishing middle, and end—and that *qian* and *kun* generate all things. Finally, the emergence of the hexagrams is described in the same terms as the emergence of the cosmos, moving through the stages of the nonexistence of *qi*, to the emergence of unformed *qi*, to forms (*xing* 形), substance (*zhi* 質), and finally the appearance of objects by means of division.[51]

The hexagrams were also linked to fertility in the generation of the human form and the propagation of humankind. One passage identifies each trigram with a different part of the body, so that collectively they constitute a full human form. Another states that humans are born in response to the trigrams. A discussion of the *Yi* text notes that it is divided into two halves, with the first half corresponding to the Way of Heaven and the second to that of man. The two hexagrams that begin the second half are said to be "the origin of male and female, the Way of husband and wife," and it is from this that the entire Way of man arises. Another attributes "the duties of husband and wife" to Fu Xi's invention of the trigrams.[52] Finally, one passage states that the initial hexagram *qian* was both a dragon and a father.[53]

Fu Xi as inventor of the hexagrams and as the dragon spirit that coupled with Nü Wa was thus two formulations of the same process. Indeed the link of dragon and hexagram is elaborated in one explanation of the yarrow's power. Just as turtles were employed in divination because of their longevity, so the yarrow was efficacious because it lived to a great age. After one thousand years, it had a purple cloud above it and a "numinous dragon and spirit turtle" (*ling long shen gui* 靈龍神龜) beneath. Another text says that it had "five dragons" beneath it. The spirit power of yarrow was marked by the presence of dragons at its base, or of the dragon and turtle pair associated with the divine revelation of writing.[54] The ability of tortoises and yarrow to reveal cosmic patterns was due to their uniquely potent vital energies, and the yarrow's vitality was connected to the presence of dragons at its roots.

Another link between fertility and the mythology of Fu Xi and Nü Wa is the fact that both of them are in different texts given credit for the invention of marriage. In the Chu silk manuscript, as noted above, Fu Xi was the father of the four seasons. The reference to Fu Xi and the hexagrams as creators of the "way of husband and wife" also signals this role. Moreover, the *Shi ben* identifies Fu Xi as inventor of the *li pi* (儷皮) ritual, a presentation of animal skins that was part of the marriage ceremony.[55] Later texts state simply that he was the creator of marriage.[56] Nü Wa was the mythic inventor of the *ji* (笄), the hair ornament that marked a woman's nubility and hence immediately prefigured marriage.[57] Moreover, as bride of Yu and hence ultimate female ancestor of the Xia dynasty, Nü Wa was one of the versions of the "High Matchmaker" (*gao mei* 高媒, also called "Spirit Match-maker" *shen mei* 神媒, "Suburban [i.e., with an altar outside the city walls] Match-maker," and other titles), a female divinity who was offered sacrifice in mid-Spring as the patron of marriage.[58] Finally, the late Han writer Ying Shao stated simply that Nü Wa had created marriage and first brought together husbands and wives.[59]

Some scholars argue that Fu Xi and Nü Wa derived from a myth of a couple that survived the flood and became the ancestors of humankind. Versions of this myth appear across Southeast Asia and among the minorities of southern China. In a classic essay, Wen Yiduo linked these myths with later versions of the story of Fu Xi and Nü Wa in which they were a brother and sister who survived the flood by floating in a gourd and then restored the human race through incest. He argues that the names Fu Xi and Nü Wa both originally referred to the gourd in which they survived. The gourd is also a symbol of fecundity.[60] While it is not impossible that the early accounts of Fu Xi and Nü Wa are based on the myth of the primal couple, it is difficult to reconcile their appearance in art and literature as snake-bodied creator deities with accounts of them as a human couple who were mythic transformations of gourds. In all likelihood the gourd myth was a separate body of tales, prevalent largely among southern peoples, that was conflated with the myths of Fu Xi and Nü Wa through the shared themes of the flood, the creation of hu-manity, and fertility.[61]

The gourd *is* linked to the earlier myths of Fu Xi and Nü Wa in their roles as inventors of musical instruments. Nü Wa or one of her servants created two closely related musical instruments made from gourds, the *sheng* (笙) and the *huang* (簧).[62] The *sheng* was associated by homophony with birth (*sheng* 生), and the Han dynasty dictionary *Shi ming* says that it was patterned on the image of things growing from the earth.[63] A late text states that Nü Wa invented the *sheng* and *huang* after the flood to cause humankind to multiply.[64] While Nü Wa created instruments linked with generation and fecundity, Fu Xi invented stringed instruments, the *se* (瑟) and in some texts the *qin* (琴). The former was noted in early texts as an instrument that produced sorrowful tones and was capable of triggering storms and droughts.[65] In the expanded versions of his myth the invention of the *qin* follows immediately on his discovery of the trigrams. The instrument, like the trigrams, is directly patterned on nature, for in one version of the story the *qin* was manufactured from the wood of the *tong* tree, the phoenix's only perch, and it was copied by Fu Xi from the body of the phoenix. Just as Fu Xi was the first of the sages, so the *qin* was both the oldest of instruments and the supreme form of music. The central posi-tion of the *qin* and its relation to Fu Xi was described by the Eastern Han scholar Cai Yong.

> The tone of the *qin* is the true tone of Heaven and Earth. If the right materials are found, they will provide a true instrument for harmonizing Heaven and Earth. If the right person is found, it can provide him the correct Way of harmonizing Heaven and Earth. If the exact pitch is found, it will make correct tones for harmonizing Heaven and Earth. Fu Xi made the *qin* in order to make perceptible the systems of Heaven and Earth and to harmonize the powers of the spirits.[66]

Here the role of the *qin* is the same as that of Fu Xi as dragon spirit and inventor of the hexagrams, to link together Heaven and Earth in a harmonious whole.

As the first of the sage kings Fu Xi also "initiated leadership" and invented the kingly Way. This achievement figures prominently in the inscription to his image at the Wu Liang shrine, and it appears in the apocryphal literature.[67] The *Di wang shi ji* states simply that Fu Xi was the "first of the hundred kings" (*bai wang zhi xian* 百王之先).[68] Other texts argue that all political order depends on the proper ordering of the trigrams, sometimes linked with the dragons who present charts signifying the rise of kings.[69] One passage traces a direct link from Fu Xi's creation of the trigrams, through King Wen's addition of the line formulae that "attach the auspicious signs of the royal mandate" (*xi wang ming zhi rui* 繫王命之瑞) to the *feng* and *shan* sacrifices that mark the king's attainment of the Great Peace through carving an inscription on Mount Tai.[70] In the Han dynasty the *feng* and *shan* were the highest of all sacrifices, and their performance was the privilege and hallmark of the succession of sages who defined the kingly way. The inscriptions by the seventy-two sages who had performed the sacrifices were each done in a different script, so they constituted a lineage of writing forms paralleling the political lineage of sage kings. This lineage of writing is emphasized in the history of Chinese script in the postface to the *Shuo wen jie zi*.[71]

In summary, Fu Xi in isolation was the inventor of the trigrams, and by extension the creator of writing and of kingship. In association with Nü Wa he was a powerful spirit associated with the creation and maintenance of cosmic order and the regeneration of life. That the two themes of visual signs/writing and generation should be united in a single figure is significant, for at least by the late Warring States and early imperial periods, literati thought of written symbols and graphs as objects capable of generation and growth. We have already seen this above, in the idea that the trigrams produced the world. The gradual emergence of the *Yi* across the generations of sages entails a vision of signs as dynamic and growing. In a *Zuo zhuan* passage cited above, the creation of "images" (*xiang* 象) which were definitive of the role of graphs (see chapter 6) led directly to "increase" or "multiplication" (*ci* 滋).[72] The *feng* inscriptions on Mount Tai also demonstrated the development of graphs in the form of a genealogy. The clearest expression of the theory of written graphs as generated, living forms appears in the *Shuo wen jie zi*.

> When Cang Jie first made written graphs, he relied on the categories [of things] and imitated their forms. Therefore he called them "patterns" [*wen* 文]. After that

the forms and sounds mutually increased, and then he called them "characters" [*zi* 字, glossed in the *Shuo wen* as "generate, multiply"]. "Patterns" are based on resembling objects. "Characters" refers to bearing children and multiplying. When written on bamboo and silk they are called "writing." "Writing" means "to resemble." In the generations of the Five Emperors and the Three Kings they changed and had different forms. Seventy-two generations inscribed the *feng* sacrifice at Mount Tai, and none of them were identical.[73]

The distinction between *wen* and *zi* assumes that the latter are generated through the combination of the former. This emphasis reflects a historical reality, for the centuries immediately preceding and following Xu Shen's work witnessed an unparalleled rate of creating new characters through the combination of existing graphs.[74] Moreover, in clustering characters under the primal graphic form from which they derive, the organization of the book adopts a genetic approach to characters. Finally, four of the six graphic structural types (*liu shu* 六書) posited by Xu Shen assume that characters are created from prior characters.

This generative model of writing, in which characters are assimilated to organic entities that reproduced and multiplied, is embodied in the figure of Fu Xi. It was fundamental to later Chinese thought about writing. First, this theory was essential to the derivation of written graphs from the *Yi* hexagrams, a derivation that gave them a privileged status as a mode of discourse. Second, as will be discussed in the next chapter, it underpinned the theory that writing was not simply a transcription of a spoken language but an independent realm of signification that offered direct insight into the world. Finally, although not relevant to the period being discussed here, the idea also underlies the fact that later Chinese calligraphic theory would draw heavily on physiological terms such as "bone," "breath/wind," and "energy" to describe graphs.

THE MYTHOLOGY OF THE DUKE OF ZHOU

The relation of the Zhou founders to Fu Xi was mythically expressed through their development of the trigrams and hexagrams into a text. The *Di wang shi ji* treats the history of the *Yi* as equivalent to the transmission of the mandate, with each of the Five Emperors and Three Dynasties extending and developing it.[75] The consensus, however, was that the next step, the addition of texts to the hexagrams, was made by either King Wen or the Duke of Zhou.[76] These figures stand in the same relation to Fu Xi as did the later kings to the earlier kings in the *Xunzi*. The latter represent a time of origins, when meaningful patterns first emerged, while the former enter the realm of documented history. Just as the later kings differed from the earlier through the existence of documents, so the difference between the Zhou founders and Fu Xi was that they turned the archetypal symbols into a text, explaining the hexagrams through language.

King Wen's links to the *Yi* and to writing stem in no small part from his posthumous title *wen* 文, which came to mean "pattern" or "writing."

> Confucius was threatened in Kuang. He said, "Since King Wen has died is not the true civilization/writing (*wen*) here? If Heaven were going to destroy this civilization/writing, then those who came after him could not participate in it. But since Heaven has not yet destroyed this civilization/writing, then what can the men of Kuang do to me?"[77]

Here King Wen, on the basis of his posthumous title, embodies the entire heritage of the Zhou.

In the later masters he is celebrated as a model king and dynastic founder, but has no special links to writing or visual symbols. Only one passage in the "Great Tradition" refers to the *Yi* arising at the time when the mandate was shifting from the Shang to King Wen, in order to explain why "King Wen's phrases," that is, the judgments (*tuan* 彖), deal with danger. This passage follows directly on a discussion of the emergence of pattern (*wen*) from the interaction of objects.[78] This appears to be the origin of the tradition that the text of the *Yi* proper was composed at the time of the Zhou foundation, but it is not elaborated.

If King Wen remains a shadowy figure in the context of the mythology of writing, the Duke of Zhou plays a much clearer role. First, he appears as a double of King Wen, replacing him as father to King Cheng. In this way their pairing to form the second link in the evolution of the *Yi* is not surprising. Moreover, from at least the late Western Zhou he began to emerge as the model of the virtuous minister. As regent for the young King Cheng he embodied the idea that authority belonged to the wisest and the best, rather than to the firstborn. This ideal later evolved into the tradition of royal abdication in favor of virtuous ministers or world-renouncing hermits.[79] He was also a major figure in the history of writing, for Warring States texts presented him as an archetype of the scholar, a founder of textual traditions, and a predecessor of Confucius. By the late Warring States period the *ru* textual corpus had become linked to the Duke of Zhou.

The Duke of Zhou does not figure prominently in the records left by bronze inscriptions, and his rise to prominence comes in association with the increasing importance of written texts.[80] From the earliest portrayals in the *Documents* the speeches insist on the importance of placing trust in ministers and honoring them, and that the kings should be humble and listen to instruction.[81] In a recent article Edward Shaughnessy has argued that two chapters of the *Shang shu* constitute a debate in which the Duke of Zhou argues for the importance of ministers in assuring dynastic prosperity, while the Duke of Shao insists on the priority of royal power.[82] In the "Luo gao" the Duke of Zhou instructs King Cheng in how to conduct himself, while the latter pledges to obey the Duke, lauds his virtue, and gives him credit for the establishment of order. In the later chapter "Li zheng" this pattern has developed further. It opens with the phrase "the Duke of Zhou spoke thus" (*Zhou Gong ruo yue* 周公若曰), a formula that equates him with a ruler, and the entire chapter is devoted to the importance of appointing good officials and listening to their advice.[83] Almost certainly an Eastern Zhou composition, the "Li zheng" proclaims the policy of making appointments on the basis of worth and assigns the origins of this policy in high antiquity to the great lineages who assisted the rulers, rather than to the rulers themselves. In this way it reads the political situation of the Spring and Autumn period back into the origins of the state, placing this argument in the voice of the Duke of Zhou. These chapters suggest that the emphasis on the Duke of Zhou at the expense of the Duke of Shao and King Cheng, who are more prominent in the bronze records, reflected the decline of royal power in later reigns and the rise of ducal and ministerial lines who sought to claim for themselves a place in the Zhou foundation on a par with that of direct descendants of the king. These texts thus acted as charters for the rising power of the nobility.[84]

The Duke of Zhou is not only the archetype and supposed exponent of the virtuous adviser, but also a figure closely associated with the power of writing. First, he is often depicted as practicing tortoise shell divination, an activity that used writing to communicate with the spirits and that was closely linked to his later role as developer of the *Yi*.[85] The *Documents* attribute to the Duke of Zhou instructions to observe earlier laws and to respect written statutes, and also to use written registers of merit both to judge the work of officials and to make a public display of this judgment.[86] The Duke of Zhou also cites as exemplary the Shang's respect for written records and statutes that both allowed them to gain the Mandate and proved that they had received it.[87] Finally, the Duke of Zhou is involved in the activity of writing invocations to the gods that are then read aloud at sacrificial ceremonies.[88] In all these ways he espouses a program of using writing to administer a state and to communicate with the spirits. The "Luo gao" also refers to the act of recording the dialogue that constitutes the chapter, so the chapters were probably considered to be written transcripts of oral performance. Since the Duke of Zhou is the central figure in the Zhou chapters, he is the putative initiator of the recorded speech as literary or historical genre.

Writing invocations to the gods also figures prominently in "Jin teng" (金縢), the chapter that constitutes the most fully developed version of the Duke of Zhou as adviser and master of texts.[89] This chapter is virtually a short story tracing the career of the Duke of Zhou from the immediate aftermath of the conquest to his death. It is divided into two halves that occur several years apart. Both sections revolve around the Duke of Zhou's writing a text and the problem of how it is to be read.

The first half of the story takes place two years after the Zhou defeat of the Shang. While the Zhou's position had yet to be secured, King Wu fell ill. Dukes Tai and Shao suggested a divination, following the conventional practice to identify the spirit causing the disease and the number of sacrifices necessary to obtain a cure. The Duke of Zhou rejected this idea, and on his own initiative prepared a ritual in which he offered himself in lieu of the conventional sacrifice. For this purpose he erected three altars, one for each of the three preceding monarchs. He had his scribe write an invocation that was then read to the spirits. In this speech he announced the king's illness and offered himself as a substitute. He explained that he had more talents and arts than King Wu and hence was better able to serve the spirits. King Wu was the holder of the Mandate and his death would lead to the collapse of Zhou's newly won suzerainty. Finally, he announced that he would divine in order to learn the decision of the ancestral spirits. He made three divinations, all favorable, and also obtained a positive response from a written oracle extracted from a box. He then placed the tablets with the text of the invocation in a metal-bound box. The next day the king recovered.

The second part of the story follows immediately on the death of King Wu some years later. Several of the Duke of Zhou's brothers spread the rumor that he was planning to usurp the throne from the young King Cheng. The duke vowed to punish the malefactors in order to be able to "report to the former kings." He then "resided in the east" for two years—usually understood as his expedition, although Shaughnessy suggests it was the exile mentioned in later texts—and the culprits were captured. The Duke of Zhou composed the poem "The Owl" and presented it to the king, who "did not dare to criticize the duke," a phrase that suggests he did not understand the import of the poem and remained suspicious. At this time a great storm flattened both the ripened harvest and great trees. The king then had the metal-bound box opened, and discovered the text in which the Duke of Zhou had offered his life in exchange for that of King Wu. The king proclaimed that there was no need to divine regarding the import of the storm, which was recognized as a response to the duke's virtue. The king personally went out to receive the returning duke, a "reverse" wind miraculously restored the harvest, and Dukes Shao and Tai led the people to replant the trees.

Given the importance of this story in the mythology of the Duke of Zhou and the centrality of the issue of writing, it requires some discussion. The story is an elaborate parable on the powers and dangers of texts. The most important writing is the invocation (*zhu ci* 祝辭) that dominates the first half and leads to the resolution in the second. This text is generally regarded as a literary version of actual religious practice, and scholars have analyzed it for insights into the religious beliefs and practices of the Eastern Zhou, as well as the religious origins of certain features of the literature of the period.[90] Fujino Iwatomo has pointed out three features that are significant in literary developments: (1) use of the first-person, (2) relation to ancestors, and (3) a vaunting of one's own talents and depreciation of others. This last feature was problematic for later Chinese readers, but it was probably important for establishing one's credentials to make claims on the spirits. It and the other two features figure prominently in works such as the "Li sao." In this way the Duke of Zhou appears here as a precedent for subsequent developments in writing the self. The specific nature of his talent (*cai* 材) and arts (*yi* 藝) is not specified, and since they are related to "serving the spirits" they might well refer to his abilities as a religious intermediary. However, by the late Warring States period *yi* had come to refer to the social arts embodied in the Confucian literary canon. Whatever the intent of the author, the story thus provided a *locus classicus* for identifying the Duke of Zhou as a scholarly predecessor of Confucius.

The text is also notable in that it consists of an appeal by the Duke of Zhou to substitute himself for King Wu. It is closely related to stories of King Tang offering to immolate himself in order to obtain relief from a drought, and textual versions of Tang's address to the spirits are linked to that of the Duke of Zhou.[91] Since the Duke of Zhou plays the role of Tang, offers himself as a substitute for the king, and claims superiority in talent and arts to the king, the invocation insists on the Duke of Zhou's status as equivalent to a king and anticipates the doctrine of Confucius as the "king without attributes." The substitution is also noteworthy in that the Duke of Zhou does not in fact die. It is the text, and not the duke, that takes the place of King Wu and is sealed in the box. In this way writing is able to guide the spirits and to stand for the person of the one who composes it.

Writing also figures prominently in the first half of the story in the act of divination. The three divinations by tortoise shell require the reading of the cracks as visual signs composed of lines, and may have involved a process of inscription. More important, the divination by shell is paralleled by a divination through extracting written documents, almost certainly on strips, from a locked chamber. This process of removing writing from a sealed place is the reverse of the sealing up of the invocation that immediately follows, and the process of unlocking writing will recur in the second half. Such processes of hiding or disclosing writing—as in the burying of covenant texts or the address to the spirits at the *feng* and *shan* sacrifices or the receiving of revealed texts—were fundamental to communications with spirits in the period.

In the second half of the story writing figures twice, first in the poem and second in the inspection of the contents of the sealed box. The poem supposedly written by the Duke of Zhou is preserved in the *Odes*, and in attributing it to him on this occasion the authors anticipate the strategy of the Mao commentary by explaining the meaning of poems through inserting them in a historical narrative.[92] The applicability of the poem to the duke's situation is not immediately apparent, but it could be read as a plaint of being subjected to slander and abuse. The story echoes the *Zuo zhuan*'s accounts of presenting odes in order to express one's intent, but there are two major differences. First, the Duke of Zhou does not quote a poem but *composes* one. Second, he does not recite it but *writes* it and sends it to the king. The first difference reflects the fact that the duke was one of the creators of the Zhou order. His role as *author* of an ode anticipates the later belief that he created many of the texts that Confucius transmitted. The second strengthens the tendency of the story to portray the Duke of Zhou as a man who acted through writing, and to emphasize the powers of writing as a mode of control and of testimony. This point is emphasized by the fact that the duke's writing serves to combat "speech" (*yan* 言) spread by his rivals.

This last point, however, requires a qualification, for the poem does not achieve its goal. The king cannot read the duke's character or intent in his verse. In the *Zuo zhuan* stories on the uses of verse such failures are indicative of the ignorance and moral failings of the auditor/reader, and such seems to be the case here. King Cheng in this story cannot recognize the virtue of the Duke of Zhou but gives credence to slanders. In this he is like the kings bemoaned in the odes of isolation and the "Li sao." The story emphasizes his failures as a reader by narrating that even after he has opened the box and read the text of the duke's invocation, he insists on having oral confirmation from the scribe and other participants that the actions indicated in the writing actually took place. These witnesses confirm the event, but state that the Duke of Zhou had forbidden them to speak of it. Thus the duke always relies on writing and forbids speech, while the slanderers rely on speech, which the king trusts. After the oral confirmation the king confesses his own ignorance, orally confirming what his double failure to read has already made clear. He also states that there is now no need to divine the meaning of the storm, thus directly equating the opening of the chest and the reading of the invocation text with the Duke of Zhou's opening of the locked chamber and reading of the divinatory text.[93] Although King Cheng chooses not to divine, Heaven sends its own message in the form of the reverse wind. This gratuitous underlining of the duke's virtue—Heaven has already displayed the duke's virtue in the earlier storm, as King Cheng himself notes—emphasizes the inadequacy of the king's reading.

It is worth noting that the division of the story into two halves obscures its mechanics and thus hides away its message to be revealed at the end to those capable of reading it. In the story the Duke of Zhou writes the invocation in the first half to rescue King Wu and the poem in the second to justify himself. However, within the complete narrative, the beneficiary of the invocation is not King Wu but rather the Duke of Zhou. This is marked by the fact that due to the ellipsis of several years, the report of King Wu's recovery is followed immediately by the proclamation of his burial as an accomplished fact. Within the economy of the narrative, the king's recovery was equivalent to his death, because it ended his sole raison d'être. This indecent haste to get the king out of the way indicates that he was simply a (literal) *pretext* for the invocation, and the whole first half simply serves to account for the existence of the hidden text that will magically appear in the second to rescue the Duke of Zhou's reputation from the incompetence of his readers. Although King Cheng declares the moral of the story to be the Duke of Zhou's diligence in the cause of the royal house, the narrative reduces the royal father and son to the role of props in the duke's repeated inscription of his own excellence. The story thus covertly echoes the duke's overt claims to be superior to the king, or rather both kings, and in some sense it justifies the slanderers in their assertions of the Duke of Zhou's royal ambitions. This doubled conclusion, in which the duke is both loyal servitor and king by right, reflects the basic commitment of the authors, for whom the Duke of Zhou's refusal to seek the title of king proves his possession of the substance. This kingship in turn is doubly textual, for it is marked in the story through the texts he writes, and marked in the broader intellectual sphere through the text of the "Jin teng."

As archetypal minister and royal double, the Duke of Zhou was adopted by the *ru* and the Mohists as a prescholastic precedent for claims to the authority of wise men and masters of text. This position is only hinted at in the *Lun yu*, where in the early chapters Confucius recognizes his personal decline because he no longer sees the Duke of Zhou in his dreams and uses him as the archetype of the "talented" (*cai* 才) man.[94] The *Mencius* invokes the figure of the Duke of Zhou in several passages. A disciple pairs the Duke of Zhou with King Wen as reliable teachers. This reiterates the idea that the duke was a double for the king and associates both of them with scholarship.[95] The close links to Confucius noted in the *Lun yu* are likewise developed. One passage identifies the *ru* cultural and literary tradition as the "Way of the Duke of Zhou and Confucius." Another summarizes the restoration of order after the flood in the sequential work of three sages: Yu, the Duke of Zhou, and Confucius. A third pairs Confucius and the Duke of Zhou as two "men who possess the virtue of a Shun or a Yu" but do not become rulers.[96] A final passage emphasizes the role of the Duke of Zhou as a scholar. It lists the virtues of the founders of the Three Dynasties and states that the Duke of Zhou tried to combine all their achievements and administrations through study and reflection.[97]

The *Mozi* cites the Duke of Zhou less frequently, but the passages are significant. One cites the story of the Duke of Zhou's retirement to the east to demonstrate that sages do not fear slander or covet rewards. This develops the theme of the Duke of Zhou's response to slander that figured so prominently above. Ultimately it develops into an argument that for scholars righteousness (*yi* 義) is more important than seeking a salary through state service.[98] The Duke of Zhou as a model for scholars is developed further in a passage that describes him reading one hundred strips every morning, which enabled him to become the servant of kings and be known in later ages.[99] This passage is attributed to Mo Di himself, who cites it to justify the large numbers of texts that he carries on his travels. Even the arch-critic of the *ru* was believed by his disciples to have patterned himself and his reading practices on the Duke of Zhou.

The fullest development of the Duke of Zhou as both figure of the virtuous minister and archetype of the textual scholar appears in the *Zuo zhuan*. He most frequently is mentioned in the text, which is centered on Lu, as the first lord of that state. However, several passages cite him as the image of the virtuous minister, and others treat him as the founding genius of the dynasty who created the major Zhou institutions.[100] The passages that reflect on his virtues as minister often note his willingness to kill his own brothers in the service of the dynasty.[101] Since the celebration of the Duke of Zhou as a model minister is often associated with the rise of the ducal and ministerial lines, it is significant that the *Zuo zhuan* refers to sacrifices being offered to the Duke of Zhou by states other than his own fief of

Lu.[102] Such sacrifices were the counterpart in the religious realm of the theory of collective ministerial power as the rule of virtue that was articulated in several chapters of the *Shang shu*. They also anticipate the sacrifices of scholars to Confucius that figure prominently at the end of his *Shi ji* biography (see below).

While not specifically devoted to the Duke of Zhou, several passages in the *Zuo zhuan* also discuss the theory of ministerial power. Perhaps the most notable is a discussion by the Astrologer Mo as to why the people of Lu and rulers of other states accepted the ministerial houses' expulsion of the duke.

> Things are born in two's, three's, five's, and in doubles (*pei er* 陪貳). So Heaven has the three lights, Earth has the five phases, the body has left and right, and everyone has his or her mate. The king has his dukes, and the dukes their ministers, so each has his double. Heaven produced the Ji clan to assist/double the Duke of Lu, and they have done this for a long time. So is it not right for the people to submit [to the usurpation]? For generations the princes of Lu have abandoned themselves to their errors, and the Ji clan for generations have cultivated their diligence. So the people have forgotten their ruler. Even though he dies in exile, who will grieve for him? Rulers and ministers have no constant positions, and it has been thus since antiquity.[103]

Mo cites the *Odes* and the *Changes* to prove his point. This argument that the minister is the double of the ruler gives a theoretical form to the role of the Duke of Zhou in the "Jin teng" and other chapters of the *Shang shu*. The same argument appears elsewhere, where it is extended to cover the relation of the collateral lines to the central one. The character *er* 貳 figures in nonpolitical uses to refer to a second or reserve chariot that accompanied the primary chariot in case of emergencies, and a second individual who assisted the man in charge of "seeing off the funeral" (*song zang* 送葬).[104] The term "double" (*er*) also was applied to sons, and more ominously to rebels.[105] This complex of minister, assistant, collateral line, son, and rebel combines all the roles of the Duke of Zhou, for in the *Xiao jing* he is celebrated as the model of filiality in that he created the procedure of sacrificing to one's ultimate ancestor as the ritual "partner/mate" (*pei* 配) of Heaven, and to one's father as the *pei* of God-on-High.[106] While he was not a rebel in the *ru* tradition, he was accused of being so in several contexts, such as the "Jin teng" or the legalist tradition. Moreover, as patron of the ducal lines and ministerial houses that claimed to represent the rule of the most worthy, he was implicated in the dismantling of the Zhou order that he was also credited with creating.

In addition to being the patron of nonroyal power, the Duke of Zhou also appears in the *Zuo zhuan* as the founder of Zhou institutions. One passage credits him with the invention of the practice of "enfeoffment" (*feng jian* 封建) in response to the rebellion of Shang subjects in the east.[107] Another refers to a covenant between the Duke of Zhou and Duke Tai of Qi, one of the earliest, if not the earliest, recorded covenants for interstate relations.[108] So the Duke of Zhou figures as an initiator not only of the feudal structure, but also the basic mechanism of interstate relations.

The reference to the covenant is significant because it is a form of writing, and the Duke of Zhou's role as founder and embodiment of the Zhou state is often linked to his textual activities. One passage cites him as the creator of the Zhou ritual system, and it attributes a book named the "Rituals of Zhou" (*Zhou li* 周禮) to him.[109] This is probably not the received text of that name, but because of the tradition that the Duke of Zhou had instituted Zhou rites, the latter was often treated as his work. The clearest linkage of the Duke of Zhou as dynastic founder and master of texts appears in the story of the mission to Lu by Han Xuanzi of Jin, a story of interest in that it depicts men traveling long distances to examine texts.

> He examined the writing in the charge of the Grand Astrologer (*tai shi* 太史). He saw the *Yi*, the *Images*, and the Lu *Spring and Autumn Annals*. He said, "The rituals of Zhou [or '*Rituals of Zhou*'] all survive in Lu. I only now know the virtue of the Duke of Zhou and the reason that the Zhou became kings."[110]

The speaker in this passage links the Duke of Zhou's virtue with the Zhou's ability to establish their dynasty, and both are revealed through a list of texts preserved in the duke's fief. At the head of the list are the *Yi* and the *Xiang*, which probably refer to some version of the line and image judgments in the *Zhou yi*. This is probably the earliest evidence of the belief that the *Yi* text was created at the foundation of the Zhou. In his role as putative author of the literary heritage of the Zhou, the Duke of Zhou came to stand not only for the political institutions but also for the Zhou civilization as a whole. In a quarrel that pitted Lu against the states of Zhu (邾) and Ju (莒), the spokesman for Lu describes the conflict as one between "the descendants of the Duke of Zhou," on the one hand, and the "barbarians" (*man yi* 蠻夷) on the other.[111] In addition to being the putative creator of the Zhou institutions, the author of texts that preserved the memory of these institutions after they had fallen into decay, and the embodiment of civilization, the Duke of Zhou was also the first lord of Lu. Statutes that he had written are cited by Confucius in the *Zuo zhuan*.[112]

All these passages mark a major development in ideas about writing. In a world where the Zhou monarchy had all but disappeared, it survived in the form of a body of texts: the *Changes*, the *Spring and Autumn Annals*, the *Ritual*, and the statutes of Lu. To this list we can add the *Odes*, for in the story of Ji Zha's visit to Lu, which in many ways anticipates that of Han Xuanzi, the entire history of the Zhou is revealed in the musical performance of the odes. Just as it is the Duke of Zhou whose virtue appears in the other texts, so the glory of the Zhou in the early odes reveals the virtues of the Duke of Zhou, Duke Tai, and King Wen.[113] Simultaneously the servant of kings, the patron sage of the ducal and ministerial houses, the archetype of the man who governs through the mastery of texts, and the embodiment of the civilizing process, the Duke of Zhou formed a human bridge linking theories of monarchy as the rule of virtue and the ideal of rule by the master of textual traditions. As regent and royal brother who textually generated the Zhou state, he plays the same role in the mythology of governance through texts as he does in the mythology of the *Yi*, to act as the transition between Fu Xi—where wisdom and political authority were united in the figure of the actual king who was also a sage—and Confucius—where wisdom and political authority were divided in reality but united in the realm of texts.

THE MYTHOLOGY OF CONFUCIUS

By the late Warring States period Confucius was the archteype of the scholar and the master of textual authority. He was the patron sage of the *ru* textual traditions and the figure against whom the Mohists defined themselves. The *Zhuangzi* invoked his authority to sanction its gallery of anonymous sages, and the *Han Feizi* and *Lü shi chun qiu* likewise placed teachings in his mouth. He was the ultimate authority for the authors of the *Zuo zhuan*, and the *Gongyang* commentary put him at the center of its theory of a text-based kingship. This elevation of Confucius culminated in the Han, and the triumph of Confucianism after the middle of the first century B.C. made him the most exalted figure in Chinese civilization.

While the earliest texts pertaining to Confucius were quotations attributed to him or remarks about him, a body of anecdotes about his life had emerged by the middle of the Warring States period. These accumulated into a substantial body of materials that formed a mythology of Confucius, which dealt with the relations of textual authority and political power. The earliest narrative (ca. 100 B.C.) that covers his entire life appears in Sima Qian's *Shi ji*. This is an episodic compilation from earlier sources of anecdotes which were adjusted, combined, and reworked by Sima Qian to convey his understanding of the sage. It is of limited value as a history of Confucius, but of tremendous importance for an understanding of Sima Qian's literary project. When combined with references in other sources it offers invaluable insights into the image of the scholar and his political role in the late Warring States and early imperial periods.

As Stephen Durrant has argued in his recent book, Sima Qian sees in Confucius above all a pattern for his own life, with a failed political career being redeemed by literary labors in his final years.[114] Although this interpretation is certainly true for Sima Qian's account of Confucius taken as a whole, the use of earlier sources means that it is also an anthology of Confucius anecdotes from the Warring States, and many of the episodes can be found in alternate versions in texts prior to or contemporary with the *Shi ji*. Many voices speak through Sima Qian's account, and when combined with fragmentary anecdotes from other sources it offers a useful template for studying the way in which Confucius was understood, and the manner in which accounts of him were employed, at the beginning of the imperial period.

Sima Qian's presentation of Confucius can be divided into four parts: tales of birth and childhood, tales of his government career, tales of travels and travails, and the final account of his literary works.[115] The first section is the briefest, but it contains a significant birth legend that announces Confucius' nature as a sage ruler and dynastic founder.

[Shuliang] He had intercourse with Lady Yan in the wilds [*ye he* 野合] and she gave birth to Confucius. They prayed at Ni Hill [*ni qiu* 尼丘] and obtained Confucius. . . . When he was born his head was indented in the center and rose up on all sides, so they called him Qiu [丘 "hill" or "tomb mound"]. His style was Zhong Ni 仲尼, and his surname Kong.

When Qiu was born his father died and was buried at Mt. Fang. Mt. Fang is east of Lu, so Confucius was uncertain about where his father was buried. His mother refused to speak of it. When a boy, Confucius loved to play at setting out ritual vessels and adopting ritual postures.[116]

Chinese commentators have devoted considerable energies to explaining away or suppressing the reference to "intercourse in the wilds." However, in most accounts of the divine paternity of sages the mother encounters the spirit outside the regions of human habitation. The reference to the prayer for a child is also a common feature in such stories.[117] The magical impregnation of the sage's mother is confirmed by the fact that Confucius has the physical attributes of the hill or tomb mound where the prayer took place, and that both his name and style are derived from it. The immediate removal of his human father through death and a hidden burial site strengthens the case for divine paternity. His youthful love of ritual performance bespeaks the influence of the funerary mound whose spirit was his sire.[118] The theme of Confucius as a [super]natural prodigy is emphasized in an anecdote that when he was only seventeen a dying nobleman instructed his sons to study rituals with the future sage.[119] The apocryphal literature presents Confucius' spirit paternity in detail, and the linkage of spirit conception and unusual physical appearance found in the *Shi ji* remains standard in later accounts.[120] In this way the *Shi ji* story assimilates Confucius to the status of the earlier sage kings and dynastic founders, but makes him distinctively a sage of ritual and cult.

The account of Confucius' public career begins with a story emphasizing his sagehood by noting that when he served as a low-level keeper of records for the Ji lineage, their livestock flourished.[121] The *Shi ji* account also marks Confucius' sage nature by including the stories from the *Guo yu* in which he names and glosses natural prodigies, ancient bones, and objects from the distant reaches of the earth.[122] However, the account of Confucius' service focuses not on his semimagical powers, but rather on his brilliance as a ritualist and adviser, on his devotion to reinforcing the ruler's power and the rule of law, and on his severity as a judge. These themes are marked in several incidents that appear in numerous early sources.

The most important of these is the meeting of the rulers of Lu and Qi at Jiagu.[123]

In the summer, the Qi minister Li Ju said to Duke Jing [of Qi], "If Lu employs Kong Qiu, its power will threaten Qi." So they sent an emissary to tell Lu that there would be a meeting for peace, and they met at Jiagu. When Duke Ding of Lu was about to mount and depart, Confucius, acting as the duke's assistant for the event, said, "I have heard that in civil [*wen* 文] matters one must have military [*wu* 武] preparations, and in military matters one must have civil preparations. In ancient times when feudal lords went outside their frontiers, they invariably were accompanied by a full complement of officials. I request that you bring along the marshals of the right and the left." Duke Ding said, "Excellent," and they brought along the two marshals. They met with the Duke of Qi at Jiagu, and set out the positions on an altar, with three earthen steps. They met with the ceremonies of greeting, and bowing with their hands clasped they ascended the altar. When the presentations of wine were completed, a Qi official hastened forward and said, "Perform the music of the [barbarians of] the four quarters." Duke Jing said, "Excellent." Thereupon with pennants, banners, feathers, barbarian costumes, lances, swords, and shields, they arrived in a tumult of drums. Confucius hastened up the steps, stopped at the penultimate one [because the last was reserved for the rulers], raised his sleeves, and said, "Our two princes have met for peace, what business has barbarian music here! Command the officials [to remove them]." The officials repelled them, but they did not depart. Confucius gazed to the left and the right at Master Yan and Duke Jing. Duke Jing was embarrassed, so he signalled with his banner and sent them off.

A Qi official hastened in and said, "I request a performance of the music of the inner chambers." Duke Jing said, "Good." The clowns and dwarves mockingly advanced. Confucius hastened up the steps, stopped at the penultimate one, and said, "For commoners who confuse feudal lords, the punishment is death. I request that you order the officials [to execute them]." The officials applied the law, and [the entertainers] were drawn and quartered. Duke Jing was frightened and set out. He knew that he was not as righteous [as Confucius], and he returned home greatly afraid. He told his assembled officials, "Lu guides its prince in the Way of the gentleman, but you only instruct me in the ways of barbarians. Having caused offence to the prince of Lu, what can be done about it?" The officials advanced and replied, "If a gentleman commits a fault, he apologizes with some substance; if a petty man commits a fault he apologizes with words [*wen* 文 'empty form']. If you regret it, then apologize with substance." So the Duke of Qi, in order to apologize, returned the territories of Yun, Wenyang, and Guiyin that had been taken from Lu.[124]

Alternative versions of the story appear in each of the three commentaries to the *Chun qiu* chronicle, in the early Han *Xin yu*, and in two other chapters of the *Shi ji*.[125] All versions credit Confucius with gaining the return of the territory, but they differ in the details. Collectively they depict several important elements in the late Warring States and early Han image of Confucius.

The most important point is that Confucius is depicted as a brilliant *official*, rather than a scholar. This insistence on his political activities dominates the chapter, and is essential to the mythology of Confucius in the period. His role as a teacher or head of a school is shifted to a separate chapter devoted to his disciples. Emphasis on Confucius as a model official takes several forms. First, the story highlights his combining the civil arts (*wen* 文) with the martial (*wu* 武). These virtues were definitive of the increasingly specialized servants of the territorial lords, but by combining both Confucius shows himself to be more like a ruler than an ordinary official. His excellence as an official is also marked by the ruthlessness with which he enforces the law by having the executions carried out. This devotion to law was not characteristic of the Confucius depicted in the *Lun yu* or the *Zuo zhuan*, but in this story Confucius has become a model practitioner of late Warring States or early imperial administration. It is as an officer in the ducal service, and one who resembles the "cruel officials" (*ku li* 酷吏) of the Emperor Wu, that Confucius is celebrated. As such he becomes the direct heir of previous sages such as Fu Xi and the Duke of Zhou, who combined actual or de facto rulership with mastery of visual signs, but Confucius is the model minister of the new imperium with its bureaucratic agents and legal codes.

The necessity of combining civil and military skills is asserted at the beginning of the story, and the balance of the account serves to demonstrate that Confucius in fact fulfills this ideal. The point is made even more clearly in other versions of the meeting, which state that the Qi entertainers were in fact intending to kidnap the Duke of Lu. As Sima Qian himself refers to the intended abduction in the "Hereditary Household" chapters of Lu and Qi, he clearly was aware of this tradition and accepted it as accurate. Confucius' insistence on the armed guard, and the listing of the weapons wielded by the first group of musicians, also indicate that a threat was being posed. Confucius was able to thwart it both through advance preparation and an immediate response. However, the theme of the attempted abduction is muted, as is explicit military action, because Sima Qian insists on the need for *civil* or ritual skills as well as military ones. This can be demonstrated through an examination of earlier versions, as well as related stories.

The oldest version of the story, that in the *Zuo zhuan*, divides the narrative into three parts. In the first part the men of Lai, barbarian subjects of Qi, attempt to seize the Duke of Lu. Confucius, however, pulls the duke back and commands the Lu troops to strike. With the threat ended, the covenant proceeds. The men of Qi at the last moment append a clause to the covenant text that requires Lu to provide military support to Qi, but Confucius takes this opening to append a further clause that makes Lu's support conditional on the return of the occupied territories. This rapid ritual response echoes his swift military reaction, and together they allow Lu to thwart Qi's designs. In the final episode the Qi party invite the men from Lu to a banquet, and Confucius delivers an oration explaining why a banquet is ritually inappropriate. On the assumption that the banquet was yet another trap, Confucius' knowledge of ritual permits him to thwart Qi a third time, and also permits the authors to deliver a lesson on aspects of ritual procedure. Here Confucius' textual mastery is indispensable to his efficacy as an official.

The *Shi ji* version cites balancing *wen* and *wu* as a theoretical maxim, but preparation and rapid response eliminate the need for actual military action. This contrasts not only with the explicitly military version in the *Zuo zhuan*, but also with several tales of the use of force during interstate meetings. Most clearly invoked is the story of Cao Mo, who forced Duke Huan of Qi to return territory to Lu by holding a knife to his throat on the altar of a covenant ceremony.[126] Other stories of violence to extract objects, territory, or actions from rulers include those of Mao Sui and Lin Xiangru.[127] Confucius, in contrast, protects his ruler and secures the return of the territory entirely through his mastery of ritual and law.

The theme of ritual correctness, present in the *Zuo zhuan* version, moves to the center of the *Shi ji* narrative. Here two ritual errors function like the paired extremes discussed in chapter 2, which defined a continuum and marked Confucius as holding the middle position. The first dancers, whose armaments and accoutrements mark them as a transformation of the men of Lai, represent the extreme of outside, as they depict the edges of the earth. The second group, who substitute for the abortive banquet, represent the extreme of inside, being music from the inner chambers. Both are inappropriate to a state occasion. In thwarting the first group, Confucius defends civilization from the barbarians, thus playing the role noted earlier for the Duke of Zhou and Guan Zhong. This theme is also emphasized in the versions in the *Guliang zhuan* and the *Xin yu*. In blocking the second group, Confucius defeats a state notorious for its dwarves and entertainers. He thus signals the ritual superiority of Lu over Qi, and by extension of the Duke of Zhou over Duke Tai. The presence of dwarves among the dancers may also be a veiled reference to Yan Ying, who was extremely short. Confucius, in contrast, was very tall. Yan Ying appears in this story as Confucius' rival, standing in the same relation to the Duke of Qi as Confucius does to the Duke of Lu, and in an earlier anecdote he persuaded Duke Jing not to employ Confucius. Thus it is fitting that Confucius' victory should be obtained by halting dwarves.[128]

However, Confucius does much more than halt the dwarves, and the brutality of their punishment has shocked many readers. The version in the *Guliang zhuan* is even harsher, for while the clowns and dwarves in the *Shi ji* might in theory have menaced the Duke of Lu, the *Guliang* speaks of only a single clown. The punishment, nevertheless, is identical. The severity of these punishments, however, is yet another sign of Confucius' role as an exemplary official combining *wen* and *wu*. While *wen* and *wu* were categories of officials and political action, they also defined the realm of law. Throughout the *Shi ji* the character *wen* either by itself or in compound with *fa* 法 means "laws" or "written regulations."[129] Since military actions were explained as a form of punishment, *wu* also included the idea of legal penalties. Consequently *wen*/*wu* meant not only "civil and martial" but also "written statutes and punishments." The *Shang Jun shu* stated, "In all cases rewards are *wen* and punishments are *wu*. *Wen* and *wu* are the epitome of law." Other texts from the period also identify *wen/wu* with law and punishments.[130] While Confucius in the *Shi ji* version no longer commands troops, he demonstrates himself to be *wu* through the severity of his punishments. The execution of the dwarves is a mock battle that succeeds in gaining back territory lost in actual warfare.

This vision of Confucius as legalist administrator was directly rooted in the more conventional *ru* image of the sage as one who passed judgment in texts. In the *Shi ji* narrative Confucius' punishments inspire *fear* in Duke Jing. As noted in chapter 3, the *Mencius* states that in writing the *Chun qiu* Confucius passed judgment on the usurping lords and officials of his age and thereby inspired fear in their hearts. In making Confucius an official who imposed punishments and thereby inspired fear in the feudal lords, Sima Qian has transformed the *Mencius*'s account of textual kingship into a political reality.

Emphasis on Confucius as an enforcer of law figures in different form in the *Gongyang zhuan*, the *Yan tie lun*, and the *Huainanzi*, which do not attribute the return of the territory to events at Jiagu.[131] These texts state that Confucius was serving as an administrator for the Ji clan, and that after only three months in office all violations of the law had ceased. Respect or fear elicited by this extraordinary administrative feat led Qi to return the occupied territories.[132] Details of his administration are not discussed, but the achievements, such as "lost objects on the roads were not picked up," are also used to describe the results obtained by the ruthless enforcement of laws practiced by a cruel official under Emperor Wu.[133]

Confucius' role as judge is also marked in the *Shi ji* through a reference to his execution of Deputy Mao.[134] This is the only specific action credited to Confucius as chief minister. Moreover, like the meeting at Jiagu, the execution of Mao is cited in many late Warring States and early Han sources. It was clearly an important element in the image of Confucius at that time.[135] Once again the portrayal of Confucius as an ideal minister focuses on his use of executions.

The earliest and most detailed account appears in the *Xunzi*. Seven days after becoming minister, Confucius executed Deputy Mao. His disciples protested that Mao was an eminent man in Lu and that his execution could jeopardize Confucius' newly won position. In response Confucius listed Mao's crimes.

> Men possess five true evils, and banditry and theft are not among them. The first is to be treacherous with a mind that widely comprehends. The second is to be resolute in perverse conduct. The third is to engage in disputation using contrived language. The fourth is to have a capacious memory that retains the uncanny. The fifth is to make things smooth when following error. A person who has one of these five cannot escape execution at the hands of the gentleman, and Deputy Mao combines them all. Where he resides he can gather crowds of followers, and his speech is able to disguise heterodoxy and delude the masses. He was strong enough to overturn the right and stand alone [against conventional opinion]. This made him the hero of the petty men. He had to be executed.

This arch-criminal is a non-*ru* philosopher, who preaches doctrines contrary to those espoused by the *Xunzi*, engages in disputation, and gathers crowds of followers.[136] This is demonstrated not only by the crimes, which all are related to comprehension, to speech, and to memory, but also by the initial reference to "banditry and theft" not being among the true evils. This echoes a passage in an earlier chapter.

> This is called the hero of the wicked men [*jian ren* 姦人, the same as the "hero of the petty men"]. When the sage arises he is the first to be executed. Only after that are bandits and thieves [executed]. Bandits and thieves can still reform, but these people cannot change.[137]

This theoretical principle became a historical event in the execution of Mao. Confucius is the sage who arose to punish the prophets of error and re-impose the rule of the Zhou textual heritage. As noted in chapter 3, the *Mencius* argued that the next sage would suppress the doctrines of Yang and Mo, and here the *Xunzi* cast Confucius in that role. Thus the *Shi ji* vision of Confucius as merciless punisher of ritual error and intellectual heterodoxy emerged from the historical visions of the Warring States *ru*.

To emphasize punishment the *Shi ji* and other Han sources engage in censorship. In the *Xunzi* the story of the execution of Deputy Mao is paired with an anecdote in which Confucius releases a son who had engaged in a legal dispute with his father. When the head of the Ji clan protests against this leniency, Confucius argues that such behavior shows that the officials have not instructed the people. Only after they have been carefully instructed should punishment be employed.[138] These two stories demonstrate the distinction, articulated elsewhere in the *Xunzi*, between the irredeemably evil and the educable.[139] However, while the execution of Mao figures prominently in the *Shi ji*, the story of pardoning the son with its appeal to education is omitted. The same is true in most Han sources, for while references to Deputy Mao are frequent, those to the companion story are quite rare.[140] Conventional accounts of Confucius insist that he privileged education and ritual over punishment, but Sima Qian and other Han authors reverse this depiction.

The execution of Deputy Mao is followed by the statement that after three months of Confucius' ministry people no longer charged excessive prices in markets, men and women did not travel together, objects lost in the streets were not picked up, and foreigners no longer sought office in Lu. As noted earlier, the three-month span and the great achievements both figure in the *Gongyang zhuan* and the *Yan tie lun*, where they explain Qi's return of occupied territory.[141] Since they follow immediately on the execution, play the same role as Confucius' actions at Jiagu, and elsewhere are employed to describe the impact of the punishments of cruel officials, the *Shi ji* account indicates that the creation of public order was a result of the ruthless efficiency of his judgments and punishments.

A final story of Confucius as an administrator that appears in several versions concerns his attempt to disarm the leading ministerial lineages, the "Three Huan" (*san huan* 三桓), and to tear down their city walls.[142] As in the drama at Jiagu and the execution of Deputy Mao, the *Shi ji* version of this action depicts Confucius as a bold administrator working in the service of centralism and the absolute power of the ruler. However, the earlier *Gongyang zhuan* provides a different picture of these events. It describes how the Jisun and the Zhongsun lineages besieged two of the cities mentioned in the *Shi ji* account. To explain the significance of this record, the text notes that Confucius was serving the Jisun clan, and that after three months no violations of the law were committed. At that point he advised the Jisun to disarm the rebellious sublineages. Other entries indicate frequent campaigns by the Three Huan lineages to subdue the cities of recalcitrant subordinates.[143] These indicate that Confucius was in the service of the Jisun clan, and that his advice on the disarmament of subordinates was given to a ministerial lineage and not the duke. The *Shi ji* account is unique in making him an adviser of Duke Ding.[144]

The reasons for Sima Qian's revision of the received traditions are clear. Writing in a united empire, he could not present Confucius as a defender of local interests and a servant of usurping nobles. In line with his depiction of Confucius as an exponent of legal administration, he also portrayed the sage as a committed defender of centralized absolutism. Since the meeting at Jiagu took place under Duke Ding, and the *Gongyang* recorded sieges conducted by that ruler at the same time as those staged by the Three Huan, it was easy to make him the recipient of Confucius' proposals for local demilitarization. The content of the advice was unchanged, but it was now addressed to the state's ruler. In this way the meeting at Jiagu, the attempt to reduce the city walls, the execution of Deputy Mao, and the almost miraculous achievement of order formed a single complex in which Confucius figured as the ideal centralizing administrator.

Although Sima Qian was sympathetic to military men and convinced of the importance of military affairs, these anecdotes demonstrating Confucius to have been *wu* as well as *wen* are not simple reflections of the historian's personal sentiments. If that were the case then the stories would not have appeared in so many different sources, some prior to or contemporary with the *Shi ji*. The terms *wen* and *wu* had come to stand for the entire administrative apparatus of the Chinese state, divided between its literary, life-enhancing aspects and its martial, punishing power. Particularly in the great encyclopedic compendia composed under state sponsorship in the Qin and early Han, the appeal for the government to be both civil and military was part of the general aim to be all-inclusive. This was closely linked to the calendrical model of kingship, in which the king practiced virtue in the spring and summer, but engaged in punishments and warfare in the autumn and winter. Ordinary people could only be either *wen* or *wu*, but the sage or the ruler had to be both.[145] The necessity of combining *wen* and *wu* was presented to the Han founder in Lu Jia's observation on the difficulty of ruling the empire on horseback, and references to it are scattered throughout the histories and other Han texts.[146] Emperor Wu proclaimed the combination as an ideal, and Sima Qian declared that the emperor had achieved the desired balance.[147] In insisting on Confucius' combination of *wen* and *wu*, Sima Qian equated the sage to the ideal ruler and assimilated his character to that of the Han emperors.

Confucius' achievements mark the apogee of his public career and the end of the second section of the narrative. In four decades of service he had advanced from a humble background through low administrative posts in the service of the Jisun clan to being chief minister. His administrative successes, like his punishments at Jiagu, inspired fear in the men of Qi.

> They selected eighty of the most beautiful of the women of Qi. They dressed them in patterned [*wen* 文] garments and had them dance the "Music of Kang." With thirty teams of dappled [*wen* 文] horses they sent them as a gift to the Duke of Lu. They displayed the women dancers and the dappled horses outside the Gaomen Gate in the south wall of the city. Ji Huanzi in disguise repeatedly went to look at them. He was going to accept them, so he talked the Duke of Lu into making an excursion along the road. They went to look, and spent the whole day out, thus neglecting government business. Zi Lu said, "Master, you ought to depart." Confucius said, "Lu is about to perform the suburban sacrifice. If they present the portions of meat to the officials, then I will still be able to stay."
>
> Huanzi in the end accepted the gift of the dancers, and for three days did not attend to government. They conducted the suburban sacrifice, but did not give the portions of meat to the officials. Consequently Confucius departed. He spent the night at Chun. Music Master Ji saw him off saying, "Then you do not blame [*zui* 罪] them?" Confucius said, "Would it be all right if I sang the reply?" He sang, "The mouths of women can expel and drive off; the presentation of women can kill and ruin. Sorrow, alas! Wandering, alas! Thus to the end of my days."[148]

Again the account is based on earlier traditions, but carefully reworked to present a version suitable to new political circumstances. The story is spliced together from two narratives that attributed Confucius' departure either to the dancers from Qi or to the failure to receive meat from the suburban sacrifice. To understand Sima Qian's message one must study these accounts and the ways in which he altered them.

The story of the presentation of the dancers appears first in the *Lun yu* and is developed in the *Han Feizi*.[149] The former refers only to the dancers being received by Ji Huanzi and Confucius departing. This account is part of the earlier tradition in which Confucius served the Jisun lineage rather than the ruling house. The *Han Feizi* makes Confucius chief minister and has the dancers received by the duke. It also resembles the *Shiji* version in beginning with an account of Confucius' achievements, noting the fear of the men of Qi, and naming the same man as creator of the stratagem of sending the dancers. It differs, however, in several ways. First, it identifies the duke as Ai rather than Ding. Second, it omits all reference to Ji Huanzi. Third, it omits the suburban sacrifice. Finally, in this version Confucius first remonstrates, and only after the duke refuses to listen does he depart.

Before analyzing the reasons for these differences, one should note the significance of stories of separating rulers from ministers by sending female dancers. The story occurs in several contexts, but the first and most widespread deals with Qin state and the Rong barbarians.[150] In one version from the *Lü shi chun qiu* the Rong are too powerful, so Qin sends female dancers and fine chefs to their king. He loses himself in the pleasures of food and women, kills advisers who remonstrate, and in the end is captured by the Qin army while lying in a drunken stupor. In a second version the Rong king has a brilliant adviser, and the purpose of the stratagem is to lead the king to ignore this official's advice and thereby drive him from the court. This version is adopted in the *Han Feizi* and the *Shiji*. Other versions of the story focus on the theme of alienating a ruler from his best adviser, and this is adopted by the *Shiji* chapter on Confucius.[151]

These stories have several elements relevant to the mythology of Confucius. First, three of the four versions dealing with the Rong king note that he lives at the frontiers of civilization and knows nothing of music. This suggests that women and fine cuisine are particularly dangerous to primitives who lack the ritual cultivation necessary to safely handle physical pleasures.[152] Barbarism and the pleasures of the bed chamber are also the menaces ritually thwarted by Confucius at the Jiagu meeting. However, the opposition between women and advisers that is central to most of the versions has a different origin. In the new political order, dependent ministers replaced autonomous nobles, so the relation of ruler to official was assimilated to that of man to wife or concubine. This idea was articulated in parables on the opposition between men in political service and the ruler's harem or his dancers.[153] This aspect of the story is highlighted by the inclusion of Confucius' song dealing with the danger of women.[154] Thus the story further demonstrates Confucius' role as defender of civilization against the forces of the primitive and of raw physicality, and it links his sagehood with his role as an administrator devoted to the service of his lord.

The analysis must still account for the role of Ji Huanzi, the suburban sacrifice, and the absence of remonstrance. One could argue that the first two are present because they appeared in the earlier sources, but Sima Qian was always free to omit or re-work, as is demonstrated by the omission of remonstrance. Once Sima Qian had changed Confucius from a servant of the Ji clan to a minister of the duke, Ji Huanzi could no longer play the role indicated in the *Lun yu*, but the very reasons for changing the identity of Confucius' lord necessitated the re-introduction of Ji Huanzi in the new guise of internal enemy. Once Confucius became an administrator working for absolutism, and Duke Ding his appreciative sponsor, then the leader of the nobility re-appeared as the chief enemy of Confucius, the internal agent who supported external foes.[155] It is he who first observes the dancers, persuades the duke to go and view them, and thereby lures the ruler away from his duties. Likewise it is he who at the end of the episode acknowledges himself to be the target of Confucius' blame.[156] The importance to Sima Qian of Ji Huanzi's role in the story is marked by the fact that he is given pride of place in the radically abbreviated version in the *Shi ji* chapter on the Lu ruling house.[157]

Like Confucius and masculine officialdom, the sacrifice is opposed to the dancers through their identical relation to the lord.[158] This identity is marked in the text both geographically—the women, like the sacrifice, are located outside the walls of the city—and temporally—the women divert Ji Huanzi and the duke for three days, the period of purification for a sacrifice. However, the sacrifice offers above all a *pretext* for departure without blaming the duke. This is noted in the *Mencius*.

> Those who did not understand [Confucius] thought that it was on account of the meat. Those who understood him thought that it was because [the duke] acted without ritual. Confucius desired to leave on the pretext of a minor fault [*wei zui* 微罪]. He did not desire to depart on account of [the duke's] negligence.[159]

By making the issue a minor ritual failing, Confucius does not condemn the ruler for dereliction of duty. That Sima Qian had this passage in mind is indicated by the repeated use of the character *zui* 罪 in the immediate aftermath of the departure. First the music master asks if Confucius "blames" (*zui*) someone, and at the end Ji Huanzi states that Confucius "blames" (*zui*) him for the dancing girls. Just as Ji Huanzi serves to transfer the blame from Duke Ding, so the introduction of the sacrifice frees Confucius from the onus of condemning his ruler in the act of departing. This also explains why Confucius does not remonstrate about the dancing girls, as he does in the *Han Feizi*, since the pretext of the presentation of meat shifts the issue from general negligence to a specific, minor omission. Each modification in Sima Qian's narrative serves to emphasize Confucius' unswerving devotion to his lord as the embodiment of centralized authority. It also places the story within a broader *ru* tradition of eschewing overt criticism of one's superiors.[160]

The third section of the chapter is devoted to an account of Confucius' travels from state to state, sometimes in search of a ruler who will employ him, sometimes fleeing for his life. As the Chinese scholar Chen Renxi argued, the entire chapter could be said to hinge on the two words "not employed" (*bu yong* 不用). The third section deals primarily with this theme.[161] Stories of Confucius' wandering in search of employment have several origins. First, they explain anecdotes in the *Lun yu* that place Confucius in other states. Second, they reflect the fact that Warring States scholastics increasingly moved from state to state in search of patronage. Several passages in the *Mencius* indicate that he identified the travels of Confucius with his own journeys.[162] Finally, the theme of being alienated from a ruler through the machinations of rivals and of wandering through the world in a fruitless search for justification also echoes the story of Qu Yuan. The section also contains large numbers of lines from the *Lun yu*, and thus demonstrates how Sima Qian converted anthology into biography. Just as the *Mao Commentary* explained the odes by assigning them a place in the history of the Zhou, and as commentators would explain much of the *Chu ci* by linking poems to Qu Yuan's career, so Sima Qian explained quotations in the *Lun yu* by inserting them into his narrative of Confucius' life. The insertion of dialogues with disciples also emphasises Confucius' ability to attract men to him, one of the hallmarks of the ruler.

The section is also marked by the prevalence of stories dealing with physical attacks on Confucius. These figure prominently in several Warring States sources, and versions appear in Western Han anthologies such as the *Han shi wai zhuan* and the *Shuo yuan*. Clearly these anecdotes were of great interest to scholars of the period, including Sima Qian himself. They are relevant here because they develop further the theme of Confucius as a man of both *wen* and *wu*. There are four such stories: the arrest of Confucius in Kuang, the assassination attempt in Song, the battle in Pu, and the siege in the wilds between Chen and Cai.[163]

The first two are versions of a single incident, as suggested in the *Lun yu*:

The Master said, "Heaven has produced this virtue in me, so what can Huan Tui do to me [*qi ru yu he* 其如予何]?"

Confucius was threatened (*wei* 畏) in Kuang. He said, "Since King Wen has died is not the true civilization/writing (*wen*) here with me? If Heaven were going to destroy this civilization/writing, then those who came after him could not participate in it. But since Heaven has not yet destroyed this civilization/writing, then what can the men of Kuang do to me [*qi ru yu he* 其如予何]?"[164]

The use of identical patterns and phrases indicates that the stories are two versions of a single, earlier narrative. While the first quotation lacks a context, a passage in the *Mencius* refers to a Marshal Huan of Song who attempted to kill Confucius. Another passage in the *Lun yu* also indicates that the incident in Kuang involved the threat of death.[165] Thus in both cases Confucius is threatened with death, evokes a special relation to Heaven marked by the receipt of virtue or civilization/texts, and concludes with an identical phrase asserting that those who threaten him cannot succeed. This extends Confucius' character as a man of *wu* to include defiance of death in the service of his intellectual and moral commitments.

While the early *ru* texts contained vague references to assaults on Confucius, more detailed versions appeared in later Warring States and early Han texts. Some of these were used in non-*ru* traditions to mock Confucius' failure. The assault in Song figures in a list of attacks on Confucius in several chapters of the *Zhuangzi*.[166] The attack in Kuang by the late Warring States is described as an "encirclement" (*wei* 圍) or "being seized" (*ju* 拘).[167] A version in the "Autumn Floods" (*qiu shui* 秋水) chapter of the *Zhuangzi* introduces important new elements. First, when surrounded Confucius continued to play on a stringed instrument and to sing. The story also explains that Confucius was attacked because he was mistaken for Yang

Hu, a noble of Lu who had previously assaulted Kuang. Finally, the fact that the misfortune was a matter of chance is used to demonstrate that one's fate is a question of "destiny" (*ming* 命) and of the "time" (*shi* 時). Confucius proclaims, "To know that ruin is 'destiny' and attainment is 'occasion' and thus to have no fear when confronting calamity, this is the heroism of the sage." Mistaken identity, music as an act of defiance, and recognition of destiny became standard elements in Han versions—*Shiji, Huainanzi, Han shi wai zhuan,* and *Shuo yuan*—which insisted more and more on the sage's heroism.

The assault at Pu figures in no early sources. In the *Shiji* Confucius is seized, a disciple cites the incident at Kuang, and once again destiny is invoked as an explanation. A new theme is introduced when the disciple declares that he would rather fight and die than suffer another calamity. A fierce battle ensues, and the men of Pu agree to let Confucius depart if he swears a blood oath not to go to Wey. He immediately violates the oath, and the story concludes with a statement by Confucius that the spirits do not listen to oaths made under duress. This statement does not survive in the literature attributed to Confucius, but it appears to be a quotation and is probably the reason for the creation of the story.[168]

The story of the encirclement at Kuang seems to have developed from that of the assassination attempt in Song, and the battle at Pu was fashioned in turn from the events at Kuang. The siege in the wilds between Chen and Cai, however, was an independent tradition with its own themes. While the other accounts tell of an assault, in its earliest versions this story deals with the theme of hunger. Several late Warring States and early Han texts contain variations of the statement that Confucius was in desperate straits between Chen and Cai, and that for seven or ten days—depending on the text—he and his disciples had nothing to eat.[169]

The theme of hunger appears as an issue in several passages in the *Lun yu* and the *Mencius* that provide a background to the later accounts. Thus a passage in one of the later chapters of the *Lun yu* states,

> In Chen [陳] their grain supply was cut off. All his followers fell ill, and none was able to get up. Zi Lu angrily said, "Does the true gentleman likewise fall into desperate straits?" The Master said, "The gentleman *inevitably* gets into desperate straits, but [the difference is that] when the petty man gets into desperate straits, then he becomes reckless."[170]

This passage is preceded immediately by one in which Duke Ling of Wei asks Confucius about military formations (*chen* 陳). Confucius replies that he knows about ritual vessels but has not studied military affairs, and then departs. The reply plays on the word *chen* 陳, which applied both to maneuvering troops in the field and to laying out vessels for a ceremony. Since the first passage ends with Confucius departing, the next one begins with no speaker, and the two are linked by the character 陳 *chen,* it is possible that they form a single narrative. In this case, the straits of Confucius and his disciples are a direct consequence of his refusal to assist a militarist lord in his ambitions. The inevitability of the true gentleman suffering would then be a consequence of his refusal to comply with immoral demands for the sake of money or position.[171]

The link between integrity and the willingness to suffer hunger was developed in later texts. The *Mencius* described the relation of Confucius to Duke Xiao of Wei as "service because of being nourished by the duke" (*gong yang zhi shi* 公養之仕), in contrast to service where there was a real possibility of putting his Way into practice or where the ruler treated him with great decorum.[172] Another passage presents these as the three reasons for taking service, and the last reason is described as follows.

> He has nothing to eat morning or night, and is so hungry that he cannot get beyond his own door. The ruler hearing of it says, "Although I cannot carry out his Way or follow his words, I would be ashamed to let him die in my territory. Take care of him." This likewise can be accepted, but only to avoid death.[173]

The terms employed here to describe the starving scholar are virtually identical with those applied to Confucius' disciples in certain versions of their starvation between Chen and Cai, so the anecdote probably developed from such discussions of under what conditions one could accept service.

Linking hunger to accepting service leads to the broader issue of eremitism.[174] Within the mythology of the Confucian tradition the theme of eremitism was introduced first through references to Bo Yi and Shu Qi, who became the ultimate exemplars of starvation as a result of refusal to take office, and then through tales of the incident between Chen and Cai. The links of this story to the debate on eremetism are signaled not only in discussions of the propriety of service, but also in repeated references to the disciples being reduced to eating a "stew of pigweed" (*li geng* 藜羹).[175] Warring States and early Han texts use this dish to suggest the coarse fare of the pauper or hermit. It figures as part of an argument in the Han dynasty *Da Dai li ji* on the links of the avoidance of service, an abstemious diet, and moral virtue.

> The benevolent man is endangered, the respectful one does not enter [the court?], the careful one is not sent on missions, the honest and direct have a brush with punishment, those who do not violate principles are in peril of condemnation. Therefore the gentleman stays on the heights of mountains or in the filth of swamps. He gathers acorns, chestnuts, and pigweed to eat, or he lives by means of agriculture in a hamlet of ten households.[176]

Against the background of this debate on the propriety of taking service for the sake of nourishment, the anecdote of Confucius' hunger in the wilds served as a means of attacking or defending his moral character. The *Mozi* states that when starving between Chen and Cai, Confucius accepted food and wine procured for him by his disciples without bothering to ascertain where it had come from or how it had been prepared. Once back in Lu, however, he became punctilious over eating only that which was properly prepared and served. When asked to explain this behavior he replied:

> When one is hungry and in want, then one does not refuse to recklessly take whatever is necessary to survive. When one is satiated, then one puts on a facade of proper conduct in order to give oneself an attractive veneer.[177]

A version in the *Lü shi chun qiu* depicts Confucius mistakenly criticizing a disciple whom he suspects of sampling from the pot before he himself has been served. This likewise shows him degrading himself out of his concern for food.[178]

Other versions argue the opposite case. Assimilating the story to those set at Song, Kuang, and Pu, they insist on Confucius' integrity and heroism in the face of hunger. A second account in the *Lü shi chun qiu* depicts Confucius strumming his *qin* and singing while Yan Hui gathers wild plants to eat. When asked by his disciples how he can sing in the face of adversity, he replies that the only true destitution is to be without virtue. So long as he finds no flaws in his conduct, the gentleman will shrug off calamity like the pine tree passing through winter. He compares himself to the hegemons Duke Huan of Qi, Duke Wen of Jin, and King Gou Jian of Yue, who passed through trials and suffering before rising to eminence.[179] In its use of music, this story adapts from the other incidents. It also shares with them an emphasis on fate, and a program of resignation and self-cultivation in the face of adversity. It differs only in treating suffering as a trial or discipline that leads to later success. Interestingly it employs the hegemons, rather than the earlier kings, as the images of triumph through endurance. This choice of ideal figures gives the story a highly political, rather than an overtly moral stance. It indicates the Warring States origins of the *Shi ji*'s vision of Confucius as a man who combined a belief in law, punishments, and military force with his devotion to ritual. The same themes and exemplary historical personalities are invoked in the *Xunzi*'s version of the story.[180]

A final version of the story asserted that the starvation of Confucius and his disciples was due to an assault by the men of Chen or Cai. The versions above simply noted that they had run out of food or been cut off from supplies, without offering any explanation.[181] By the late Warring States period several texts speak of a "siege" or "encirclement" (*wei* 圍). This is particularly notable in the *Zhuangzi*, where the story figures in a list of assaults on Confucius that is used sometimes in criticism, and sometimes to celebrate Confucius as a Daoist sage who has risen above such worldly concerns as satiety and hunger, or life and death.[182] This version was probably created through the influence of the list of assaults that had already developed. It had the advantage that a story of an attack could lend either sharpness to the critique of Confucian doctrine or glory to the heroism of Confucius, depending on the choice of the author.

The *Shi ji* account includes the earlier versions with a few modifications. First, it identifies the men who encircle Confucius—the nobles of Chen and Cai—and provides them with a motive—to prevent Confucius from going to Chu. It adds an episode in which Confucius recites two lines of verse that evoke his situation to three disciples in turn and asks them to comment. As Durrant has shown, the replies form an inventory of "possible responses to personal trial and frustration."[183] The scene also adapts the stories in the *Lun yu* and *Zuo zhuan* where people are asked to each present a poem, and the listener assesses their choices. It differs in that the poem is assigned by the questioner, and the interpretation is to be judged. Moreover, it shifts the focus from the reading of character to a discussion of the appropriate response to suffering. Yan Hui's answer echoes Confucius' own self-justification in the accounts in the *Xunzi*, the *Lü shi chun qiu* "Shen ren" chapter, the "Qiu shui" and "Rang wang" chapters of the *Zhuangzi*, and the account in the *Han shi wai zhuan*. It could serve as an epitome or moral to the entire third section of the *Shi ji* account.

With its depiction of Confucius singing in the face of adversity, phrases on the inevitable suffering of the gentleman, and the ultimate justification through self-cultivation offered in the response of Yan Hui, the story contains the basic elements of the celebratory reading of the incident that had developed in the late Warring States. The one theme missing is the idea of suffering as a trial through which one passes to attain power in the manner of the hegemons. Although absent from the chapter on Confucius, it appears in references to the Chen-Cai incident elsewhere in the *Shi ji*. Sima Qian includes the encirclement of Confucius in a list of the sufferings undergone by leading ministers in the past, including Shun, Yi Yin, Fu Yue, Lü Shang (Tai Gong), Guan Zhong, and Baili Xi. The later names on the list clearly identify Confucius with the centralizing administrators. In the chapter on Mencius and Xun Kuang, the incident is cited, along with Mencius' difficulties in Qi and Liang, as a counterexample to the lavish patronage enjoyed by Zou Yan. Finally, in Sima Qian's postface the incident between Chen and Cai leads directly to the composition of the *Chun qiu*.[184] Since writing this text was identified as the action of a king, linking its composition to the suffering between Chen and Cai fulfills Confucius' prophecy in the *Xunzi* and the *Lü shi chun qiu*, where he identified himself with the historical hegemons who had endured trials only to triumph as rulers.[185]

The theme of writing defines the fourth section of the chapter. When recalled to Lu Confucius received no office, so he devoted himself to texts for the last three years of his life. Durrant has written a chapter on the emergence of the curriculum of the "Six Arts" defined by the texts associated with Confucius. I will here summarize his presentation and suggest some modifications.[186]

The Confucius of the *Lun yu* cited certain texts or disciplines—*Odes, Documents, Ritual, Music*—as authorities for conduct and the bases of a curriculum. Subsequent *ru* textual traditions cited these with greater frequency, and added quotations from Confucius. The *Mencius* was the first text to cite the *Chun qiu* as a work in which

Confucius played the role of Son of Heaven by rewarding and punishing the nobles of the Spring and Autumn period through his coded judgments. The *Xunzi* was the first to list these five texts (described as *yi* 藝 "social arts") as a curriculum, and it cites the *Yi* (*Changes*) without including it in the list. The *Xunzi* never links Confucius to the texts, but it treats him as a great sage and cites him as an authority equal to the texts. The *Gongyang zhuan*, which treats Confucius as the author of the *Chun qiu*, traced its teacher-disciple transmission back to the *Xunzi*. Finally, several late Warring States texts in other traditions, including the *Han Feizi* and the *Zhuangzi*, refer to Confucius' composition of the *Chun qiu*.[187] Since Han Fei was also a student of Xun Kuang's, it is likely that the latter espoused the theory of Confucius' authorship of the *Chun qiu*. At any rate, the idea was widely held by the late Warring States period.

By the early Han dynasty the *Yi* regularly appeared on lists of the canonical texts, now identified as the "Six Arts" or "Six Classics" (*liu jing* 六經).[188] This was the immediate background to Sima Qian's chapter on Confucius in the *Shi ji*, which contains the earliest surviving explicit assertion that the six classics were all edited or written by Confucius. Moreover, as Durrant notes, it was in this chapter that "the relationship of Confucius to the Six Arts is finally given a specific, biographical shape." That shape, inspired in part by Sima Qian's own experiences, treated literary activity as a consequence of personal sorrow and frustration. Blocked in his attempts to realize his Way, Confucius collected and edited the works of earlier rulers, and himself composed the *Chun qiu*, in order to "complete the Way of the king" and preserve it for the future. The accumulated wisdom of the ancients would not be lost, and Confucius would find in later times the recognition that had escaped him in his own lifetime.

Although these literary activities are the climax of the life and the justification of the biography as explained in the historian's remarks and the postface, the account is quite brief. It begins:

> At the time of Confucius, the Zhou house having declined, ritual and music had been abandoned and the *Odes* and *Documents* were fragmentary. Following the traces of the rites of the Three Dynasties and putting in order the *Documents* and *Traditions*, he went back in time as far as the age of Yao and Shun, and down to [the reign of] Duke Mu of Qin [a reference to the "Qin shi" 秦誓 chapter of the *Shang shu*, recording a speech supposedly delivered in 627 B.C.].

It then describes in a few sentences, largely assembled from the *Lun yu*, how he evaluated and put in order the ritual and historical texts, the odes, and the music. Recalling the stories of Confucius' heroism when under assault, it mentions his strumming the *qin* and singing the odes. Finally it concludes,

> From this time the ritual and music could be presented, and he thereby completed the kingly Way and perfected the Six Arts.[189]

Confucius is credited with collecting and editing the literary remains of earlier rulers, a task made necessary by the deterioration of the ruling Zhou house. His work was a response to the decline of the current kings, and his achievement was to perfect the kingly Way in the guise of the major social arts. This literary work was a substitute for the political path that had been blocked to him.

The sentence on the completion of the kingly Way is followed immediately by the statement that Confucius put in order sections of the *Yi*, followed by a quotation about the *Yi* from the *Lun yu*. This separation of the *Yi* from the rest of his editorial work reflects the fact that the text is not cited as an authority in the *Lun yu*, nor does it figure as part of the curriculum indicated in that work. This is emphasized in the next sentence, which lists the texts which he taught as the *Odes*, *Documents*, *Ritual*, and *Music*.

This summary of his editorial and teaching activities is followed by quotations from the *Lun yu* pertaining to his ritual conduct and his speech. These are followed in turn by the capture of the *qilin*, the event which conventionally served as the immediate impetus for Confucius' composition of the *Chun qiu*.[190]

> They hunted at Daye, and a charioteer of the Shusun clan, Ju Shang, captured a beast. They thought it was inauspicious. Confucius looked at it and said, "It is a *qilin*." So they took it. Confucius said, "The Yellow River produces no chart and the Luo River no writing. I am finished!" Yan Yuan died, and Confucius said, "Heaven is slaying me." When he went hunting in the west and saw the *qilin* he said, "My Way is used up."

The version is adapted from the concluding passage of the *Gongyang zhuan*.[191] It differs in the addition of the motif derived from the *Guo yu* of the identification of the prodigy, the reference from the *Lun yu* to the chart and the writing, and the deferral of a reference to the death of a second disciple.

Nevertheless, both treat the composition of the *Chun qiu*, the sole text of which Confucius is the putative author, as an expression of despair. Either preceded or framed by the deaths of his favorite disciples, begun with the proclamation of his own imminent end, his writing apppears as a form of final testament or suicide note. The *Shi ji* follows with the statement that the *Chun qiu* was written to be read by later generations (*hou shi* 後世), quoting the *Mencius*'s remark about those who would recognize Confucius, or blame his hubris, through reading the *Chun qiu*.[192] Nor is the comparison to a suicide note excessive, for in his postface Sima Qian assimilates Confucius' writing the *Chun qiu* to Qu Yuan's writing the "Li sao."

> Previously the Earl of the West [King Wen] was imprisoned at Youli and elaborated the *Zhou yi*. Confucius was starved between Chen and Cai and wrote the *Chun qiu*. Qu Yuan was banished and wrote the "Li sao." Zuo Qiu lost his sight and produced the *Guo yu*. Master Sun [Bin] had his leg cut off and discoursed on military methods.

Lü Buwei was exiled to Shu, and the ages transmit the *Lü shi chun qiu*. Han Fei was imprisoned in Qin and wrote the chapters "Shuo nan" and "Gu fen." The three hundred odes in general were composed by worthies and sages who vented their rage. These people had intentions that were blocked up, and they were unable to carry out their Way. So they narrated things past, while thinking of those yet to come.[193]

Behind these executions, suicides, and mutilations lay Sima Qian's own castration and his decision to complete his work in order to justify himself and his father, rather than commit suicide as expected. Once again authorship is a sign of disaster and the rupture of proper human ties. Far from being the hero's prize, the Golden Fleece suggested by Durrant's misapplication of Campbell's hero myth, Confucius' composition was interpreted by the *Gongyang* and by Sima Qian as a cry of despair cast into the void in the hope that someone might read it and grasp the author's intentions. Sima Qian's vision here of the Confucian texts is not far from that of the *Huainanzi*, which noted that they were written to counter the disappearance of the kingly way, but as mere written vestiges they were hollow counterfeits of true kingship.[194]

However, if writing was the action of the outcast, the cripple, and the man of sorrows, it was also a transformation of kingship. This was seen in the figure of the Duke of Zhou, who fashioned the literary heritage of the state that he shaped without ruling, and it is echoed in the figure of his double, King Wen, who here writes as a prelude to assuming the kingship. It is also, as was discussed in chapter 3, the form of Confucius' kingship. This idea figured in the *Mencius*, where the writing of the *Chun qiu* was Confucius' version of the punishment of the guilty and the expulsion of the beasts performed earlier by Yu and the Duke of Zhou. It was developed into the doctrine of the "king without attributes" of the *Gongyang*, as well as the opposition of "text" (*wen* 文) and "reality" (*shi* 實) in the same work. It underlay the theory, discussed in chapter 3, of the *Chun qiu* as model for legal judgment, a theory also developed in the *Shi ji* and the *Huainanzi*.[195] Similarly, the Mao commentary reads the *Odes* anthology as a textual version of the Zhou state. Finally, the theory of the *Chun qiu* as a form of rule was expressed as a model of history, in which its textual kingship was the successor to the actual kingship of the Three Dynasties. Thus the *Huainanzi* stated, "The Yin [Shang] changed the Xia, the Zhou changed the Yin, and the *Chun qiu* changed the Zhou."[196] The *Shi ji* articulates a much more elaborate theory in which the Six Arts are mapped onto the succession of rulers, with the *Chun qiu* being the final text in the chain.

Fu Xi was supremely pure and generous, so he created the hexagrams of the *Yi*. As for the apogee of Yao and Shun, the *Shu* records it, and the *Li* and *Yue* were created then. At the peak of Tang and Wu, the poets [*shi ren* 詩人] sang their praises. The *Chun qiu* adopts the good and condemns the bad. It extends the virtues of the Three Dynasties and praises the Zhou house.[197]

This same idea appears in the apocryphal literature of the Han dynasty in the theory that Confucius had been the ruler who corresponded to the phase "water," and hence was known as the "black" Confucius.

However, the theory of a purely textual kingship easily turns into an empty fantasy of royalty, as both the *Gongyang zhuan* and the *Huainanzi* suggest. This difficulty probably explains the structure of the *Shi ji* chapter on Confucius. The bulk of the text is devoted not to the textual activities that ultimately justify its inclusion, but rather to Confucius' actions in the world, first as a wielder of punishments in the name of central authority and then as a leader of disciples and a model of endurance in the face of physical assault. Because Confucius' role as the leading exponent of *wen* was common knowledge, the task of the author was to show his *wu* aspect. Placing his chapter apart from those of all other scholars in the category of the hereditary households made sense only to the extent that he was a political figure and a dynastic founder, so Sima Qian devoted himself to showing Confucius as a man of action in the world.

No amount of literary dexterity could convert Confucius into an actual king, so the chapter closes with an element of the myth of Confucius that lent substance to his textual kingship. Contemplating writing the *Chun qiu*, Confucius first asks how he can reveal himself to later ages, and then closes with a prophecy.

> As for the meaning of [the *Chun qiu*'s] condemnations, later there will be a king who will take it and open it. The righteousness of the *Chun qiu* will be put into practice, and the world's rebellious ministers and criminal sons will fear it.[198]

The fear inspired by the *Chun qiu* is borrowed from the *Mencius*, but there it was treated as a reality of Confucius' day, whereas Sima Qian takes the more plausible position that it will inspire fear only when put into practice by a later ruler. The future invoked in the prophecy was Sima Qian's present, and the king who would wield the *Chun qiu* and strike fear into the hearts of ministers and sons was Emperor Wu. This ruler's sponsorship of *ru* scholasticism and his establishment of erudites for each of the classics gave political substance to the empty patterns of Confucius' textual kingship. It was as a prophet of the Han, and the spiritual ancestor of the Han literati, that Confucius' text-based authority became a reality in the world.

The theory of Confucius as a prophet of the Han had been formulated in the *Gongyang* tradition, and Sima Qian incorporated it into his own account. It comes to fruition in two passages that follow Confucius' death in the narrative. The first gives an elaborate account of the emerging cult of Confucius. It describes how the disciples observed a three-year period of mourning by his tomb, a village of more than one hundred households grew up around it, the state of Lu began to offer seasonal sacrifices, and associations of *ru* began to perform rituals in its vicinity. A temple was established that contained Confucius' clothing, the *qin* that he had played in so many stories, his carriage, and his texts. The Han founder had offered sacrifice there, and officials paid their respects at the tomb before taking office.

In the second passage Sima Qian exclaims that in reading Confucius' works he can see what sort of man he was. This shows that the prophetic intent of Confucius was fulfilled also in Sima Qian himself, who recognizes the sagehood of the master through the works written in hope of such a future reading. Sima Qian describes a visit to the tomb of Confucius where he witnessed the activities of scholars. He concludes:

> There have been many princes and worthies in the world. Glorious in their own day, they died and that was the end of them. Confucius was a commoner, but his name has been transmitted for more than ten generations, and scholars treat him as their fixed, ultimate ancestor. From the Son of Heaven and the nobility [on down], all those in the Middle Kingdom who speak of the Six Arts find the correct, "middle way" in the Master. He can be called the supreme sage.[199]

Kingship is demonstrated by the ability to draw men to oneself, to receive their tribute, to command their actions, and to guide their speech. In all these ways the deceased Confucius and his tomb had emerged as a force in the world. The role of Confucius as founder of a dynastic line is realized in his establishment as the ultimate ancestor of Han scholarship in a cult that turned textual traditions into a lineage. This ability to endure through time and to summon men across space depended on the power of the texts disseminated under Confucius' name. Having been transformed from a teacher into a ruler of empty pattern, he became a true ruler of men through the capacity of the texts to make him once again a teacher.

CONCLUSION

The sequence of Fu Xi, the Duke of Zhou, and Confucius traced out a history of the relation between texts and political authority. Fu Xi combined the roles of creator of kingship, inventor of the graphic signs that evolved into writing, and father of the human race. The overlap of these three roles mythically marked the unique status increasingly attributed to writing, which was both the ultimate foundation of civilization and a parallel world with its own dynamism and reproductive powers. The Duke of Zhou embodied the first split between mastery of signs and political authority. Invented as a political philosopher in texts that asserted the power of the nobility vis-à-vis the king, he became the classic figure of the textual sage who ruled in fact without having the royal office. Cast in the role of royal double and regent, he ultimately developed into the mythic creator and patron of the textual heritage of the Zhou. In this guise he became a model for scholars. The process of the separation of text from state was completed in the figure of Confucius. First a model of the teacher, he became an uncrowned king who legislated and passed judgment in the form of the writing of history or commentary. This vision of a purely textual kingship was in turn rewritten as a biography in which Confucius first acted as ruling minister and high judge, and when cut off from the possibility of government transferred his efforts to the editing and composition of texts. In this biography textual authority became a substitute for actual rulership. This substitute formed of empty words was finally given substance by a sacrificial cult that established Confucius as founder of the lineage of scholars. The kingship of Confucius also served as a prophecy of the re-unification of textual authority and political power in the person of an emperor who would also be a sage.

Although three-stage models of history were conventional in Warring States and early Han China, no single text presents this model of the evolving links of writing and political power. However, Fu Xi, the Duke of Zhou, and Confucius were linked in the tradition, noted in the introduction to this chapter, that they together over the centuries produced the *Yi jing*. This text was regarded as the ultimate origin of writing and the fundamental treatment of the powers of visual signs. The conflation in a single text of the primal visual signs, linguistic notation of their meanings, and extended essays on their significance led the first commentators to seek underlying coherence through the hypothesis of a sequential composition. In this model the text recapitulated the cultural history that the schoolmen had created in order to link themselves to the originary moment of the cosmos. The exact number of authors and their respective roles was the object of debate in the later history of "classical studies" (*jingxue* 經學), but the basic outlines had been established by the end of the Warring States period. This schema consisted of three stages that paralleled the political history of textual power sketched above.

First, the trigrams were discovered in the natural patterns of the world by the first of the sages, Fu Xi. That this figure was placed at the beginning of the genealogy of sages indicates that the trigrams were the ultimate root of all culture and civilization. The second step was taken by the Zhou founders, and it is for this reason that the text was also called the *Zhou yi* 周易. Some writers attribute the work to King Wen, some to the Duke of Zhou, and some to both. They doubled the trigrams to form hexagrams and added the "judgments" to the lines and the hexagrams. They thus were the first to add actual characters to the primal, pre-linguistic signs. Traditions also specifically link King Wen's work on the hexagrams to the period of his imprisonment at the hands of King Zhou of the Shang. This link of writing to failure or suffering also figured prominently in the myths of Qu Yuan and Confucius. The completion of the work is attributed to the latter, to whom are ascribed the commentarial chapters that appear at the end of the received edition.

In all likelihood, the order presented here reverses the process by which the tale of origin developed. When the *ru* schoolmen adopted the *Yi* as a classic, they gave it a status equivalent to their other sacred texts. In order to do this they named Confucius as editor and transmitter, and asserted that like the *Odes, Documents, Music,* and *Ritual* it was an element of the heritage received from the Zhou kings. Finally, the text was read back into the origins of civilization through assigning its advent to the inspired perceptions of natural patterns achieved by the great sage Fu Xi. In this way the *Yi jing* commentators discovered the roots of writing in nature, found the principles common to objects and signs, and thereby created a natural philosophy of writing.

Chapter Six
THE NATURAL PHILOSOPHY
OF WRITING

The *Yi jing* (易經 "Classic of Changes") was the last text to enter the *ru* canon at the end of the Warring States, but it was first in Sima Qian's curriculum and in the *Han shu* bibliographic monograph.[1] This priority was due to its grounding of writing and philosophy in cosmic principles. It thus served as the *ru* response to proto-Daoist texts tracing their doctrines to a vision of the primal unity and the first stages of its division. It also foreshadowed and made possible Dong Zhongshu's grounding of Confucian philosophy in natural correlations. The *Yi*'s prominence thus lay in its attempt to ground writing and the scholastic enterprise in the world of nature through creating a protoscience of graphic signs.

Despite its lofty destiny, the *Yi* began as a simple manual of divination, and its incorporation into scholastic discourse took centuries. Like the theories of *yin* and *yang* and the Five Phases, it developed within the mantic traditions, and it was employed as a tool of the trade by professional diviners.[2] As discussed in chapter 2, such traditions were rivals of the philosophical schools within the intellectual field of the Eastern Zhou, so the cooptation of the *Yi* text by philosophers entailed a protracted debate over the nature and uses of divination, and an eventual redefinition of the process. The earliest evidence of this appears in anecdotes about divination with yarrow stalks in the *Zuo zhuan*. The intellectual interests and patterns of quotation in this text suggest close ties to court musicians and astrologers, so it is not surprising that it contains many anecdotes dealing with divination and the *Yi* text. The *Zuo zhuan* portrays a world in which the *Yi* is still used as a divination manual, but some had begun to treat it as a source of philosophical wisdom, or to subsume the process of divination under an encompassing moral or ritual wisdom.

However, even while philosophers treated the *Yi* as a source of wisdom, divination remained a mantic art practiced by professionals. It thus became a point of tension between the philosophical traditions and their technical rivals. Texts from tombs provide evidence of the survival of Shang-style divination largely unchanged through the fourth century B.C., and the development of new techniques for utilitarian divination in the third. Moreover, texts found in tombs indicate an active rivalry between the *ru* and diviners in the early Han, and the two chapters on divination in the *Shi ji* showed that this debate continued well into the dynasty.

The evidence for the next stage of the transformation of the *Yi* into a philosophical classic comes from the text itself. The attributions of sequential authorship traced in the last chapter belong to the realm of myth, but the hypothetical stages probably correspond to actual history. The essays and abstracting commentaries attributed to Confucius, the so-called "Ten Wings," and the commentaries discovered at Mawangdui are almost certainly Warring States compositions. They show how *ru* scholastics adapted the divination manual as a philosophic work on images or signs and their relations to natural phenomena.

The natural philosophy articulated in the "Ten Wings" and related texts hinges on two key concepts: image (*xiang* 象) and number (*shu* 數). Both can be traced back to the *Zuo zhuan*, and there are hints that they played a crucial role in earlier stages of *Yi* divination. However, in the "Ten Wings" and later Han theories of the *Yi* they took on an entirely new meaning. The relation of line to image elaborated within the *Yi* provided a philosophical underpinning to the project of making the world intelligible by establishing correspondences between the natural and human spheres. Within this context the character *xiang* 象 also referred to astral correlates of earthly phenomena, or human correlates of processes in nature. In the mythology of the sage kings, mastery of the *xiang* figured as an attribute of kingship. Finally, the term became fundamental to early poetic practice, and to theories of the origins of characters.

Shu 數 likewise was a crucial term in the period. Under the influence of Greek philosophy and modern science, Westerners treat numbers as the key to all law in nature. Although not so privileged in China, the concept of number was crucial to the system of correlations by which thinkers of the late Warring States period and the early empires made sense of their world. A series of numerical categories—the duality of *yin* and *yang*; the triad of man, Heaven, and Earth; the four seasons; the Five Phases; the six lines of a hexagram; the eight trigrams—was employed to tie disparate phenomena together into intelligible systems. As discussed in chapter 1, ordering through number figured prominently in the political realm, where both population and army were divided into numbered units, the male populace numerically ranked, rewards and punishments numerically graded, and administrative reports built around sets of key numbers. Accounts of the philosophical traditions sometimes identified the philosophers of statecraft with number.

"Image" and "number" combined to form a comprehensive model in which the hexagrams linked principles of cosmic order, the human ability to recognize patterns, the capacity of written characters to communicate meanings, and the possibility of proper government. The first text in the state-sponsored canon established in the Western Han, the source of writing and intelligible pattern, the *Yi* became the foundation of a theory in which the authority of texts was grounded in the privileged relationship of written graphs to the fundamental dyad of *yin* and *yang*, and by extension to the regularities of Heaven and Earth.

BETWEEN DIVINATION AND PHILOSOPHY

The *Zuo zhuan* anecdotes about yarrow stalk divination, often in association with the cracking of tortoise shells or the interpretation of dreams, have been the subject of much study. This has concentrated on reconstructing the techniques of divination.[3] More important here are the questions of who divines, how divination is combined with other forms of prediction, and how the *Yi* text is used for purposes other than divination. It is also worth asking whether there is any evidence of changes over time, for although the *Zuo zhuan* was probably largely written in the late fourth century, its author(s) had access to earlier records, and these may have served as the basis of anecdotes.[4]

The first topic has been analyzed by Kidder Smith. His figures indicate that less than half the cases of using the *Yi* involve the participation of specialized "crackmakers" (*bu* 卜, tortoise shell diviners) or astrologers (*shi* 史). The latter were the specialists in *yi* divination, but the former also read the results of casting yarrow stalks. However, most interpreters of divinations were not these specialists, but ordinary noblemen (or in one case woman) and political advisers. Moreover, while the mantic specialists predominate in the earlier period, by the middle of the sixth century B.C. they disappear from accounts of *Yi* divination and uses of the *Yi* text.[5] Thus the *Zuo zhuan* suggests that by the late Spring and Autumn period knowledge of the use of the *Yi* was spread throughout the politically active nobility and, at least in political questions, it was applied by a wide range of individuals.

A precondition of such dissemination is the increasing prominence of the *Yi* as a *text*. A specialized body of technical lore, transmitted from generation to generation, relied on a protracted apprenticeship.[6] Education in such a context relied on oral instruction and demonstrations, with writing playing an auxiliary role for storing information to be consulted when necessary. In some stories diviners extemporize verses on their reading of the divination, rather than mechanically reciting a fixed text.[7] Moreover, in the first seven examples of yarrow-stalk casting the prognosticator never cites the name of a text. In the next seven cases the text is mentioned four times and is always called the *Zhou yi*. In the last eight cases the text is named seven times, but in addition to being called the *Zhou yi* it is also referred to as the *Yi*, the *Yi xiang* (易象) and the *Yi gua* (易卦).[8] Thus the dissemination of *Yi* lore is associated with an increasing tendency to name the text and to quote directly. This indicates that transmission throughout a broader group depended on written texts, and that people no longer able to appeal to the authority of an office and a family tradition had to quote chapter and verse in order to gain acceptance for their interpretations. As divination lore became part of a general heritage of the literate, authority shifted from person to text.

The changing identity of prognosticators and evolving role of the text was linked to a new understanding of divination. To summarize, the *Zuo zhuan* incorporated accounts of divination into the world sketched in chapter 3, in which destiny was determined by the individual's adherence to ritual. Here divination appears as at best a supplement to percipient analysis of action. It parallels or doubles predictions made by other means, and the ability to correctly prophesy depends on the moral character of the prognosticator. This indicates the denial of divination as an independently efficacious technique, if such a belief had existed. Instead it was an extension of the rules of action and forms of intelligence that characterized the educated nobleman, or the scholar who later took him as a model. In addition, the increasing reliance on the *text* of the *Yi* led to its assimilation to the status of works such as the *Odes* and *Documents*. It was increasingly cited as a source of lore or wisdom, and the ability to recognize its true meanings became a hallmark of percipience and testimony to moral character. By contrast, the misreading of the *Yi*, like the failure to recognize poetic allusions, demonstrated a moral obtuseness that entailed inevitable doom. The *Yi* became more a test of moral acuteness than a means of receiving messages from the spirits.

This attitude toward divination and the social tensions underlying it are best demonstrated by two anecdotes in the *Guo yu*, both featuring Duke Xiang of Dan. In the first Duke Xiang observes the Duke of Jin and three of his nobles, and then tells the Marquis of Lu that Jin will have civil war.

> The Marquis of Lu said, "I fear I cannot escape the threat of Jin, and now you say, 'They will have a civil war.' Might I ask you whether you know this from the Way of Heaven, or from the affairs of men?" Duke Xiang replied, "I am not a blind musician nor an astrologer. How should I know the Way of Heaven? I observed the appearance of the Prince of Jin and listened to the words of the three Xi [noblemen]. They are men whom calamity will inevitably befall. A gentleman's eyes fix his body and his legs follow, so if you observe his appearance you can know his heart."[9]

Duke Xiang then describes the improper bearing of the three men in question, explains what it reveals, and prophesies their destruction. The story concludes by noting how the prophecy was fulfilled.

This story resembles those in the *Zuo zhuan* discussed in chapter 3, where a keen observer prophesies defeat or death by noting errors in ritual deportment. However, it is noteworthy because it explicitly challenges dependence on traditional divination. The Marquis of Lu's question poses the alternative of prophecy through divining the intent of Heaven versus prophecy through observing human conduct. Duke Xiang insists on the latter, and he does so by denying for himself the status of a specialist in divination. The shift deduced above from the changing pattern of divination in the *Zuo zhuan* is here proclaimed as the principle that observing conduct is superior to the manipulation of tortoise shell and yarrow stalks.

The other story in the *Guo yu* develops this theme. Zhou, a collateral descendant of the Jin rulers, comes as a hostage to the Zhou court where he serves Duke Xiang. The duke predicts that he will become ruler of Jin. He lists eleven virtues of the future ruler, all aspects of "culture" (*wen* 文), and then proceeds:

Heaven has six [*qi*] and Earth five [phases]. These are what are constant in numbers [*shu* 數]. We use Heaven as the warp and Earth as the weft. When the warp and weft have no error, this is the image [*xiang* 象] of culture [*wen* 文]. King Wen [文] had both substance and culture, so Heaven bestowed the world upon him like a portion of sacrificial meat. This man [Zhou] has received it [the substance and culture of King Wen]. Moreover, he is near in the ancestral line. It is suitable that he should obtain the state.[10]

Zhou's eleven virtues are numerologically equated with the fundamental powers of Heaven and Earth. These are the constant numbers, and their visible manifestations yield images. These terms became fundamental to *Yi* philosophy in the late Warring States, and as a pair they were already metonyms for divination in the *Zuo zhuan*.[11] Thus Duke Xiang coopts the basic categories of conventional divination to give a naturalistic underpinning to his prophecies derived from the observation of decorum.

This incorporation of divination into philosophic analysis is immediately reinforced by Duke Xiang's citation of a divination made several generations earlier that predicted a change in the present generation. This is supported by an interpretation of a dream dating to the same generation as the divination. The argument concludes with a citation from the *Shang shu* in which King Wu declares his certainty of victory because his dreams have coincided with the tortoise shell divination and the omens.[12] Duke Xiang will cite divinations in his argument only as an adjunct of his observations and with the imprimatur of a classic text. Divination here supplements the ritual-based percipience and textual learning of the scholar. One reads the will of the spirits as one reads the intent of a man in his verse, or his virtue in his ritual conduct.

The same denial of divination as an independent technique of specialists, and redefinition of it as an extension of the repertoire of the generalist nobleman or scholar, appear in the *Zuo zhuan*. The characteristic most often noted of *Yi* lore in the *Zuo zhuan* is its moralization. This takes two major forms. First, some stories indicate that divination only confirms a fate already determined by conduct. Second, the ability to interpret a divination hinges on the moral character of the prognosticator. The wise and virtuous man understands the sense of the stalks, because they confirm what he already knows, while the evil man cannot perceive the warning implicit in the prognostication, and will proceed blindly to his doom.

The most frequently cited story indicating this moralization is that of Mu Jiang, who was imprisoned in a secondary palace for having conspired with a lover to supplant her son, Duke Cheng of Lu. A divination was conducted when she was first sent into captivity, and the astrologer foretold a rapid release. She replied,

No. Of this the *Zhou yi* says, "*Sui* [name of hexagram] eminent, penetrating, beneficial, sincere. Without blame [*yuan heng li zhen wu jiu* 元亨利貞無咎]." The eminent is what is superior in the self. The penetrating is the gathering of the auspicious. The beneficial is the harmonizing of duties. The sincere is the trunk of affairs. If the self is benevolent one can be superior to others. If the auspicious is gathered, one can unite the rituals. If one benefits things one can harmonize duties. If sincerity is firm one can manage affairs. It being so, one certainly cannot deceive. Therefore, even though "Sui" says "no blame," I am a woman and have participated in rebellion. I am certainly in a low position and lacking benevolence, so I cannot be called "eminent." I have not brought peace to state or family, so I cannot be called "penetrating." In acting I have harmed myself, so I cannot be called "beneficial." I have abandoned my proper place to engage in intrigue, so I cannot be called "sincere." If one has the four virtues, then one is "Sui" and "without blame." I have none of them, so how could I be "Sui?" Having chosen evil, can I be "without blame?"[13]

This story in fact signifies more than moralization. First, it is framed by a dispute over interpretation between an astrologer and an amateur. The astrologer mechanically reads the results to predict good fortune. The nonspecialist, on the other hand, reads the prognostication as a conditional sentence: *if* one is eminent, penetrating, beneficial, and sincere, *then* one is without blame. This reads the line not as a reference to the situation in question, but as a general rule that moral actions determine results.[14] Again divination is reduced to an adjunct that reiterates the centrality of virtue and ritual in human conduct.

This tension between diviners and officials also figures in stories of diviners altering or suppressing the results of divination, and thereby leading the ruler to disaster.[15] These stories pertain to a bad ruler who is ultimately responsible for his own ruin, but they suggest the danger of delegating decisions to mantic specialists. They might also indicate that a better ruler would handle his own divinations.[16]

Mu Jiang's story also highlights the importance of the *Yi* as *text*. Rather than extemporizing a verse, she simply quotes the text, glosses its terms, shows that these do not fit her case, and concludes that the auspicious result does not apply. As Kidder Smith has noted, this practice of listing and glossing terms appears elsewhere in the *Zuo zhuan*, and it serves to re-interpret received concepts.[17] This is the first case in which any figure reads an *Yi* prognostication in this character-by-character manner and thereby transforms the original sense into a moral message.[18] Emphasis on the sense of words appears in several anecdotes, where divination depends on choosing the appropriate sense of a multivalent term, or recognizing a play of multiple meanings.[19] Here the process of divination becomes an exercise in textual scholarship.

Another anecdote implicates the *Yi* in its own moralization. Nankuai divines for his planned rebellion and obtains the prognostication, "Yellow skirt, greatly auspicious" (*huang shang yuan ji* 黃裳元吉). He asks Zi Fu Huibo how this prognostication would apply to undertaking a great affair. Huibo replies,

> I have studied this [the Yi]. If it is an affair of loyalty and good faith, then you should do it. Otherwise you will certainly fail. Strong on the outside and accommo-

dating on the inside [one of the two hexagrams obtained is composed of the trigram *kan*—pit, earth, danger, strength—above, which equals outside, and the trigram *kun*—*yin*, water, yielding, obedience—below], this is loyalty. Blended by guiding sincerity, this is good faith. Therefore it says, "[If] yellow, skirt, and eminent, [then] auspicious." "Yellow" is the color of the center. "Skirt" is the ornament of the lower [body]. "Eminent" is the highest excellence. If the center is not loyal, it does not get its proper color [this statement—based on the phonetic identity and graphic link of *zhong* 中 "center" and *zhong* 忠 "loyal"—derives the first character of the prognostication from the hexagram]. If the "lower" [the "skirt," but also Nankuai] is not respectful, it does not obtain its ornament. If the affair is not good, it does not reach its goal [*ji* 極 "limit," equated with *yuan* 元, "original," "highest," or "best"]. For inner and outer to flourish and harmonize is loyalty. To conduct affairs with good faith is respect. If one nourishes these three virtues then it is a good [result]. If it is not a case of these three, then it [the hexagram] does not match. The *Yi* cannot be used to prognosticate on danger. What affair is it? Does it bear ornamentation? Inner excellence can be "yellow," upper excellence can be "eminent," and lower excellence can be "skirt." When the three are complete then one can cast stalks. If any are still lacking, then even if it says "auspicious," it is not.[20]

As for Mu Jiang, the prognostication is glossed as an "if . . . then . . . " sentence where the conditional phrase indicates necessary virtues and the consequence indicates results obtained. It also uses elaborate definitions. However, it goes further in the moralization of the text by deriving the virtues from the structure of the hexagram. The interplay of *yin* and *yang* lines indicates natural images which themselves stand for certain virtues. The structure of the cosmos thus dictates rules of conduct revealed in the line text. The divination yields not a forecast but rather a standard against which the participant measures himself and thereby assesses his prospects. Consequently the *Yi* text doubles the moral or ritual virtues already known to the nobleman or scholar, and it grounds these in the basic images of nature.[21]

Tales in which literati nobles surpass technical specialists or remonstrate with rebels indicate that the moralization of the *Yi* also entailed the claim that the superior man made the better diviner. As in the cases of succeeding through the skillful citation of verse, perishing through a failure of recognition, or foretelling the future through observing others' conduct, the skillful reading and manipulation of the *Yi* text became a proof of percipience and character, both with a strong class bias. The clearest example of morality as a precondition of divination is the story of the dispute over Cui Wuzi's marriage. Cui Wuzi—a reprobate who ultimately killed himself after all his sons were slain for massacring their own stepbrothers— desired to marry a woman who shared his surname and was in mourning for her first husband. Rejecting the argument against incest, he cast stalks for the marriage. The astrologer proclaimed the result to be auspicious. He showed it to Chen Wenzi, who in several anecdotes foretells the future through examining moral conduct.[22]

Wenzi said, "The man is followed by wind [referring to the lower trigram and the trigram into which it mutated in the second hexagram]. The wind brings down the wife [the trigram *dui*, which corresponds to 'wife,' is the upper trigram in both hexagrams]. You cannot marry her. Moreover, its oracle-text says, 'Difficulties in the rocks, clutching the caltrop. Entering his house he does not see his wife. Inauspicious.' 'Difficulties in the rocks' means he goes but does not get through. 'Clutching the caltrop [which has sharp seeds]' means that what he relies on harms him. 'Entering his house he does not see his wife. Inauspicious,' means that he has no home." Cuizi said, "She is a widow. What harm is there? Her first husband matched it [i.e., the prophecy was fulfilled by the first husband, so there is no longer danger]." Consequently he married her.[23]

Here again the scholar-official proves more perceptive than the astrologer, but his interlocutor will not listen. Blinded by lust, Cui Wuzi joins in the game of interpretation. He accepts Chen Wenzi's reading that the woman is inauspicious as a wife, but uses her earlier marriage to deny its applicability to him. The results of divination invariably required interpretation, and many hermeneutic moves were possible, but in the *Zuo zhuan* the true reading is that which reiterates the teachings of morality and ritual.[24]

The assimilation of the *Yi* to the status of a classic text like the *Odes* and *Documents* is also marked by the fact that in several anecdotes it is not used for divination, but rather as a source of doctrine or information. In one story references to dragons in the line-texts of the first two hexagrams are used to prove the presence of dragons in earlier times.[25] The *Yi* is also quoted to provide historical information, with reference to a divination anecdote that appeared earlier in the *Zuo zhuan*.[26] More commonly it is used as a source of moral principles or practical wisdom. It demonstrates that ambition is dangerous, that observance of regulations is crucial for an army, and that abandoning the fundamental in pursuit of the peripheral leads to disaster.[27] These stories all involve predictions, but they are based on observations of behavior, while the *Yi* is cited simply as a textual authority for the principles invoked.

One prediction based on lore from the *Zhou yi* and observation of conduct includes graphic analysis. The case is also of interest because the predictions, citations, and analysis are performed by a doctor (*yi* 醫).

The Marquis of Jin sought a doctor from Qin. The Earl of Qin sent Doctor He to examine him. He said, "There is nothing to be done about the illness. It is called [in verse]

Proximity to women
Produces a disease like *gu* 蠱.
Neither demons nor diet;
Led astray, he has lost all will.

. . . Heaven has six energies [*qi* 氣]. These are *yin*, *yang*, wind, rain, dark, and light. These are divided into the four times of day [or 'seasons' *shi* 時], and put in order through the five rhythms. If there is excess then they produce disaster. Excess of *yin* means cold illness; excess of *yang* means hot illness; excess of wind means illness of the limbs; excess of rain means illness of the belly; excess of dark means delusional illness; excess of light means disease of the heart/mind. Woman is an object [of desire] for the *yang* in the times of darkness. If there is excess, then it produces a disease of overheated flesh and delusional *gu*. Now the prince observes no rhythms and no times. Could he not arrive at this [disease]?" . . . Zhao Meng [chief minister of Jin] said, "What is meant by *gu*?" [Doctor He] replied, "It is that which is produced by sinking into excess and delusional disorders. As for the graph, a 'basin' [*min* 皿] and 'insects' [*chong* 蟲] form *gu* [蠱]. Insects in grain also are *gu*.[28] In the *Zhou yi* a woman deluding a man or wind blowing down a mountain are called *gu* [name of hexagram #18]. They are all the same category."

Zhao Meng said, "Excellent doctor!" He gave him generous presents and sent him home.[29]

The analysis and prediction are based on numerological theory and observation of conduct, while the *Yi* text is linked with character analysis to demonstrate different aspects of the ailment and its relation to natural phenomena. It seems to be the textual grounding of his diagnosis that proves him to be an excellent doctor, and leads to his receiving the ritual bestowal of gifts rather than a simple payment.

The *Zuo zhuan* thus included cases in which predictions through divination doubled or reinforced those made through observation of conduct, and others in which the *Yi* text offered textual authority for principles underlying empirical predictions. Their common ground is the rejection of divination as an independent source of wisdom. This is the intellectual correlate of the rejection of mantic specialists as possessors of an esoteric *gnosis* denied to ordinary men, or rather to men of general, literary cultivation. It appears most clearly where the speaker rejects any need for cracking tortoise shells or casting yarrow stalks. One arena of such rejections is military affairs. When a Chu commander is asked before a battle if he wishes to divine he replies, "One divines in order to resolve doubts. If one does not doubt, why divine?" Other stories depict the rejection of divination before a combat judged to be righteous. Refusal to divine military affairs became a matter of principle in several military treatises.[30]

Another story features Duke Hui of Jin, who had been taken prisoner by Qin after repeatedly violating the obligations that he had incurred toward that state.

When Duke Hui was in Qin, he said, "If the previous ruler had followed the prognostication of Astrologer Su, I would not have come to this." Han Jian was in attendance, and he said, "Tortoises are 'image,' and yarrow 'number.' Only after objects appear are there 'images.' Only after there are images is there growth. Only after there is growth is there 'number.' Would the previous ruler's ruin of virtue have been reached by 'number' [which appears so late in the process]? What gain would there have been if he had followed Astrologer Su's prognostication? The *Odes* says, 'The calamities of men are not sent down by Heaven. Whether they come together with civil speech or turn from one another in hatred, the responsibility lies with men.'"[31]

This passage, sanctioned by a quotation from the Zhou odes, makes moral conduct decisive and relegates divination to the role of revealing circumstances that have already taken shape. Consequently it is of benefit neither to men of discernment, who follow the dictates of ritual in any case, or to reprobates who violate them.

An appeal to authoritative texts to reject divination also figures in the story of King Hui of Chu, who chose when invaded not to divine for a new commander. After Chu triumphs, the narrative concludes

> The gentleman says, "King Hui knew true resolve. The *Documents of Xia* says, 'Only after he fixes his will does the diviner make his charge to the primal tortoise.' The *Record* says, 'The sage does not trouble himself with crack-making and the casting of stalks.' So it was with King Hui."[32]

Stories proving that divination was superfluous were part of the same literary culture that first rejected stalk casting as the highest mode of prophecy, and then absorbed a modified version as an adjunct mode of analysis. In this new schema the text of the *Yi* was increasingly divorced from its old function as a divination manual, and instead assimilated to the roles hitherto played by the *Odes* or *Documents*. Thus the *Xunzi* would later argue, "He who is skilled in the *Yi* does not divine."[33]

The cooptation of the *Yi* by nobles and philosophical traditions did not mean that divination ceased to be a technical discipline of specialists employed for their mantic skills. As discussed in chapter 2, the Baoshan divinatory materials, roughly contemporary with the composition of the *Zuo zhuan*, record procedures used by professional diviners to identify spirits causing illness and fix the type and number of sacrifices necessary to assuage them. The style and assumptions of these practices are continuous with those found in the Shang oracle texts. Less than a century later, the almanac found at Shuihudi offers a theory of illness based on the Five Phases. The origin and course of the disease is mechanically determined by the date on which it was contracted. Although this theory of divinatory diagnosis is distinct from that at Baoshan, it is likewise opposed to the moral/ritual etiology of diseases and death found in the *Zuo zhuan*. Again, as noted in chapter 2, the Mawangdui text entitled "Yao" (要) depicts Confucius advocating the *Yi* as a source of wisdom, but still at pains to distinguish his use of it from that of the technical diviners. The struggle between diviners and officials/scholars to claim the text is also the theme of the *Shiji* chapter "The Diviners of Auspicious Days."[34] This last sides with the diviners against the scholars, but it takes for granted the cooptation initiated by the *Zuo zhuan* and carried through in the later chapters of the *Yi*.

The story begins with two scholar officials, Song Zhong and Jia Yi, discussing the *Yi* as the ruling art of the former kings and a complete inventory of human nature. Jia Yi remarks that he has heard that when the ancient sages were not at court, they were invariably to be found among the diviners and doctors (echoing the story in the *Zuo zhuan* of the doctor employing the *Yi*). They go to the diviners in the market, listen to the discourse of one, and are so impressed by the brilliance of his exposition of cosmic principles that they ask him why he is in such a humble position. This question triggers a lengthy lecture in two parts. First he ridicules officials as sycophants who risk their lives in order to make themselves slaves of the ruler, lacking the integrity to retire when their advice is ignored. By contrast, diviners exemplify the way of the true scholar in refusing to compromise for the sake of position. They pattern themselves on Heaven and Earth, and carry forward the Way of kings created by Fu Xi and King Wen. The way in which they conduct themselves in the market is a model for the common people. He cites *Laozi* and *Zhuangzi* to justify the benefits of obscurity, and notes that the occupation does not endanger its practitioners. He closes by celebrating the superior man who hides from the world but nevertheless achieves great merit through his unnoticed influence.

This leaves the two scholars speechless and dazed, like the recipients of a discourse in the *Zhuangzi* or the loser in a Han rhapsody. Several days later they meet again and agree that as high officials they live in constant peril of death. By contrast the diviner lives at ease and collects his money whether or not he is correct. The story concludes by narrating how both Song Zhong and Jia Yi died in service, confirming the diviner's prophecy. Thus this debate, like many stories dealing with the *Yi*, is a tale of the fulfillment of prophecy, in which the death of one party validates the other's reading of the text.

This anecdote espouses Daoist philosophy through references to key texts, insistence on the virtues of retirement and the role of hidden sages, and the theme of preserving life. Nevertheless, as a staged confrontation between scholars who treat the *Yi* as a source of wisdom and a diviner who lives by using it as a manual of prophecy, it carries on the earlier debate. Rather than defending the uses of the *Yi* as a manual, it accepts the scholastic position, while mockingly insisting that the humble diviner in the market place comes closer to the scholastic ideal than the scholar officials. The diviner defends his art as a natural philosophy applying the Way of Heaven to human affairs, as the Way of the sage kings, and as a means of inculcating morality among the people. His critique of the scholars, and the veiled prophecy of their deaths, is based entirely on the observation of their conduct and the world in which they live. In short the diviner is not a diviner at all, but a satiric double who embraces the theoretical positions of the scholars only to show their failure to practice them. Thus the anecdote accepts the moral reading of the *Yi* as a given, and uses it to denounce the very group who supposedly espoused it. Like an oracle-text from the *Yi*, the scholastic interpretation of the text had become a ground of disputed readings among conflicting parties.

THE NATURAL PHILOSOPHY OF SIGNS

The *Zuo zhuan* and *Guo yu* anecdotes dramatize the transformation of the *Yi* into a text of wisdom wielded by statesmen and scholars, as indicated in chapter 5 by its links to the Duke of Zhou and Confucius. The wisdom of the *Yi* took the form of a natural philosophy of signs, in which energetic processes were transformed into patterns of lines that allowed the course of events to be read and guided. The basic assumptions and details of this theory were developed in the Warring States commentaries to the *Yi*, the so-called "Ten Wings" (*shi yi* 十翼) and the texts discovered at Mawangdui. The most extensive of these, and one of the last composed, is the "Great Tradition," (*da zhuan* 大傳) or "Tradition on the Appended Texts" (*xi ci zhuan* 繫辭傳). This was probably an independent essay, or rather set of essays, presenting the basic philosophical concepts of the *Yi*. It is the culmination of pre-imperial scholastic studies of the *Yi* and shows how this divination manual was incorporated into philosophical discourse and established as the primal writing from which all authoritative texts, the written language, and civilization itself derived.[35]

The "Great Tradition" represents the culmination of the process suggested in the *Zuo zhuan* anecdotes, for it explains the creation of the text by sage kings and their use of it to maintain civilization through the correct reading of signs. As the origin of sagely rule and meaningful signs, the *Yi* figures as the fountainhead of both kingship and scholarship, and hence a tool of scholars and men of government. This moralized, politically oriented reading of the text is expounded in a set of attributes which, for purposes of exposition, I will discuss under seven rubrics: (1) the *Yi* as the product of sages and model for gentlemen, (2) the *Yi* as a microcosm of the universe, (3) the *Yi* as a revelation of the structure of time, (4) the *Yi* as a revelation of the structure of hierarchized space, (5) the *Yi* as model of the vitalistic or generative aspect of signs, (6) the *Yi* as a repertoire of "images" (*xiang* 象) linking natural processes to their representations, and (7) the *Yi* as the source of the "numbers" (*shu* 數) that underlie the world's order. Rubrics six and seven are sufficiently important to be allotted independent sections.

[1] As discussed in chapter 3, the sages were mythic figures who provided the historical model for scholastic projects and the grounds for claims to textual authority. The redefinition of the *Yi* as a book of social wisdom entailed linking it to the sages of antiquity. This link runs throughout the "Great Commentary." First, it states that the sage—specifically Fu Xi—established the hexagrams, or that he created the *Yi*.[36] It also tells how the percipience of the sages both created the text—including the lines, images, and appended commentaries—and used it to order the world.

> The sages had the means to perceive the world's arcana and to measure out their forms. They made images of what was appropriate to each object, and therefore we

call them "images" [*xiang* 象]. The sages had the means to perceive the world's movements and observe where they converged and penetrated [*hui tong* 會通], and they thereby put into practice their standard rituals. They attached phrases to them in order to determine good and bad fortune, and therefore called them "lines" [*yao* 爻, here glossed as *jiao* 交 "to match" or *xiao* 效 "to imitate"]. Reaching to the limits of the arcana lies in the hexagrams. Stirring and guiding the movements of the world lies in the phrases.[37]

The *Yi* is not merely the creation of the sage and the textual form of his powers of perception and response, but also the instrument of sagely authority. It is the means by which the sage "exalts potency and broadens his enterprise," or "plumbs the hidden depths and examines the pivotal moments of change." The sage uses it to "completely understand the aspirations (*zhi* 志) of the world, fix the enterprises of the world, and resolve the doubts of the world."[38] The text embodies the entire sagely Way.

> The *Yi* has the four aspects of the sagely Way within itself. For language one exalts its "phrases." For movement one exalts its "alternations" (*bian* 變).[39] For creating implements one exalts its "images." For crack-making and stalk-casting one exalts its prognostications.[40]

The sages' language and actions both take their models from the *Yi*. "Creating implements" refers to the account translated in chapter 5, in which the tools and practices of civilization were introduced by the sages through the inspiration of the hexagrams. The final sentence acknowledges the use of the *Yi* as a divination manual, but this now finds its place only within the larger ideal of sagehood.

The theme of the sages as innovators inspired by the *Yi* appears in another passage equating man and text. After describing the generation of the *Yi* text through repeated mathematical divisions of an original unity, it equates the *Yi* with the principle elements of the universe. Echoing the mythology of Fu Xi, it conflates the generation of visual signs with that of the physical objects they represent, and places the sages among these objects. Whereas the passages above indicated that the sages had created the *Yi*, this suggests that the text had created the sages.

> Of "models" and "images," nothing is greater than Heaven and Earth [Fu Xi made the trigrams from the "models" of Earth and the "images" of Heaven.]. Of "alternations" and "moving throughout," nothing is greater than the four seasons. Of "suspended images" and shining objects, nothing is greater than the sun and moon. Of the "exalted" and "high," nothing is greater than wealth and honor [These are attributed to the hexagrams at the beginning of the "Great Tradition."]. For completing objects and making them useful, for establishing perfected implements in order to benefit the world, nothing is greater than the sage. For exploring the arcana,

searching out the hidden, fishing in the depths, and causing the distant to come, thereby fixing what is auspicious and inauspicious for the world and completing its labors, nothing is greater than the yarrow and tortoise shell.[41]

This passage maps images, signs, or categories defined by the *Yi* onto the major categories of the natural and social worlds. The sages, like Heaven and Earth, the four seasons, the sun and moon, or the implements of divination, figure as agents by which principles developed within the *Yi* text are realized in the world. The changes of Heaven and Earth, the celestial images suspended in the sky, and the writings revealed by the rivers provide patterns of meaningful signs formulated in the *Yi*, and the sage simply copies them.[42]

While the text usually refers only to the sages as a generic term, the tradition of sequential composition figures in scattered passages. The role of Fu Xi as inventor of the trigrams or hexagrams is asserted in the account of the invention of civilization. Other passages state that the *Yi* as a finished text reflects "the ideas of a declining world," arose "in middle antiquity," and indicates the "worries and anxieties" of its author. These veiled references are finally specified.

> As for the rise of the Yi, did it correspond to the declining age of the Yin and the flourishing power of the Zhou? Did it correspond to the affairs of King Wen and King Zhou [of the Shang]? For that reason its phrases deal with danger.[43]

Here the phrases of the *Yi* and perhaps the doubling of the trigrams were products of the Shang-Zhou transition and grew out of the concerns of that period. If the passages that begin with the phrase "the master said" refer to Confucius, as later interpreted, then the authors of the "Great Tradition" espoused the theory of a text composed in three stages by the sages of high, middle, and late antiquity.

A final hallmark of the sage in the *Yi* text is his recognition of the inadequacy of language. This problem, noted in chapter 2 in the philosophical traditions, received its classical formulation in the "Great Tradition," and a tentative solution was offered through the hexagrams and images.

> The Master said, "Writing cannot exhaust words, and words cannot exhaust meanings." That being so, then can the meanings of the sages not be observed? The Master said, "The sages established the images in order to exhaust ['fully express'] their meanings. They established the hexagrams in order to exhaust ['fully describe'] the true nature of things and artifice. They attached the phrases in order to exhaust their words. They alternated them and caused them to go through [a cycle] in order to exhaust benefit."[44]

Here the system of visual signs and natural referents formed by the images, hexagrams, and appended phrases figures as an alternative to conventional speech. This fullness of meaning offered by the *Yi* is possible because it is directly rooted in

[handwritten margin note: of visuality versus the power of language]

the patterns of the cosmos, and hence is not translatable into ordinary language. It remains the province of the sages and those who imitate them.

For while the *Yi* is explained as the product of and pattern for the sages, it is not reserved for them alone. Those who emulate them, known either as "worthies" (*xian ren* 賢人) or "gentlemen" (*junzi* 君子), can use the text as a means of access to sagely wisdom. Such men are urged to study or contemplate the text when at leisure, and to follow it when engaged in worldly affairs.

> That in which the gentleman dwells and finds peace is the sequence of the *Yi*. That in which he delights and manipulates is the line phrases. Therefore when the gentleman is at rest he observes its images and manipulates its phrases. When he acts then he observes its alternations and manipulates its prognostications. Thus with the good fortune of Heaven's assistance, there is nothing which is not beneficial.[45]

This passage follows the *Zuo* anecdotes, treating the divinatory function of the text as an extension of its analytic or contemplative uses. Elsewhere the words and actions of the gentleman, the means by which he secures honor and guides the people, are compared to the trigger of the crossbow. This is the mechanical equivalent of the moments of incipient change revealed through the *Yi*. Guiding his actions by the principles revealed in the text and the divinations he obtains from it, the gentleman attains the adherence of the people and success in the world. As the text points out, conduct follows the principles revealed in the *Yi*, but only the gentleman recognizes this. The efficacy of the *Yi* depended on the men who used it, and those who grasped its truths were few.[46]

[2] The power of the *Yi* depended on correspondences between the text and the world. The trigrams, hexagrams, and images constituted a microcosm of Heaven and Earth, so that one who understood the text also grasped the processes of the world and could guide these toward desired results. This correspondence of the hexagrams to the cosmos and the social order is announced at the beginning of the "Great Tradition."

> Heaven is exalted and Earth lowly; thus *qian* and *kun* are fixed. The humble and lofty being laid out, the noble and base are positioned. Movement and stillness having constancy, the hard and the soft [equivalent to *yang* and *yin* or the broken and unbroken lines] are divided. The models being divided by kinds and objects divided into classes, good and bad fortune is set forth. Images being formed in Heaven and models on Earth, alternation and transformation appear.[47]

Here the elements of the text and the concepts it reveals develop in correspondence with processes in the natural world. This insistence on the parallels of cosmos and text, often indicated through verbal parallelism or explicit analogy, is summarized in the simple statement, "The *Yi* is the paradigm of Heaven and Earth."[48]

The most elaborate correspondence between the microcosm of the text and macrocosm of the world is developed in the only passage that describes the practice of divination. The steps in the manipulation of the stalks are said to represent first the appearance of division within the primal unity, and then the progress of the cosmos through the annual cycle. The initial number of stalks represents the primal unity. Their division into two groups represents *yin* and *yang*. The discarding of one stalk creates three groups that match Heaven, Earth, and man. Their counting into groups of four matches the four seasons. The placing of residual stalks between the fingers matches intercalary months.[49] Just as the text represented the cosmos, its manipulation in divination recapitulated the processes that guided the world's movements.

The *Yi* thus claimed to offer a comprehensive, encompassing schema of the universe. Heaven and Earth, which stand for the universe, are matched with *qian* and *kun*, which stand for all the hexagrams and by extension, the entire *Yi*. The other complementary pairs in terms of which the function of the text is defined—hard and soft, motion and stillness—indicate the same claim to universality. The most explicit formulation of this idea states,

> The *Yi*'s nature as writing is that it is vast and complete. The Way of Heaven is within it. The Way of man is within it. The Way of Earth is within it. It combines these Three Powers and doubles them [through *yin* and *yang*]. Therefore there are six [lines]. The fact of there being six is nothing other than the Three Powers.[50]

The "Great Tradition" employs many verbs indicating that the action of the *Yi* is comprehensive, that it embraces all things, or that its nature is to complete. Among these verbs the most common are *tong* 通 "to go throughout, to penetrate," *ji* 極 "to reach the limits of," *bei* 備 "to complete," and *cheng* 成 "to finish, to perfect." Less frequent but still important are *jin* 盡 or *qiong* 窮 "to exhaust, to use up," as well as *zhou* 周 or *wei* 圍, "to encircle, to encompass."[51] Finally, the attempt to present a complete list of the hexagrams and establish a *necessary* sequence between them also derives from the idea that the text sketches the structure of the cosmos and depicts its operations.[52] Similar claims to schematic completeness have been noted also in such texts as the *Zhou li*, the "Yao dian," the "Yu gong," the "Hong fan," the "Tian wen," and the Mao tradition of the odes. The significance of this to textual authority in the late Warring States and early empires forms the subject of the next chapter.

[3] The text's project of encompassing the universe includes a claim to depict the structure of time. This claim focuses on the notion of change. This is the name and theme of the text, and it entails a model of the world based on evolution over time. References to charting *bian* 變 "alternation," *hua* 化 "transformation," *tong* 通 "going throughout [time]," and *yi* 易 "change" all reiterate the text's claim to offer mastery of the fluctuations of time.

The *Yi*'s nature as writing is that it cannot be kept at a distance. Its nature as a Way [of acting] is that it repeatedly shifts; it alternates and moves without resting in place. It completely flows through the six positions [filled by lines to form hexagrams]. The upper and lower [trigrams] are inconstant. The hard and soft [lines] change into one another. It cannot be a fixed rule, but accords only with alternation.[53]

The *Yi* offers the wisdom of the sage not in the form of invariant principles but as a set of written signs that enact or reproduce the changes underlying the processes of the physical world.

The most detailed discussion of how the signs of the *Yi* can recapitulate physical change occurs at the beginning of the second part of the "Great Tradition."

The eight trigrams form a series [*lie* 列] and the images are among them. When these are followed upon and doubled [forming hexagrams], the judgment statements are among them. When the hard and soft [lines] displace one another, the alternations are among them. When phrases are attached to them and they are charged [*ming* 命, i.e., the subject of the divination proclaimed], movement is among them. "Good fortune," "evil fortune," "remorse," and "humiliation" [formulaic results of divinations] are produced by this movement. The hard and soft establish the base. Alternation [of lines] and going through [a process] follow the time [*shi* 時 "season, occasion"].[54]

Since this dense passage is filled with technical terms of *Yi* lore, it can be developed only through reference to other sections of the text. The reference to the series of the eight trigrams and their images in the first line is explained in the "Shuo gua" commentary.[55] It identifies each trigram with its natural image: *qian*/Heaven, *kun*/Earth, *gen*/mountain, *dui*/lake, *zhen*/thunder, *sun*/wind, *kan*/water, and *li*/fire. It then presents them in two different fixed orders. In the first, the "prior to Heaven" (*xian tian* 先天), the trigrams are divided into four complementary pairs wherein each *yang* line is replaced by *yin* in its complement and vice versa. This series explains the play of correlates in nature—Heaven and Earth, mountain and lake, thunder and wind, water and fire—by the systematic reversal of the *yin* and *yang* elements that go into their makeup. It thereby explains alternation (*bian* 變) in the world as a necessary consequence of the first emergence of polarity, and creates an underlying typology of polarities in terms of the physical and moral attributes of the images.

The second sequence, the "posterior to Heaven" (*hou tian* 後天), presents the eight trigrams in a cycle in which each trigram is followed by one that represents the next stage in development. It begins with the trigram *zhen*, which depicts thunder and the first stirrings of life in the spring, and it ends with *gen*, which represents the mountain and fixity. Each image is also correlated with a direction, so this sequence depicts the cycle of directional winds that form the year.[56] Whereas the *xian tian* sequence is the image of alternation, of change explained in terms of *yin* and *yang*, the *hou tian* sequence is the image of cycles, of change described by the term *tong* 通 "to go throughout," and elsewhere depicted by the Five Phases.

The next sentences refer to the formation of the hexagrams and the addition of the judgments. These and the trigram images provide the basic tools for applying the visual signs of the *Yi* to the world. In the *Zuo zhuan*, most interpretations are based on the interplay of the two images in a hexagram ("wind over the lake," "mountain on the earth"), whereas later divination relied more on the judgment statements. References to the alternation of hard and soft lines indicate development within a hexagram. Each hexagram began with a line that was either *yin* or *yang*, and the subsequent lines of the hexagram depicted the unfolding of a process over time. This idea antedates the "Great Tradition," as is indicated in the "Tradition on the Judgments" of the first hexagram.

> Greatly illumined on the end and the beginning, the six positions in their time are completed. In the proper time ride the six dragons [the line judgments in the first hexagram all refer to dragons] to soar up to Heaven.

This is further elaborated in the "Tradition on the Words of the Text" appended to the same hexagram.

> How great is *qian*! . . . Its six lines open up and display, going through each aspect of the circumstances. "In the proper time ride the six dragons to soar up to Heaven." The clouds move, the rain falls, and the world is pacified.[57]

Here the sequence of six lines is a temporal sequence which progressively opens up and thereby reveals the dynamic tendency of present circumstances.

The manipulation of the yarrow stalks, which reproduced the annual cycle, selected the hexagram whose tendencies matched those of the present moment. The phrases appended to each line verbally explicated that line within the process schematized by the entire hexagram. These phrases included physical images (for example, "biting through dried gristle, he obtains a metal arrowhead"), moral maxims (for example, "exercise constancy in the face of difficulties"), or divination formulae such as those sketched in the passage ("good fortune," "evil fortune"). The hexagrams also had their own texts composed of similar elements.

The passage finishes with the assertion that the temporal process marked by alternation of *yin* and *yang* between the lines will accord with the occasion or season. This reference to "season" is crucial, because the annual cycle was the principle image for all patterns that underlay temporal sequences. The "Great Tradition" states that all "alternating and going through [cycles]" (*bian tong* 變通) are matched with the four seasons, or that the four seasons are the highest form of alternating and going through cycles.[58]

It is because the signs in the *Yi* and their appended phrases recapitulated the processes of the physical world that it could be used as a divination manual. The text contains all possible processes, and one has only to identify which is appropriate to the present moment in order to grasp the tendency of events. Although the commentaries acknowledge the use of the text for prognostication, in order to claim the *Yi* for sages and rulers and downplay its use as a technical manual, they place divination within a project of mastering all time, both past and future. While one or two passages refer to knowing the future, most speak of both knowing the future and mastering (or "storing up") the past.[59] The discussions in the "Shuo gua" of the sequences of trigrams also insist that they allow for comprehension of processes in both directions.

> Given the arrangement of the trigrams, one counts [*shu* 數] back into the past in the order of the sequence, and one knows the future through reversing the order. Therefore the *Yi* goes against the sequence [for divination] and counts with it [to know the past].[60]

This reading of process in both directions is essential to claims of comprehensive knowledge. It also links the *Yi* as a text with the chronicles, documents, odes, and philosophical texts that found authority in the past.

[4] In addition to offering mastery of time, the *Yi* also generated comprehensive models of space, in the form of a structure of vertically ranked positions (*wei* 位) and horizontally ordered sequences. The former appeared in the opening passage, where the hexagrams *qian* and *kun*—in parallel to Heaven and Earth—defined the hierarchy of noble and base. Whereas the temporal sequence of lines moved from the bottom up, the spatial/hierarchical series moved from the top down. A horizontal sequence has likewise been previously cited, in the series of the trigrams. Other passages refer to the "positions" established by the hexagrams, which are derived from the principles of the cosmos.[61] Some state that the *Yi* exists and operates entirely as a function of vertical and horizontal sequences.

> The exalted imitates Heaven, the lowly imitates Earth. Heaven and Earth establish their positions, and the *Yi* [or "the changes"] moves between them.

> *Qian* and *kun* complete their sequence, and the *Yi* is established between them.[62]

The idea of parallel hierarchies of positions in the cosmos and the text is also implicit in the reference to Fu Xi gazing up to Heaven and down to Earth to find the patterns for the trigrams.[63] Accounts of the *Yi* using the positions of the hexagrams to move between Heaven and Earth attribute the same role to the text as the myths did to its inventor.

The idea that the position of lines defines a hierarchy is also incorporated into the line texts. Since *yang* numbers are odd and *yin* even, it is appropriate to have solid lines in the first, third, and fifth positions and broken ones in the others.[64]

Consequently, the significance of the lines depends on their positions in the vertical scale, which are equated with and provide a model for ranking in society.

> The second and fourth lines have the same [*yin*] function but their positions are different, so their excellence is different. Line two is mostly praised, while line four is mostly feared. This is because it is too near [the ruler]. . . . The third and fifth lines have the same function but their positions are different. Line three is mostly inauspicious, while line five is mostly meritorious. This is because of the rankings of noble and base.[65]

The fifth line is the "ruler" of both the upper trigram and the hexagram as a whole, so the value of particular lines is interpreted in terms of their relation to it. This idea of the hexagrams as analogous to the social order appears already in the judgments appended to some hexagrams.[66]

The "Great Tradition" also applies the social reading of lines to the trigrams on the basis of their structure. It distinguishes *yang* trigrams (with one *yang* line) from *yin* trigrams (one *yin* line) and ranks them.

> The *yang* trigram has one ruler [*yang* line] and two subjects [*yin* lines]. This is the Way of the gentleman. The *yin* trigram has two rulers and one subject. This is the Way of the petty man.[67]

The individual lines relate as ruler and subject, and on the basis of this relation the trigram is ranked as noble or base. Thus not only individual lines but clusters of lines are spatially arranged in ranks of honor.

[5] The parallel between nature, society, and the *Yi* also figures in passages that credit the hexagrams with vitality and generative powers. Chapter 5 discussed the generative power of written signs in the mythology of Fu Xi and Nü Wa, as well as the homophone glosses in Han dictionaries. This same theme is theoretically elaborated in the "Great Tradition," where the correlation of the hexagrams with nature entails the former's ability to move and to reproduce. The vitality of the hexagrams was implicit in the idea that the sequence of the six lines enacted a dynamic process in which the lines "opened" or "developed" (*fa* 發), "brandished" or "displayed" (*hui* 揮), and "went [to a destination]" (*zhi* 之). However, other passages explicitly assert the dynamism and fecundity of the hexagrams.

The first follows immediately on the opening discussion of the hexagrams *qian* and *kun*.

> Therefore the hard and soft [lines] press one another. The eight trigrams agitate one another. Drum them with thunder and lightning. Moisten them with wind and rain. The sun and moon move in cycles, now cold now hot. The Way of *qian* forms the male, the Way of *kun* forms the female. *Qian* has mastery of the great beginnings, and *kun* achieves the completion of things.[68]

The elements of the *Yi* appear as dynamic, living agents that push and move on their own accord. They are the constant correlates of natural processes and underlie the sexual division that allows generation and maturation. Consequently they are responsible for the birth and death of all things.

The image of the trigrams and hexagrams as motors of natural process recurs throughout the "Great Tradition," often expressed in the character *dong* 動 "movement." It states, "The movements of the six lines are the Way of the Three Powers," so the *Yi* contained the principle of all activity in the universe. Other passages state that the elements of the *Yi* move, that they elicit motion from objects in the world, or that they allow men to guide motion. "Alternation" and "change" are directly linked to movement.[69]

The lines, trigrams, and hexagrams also generate life. This is implicit in the identification of *qian* and *kun* with the male and the female, but it is also explicitly stated.

> To daily renew is called "flourishing virtue." To produce life is called "change" [*yi* 易]. To complete the [Heavenly] images is called *qian*. To imitate the Earthly models is called *kun*. To trace the numbers to their limit and know the future is called "prognostication."[70]

The defining attribute of the *Yi*, encompassing the division into *qian* and *kun* and the act of prognostication, is the generation of life. Other passages identify the *Yi* and its elements with the generation of life and the development of living things, or treat the trigrams and lines as living things that are born and grow.[71]

As a generated text, the *Yi* offered unique insights into life and death, and thus served to link the world of men with that of the spirits.

> [The *Yi*] traces back to beginnings and returns to ends. Therefore it masters the explanations of life and death. Refined energies form objects, and wandering souls [*hun* 魂] work changes. Therefore it masters the nature of ghosts and spirits.[72]

Here the ability of the *Yi* to guide divination and give a comprehensive account of the world is linked directly to vital energy and to the associated theories of life and afterlife.

One of the most striking images of generation adapts the proto-Daoist account of cosmogony through numerical division to the structure of the *Yi*.

> Therefore the *Yi* [or "changes"] possesses the Supreme Ultimate. This gives birth to the Two Standards [*liang yi* 兩儀, *yin* and *yang*]. The Two Standards give birth to the Four Images [the four possible combinations of broken and unbroken lines]. The Four Images give birth to the eight trigrams. The eight trigrams fix the auspicious and inauspicious. The auspicious and inauspicious give birth to the Great Enterprise [usually the founding of a dynasty].[73]

This account conflates the proto-Daoist account of the emergence of the world with a history of the development of the *Yi* text. It thus reinforces the relation of the text to the world as that of microcosm to macrocosm, but does so in a cosmogonic narrative that centers on the generation of the text, and its ability to generate order in the world.

IMAGES AND WRITING

This account of the origins of the text in the form of the origins of the world highlights another feature of the "Great Tradition." Due to its elaboration of the microcosm-macrocosm relation between text and world, the "Tradition" both *insists on* the nature of the *Yi* as text and *denies* that same nature by making its operations indistinguishable from natural phenomena. The most notable examples of this are the passages, two of which were translated above, that discuss "the *Yi*'s nature as writing" (*Yi zhi wei shu* 易之爲書). The first proclaims the *Yi* to be vast and all-encompassing, including within itself Heaven, Earth, and man. Another phrase introduced by the same formula states that as something that traces natural process, the *Yi* "is regarded as a substance" (*yi wei zhi* 以爲質).[74] The conflation of text *qua* text with substance and process in the world is marked by the fact that certain terms, for example, *ji* 吉 "auspicious" and *xiong* 凶 "inauspicious," can refer either to phrases in the text or features of the natural world.[75] The character *yi* 易 likewise refers to the text, to change in the world, and sometimes (as in the quote immediately above) possibly to either. This conflation of sign and reality is central to the project of elaborating a natural philosophy of writing, a project in which the *Yi* was the central text.

The blurring of text and object is linked ultimately to the concept of "image" (*xiang* 象), one of the key terms in the situating of visual signs within the natural world. This character figures in the names of two of the earlier commentaries on the *Yi*, it runs throughout the "Great Tradition," and it plays a central role in early accounts of kingship, punishments, and the nature of writing.

Before examining the development of the notion of image within the *Yi* commentaries, one should note that earlier sections of the text, notably the line statements, often begin with a natural image as a "topic" or "omen."[76] As Richard Kunst and Edward Shaughnessy have argued, these images are related to the "evocations" (*xing* 興) that begin many Zhou odes. The clearest example of this relationship is the identical use of the image of the wild goose in hexagram #53 "Gradual Advance" (*jian* 漸) and in several of the odes.

> "Jian," line statement 3: The wild goose advances across the land;
> the man campaigns and does not return;
> the wife becomes pregnant but does not give birth;
> Inauspicious. Beneficial to ward off bandits.

Mao #159, "Jiu yu" (九罭): The wild goose flies across the land;
                      The lord heads home but does not return.

Mao #181, "Hong yan" (鴻鴈): The wild goose in flight
                     'Flap, flap' go his wings;
                     These men on campaign
                     Toiling in the wilds.[77]

The above examples all have an opening line evoking some phenomenon in the natural world, followed by a rejoinder taken from the human world. While no explicit connection is made, the analogy between the passage of the wild goose across the landscape and the movement of soldiers on campaign is easily discerned. The recurrence of the link in several poems and a divination text confirms that the association between flying geese and men sent far from home was intentional, and probably a convention. Other phrases from the *Yi* can also be explained by reference to couplets in the *Odes* indicating parallels between nature and society. Although most natural images evoked in the *Yi* line statements are not paired with any immediate equivalent from the world of men, it is likely that the Western Zhou diviners who created the text knew the relevant associations and employed them to link omens to prognostications.[78]

This suggests that the idea of a correspondence between the natural and human realms emerged out of the ancient social and religious milieu in which the phenomena of the natural world were scrutinized and recorded as guides to human actions. Omens were collected by court diviners or astrologers and developed into an oral corpus of verse formulae and homilies. As ritual hymns developed into songs for entertainment or protest, the omen lore provided images evoking particular ideas or emotions. At roughly the same time the oral divination formulae were set down in texts. Natural images were compiled together with prognostications in a catalog of hexagram and line statements that could be applied to any situation through the use of stalk casting. When the divination manual was read as an exposition of the principles of the cosmos, correspondences between the natural and human worlds were developed into elaborate systems that gave intelligible form to both domains. Moreover, when hexagrams were imagined as the origins of script, reading natural phenomena as signs became the prototype of reading graphs. This was facilitated by the fact that many *Yi* line statements derived meaning from plays on words or graphic manipulation.[79]

The role of natural images in the earliest sections of the *Yi* offered material for more theoretical treatment in the commentaries. Those under the rubric "image" are divided into "greater" and "lesser." In fact, these two are separated not by scale but by a different approach to the nature of the hexagram. The "Greater Images Tradition" explains the meaning of hexagrams through dividing them into trigrams. Each of the eight trigrams is assigned a different natural phenomenon— Heaven, Earth, thunder, wind, water, fire, mountain, and lake (or "swamp")—and the powers or actions associated with that phenomenon. The sense of the hexagram is explained through the interaction of the phenomena evoked by its trigrams. Thus the commentary to hexagram #8 *bi* 比, composed of the trigrams *kan* "water" and *kun* "earth" reads:

> On the earth there is water. *Bi.* The former kings thereby established the myriad states and formed intimate ties with the feudal lords.[80]

The commentator argues that the image is of the king's influence flowing across the earth like water, covering its surface with loyal feudatories. The same pattern— the interplay of two natural images suggesting a moral or political lesson—is repeated for most of the hexagrams. This model of divination figures in many examples in the *Zuo zhuan* and *Guo yu*, and it could well be the earliest form of divination preserved in the *Yi* tradition. The lessons provided in the text are aimed at heads of state and high political figures, and they emphasize the role of ruler as teacher or moral exemplar. This indicates that the politicization of the *Yi* drama-tized in the *Zuo zhuan* had become an underlying assumption of the later commentarial tradition.[81]

The "Lesser Images Tradition" is based on the individual lines, consisting of glosses on their appended statements. Whereas the images of the "Greater Images" were dynamic natural forces, those of the "Lesser" tradition are disembodied, hier-archical relations—depicted in spatial terms—and their associated social roles. As an example, the "Lesser Images" commentary of the hexagram #30, *li* 離 reads:

> First [line, reading from bottom to top] nine [i.e., *yang*]. Treads carefully to rever-ence it. No blame. The "Images" says, "Through the reverence of treading carefully, one thereby avoids blame."
>
> Second, six [i.e., *yin*]. Yellow, encounters fundamental good fortune. The "Images" says, "'Yellow, encounters fundamental good fortune.' This is obtaining the middle Way."
>
> Third, nine. Encounter with the setting sun. If one does not drum the pot and sing, then it will be the sighing of the aged. Inauspicious. The "Images" says, "'Encounter of the setting sun.' How could it last long?"
>
> Fourth, nine. Sudden is its coming. Like burning, like death, like abandonment. The "Images" says, "'Sudden is its coming.' There is nothing that accepts it."
>
> Fifth, six. Emits a flood of tears, sad and sighing. Auspicious. The "Images" says, "The auspiciousness of six [*yin*] in the fifth comes from encountering the king and duke."
>
> Sixth, nine. The king employs it to launch punitive expeditions. There is blessing. Chop off heads and capture those who are not of the right kind. No blame. The "Images" says, "'The king employs it to launch punitive expeditions.' This is to correct the state."[82]

Here the image is not linked to any recurring unit, such as the trigram, but rather to the place of the line within the hexagram. The most notable feature in this commentary is the importance of lines two and five. As the central lines of the two trigrams, these are regularly the most important in the "Lesser Images" and are often associated with the ruler. This is especially true of line five. Here line two is auspicious because it is the middle and associated with the color yellow. Line five corresponds to the ruler, hence it indicates "encountering the king and duke," and is also auspicious. Line three, the last and highest of the lower trigram, is matched with the setting sun. Line four, the first line of the second trigram, indicates an arrival. Line six, the end of the hexagram, is associated with setting out. It thus interprets the images primarily in spatial terms as a depiction of hierarchical relations, and secondarily in temporal terms as comings and goings.

The "Lesser Images" commentary also often refers to the match between the line and its position. *Yin* lines match the even positions while *yang* lines match the odd. Commentaries on some hexagrams discuss the relation between the corresponding lines of the two trigrams—one and four, two and five, three and six. When this issue is discussed, it is considered auspicious to have one *yin* and one *yang* in the two positions, thereby forming a matching pair.[83] However, the association of phrases with lines preceded the commentaries, and the principles enunciated by the authors of the latter often fail to explain the former.

The commentaries explain the meanings of hexagrams, and by extension that of the entire *Yi*, through the assumption that their constituent elements have an unmediated correspondence to the world. In the case of the "Greater Images" the trigrams symbolize natural processes, and the sense of the hexagram derives from their interplay. The "Shuo gua" commentary, in turn, linked each trigram to its natural referent through the interplay of its *yin* and *yang* lines. In the case of the "Lesser Images" the hexagram defines a set of hierarchical positions occupied by one of the two types of lines. The relations of the lines to their position and to each other define the total situation and the status of each line, which are interpreted in terms of social roles. Thus the images in all cases are understood as visual signs that through their correspondence to the natural and social worlds allow insights into the structure of reality and its inherent tendencies.

Images are, however, neither linguistic units (names) nor direct representations (pictures). Names and pictures give an account of the world through one-to-one correspondences with their objects. The images, in contrast, constitute a delimited number of fundamental units—eight trigrams, two types of line—in a fixed number of possible relations—upper or lower for the trigrams, one of the six positions for the lines. The commentators claim to explain all phenomena through appeal to the possible combinations of these elements and relations. Thus the "Image" commentaries turn the *Yi* into a natural philosophy of signs by developing a calculus in which the processes of the world can be accounted for by the manipulation of a limited number of basic units. They give pride of place to *interactions* between the units, which are inherently moving and dynamic, rather than their nature. They thus create a proto-science of generating and mutating signs, rather than fixed essences, to account for the patterns that underlie change in the world.

However, the units and their relations are adopted directly from the observable world they seek to explain. They remain images in that they are not purely abstract quantities or formal relations, but rather schematized forms of real entities. The trigrams use natural phenomena as types for all possible energies or processes in the world. The hexagrams and lines use certain relations—center versus periphery, matching correlates versus mutually repelling identities—as types for all social bonds. Because they are, on the one hand, a fixed repertoire of signs and interactions and, on the other, abstracted representations of natural or social phenomena, the elements of the *Yi* are interchangeably (or indistinguishably) text and reality. In defining these elements and relations, the authors of the text smuggle the phenomenal world into their proto-mathematical system, and then claim to derive that world from their calculations. This identity of text and world, or rather their mutual generation, reinforces the idea that the former allows a direct perception of the structure of the latter. This validates the science and authorizes its practitioners as masters of wisdom.

The "Great Tradition" develops these ideas in several ways. It increasingly associates the images with astral phenomena, which are paired with the "models" of the terrestrial realm. This link appeared already in the account of Fu Xi looking up to see the images in Heaven and down to see the models on Earth. It appears in several other passages, being given its most explicit formulation as follows.

> In Heaven it becomes images, on Earth it becomes "forms" (*xing* 形), and the alternations and transformations become visible.[84]

The association with Heaven was reinforced by describing glowing astral bodies as "suspended images" (*xuan xiang* 懸象).

Of the suspended images and visibly bright [objects], none are greater than the sun and moon.[85] This identification with astral phenomena influenced astrology, in which *xiang* 象 became the standard term for celestial counterparts to earthly events.[86] These celestial images formed a parallel realm offering signs for reading the world of man, and the *Yi* was a textual adaptation of such signs.

The images were also fundamental to the work of the sages. Thus in the account of the sage's work translated above, his perception of the hidden patterns of the world and measuring of their forms culminates in the creation of images that reveal their character. The sages' creation of implements also depended on the translation of the images of Heaven into trigrams and hexagrams, and then the application of these to the transformation of brute nature. This idea was most elaborately developed in the myth of the sage's invention of civilization, but the translation of images into implements figures in several other passages.[87]

The images are also fundamental to the sage's distinctive use of written signs. The most important passage on this question is the discussion of the limits of language cited earlier. The sage uses the images, which directly capture the truth of the world, to overcome the inability of written and spoken language to exhaustively represent things. With knowledge based on the images, he can achieve an adequate language in the form of the appended phrases. A variation on this idea is developed elsewhere.

> Heaven produces numinous things, and the sage takes them as pattern. Heaven and Earth alternate and transform, and the sage copies them. Heaven hangs down its images to reveal the auspicious and inauspicious, and the sage imitates them. The [Yellow] River produces the Chart and the Luo [River] produces the Writings, and the sage takes them as his pattern.[88]

The sage's actions are defined through the imitation of Heaven and natural process. They culminate in his imitation of the celestial images and in his copying of the revealed natural patterns that produce writing. This link of the natural signs in Heaven to written graphs is reinforced by the next passage, which transfers this parallel from the world to the *Yi*.

> The *Yi* has the four images. These are the means by which it shows. It appends phrases to them. These are the means by which it announces.[89]

In the parallelism of the text the suspended images in the sky correspond to the "four images" of the *Yi*, while the graphic forms revealed by the rivers match the appended phrases of the text. Thus the *Yi* links yarrow divination, astrology, and writing in the natural correspondences that underlie accurate representation. Recognition of these links is based on perception of the images, and this perception defines the sage.

The images define not only the sage, but also the *Yi*. The above passage indicates the central role of the images, which stand for the preverbal apparatus of the *Yi*—the trigrams and hexagrams—parallel to the linguistic element of the appended phrases. As all possible pairs of lines, the images encompass the trigrams and hexagrams. This idea is reiterated in the assertion, "The eight trigrams use the images to inform." An account of the development of the *Yi* through progressive incrementation likewise begins with the statement, "The eight trigrams form a series and the images are among them."

The structure of the *Yi*, like the trigrams and hexagrams, is defined through the images. Thus one passage asserts, "The hexagram statements speak of the images." Another, playing on homophone glosses, pairs the lines and images as the two entities that form the *Yi* through their nature as correlates of the natural world.[90] The most elaborate equation of the *Yi* with images is the following.

> The sage established the hexagrams and observed the images. He appended phrases to them and made clear the auspicious and inauspicious. The hard and soft displaced one another and produced alternation and transformation.
>
> Therefore "auspicious" and "inauspicious" are the images of success and failure. "Regret" and "harm" are the images of concern and worry. Alternation and transformation are the images of advance and retreat. Hard and soft are the images of day and night.[91]

Here the images are paired with hexagrams as the foundations of the *Yi*, while the basic concepts and technical vocabulary of the text are all glossed as images. These passages are summed up in the assertion, "The *Yi* is the images. The images are imitation."[92] Having begun as elements of divination formulae and developed into the core of the *Yi*'s theory of correspondences, the images emerged as the core of the text, the key to the possibility of representation, and the foundation of the sages' wisdom.

Xiang 象 was also a key term in other writings on the sage kings and the natural foundations of writing. The clearest example of the former is the story (cited in chapter 1) of the tripods of Yu.

> In the past when the Xia had virtuous potency, the distant regions made illustrations [*tu* 'I] of their objects, they had tribute of metal sent in by the Nine Shepherds, and they cast tripods with images of the objects. They included all objects, so the people could recognize spirits and demons. Therefore when the people entered the rivers and swamps, or mountain forests, they would encounter nothing untoward. None of the evil spirits of the wilds could come against them. They used them to harmonize those above and below, in order to receive the blessings of Heaven. Jie [the last Xia king] had benighted virtue, so the tripods passed to the Shang and stayed there six hundred years. Zhou of the Shang was violent and cruel, so the tripods passed to the Zhou.[93]

In this story world rulership is marked by the collection of illustrations—identified by the same character as the prototypes of writing revealed by the Yellow River—of all the objects in the world and their casting as images on bronze tripods. The links of tripods to political authority had roots in practice as well as ritual theory, for the number of tripods in funerary sets had marked the deceased's ranking in the lineage law.[94] Here the tripods cease to be actual vessels used for offerings of food to ancestral spirits from whom power is derived, and become instead the repository of images that generate authority.

These images produce authority in several ways. First, like the metal in which they are cast, they are tribute, the receiving of which marks the Xia's power over distant regions. Images as power-generating tribute figure in chapter 7, in the poetry of Sima Xiangru. Second, the images provide an inventory of the objects of the world. In this they anticipate the images of the *Yi*, which mark the sages as kings through their encompassment of the cosmos. Although this passage does not mention the number of tripods, later traditions stipulate that there were nine, corresponding to the nine provinces into which Yu divided the world. This number links the theme of the images as tribute to the idea that the images include the world. Third, as noted in chapter 1, they grant the power to identify and presumably to name rare objects and denizens of the spirit world. Although, here, this is a means of protecting the people, such powers of identification and naming were a hallmark of the sage ruler. This royal function of the tripods is marked by the reference to their harmonizing "those above and below," and marking possession of Heaven's Mandate.

Links of tripods to rulership figure also in the *Lü shi chun qiu*. Though referred to as the "tripods of Zhou," references to their images show that these passages are based on the same tradition.

> On the Zhou tripods they applied images, and these allowed a comprehensive knowledge of principles. Comprehensive knowledge of principles is the Way of the ruler.

> On the Zhou tripods they applied Taotie. He has a head with no body. He ate a man, but before he had even swallowed, the harm befell his own body. This is in order to tell of retribution.

> On the Zhou bronzes they applied Chui with his fingers bitten off. The former kings had the means thereby to show that great craft could not be practiced.

> On the Zhou bronzes they applied worms [or "snakes"]. Their twisting appearance was very long. They curled both upward and downward. They thereby revealed the ruin brought about by going to extremes.

> On the Zhou tripods they applied rats with horses treading upon them. This means that they do not rise up. "Not rising up" is the custom of a doomed state.[95]

One passage states that the images on Zhou bronzes allowed a comprehensive knowledge of principles that defined the Way of the ruler. The rest give specific examples of images and explain the principles they demonstrate. Many of the images discussed indicate attempts in the Warring States period to account for the decor on Shang and Zhou vessels, but the explanations rely on the tradition of Yu's casting of images.[96] These passages echo the line statements of the *Yi*, beginning with a graphic image and concluding with a moral lesson or advice. The links between the images and the lessons are clearer than many of those in the *Yi*, but they share the assumption that the sages discerned true principles and derived appropriate actions through the contemplation of images.

Another link between the *Yi* and the tripods is that trigram #50 is named "Tripod" (*ding* 鼎). This hexagram has two distinctive features. First, it is the only hexagram in the received *Yi* that is named for an implement, and one of only three possibly named for artificial objects.[97] Since the "Great Tradition" repeatedly linked "images" to the sages' invention of implements, the fact that the one hexagram certainly named for an implement is linked to the central myth of the political role of images might not be accidental. Second, as Edward Shaughnessy has noted, "Tripod" is the only hexagram where the line statements explicitly assert that the lines taken together suggest an image of the object for which it is named. Thus "Tripod" may be the only hexagram which the earliest authors understood as a direct visual image of its name. However, late Warring States commentators were clearly convinced that the hexagrams *should* have presented visual images, since the "Great Tradition" tries to prove the imagistic basis of no less then thirteen hexagrams.[98]

A second myth linking images to the sage kings was the tradition that Shun and Yu had employed "punishments through images" (*xiang xing* 象刑).

> The vulgar persuaders of the present day say, "In well-regulated antiquity there were no mutilating punishments [*rou xing* 肉刑] but instead there were punishments through images."[99]

The description of these punishments is corrupt, and has been reconstructed from passages from the *Shenzi*, the *Shang shu da zhuan*, and the *Han shu*. The reconstructed passage suggests that tattooing was replaced by drawings on the face or the wearing of a face covering, cutting off the nose by the wearing of bleached cap strings, amputation of the feet by the wearing of straw sandals, castration by the wearing of an apron with a piece cut off, and the death penalty by the wearing of a collarless jacket stained red. Rather than being carved into the flesh, the punishments were drawn on the face or marked on specified pieces of clothing. They were images because they were purely visual and without fleshly substance.

The *Xunzi* denies the possibility of punishment through images, but this indicates that the tradition had some currency in the late Warring States period. This is supported by references in the *Shenzi* and the *Shang shu da zhuan*. The tradition later became enmeshed in Han debates on mutilating punishments, and it was cited in several Han sources as evidence of the sagehood of the early rulers and the potency of their regimes.[100] Since distinctive clothing and haircuts were used in the Qin and Han to mark categories of criminals, the myth of "punishment through images" was related to actual practice in the period.

A final reference to "punishment through images" occurs in the *Shang shu*. The chapter is a later old text forgery, but the sentence is cited in Han discussions of the practice. Thus it is likely that a version of the chapter existed in Han times. The reference to punishments adds nothing, but the same chapter discusses the use of images by the ruler.

I [Shun] wish to spread my power through the four quarters. You [Yu] will do this. I wish to observe the images used by the ancients. The sun, moon, constellations, mountains, dragons, flowers, and snakes shall be depicted on vessels in the ancestral temple. The pondweed, flames, grains of rice, white and black axes, and ornamental characters shall be embroidered. With all colors these patterns shall be displayed on the five ranks of clothing. You shall make these clear.[101]

Here images on vessels, closely related to images in the *Yi* and perhaps suggesting the tripods of Yu, are linked immediately with those on official robes. Like the use of images to punish, this myth of the ancient rulers' having images embroidered on their robes reflects actual practice in the Warring States and early empires.[102] This passage became a classic precedent for such regulations in early imperial China and was cited in the first monograph on imperial robes and chariots, written by Sima Biao (ca. 240–ca. 306 A.D.).[103] Rule through images thus became the foundation myth for using clothing and hair style to mark both convicts and courtiers. The images visibly represented the "twin handles" of government, reward and punishment.

The opposition between *rou xing* 肉刑, literally "punishments in the flesh" and *xiang xing* 象刑, "punishments through images," suggests another anecdote dealing with images. The character for image was derived by homophony from that for "elephant." On this basis the authors of the *Han Feizi* explained "image" as follows:

> Men rarely see a living elephant, but they can see the bones of dead elephants. On the basis of this representation [*tu* 圖 "chart," the naturally revealed patterns of writing] they think of [what it was] in life. Therefore the means by which people are able to have an idea of or think about something are all called "elephants/images." Although the Way cannot be heard or seen, the sage grasps its visible functions to fix a vision of its "form." Therefore it [the *Dao de jing*] says, "The formless form, the 'thingless' image."[104]

Here the flesh of the elephant has vanished and can only be deduced from its skeletal image. This gloss makes at least three points. First, an image suggests something that is absent. Second, it is not an arbitrary symbol but linked to what it represents. In this way it is an "icon" in Pierce's sense of a nonarbitrary sign, as well as in the etymological sense of its Greek origins.[105] Third, it is tied to writing, both through its description as a "chart" (*tu* 圖) and through its consisting of a set of lines, in this case bones, that indicate the vanished object.[106] This exercise in popular etymology thus recapitulates many of the ideas underlying the images in the *Yi* text and associated myths.

In the above uses the term "image" (*xiang*) does not, however, refer to a mimetic representation or picture. Bones do not depict an elephant, stars are not a picture of the earthly phenomena to which they correspond, and punishments by images did not offer a likeness of the mutilation that they replaced. These images are defined by being visual, fleshless, and indicating the meaning or structure of the phenomena for which they stand. It is for this reason that the abstract relations of lines in the *Yi* text could be described as images. This must be kept in mind when analyzing the application of the term to written graphs.

If images were identified with the power of the ruler as forms of tribute, modes of knowledge, and instruments of control, their chief importance was as the source of writing. The role of images as the basis of writing already figured in the mythology of inventions, but it was developed into a general account of the creation of graphs. The clearest form of this was the hypothesis of the "six [types of] graphs" (*liu shu* 六書), first mentioned in the *Zhou li*, but the details of which we know only from the late Western Han writings of Liu Xiang and the Eastern Han *Shuo wen jie zi*.[107] The figure "six" was selected for purposes of making correlations, so several of the types may be little more than attempts to fill out the number.[108] This theory is the subject of a massive literature, but here I will simply examine those elements of it that are related to the idea of image and the accounts of the origin and role of writing. Since the *Zhou li* provides no list of types, and what is left of Liu Xiang's essay contains only the names, the analysis must begin with Xu Shen's definitions in the postface to the *Shuo wen*.

Xu Shen offers a typology based on origins. He prefaces the discussion of the "six types" with a history of writing, beginning with an extended quotation of the "Great Tradition" account of Fu Xi's examination of the "images of Heaven" and the "models of Earth."[109] This concludes:

> Thereupon he first made the eight trigrams of the *Yi*, in order to hand down exemplary images (*xian xiang* 憲象).

Thus the trigrams are not only copied from images, but they in turn furnish images for the later development of graphic signs.

After a brief account of Shen Nong keeping records with knotted cords, he narrates the invention of written graphs by Cang Jie.

> He observed the footprints of birds and beasts, and recognized that meaningful patterns could be distinguished. For the first time he created graphs and tallies [*qie* 契, a word which referred to tallies, contracts, and Shang oracle script]. All types of craftsmen were thereby put in order, and all types of products were thereby examined. He probably took this from the hexagram #43 *Kuai* [夬]. . . . When Cang Jie first made graphs, he relied on categories and the imaging of shapes [i.e., "pictographs"]. Therefore they were called *wen* 文 ["patterns"; simple, nonanalyzable graphs]. Later the "form and sound" graphs increased, and these were called *zi* 字 ["compound graphs"]. "*Wen*" are the roots of all images of things. "*Zi*" means to be fruitful, multiply, and gradually increase. When written on bamboo and silk they

were called *shu* 書 ["writing"]. "Writing" means "to resemble." The ages of the Five Emperors and Three Kings changed their forms. Seventy-two ruling houses made the *feng* sacrifice at Mt. Tai and none of them used the same [graphs].

Here Cang Jie repeats the examination of natural patterns by which Fu Xi invented the trigrams, but he focuses on footprints. These physical traces of departed creatures echo the *Han Feizi*'s account of elephant bones as the origins of the term "image," and also are linked to stories that will be discussed below. The reference to craftsmen and their products likewise echoes the links between images and implements, with the craftsmen standing in for the sages who were their mythic prototypes.[110] Xu Shen then distinguishes between simple graphs formed from the images of things, and compound graphs derived by combining the simple ones. In this model all graphs ultimately derive from images, and they multiply through the mating of simple graphs. This history—and the six types of graphs that derive from it—gives theoretical form to Fu Xi's mythic embodiment of both visual signs and the process of generation. The definition of *wen* reiterates the derivation of graphs from natural images, as does that of *shu* 書, which makes resemblance to the world the hallmark of writing. The final passage draws the history of writing into the more general theory—discussed in chapter 1—of the evolution of rites and the identification of authority with change.

Xu Shen then defines the six types of graphs. He posits two types of simple graphs (*wen* 文): "indicators of function" (*zhi shi* 指事, literally "pointing at affairs/ tasks") and "form imaging" (*xiang xing* 象形). The latter are what Westerners commonly call "pictographs," such as characters that indicate "sun," "moon," "mountain," or "river" by simplified pictures.[111] The former depict a relation or function, such as graphs that indicate "above" and "below" with a long horizontal line and a shorter line either above or below it. It is interesting that Xu Shen begins not with pictographs, but with graphs indicating abstract relations through the disposition of lines in space. In fact, his examples evoke the "Lesser Image Tradition" of the *Yi*, which also focuses on the derivation of meaning from abstracted relations of lines. Indeed the older form of the graphs "above" and "below" could stand as two-line images in the *Yi*'s technical sense. His beginning with "indicators of function" probably stems from his belief, announced earlier in the postface, that the graphs ultimately derive from Fu Xi's trigrams.

Xu Shen next introduces the two means of generating compound graphs. The most common, covering roughly 90 percent of the graphs in the *Shuo wen*, is "form and sound [or 'giving form to sound']" (*xing sheng* 形聲). These are formed from two simple graphs, one indicating the pronunciation and the other the semantic category to which the graph belongs, for example, language, liquid, plants, metals, and so on.[112] The second means of generating compound characters was "combining meaning" (*hui yi* 會意). Here the sense was indicated by the common feature of the simple graphs, or the relation of one to the other. Examples of this include the character for "bright" formed by the combination of "sun" and "moon," the character for "herdsman" formed by the combination of "ox" and a "hand with a whip," and the character for "trust" by the combination of the characters "man" and "speech."

The final two categories are not means of forming graphs, but ways of extending existing graphs to perform new functions. The first of these, "reciprocally glossing" (*zhuan zhu* 轉注), is the most obscure category. Judging from the examples provided by Xu Shen, it refers to characters that are graphically related, phonetically similar, and etymologically linked, such as the characters *kao* 考 and *lao* 老. They may be derivatives of a single character that has split over time.[113] The final category is "loaning" (*jia jie* 假借). Xu Shen's examples involve extended meanings (*zhang* 長 "eldest"—or *chang* 長 "long"—used to mean "chief, leader"). More broadly, it refers to cases where one indicated an unrepresentable idea or grammatical function by using a character that had the same sound.

This typology of characters derives from the history of writing with which the postface began, and like the latter it treats visual images as the foundation of writing and definitive of its nature. This has two consequences: first, writing is separated from the spoken language as an autonomous system; second, writing is treated as a dynamic entity that generates and multiplies. I will discuss each of these in turn.

That writing derives directly from the contemplation of the world without passing through the medium of spoken language is central to both the myth of origin and the typology of characters. In the former, Fu Xi derives the trigrams from the contemplation of visual patterns, and Cang Jie turns these into characters through the examination of visible traces. In the latter, all simple graphs are derived from the visual depiction of relationships or forms, and all compound graphs are created through combining simple ones. Speech figures not at all in the myths, and it is introduced into the typology only at the stage of the compound characters. Even there its role is muted in Xu Shen's definitions, which always subsume indications of sound under a prior semantic role derived from visual depiction. Thus his definition of the "form and sound" characters indicates that the sound element also indicates the meaning of the character (see note 112). Many etymologies in the *Shuo wen* indicate that the choice of phonetic elements prefers those that contribute to meaning, and later scholars elaborated this point.[114] Moreover, the privileging of paronomastic glosses in the *Shuo wen*, the *Shi ming*, and Han commentaries clearly indicates a commitment to the belief that sounds included a semantic element. Consequently phonetic elements in characters were viewed as full characters in their own right, contributing both sound and meaning to the composite graphs.

The stress on the visual over the oral is even clearer in his definition of "loan" characters.

> "Loans": originally there is no character, so on the basis of the sound one entrusts the matter/affair (*shi* 事).

One must note carefully what this says. Xu Shen views it not as a case of using an existing character to stand for a homophonous word for which no character exists, but rather of using homophony to attribute a new meaning to an existing character. The character is taken as the fixed entity to which the meaning is "entrusted."[115] Just as for "form and sound" characters, he rejects—or cannot conceive of—the possibility that the written graph is to be understood as a depiction of spoken language.

While in both myth and theory Xu Shen denies the links of writing to speech, the earlier discussion of the six types of characters by Liu Xiang seems to have gone even further. The bibliographic chapter of the *Han shu* preserves only the six rubrics, but these can be identified with those of Xu Shen. Notably, all four types relating to the creation of graphs are named with the word "image." Thus Liu Xiang begins his list with "form imaging," which was adopted by Xu Shen. However, rather than "indicating function/affairs" (*zhi shi* 指事), Liu Xiang refers to "imaging function/affairs" (*xiang shi* 象事). In the third position he puts "imaging meaning" (*xiang yi* 象意), rather than Xu Shen's later "combining meaning." Finally, rather than "form and sound," he refers to "imaging sound" (*xiang sheng* 象聲). Thus Liu Xiang argued that not merely all simple graphs but all compound graphs as well were formed from images. Some depicted the shape, some the function or role, and some the meaning. Even characters with phonetic elements were regarded as direct visual images of sound. This again clearly shows that the notion of image was not defined by or restricted to physical resemblance.

The second feature of Xu Shen's typology is that it assumes that all graphs derived directly from the world or were produced by other graphs. Words cannot, as in an alphabetic system, be decomposed into a set of smaller units that exist at a presemantic level, nor can new words be generated through the recombination of such units. The simple graph depicting an object or relation is the lowest level, and new graphs appear through the combination of old ones. Graphs, and the elements of which they are composed, are thus irreducibly meaningful entities which cannot be taken apart without dying, and they reproduce themselves in an almost sexual manner. This insistence that graphs cannot be reduced below the semantic level reproduces as a theoretical proposition the tendency of the "Great Tradition" to identify written language with its topic, that is, to conflate the character with the object or the text with the world. The theme of characters as organic is likewise reflected in the *Han Feizi*'s use of skeletal remains as the prototype of the image, and Xu Shen's derivation of characters from the footprints of birds and beasts, the traces of living creatures, rather than from inanimate, tangible objects.

An alternative line of argument would suggest that since all simple graphs are composed of lines, the truly irreducible unit is the line. Taking the single line as the beginning, one would combine two lines to form the character "two," which in turn would combine with the single line to form "three," and so on. Such a structure reproduces the accounts in the *Dao de jing* and the "Great Tradition" of cosmic origins by division from a primal unity, only now it is the graphic system that is generated rather than the universe. Such a schematic account would reproduce the theories of the origins of graphs from the trigrams.

This theory of written graphs as a direct depiction of the structure of reality detached from the spoken language has had a tremendous influence on accounts, both native and foreign, of the Chinese script.[116] It is clearly an ideological construct or myth, and any study of the role of writing in the Warring States and early empires must consider its origins. As discussed in chapter 2, the forms of teaching and the generation of texts within the schools fostered a general suspicion of language, a tendency heightened in the rejection of paradoxes and rules of argument. This generalized suspicion of the possibility of establishing truth within language pushed thinkers to try to ground their claims to authority in a perception of the world not contingent on verbal manipulation. One result of this was the elaboration of the meditation-derived theories of mental tranquility leading to clear and immediate perception of truth (see chapter 1). Another rival claim was that written graphs, like the mirroring mind of the sage, were either direct images of the world, or derivatives of the hexagrams revealing the underlying structures of natural process.[117]

Apart from rescuing texts from the general disrepute of language, and lending greater authority to texts nearer the foundation times, the myths of Fu Xi and the *Shuo wen*'s account of the origins of graphs also responded to a specific critique of reliance on texts. This is marked by the reference to "footprints" in the *Shuo wen*, because some writers had used the analogy of writing to "footprints" as a form of condemnation. They had argued that texts were the remains of a past reality, the residue of a vanished plenitude, and that one should seek the reality and the fullness rather than its remnants.

The clearest example appears in the *Zhuangzi*:

> Confucius said to Laozi, "I have studied the six classics—the *Odes*, the *Documents*, the *Rites*, the *Music*, the *Changes*, and the *Spring and Autumn Annals*—for what seems to me to be a long time. I thoroughly know their contents. With them I have confronted seventy-two rulers. I have discussed the Ways of the Former Kings and made clear the path [*ji* 迹, literally "footprints, traces"] of the Duke of Zhou and Duke Shao. Yet not one of them has ever employed me. How difficult it is to persuade people! How difficult it is to make clear the Way!"
>
> Laozi said, "You are lucky indeed that you did not meet the ruler of an ordered age. The six classics are the old footprints [*ji* 迹] of the Former Kings. How could they be the means by which they made those footprints? Now what you speak of are like footprints. Footprints are produced by stepping [or "shoes" *lü* 履, a character often used as a homophone gloss for "ritual," here indicating efficacious action], but how could they be stepping?
>
> If white fish-hawks gaze at one another without moving their eyeballs, fertilization occurs [*feng hua* 風化, a term that also meant "transform through moral influence"]. With insects the male calls on the wind above and the female responds

on the wind below, and fertilization occurs. Categories spontaneously divide into male and female, and therefore there is fertilization."[118]

Both Confucius and Laozi describe the texts of the ancient kings as "footprints" or "traces," but the latter uses it specifically to suggest the lifeless remains of what was once vital and moving. This contrast of the quick and the dead is then carried forward in a portrayal of the spontaneous vitality of nature that mocks the Confucian textual program through its punning on the word "wind" (*feng* 風), which also meant "song," "moral influence," or "sexual arousal," and "transformation" (*hua* 化), which meant moral transformation through education, as well as generation and growth. Here the natural generation of living things, which routinely *feng hua*, contrasts with the dead Confucian texts, which singularly fail to do so.

Another anecdote on the limitation of writing deals not with footprints, but rather with a model of the foot. It is the last in a series of stories in the *Han Feizi* on the folly of relying on writings rather than direct perception of the world.[119] The first two stories tell of men who mechanically apply literal readings of ancient texts to their own lives and thereby become ridiculous. The next two are as follows.

> There was a man from Ying [in Chu, in the far south] who wrote a letter [*shu* 書] to the chief minister of Yan [in the far north]. He wrote at night, the fire was dim, so he addressed the one holding the candle, "Raise the light." As he was speaking he accidentally wrote, "Raise the light." "Raise the light" was not the meaning of the letter, but when the minister of Yan received it, he delighted in it. He said, "'Raise the light' means 'honor the enlightened.' 'Honor the enlightened' means 'promote the worthy and employ them.'" The minister of Yan told the king, and the king was greatly pleased. The state thereby was regulated. It is true it was regulated, but this was not the intent of the letter. Those of the present generation who employ scholars are largely of this kind.
>
> There was a man from Zheng who was going to buy shoes [*lü* 履]. He first measured his own feet, and then set the measurements on his seat. When he reached the market, he found that he had forgotten to bring the measurements. He had already found the shoes, and he said, "I forgot to bring the measurements." He returned home to get them. When he returned the market had closed, so he did not get the shoes. Someone said, "Why didn't you try them on your feet?" He replied, "I would rather trust the measurements, and not trust myself."[120]

The first anecdote argues that writings are a record of speech, to the extent that the writer mechanically inserts his own peripheral words into the text. Speech, however, is situational and hence not necessarily applicable to distant places or times. The meaning of the phrase in its original circumstances is lost when preserved in a text, and hence becomes subject to misreadings. This loss of the original intent of the author, according to the *Han Feizi*, is the problem that afflicted the *ru* and the Mohists, causing them to split into factions.[121]

Although the second story does not specifically refer to writing, the account of it at the beginning of the chapter reads:

> To not devote oneself to the service of the state and to make plans for the Former Kings are cases of returning home to fetch the measure [of one's own foot].

This image of writings about the Former Kings as the traces of a shoe that supplants both the foot and its shoe (*lü* 履) is identical with that of the *Zhuangzi* anecdote even to the point of using the same vocabulary. Like the reply of Laozi to Confucius, the anecdote assumes that writings are vestiges of words and actions. They are destructive because they inhibit further words and actions, and trap the reader in a mindless repetition of a past reality that he no longer understands.[122]

These anecdotes reveal the significance of the ideas about written characters developed in the myths of Fu Xi, the theory of writing's derivation from the trigrams, and the insistence on graphs' status as images independent of the spoken language. The condemnation of writing stresses two points: that it is a record of words and that it is a substitute for reality. As a record of words it is at best derivative and at worst inaccurate and void of the wisdom embodied in the master. As a substitute for reality it is dead and an obstacle to action. The mythology of Fu Xi and the theoretical derivation of written characters from the trigrams answer these charges. Writing is not a simple record of language, but an independent system of signs directly derived from natural processes. Graphs are images that like the stars actively correlate with the world of man, or like the bones of the elephant indicate the object of which they are a part. They are vital and dynamic objects that generate and grow over time. They mutate together with the sages who inscribe them on the peak of Mount Tai, adapting like rites and music to changing circumstances. As a parallel world, distinct from material reality yet inextricably linked to it, characters assume the powers of the divinatory signs from which they emerged, and the astrological images with which they share a common nature.

NUMBERS AND WRITING

As a system of signs correlating with tangible reality in the same manner as divinatory signs and celestial images, writing was linked with the world of numbers. Marcel Granet demonstrated that early Chinese numbers were not limited to counting and calculating, but functioned as polyvalent "emblems" or "emblematic rubrics" that were applied to many disparate fields. They served to classify and hierarchize, creating order within what otherwise would remain an undefined mass.[123] In an account of the use of numbers in Shang inscriptions, published in an issue of *Extrême-Orient, Extrême-Occident* devoted to numbers, Redouane Djamouri argued that "numbers do not in themselves correspond to a numbering that refers back to objects, real or imaginary, but rather they show how a language permits one to separate discrete realities from the space-time continuum." He cited R. Laffont's assertion that "[numbering] is not representative of the world, but rather of the activity of choice that the mind [*l'esprit*] applies to it."[124] In the conclusion of an article on the significance of the fact that the character *shu* 數 could mean both "number" and "procedure," Karine Chemla posits that,

> the term *shu* would designate here a quantity, to the extent that it is structured by the application of some procedure of measurement. . . . One could not, in fact, make effective calculations on raw quantities. A procedure must structure them, furnish them with a category [in the case that Chemla is studying, a denominator]. All operations that employ them as a term are free to again borrow this procedure in order to change their category in a suitable manner: *shu* are reborn each time they are put to use.[125]

All these formulations define number as a means of ordering the world by dividing it into units that allow for finite representations of potentially infinite phenomena. G. E. R. Lloyd summarized these arguments by suggesting three uses for numbers in early China, apart from their role in calculation. First, they "enabled correlations to be suggested between widely disparate phenomena." Second, they allowed the "standardisation of the number system, and of weights and measures" in the service of "the establishment of political and moral order." Finally, they served as "a sign of the learning of the learned," a means of "securing the position of the elite officials who were in charge of these systems."[126]

One modification that must be made in Professor Lloyd's formulation is the focus on officials. Numbers were employed as a token of authority not only by officials—in the statistical reports, records of stores, and population registers sketched in chapter 1—but by scholars in the systems of correlations noted in Lloyd's first point. The history of the uses of numbers paralleled that of divination discussed in the first section of this chapter. Numbers as a mode of dividing and describing the world figured most prominently among the technical traditions that developed apart from the philosophical traditions, notably the traditions of astrology/astronomy and music. As late Warring States thinkers increasingly grounded themselves in natural patterns—a process noted above in the philosophical cooptation of divination and the defense of written graphs through links to the natural world—they also incorporated elements of the numerical methods that were fundamental to astronomy, calendrics, music, and even medicine.[127]

As discussed earlier, the philosophical traditions' claim to superiority over the technical ones was based on their supposed possession of an encompassing, generalizing wisdom. This was exemplified in their cooptation of the *Yi*, wherein a technique for divining was read into a moral-ritual depiction of the world. The casting of yarrow stalks was employed as a supplement to percipient analysis of circumstance and character, the trigrams and hexagrams were interpreted as an exhaustive depiction of potential developments derived from first principles, and the lines of the divination manual were read as an esoteric wisdom grounded in the cosmic order. In the same way, mathematical calculations of calendars, pitchpipes, or the progress of diseases were absorbed into the project of defining the entire universe through breaking it into sets of enumerated entities, and then linking these together under the emblematic rubrics of the integers. Thus the correlations were part of the larger project of the philosophical schools of incorporating key elements of the technical traditions by transforming numbers from tools of technical calculations into a system for creating schematic, graphic accounts of the cosmos. Seen in this light, the rise to prominence of numerology—*yin/yang*, the Three Powers, the four seasons, the Five Phases, the six lines of the hexagram, the eight trigrams—was an outgrowth of the philosophical traditions' attempt to achieve intellectual supremacy by bringing the entire universe within their discourse.

This is demonstrated by the fact that the different numerical categories were all ways of talking about the whole cosmos. The application of numbers—the three x, the five y—showed that the author was giving an exhaustive list of the elements of a closed system. Thus accounts of the generation of the world through division begin with the one, which divides to form the two, which in turn forms the three, the four, the eight, and so on. Nevertheless, at each step the number still represents the totality of things, only divided into ever smaller units with consequent changes in their identities and attributes.[128]

The one divides to form two—*yin* and *yang*—but the two combined make up the one; as the "Great Tradition" notes, "One *yin* and one *yang* is the Way."[129] Any complementary pair forming a whole could be labeled *yin* and *yang*—the cold and warm seasons of the year, Heaven and Earth, man and woman. Three—as the triad of Heaven, Earth, and man—also represented a totality, but understood as a hierarchy. The trigrams represented the same phenomenon in the "Lesser Images Tradition," where they were hierarchical structures. In addition the triad symbolized the generative aspect of the universe, in which two "parents" produced an offspring. The four (seasons) or five (phases) represented a totality understood as a cycle, with the latter also introducing the notion of a center. The number six, though less commonly used, could stand for the lines of the hexagram or for Heaven, Earth, and the four seasons. It was employed, as we will see below, in certain totalizing enumerations. The number nine, as in the poem sets of the *Chu ci* anthology, represented completeness through being the culminating integer. It functions in this manner in the division of the world into nine provinces, the representation of sovereignty in nine tripods, or the presentation of the "Great Plan" of Yu in nine sections. Finally, the totality of objects was named with the numerical rubric 10,000.[130]

This practice of using different numbers to talk about the same reality from divergent perspectives is discussed in the *Zhuangzi*. In several passages the text acknowledges that 10,000 is a conventional number chosen to represent all things taken as individuals, and links this to using the numbers "nine" or "two" to express totality in different forms.

As a designation for the number [*shu* 數] of things, we say "10,000," and man is only one of them. Speaking generally, there are "Nine Continents" where grain grows and boats or carts reach, but man occupies only one of them.

Now if we calculate the number [*shu* 數] of things, it will not stop at 10,000. But we fix it and say, "the 10,000 things." We take the biggest of numbers to designate it and speak of it. Thus Heaven and Earth are the largest of forms, *yin* and *yang* are the greatest *qi*, the "Way" is what embraces them. To use what is biggest as a designation in order to speak of them is acceptable.[131]

These passages agree that "10,000 things" is a conventional means of speaking of all things. Similarly, the "Nine Continents" is a numerical figure for the surface of the world, while the pairs "Heaven and Earth" and "*yin* and *yang*"—both nothing more than "acceptable" designations for want of a proper one—are encompassed in the Way. The *Zhuangzi* repeatedly insists that the "10,000" also are truly one, and that they are absorbed in the Way or in the primal *qi*.[132] To explain the constant transformations of the 10,000 things, however, it describes them in terms of *yin* and *yang*.[133] Thus the numerical rubrics applied depend upon the types of analyses or arguments that an author wishes to perform. This process of carving up the world in different manners according to one's needs is summarized in the *Xunzi*.

Although the 10,000 things are numerous, there are times when one desires to refer to them all, and thus one calls them "things." "Thing" is the great common name. . . . There are times when one wishes to selectively refer to them, so one says, "birds" or "beasts." "Birds" and "beasts" are the names of the great divisions. One extends the process and divides them, divides them, and again divides them. When one reaches the point of no further [possible] divisions, then one stops.[134]

Again the mode of division and numbering depends on the subject who is performing the operation.

The analysis of reality through the application of numbers converged with that through images and graphic signs in the text of the *Yi*. Recent archeological finds have shown that the links of the *Yi* to number are ancient. Among the fragments of inscribed, divinatory tortoise plastrons from the preconquest Zhou palace at Qishan were several sets of symbols that had previously been found on Western Zhou bronzes and explained as clan insignia. Zhang Zhenglang demonstrated that they were numerals arranged vertically in sets of three or six. He concluded that they were the earliest form of the later hexagrams and trigrams, and he developed a model by which these numerical hexagrams evolved into those composed of broken and unbroken lines. While the latter remains open to question, the idea that these were hexagrams has been confirmed by the fact that manuscript versions of *Yi* divination from the fourth to second centuries B.C. also employ hexagrams formed entirely from numbers.[135]

Even after the hexagrams were converted into emblems composed of lines rather than numerals, as they appear in the early Han tomb at Mawangdui, the accompanying text continued to analyze them in terms of number. Each line statement begins by identifying the number of the line and then stating whether it is a "six" (*yin*, broken) or a "nine" (*yang*, unbroken).[136] Thus the hexagrams are presented as a matrix in which both the position and nature of the line is identified in numerical terms.

While the numerical character of the hexagrams is ancient, only in the "Great Tradition" and the "Shuo gua" commentaries were the numbers theoretically articulated and worked into the analysis of the cosmos through numerical correlations. At the beginning of the "Great Tradition" the two primal hexagrams are equated with Heaven and Earth and thus drawn into the definition of totality through bipolar coordinates. A later passage states, "The movements of the six lines are the Way of the Three Limits [*san ji* 三極, Heaven, Earth, and man]," thereby giving a different numerical depiction of a similar idea.[137] Passages define both the process of divination and the understanding of the cosmos as the manipulation of numbers, and they employ numerology to explain the structure of the text. Finally, the passage on the casting of yarrow stalks defines the structure of the universe through numbers, and then duplicates those numbers in the manipulation of the stalks.[138] Since the hexagrams are generated by numbers, it is the power of number to reproduce the structure of the universe in a visual emblem that makes possible the *Yi*'s creation of images.

> [The *Yi*] alternates the "three" and "five," intertwines the numbers, masters their alternations, and thereby completes the patterns of the world. It traces the numbers to their limits and thereby fixes the images of the world.[139]

The manipulation of stalks to numerically analyze a situation was not limited to the *Yi*. The *Sunzi* military treatise describes the use of counting rods to calculate the balance of strategic advantage at the beginning of a campaign. This procedure was performed in the ancestral temple, in place of sacrifices and divinations. Such counting rods became a basic tool for mathematical calculation in early imperial China.[140] Another use of rods for calculation was in the early version of the board game "Liu bo," where six rods were cast to determine the movement of the pieces on the main board. The six rods are equal to the number of lines in a hexagram, and some Han illustrations of the game being played by immortals depict a second board on which the six rods are laid out in the primal hexagram *qian*.[141] Most scholars agree that there was a divinatory element or origin to the game, so the link with the *Yi* hexagrams might not be accidental.

As a source of numerical lore the *Yi* was fundamental to uses of numbers by the imperial state. One example was the preparation of calendars, which was based on "calendrical numbers" (*li shu* 曆數).[142] The creators of the *Tai chu* 太初 calendar under Emperor Wu of the Han in 104 B.C. claimed to derive their numbers from the pitchpipes. The account of the reform states, "The pitchpipes are *yin* and *yang*, nine and six. They arise from the [*Yi's*] lines and images." The *San tong li* 三統曆 calendar compiled by Liu Xin at the end of the Western Han was also based on numerical constants from the *Yi jing*, as was the *Qian xiang fa* 乾象法 calendar compiled by Liu Hong in 187–89 A.D.[143] Thus the *Yi* was regarded as the foundation text for the state-sponsored calendrics of the Han empire.

This link is further demonstrated by the fact that the "Great Tradition" is one of the most frequently cited texts in the *Han shu* monograph on the pitchpipes and the calendar. This monograph is "the first surviving text that gives evidence of a system integrating metrology [knowledge of weights and measures] with such diverse fields as numerology, musical pitch, astronomical phenomenons [*sic*], astronomy, cosmology, as well as historiography, and political, ethical, and moral thought."[144] In addition to their importance in calendrics, the monograph also links the *Yi* numbers to the creation of measures. The first section is divided into five rubrics: number, pitchpipes, measures of length, measures of capacity, and measures of weight. These are listed in a hierarchical order, since numbers furnish the basic units for the subsequent four categories, and all the other forms of measure are derived from the size of the *huangzhong* (黃鐘) pitchpipe, as measured by the grains of black millet required to fill it.

The monograph deals not only with the derivation of the units of measure, but also with the "six standardizing instruments." These instruments, first listed together in the *Huainanzi* where they are said to correspond to Heaven, Earth, and the four seasons, were the weights, the balance, the marking-line, the water-level, the compasses, and the carpenter's square. These last two figure prominently in the mythology of Fu Xi, and the account of the instruments echoes this mythology in that, like the written characters, the standardizing instruments generate one another.

> The equilibrium of the weights and their objects generates the balance. The balance revolving generates the compass. The compass circling generates the carpenter's square. The rectangularity of the carpenter's square generates the marking-line. The straightness of the marking-line generates the water-balance. When the water-level is correct then it levels the balance and brings the weights into equilibrium. These act as the Five Patterns.[145]

In this adaptation of the Five Phases cycle, the instruments as well as the units of measure are linked to the cosmic order, and both are ultimately traced back to the numerical constants established by the *Yi*.

This absorption of the state-imposed standards into a system of numerical correlations derived from the *Yi*, the Five Phases, and related systems had a social import similar to that traced in the first section of this chapter, but in relation to a different group. The first section showed how the philosophical traditions adapted a central text of the diviners' art as part of their own universalizing program. The transformation of the *Yi* into a cosmological text applied to diverse realms of human experience entailed the development of its numerical features as an element in the theories of universal correlations formulated in the period. The incorporation of such features of state practice as the calendar, pitchpipes, measures, and weights into these correlations subjected fundamental aspects of administration to the expertise and text-based programs of the philosophical traditions. These policies were also closely linked to the imperial unification of script. In this way the schoolmen claimed ultimate mastery not only over the arts of the technical traditions but also over those of the men in state service. To the extent that the *Shi ji* record of Qin is reliable, this adaptation of administration to numerology figured prominently in the Qin unification, and the *Han shu* monograph shows how it became more pronounced during the Western Han and triumphed in the time of Wang Mang.[146]

This triumph of numerology and the establishment of the *Yi* as the foundation of certain aspects of administration was part of a broader tendency to make textual arts essential to government service. We have already observed this in the Eastern Han practice of using the *Chun qiu* as a source for judicial decisions. Another aspect of the same process appears in Xu Shen's history of the emergence of the Chinese script. After the myths of origins, the account moves into the realm of history with a narrative of state-sponsored textual reforms and the books produced to establish standard script forms. It then sketches all the different types of script still encountered in Xu Shen's day, including the old script versions. It concludes with a condemnation of ill-trained officials, including examples in which the muddling of etymologies and script forms leads to misinterpretation of texts and consequent errors in the execution of the law.[147] This provides clear evidence for the scholastic transformation of government service, noteworthy for emphasizing the mastery of the entire history of the written script as the basis of good government. To the extent that knowledge of ancient, esoteric texts and their mathematizing interpretations had become crucial to administration, government officials could come only from the scholastic traditions.

CONCLUSION

The *Yi* text, the development of which was a central theme in the mythic history of scholarship and writing, was crucial to the articulation of a theory of writing in Warring States China. Originally a divination manual based on the manipulation of numeric and graphic emblems, it was adopted by exponents of certain philosophical traditions as a means of grounding visual signs in cosmic principles. The first stage of this process, as indicated in the *Zuo zhuan* and the *Guo yu*, entailed reinterpreting divination as a formalization of or supplement to the cultivated percipience of one already wise in the principles of ritual and the patterns of political success. At the same time, the divinatory formulae of the *Yi* manual were read as a form of wisdom literature parallel to the *Odes*, the *Documents*, and the ritual texts.

While the earlier sections of the *Yi* were re-interpreted as sources of esoteric wisdom, the later commentarial texts developed this rereading of the hexagrams and line statements into a theory of signs. These texts, notably the "Great Tradition," argued that the *Yi* had been written by sages who had discerned the patterns underlying natural processes and then epitomized those processes in a set of visual signs. The signs were themselves analyzable into smaller units, based on the interplay of the complementary pairs that had emerged from the first division of the primal unity. Because the hexagrams depicted all possible processes, the text was read as a microcosm in which the adept could discern the entire cosmos. This included both a depiction of temporal processes, understood through the model of the four seasons, and the hierarchical construction of space, understood through the model of the triad of Heaven, man, and Earth. Through its claims to offer a schematic model of the entire universe and of all possible circumstances, the text claimed intellectual authority over lesser, derivative writings.

The use of the term "image" (*xiang* 象) in the "Great Tradition" also suggested a model of the relation of written signs to the world. This term, which indicated those features of the world used by the sages to compose the *Yi* and to make their inventions, also named the two-lined substrate of the trigrams that mediated between the primal complementary pair—*yin* and *yang*—and the fully developed sets of three lines. Earlier commentaries used the term to indicate a natural referent with a characteristic mode of action for each trigram and elaborated a theory of the hexagrams as internally differentiated entities with their own hierarchical structures and dynamic tendencies. The use of the same term to identify the astral correspondents of terrestrial phenomena likewise indicated that the hexagrams, and the characters derived from them, formed an alternate plane of reality that indicated developments in the world through powers of sympathetic correlation. The idea of written signs as analogous to natural ones and directly tied to reality also underlay the emergence of a theory of writing in which graphs were ultimately based on simple patterns derived from natural images. These fundamental, indissociable patterns then joined together to multiply through the formation of compound characters. This theory sought to escape the perceived inadequacies of language by privileging writing as an extralinguistic phenomenon directly reproducing the structure of reality.

A final element of a natural philosophy of writing developed in the comentarial traditions of the *Yi* was the linkage of number to writing through common origins in the hexagrams. Archeological evidence has revealed that the earliest hexagrams were composed of numbers, and that they continued to be written in this form to the end of the Warring States period. Even when rewritten as sets of lines, the written accounts of the hexagrams in the line statements continued to present them in the form of numbers. The "Great Tradition" and the "Shuo gua" commentary developed theories in which the text emerged through the numerical process of repeated division, the organization of the hexagrams was explained through numerical correlations with the structure of the world, the use of the text was described in terms of counting or calculation, and the process of constructing a hexagram through casting yarrow stalks was explained as a mathematical reenactment of basic natural processes. These commentaries established the *Yi* as fundamental not only to the origins of writing but also to the numerical correspondences through which scholastics analyzed the world. In this role the text was treated as the foundation of a range of number-based aspects of the state: calendars, pitchpipes, units of weight, units of volume, and units of measure. The scholastic project of absorbing the technical tradition of divination through rewriting a manual as a work of philosophy culminated in the similar absorption of many of the basic functions of state administration. In this way the *Yi* became a foundation text to the project of forging a unitary world in written form, and creating a unified body of intellectuals around the all-encompassing texts.

Chapter Seven
THE ENCYCLOPEDIC EPOCH

The writings discussed in the first four chapters—administrative and legal documents, collective compositions of intellectual traditions, accounts of the past, and verse—all created groups or social roles claiming authority through their text-based wisdom. In the late Warring States period, developments within the textual traditions and the political realm coincided to produce new forms of writing intended to encompass the world in writing. Several of these works have been discussed earlier: the *Zhou li*, portraying society in the form of an all-inclusive state mapped onto space (Heaven-Earth) and time (the seasons); the Mao odes, depicting the temporal (the cycle of the Zhou's rise and fall) and spatial (moving inward from the songs of the states to the hymns of the royal temple) dimensions of moral-political order; the "Tian wen," tracing nature and man from their emergence to the author's day; and the *Zhou yi*, representing the dynamic structures of all possible circumstances within the sequence of its sixty-four hexagrams.

These works were part of a general trend proclaiming completeness or totality as the highest form of textual authority. This dream of writing the world in a single text prefigured, in turn, the enterprise of uniting the world in a single state. The close links in imperial China of political authority with textual mastery or patronage emerged out of this conflation of the intellectual and political realms in a shared ideal of a single, comprehensive authority. I call the texts reflecting this development "encyclopedic," not in the modern sense of a reference work consulted for basic information on all matters of concern, but in its original sense of "cycle of learning," grand schemes that led the reader through an ordered, often hierarchical sequence including all essential knowledge. While only a few of these works actually took the form of a cycle, they all sought to create a sense of completeness through appeals to schemata of recurrent patterns, ultimate origins, numerical categories implying totality (see chapter 6), or related models.

This trend emerged from the interschool polemics. As discussed in chapters 2 and 3, all traditions except the late Mohists and logicians condemned argumentation as corrupting, and claimed authority as heirs of the sages who stood above the fray. In the late third century, several texts developed this position into the argument that others defended one aspect of the truth, while the authors of the texts in question possessed the encompassing wisdom in which all lesser truths found their place. Disputations between schools were proof of their partiality, while the comprehensive truth had no need to refute positions based on limited perspectives. Such arguments informed not only interschool polemics, but also discussions of the nature of knowledge, and historical accounts in which the Way of wisdom and government embodied in the sage kings fragmented into a world of competing schools and states. At the end of the Warring States period these intellectual debates and historical models were transferred into the political sphere by schoolmen who had gained high political office. The most notable of these was Li Si, who used scholastic models in his arguments that Qin should establish a textual monopoly within its newly unified empire.

A related development was the claim that certain texts expressed constant truths underlying all change. Identified with the label *jing* 經, which emphasized their universality, such writings appeared within the different philosophical traditions. In the *ru* tradition the term was applied to the major texts of the "arts" (*yi* 藝) established as a curriculum within the *Xunzi*. The traditions that fused in Han Daoism applied the rubric to texts that either propounded the fundamental mysteries in verse and paradox, such as the *Dao de jing*, or explained society and politics through natural patterns or cosmic origins perceived by the sage, such as the *Jing fa* and the *Shi liu jing*. The term *jing* figured in the legalist traditions not as the title of independent texts but rather in chapters that paired obscure, gnomic dicta with explanations or anecdotes (*shuo* 說) that made them intelligible to the reader.

Another model for comprehensive texts was the collective essay collection sponsored by a leading political figure. The major examples are the *Lü shi chun qiu*, sponsored by Lü Buwei as chief minister in Qin, and the *Huainanzi*, composed under the auspices of the king of Huainan, Liu An. Producing these works involved assembling numerous scholars from many regions and diverse intellectual traditions. Thus the composition of the texts demonstrated the sponsor's charisma—which drew men to him—and the range of his influence. Just as the competing philosophical traditions of the period claimed to encompass their rivals, so these collections reconciled divergent intellectual tendencies by situating them within larger structures. Both works were also organized according to patterns drawn from nature, thus serving as microcosms of the world that they claimed to doctrinally encompass.

Another totalizing work from the same period was Sima Qian's history of the known world from the Yellow Emperor until his own day. In addition to tracing all of history, the work included "monographs" (*shu* 書) on such topics as ritual, sacrifice, music, the pitchpipes, the calendar, astronomy/astrology, rivers and canals, and the flow of commodities. It thus served as a general compendium of politically significant knowledge. Finally, it was structured as a reproduction of the social order, placing the ruler at the center in the form of the "Fundamental Chronicles" (*ben ji* 本紀), moving out through the "Hereditary Households" of the nobility and close servants of the rulers (*shi jia* 世家), and finishing with "Traditions" (*zhuan* 傳) relating to officials, commoners, and foreign peoples.

Slightly earlier the poet Sima Xiangru (no relation) had sought to frame the world in verse. His rhapsodies on the imperial hunting park, the cosmic journeys of the "Great Man," and the *feng* and *shan* sacrifices celebrated the imperial vision through an exhaustive enumeration of its physical attributes and its spacial and temporal range. Having begun his poetic career with verse encomia on a feudal monarch, he incorporated his earlier work into a larger opus glorifying the imperial absorption of the feudatories in a poem that equated the imperial hunting park with the world. In rare and obscure characters it inventoried the marvelous signs and items of tribute that proved the universal character of Han rule. In a subsequent poem on Emperor Wu's journeys through space and his conquest of Heaven, he extended the poetic portrayal of universal rule from the terrestrial to the celestial sphere. The theme also recurred in his posthumous essay and poem on the *feng* and *shan* sacrifices, which ritually marked the themes of universal lordship and the linking of Earth to Heaven. Sima Xiangru was also a lexicographer, and though none of his writings on characters have survived, the rich vocabulary of his verse bears testimony to the range of his studies, and to the manner in which a comprehensive knowledge of written forms served to create literary versions of a universal empire containing all the species and genera of the natural world.

A final example of totalizing writing that demonstrates the conflation of literary and political authority was the catalog of the imperial library produced by Liu Xiang in the late Western Han and preserved in the *Han shu*. This presented a *catalogue raisonné* of all writing deemed to be significant. It not only aimed to be comprehensive, but in its title and organization it enshrined the distinction between the privileged sphere of the universal, in the form of the *ru* canon, and the particular, in the form of the other categories of writings. In tracing each type of text back to an office in an imaginary ancient state, it also demonstrated the identity of political and textual authority, and generated an ideal state through the backward projection of the range of texts existing in the Han. In this way it drew together the twin ideals of comprehensive knowledge as the highest form of truth, and the identity of political and textual authority.

TOTALITY AND TRUTH

Earlier chapters examined arguments claiming superiority for a given position because it was more comprehensive than its rivals. The critique of the technical traditions discussed in chapter 2 was based on the presumptive superiority of a flexible, generalized intellect over specific skills in limited domains. This critique was developed in the parables in the *Zuo zhuan*—discussed in chapter 6—on the superiority of divination through general analysis over that based on yarrow stalks. It also figured in the models of the past discussed in chapter 3, wherein different schools claimed to be heirs of the unitary Way of the sages, while their rivals expounded deviant teachings that threatened social harmony. This culminated in the *Mencius*, in which philosophical disputation resulted from the collapse of political unity, and the anticipated return of the sage would bring an end to the fractiousness incarnated in Yang Zhu and Mo Di.

In the third century B.C. these arguments developed into a common polemical stance wherein each tradition claimed to represent the all-encompassing wisdom, while rivals espoused partial or fragmentary truths of limited applicability. This stance, closely linked to the historical models developed in the fourth century, equated encompassing truth with the era of the ancient kings, when the universal monarchs had also been the doctrinal masters. It linked the appearance of competing traditions in the intellectual realm with political fragmentation into competing states.

The evolution from the fourth-century models to those of the third century can be traced within the *Xunzi*. This books contains two systematic critiques of rival traditions. The first, in the chapter "Contra [or 'Condemnation of'] Twelve Masters" (*fei shi er zi* 非十二子), follows the pattern established by the *Mencius*, except for recognizing a superficial reason and plausibility in each of the rivals and attempting an exhaustive list. The second, in "Dispelling Ignorance" (*jie bi* 解蔽), systematically develops the theme of partiality versus universality, elaborates the parallel of political and intellectual authority, and includes an explicit assertion of the ideal identity of the sage and the king.[1]

The "Condemnation of Twelve Masters" is structured according to a simple, recurring pattern. Six philosophical errors are presented. The author then explains why these doctrines cannot provide norms for government or establish social hierarchy. He concedes that the argument "has its reasons" (*you gu* 有故) and is "coherent" or "rational" (*cheng li* 成理) and consequently is able to delude people. Finally, he names philosophers who exemplify each error.

Against these twelve sectarians the author sketches the ideal of the sage, uncrowned or crowned. The former, exemplified by Confucius or Zi Gong, "combines" (*zong* 總) practical methods with general principles, "makes equal" (*qi* 齊) words and actions, "unites" (*yi* 壹) guiding principles and categories, and "assembles" (*qun* 群) the world's heroes. He "completes" (*ju* 具) within himself all the patterns or marks (*wen zhang* 文章) of the sage. The latter, exemplified by Yao or Shun, "unites the world" (*yi tian xia* 一天下), "regulates the myriad objects" (*cai wan wu* 財 [=裁] 萬物), "universally benefits the world" (*jian li tian xia* 兼利天下) and makes everyone within his "universal reach" (*tong da* 通達) submit.[2] Thus the chapter opposes the fractious, partial doctrines of the schoolmen—condemned for their social and political consequences—with the power of the sage to unite all things. It also defines the philosophical master as the "sage who does not gain position [or 'power']" (*sheng ren zhi bu de shi zhe* 聖人之不得勢者), paired with "the sage who gains position [or 'power']" (*sheng ren zhi de shi zhe* 聖人之得勢者), that is, the sage king. The former bans the six doctrines and twelve masters from his presence, while the latter silences the doctrines and converts their exponents.[3]

The contrast between universal truth and particularist error, with the parallel of political and intellectual authority, is developed in "Dispelling Ignorance." The character here translated as "ignorance" (*bi* 蔽) means "to cover," "to conceal," or "to screen off." It suggests ignorance, in contrast with characters indicating comprehensive wisdom such as *tong* 通 "universally penetrating," or *da* 達 "reaching to the ultimate." The chapter begins by contrasting the perceptions of petty men, limited to one small corner and hence in conflict with other partial views, with the Way of the sage which is universal and thus true for all.

> The calamity of common men is to be blocked off by one corner [*yi qu* 一曲] and thus blind to the great principle. When there is order they return to the constant norm [*jing* 經], but when there are doubled, similar [*liang ni* 兩疑=擬, sources of authority] then they are in doubt. The world has only one Way and the sage only one mind. Now the feudal lords have different governments and the hundred schools different theories, so inevitably some are right and others wrong, some well-governed and some in chaos. . . . Each is partial to what he has accumulated, and fears hearing ill of it. Relying on their partiality to regard different methods, they fear hearing something good of them. Therefore they hurriedly depart from order and never cease to consider themselves correct.[4]

Political and intellectual divisions make error and disorder inevitable, and where each party takes his own position as correct there is no standard or judge to decide between them. In such a world, one who attains the way will be denounced by "the rulers of chaotic states" and the "men of chaotic schools."

The next section proclaims that any object or position, if made the exclusive object of attention or assertion, produces ignorance. It first discusses ignorance due to partiality or obsession in the political realm. It lists evil rulers of antiquity, victims of listening exclusively to evil ministers, and contrasts them with virtuous rulers who listened to advice and remonstrance and hence achieved an impartial correctness. It follows with a list of evil ministers whose blind obsession with their desires ruined their rulers, in contrast with virtuous ministers who were benevolent and free from particularist obsessions.

The chapter then traces the same phenomenon in the intellectual realm.

> Master Mo was blocked by the idea of utility [*yong* 用] and consequently was insensible to refined culture [*wen* 文]. Master Song [Xing] was blocked by the idea of [limiting] desires, and consequently was insensible to fulfillment. Master Shen [Dao] was blocked by the idea of law [*fa* 法] and consequently was insensible to worthy men [*xian* 賢]. Master Shen [Buhai] was blocked by the idea of the force of position [*shi* 勢] and consequently was insensible to wisdom. Master Hui was blocked by the idea of fine words [*ci* 辭] and consequently was insensible to realities [*shi* 實]. Master Zhuang was blocked by the idea of Heaven and consequently was insensible to the human. . . . Each of these "tools" [*ju* 具] is one corner of the Way. The Way

embodies the constant and exhausts all changes. A single corner is not sufficient to give an idea of it. Men of limited knowledge, observing one corner of the Way, are not yet able to recognize [the whole]. Therefore they regard [their own ideas] as sufficient, and elaborate on them. Within they confuse themselves, and on the outside they delude others. Superiors thereby block up subordinates, and subordinates thereby block up superiors. This is the calamity of obstruction.

Confucius was benevolent, wise, and not blocked. Therefore, though studying confused methods he was still sufficient to have been one of the ancient kings. His single school obtained the Way of Zhou [*zhou dao* 周道, also "the complete Way"]. He took and employed it, and was not blocked by his accumulated learning. Therefore his virtue equalled that of the Duke of Zhou, and his fame that of the rulers of the Three Dynasties. This is the blessing of not being obstructed.[5]

Confucius was the only master not obstructed by a commitment to private doctrines. His wisdom made him an equal of the textual creator of the Zhou, as well as the kings of Xia, Shang, and Zhou. Thus the comprehensive Way culminates in the merging of the intellectual and the political.

This passage is followed by a discussion of the mental techniques that allow the sage to recognize all the aspects of the Way. These techniques—holding the mind still to respond to all things while clinging to none—and their background were discussed in chapter 1. This discussion also contains the passage cited in chapter 2, contrasting men of partial skills such as farmers, craftsmen, and merchants with the gentleman who, knowing the Way, can thus combine the skills and administer them. Near the conclusion the author notes that no accumulation of knowledge could ever thoroughly account for all the transformations of the world, so that knowledge must have a standard that defines its limits.

Therefore studying necessarily studies that which brings it to an end. What brings it to an end? One ends it at "supreme sufficiency." What is meant by "supreme sufficiency?" The sage [and the king]. The sage exhausts human relationships. The king exhausts all regulations. These two are sufficient to provide a standard for the entire world. Therefore students take the sage king as their teacher and the regulations of the sage king as their law/model [*fa* 法].[6]

Here the ideal of a comprehensive truth encompassing all particularist doctrines could exist only in the fusion of the sage and the king, the textual and the political.

This idea also figures in the final chapter of the *Zhuangzi*. This begins with the observation that there are many "limited techniques" (*fang shu* 方術) whose exponents believe their own arts to be supreme. Although elements of the ancient Way exist in all of them, none are like the men of old who completed (*bei* 備) the Way. After a brief discussion of the documentary heritage of Zhou preserved by the *ru*, who as noted in chapter 2 are distinguished from the schools, the chapter proceeds,

The world is in total chaos. The sage and the worthy are not clear/eminent. The Way and its Power are not united. In the world many obtain one element which they examine carefully and in which they delight as their own. Like ears, eyes, nose, and mouth, which each make something clear but cannot combine each other's functions, so the multiple techniques of the Hundred Schools each have their own strengths and sometimes are useful. However, they are neither inclusive nor comprehensive. They are scholars of a single corner. They divide up the beauties of Heaven and Earth, break up for analysis the principles of the myriad things, and thus examine what for the ancients was a totality. Few are able to completely master the beauties of Heaven and Earth, or speak of the fullness of the spirit illuminations. Therefore the Way of being a sage on the inside and a king on the outside is obscure and dark. It is blocked up and does not come forth. In the world each man pursues his own desires and makes them into his own technique. Alas! The Hundred Schools set out but do not return, so inevitably they cannot join together. Scholars of this later age unfortunately do not perceive the purity of Heaven and Earth nor the great corpus of the ancients, so the art of the Way is torn to pieces by the world.[7]

The comprehensive Way of the ancients, expressed in the unity of the world, the unity of doctrine, and the unity of the sage and the king, has been ripped apart by the particularist doctrines of the scholastic traditions.

The chapter develops this vision of a lost unity into an analysis of the intellectual realm of its day. It describes the fragment of the original, encompassing Way preserved by each tradition, lists their founders, and then shows how their partiality led to error. This criticism for partiality includes even Zhuang Zhou, the eponymous founder of the tradition in which this chapter was included. This indicates that the syncretist authors of the later chapters no longer saw themselves as disciples in the line of Zhuang Zhou, but adepts of a new, comprehensive mode of thinking that included the best of all the traditions. The only exception to the recurring pattern is the final section on the rhetoricians. No share of the ancient Way is attributed to these thinkers, who are utterly condemned, just as they are in the *Xunzi*.[8] Disputation and rules of argument had no place in the grand scholastic synthesis proclaimed by the traditions of the late Warring States.[9]

The chapters "Five Vermin" and "Eminence in Learning" in the *Han Feizi* follow a similar rhetorical strategy with one significant difference. Whereas the chapters in the *Xunzi* and the *Zhuangzi* identify the encompassing Way with the sages of antiquity and their own teachings, the *Han Feizi* identifies the Way of the sage ruler as constant adaptation to demographic and economic circumstances. It is comprehensive in its inclusion of the whole history of human government. Rule through virtue under Yao and Shun was appropriate to a time of primitive plenty, while the use of rewards and punishment to encourage agriculture and bellicosity is appropriate to the scarcity of later times. In contrast, the *ru* cling to outmoded models and celebrate particularist virtues such as filial piety at the expense of devotion to public order. Similarly the teachings of Yang Zhu are dismissed as concern with private benefit at the expense of the general good. The schools are divided not only against one another, but also internally, with the *ru* split into eight traditions and the Mohists into three. The rhetoricians, advocates of alliance, writers on administration, and writers on warfare are all condemned for limited doctrines pernicious to the general good, or for undermining the state by using learning as the road to a private eminence and wealth that undermines public devotion to agriculture and combat. The conclusion, as noted in chapter 2, is that in the state of the enlightened ruler the only texts studied will be the law, and the only teachers the officials.[10] Thus the text uses the same rhetoric of the superiority of the universal and encompassing over the particular and limited, but it equates the former with the state and its officials, and the latter with the scholarly traditions.

This doctrine figures prominently in the proposal of Han Fei's classmate, Li Si, that Qin should suppress the private ownership of nontechnical writings and make the state the sole source of education.

In ancient times the world was fragmented, and none was able to unite it. Therefore feudal lords arose side by side. They all spoke of antiquity as the true Way in order to disparage the present. They adorned empty words in order to confuse substantial realities. People regarded their partial, private [*si* 私] teachings as the best, and thereby criticized what was established by their superiors. Now Your Majesty has united the world, distinguished white from black, and established a single locus of honor, but the exponents of private teachings band together to criticize the institutions of law and instruction [*fa jiao zhi zhi* 法教之制]. When they hear that a regulation has been sent down, then each one criticizes it in the light of his private teaching. On the inside they condemn it in their minds, when they go out they criticize it in the alleys. They condemn the ruler to make themselves famous, and dissent to make themselves lofty. They lead their assembled followers in creating slanders. If this is not banned, then the ruler's authority will diminish above, and factions will form below. It should be banned.

I request that anyone who possesses literary teachings, the *Odes*, the *Documents*, or the words of the Hundred Schools should abandon them. Anyone who has not done so within thirty days from the time that this decree reaches them shall be tattooed and become a convict laborer. The books not to be abandoned are those on medicine, divination, agriculture, and forestry. Should any desire to study, they will take the minor officials as their teachers.

The First Emperor approved his proposal. They collected the *Odes*, the *Documents*, and the words of the Hundred Schools to keep the people ignorant, and caused the world to no longer use antiquity to criticize the present. Making clear laws and measures, and fixing codes and statutes all began with the First Emperor. He unified the writing system, and placed detached palaces and halls all across the empire.[11]

Here the existence of rival philosophical traditions is equated with the division of the world into competing states, and set against the unity achieved by the

First Emperor. Like the earlier texts it assumes the superiority of the comprehensive over the partial but, as in the *Han Feizi*, the former is identified with the state and assigned to the present time. With the state cast as the single, unitary tradition fixing linguistic standards of "black and white" and instituting "law and instruction," the philosophical traditions appear as self-seeking factions that threaten public order through the pursuit of private glory. Truth, like laws, measures, and script, should be dictated from the center and enforced by the emperor's servants.

This treatment of rival philosophical traditions as fragments of a whole preserved only by one tradition or institution continued into the early Han. Sima Tan's division of the intellectual field into a delimited number of doctrinally defined schools, the first such analysis that did not simply list masters, follows the pattern established in the texts noted above.

> The "Great Tradition" of the *Yi* says, "The world has a single end but a hundred ways of thinking of it, a common destination but different roads." The traditions of Yin/Yang, the *Ru*, the Mohists, Names, Law, and the Way and its Power all devote themselves to public order. It is only that the different roads that they follow and advocate are discerning or they are not. I examined the techniques of Yin/Yang. They are excessively detailed and have numerous taboos, so causing people to be immobile and full of fear. But the way they put in order the harmonious course of the four seasons cannot be lost. The *Ru* are broadly learned but lack essential points, so they toil hard but achieve little. Therefore it is difficult to completely follow their regimen. But the way they put in order the rituals of ruler and minister or father and son, and establish the divisions of husband and wife or elder and junior cannot be changed. The Mohists are frugal and difficult to follow, so their regimen cannot be entirely obeyed. But their manner of strengthening the root and being economical in consumption cannot be abandoned. The Legalists are severe and show little mercy, but the way they correct the divisions between ruler and minister or superior and subordinate cannot be modified. The School of Names causes people to investigate [reading *jian* 檢 for *jian* 儉] and be prone to lose the truth, but the way that they correct [the relation of] name and reality must be examined. The Daoists cause people's refined spirit energies to be undivided, their actions to accord with the formless, and nourish all things. Their technique follows the general order of the Yin/Yang, selects the good points of the *Ru* and the Mohists, and extracts the essential points of the School of Names and the Legalists. Moving with the seasons, changing in response to things, it establishes customs and bestows tasks, and there is nothing which is not appropriate.[12]

The discussion further elaborates the strengths and weaknesses of the schools, but the argument is epitomized in this opening section. Like the *Xunzi* it credits each school with mastery of some element of the Way, but sees this partiality as resulting in errors. Unlike the *Xunzi* it is the Daoist tradition and not the *ru* that escapes from the trap of incompleteness. It does this in two ways. First, it incorporates the best features of all the other traditions. Second, it embraces the necessity of constant change and adaptation, responding to each new situation rather than clinging to a single set of rules or principles.

The theme of universal versus partial also appears at the end of the *Huainanzi*, in a passage presenting this work as the culmination of all the traditions that preceded it. This account introduces each tradition in terms of the historical circumstances in which it appeared and the problems to which it responded. It begins with the depravity of the last Shang king and the plans of the Zhou to overthrow him, so the first tradition to appear was that of the military texts, identified with the mythicized figure of Duke Tai. After the Zhou victory the Duke of Zhou brought an end to the threat of rebellion and civil war, thereby establishing civil government. Confucius and the *ru* transmitted the teachings of the Duke of Zhou and studied his writings. By contrast the Mohists with their emphasis on frugality and simple funerals carried forward the teachings of Yu and the more rustic Xia dynasty. Evolving political circumstances and new crises elicited such works as the *Guanzi*, the *Yanzi chun qiu*, the writings on diplomacy and alliances, the *xing ming* theories of Shen Buhai, and the writings on law of Shang Yang. Each of these textual traditions is explained as the product of a particular political situation, the customs of a particular state, or the character of an individual ruler to whom they were addressed.

The passage concludes with an account of the *Huainanzi* itself.

> The writings of Master Liu [An] observe the images [*xiang* 象] of Heaven and Earth, and comprehensively penetrate [*tong* 通] affairs from ancient times to the present. They assess affairs to establish institutions, and measure forms to dispense what is suitable. They trace the heart of the Way back to its origins and unite the moral influences of the Three Dynasties in order to assemble the most vast. In the midst of the obscurest subtlety they discerningly advance to observe the most minute. They cast out the impure to pour forth the still and silent. Thereby they unite the world, bring order to all things, respond to changes, and comprehensively penetrate the distinct classes or categories. They do not follow a single, established path, cling to what is indicated by one corner, let themselves be bound by material things so that they will not change with the times. Therefore if you apply them to the common they will not block it up, and if you apply it to the world it will leave no gap.[13]

The text covers all of space and time. It includes cosmic origins and human history, responds appropriately to all changes, and can regulate the entire world. The last two parallel phrases are a variation of a standard description of the Way, small enough to fit into the most minute object and still leave room, but large enough to fill the universe and leave no empty space. Corresponding to the all-encompassing Han empire just as the earlier texts matched the political circumstances of their own day, the text subsumes all the partial traditions which preceded it. Like Sima Tan's categorization of the schools, it indicates the dominance of the trope of whole versus part in the intellectual debates at the time of Emperor Wu of the Han, and it shows the close links of this vision with the conflation of textual and political authority.

CANON AND COMMENTARY

The late Warring States and early imperial practice of claiming authority through possession of a comprehensive wisdom was doubled by the practice of identifying texts or passages as uniquely important through their all-penetrating nature. These were identified with the character *jing* 經, which came to define a category of writing as canonical or classic, but which originally indicated something running throughout an area and serving to define or regulate it.

The earliest gloss on this character appears in the *Shuo wen jie zi*.

> The vertical line [i.e., warp] of weaving. It is derived from *si* 糸 "silk" and pronounced *jing* 巠.[14]

This derives the sense of the character from the silk signific, and identifies it with the warp thread that provides the structure for the fabric. It inspired Zhang Binglin's explanation that the character had originally referred to the thread that bound strips together to form texts in early China.[15]

However, the emphasis on silk is probably mistaken, because the *jing* 巠 element that Xu Shen treats as a phonetic figures in a set of characters with meanings related to the idea of "running through" or "linking together." Thus the element *jing* 巠 itself is glossed in the *Shuo wen* as either a "subterranean channel of water" or a "vast body [of water]."[16] This, however, seems to be a misreading based on the seal script form, and Karlgren has argued that the form of the character on bronzes suggests a device used in weaving, with threads coiling around a staff.[17] With the "stepping" radical it forms the character *jing* 徑 "road, direct path" which the Han dictionary *Shi ming* uses as the homophone gloss for *jing* 經.

> *Jing* 經 "classic" means *jing* 徑 "road." It means the "constant standard" [*chang dian* 常典]. Like a road, there is nothing it does not pass through, and it may be constantly employed.[18]

With the "grass" radical it forms *jing* 莖 "stalk" of grass or "trunk" of tree. Applied to the human body, it figures with the "head" radical in *jing* 頸 "neck," and with the "meat" radical in *jing* 脛 "the calf, the part of the leg linking the knee to the ankle." With the addition of the "strength" radical it forms *jing* 勁 "strong," originally in the sense of "stiff, unbending," as indicated by its use in the character *jing* 痙 "convulsive contractions" in which the muscles lock up.[19] In short, virtually all the characters containing the element *jing* 巠 indicate the central element running through something or holding it together, with the associated sense of "strong" and "unbending." *Jing* 巠 in the sense of "warp [of a fabric]" is only a particular version of this broader, overarching meaning.

The *jing* 巠 element also appears as an independent character in several bronze inscriptions. It functions as a verb or adjective in association with the ancestors, their potent virtue (*de* 德), or their commands/mandate (*ming* 命). It also appears once in association with the "four directions" (*si fang* 四方).[20] While the meaning of the character is uncertain, in the light of the senses of the characters that evolved from it, it apparently meant "take as guiding/unifying principle," or—when applied to the four directions—"to link together" or "to go throughout."

This word cluster indicates the semantic field within which the character *jing* 經 "classic/canon" appeared. The meanings of this cluster also figure in the uses of the character prior to its emergence as a bibliographic category. One of the most significant was the sense of *jing* as "boundary" or "demarcation." In its discussion of the "well-field" system the *Mencius* asserts that "benevolent government must begin with establishing boundaries" so that land and salaries will be equitably distributed.[21] After the flood Yu divided the world into nine provinces by "demarcating and opening up" (*jing qi* 經啓) nine roads.[22] The *Zhou li* states that the "Supervisor of Markets" (*si shi* 司市) "divides the land and demarcates [*jing* 經] the market place," that is, establishes the rows in which different goods were sold.[23] Thus *jing* 經 applied to space indicated making divisions to create order and equity in what would otherwise be chaos.

This use of *jing* 經 to indicate dividing lines that establish order or create structure is closely related to its sense as the warp of a fabric. Consequently, when indicating spatial demarcation it is sometimes paired with the character *wei* 緯 "weft." The "Kao gong ji 考工記" describes the office of "Builder" (*jiang ren* 匠 人) who was responsible for erecting a capital city. It specifies that there should be nine "vertical boulevards" (*jing* 經) and nine horizontal ones (*wei* 緯) and that each of these major, demarcating roads (*jing tu* 經涂 = 途) should be as wide as nine axles.[24] The intersection of *jing* and *wei* defines the city by dividing it into squares in an urban version of the *Mencius's* well-fields. This same schema is applied to the world in early Han texts, such as the *Huainanzi*, where north-south lines that divide the earth are described as *jing* and east-west ones as *wei*.[25] These characters would ultimately be used to translate the terms "longitude" and "latitude."

This sense of *jing* 經 was extended to mean "put in order" without explicit reference to the demarcation of space. One of the *Zuo zhuan's* definitions of ritual discussed in chapter 3 stated that it "put in order [*jing* 經] state and lineage, fixed in position [*ding* 定] the altars, and placed in sequence [*xu* 序] the people."[26] All these verbs suggest creating order through proper spatial distribution, but there is no indication of physical demarcations. In the *Guo yu* a scribe identifies the actions of an official as "ordering and organizing [*jing ying* 經營] the state."[27] The link with the verb *ying* 營, which meant to "set up a military camp or walled compound" suggests spatial organization but here, as in the modern bisyllabic compound formed by these characters, the concrete meanings seem largely superceded by a general sense of "organizing" or "administering." In other passages there is no suggestion of structuring space, and the character *jing* 經 seems to function simply as a verb meaning "to rule."[28]

In addition to verbal uses derived from the senses of "demarcation" or "structuring" suggested by the cluster marked by *jing* 巠, the character *jing* 經 also functioned as a noun meaning "guiding principle" or "constant norm." This usage was noted in chapter 3, in the discussion of the *Gongyang* tradition's use of the opposition between *jing* and *quan* 權 "expedient assessment." It appears in this sense in many Warring States texts, such as a passage in the *Mencius* that defines the gentleman as the one who "returns to the constant norm" (*fan jing* 反經) or a similar phrase in the *Xunzi* that describes good order as "return to the constant norm" (*fu jing* 復經).[29] In other passages it signifies the constant norm or principle of some phenomenon, such as "ritual" (*li* 禮), "duty" (*yi* 義), or "public order" (*zhi* 治).[30] Elsewhere the sense of "constant norm" entails the idea of division or demarcation, such as the constant norm of *yin* and *yang*, life and death, or right and wrong.[31] Finally, some passages note that *jing* 經 is distinguished by being universal and without "partiality" or "faction."[32]

In the late Warring States period the character *jing* 經 began to appear in titles of texts or chapters, or to be applied to a certain body of works. Presumably this entailed claims that the texts were constant or universal, and that they provided the key to structuring or giving order to the world. The use of the term as a bibliographic category appeared at the same time that schoolmen began to claim superiority on the grounds of the universality of their own tradition's doctrines and to condemn their adversaries for partiality. This was also the age when textual authority was increasingly conflated with an ideal of monarchy, whether that of ancient sage kings, a "king without attributes," or actual rulers.

The final chapter of the *Zhuangzi*, which posited an ancient unity of monarchy and sagehood that had been fragmented by the schools, states that the Mohists "all recite the Mohist canon [*Mo ching* 墨經]," but each of them has a different version.[33] This passage almost certainly refers to the earlier chapters, each preserved in three versions, but the later chapters dealing with logic are all entitled either "canon" (*jing* 經) or "canon and explanation" (*jing shuo* 經說).[34] The first nine chapters of the *Guanzi* are entitled "Discussion of Constant Principles" (*Jing yan* 經言) and deal with methods for obtaining and using power. The character *jing* 經 appears frequently in the text preceded by a numeral, and these serve as rubrics for enumerating the principles of statecraft.[35] In the *Han Feizi* a chapter entitled the "Eight Constant Principles" (*Ba jing* 八經) deals with maxims for controlling subordinates.[36]

The character was also employed in the title of the texts associated with Laozi and the Yellow Emperor found at Mawangdui. These include the "Constant Model" (*Jing fa* 經法), the "Sixteen Canons" (*Shi liu jing* 十六經), the "Canon of the Way" (*Dao jing* 道經), and the "Canon of Virtuous Power" (*De jing* 德經). Like the texts on administrative theory, these classics of what became Daoism present principles of social order, but they trace these back to their origins in the cosmic Way. The first two works are probably the text identified in the *Han shu* bibliographic monograph as the "Four Canons [*jing*] of the Yellow Emperor," so they assume the identification of *jing* 經 with the rule of the early sages. This also occurs in the major medical texts of the period which were identified as *jing* 經, at least by the time of the compilation of the catalog of the imperial library, and sometimes linked to the Yellow Emperor.[37] Likewise several geographic works of the period, such as the *Canon of the Mountains and Seas* (*Shan hai jing* 山海經) and the "Yu gong" chapter of the *Shang shu*, part of the *ru* canon, were attributed to Yu.

Another feature of the texts or chapters entitled *jing* was that they were frequently accompanied by texts called *zhuan* 傳 "transmission, tradition" or *shuo* 說 "explanation." The latter term was already noted in the titles of chapters on logic in the Mohist canon. It also figures in six chapters of the *Han Feizi* entitled "Collected Explanations" (*chu shuo* 儲說). These begin with lists of techniques or subtleties of government described in brief formulae and with references to anecdotes. The introductions conclude with the statement, "The above are the constant principles" (*you jing* 右經. *You* here means "[to the] right," i.e., "the above"). The anecdotes which demonstrate the principles are listed as "explanations" (*shuo* 說).[38] In addition, the character *shuo* 說 appears in many titles listed in the *Han shu* bibliographic monograph, both commentaries on the *ru* canon and such works as *Master Lao, Mister Xu's Canon and Explanations* (*Laozi Xu shi jing shuo* 老子徐氏經說).[39]

However, the primary rubric for commentaries was *zhuan* 傳. The *Shuo wen* glosses this character as a carriage used in relays to deliver messages, while the *Shi ming* defines it as the stations at which such carriages changed horses. The latter also states that as a literary term it means "to hand down and show to later men."[40] This indicates that the term derived from a figurative sense in which the message of the canon, difficult to understand because of its brevity and subtle language, was delivered to the world at large. The term also marks the hierarchical relationship between the canonical text and its commentary, for early texts insist on the low status of officers who delivered messages through the relay system, even prescribing the title as a humble self-referent for the lowest rank of nobility when addressing the Son of Heaven.[41] This idea of the *zhuan* 傳 as a means of relaying the hidden, manifold meanings of the eternal canon was also marked in the attributes of their putative authors. Thus the Eastern Han scholar Wang Chong argued:

> The sages make the canonical texts [*jing* 經]. The worthies create commentaries [*zhuan* 傳] for them. They transmit the ideas of those who made them, and adopt the fixed intent [*zhi* 志] of the sages. Therefore the canonical texts need the commentaries.[42]

The sages possess supreme intelligence, and the canons are their textual equivalents. The commentaries, in contrast, derive from the worthies, who devote themselves to transmitting the ideas and intentions of the sages. Neither form of text had meaning without the other.

The mutual reliance of canon and commentary can best be demonstrated through an examination of what would become the official canon of imperial China, the "Five Canons" of the *ru* tradition. The texts mentioned above under the rubric *jing* 經 were all recent compositions, many written together with their appended explanations to serve as the textual norm of a tradition. The central texts of the *ru* tradition, however, had originated centuries before the notion of a written canon existed. The Zhou *Odes*, the *Documents*, the central parts of the *Yi*, and the *Chun qiu* have all been discussed earlier. The last of the five *ru* canons, the ritual texts, were themselves more recent compilations, but references to ritual texts date back to the *Lun yu*. The origins of these texts outside the *jing/zhuan* complex is indicated by the fact that only in two late Warring States period texts are they described as *jing*.[43] Well into the Han dynasty they were routinely identified as the "Six Arts" (*liu yi* 六 藝, the sixth art being music, for which no canonical text existed) rather than or in addition to the later standard rubric of the "Five Canons."[44]

The fact that existing works were *transformed* into "canon/classic" indicates a crucial point about the emergence of *jing* as a textual category. Virtually any text could in theory have been established as a *jing* through the addition of a *zhuan*. When Wang Chong argued that *jing* need *zhuan*, he meant that only with a commentary could a canon/classic be understood, but in practice the addition of a commentary certified a text as a constant, fundamental norm by showing its hidden depths or polyvalent application to many situations. Thus the Zhou *Odes* were interpreted by the *Xunzi* as the preserved wisdom of ancient sages that revealed philosophical truths regarding institutions and practices of his own day. The Mao tradition, in turn, read them as an anthology depicting the nature of kingship, the rise and fall of royal power, and the geographic hierarchy of a state. Commentaries on the *Chun qiu* explained a chronicle compiled at the court of Lu as a philosophy of government expressed through a coded set of quasi-legal judgments. Similarly the commentators on the *Documents* reread political speeches dealing with particular issues as depictions of a model of kingship.[45] The *Zuo zhuan*'s use of historical anecdotes to elaborate principles derived from the primary *ru* texts is also an example of canonization through the addition of commentary.

The establishment through the addition of commentaries of a privileged category of texts indicates a major development in the definition of textual authority in the late Warring States. As noted in chapter 2, the philosophical traditions condemned disputation as a form of social breakdown. In contrast they claimed, as discussed in chapter 3, that their doctrines were methods of creating social order that had been employed by earlier sages. These claims took mythic form in accounts of successive eras of text-based sages who were actual kings or who acted as rulers in text-based, parallel worlds. They also justified the arguments discussed in the first section of this chapter, which transformed disputation over right and wrong into claims of encompassment, and identified the totalizing wisdom claimed by each tradition with a prior unity of political and intellectual authority embodied in the sage kings.

The textual category of *jing* emerges at the confluence of these intellectual developments. These texts supposedly offered constant principles that were the key to social order. They were identified as the work of sages or those preserving their influence: the Zhou kings and their historians, great ministers such as the Duke of Zhou or Guan Zhong, sage kings like the Yellow Emperor or Yu, or hidden masters like Lao Dan. They employed a uniquely subtle or profound language requiring constant re-interpretation and application to specific circumstances. In this context the addition of commentaries became crucial, for the need for explication demonstrated the profundity of the canon and removed it from the arena of debate.[46] The writing of commentaries established the *jing* as authoritative texts, and began the process of decentering the philosopher's textual traditions in the intellectual field. As the constant, efficacious testaments of the sages, the *jing* embodied the vision of history articulated by the schools, and also conformed to the textual ideals suggested in their mutual criticisms. They were not, however, the only kind of text to do so.

STATE-SPONSORED COMPENDIA

As an alternative to canons that presented constant principles in abstracted, gnomic language requiring explication, or used commentaries to read evolving, hidden meanings into archaic texts, several major works claimed to be universal encyclopedia containing everything worth knowing. The major examples are the *Lü shi chun qiu* and the *Huainanzi*.[47] Although composed more than a century apart, the two texts share many common features of the encyclopedic tendency. Among these are: (1) the texts are the collective works of numerous scholars gathered around an eponymous political patron for whom the text is named, (2) they adopted maxims and principles from all known philosophic traditions and tried to synthesize them into a coherent whole, (3) this coherent whole was adapted from natural models, so that the text acts as a microcosm, (4) the incorporation of multiple doctrines into a comprehensive structure used the dimension of time as an organizing principle, and (5) both texts insisted on the ideal of political and doctrinal unity.

The intellectual traditions discussed in chapter 2 shifted from an early reliance on face-to-face transmission from teacher to disciple outside the state sphere toward a transmission based primarily on texts, debates between philosophic traditions in the courts, and patronage by leading political figures. Patronage of scholars was part of a social development in which eminent men competed for prestige by surrounding themselves with figures who possessed all sorts of useful or amusing talents. The great sponsored compendia of the late Warring States and early Han were a further step in this process. The patrons of these works not only attracted large numbers of scholars to their courts to increase their prestige, but also actively intervened in scholarly activities through organizing the writing of large texts that took their names.

The collective nature of these works is emphasized in accounts of their composition. Both the biography of Lü Buwei and that of Liu An state that they assembled thousands of scholars. Gao You's preface to his commentary on the *Huainanzi* likewise insists on the large number of scholars gathered at Liu An's court, and lists eight men who shared in organizing the project.[48] Some modern scholars, convinced that serious philosophy can only be written by individuals, assert that Liu An composed the work. This position, however, not only ignores the statements of the earliest Chinese historians, but also runs counter to the work itself, which repeatedly insists on the limits of the individual mind and the necessity of attaining mass participation in order to secure comprehensive wisdom.[49] This insistence on the large numbers of people who participated in the writing of the texts is part of the program of comprehensiveness that defined the project of composing such encyclopedia.

Naming the books for a political patron rather than a teacher likewise indicates their public, collective nature. The philosophers associated comprehensive philosophy with political and intellectual unification under the sages, and identified competing traditions as a sign of decay. Many thinkers, primarily those of a legalist bent, called for the abolition of scholastic disputation through the re-assertion of the intellectual hegemony of the state. The pattern of the *Lü shi chun qiu* and the *Huainanzi*, in which a chief minister or a king assembled scholars from the competing traditions and produced a collective work synthesizing their positions into a harmonious whole, represented one response to these calls.

Another common point was that the sponsors of these texts were both established political figures confronted with a young ruler who had acceded to the throne before being able to rule. Some scholars have suggested that sponsorship of textual composition by Lü Buwei and Liu An was a preliminary to rebellion. However, no historical text suggests that the former plotted revolt, and if he had wanted to do so it would have made more sense to move while he was at the peak of his powers and the emperor still a youth of thirteen. In fact, the explanatory postface to the calendrical section of the *Lü shi chun qiu* quotes Lü Buwei as saying that he had "been able to study that which the Yellow Emperor had taught to Zhuan Xu."[50] This indicates that the work was intended as instruction in the methods of kingship for a young ruler. As for Liu An, even the hostile historical record does not pretend that a rebellion took place, and the accusations against him are supported only by the testimony of a former supporter who was seeking to preserve his own life by denouncing his erstwhile patron. Moreover, the *Han shu* states that Liu An presented the *Huainanzi* to the young Emperor Wu, apparently at the beginning of the latter's reign. In short, both books were in all likelihood written to guide the conduct of a young ruler. Their respective patrons thus cast themselves in the role of the Duke of Zhou as authors of texts containing a comprehensive political wisdom and as advisers or regents who showed the monarch how to be a true king.

As comprehensive treatises produced by large numbers of scholars under the aegis of a leading political figure who aspired to guide a young ruler, both texts aimed to bring together all the competing doctrines of the period. The account in the *Shi ji* of the *Lü shi chun qiu*'s composition states that Lü Buwei had each of his 3,000 retainers write down the doctrines and theories that he knew and then edited them into a work that would "embrace all the affairs of Heaven, Earth, the ten thousand things, the past, and the present." He offered a fortune in gold to any wandering scholar or scholastic retainer of another feudal lord who could "add or subtract a single character." This shows that the book was intended to encompass all the traditions of the period and to contain everything worth knowing. The text itself also states the necessity of combining the strengths of each of the philosophical traditions.[51] The final chapter of the *Huainanzi* points to similar aspirations. As noted in the first section above, the conclusion lists the historical and geographic factors that produced each of the philosophical traditions, and then praises the *Huainanzi* as a universally applicable work that surpasses or includes all the previous, limited texts. The syncretic nature of the two compendia was indicated by their classification as works that "mixed" or "combined" (*za* 雜) the schools.[52] Many modern scholarly studies have examined how these texts combine and attempt to reconcile the competing traditions of the Warring States.[53]

To allow multiple authors to create a synthesis of the philosophical traditions, both the *Lü shi chun qiu* and the *Huainanzi* were written as collections of essays. To demonstrate their comprehensive character, however, they worked the essays into more elaborate structures that suggested both totality and natural foundations. The *Lü shi chun qiu*'s structure was modeled on the annual cycle, as indicated in its title and the structure of its first section. The *Huainanzi* took its structure from the cosmogonic models sketched in the *Dao de jing*, the *Zhuangzi*, and the Mawangdui manuscripts. In both cases the structure breaks down in later sections of the book, which are devoted to filling in omissions or elaborating points already made. Nevertheless, it is clear that the authors attempted to find natural models and thereby establish the texts as replications of the universe.

The title of the *Lü shi chun qiu* points to its calendrical structure. The book is composed of three sections—twelve "registers" *ji* 紀, eight "overviews" *lan* 覽, and six "assessments" *lun* 論—and only the *ji* are strictly calendrical. However, these chapters are the core of the book and were probably written first as an independent work. This is indicated by the presence of a postface (*xu* 序) discussing the nature of the work immediately after the last *ji*. It was a common practice from the late Warring States through the Han to add such chapters at the end of a work. Moreover, the postface itself refers to the work as the "Twelve Registers" and argues that it forms a totality encompassing the triad of Heaven, Earth, and man.

A freeman asked about the "Twelve Registers." The Marquis of Wenxin [Lü Buwei] said, "I have been able to study that which the Yellow Emperor taught to Zhuan Xu. There is a great circle [Heaven] above and a great square [Earth] below.

If you can imitate them, you will be the parent of the people. I have heard that the pure times of antiquity were a case of imitating Heaven and Earth. In all cases the 'Twelve Registers' provide a register of order and chaos, preservation and destruction. They are the means by which one knows longevity or premature death, good fortune or misfortune. Above they investigate in Heaven, below they verify in Earth, and in the middle they examine in men. Thus in questions of right or wrong or proper and improper, nothing is hidden.

Heaven means 'to accord,' and 'to accord' means to give life. Earth means 'to stabilize,' and 'to stabilize' means to make peaceful. Man means 'good faith,' and 'good faith' means to be obedient. If these three are all proper, then things proceed without conscious contrivance. 'Proceed' means to carry out their principles. If one carries out the numbers [of Heaven] and follows the principles [of Earth], then this eliminates bias [*si* 私]. Biased vision blinds the eye, biased hearing deafens the ear, and biased reflection crazes the mind. If these three biases are all established, then one's wisdom has no means to be public minded/universal [*gong* 公]. If wisdom is not universal, then good fortune daily declines and disaster daily increases."[54]

According to this, the first twelve chapters formed an independent work that contained within itself the principles for imitating Heaven and Earth, doing away with bias or partiality, and attaining a universal wisdom based on cosmic principle. Consequently this block of text forms the essential core of the *Lü shi chun qiu*, with the remainder consisting of elaboration, repetition, and the filling of lacunae.[55]

The "Twelve Registers" follow the pattern of other univeralizing works by placing the program for a comprehensive intellectual synthesis under the aegis of the ruler. The "Registers" are named according to the months of the year, and each begins with the relevant section from the calendar of royal activities commonly known as the "Monthly Ordinances" (*yue ling* 月令), a work which also appears in modified form in the *Li ji* and the *Huainanzi*.[56] Each section begins by identifying the position of the sun in the heavens, identifies the cyclic characters, and then gives an inventory of relevant correlations such as the active god, his assistant, the seasonal class of creatures, the seasonal note of the pentatonic scale, the monthly pitchpipe, the number, the taste, the smell, the appropriate sacrifices, and the signs from the natural world. After this listing of relevant celestial and earthly characteristics, the chapters describe the conduct of the ruler and the policies he should pursue. These are based on the principle that the ruler must imitate natural pattern and bring his conduct into accord with the seasons. Thus he gives life in the spring and causes it to flourish in the summer, but in the autumn and winter he takes life through war and punishments, stores things away, and seals them up. The text also stipulates the natural calamities that would result should he perform actions inappropriate to the season.

These opening sections are followed by essays extending the strictures of the royal, ritual calendar into a theory of kingship. The sections on spring are followed by essays on the supreme importance of life, the necessity that the ruler value his own health, and his duty to impartially further the lives of other beings. The essays appended to summer deal primarily with the need to further life through respect for teachers, the cultivation of ritual, and the practice of music. The essays of autumn deal largely with military affairs. Those of winter begin with discussions of funerals, and then switch toward advocacy of personal austerity, the checking of accounts, the selection and rewarding of personnel, and the making of long-range plans.

As James Sellman has argued, the ruler's adaptation to the shifting character of the seasons provides a frame in which the theories advocated by the philosophical traditions all find their place. While ideas from the different traditions are scattered throughout the text, the spring section is dominated by theories adapted from the Yangist and syncretist chapters of the *Zhuangzi*, the summer months by the educational program of the *ru*, the autumn by the military treatises and chapters on warfare from the philosophical schools, and the winter by Mohist strictures on funerals and economy, and legalist teachings on the assessment and employment of talent.[57] Here the ideal of a comprehensive doctrine in which the limited teachings of each school find their place is achieved by subsuming them under the calendar of royal activities. The king, who embodies and enacts the cycle fixed by Heaven, and who is obliged to secure every object its place, becomes the locus in which the schools converge and form a total program of social order. This is the role attributed to the ancient sages in the final chapter of the *Zhuangzi*, and which Li Si would proclaim as the ideal in his memorial on doctrinal unification.

In addition to the calendar, the *Lü shi chun qiu* also appeals to numerology to suggest totality. Each of the twelve "Registers" has four appended essays. The second section consists of eight "Overviews," each of which contains eight essays, for a total of sixty-four. The number eight corresponds to the winds and the directions, perhaps suggesting a model of space to follow that of time, while eight and sixty-four also correspond to the trigrams and hexagrams. The third section consists of six "Assessments," each containing six essays. The number six corresponds to the four directions along with up and down, thus suggesting the three dimensions. The importance of the numbers is demonstrated by the frequency of repetition, indicating the authors' insistence on having a meaningful number of essays. In addition to numerical symbolism, both the second and third sections begin with essays indicating natural beginnings. The "Overviews" begin with the essay "Having an Origin" (*you shi* 有始), which takes as its theme the origins and structure of Heaven and Earth. The "Assessments" begin with the essay "Opening Spring" (*kai chun* 開春).

While the *Lü shi chun qiu* finds a model in the cycle of the seasons, the *Huainanzi* adopts its pattern from the proto-Daoist cosmogonies sketched in the *Dao de jing* and the Mawangdui manuscripts. These cosmogonies, as discussed in chapter 3, operate according to the principle of mathematical division, with one forming two, two forming three or four, and so on. The first chapter of the *Huainanzi* deals with the universal Way, which is both the origin of all things and the model for comprehensiveness. The second chapter elaborates the cosmogonic account from the *Zhuangzi*, and then develops the principles of division and transformation by which the universe and all things within it were formed. The third chapter presents the structure of Heaven, the fourth chapter that of Earth, and the fifth traces the annual cycle in a version of the "Monthly Ordinances." The sixth chapter then presents the principle of "resonance" that links Heaven and Earth, as well as other natural phenomena. The seventh deals with the origin and nature of the human body, the eighth with the all-penetrating virtue of the sage, and the ninth with the ruler. Having ascended from the primal unity, through first divisions, the structure of space and time, and the origins of man, to the highest forms of men in the sage and ruler, the text, like the *Lü shi chun qiu*, loses a clear sense of structure. Nevertheless, the passage in the early chapters from primal unity to the sage provides a natural model for the ideal of an all-encompassing textual unity incorporating all philosophical and technical traditions.

This ideal is described in the opening passage of the final chapter.

> Making these written expositions is the means by which we provide guiding cords [*ji gang* 紀綱] for the Way and its power, and a warp and weft [*jing wei* 經緯] for human affairs. Above we check it in Heaven, below measure it in the Earth, and in the middle trace it throughout all principles. Even if it is not able to fully draw out the central matter of the hidden and marvelous, it is sufficient to, in a prolix manner, observe the beginnings and the ends. If we drew together and summarized everything with a language that did not destroy the pure, uncarved block and scatter the great origins, we feared that people would stupidly not be able to understand. Therefore we made elaborate language [*ci* 辭] for it and broad explanations [*shuo* 說]. Again we feared that people would abandon the fundamental and pursue the peripheral. Therefore if we spoke of the Way and not of affairs, then there would be no way to rise and fall with the generations. If we spoke of affairs and not of the Way, then there would be no way to freely wander and grow with the transformations [*hua* 化]. Therefore we wrote these twenty chapters.[58]

The text thus justifies its repetitions and loose structure through the need to present both the underlying unity and its manifestations as they change across time.

While the *Lü shi chun qiu* presents totality through the image of the annual cycle and the *Huainanzi* through the cosmogonic derivation of the many from the One, both reinforce their claims to comprehensiveness through the inclusion of all human history. The *Lü shi chun qiu* provides the earliest surviving account of natural underpinnings to the sequence of dynasties.[59] It insists that the ruler must be able to situate himself in time through his comprehensive knowledge of both natural phenomena and human events. The *Huainanzi* similarly refers to the full range of both ancient times and recent history, and insists on the the ruler's knowing such matters.[60]

The vision of intellectual unity was also linked with the ambition of political unification. This is particularly true for the *Lü shi chun qiu*, which was composed just two decades before Qin's final campaigns of conquest. The text insists repeatedly on the importance of rulers and the value of unification. First, it argues that in antiquity before the appearance of rulers, or in distant lands that have no monarchs, people lived like animals. Kin ties, hierarchical relations, ritual conduct, implements and tools, and all other features of civilization depended on rulers for their introduction and maintenance. Second, the functions of the ruler could be carried out only if one man ruled over all, the absence of such a ruler leading to chaos and war.[61] Such a ruler with his comprehensive laws and measures was also essential to the unification of the schools and their divergent standards of judgment.[62] Written in a feudatory state decades after the Han had established a unified empire, the *Huainanzi* placed less stress on the theme of unification. However, it assumes unity as an ideal and echoes arguments from the *Lü shi chun qiu*.[63]

The *Lü shi chun qiu* and the *Huainanzi* developed several of the features noted in the preceding sections, although they differed from *jing* in avoiding a hierarchical division into a central text and appended explications. First, they claimed authority through being comprehensive, as demonstrated by the inclusion of doctrines borrowed and adapted from all the leading philosophical schools. Second, the writing of a comprehensive work in which all the schools were reconciled was held to be possible only under the guidance of a ruler. Third, the doctrines of the competing schools were both affirmed and transcended through their incorporation into an overarching, temporal structure. In both texts this temporal frame included both a model of history that explained the appearance of the schools and set the terms for their abolition, and a trans-historical, temporal frame offering a model for the conciliation of contradictions in a higher unity. These works were thus the textual forms of political unification.

SIMA QIAN AND UNIVERSAL HISTORY

Composed in the decades following the presentation of the *Huainanzi*, the *Shi ji* also aimed to give a textual form to a world empire. In his letter to Ren An justifying his decision not to commit suicide after his castration because of his desire to finish the history, Sima Qian first described it as follows:

> These men [King Wen, Confucius, Qu Yuan, Zuo Qiuming, Sun Bin, Lü Buwei, Han Fei, authors of the Zhou *Odes*] all were frustrated in their intentions and were unable to fully carry out [*tong* 通] their Way. So they narrated past affairs, while thinking of those to come. Such people as Zuo Qiuming, who had gone blind, and Sun Bin, whose leg had been cut off, could not be employed. They retired and put judgments in writing in order to vent their frustrations, thinking to hand down empty writings to make themselves known. Daring to be arrogant, I have recently entrusted myself to such impotent words. I have gathered together old traditions abandoned by the world, examined their conduct, and investigated the principles

of success and failure or rise and decline. In total there are 130 chapters. I desire thereby to exhaust [*jiu* 究] the interchanges between Heaven and man, completely trace [*tong* 通] the changes from ancient times to the present, and thus complete [*cheng* 成] the words of a single school/family [*yi jia zhi yan* 一家之言].[64]

While scholars studying this passage have concentrated on Sima Qian's theory of the relation between Heaven and man or the existence of cycles in history, one should note the frequency of verbs insisting on the spatial and temporal comprehensiveness of the work. The sole exception is the final phrase, where Sima Qian with formulaic modesty states that he offers nothing more than the limited teachings of a school. If one translates it as "words of a single family," rather than "school" than it again has a universal sweep, for Sima Qian traced his family's links to the office of astrologer/historian (*shi*) back to the beginning of time. It is the aspiration to cover all human history and society that repeatedly comes to the fore in the *Shi ji*.

First, the work is comprehensive in that it offers a history of human society from the creation of the state by the Yellow Emperor down to Sima Qian's own day. Sima Qian thus included the periods both before and after those covered in his historical models, the *Documents* and above all the *Chun qiu*. While he does not explicitly explain this, apart from his remark to Ren An that he hopes to completely trace the course of history, he suggests a motive by the inclusion of his father's essay on the "Six Schools" near the beginning of the postface that tells how he came to write the *Shi ji*. This essay, as noted above, celebrated the Daoists for including the good points of all other schools, "evolving with the times," "changing in response to things," and hence "being suitable to all affairs." In contrast the *ru*, from whom the models of historical writing were derived, had too many texts to be fully mastered.[65] Among the schools, the Daoists thus come closest to the ideal of comprehensive wisdom to which Sima Qian aspires for his own work, and he marks this by going beyond the patron sages of the *ru* to begin with the Daoist sage king, the Yellow Emperor.[66] He also, as he explains in the postface, fills in the centuries between the end of the *Chun qiu* and his own lifetime.

In addition to its temporal range, the *Shi ji* employed a novel structure to suggest a comprehensive, hierarchical ordering of space. Rather than providing a single chronicle with incidents and speeches appended under their respective years, Sima Qian divides his chapters into ranked categories that textually replicate the social order. The principles for each category are described at the end of the postface:

> Where the kingly traces [*ji* 迹] arise, I trace them back to their origins and examine their ends, regard their flourishing and observe their decline. I assess and check their conduct, in general extrapolating back for the Three Dynasties and recording Qin and Han. Above I record from the Yellow Emperor and come down to the present. I have composed the twelve "Fundamental Chronicles" to completely establish a thread for it.[67]

At the same time there are different [noble] lineages, so the years are discrepant and unclear [i.e., each state or principality had a different calendar]. So I made ten "Tables" [*biao* 表].

Ritual and music are reduced or increased. The pitchpipes and calendar are changed [formulae for the adaptation of rites by dynasties]. Military strategems, mountains and rivers, ghosts and spirits, the interchanges between Heaven and man, following on a time of decline [a new dynasty arising when its predecessor is exhausted] I thoroughly traced [*tong* 通] their changes, and made the eight "Monographs" [*shu* 書].

The twenty-eight Lunar Lodgings revolve around the Northern Dipper; thirty spokes converge on a single hub, revolving inexhaustibly. Ministers who assist like limbs are paired [with rulers]. Loyally and faithfully they practice the Way, in order to assist their masters. So I made the thirty "Hereditary Households" [*shi jia* 世家].

Aiding the right but not bound by conventions, not allowing themselves to miss the time, they established merit and fame throughout the world. So I made the seventy "Arrayed Traditions" [*lie zhuan* 列傳].[68]

As in the works discussed above, the project of creating a comprehensive text is placed under the aegis of a single, supreme ruler. The traces of the kingly Way create a chronicle of dynastic rise and fall to serve as a guiding thread for the entire work. This reads the unified empire created by Qin back into the beginning of history and assumes that this undivided "sovereignty" passed from king to king or dynasty to dynasty without break from the Yellow Emperor to Emperor Wu. The single ruler advocated in late Warring States polemics as the ground of intellectual unity and inscribed in the state-sponsored compendia here reappears as the unifying principle of history. Making the monarch the organizing principle of history absorbs the contentions of the Warring States and the schools into the original harmony imagined by the schoolmen, and allows the application of the model of the *Chun qiu*, the chronicle of a single state, to the entire known world.

All other categories of chapters are defined in terms of their relation to the ruler. Thus the "Tables" are identified with the noble lineages. They reconcile the assumption of perpetual unity with the facts of political division. A chronicle of rulers has no place for the divergent calendars of the Zhou feudatories and the competing states, so the initial thread must be supplemented with charts to link the history of each principality back to the sequence of presumptive kings.

The "Monographs" in turn, trace the evolution of ritual, music, pitchpipes, calendars, and sacrifices. These are the visible and audible forms of the thread of sovereignty running through the "Fundamental Chronicles," since each new dynasty modified rites, music, and other activities to mark both continuity and adaptation.[69] They thus treat topically the history that appears as a series of dated events in the first twelve chapters. They also incorporate topics dealt with in the *ru* canon.

The "Hereditary Households" deal with holders of fiefs, thus representing the nobility. Sima Qian describes them as loyal servants assisting their masters, but he includes chapters for the ruling houses of the major states of the Eastern Zhou period, as well as the major followers of the Han founder. Like the "Tables" this category allows for the incorporation of a multistate reality into a history defined by the assumption of a single ruler or ruling house. It also includes the account of Confucius discussed in chapter 6. This is justified by the fact that Confucius had become a recipient of cult from Han scholars, and it may constitute a veiled acknowledgment of his status as "king without attributes."[70]

The "Arrayed Traditions" are described only in general terms as including those who "established merit and fame." Since the preceding categories are determined by links to the political structure, the "Traditions" are by implication equated with the commoners. They deal with those who in any field achieved a distinction that Sima Qian regarded as worthy of note. Dealing with officials, diplomats, generals, merchants, manufacturers, philosophical masters, scholars, poets, diviners, assassins, and gangsters, they provide a portrait of the society of the Warring States and early Han.[71]

The organization of the history also universalizes through adopting the structure of canon and commentary. Sima Qian states that his work was a continuation of the *Chun qiu*, which he employed as a structural model. The latter consisted of the Lu chronicle, now called a canon (*jing* 經), and appended commentaries (*zhuan* 傳). For Han scholars the two levels were inseparable, and one could not read the canon without its commentary, or vice versa. Sima Qian could scarcely describe his history as a canon, and his proclaimed intent of establishing a school or completing a family work denied such an ambition. However his opening twelve chapters formed a chronicle of events in the image of the *Chun qiu*. Moreover the rubric *ji* 紀 *kieg which he applied to these chapters was nearly homophonous with *jing* 經 *kieng, and shared a common range of meanings—"guiding thread," "regulate," "rule, norm." Sometimes the two characters were linked in a synonym compound.[72] Thus Sima Qian's royal chronicle stands in the place of the *Chun qiu*, a substitution anticipated by the doctrine that the *Chun qiu* performed the function of the monarch and established a model of kingship. Here Confucius' textual kingship was translated into a text of kings. Moreover, the defining traits of a *jing* 經 were to be universal, to regulate, and to provide a guiding thread, the roles attributed both to a true monarch and Sima Qian's chronicle.

While the chronicle of sovereigns is a homophonous equivalent of the canon, most of the remaining chapters bear the rubric *zhuan* 傳, the character applied to commentaries. The narratives and anecdotes in Sima Qian's *zhuan* have little in common with the explication of graphs of the *Gongyang* tradition, but they resemble the material of the *Zuo zhuan*, which Sima Qian describes as the most accurate record of Confucius' explanation of the *Chun qiu*.[73] The biographies of commoners in the *Shi ji* thus play the role of commentary to canon, adding substance, detail, and drama to the briefer, drier presentation in the chronicles. They also stand in the subordinate position of commoner to ruler. The "Tables" and "Hereditary Houses" were needed to accommodate both chronicle and tradition to the fact of historical divisions, and the latter highlighted the hierarchical structure of the work by introducing an intermediate textual/social category between the ruler and the rest. They thus functioned like the nobility and privileged officialdom in Jia Yi's social metaphor, as steps elevating the temple of the ruler above the ground of the common people.

The "Monographs" give an evolving, institutional frame to the bare chronicle of rulership, but they also serve another function in the vision of an all-inclusive text. As noted in chapter 5, Sima Qian regarded Confucius not only as the author of the *Chun qiu* but also the editor of the other five canonical texts. Since Confucius was Sima Qian's model, his history not only carried forward the chronicle of Lu but also incorporated the other canonical arts in the "Monographs."

> The Grand Historian [Sima Qian] said, "My predecessor [Sima Tan] said, 'From the death of the Duke of Zhou it was five hundred years to Confucius. From Confucius' death to the present is also five hundred years. Is there someone who can link these enlightened ages, correct the *Changes*, continue the *Chun qiu*, and base themselves on the common points of the *Odes*, the *Documents*, the *Rites*, and the *Music?*' My intention lies in this! My intention lies in this! How would this little son dare to decline?"[74]

The monographs on ritual and imperial sacrifices thus correspond to the canonical texts on ritual, those on music and the pitchpipes to music, and those on the calendar and astrology to divination. While the monographs on waterways and merchants have no exact canonical analogue, they are closely related to the "Yu gong" chapter of the *Documents*.

Sima Qian's work also aims to be comprehensive as an anthology of earlier texts. As noted in chapter 5, the account of Confucius includes many *Lun yu* passages, historically situated to provide a context. Other biographies, such as those of Qu Yuan, Jia Yi, and Sima Xiangru, consist almost entirely of works composed by these figures. Sima Qian also borrowed much material from the *Zuo zhuan*, although he rewrote its archaic language, and his history of the Warring States period is formed from extensive quotations from the works later edited to form the *Zhan guo ce*. Philosophical works such as the *Mencius* are quoted or adapted to provide material. In short, although composed by Sima Tan and Sima Qian, the frequent use of quotation and the wholesale incorporation of other works turns the *Shi ji* into an authoritative, multivoiced "encyclopedia" of the literature known in the early Han.

The multivoiced nature of the work, which marks it as universal, is also employed in several ways to create authoritative speech. First, the incorporation of others' words can suggest truth through an ironic interplay between quoted assertions and factual narrative. Examples of this are the contrast between the inflated claims of the First Emperor's inscriptions and Sima Qian's narration of his policies, or that between promises of the Masters of Esoteric Arts (*fang shi* 方士) to

Emperor Wu and results obtained. Similarly, the *Shi ji* marks its objectivity by describing historical figures primarily in the voices of actors, rather than that of Sima Qian, and its universalism by dividing narratives into multiple chapters written from the perspective of different participants.[75] Finally, quoting earlier works gives the *Shi ji* historical depth through internal references and echoes, as well as the authority of past masters whose words are borrowed.

The encyclopedic nature of Sima Qian's work may also be marked by having the numbers of chapters correspond to the calendar in the manner of the *Lü shi chun qiu*. The most elaborate hypothesis of such correlations was that of the Tang commentator Zhang Shoujie (張守節).

> He made twelve "Fundamental Chronicles" as the image [*xiang* 象] of the year having twelve months. He made ten "Tables" as the image of Heaven alternating "hard" and "soft" in ten-day intervals [the Chinese "week"] to record the generations of the enfeoffed houses from beginning to end. He made eight "Monographs" as the image of the year having eight "segments" [*jie* 節, first day of each season, solstices, and equinoxes], to record Heaven, Earth, the sun, the moon, the mountains, the rivers, ritual, and music. He made thirty "Hereditary Houses" as the image of a month's having thirty days, "thirty spokes converging in one hub," in order to record success and failure in terms of the loyalty of houses with hereditary salaries and ministers who assisted as limbs. He made seventy "Arrayed Traditions" as the image of the seventy-two days that make up one-fifth of a year [significant in five-phases theory], but uses seventy as a round number with the remaining two days as the image of the intercalary periods, in order to record princes, marquises, generals, ministers, heroes, and worthies who established merit and fame throughout the world, and can hence be arrayed in sequence. These combine to make 130 chapters in the image of the twelve months plus one intercalary month. The Grand Historian made these five categories, and not one can be omitted. He thereby comprehensively traced the principles of Heaven and Earth, provided encouragement and warning, and created a model for later generations.[76]

It is unlikely that all these correspondences were conceived in this way by Sima Qian, and virtually any number has some correspondent in Han numerology. Sima Qian himself asserts such a referent only for the hereditary households, and there it is to the "lunar lodgings" (*su* 宿) rather than the days of the month. However, even this one case announces the possibility of such correspondences, and in the mental universe of the Han many readers would have noticed them, whatever the author intended or announced.

Sima Qian also asserts the comprehensive nature of his history in the genealogy of his family at the beginning of the postface. He traces his clan and their office as astrologers/historians back to the mythical Chong and Li who presided over the separation of Heaven and Earth. This act is here described as an appointment to office in the time of Zhuan Xu, but other texts show that Chong and Li derive from a myth explaining the origins of sacrifice as a consequence of a rupture between gods and men.[77] In tracing the origins of his family and his office as historian back to the earliest times, Sima Qian links his own story with the full sweep of the history which he narrates. The final chapter of the *Shi ji* thus returns to the point where the chronicle began, and Sima Qian's account of his family, his father, and himself becomes the ground in which the entire history is drawn together. As Jean Levi has suggested, this account of the ancient origins of the Sima clan might also be a veiled attack on Emperor Wu, whose unjust punishment menaced the ancient Sima line. In contrast to his historians, whose calling dated back to the origins of civilization, Emperor Wu could trace his sovereignty back only two generations. Moreover, in the *Zuo zhuan* the Liu clan was linked to the myth of Chong and Li in an account of the disappearance of the office in charge of rearing dragons. In this story dragons disappear from the human realm because of the dereliction of Liu Lei (劉累), thus implicating the later imperial clan in the disappearance of the magic beast most closely associated with the power of the sovereign.[78] In writing the work that would immortalize himself and his clan, Sima Qian defied the emperor who threatened both.

Emperor Wu's quest for immortality points to another form in which Sima Qian made his history a comprehensive work. Accounts of this quest are concentrated in the "Monograph on the *Feng* and *Shan* Sacrifices," from which they were transferred into the "Fundamental Chronicle of Emperor Wu" pieced together to replace the missing original. The *feng* and *shan* sacrifices were a major issue of the reign of Emperor Wu, and they inspired writings by the leading literary figures of the day. Sima Qian not only devoted a monograph to these sacrifices, which he portrayed as the culmination of the state's sacrificial cult, but also placed it prominently in the account of how he came to write his *magnum opus*. In this way, Sima Qian's treatment of the sacrifices offers an insight into his vision of history.[79]

The *feng* and *shan* sacrifices were first conceived in the late Warring States or Qin through a fusion of several earlier rituals—sacrifices of conquest or territorial lordship, royal processions, and mountain sacrifices. As the ritual form of the new vision of a unitary empire, they signaled the attainment of world rulership and universal peace. In addition to their all-encompassing geographic scope, they included all of time, for a belief widely attested by the second century B.C. held that they had been performed by seventy-two monarchs, from the beginning of time to the Three Dynasties. The *feng* and *shan* constituted a political genealogy, a series of sacrifices that created a line of public authority linking sage to sage through the centuries, a continuous transmission marking the survival of rulership and civilization in the world. They thus offered a latent model for Sima Qian's "Fundamental Chronicles," and by extension his entire work. Indeed, the list of the last twelve monarchs to have supposedly performed the *feng* and *shan*, the only rulers named, is identical with Sima Qian's "Chronicles" through the foundation of the Zhou.

This link of the *feng* and *shan* to the writing of history is strengthened by the fact that it was part of the complex of written communication with the spirits that was described in chapter 1. The central act of the *feng* sacrifice was to place a written message to the god in a sealed chest (one meaning of *feng* 封 is "to seal") like the one in the story of the Duke of Zhou. In their Qin versions, the *feng*, *shan*, and other mountain sacrifices that punctuated imperial processions were also recorded in stone inscriptions, which made them acts of writing history. Among the literary forms that established parallels between human and spirit realms, the spirit form of history was the commemorative inscription. A series of such inscriptions from the *feng* sacrifices would have mapped out the succession of monarchs that formed the backbone of a court-based history like Sima Qian's "Chronicles." Indeed the archive in which he deposited his completed work was called the "Famous Mountain" (*ming shan* 名山). This suggests the close links between Sima Qian's history and the inscriptions of mountain sacrifices, for both of them were placed in "famous mountains" in hopes of lasting for all time.[80]

The *feng* and *shan* sacrifices also acted as an immediate impetus for Sima Qian's writing. Sima Qian states that his father could not accompany Emperor Wu to Mt. Tai for the performance of the sacrifices, and that his consequent anger and despair led to his death. On his deathbed Sima Tan recounted how their clan had been royal astrologers/historians since ancient times, and that Sima Qian must now take up the family calling or the tradition would be lost. He noted that in performing the *feng* sacrifice Emperor Wu was extending the millennial line of sovereignty. Sima Tan then links the sacrifices to written accounts of the past through reference to the Duke of Zhou writing hymns to Kings Wen and Wu, the transmission of the *Odes* and *Documents* by Confucius, and the writing of the *Chun qiu* by the latter. These texts proclaimed the Zhou to later times, and Sima Tan had hoped to carry on this tradition in his chronicle. Death, however, had thwarted his plans, and he charged his son to prevent the historical record from being cut off.[81]

In this speech Sima Tan presents the inherited calling of the Sima clan, the political genealogy of the sage kings inscribed in the *feng* sacrifices, and the sequential record of the past as three threads converging in his person. His imminent death threatens the continuation of all these lines, charging the deathbed laying on of hands with an epochal significance. In placing this scene at the center of his account of writing the *Shi ji*, Sima Qian links the *feng* and *shan* sacrifices, his family history, his personal fate, and his life's work as variant forms of a common duty to save and transmit the achievements of those who had come before. To take up the office of Grand Astrologer, act as witness to the *feng* and *shan* (admittedly a critical one), and write the *Shi ji* became three aspects of a single filial duty that covered all of history.

In the next section of the postface Sima Qian again justifies his life's work with reference to the sacrifices. After citing Dong Zhongshu's assertion that Confucius used history in a dark age to preserve moral truth and ritual correctness, he responds to a hypothetical questioner by asserting that even in good times history must be written to proclaim the glory of the rulers. He gives a brief panegyric of the Han's achievements, and the *feng* and *shan* are again given pride of place. This is followed immediately by an account of his castration, and his resolve to complete the work inspired by the aforementioned list of men who wrote as a response to personal failure and catastrophe.[82]

This final justification of his work, however, calls into question that which precedes it, and highlights his critical intent. Sima Qian's citation of the *feng* and *shan* sacrifices as proof of Han glory is ironic, for his monograph is a thinly veiled criticism of Emperor Wu's decision to perform them. From the beginning the chapter intimates this criticism, for it starts by discussing why the sacrifices were so seldom performed.[83] Most of the chapter deals with their performance by the monstrous Qin Shihuang, with sorcerers who dupe Emperor Wu by promising him immortality through performing the sacrifices, and with the absence of any response from the spirits.[84] References to Confucius, Qu Yuan, the authors of the *Odes*, and the rest as precedents for his writing likewise undercut his suggestion that he is writing in praise of the Han, for these are all examples of virtuous men unjustly ignored or punished by mediocre rulers.

In fact the author of the *Shi ji* criticizes most aspects of the reign of his master, and finds little to celebrate in any member of the Liu house. Jean Levi has gone so far as to argue that Sima Qian entered into "a competition for immortality with his master," and that his history "was transformed from an act of piety that a son owed his father into an engine of war of a subject against his prince. The *Shi ji* is the instrument and the product of this struggle." His criticisms of the emperor's policies, celebrations of failures who turn to literature or accept humiliation in order to complete great tasks, and the missing "Chronicle" of Emperor Wu are all tied to Sima Qian's desire for self-justification and triumph over his adversary. He thus achieved for himself in his writing the immortality that Emperor Wu had failed to attain in his sacrifices.[85]

This adversarial stance of the historian, however, was not an accident of biography but grew directly out of Warring States ideas of historiography. In adopting the model of Confucius as historian, Sima Qian directly incorporated the *Gongyang*'s theory of the historian as a "literary" (*wen* 文) ruler passing judgments in the absence of a "real" (*shi* 實) Son of Heaven. In the vision of a monarchy traced back to the Yellow Emperor he also inherited the model of the past forged in the scholarly traditions as the ground for their critiques of political authorities (see chapter 3). Literary accounts of the past, as opposed to court chronicles, had been a tool of criticism and opposition, and this function was carried forward in Sima Qian's work. As the writer of a comprehensive history, and the heir to a family tradition stretching back to the origins of the state, he adapted the model of Confucius as king and judge to the encyclopedic ideal in which authority was defined by universality and the monarch was the image of the universal man. The *Shi ji* not only contained criticisms of Emperor Wu, but also established a literary universe that doubled and replaced the real world of events. In this parallel world the historian mastered the monarch, and the castrated Sima Qian passed judgment on the man who had condemned him.[86] The new historiographic structure functioned only in assuming the status and image of the monarch, the very figure from whom it drew its authority.

SIMA XIANGRU AND UNIVERSAL POETRY

The other great writer of the age of Emperor Wu, Sima Xiangru, was also an exemplar of the encyclopedic epoch, for he developed the poetry of the period into a language that gained authority through its all-inclusiveness. Like the works discussed above, the "rhapsodies" (*fu* 賦) of Sima Xiangru encompassed time and space in words, adopting the ruler as the emblematic figure of totality. They also promoted an ideal of the recently created empire as the image of the all-inclusive state.

The writings are closely related to those of Sima Qian, a younger contemporary in whose history the poetry and prose of Sima Xiangru were preserved. Sima Xiangru gave a central place to the *feng* and *shan* sacrifices, and emphasized the role of writing within this supreme rite of empire. He also resembled Sima Qian in that through re-creating the empire and its ruler in the form of language, he absorbed Emperor Wu into the realm of graphic signs. There is no evidence that Sima Xiangru had an animus against Emperor Wu in the manner of Sima Qian, and he fills his writings with advice rather than criticism. Nevertheless, as in the works of Sima Qian, the composition of an encyclopedic work created a literary alternative to the political reality, an alternative that outdid the ruler, if it did not condemn him.

The work of Sima Xiangru, however, is distinctive in two ways other than genre. First, its incorporation of elements from the *Chu ci*, most prominently the theme of flights in the company of gods and immortals, gives it a broader spatial range. By contrast, the temporal element is less central, except in the discussion of the *feng* and *shan* sacrifices and references to ancient sages. Second, the use of rare characters and their clustering in groups sharing a signific calls attention to the role of the *written* character in re-creating the world, and anticipates the theory of characters in the *Shuo wen jie zi*.

The works of Sima Xiangru, accepting as genuine only those preserved in his *Shiji* biography, consist of two major rhapsodies, one essay with a linked rhapsody, a brief lament for the second Qin emperor, two prose pieces growing out of his political activities in the southwest, and a brief memorial attempting to restrain the emperor's fondness for hunting.[87] This discussion will concentrate on the first three pieces, his most ambitious poetic works, and make reference to the others and to the *Shiji* account of Sima Xiangru's career only where these cast light on themes of the major works.

The longest and most influential composition of Sima Xiangru is the "Rhapsody on the Imperial Hunt" (also known as the "Sir Fantasy Rhapsody" or the "Rhapsody on the Shanglin Park"). This poem takes the form of a debate between three fictional figures who describe the hunting parks and hunts of the kings of Chu and Qi, and then those of the emperor. It thus dramatizes the empire as a world state encompassing the lesser kingdoms. It also reenacts Sima Xiangru's own career, for after an unhappy start at the court of Emperor Jing he had joined a circle of literary men who were clients of King Xiao of Liang, where he composed the first section of the poem. Only years later, when Emperor Wu read the work and had its author summoned to his court, did Sima Xiangru add the second half dealing with the imperial park. Thus his career as court poet led him from the realm of a feudatory monarch to the court of the emperor, and the rhapsody on the hunting parks traced the same progression.

In the first part of the poem the emissary from Chu describes the hunt that he has witnessed in Qi, and in response to questioning he delivers an elaborate account of the Yunmeng park in Chu and the much larger hunts held there. The account begins with a description of a mountain that towers as an *axis mundi* between Heaven and Earth, blotting out the sun and moon. It lists the rare minerals, plants, and animals that fill the park, and describes its strange geographic features. With the mountain defining the center, the account of the park is schematically distributed according to the four cardinal directions, thereby suggesting the inclusion of the world. It is filled with obscure characters, both the names of exotic objects found in the park and rhyming or alliterative binomes that evoke their characters or actions.[88] This is followed by a description of the splendors of the hunt, and the skills of the men and women who participate. Once again the depictions feature numerous rare words evoking the apparel and weaponry of the participants, and images from the natural world and the realms of the spirits are invoked to suggest their actions. In response the spokesman for Qi briefly sketches the size of his state and its hunting park. He insists that all kinds of rare creatures are also assembled in Qi, but that he "could not record them all, nor could Yu name them."[89] He concludes that as a vassal of the emperor the king of Qi did not think it proper to boast of his own park.

This reference to Yu is significant, for as discussed in chapter 1 he was the sage who named the animals and plants, and thus epitomized the power of the sage ruler as master of names. In saying that Yu could not name all the exotic creatures in the park, the spokesman of Qi sets the stage for the second half of the poem, in which Sima Xiangru, in the voice of the emperor's representative, plays the role of Yu in offering exhaustive lists of the rare minerals, plants, and animals that fill the imperial park. The fact that the second half of the poem is conducted under the aegis of Yu means that it is a re-creation of the world.

The elaborate language and protracted lists used to describe the hunt in Chu pale into insignificance, as the author intended, before the account of the Shanglin park. It defines the limits of the park in each of the four directions, echoing the cosmological schema of the Chu account. It follows with long lists of rivers and line after line of binomes and onamatopoeia evoking the surging of their currents and swirling of their eddies. Then come enumerations of the rare creatures that fill the waters, and in turn the precious stones and the varieties of birds. Having dealt with waters it moves on to describe the mountains with their twisting shapes and precipitous cliffs, and then the types of plants that cover them. It next equates the park with the world, describing the sun rising in its east and setting in its west, while its northern extremes are locked in eternal ice and its southern reaches know no winter. This is followed by accounts of the elaborate palaces and other buildings that fill the park, structures that reach up to the heavens and to which immortals come to dine. These descriptions include long lists of the precious substances from which they are built, the fruits and trees that fill their courtyards, and the exotic apes that fill the trees.

As in the account of the emissary from Chu, the description of the park is followed by a lengthy account of the hunt that dwells on the marvelous apparel and skills of the participants, as well as the number and variety of the animals slaughtered. In one scene the huntsmen soar up into the void "together with the spirits" and crush the birds of the air beneath their wheels.[90] The hunt is followed by a scene in which the emperor observes the numbers killed by each huntsman, and then an account of a musical performance. As with other elements, emphasis is placed on the variety of the music and its diverse geographic origins.

At this point the verse shifts back into prose, and the emperor speaks in his own voice. He decries the waste, indicates that he engages in hunting only to imitate Heaven's autumnal killing, but denounces all excess. He then orders that the hunting park should be opened for cultivation. A final verse passage describes how after proper purification he mounts the carriage of state and undertakes a new hunt in the "park of the Six Arts," the "forest of the *Chun qiu.*" The activities of hunting reappear as images of moving through a textual realm and snaring literary objects.[91] The poem closes with praise for the ruler who devotes himself to his people rather than the hunt, and denunciations of the kings of Chu and Qi for their inability to match the emperor's virtue. The spokesmen for the kings, in the manner of those overwhelmed by Daoist imagery (see chapter 2) or rhapsodic language are dumbfounded and can only stammer their apologies.

The poem's major theme is the all-inclusive power of the ruler, and it treats totality as the defining attribute of power. The poem regards the equation of the hunting park with the world as fundamental to the emperor's claims to lordship. Microcosm and macrocosm were central tropes in the imagery of power in this period, as in Qin Shihuang's rebuilding Xianyang as a replica of Heaven, making copies of the palaces of conquered states, and melting down the weapons of defeated adversaries to make statues laid out in imitation of a constellation. The equation of the hunting park with the world derived from the same mode of thought.

A second feature of the poems linking authority to all-inclusiveness is the listing of the rare objects that fill the parks or accompany the hunts. Enumeration in lists, as Helen Vendler has noted, is the standard "trope of plenitude."[92] The lists in the verse of Sima Xiangru, and in the other major Han rhapsodies, function in just this manner, suggesting that the realm of the emperor contains everything that the world has to offer. This possession of exotic objects was another fundamental feature of Han political power, leading to the notion of "tribute." Each region of the empire demonstrated its loyalty by offering its distinctive products, and the submission of distant peoples was marked through their presentation of exotica. The range of the emperor's power was proven by his ability to secure rare products from distant regions, and the listing of such objects transformed the poem into a form of tribute. This is indicated by the name *fu* 賦 "to present, to offer." The emperor's spokesman's prefacing of his criticism of the two kings with a discussion of the significance of tribute shows the importance of the theme.[93] This is also indicated by the importance of tribute in Sima Xiangru's prose essays, which make the submission of distant peoples and their offerings central to his claims for the greatness of the Han.[94] Tribute in the form of precious plants and animals also merged with the apparition of magic animals and plants as signs from Heaven in recognition of imperial virtue.[95] In this way the imagery of geographic inclusiveness and the exhaustive lists of contents converge in celebrating the possession of rare varieties of plants and animals as proof of world mastery.

The spatial range of the hunting rhapsody is extended to include the cosmos in the "Great Man Rhapsody." Here a figure representing Emperor Wu mounts a dragon chariot and travels to the edges of the earth. He assembles a cortege of immortals, commands the highest gods to do his biddings, and then travels to many of the sacred sites mentioned in the "Li sao" and the *Shan hai jing*. Unlike Ling Jun, who was thwarted by Heaven's gate keeper, the "Great Man" storms the gates of Heaven and carries off the Jade Maiden(s). He travels to the realm of the Queen Mother of the West and mocks her miserable existence, before finally ascending into the heights to dwell in isolation above all other beings.

The most frequently discussed feature of this rhapsody is its relation to the poem "Far Roaming" ("Yuan you" 遠遊) in the *Chu ci*. The two poems tell similar stories, and they share many individual lines and complete couplets. Some scholars have argued that the "Great Man" is largely adapted from the "Far Roaming," others have reversed the affiliation, and still others have argued that the latter is the rough draft of the former. Paul Kroll has recently pointed out that the author of "Far Roaming" evinces much more knowledge of and interest in Daoist concepts and techniques than does Sima Xiangru.[96] Whatever their relation, both poems clearly borrow the theme of celestial travel and many of their images from the "Li sao." What is perhaps most significant is the ease with which the same theme and images can be adapted to three radically different purposes. In the "Li sao" the spirit journey figures as a search for a place where the author's talents are recognized, and as a shamanic ritual that does not generate the power that was its traditional purpose but serves to validate the character of the poet. In the "Far Roaming" it takes the form of a Daoist *bildung* that ends in the attainment of immortality. In the "Great Man" it appears as a celestial version of an imperial progress, an armed procession of conquest throughout the cosmos that culminates in universal dominion. Thus a *topos* and repertoire of images that originally sought a ground of authority for a poet who had lost all place in the world re-appears as an account of the cosmic apotheosis of the ruler. Just as the failed Confucius became the double of the ruler in the textual realm of the chronicle, so in the sphere of verse Qu Yuan became the template for the highest lordship.

Sima Xiangru's last major piece of writing, his essay and poem on the *feng* and *shan* sacrifices, was also devoted to the theme of creating power through all-inclusive writing. As noted in the discussion of Sima Qian, the sacrifices were traced back to the first sages. Sima Xiangru begins his essay with remarks on these ancient roots and a citation of the seventy-two known monarchs who had performed it.[97] This is followed by a panegyric for the all-encompassing virtue of the Han, which reaches every corner of the world, the heights of Heaven, the depths of the Earth, and includes the lowest animals.[98] The reference to animals leads to an account of the miraculous beasts and plants that have appeared as signs from Heaven that the ruler's virtue is complete and that he should perform the sacrifices. The author then presents a speech attributed to the grand marshal elaborating the above themes, and cites the receipt of tribute from alien peoples. After a lengthy passage that I will discuss below because it deals with the pivotal role of writing, the poem begins with a speech attributed to the emperor in which he proclaims how his virtue falls like rain on all creatures and has brought forth magical omens. It concludes with more discussion of the omens, and the prose piece finishes with a call for the emperor to perform the sacrifices.

In summary, all the major rhapsodies of Sima Xiangru explore the uses of language to invoke the power and glory of the Han through versions of the theme of universality. This appears in the equation of the ruler's park with the limits of the world; the exhaustive lists of rare plants, animals, and minerals in a literary epiphany of the theory of tribute; the extension of this tribute to include the magical signs from Heaven; the depiction of the emperor's journey around the edges of the world and to the heights of space; and the tracing of emperorship back to the beginning of time in the *feng* and *shan*. These sacrifices, intended as the culmination of the Han world dominion to which Sima Xiangru devoted his political work in the southwest, provided a ritual form to the themes of his writing, and his posthumous essay-poem gave a literary rendition of the sacrifice that summarized his writing.[99] Like the history of his near contemporary Sima Qian, the verse of Sima Xiangru found its model and culmination in the central political ritual of his day, and it thus appeared as a literary doubling of the emperor whom he served.

In addition to offering the major poetic expression of the dream of an encyclopedic writing that gave literary form to the emergent state, Sima Xiangru's work and accounts of the poet's career highlight aspects of the role of writing in the period. First, the bibliographic monograph of the *Han shu* lists Sima Xiangru as the author of a lexicographic work.[100] From the surviving fragments, it appears to have been a lexicon composed of sets of six or seven characters that sometimes formed sentences and sometimes constituted lists of words belonging to a single category. According to Ban Gu it repeated no characters and had a larger vocabulary

than the *Cang jie pian* 蒼頡篇 compiled by Li Si that had defined forms of characters for the imperial script established by Qin. Sometimes it adds a description
roughly in the manner later employed by the *Shuo wen jie zi.*

Sima Xiangru's work as a lexicographer was related to his poetic oeuvre,
because the use of rare characters and the clustering of characters by category—
plants, fruits, birds, aquatic animals, precious stones, and so on—were fundamental
to his work. The fact that his poems evinced features of a lexicon also shows how
his work expressed or anticipated Han theories of writing. Nouns of a common
category as well as binomes depicting action or character, for example, clusters of
words describing the movement of water, are characterized by shared signific elements. Consequently the poems brought together characters with the same radical
in the same manner that the *Shuo wen* would later group characters. In the theory
articulated in the *Shuo wen* and the *Shi ming* such groups of characters were organi-
cally related as "offspring" (*zi* 字 "character" = *zi* 子 "son, child") of an original
pattern. We do not know if Sima Xiangru conceived of characters in this manner,
but the theory of writing as a dynamic realm paralleling the world of objects already
existed, and it was fundamental to Sima Xiangru's theory of poetry. Thus his verse
constituted an exploration or demonstration of the operating principles of the
formation of graphs and the manner in which these principles allowed written
forms to double the world they represented.

In addition to exploring the manner in which written characters worked as
visual images, the writing of Sima Xiangru also emphasized their aural qualities.
The rhapsody form, particularly as he defined it, placed great emphasis on the use
of binomes to evoke features of the natural world. These binomes involved repeated
characters, alliteration, or internal rhymes. The only gloss for most of them is that
they describe the sound or character of the object to which they are applied in the
poem. This indicates that many of them were either onomatopoeia or sounds
intended to evoke a sense of motion or a type of emotional response. In close
succession they would have constituted an aural barrage intended to dazzle or
stun the reader and leave him in the state of speechless amazement attributed to
the fictional listeners within the rhapsody itself.[101]

The works themselves also speak of the role of writing. Thus in the final
poetic section of the "Rhapsody on the Imperial Hunt" the emperor abandons his
park for hunting in the realm of written symbols. The verses repeatedly apply
verbs and nouns derived from the chase to the literary works of the "Six Arts" and
to named songs and dances. While this account of hunting in text and song is
applied to the classics of Sima Xiangru's day, it is also a veiled reference to the
rhapsody that it concludes, a poem that allows the reader to wander, hunt, trap,
and snare within a world created entirely through the magic of words. The concluding verse section of the rhapsody thus explains and justifies the entire work. It
shows how the visual and aural powers of written characters can create a literary
hunting park far greater than the real one, fill it with more exotic wonders than
exist anywhere on earth, and offer the reader the thrill and spectacle of a hunt

more magnificent than any that the emperor could actually stage. Given this capacity of writing to duplicate or to surpass the world, the emperor finds his true role and highest pleasures within the world of texts created by the men of letters.

Writing is also given a central role in the essay-poem on the *feng* and *shan* sacrifices, for as noted above, these sacrifices entailed creating texts. Sima Xiangru cites a shadowy antiquity from which no names have survived, save those of the seventy-two monarchs preserved in the writing generated in the sacrifices. In the next era some details as well as names were preserved in the canonical texts. This is repeated by the grand marshal, who argues:

> Some say that Heaven is without meaningful patterns and mute, so the precious signs [indicating the propriety of performing the sacrifices] cetainly cannot be refused. If they were refused, then Mt. Tai would have no records [of the *feng*] and Liangfu none [of the *shan*]. If each had been glorious in his own time and shrunk away after his death, then how could persuaders have praised them to later ages or spoken of the seventy-two rulers?
>
> Cultivating one's virtue to receive signs and then obeying the signs to carry out the sacrifices is not being forward or overstepping bounds. Therefore the sage kings do not cast duty aside but carry out the rituals to the God of Earth, report their sincerity to the Spirit of Heaven, and record their merit on the Central Peak [Mt. Tai, here "central" between Earth and Heaven] in order to make clear that they are most honored, unleash their flourishing virtue, send forth their titles and glory, and receive generous blessings that they may bestow on the common people. . . .
>
> We beg your majesty to complete [this ritual]. . . . , and lay out a correct account of it, ornamenting its writing, to create another *Chun qiu* as a new canon that will be added to the old six to form a seventh.[102]

Writing is the sole means of preserving the sages and the sagely way across time, and its ultimate sources are the records created in the *feng* and *shan* sacrifices. These underpin the canonical texts themselves, which are defined as the works of the sages or those writing under their influence. In placing a written account of the ritual at Mt. Tai, the Emperor would write a seventh classic and thereby join the company of sages. Since Sima Xiangru has already written such an account, the proclamation of a new classic is a veiled reference to his own work. After a formula of acceptance and a hymn of praise placed in the mouth of the emperor, Sima Xiangru concludes with another reference to the canonical texts on the importance of the sacrifices.[103]

In addition to the central place that Sima Xiangru accords to writing in his own works, his biography in the *Shi ji* contains anecdotes defining him as an exemplar of the role of writing. First, as noted in chapter 4, Emperor Wu first encounters Sima Xiangru in the form of a written version of the "Rhapsody on Sir Fantasy." The emperor laments that he was not alive at the same time as the author, and is startled to be informed that the author is alive. Summoned to court, Sima Xiangru confirms that he is the author, and offers to compose a further rhapsody that will serve both as an initial offering and proof of his claim to authorship. The emperor orders that Sima Xiangru "be provided with writing tablets," and he confirms his identity in the same medium through which he was discovered. A second anecdote extends this theme with the information that Sima Xiangru stuttered and thus depended on his skill in writing to communicate.[104]

A final story dealing with writing is set at the time of Sima Xiangru's death.

> The Son of Heaven said, "Sima Xiangru is very ill. We should send someone to go and collect his writings. Otherwise, they will afterward be lost." He sent Suo Zhong, but Xiangru had already died, and there were no writings in his house. He asked his wife, and she replied, "Changqing [Sima Xiangru] certainly never possessed any writings. Occasionally he would write something, but others took them and departed, so he lived with no texts. When he had not yet died he wrote one scroll and said, 'There will be a messenger who comes to look for writings, present [*zou* 奏] this.' There are no other writings." These writing tablets that he had left behind spoke of the *feng* and *shan* sacrifices, and they were presented to Suo Zhong. Suo Zhong presented them to the emperor, who marveled at them.[105]

This story illustrates several points. First, it indicates that Sima Xiangru used writing strictly as a form of social interchange, giving away his compositions as soon as they were finished. Second, it forms a pendant to the story of Emperor Wu first discovering him in the form of a text and imagining him already dead, for here he takes his leave in the same form when he has actually died. Knowing that the emperor would try to retrieve what he had written, he left behind only a single piece addressed specifically to the ruler on the subject of the *feng* and *shan*. These sacrifices were the culmination of the glory of the dynasty to which he had devoted much of his life, and the text summarized his own work. Since a major topic of the piece was how the writings employed in the sacrifices preserved names and deeds after death, it made a fitting theme for the message in which he recalled himself to the emperor from beyond the grave. The identification of the text with the sacrifice is also indicated by the final dramatization in which the poet takes on the voice of the emperor, declares that the sacrifices will be performed, and chants a poem in celebration of them.

The relation between the poet and the emperor is central to the work of Sima Xiangru. He was a court poet, and all the poetry preserved in the *Shi ji* biography was addressed to the emperor, as was the memorial on hunting. Moreover, the emperor was the central subject of his writings. The two major prose pieces communicate the emperor's wishes to his people, and they deal with the glory of the empire and the achievements of its ruler.[106] Similarly, the rhapsodies on the imperial hunt, the "Great Man," and the *feng* and *shan* define and celebrate emperorship. Each also introduces the emperor as a dramatic figure who acts and speaks at the behest of the poet. As in the works discussed above, Sima Xiangru's textual ruler spans all time and space and thereby achieves the universality that defines true wisdom.

While it is largely panegyric and lacks the critical tone of the *Shi ji*, Sima Xiangru's oeuvre resembles Sima Qian's history in that it creates a literary double of the empire as an imagined structure embracing time and space. Such a doubling provides grounds for criticism of the actual ruler. As noted above, the "Rhapsody on the Imperial Hunt" suggests the superiority of the poem to the emperor's park and hunts, and stipulates a model for his conduct based on that superiority. Similarly, the "Rhapsody of the Great Man" depicts a cosmic triumph and an attainment of immortality that defied the historical Emperor Wu.[107] The essay on the *feng* and *shan* dramatized the performance of a rite of emperorship that the ruler himself had not yet resolved upon, and celebrated a celestial response that would not be forthcoming. In each case the written text creates a parallel realm of ideal rulership against which the historical career of Emperor Wu would be found wanting. As in the theory of "the king without attributes," the creation of a realm of literary meaning (*wen* 文) implied the absence of a Son of Heaven in the real (*shi* 實) world.

THE LIU FAMILY AND THE UNIVERSAL LIBRARY

The last great encyclopedic endeavor of the Western Han was the catalog of the imperial collection composed by Liu Xiang and his son Liu Xin, and included in modified form in the *Han shu* as the "Monograph on the Arts and Letters" (*yi wen zhi* 藝文誌). It resembles the earlier works in identifying universality with the ideal government of the ancient sages, and in culminating in a textual doubling of the world. It also echoes late Warring States philosophical traditions and the *Huainanzi* in portraying the world that generated the texts with which it deals as a falling away from the earlier, ideal state. Unlike the other works discussed in this chapter, it was composed when the *ru* tradition had come to dominate the intellectual field. Consequently it builds its textual universe around the assumption that the officially canonized *ru* texts were both the exemplary models of proper writing and the origin of all other categories of text.

The appearance of the library, a documented and categorized collection that aims to cover and define some field of writing, represents a major step in the evolving relation between men and texts. It occurs when the amount of written material grows too great to be mastered by any individual or group, and when some organization has the interest and resources to collect the products of numerous previously isolated groups. It is the product of a world where works are seen as traces of a vanished or vanishing era that must be maintained through active *scholarly* work.

The development of libraries is thus often a feature of times of major social change, as in the eastern Mediterranean where the disappearance of the city-state and the rise of Alexander's empire destroyed the social bases of much earlier literature while increasing the reverence in which it was held as the heritage of a golden age. This inspired the development of new scholarly approaches to the creation, correction, and preservation of literature in written form, and it culminated in the formation of the great libraries of the Alexandrian period.[108] A similar response followed the creation of the Chinese empire and the Qin burning of the books. A large-scale effort was undertaken to retrieve and restore lost manuscripts, which became the center of scholarly debate and criticism. With the establishment of a state-sponsored canon the definition of correct texts became a matter of official concern, and orally transmitted commentaries were set down in writing. At the same time, the recovery of texts written in pre-unification scripts called into question many of these oral traditions and intensified the debate over the true forms of the canonical texts and other writings inherited from the Warring States period.[109]

An exposition of all the textual discoveries and debates involved in the composition of the Lius' catalog would have to recapitulate the scholarly history of the Western Han. Here I will simply use the catalog as a key to the structure of the textual field, and by extension the intellectual universe, in the immediate aftermath of the triumph of Confucianism. Libraries and their arrangements are an important means of investigating such questions.

> Actual and imaginary libraries such as these are important parts of our culture, one of the few points at which we can actually examine print society's conception of knowledge and its organization. There are other places as well at which the "knowledge tree" becomes visible . . . but the library is particularly revealing because it contains the primary sources of information—printed books—dictates the methods by which they can be approached and studied, and schematizes their principal modes of organization in the shelving arrangements and the catalogue. The library focuses the intellectual world and provides a paradigm of consciousness, what a society knows and how it knows it. Not to be a category in this official scheme of knowledge, as alchemy or astrology no longer are, or to get into the wrong classification group, the "practical," say, rather than the "fine arts," or to get the wrong name, belles-lettres rather than "literature," has fatal consequences for any mode of knowledge and its practioners.[110]

References to printing and to arrangement on shelves are not relevant to the Han case, but the observations about library organization as a key to the structure of the "knowledge tree" remain valid. The Lius' account of the imperial collection, which involved the participation of other individuals and received the imprimatur of Ban Gu, serves as both a useful indicator of the structure of knowledge in the late Western Han, and an end point for the history of textual authority in early China.

The catalog exhibits several features. First, it presumes unity of knowledge as the ideal and treats multiplicity of versions and texts as a problem to be corrected. Second, it sets apart the official canon and related texts as uniquely authoritative.

These texts are granted a hierarchical and a temporal preeminence, as both models for all forms of writing and the origin from which the lesser categories derived. Third, the structure of the textual field is derived from the state apparatus. The canons are identified with the sage king and each category of texts traced back to a department or office. Fourth, each section explains the existence of corrupt texts within the category. These explanations adopt the rhetoric of the interschool polemics, noting the strength of each partial position and its counterbalancing weakness. Fifth, the account of the composition of the catalog emphasizes its collective nature, and it reproduces the division between the general, encompassing skills claimed by the philosophical traditions and the specific, limited skills attributed to the technical ones. Thus the principles underlying the catalog derive directly from ideas about texts developed in the interschool debates and the production of encyclopedic works in the preceding centuries. The catalog accepts unity as an ideal, treats diversity as proof of partiality, locates the possibility of unity in the figure of the king, and posits a model of history in which early unity was shattered, but is to be restored by the project of the present authors.

The theme of a lost unity and its restoration through comprehensive bibliography is announced in the opening section of the monograph that explains how it came to be written.

> Long ago Zhongni [Confucius] died and the subtle words [*wei yan* 微言] were cut off. His seventy disciples perished, and the great truth was perverted. Therefore the *Chun qiu* divided into five versions, the *Odes* into four, and the *Changes* was transmitted in variant traditions. In the Warring States period diplomats and persuaders quarreled over what was true and false, and the words of the masters were a confused, jumbled chaos. The Qin state was disturbed by this, so it burned and destroyed writings in order to make idiots of the common people. The Han arose and reformed the damage wrought by Qin. On a large scale they assembled texts and strips, and they broadly opened the path for the offering up of documents.
>
> When it reached the time of Emperor Wu, the writings had lacunae and strips were missing. The rituals were in ruins and music in a state of collapse. The sage emperor sighed and said, "I am deeply grieved over this!" Thereupon he established a policy of storing writings and set up officials to copy them, including even the [writings of] the various masters and transmitted sayings. They were all stored in the secret archives.
>
> When it reached the time of Emperor Cheng, because the writings were dispersed or lost, he sent the Internuncio Chen Nong to seek for missing books throughout the empire. He summoned the Imperial Household Grandee Liu Xiang to check the canons, their commentaries, the masters, lyric verse, and rhapsodies; the Commandant of Infantry Ren Hong to check the military writings; the Grand Historian/Astrologer Yi Xiang to check [writings on] numbers and divination [*shu shu* 數術], and the Attendant Physician Li Zhuguo to check [writings on] formulae and techniques [for health and immortality, *fang ji* 方技]. When a text was completed, Liu

Xiang would fix its number of chapters and title, summarize its essential meaning, record it, and present it to the emperor.

When Liu Xiang died Emperor Ai ordered his son, the Commandant of the Imperial Equipage of the Palace Attendants, Liu Xin, to complete his father's work. Xin thereupon gathered together all the books and presented his "Seven Epitomes" (*qi lüe* 七略): the "Collective Epitome," "Epitome of the Six Arts," "Epitome of the Masters," "Epitome of Lyrics and Rhapsodies," "Epitome of Military Texts," "Epitome of Numbers and Divination," and "Epitome of Formulae and Techniques." Now we have cut it away to its essentials, in order to completely list (*bei* 備) the texts and writings.[111]

In this narrative of decline and rebirth, the words of the sages ended with Confucius and fragmented into competing doctrines with the death of his immediate disciples.[112] Divisions within the canonical traditions led to chaos with the appearance of theoreticians of language and philosophical traditions. The decline reached its nadir in Qin's destruction of texts. The balance of the introduction traces the gradual recovery of philological studies under the aegis of the Han dynasty. It credits a series of emperors—the unnamed Wen, followed by Wu, Cheng, and Ai—for taking the lead in gathering books, and lists the leading scholars who worked in the compilation of the final catalog. The account thus echoes the creation of such works as the *Lü shi chun qiu* and *Huainanzi*, in which the completeness which it claims for itself was achieved by rulers who gathered the scholars needed to put together a comprehensive, composite work.

The second major feature of the catalog is the centrality accorded to the canonical texts as the basis of all writing. This point is made in the title of the monograph, which divides the textual realm into canonical "arts" (*yi* 藝) on the one hand, and all other "writings" (*wen* 文) on the other. This is reiterated in the brief history of texts with which the monograph begins. It is also indicated by the fact that whereas all other categories of writing are attributed to offices in an imagined early state, the canons derive from no office but rather from the sage rulers.[113] Just as officers derived their authority from the monarch, so the lesser forms of writing traced their limited share of the truth back to the textual traces of the sages. This relation of dependence is also marked by the fact that the noncanonical categories were usually justified by a quotation from one of the classics or from the writings of Confucius.[114]

Indeed the textual forms of philosophy and verse that emerged in the Eastern Zhou are all treated as derivations from the earlier, canonical works. The summary of the category of the masters states:

> The masters form ten traditions, of which nine can be observed. They all arose from the fact that the Way of kings had grown obscure, and the feudal lords governed through force. Recent rulers loved or hated different methods, so the techniques of

the nine traditions arose together. Each took one thread and exalted what they preferred. They rode about using these for persuasions in order to join with the feudal lords. Although their words differed, like fire and water they both destroyed and gave birth to one another. [Like] benevolence and duty, respect and harmony, they were both opposed and complementary. The *Yi* says, "The whole world converges on the same goal, but the roads differ. There is one destination but a hundred ways of thinking about it." Now the different traditions all cling to their own strong points. They know them thoroughly and reflect on them exhaustively in order to make clear their meanings. Although they are obstructed or weak, if you join their essential conclusions they are all branches or channels of the Six Canons. If their followers encounter an enlightened king or sage ruler who finds their common points, then they all have the ability to serve as his limbs. Confucius said, "If the rituals are lost, then seek for them in the wilds." Now we are far removed from the sages, and the methods of the Way are deficient or abandoned. There is no place in the world where they can be sought. Are not the nine traditions better than the "wilds?" If one can cultivate the methods of the Six Arts and observe the words of the nine traditions, eliminate their weakness and take their strong points, then one can thoroughly comprehend the epitome of the myriad methods [*tong wan fang zhi lüe* 通萬方之略].¹¹⁵

From the historical model developed in interschool polemics and the assumption that writing and government are parallel realms, the writer concludes that the texts of the masters were the literary expression of the fragmentation of power. Canons correspond to kingship, and the writings of the philosophers derive from the breaking up of the canon, just as the feudal lords emerged from the disintegration of the Zhou state. As written fragments of the canon, the writings of the masters preserved elements of its truth and should a true king return to the world he would draw them back into the original unity from which they had split off.

The same model informs the discussion of poetry.

In ancient times when the feudal lords and hereditary officials had interchanges with neighboring states they used subtle words [*wei yan* 微言] to move one another. When saluting with bows they invariably cited an *Ode* to make known their deepest aspirations [*zhi* 志], and they thereby separated the worthy from the unworthy and observed flourishing or decline. After the Spring and Autumn period, the Way of Zhou was gradually ruined, and odes of paying respects and making inquiries were no longer practiced among the states. Men of honor who studied the *Odes* were lost among the commoners, so the *fu* of worthy men disappointed in their aspirations arose. The great *ru* Xun Qing and the Chu minister Qu Yuan were separated [from rulers] by slanderers and worried for their state, so they wrote *fu* to covertly criticize or influence [*feng* 風]. They both had a righteousness that included concern for the ancient odes.¹¹⁶

The passage cites Yang Xiong's praise for the "rhapsodies of the man of *Odes*" [*shi ren zhi fu* 詩人之賦] over the "rhapsodies of the man of beautiful phrases" [*ci ren zhi fu* 辭人之賦] and calls for the restoration of the canonical ideal of morally serious verse under the Han emperors.[117] Here again recent writings were treated as decadent genres that in ages of decline preserved distorted memories of canonical models. Only after the return of virtuous rulers could they be made to revert toward their exemplary, ancestral forms. The absence of canonical ancestry for texts on the military, numbers and divination, and the methods of longevity will be discussed below.

The pattern of establishing relations of descent among genres, with the ancestral text as exemplar, is reproduced within the canon itself. Each of the five canons apart from the *Yi* is assigned a social function and described as the manifestation of a virtue. *Music* harmonizes with the spirits and manifests benevolence, the *Odes* correct speech and manifest duty, *Ritual* illumines the body and is the self-evident manifestation of illumination, the *Documents* spread teaching broadly and is the "technique of wisdom," while the *Annals* adjudicate affairs and is the "tally of good faith." These five form a system of mutual reliance, but "the *Yi* is their source." Unlike the other five fields of study, which evolve within human time, the *Yi* "begins and ends together with Heaven and Earth."[118] The *Yi* is the origin of the canon because it is the foundation of all insight into the cosmos and the beginning of written language. As the ultimate model, it provides quotations explaining and justifying both itself and the other canons in the monograph's summaries.[119] The exception is the *Annals* which, as a text written by Confucius, is explained by remarks from the *Lun yu*.

The third feature of the monograph is the importance of the parallel between texts and government. This is already manifest in the passages discussed and translated above. The canons, origins and model for all writing, are equated with the early kings, and the emergence of the traditions of the masters and new forms of verse are both explained in terms of political developments. The Han's rise as a dynasty patterned on earlier sages had to be reflected in the improvement of literature through the resurgence of earlier principles, if not necessarily earlier forms.

This model is extended through the textual realm by equating generic categories with political offices. As noted above, this practice figures among the canonical texts in the reference to the office of historian/astrologer as the origin of the *Annals*, although these are canonical only through Confucius' intervention. As for other categories and subcategories, *ru* texts are derived from the office of Minister of the Masses/Education (*si tu* 司徒); Daoist from the historian/astrologer; yin/yang from the calendrical office of Xi and He; legalist from judicial officials; those of the school of names from ritual officials; Mohist from officials in charge of the ancestral temple; those of the school of alliances from the office of emissary; mixed school (*za jia* 雜家) from policy officials (*yi guan* 儀官); agrarian school from agricultural officials; those of the school of "petty talk" from lowly officials; poetry from the use of odes among the nobility; military from the office of commander;

and those on number and divination from the offices pertaining to the Hall of Light, those of Xi and He, the astrologers/historians, and the diviners. Finally, the texts on formulae and techniques of longevity are derived from unspecified royal officers (*wang guan* 王官), identified only by the names of famous physicians of antiquity.[120]

Mapping texts onto government reflects not only the equation of intellectual with political authority but also the model of multiplicity emerging from, and being resolved back into, a primal unity. Offices were described as the limbs or sense organs of the ruler, so the identification of texts with offices suggests they are multiple, partial elements within a "corpus" defined by the canon or ruler. Thus the mapping of texts onto government offices plays the same role as multiple authorship in the *Lü shi chun qiu* and *Huainanzi*, or the idea that the traditions of the masters could be combined by the sage ruler to restore the original unity of the canon. The canon, in its turn, marks the completeness that was part of its etymological sense.[121] In the same way, the account of the monograph emphasizes that it was written by a group of officials whose combined expertise, under the sponsorship of sage rulers, produced a complete, annotated account of the textual realm.

The fourth feature of the monograph, derived from the idea that the imperial library was a product of the decomposition of the sages' unitary government, is the insistence on the inadequacy of texts and the fragmentation of traditions. This is true even of canonical texts, which survived in multiple versions following the death of Confucius and the Qin burning of the books. The *Yi* was best preserved because it was not suppressed by Qin, but even this fount of all textual wisdom existed in a half dozen versions in the Han, and only one of these matched the old text version espoused by Liu Xiang. Every other canonical text was divided into competing commentarial traditions, often with varying old text and new text versions.[122] The traditions of the masters were treated in the same manner as in the interschool polemics, every school recognized for preserving one element of the truth, but falling into error through their partiality.[123]

The failing of verse was that after becoming a genre for commoners, as described in the passage translated above, it lost its political role and became a competition in elaborate language and flights of fantasy. Military texts were initially imbedded in the kingly way, as indicated by the mixture of military and ritual concerns in the *Sima fa*, but during the Warring States period they became purely military and were devoted to maneuver, treachery, and deception. Supporters of the Han founder compiled partial anthologies for practical application, and these predominated until the compilation of the Lius' catalog. Similarly, divinatory techniques had been corrupted in passing from the sage kings, who recognized the links of mantic procedures to government, into the hands of technical specialists unable to understand the full range and subtlety of astronomy and calendars. Each aspect of the arts of health and longevity was described as an element of the comprehensive knowledge of the sage kings that had been corrupted by narrow specialists who employed it as a technical trick for the prolongation of life.[124]

These attacks on specialization in the last three categories indicate a final theme of the monograph, the superiority of general, encompassing skills to limited, technical ones. This theme, developed in the self-justifications of the philosophical traditions discussed in chapter 2, figures in the account of the composition of the monograph. As noted above, the work was divided into seven categories. The first four—collective, the canons, the masters, and verse—were compiled by Liu Xiang and Liu Xin. The remaining three—military, numbers and divination, and formulae and techniques of longevity—were each compiled by a specialist in the field—a military officer, the Grand Astrologer, and the emperor's attendant physician. Thus literary and generalist skills, including the vanished collective category and the all-encompassing canons, were handled by the literary officials in charge of the project, while the technical disciplines were entrusted to specialists.[125] The categories are also listed hierarchically, with the generalist headings preceding the technical ones. Moreover, writings of the masters and verse are treated as generic developments of the canon, while the technical works are not traced back to canonic models. Finally, the technical categories are marked by a distinctive form of corruption. The masters degraded canonic forms through partiality and the poets through absence of political purpose, but both remained elements of the canonic heritage redeemable under a revived sage government. The technical arts, by contrast, corrupted canonical principles by their very existence as techniques, and no program for redemption is proffered in the monograph.

However, the depiction of specialization in the bibliographic monograph is different from that during the Warring States. The philosophers had distinguished themselves from the mantic traditions through claims to a generalizing intellect that encompassed and guided individual arts. They thereby assimilated their status to that of administrators or kings. In the wake of the vision of writing comprehensive texts, or of rereading existing texts as universal, the masters were themselves demoted to the status of parts in an encompassing whole. The bibliographic monograph represents the triumph of one version of the dream of an all-encompassing textual corpus, the establishment of the major *ru* texts as a state canon. Within this new intellectual order the canons were identified with the monarch and the unity of wisdom, and all existent texts treated as fragments of this idealized unity. The older hierarchy articulated by the traditions of the masters survived in the ranking of the "literary" arts over technical disciplines, but they were now placed in a subordinate position within a larger order defined by the canon.

CONCLUSION

In the intellectual field of the Warring States period, the traditions of philosophical masters had distinguished themselves from technical traditions by claiming a generalizing wisdom that encompassed and guided particular arts. In doing this, they claimed to function in the manner of rulers and administrators. When confronted with the rules of definition and argument propounded by the later Mohists, as well as the paradoxes of the logicians, the leading philosophical traditions defended their positions by treating the new modes of argument as an attack on the social order. They thus once again assimilated their role to that of the monarch. Finally, to assert the practical utility of their social programs, the traditions claimed to derive their principles from the monarchs of high antiquity.

In the late Warring States period these positions converged in the development of a new form of argument employed in polemics between traditions. A universal Way valid across time and space was attributed to the ancient sage kings, and this Way was claimed by each of the leading traditions as the basis of its own programs. All other traditions possessed some fragment of the Way, but were blinded by their partiality. This argument developed the claim to generalizing wisdom, the assimilation of the philosopher to the king, and a model of history in which the multiplication of schools paralleled the fragmentation of the political order. It identified disputation with the political breakdown that had produced large-scale warfare. Each tradition, by contrast, identified itself with the dream of unity and an end to argument.

One result of this new vision was the appearance of a category of text called *jing* 經 "canon/classic." This graph had a range of meanings related to "delimitation," "structure," "control," "constancy," and "perpetuity." In the textual realm it figured as the rubric for works or chapters to which were attributed profound, hidden depths. Consequently the canon was regularly paired with an "explanation" (*shuo* 說) or a "tradition/commentary" (*zhuan* 傳) that articulated the significance of the master text. This exposition of principles took such varied forms as anecdotes, lists of examples, explanations of particular words, or allegorical readings of a poem or story. For the Mohists, the *jing* were defined by the central chapters containing the teachings of Master Mo, and the character *jing* was directly applied to the later chapters devoted to argumentation. In the case of proto-Daoist traditions, and some elements of late Warring States legalism, these *jing* took the form of condensed accounts of the hidden principles of the cosmic Way or of cosmogonic origins, often with political applications. The *jing* of the *ru* tradition were the texts attributed to the Zhou. The allegorical readings of the *Odes* and the derivation of principles from the *Documents*, the *Odes*, the *Rites*, and later the *Yi* and the *Annals*, developed into an extensive commentarial tradition. Here a permanent truth was attributed to the old texts with their archaic language, while the commentaries were used to successively apply this truth to changing social problems and evolving philosophical debates.

In a related development certain patrons ceased to simply support scholars as one type of client among many, and began to play a role in directing scholarship. Such patrons, most notably the Qin chief minister, Lü Buwei, and the Han King of Huainan, Liu An, gathered scholars from many traditions and supervised the composition of collective works. These carried out the programs suggested in the interschool polemics by drawing the partial opinions of conflicting traditions into a synthetic whole. Both the *Lü shi chun qiu* of Lü Buwei and the *Huainanzi* of Liu An employed temporal schemata to frame their syntheses. The latter organized its core chapters around the calendar, associating different virtues and policies with each season. It added supplementary chapters grouped according to magic numbers used as indicators of completeness. The *Huainanzi* adopted the cosmogony of the proto-Daoist traditions as its organizing principle, and organized its topics as a recapitulation of the formation of the world from an undivided unity. Many of its chapters also formed linked pairs, perhaps in an echo of *yin/yang* thought.

As political unification became an enduring reality, some writers adapted other forms of literature developed in the Warring States to compose works that encompassed the world in textual parallels of the empire. One of the most notable of these was the *Shi ji*. In this history Sima Qian adapted the canon-commentary structure of the *Annals* to both trace the entire course of history and recapitulate the political order in the structure of the text. Projecting the vision of a single ruler and a unitary state back to the earliest times, he composed "Fundamental Chronicles" tracing a political genealogy from the Yellow Emperor to his own time. The "Hereditary Houses" and the "Tables" incorporated the fact of political division into a presumptive unity, and served as the textual parallels of the old nobility and enfeoffed Han officials. Monographs traced the temporal linkage of the arts and techniques that defined the state to the succession of rulers. Many of these were directly derived from the *ru* canon that had recently been established as state orthodoxy. Most of the work took the form of individual or collective biographies of commoners and non-Han peoples. These chapters were entitled *zhuan* (傳) and thus assimilated to the status of the commentaries on the *Annals*, which in turn was the model for the "Fundamental Chronicles." This last level completed the work as a parallel state and allowed the inclusion of both the heroes and writers whom Sima Qian admired, and the opportunists and sycophants whom he scorned. The historian included numerous veiled critiques of Emperor Wu, and the total work created a textual universe in which he acted as literary king or judge who condemned the rulers of his own day in the manner attributed to the Confucius of the *Annals*.

Shortly before Sima Qian adapted history into a totalizing text that portrayed and passed judgment on the world, Sima Xiangru had adapted the recently developed verse form of the rhapsody to celebrate the unified, world empire. In his first major work, the "Rhapsody on the Imperial Hunt," he expanded an account of the royal hunts in Qi and Chu into an exhaustive presentation of the dimensions and contents of the imperial hunting park and the activities pursued therein. It dramatized both the encompassing scale of imperial power, eclipsing the lesser kings, and the all-inclusive reach of the emperor's rule. The latter was indicated through the deliberate equation of the hunting park with the world, and the enumeration of the exotic plants, animals, and minerals that filled it in the manner of the tribute from distant peoples by which the emperor manifested the range of his power. Subsequent poems on the emperor's cosmic journey and on the *feng* and *shan* sacrifices extended the reach of the ruler's power into the heavens themselves, traced his political lineage to the origins of time, and celebrated the magic signs and ritual performances that gave Heaven's seal to the Han imperium.

Sima Xiangru's poetry also explored the powers of written characters. Its long lists of characters, often forming clusters linked by a common signific, derived from Sima Xiangru's work as a lexicographer and provided a model for Xu Shen's later organization of the *Shuo wen jie zi* into characters grouped by significs as children derived from an ancestral image. Its use of binomes formed by internal repetition, rhyme, or alliteration to evoke the properties and actions of objects also emphasized the phonic aspect of written graphs and thus highlighted their dual character as images and sounds. The major works of Sima Xiangru, particularly the "Rhapsody on the Imperial Hunt" and the essay-poem on the *feng* and *shan* sacrifices also articulated a theory of the powers of writing. The former demonstrated and then asserted the power of writing to create a duplicate world that surpassed the material one. The latter portrayed writing as the primary form in which man related to Heaven, and thus as the material form of the ruler's power. The rhapsody genre which he defined thus celebrated the magic power of words to command reality.[126] While not expressing overt criticism of the ruler in the manner of Sima Qian, Sima Xiangru's verse attained a comprehensive range, grandeur, and immortality that seemingly mocked the failures of Emperor Wu.

The final encyclopedic work of the Western Han was the catalog of the imperial library compiled by a team of scholars under the direction of Liu Xiang and Liu Xin. Like the *Lü shi chun qiu* and the *Huainanzi*, this was a collective work that insisted on the multiplicity of authors while granting pride of place to its imperial patrons. Its structure combined many of the features developed in earlier works. From the interschool polemics it adopted the model of locating truth in an encompassing whole of which extant texts were fragments or corruptions. It also adopted their historical model, in which the totality was associated with the wisdom of the ancient sage kings that had fragmented with the Zhou monarchy. Composed after the officially sanctioned *ru* canon dominated the intellectual scene, it accepted these texts as the closest written approximation of the ideal unity of the sages. The canon was taken as the textual form of the king, while the other categories of texts were identified with offices from which they had supposedly derived. As officers these texts were authoritative but partial, the limbs and sense organs of the complete and perfect body of the monarch. In this way the catalog of the imperial library was read as a parallel state that contained within itself the political history of the emergence of the empire.

The interplay between part and whole in the catalog also preserved the old model in which the philosophical traditions had asserted their superiority to their "technical" rivals—medical, mantic, and military—through claims to represent a generalizing intelligence that encompassed limited arts and directed them for the public good. Adapting this model, the authors of the catalog treated the texts of the masters as literary derivatives preserving fragments of the kingly Way. Under a returned sage ruler they could be recombined to restore the full meaning of the canon. Similarly, the poetry of the Han was treated as an inferior literary form derived from the model of the *Odes*, but which like the works of the philosophers could be brought back within the sphere of the canon under a wise monarch. In contrast to these literary arts, catalogued by the Lius, the three categories of the technical traditions were not placed within a literary genealogy and not allowed the possibility of a restoration to canonicity. As lesser traditions they were placed after the literary texts and edited by officials who specialized in military activity, divination, and medicine. Thus the claims of the masters to superiority over their rivals were validated, but they in turn were now treated as inferior to the supreme unity attributed to the newly established category of the canonical text.

Chapter Eight

THE EMPIRE OF WRITING

The encyclopedic project was both encompassing and exclusive. The former attribute was discussed in chapter 7, but the rhetoric of encompassment could not abolish the tension between competing frames. While each author or master granted a limited place to others within his own schema, the debate was merely transferred to the level of who could assign places to the rest. The ultimate victor in this dispute was the body of texts that defined the curriculum of the *ru*, but the reasons for this triumph have been the subject of little serious study.[1] In this chapter I will sketch some of the reasons for the Han establishment of the *ru* texts as a state canon, the impact of that policy on attitudes toward texts, and the consequences for the history of later, imperial China.

The Han victory of Confucianism can be explained both in terms of the decisions and actions of specific individuals, that is, in terms of the history of events, and as a long-term development rooted in the evolution of social, economic, or intellectual patterns. The former deals primarily with the decision of Emperor Wu to link the offices of the erudites to the texts of the *ru* canon and to establish the Imperial Academy as a major avenue to office holding. The latter is tied to the transformation of the material bases of the Han state through the rise of landlordism and the abolition of universal military service, and the associated emergence of a new form of elite.

The actions of Emperor Wu, in turn, can be analyzed in terms of both his personal history and the divisions within the intellectual field in the early Han state. As for the former, his patronage of the *ru* arts reflects both his own educational experiences and the need to establish himself in a court dominated by the dowager empress. As for the latter, his granting pride of place to the *ru* canon can be explained in terms of the political role of the Huang-Lao tendency in the early empire, and the tension between competing centers of patronage that characterized the intellectual landscape of his day.

While the innovations of Emperor Wu were important, the triumph of Confucianism was a long-term process not completed till the abortive Xin dynasty of Wang Mang and the refoundation of the Han by Emperor Guangwu. During this period imperial attitudes toward the *ru* shifted between indifference or hostility—as in the later career of Emperor Wu, the Huo Guang regency, and the reign of Emperor Xuan—to enthusiastic support in the reign of Emperor Yuan, to vacillating patronage under Emperor Cheng. Nevertheless, the position of *ru* scholasticism within the empire steadily advanced and ultimately triumphed. This long-term evolution can be explained in terms of the changing nature of the state, and the emergence of a social elite created by new modes of access to office and patterns of landholding. The former was marked by the progressive dismantling of the society organized for war through universal military service, and its replacement by a state defined through the propagation of cultural and literary models. The latter entailed the reliance on academic institutions to fill offices, the need of families that rose to eminence in state service to secure their positions through the purchase of land, and the need of landowners to protect their families from the ravages of partible inheritance by access to the supplemental income provided by office-holding.

However, the triumph of Confucianism during the Han was also an intellectual event to be explained as the culmination of the developments sketched in the preceding chapters. The tendency to compose and read texts as alternate or parallel states and to ground political programs in an imagined antiquity led to a total reevaluation of the past in the service of the new state. The presumptive textual remains of the defunct Zhou dynasty, as reshaped and transmitted by Confucius and his followers, were promulgated as a canon of authoritative texts which defined the ideal political and social order. In a classic instance of "the imaginary institution of society" the Han Confucians created a new vision of a state by rereading the Zhou texts in terms of their own categories and values, and then using this newly imagined Zhou to criticize and reform the institutional framework received from Qin. This Han canonization of antiquity represented not only a reversal of the dominant values of the late Warring States polity, but also an attack on the institutional inheritance of Qin and a negation of the entire Warring States period, now interpreted as a dark age between two glorious summits. This model of history—wherein the Three Dynasties or the Zhou inscribed in the canon became the political ideal and the reforms of the Warring States period were interpreted as decay or usurpation—provided a crucial intellectual underpinning for the dismantling of the institutional and religious order that had developed in the world of multiple states, culminated in the Qin empire, and survived largely unchanged into the reign of Emperor Wu.

While this theory of history embodied in the new state canon justified the abandonment of the Warring States political legacy, the meanings read into canonical writings by the commentarial traditions provided the model for a text-based, cultural authority to replace the military, administrative program of the Warring States and the Qin. In this way the establishment of the canon and the idealization of an imaginary, text-based antiquity provided the foundation for the Han creation of a new political form, a unitary empire which controlled "all under Heaven." The texts, both model for and double of the empire, in turn became essential to the self-image and the livelihood of the new elite. Through this implantation of the canon among the powerful families, the dream of empire that it had come to embody was preserved among the local elite and thus able to survive the collapse of the Han empire and all subsequent dynasties. Imaginatively grounded in a body of texts, the Chinese empire became an empire of writing, and it vanished only when the texts that defined it ceased to command the hearts of men.

ESTABLISHMENT OF THE CANON

The roots of an imperial literary policy were laid in the Qin. First and foremost, the Qin created a single script for the empire. This unification of writing in a nonphonetic script was crucial to the survival of the unified Chinese state, for it allowed communication across regions that shared no common tongue. Moreover, the written script and its texts established a high culture with its own distinctive language. Initiation into this language and culture became the hallmark of the ruling elite whose members were separated from the common people and attached to the imperial system through the very words in which they expressed their thoughts or conversed with their fellows. The unification of script was also linked to that of weights and measures, and as we saw in chapter 6 both graphs and measures were by the Han traced back to a common origin in the *Yi* hexagrams. Thus the creation of a unitary state was completed in the creation of a unitary realm of signs and standards, all grounded in cosmic pattern.

The second policy of Qin in the realm of writing was the series of inscriptions that Qin Shihuang erected on the sacred peaks during his tours. As noted earlier, these texts were proclamations of his achievements both to men and, through their placement on mountain tops, to gods. In this way they carried forward the ancient linking of the realm of spirits and men in the medium of writing, but they used this link to transfer men and spirits alike into the new world of the unitary state and the godlike supreme ruler. In placing these inscriptions on peaks in the newly-conquered Eastern states, the First Emperor completed his conquest by inscribing the reality of his power, in the newly created imperial script, into the sacred landscape of his new subjects. Finally, the act of carving in stone, as noted by writers of the period, was intended to render the words, and the sovereignty that they proclaimed, eternal.[2]

The final major literary policy of the Qin was the ban on the private ownership of certain categories of texts, and the attempt to secure a monopoly of the interpretation of writings on political matters. Aspects of this policy have been discussed earlier, so here I will simply note that the insistence on the supreme authority of the state within the textual sphere was a direct outgrowth of ideas current among the scholastics, and it was much closer to later policies than Han intellectuals cared to acknowledge. Although overambitious in trying to impose a physical monopoly that the state could not enforce, and clumsy in seeking to intimidate with threats rather than coopt through rewards, the Qin concentration of intellectual authority in a body of erudites and an imperial library was the first step toward the imposition of a state canon by Emperor Wu. However, it was cut short by the rapid collapse of the Qin regime, and the next steps in the evolution of imperial literary policy were deferred for decades.

All accounts of Han intellectual history, beginning with that in the *Shi ji*, describe the first four reigns as a time in which scholars played a secondary role in the political sphere and in which the dominant tendency was Huang-Lao. Sima Qian begins his chapter on the *ru* with a survey of the relations of scholars and their texts to the state. He asserts that in the first two reigns all important officials had gained merit as military men, that the third emperor had recruited some scholars but privileged legalist (*xing ming* 刑名, the use of the character meaning "punishment" rather than "form" may be significant) thinkers, and the fourth emperor—under the influence of his mother—privileged "the techniques of Huang-Lao."[3] This sketch, which Sima Qian elaborates and defends throughout his work, has defined all discussions of the period.

The relative unimportance of scholars during the first two reigns, despite Shusun Tong's drafting of a court ritual and Lu Jia's assertion to the Han founder of the importance of civil administration, runs through all accounts of the period. Typical was Zhou Bo, one of Gaozu's most important military followers who was famous, like his imperial master, for holding scholars in contempt. He, along with another military veteran Chen Ping, took the lead in toppling the clan of the Empress Lü and placing Emperor Wen on the throne. His antischolar clique contrived the exile of Jia Yi, and he rose to the rank of chief minister.[4] Sima Qian notes the activities of several major scholars in these reigns, but they remained at the margins of the court and are treated as prefigurations of his own disaster. On the basis of such evidence, and still following Sima Qian's lead, Qian Mu has argued that scholars wielded little influence in the first decades of Han rule because the court was dominated by those who had risen to influence through military merit.[5]

The second characteristic attributed to the reigns prior to that of Emperor Wu is the predominance of Huang-Lao thought. This term, which first appears in the *Shi ji* but is never defined therein, has become a philosophical football in which modern scholars invent their own traditions by combining whatever texts meet their chosen criteria.[6] Setting aside the question of whether there was a philosophical tradition known as Huang-Lao, and not just a set of diffuse and ill-defined tendencies, it is significant that the majority of the figures to whom Sima Qian applies the term were not scholars at all but political figures. They are often military men, interested in Huang-Lao as a mode of government or a means of preserving life through retirement and self-cultivation.[7] Its use by these political figures defines the importance and nature of Huang-Lao in the *Shi ji*, and it is against the tendencies defined by these men and women that Emperor Wu acted when he elevated the *ru* canon to pre-eminence.

In its political form Huang-Lao defines the major features of the first century of Han rule. First, this was an era when the court was dominated by men who had risen through military achievements, and both the eponymous figures of Huang-Lao, the Yellow Emperor and Laozi, were linked with military theories and institutions.[8] It is also notable that this was an era when the principle that the general in his camp and the field was beyond the ruler's commands was still defended by leading figures.[9] The association of Huang-Lao with the military arts was one element in its prestige.

The major political significance of Huang-Lao as defined by Sima Qian is its association with a minimalist government. This takes three forms. First, some Huang-Lao adepts eschew politics altogether. The classic case is Zhang Liang, who retires from public life to cultivate the arts of immortality. The Song historian Sima Guang argued that Zhang sought long life not primarily through Daoist arts but rather through retirement at a time when the influence of the family of the Dowager Empress made political activity dangerous. In any case, Huang-Lao was associated with the preservation of life, and Sima Qian also associates it with Chen Ping's ability to live out his full life span.[10]

A second aspect was the avoidance of the details of administration, which were left to subordinates. The classic example was Cao Shen, a military follower of Gaozu who became chief minister in Qi. There Cao heard of a Master Gai skilled in "the words of Huang-Lao," from whom he learned that the most important thing in governing is to "be pure and tranquil, while the people stabilize themselves." Cao delegated all affairs to Master Gai, who in turn entrusted them to subordinates. On leaving Qi to become chief minister at the court of Emperor Hui, Cao advised his successor simply to not disturb the prisons or markets. As chief minister he appointed officials who were "clumsy at writing fine phrases" (*chu yu wen ci* 詘於文辭) and dismissed all those who were "punctilious in language and documents" (*yan wen ke shen* 言文刻深). He did not "devote himself to business" (*bu shi shi* 不事事) but gave himself up to drink and would not discuss political affairs with those who had audience with him. The same actions are attributed to Chen Ping, and the same words used to describe him.[11]

As in the case of Zhang Liang, this refusal to engage in administration may have been a means of self-preservation when the court was splitting into factions for or against the Lü, and any action could have resulted in death. Nevertheless, "ruling through inaction" had become a standard element in the political philosophy of the Warring States, and the delegation of tasks was central to legalist thought. The account of Cao Shen's hostility toward both skillful writing and concern with the legal or administrative texts also suggests that a theory of government was involved in his action, as well as a philosophy of survival. One of the major features of this theory was a hostility toward a reliance on texts, whether in the form of scholastic writings or the state's own legal codes and administrative documents.

The account of Cao Shen's conduct shows the third feature of the political stance associated with Huang-Lao, the avoidance of interfering with the people so that they could pursue their own activities. This idea was closely linked to the antitextual sentiments noted above. After the decades of civil war at the end of

Qin, and Gaozu's wars with enfeoffed followers whose loyalty he suspected, much of the registered population had been displaced and economic activities disrupted. The early reigns are viewed as a time when the policies of the government were devoted to stability for the sake of restoring economic vitality and wealth. Fiscal policy was marked by low taxes on land and the absence of irregular exactions, and foreign policy consisted of paying tribute to the Xiongnu in order to reduce their incursions and avoid expensive campaigns. Finally, the elaborate provisions of the Qin code had been simplified by Gaozu and Xiao He. As a theory of minimalist government, Huang-Lao provided the rationale for this era of low taxes, nonintervention, simplified legal codes, and the dispersal of authority among fiefs. Sima Qian's accounts of Cao Shen and Chen Ping—with their nonaction, delegation to clerks, and hostility to written documents—dramatize the policies and institutions that characterized the government of this period.

One of the most important elements in the reduction of government activity was the institution of the fief. Gaozu's followers had been awarded substantial territories, some of which were smaller replicas of the imperial court. Most of these followers were eliminated during Gaozu's rule, but the fiefs were restored in the hands of collateral relatives. For the first half century of Han rule, large expanses of the empire were not directly administered by the central government, and even in the areas controlled by the court much of the tax income went to holders of fiefs. The political devotees of Huang-Lao listed in the *Shiji* are clustered in the "Hereditary Households" section of the work, because they had received titles and fiefs. By contrast the leading scholars of rival intellectual currents—Jia Yi and Chao Cuo—advocated breaking up the fiefs. Indeed Jia Yi followed his calls for dividing the fiefs and conquering the Xiongnu with a mocking assault on those who espoused a policy of "not moving" (*wu dong* 毋動) or "not acting" (*wu wei* 毋爲), here referring to advocates of what Sima Qian describes as Huang-Lao.[12]

The identification of Huang-Lao with minimalist government and hostility toward devotees of writing was carried forward into the time of Emperor Wu. It figures in accounts of his grandmother, Dowager Empress Dou, who dominated the court in the first years of his reign, and those of Ji An, who appears in the *Shiji* as the primary advocate of Huang-Lao at this time. Analysis of the stories dealing with these figures provides insight into the fault lines that divided the court in the youth of Emperor Wu.

The *Shiji* describes Empress Dou as an adherent of Huang-Lao who insisted that her whole family, including Emperor Jing, study the *Dao de jing* and a text attributed to the Yellow Emperor.[13] There are also anecdotes that depict her commitment to the *Dao de jing* and hostility to the *ru* canon. One tells of a debate in the presence of Emperor Jing between Yuan Gu, founder of the Qi tradition of the *Odes* and Master Huang. This is probably the Master Huang identified elsewhere in the *Shiji* as a devotee of Huang-Lao who taught its doctrines to Sima Tan.[14] The debate begins with Master Huang's denunciation of Kings Tang and Wu as assassins and usurpers. It is brought to a halt when it touches on the establishment of the Han. More interesting for the current study is the following story.

> Dowager Empress Dou loved the book of Laozi. She summoned Yuan Gu and asked him about this book. Gu replied, "This is nothing but the words of a schoolman" [*jia ren zhi yan er* 家人之言耳]. The dowager empress angrily said, "How could I obtain the [Zhou] Master of the Masses's book on penal servitude?" She then had him enter the animal pens to fight a wild boar.[15]

Yuan Gu denounces the *Dao de jing* as the product of a school, a partial doctrine inferior to the universal *ru* canon that he espoused. The dowager empress counterattacks on two grounds. First, she mocks Yuan Gu for seeking authority from ancient writings that are no longer relevant and may no longer exist, the text suggested here being something like the material of the *Zhou li*. Second, in referring to a hypothetical Zhou work on penal laws, she associates the *ru* canon, identified with the Zhou, and the legal code. They are apparently linked by their common function as tools of social control and state power.

This linkage figures more prominently in the biography of Ji An. He is described as a student of the "words of Huang-Lao" who cultivated tranquillity, entrusted the work of government to subordinates, instructed them in basic principles, but did not worry about details. Moreover, "he was not constrained by written laws" (*bu ju wen fa* 不拘文法). Although he was frequently sick and confined to bed, his commandery was well-regulated. When Emperor Wu began to employ "*ru* versed in literary studies" [*wen xue ru zhe* 文學儒者], Ji An criticized him for "inwardly harboring many desires, outwardly making a display of benevolence and righteousness," and being unable to "imitate the good government of Yao and Shun [who had ruled through inaction]."[16] Ji An's linking of *ru* texts with elaborate legal codes as targets of attack focused on Zhang Tang, the greatest of Emperor Wu's "cruel clerks" (*ku li* 酷吏) and pioneer in the use of the *ru* canon to decide doubtful legal cases.[17] After quoting Ji An's denunciation of Zhang Tang for rewriting and elaborating the Han legal code, the *Shi ji* continues:

> An often debated with Tang. Tang, in debating, always insisted on the letter of the text and went deep into petty details, while An boldly defended principles and would not yield. Angrily he cursed, "The world says that petty clerks with their knife-erasers and brushes [*dao bi zhi li* 刀筆之吏] should not become high officials, and indeed it is so. Certainly it is you who causes the whole empire to stand heavy-footed in place and look askance at one another [for fear of arrest]."
>
> At this time the Han were attacking the Xiongnu, to bring the barbarians to submit. An devoted himself to reducing government business. Availing himself of the emperor's idle moments, he constantly advocated harmonious relations with the Xiongnu through sending princesses in marriage. The emperor at this time was tending towards the techniques of the *ru*, and honored Gongsun Hong. So government

business increased, and the clerks and people [tried to] skillfully manipulate each other. The emperor minutely analyzed the written laws, while Tang and the rest repeatedly sent up memorials requesting decisions on legal cases in order to seek favor. But An constantly attacked the *ru* and denounced Hong and the rest for harboring treachery and displaying cleverness in order to curry favor with the ruler, while the petty clerks with their knife-erasers and brushes devoted themselves to seeking out the subtleties of the written laws to skillfully accuse, trapping the people in crimes, causing them to be unable to preserve their native purity, and regarding victory as the only merit. But the emperor increasingly honored Hong and Tang, who hated An to the depths of their hearts.[18]

The passage posits a division between Ji An, who espouses minimalist government and concern for principles, and those who base their actions and claims to authority on the mastery of textual minutiae—Zhang Tang and the cruel clerks with their law codes, Gongsun Hong and others steeped in the *ru* canon, and the minor clerks who imprisoned and murdered through their skill with government documents.

These clerks with their knives and brushes—or "knifelike brushes," for the *Shiji* repeatedly insists on their ability to kill—figure prominently elsewhere in the text. Thus general Li Guang, after a life of service at the frontiers, falls afoul of military regulations and finally kills himself to escape further dealings with the clerks.[19] Li Guang was the grandfather of Li Ling, whose biography is appended to that of Guang. Since it was Sima Qian's defence of Li Ling that led to the historian's castration, the shadow of Sima Qian's personal disaster hangs over all these references to the destructive powers of writing instruments and texts.

The Huang-Lao political critique of all text-based *ru* and administrators parallels Sima Tan's support of the Daoists and condemnation of the *ru*. As discussed in chapter 7, Sima Tan celebrated the Daoist school, which is closely related to what Sima Qian calls Huang-Lao, as the flexible summation of the best features of all the other schools. "Pointing to the essentials, it is easy to handle; its affairs being few, its achievements are great." In a striking rhetorical move, he then singles out the *ru*, who have already been discussed as one of the schools, for criticism.

> As for the *ru*, they are not like this. They think that the ruler must be a model for the empire. The ruler sings the lead, and the ministers harmonize. The ruler goes first, and the ministers follow. It being so, then the ruler is worn out and the ministers at ease. As for the great essentials of the Way, the elimination of self-assertion and desire, and the blunting of cleverness, they abandon them and employ techniques (*shu* 術). If the spirit is greatly used it is exhausted. If the body is greatly wearied it breaks. For the body and spirit to be troubled and agitated and to desire to be as long-lived as Heaven and Earth is something unheard of. . . .
>
> The *ru* take the "Six Arts" as their model. The classics and their commentaries on the Six Arts are numbered in the tens of thousands. In several lifetimes one

could not completely study them, and at the present time one cannot get to the end of all their rituals. Therefore I say, "They are broad but lack the essentials, toilsome but achieving little."[20]

In singling out the *ru* for criticism, Sima Tan was probably responding to Emperor Wu's employment of men distinguished for literary studies, in the same manner that Ji An fought with Zhang Tang and Gongsun Hong. He attacks two main points: an activist ruler who takes the lead in all things, and the replacement of a minimalist government defined by broad principles with myriad regulations enshrined in texts. In this way Sima Tan's sketch of the schools anticipates his son's depiction of the political scene. Both support a party committed to inaction, broad principle, and suspicion of texts against one based on an activist ruler, minute regulation through law and ritual, and textual foundations to authority.

The reference to Li Guang above points to another aspect of the shifting nature of the Han regime associated with Emperor Wu's activism and text-based government: the reevaluation of military command. As noted earlier, men who had earned military merit with Gaozu or in the suppression of the Lü clan dominated the court in the early decades of the Han. They were sufficiently powerful to compel Emperor Wen to exile Jia Yi, and they enforced the principle that on campaign or in a military camp the commander's words took precedence over those of the ruler.[21] However, the stories of Li Guang and Li Ling highlight the increasing subjection of military commanders to civil authority during the reign of Emperor Wu, a development dramatized in the *Shi ji* account of Wei Qing.

Wei Qing was first appointed to military command because he was the brother of the emperor's favorite concubine, and when his sister gave birth to a son and became empress his position was advanced. Despite mediocre performances in the field he received rich rewards, and he and all his sons were enfeoffed. When a subordinate general lost his entire command, an expert in military law advised him to execute the culprit in order to establish his authority. Wei Qing replied,

> Because I am a relative of the empress, I have been allowed to await punishment here in the army, so I need not worry about my authority. So when Ba persuades me to make my authority clear, this totally misses my intentions. Moreover, although it is proper for me to execute a general, because of the great honor and favor shown me, I do not dare to carry out an execution on my own authority here beyond the frontier. Instead I will send him back to the emperor, and the emperor may himself pass judgment. I will show that as a servant I do not dare to act on my own authority.[22]

In this speech Wei Qing renounces the privileges of the general, and assimilates himself to the status of an imperial affine and creature of the emperor's will. Other stories indicate that Emperor Wu treated Wei Qing with a casual familiarity bordering on contempt.[23] In his servility and flattery, Wei Qing echoes Zhang Tang, Gongsun Hong, Ni Kuan, and others who rose to prominence under Emperor

Wu. Later in his reign Emperor Wu established the precedent that the highest military office, that of *da sima* (大司馬), should be held by an imperial affine and be chief of the emperor's inner court. This completed the emperor's assertion of authority over his commanders, a major development in the concentration of power in his person.

A final element in the background to Emperor Wu's establishment of the *ru* texts as a state canon was the political geography of intellectual patronage at the beginning of the Han. The existence of the feudatories preserved the late Warring States pattern in which intellectuals moved from court to court seeking patronage. Yu Yingshi has pointed out that at least five of the feudatory states or princedoms were still actively assembling men of letters at the beginning of Emperor Wu's reign. These were the King of Wu, the King of Hengshan, King Xiao of Liang, King Xian of Hejian, and Liu An, the King of Huainan.[24] The *Shiji* describes how these rulers attracted scholars with gifts of rank, salary, or land, and how their lifestyle and conduct sometimes copied that of the emperor. Indeed the grand display put on by the King of Liang led Sima Xiangru to give up his post at the imperial court and become a retainer of the feudatory lord.[25] There is no evidence that most of these kings had any particular intellectual penchants, although King Xian of Hejian wore *ru* attire, conducted himself according to *ru* ceremonial dictates, and assembled the texts that would later define the old text tradition. However, the most important intellectual patron and the one who most influenced Emperor Wu was Liu An, the King of Huainan.[26]

The *Huainanzi*, composed under the auspices of this ruler, was discussed in chapter 7. What is important to note here is that this encyclopedic work was composed in the court of a feudatory whose father had been exiled and driven to suicide for supposed imperial pretensions. Liu An, who had become king in 164 B.C. and was noted for devoting himself to literary studies since his youth, had assembled scholars from all over the empire to compose this work. It was presented as either tribute or advice to the young Emperor Wu in 139 B.C., shortly after his ascent to the throne. While the emperor is said to have been delighted with the work, a work of cosmic pretensions composed under the auspices of an older relative with possible imperial claims was doubtless disquieting to a young ruler of ambition and literary aspirations. The forced suicide of Liu An in 122 B.C., on trumped-up charges of plotting against the emperor, suggests that the spectacle of numerous scholars in Huainan producing a collection of cosmopolitical essays, only fifteen years after the rebellion of the feudatories in 154 B.C., was indeed disquieting. Combined with the fact that many scholars in Shandong chose the court of Hejian over his own, or that lowly officials in his court opted to depart for those of subordinate kings, the pretensions in literary or intellectual patronage of these potential rivals must have appeared as a challenge, and possibly a threat.

While the *Huainanzi* was a syncretic work, its organizing principles and pattern of citations clearly granted pride of place to the *Dao de jing* and the *Zhuangzi*, with an admixture of the "Five Phases" theory that had become part of the scholastic *lingua franca*. Many scholars, including recently John Major and Harold Roth, have seen the *Huainanzi* as a philosophical summation of the intellectual position that Sima Qian called Huang-Lao. Whether or not one accepts this position, there is no doubt that the *Huainanzi* and the Huang-Lao tendency shared textual roots—the *Dao de jing* and the Mawangdui "Yellow Emperor" manuscript—a cosmological theory, and a rhetoric of psychological cultivation as the basis of government. To the extent that the work was associated with a political position advocating passive rulership, minimalist government, and a dispersal of power in the feudatories, its challenge to the burgeoning ambitions of Emperor Wu would have been all the greater.

With these long-term political and intellectual elements in the background, one can situate the decision to establish the *ru* texts as state canon in the circumstances and character of Emperor Wu. First, when the emperor was young his junior tutor had been Wang Zang, a disciple of Shen Pei's "Lu" tradition of the *Odes*. Although removed from the post for unspecified reasons, on Emperor Wu's succession in 141 B.C. he was promoted to the office of Prefect of Gentlemen-of-the-Palace (*lang zhong ling* 郎中令), an important post responsible for the emperor's personal security and the provision of advice.[27] This indicates some attachment on the part of the emperor to his former tutor, which suggests that his education might have inclined him toward an interest in *ru* literary concerns. The fact that he had a *ru* tutor also indicates that the dowager empress's domination of the court was not so firm as some accounts suggest.

The emperor's educational ties to the *ru* were reinforced by his senior tutor, Wei Wan. The latter had previously served as the tutor of Liu De, the future king of Hejian who became the great patron of the *ru*, and had been enfeoffed and given imperial office for merit earned in the suppression of the rebellion of the feudatories. Sima Qian describes him as an undistinguished but loyal official who was appointed Chancellor (*cheng xiang* 丞相) by Emperor Jing at the end of his life in order that he might assist the young heir when he first became emperor. This appointment was made against the recommendations of Dowager Empress Dou that her kinsman Dou Ying be appointed.[28] On his accession, Emperor Wu called for his officials to recommend worthy men for office, and Wei Wan memorialized that those who studied the legalist teachings of Shen Buhai, Shang Yang, and Han Fei, or the alliance strategems of Su Qin and Zhang Yi should be excluded. This was approved, opening a struggle for intellectual influence with the new ruler.[29]

Soon after Emperor Wu ascended the throne, Wei Wan was dismissed and Dou Ying appointed chancellor, thus fulfilling the dowager empress's earlier request. Although, or perhaps because, he had risen as her protégé, Dou Ying formed an alliance with the Grand Commandant Tian Fen to transfer control of the court to his own hands. He did this by supporting the aforementioned promotion of the emperor's former tutor Wang Zang, as well as that of Zhao Wan, another student of Shen Pei's teaching of the *Odes*. Shen Pei was also brought to the court by his former disciples, where he immediately offended the emperor by criticizing his penchant for "elaborate phrases" (*wen ci* 文辭). These men proposed a program of ritual and political reforms that included establishing the "Bright Hall" (*ming tang* 明堂), a ceremonial hall described in *ru* ritual texts, changing the garments worn at court ceremonials, changing the calendar, performing imperial tours leading to the *feng* and *shan* sacrifices, eliminating controls and taxes on travel between directly administered territory and fiefs, and having the marquises return to their fiefs. This last policy would have removed many relatives of the Empress Dou from the imperial court. It was linked with a purge of imperial relatives who had engaged in improper conduct. Regarding the policies as an attack on her person and influence, the dowager empress had Zhao and Wang arrested for "illegally profiting from their policies." They both committed suicide, Shen Pei retired from the court under pretext of illness, and Dou Ying and Tian Fen both resigned and returned to their own fiefs.[30]

This initial failure left the literary politics of the court unchanged until the death of Dowager Empress Dou in 135 B.C.[31] After, or shortly before, her death Emperor Wu established special erudites devoted to the five *ru* classics, and in 134 he again called for the recommendation of scholars. This brought to court such leading *ru* as Gongsun Hong and Dong Zhongshu. Sometime during the first fifteen years of Emperor Wu's reign, a Grand Academy (*tai xue* 太學) was established. This had been suggested by Dong Zhongshu in his replies to questions posed by Emperor Wu, although it is unknown whether the proposal was made in 140 or in 134.[32] There is also no evidence of any relation between the proposal and the later implementation of the policy, since Dong Zhongshu alienated Emperor Wu early in his reign, was twice sent out to the courts of notoriously ill-behaved kings, never attained high office, and at no point gained the ear of the emperor.[33] The linking of the erudites to the *ru* canon and the establishment of the Academy in the capital first attained importance in 124 B.C., when a memorial from Gongsun Hong led to the recruitment of 50 disciples to attend the Academy. These men were to be tested each year for mastery of the classical texts, and appointed to office on the basis of their performance.

> "I respectfully note that the decrees and laws sent down make clear the boundaries between Heaven and man and thoroughly comprehend the truths of past and present. Their literary style is refined and abstruse [*wen zhang er ya* 文章爾雅], their instructive phrases are profound and generous [*xun ci shen hou* 訓辭深厚], and the blessings bestowed are excellent. Petty clerks are shallow in their learning and cannot understand or announce. They have no means to make clear what is being presented or to instruct the people. [Have men] study ritual and then classical precedents, use literary studies and ritual duty to become officials, and thus promote those trapped [in low positions]." . . . The emperor decreed, "It should be done." From that time on the high ministers and officials were largely scholars of literary arts.[34]

This decree marked the crucial step in establishing a close link between scholarship and office-holding. During subsequent reigns the number of disciples was steadily increased, and on several occasions the number of canonized texts with their associated erudites was also raised. By the end of the Western Han the limit on the number of disciples had reached the figure of 1,000, and since disciples were given office or dismissed on the basis of examinations, the number who passed through the Academy over the course of the years would have been considerable.[35] In this way the Academy became the primary route for access to office, and literary studies, especially those dealing with the Zhou texts, became an indispensable element of the upbringing of anyone who aspired to a career in government.

The establishment of the *ru* classics as a state canon under Emperor Wu can be explained only through a combination of the biographical, intellectual, and political factors sketched above. In part it was a consequence of his education by *ru* scholars. It was also a rebellion against his grandmother and the court faction that had dominated his early years. From his later role as founder of the Music Bureau, or the ruler who gave it unprecedented importance, and his sponsorship of the composition of temple hymns and other songs, he clearly took an active interest in music and verse. Even though his taste in these matters did not jibe with Confucian orthodoxy, the *ru* textual tradition was the only one that granted a central place to music as an aspect of government. Similarly he was responsible for the prestige at court of the epideictic rhapsody, exemplified by the works of Sima Xiangru, which combined *ru* teachings with the local traditions of Chu verse.[36] Emperor Wu was also devoted to ritual activities, and in this sphere the *ru* tradition was the most active and richest in lore. However, the emperor drew freely in his ritual reforms from several traditions, and noncanonical rites advocated by masters of esoteric techniques figured prominently.[37]

In addition to these facts of biography and temperament, the intellectual geography of the early Han empire encouraged Emperor Wu toward support of the *ru* textual tradition. Since texts associated with the Huang-Lao political tendency had been given pride of place in the literary opus of his elder kinsman and rival intellectual patron, Liu An, Emperor Wu's aspirations to eminence in this field were pushed toward rival traditions. Accepting the supremacy of the *Dao de jing* and related texts would have entailed a recognition of the priority in the realm of letters of a rival court. Similarly, the decision to grant canonical status to the Qi textual versions of what would later be known as the new text tradition was encouraged by the active support of Lu scholars for the King of Hejian, and the latter's patronage of what became old text classics.

However, the most important factor underlying Emperor Wu's recognition of the canonical status of the *ru* texts was his rejection of the positions espoused by the hitherto dominant political tendencies. First, whereas political figures linked with Huang-Lao had advocated a passive ruler who entrusted administration to officials, Emperor Wu concentrated power in his own person and delegated as little as possible. The clearest example of this was the transfer of the business of government from the official, outer court to his personal attendants in the "inner court," a policy that allowed the emperor to conduct all business without the participation of his officials.[38]

Second, while the proponents of Huang-Lao had supported the policy of paying tribute to the Xiongnu and avoiding armed conflict, Emperor Wu opted for war. His frontier campaigns became one of the hallmarks of his reign, and also led to the Han exploration and colonization of Central Asia.[39]

Third, while the Huang-Lao advocates had supported low taxation and minimal interference with people's livelihoods, Emperor Wu paid for his aggressive military policies with many new taxes and imperially controlled monopolies. Taxes were imposed on market transactions, vehicles, and property, while the rate of the poll tax on minors was increased. Private minting was banned, and monopolies on salt and iron instituted.[40] Taxes on property depended on self-assessment, and to discourage underreporting the Han state confiscated all property of any subject who reported less than his full wealth. It paid a percentage of the confiscated wealth to any informer. Several of the cruel clerks specialized in manipulating the law to destroy powerful local families, both to raise money and to eliminate threats to central authority.[41]

Fourth, while many advocates of Huang-Lao had been holders of fiefs or their clients, Emperor Wu set out to eliminate the influence of the feudatories. The failure of the rebellion of 154 had been followed by breaking up the largest states. Individual rulers were also the targets of suspicion or suppression. However, the key step of Emperor Wu was the introduction of partible inheritance in kingdoms. Proposed by Zhufu Yan in the name of imperial beneficence, a decree in 127 proclaimed that all sons of kings would be named marquises and the kingdoms divided among them.[42] This guaranteed that within the space of a generation or two, no feudatory state would be large enough to pose any threat to the imperial court.

Thus the establishment of the *ru* texts as an imperial canon was part of a larger program to create a centralized state focused on the person of the emperor and capable of intimidating neighboring peoples through force of arms. This powerful, new state entailed the production of numerous texts, including decrees, codification of ritual innovations, and the reworking of the legal code. This required officials trained in the use of thousands of written graphs to produce documents in a language increasingly removed from that of daily speech. Exponents of the *ru* canon were only one group sponsored by the emperor as part of this program, which also involved many legal or administrative specialists, as well as proponents of mantic or technical traditions. This is indicated in the *Shiji* by the repeated links of *ru* scholastics with legalist administrators as men who ruled through texts and literary arts. Imperial sponsorship of the *ru* textual tradition was largely confined to education and ritual reform, and did not extend to state policy. Even imperial ritual emphasized the cults of the Grand Unity and Sovereign Earth, and the *feng* and *shan* sacrifices, all of which derived from the teachings of the *fangshi* magicians.

Emperor Wu's establishment of the Confucian monopoly of erudites was a means of securing intellectual support for his break with the policies of the past and for instituting his grandiose vision of imperial power. It did not indicate any commitment to the Confucian program, nor did it prevent him from treating the *Chu ci* as a canonical text and ordering the king of Huainan to write a commentary for it. Although the *ru* curriculum had received state sanction, it was far from dominating the intellectual field of the Han empire.

TRIUMPH OF THE CANON

More than a century elapsed between the recognition of the *ru* texts as the curriculum of the Grand Academy and the establishment of *ru* intellectual hegemony. The court remained ambivalent towards Confucianism under the Huo Guang regency and Emperor Xuan. The latter argued that the Han had always balanced the moralistic "Way of kings" with the rule through force of the hegemons, and that his heir's devotion to the *ru* arts would bring chaos to the dynasty.[43] Only under this son, Emperor Yuan (B.C. 48–33), did Confucianism come to dominate court policy. It was not until Wang Mang that the major Confucian ritual of sovereignty, the suburban altar sacrifice to Heaven, became fixed as the center of the imperial ritual calendar. Thus while the canonization of Confucianism took place under Emperor Wu, the triumph of Confucianism as philosophy and cult emerged over a century and a half, under monarchs whose attitudes ranged from muted hostility to passionate interest. To explain this phenomenon one must look beyond individual temperaments and intellectual concerns to long-term intellectual and social developments.

The triumph of Confucianism had three major, long-term causes. First, the Confucian canon provided a schema offering both comprehensive knowledge of the universe and subordinate roles for other intellectual arts and traditions. In this it was only one candidate, but the claim to universality was a necessary precondition. Second, the *ru* canon provided a rationale for the state and a model for the ruler in the new circumstances that emerged in the wake of the unification of China and the disappearance of the Warring States polity. Third, because the Grand Academy had become the major route for access to office, and office-holding was crucial to preserving wealth and status across generations, textual studies in the *ru* canon became a fundamental feature of the new elite that emerged during the Western Han. The first point was discussed at the end of chapter 7. Here I will focus on the other two.

The Warring State as a form of political organization was based on the universal levying of taxes and military service from individual peasant households in the name of "enriching the state and making the army strong." The ruler was the supreme administrator who was responsible for establishing laws to control the peasant population, appointing officials to carry them out, and guiding the state in its constant struggles with hostile powers. This form of polity made sense only in a world of competing states. The achievement of unification under a single autocrat made obsolete the fundamental institutions of the Warring States polity and its ruler. The short-lived Qin empire remained one state ruling others from its strategic base in Guanzhong. The early Han replicated this structure, basing its power in Guanzhong while dividing the rest of the empire into semi-independent kingdoms separated from the core of the Han realm through legal and administrative measures.[44]

However, the inadequacy of the Warring States model became increasingly apparent, and with the elimination of the large feudatory states after the rebellion of 154 B.C. the need for mass, infantry armies vanished at the same time that the danger of maintaining them became apparent. The wars against the Xiongnu required skilled cavalrymen, specialists in the crossbow, and garrison troops who could spend long periods at the frontier. Service in rota for one year in the locality and one at the frontier or the capital did not provide sufficient training to achieve the requisite levels of skill. Thus records of the reign of Emperor Wu contain the first evidence of the shift from peasant levies to long-term volunteers, convicts, and non-Chinese troops. This process continued throughout the first century B.C. and culminated in the abolition of the regular peasant levy by Guangwu, the founder of the Eastern Han.[45]

The same process also transformed the social character of military command. In the Warring States generalship had frequently become a hereditary office, and the major exceptions to this principle had risen through achievements on the field of battle. Generals had been granted legal independence from the ruler while on campaign, and the office had held considerable prestige and authority at court. As noted above, this pattern had continued into the Western Han, and the court under Emperors Wen (B.C. 179–57) and Jing (B.C. 156–41) had been dominated by military men, many of them the sons of generals who had served the Han founder. Under Emperor Wu this began to change. The office of Grand Commandant was abolished, and the supreme command of the armies was granted to relatives of the emperor by marriage. This shift was institutionalized in the office of the *da sima* (大司馬), in which capacity Huo Guang ruled as regent. Under the Eastern Han it became a principle that supreme military command was the prerogative of imperial affines. As soldiers came to be primarily convicts or barbarians, and commanders creatures of the emperor, the military service which had defined the Warring States polity became the realm of the dregs of society, and the militarily based ruling group was replaced by dependent relatives through marriage.

The same century and a half which witnessed the end of universal military service and the social depreciation of the army also saw the rise of large-scale private landlordism. This was made possible by the investment of the fruits of office and merchant capital into land, investment encouraged by Han taxation policies. Although the imperial government at first resisted this development, Emperor Xuan's (B.C. 73–49) abandonment of the use of cruel clerks against local powers marked de facto government recognition of landlordism. Concessions to local sensibilities and the cult of filiality in the ritual reforms of his successor, Emperor Yuan, who eliminated local temples dedicated to imperial ancestors, marked a further yielding of authority. With the foundation of the Eastern Han, the state abandoned all attempts to restrict the development of large estates and thereby surrendered the direct extraction of taxes and service from the individual peasant household which had been the basis of the Warring State polity.[46] Thus the dismantling of the Warring State polity covered the same period as the intellectual and ritual triumph of Confucianism.

The coincidence of the triumph of Confucianism with the decline of universal military service and the development of landlordism is merely suggestive unless one can show how Confucian canonical studies presented a critique of Warring States institutions and an alternative vision of the state. This critique lies in the Confucian model of history that treated the Warring States as a dark age. It provided an alternative model for the Han empire based either on an idealized Zhou state or the mythical kingship of Confucius that was read into the texts of the *ru* canon in the commentarial tradition. For the sake of exposition I will divide this presentation under three rubrics: (1) the Confucian model of history as a critique of the Warring States, (2) the new vision of the state and ruler, and (3) an alternative idea of the role and nature of officials.

As discussed in chapter 4, the schoolmen used history to claim the sanctions of reality and proven efficacy for their critiques of the political practices of their day. The Confucian vision of history was a variant of this practice derived from remarks attributed to Confucius in the *Lun yu*. These criticized the usurpations of the feudal lords and cadet lines, and insisted on the authority of the Zhou monarch.

> When all under Heaven has the Way, then rites, music, and punitive expeditions are initiated by the Son of Heaven. When all under Heaven lacks the Way, then rites, music, and punitive expeditions are initiated by the feudal lords.[47]

The Western Zhou was accepted as an ideal state and identified with the Way, while the institutions that had begun to develop in the Spring and Autumn period were condemned as corruption or decline. The *Mencius* developed these ideas, denouncing the hegemons and military strategists as criminals. The opening set of *cheng xiang* poems and the last poem in the *fu* chapter in the *Xunzi* similarly treat his age as an inverted world of rampant criminality, while lauding the Zhou kings as models to be emulated.[48]

These ideas were developed by later Confucians in several ways. First, the "rectification of names," discussed in chapter 1, provided a model for the ideologically charged writing of history in the commentaries on the *Chun qiu*. In times of social breakdown, as Thucydides noted in his account of *stasis* in Corcyra, words change their meaning, and in the Warring States period words were changing. The questions of who was a king and what was a father were wide open, and the answers given determined how the history of the period was read. If the king was the Zhou monarch, viewed by Warring States *ru* as the model of rule through ritual and charismatic potency, then the rulers of Qin and Qi who claimed the title "king" were usurpers and their reforms criminal. If those who wielded political power and commanded mass armies were the kings they claimed to be, then the Zhou monarchy was an empty anachronism. The canonical scholars of the late Warring States and the Han adopted the former position. In works like the *Gongyang* tradition they developed systems that showed how, through the choice of topics and words, Confucius had written the critique of Eastern Zhou political developments into his chronicle of the period.

Basing themselves on the material of these chronicles and commentaries, Han *ru* developed an elaborate political rhetoric in which the idealization of the Zhou and the critique of Warring States reforms were used to articulate a model for the Han state. Thus the descriptive terms "king" and "hegemon" were transformed into ideal types for contrasting rule through ritual with rule through force, as in the remark of Emperor Xuan quoted in note 43. In general, Han Confucians abandoned the *Mencius's* denunciation of the Spring and Autumn hegemons as criminals and instead followed the *Xunzi* in accepting them as limited defenders of the Zhou order or as failed kings who relied on force to do good. However, also following the *Xunzi*, they traced a decline from the hegemons to men who relied on strategy, deceit, or naked force, and those in this category, the rulers of the Warring States, were condemned to extinction. Similar models of decline were articulated in terms of such instruments of the pre-imperial order as oaths and blood covenants—wherein the highest age had no oaths, the next oaths without blood, and the lowest blood oaths—and in every case Warring States developments were presented as the negation of order or justice.[49] In the rhetoric of the Han Confucians the Warring States period became an age of assassinated princes and murdered fathers, a topos for the abolition of hierarchy and the collapse of social order.[50]

In contrast, the ideal rulers were the ancient sages. As shown in chapter 3, these figures were developed within the schools, and they embodied the idealized convergence of sage and king. The ideal of rulership through cultural or textual mastery was embraced by the state with the establishment of an official canon. This model of kingship as read into commentaries on the *Odes*, the *Chun qiu*, and the rest of the *ru* canon became a convention of political thought. The decline of the military foundations of state power sketched above intensified this development. With the sages, of whom the Zhou kings and Confucius were the last incarnations, established as the ideal, the rulers of the Spring and Autumn period recorded in the *Chun qiu* and their Warring States successors were at best men who imposed order in the absence of a true king, and at worst criminals. In this context the writing of history, as exemplified by the *Chun qiu*, was essentially a critical enterprise. It embraced a sagehood that had existed in ancient times and would reappear under the Han, but the intervening centuries were times of darkness.

The founder of imperial historiography, Sima Qian, incorporated the idea of history as a criticism of contemporary affairs and recent centuries into the structure of his *Shiji*. First, in his postface he accepted the conventional theory that the writing of history, as shown by the *Chun qiu*, was a critical act undertaken in response to social collapse and political failure. Similarly, he repeated the formula on the large numbers of assassinated princes and destroyed states recorded in the text. So strong was the association of history with moral condemnation that Sima Qian posited an interlocutor who asked why he should write a history of a time of order and prosperity such as his own.[51] He replied that each of the classics, including the *Chun qiu*, included praise as well as condemnation, but the fact that the argument had to be made shows how widely accepted was the idea that to write a chronicle was to condemn. This idea grew directly out of the rejection of the developments of the Eastern Zhou and the idealization of the Zhou state and earlier sages.

As described in chapter 7, the organization of Sima Qian's history proclaimed the ideal of a unified state that had existed from earliest antiquity to his day. It thereby treated the political divisions and institutions of the Eastern Zhou as an aberration or a nullity. The entire period was written under the rubric of the Zhou, and the independent states of that time were reduced to "hereditary households" (*shi jia* 世家), a category which also included Confucius and the enfeoffed nobles of the early Han. As households, the states of the Eastern Zhou were by definition partial and private, so their rulers were not true kings. Sima Qian conceded the fact of political division by including tables to synchronize the events of competing calendars, but viewed in the light of the "rectification of names" and the Confucian historiography that the historian claimed as his own, the structure of the *Shiji* condemned the Warring States rulers as usurpers.

This denial of the Warring States polity was at first only a historiographic model or a commentarial convention, but during the Western Han it was introduced into political debate and ultimately into ritual and institutional reform. The clearest example is the debate over the salt and iron monopolies held in 81 B.C., of which a literary account was made. The account, which claims to be based on records kept by participants who were hostile to the monopolies, was rewritten long after the fact by a man who had not been present, so it is biased and not a verbatim record of the arguments. Nevertheless, what the text portrays is two radically different visions of the nature of the state, with one party adhering to the Warring States model of the state defined by military and fiscal power, while the other assumes the vision of the state as a defender of cultural order which makes the minimum possible disruption in the lives of the people.[52]

Sang Hongyang, chief defender of the monopolies, justifies them as a means of enriching the state, suppressing mercantile activity through state control of economic transactions, and providing money for wars. These, in turn, are justified as essential for maintaining the state's power and prestige against the Xiongnu. The provincial literary men who attack the monopolies do not refute these arguments; instead they denounce him for involving the state in commerce, exhausting the people through taxes and military service, and draining the state in foreign wars. In short, they criticize those features of policy that defined the Warring State polity: the central role of military power, the basing of the state on extracting service and taxes from the people, and the direct control of the population's activities by the state's officers.[53]

Against the Warring States tradition, the *ru* canon also provided a new theory of the ruler. In the contrast between king and hegemon, the Confucians had de-emphasized force and law, and stressed the role of the king as ritualist and embodiment of potent virtue (*de* 德). Appeals to the terminology of the Zhou and the Spring and Autumn period as a vocabulary for political philosophy pervade the debates of the period. Even when Emperor Xuan criticized Confucian calls for rule through benevolence, he did so by saying that the Han dynasty had always combined the way of the king with that of the hegemon.[54] Thus even critics of *ru* claims articulated their theory of rulership in terms of the Confucian model of antiquity. With the disappearance of interstate conflict and the declining importance of military service to the Han state, the Confucian model of the ruler as ritualist and defender of culture supplanted the antiquated Warring States vision of him as leader in a struggle for wealth and power. No longer warlords and conquerors, the Han emperors found their role as high priests whose rituals maintained cosmic balance, and sages who defended the social order embodied in the canon.

The new attitude to the past also took the form of a ritual redefinition of the relation of Han to Qin. The early Han state carried forward many Qin institutions, and as noted above it ruled from the Qin heartland. The idea had been established under Qin, as shown in a passage in the *Lü shi chun qiu*, that the rise of a new dynasty signaled the ascent of a new phase in the natural cycle. Qin had claimed to rule under the phase "water," which entailed privileging the number six, wearing black clothing at court, and other ritual actions.[55] During the first century of Han rule the imperial court continued to rule under the virtue of "water" and made no significant modifications in the calendar and related ritual matters. However in 104 B.C., in assocation with the *tai chu* (太初) calendrical reform, Emperor Wu declared that Han ruled under the phase "earth," thus breaking Han's links with Qin. During the next century some scholars argued that Han ruled under the phase "fire," born from the Zhou who were now identified with the phase "wood." This belief was given official sanction by the founder of the Eastern Han.[56] Thus over the course of the Western Han the self-image announced by the court shifted from being heir of Qin, to conqueror of Qin, to successor of Zhou.

This linking of Han to the Zhou dynasty and the relegation of Warring States history to the role of moral counterexample was facilitated by a second redefinition performed by Confucian scholars, the re-creation of the Zhou as a centralized, bureaucratic state. The clearest example of this is the ritualized, bureaucratic fantasy of the *Zhou li*, described in chapter 1. This work took the titles of Zhou offices preserved in bronzes and early texts, and worked them into a law-based state in which all aspects of human existence were brought into a natural order dictated by the pattern of the seasons.

A related idea is articulated in the commentarial remarks of the *Gongyang*. Here such features of the Qin and Han empires as the unity of the state, the absolute power of the king, the obedience of cadet lines, and the absence of a hereditary officialdom were read back into the ideal state of a true Son of Heaven. This state, however, was not identified with the Zhou, who were criticized for their failings in the Spring and Autumn period, but rather with the textual realm of Confucius, the uncrowned king. This textual kingdom was an expression of the idealization of the sages, which included the ancient kings as well as Confucius.

A third element in the Confucian reading of an idealized, textual Zhou into Han practice was the idea that officials were more than the servants of the ruler and tools for the implementation of his policies. Aided by the fact that the word *shi* (士), which identified the service elite of imperial China, had referred to the lowest level of the Zhou nobility and been used as an encompassing term for the nobility in certain ritual contexts, Confucian thinkers assimilated Han officialdom to the status of the Zhou nobility, or re-imagined the Zhou nobility on the model of Han officials.[57] This had begun in the Warring States period, when Mencius had translated the Zhou distinction of noble and commoner into a division between those who toiled with their minds and those who toiled with their bodies. Han scholars and commentators carried the process much further.

One of the earliest examples was the *Gongyang* tradition, which treated the Zhou king as an absolute monarch like the Han emperor, reducing the feudal lords and hereditary nobles to the status of Qin or Han officials. It claimed that feudal lords had no right to launch military expeditions and that nobles could take no action without orders from the king. It recognized exceptions in certain circumstances, for example, to save a state or avoid attacking a state in mourning, but even these concessions to a degree of noble autonomy, far less than what existed in reality, were condemned by the rival *Guliang* tradition.[58] Even the Chu king, who had been independent of Zhou, was reduced to the status of an officer in these accounts.

The inverse of this equation of Zhou nobility with Han officialdom was the claim of a unique status for Han officials vis-à-vis the common people. Jia Yi matched high Han officials with the nobles of the Zhou, elevating them not only over the common people but over the government clerks (*li* 吏) as well. He argued that the ruler could not be truly elevated without a stratum of seminoble officials between himself and commoners, so he carefully separated scholarly *shi* 士 from functionaries and scribes. To honor the *shi* and the ruler with whom they were associated, high officials were to be granted a range of privileges in sumptuary regulations regarding dress, numbers of chariots, and so forth. They were likewise to be exempt from imprisonment or torture, and granted the right to commit suicide in capital cases. This theory also figured in Han debates over the reading of ritual texts, such as the dispute over whether officials, as *shi*, were entitled to shrines and tablets.[59] The same idea was articulated in the oft-cited doctrine that rituals did not reach down to the common people nor punishments up to the high officials. Here the privileged status of the ritually defined Zhou elite was transferred into the legal codes that defined the imperial state. In practice the Han granted sumptuary privileges to high officials (as shown in Han burial procedures and tomb paintings), instituted the legal immunity of high officials from certain forms of interrogation and punishment, and regularly enfeoffed chief ministers and other high officials. These practices realized the text-based theories of the nobility of officialdom.

The equation of officials with Zhou nobles also informed economic debates. Dong Zhongshu argued that officials received salaries from the emperor to free them from banausic concerns with agriculture, manufacture, or trade.[60] This doctrine, which in distinguishing officials from those who worked identified them with nobles, figured in the *Yan tie lun* and other texts where it justified criticisms of government interference in trade. Since officials were bound to the ruler through the debt they owed him, they devoted themselves to public service rather than private enrichment.[61] Other texts, notably the *Han Shi wai zhuan* and the *Xin xu*, praised an "integrity of the scholar" (*shi jie* 士節) marked by unconcern for material well-being, and willingness to endure hardship or to die for the Way of virtue or the sake of the ruler.[62]

Another aspect of the equation of officials with nobles was the elevation of filiality to the highest of virtues. Within the *zong fa* (宗法) kinship system that had structured the Zhou realm, the relative seniority of kin lines and of members within a line had defined relations of authority. The rise of territorial states had undercut the authority of kinship, and legalist theoreticians of the Warring States had insisted on the precedence of political authority over kin ties. At the end of Qin or in early Han, however, the *Xiao jing* and other texts found a place for filiality within the political order as a means of inculcating respect for authority and extending state power at the local level. This idea gained official sanction at the beginning of the Han when Liu Bang, the dynasty's founder, secured his positions as Lord of Pei and then king of Guanzhong by declaring bonds with the elders of these areas. These were officially carried into the dynasty in the office of the "Thrice Venerable" (*san lao* 三老) and the cult of the aged marked by an annual ritual and the granting of sacred dove staffs to those over seventy. The Han thus identified their authority with that of the aged in the community and the father in the household, thereby reasserting the links of kinship ties and political authority. The centrality of filial piety was also marked by the addition of the epithet *xiao* (孝) to the posthumous title of every emperor.

The themes of the nobility of officialdom and the importance of filiality were also central to the emergence of a new form of social elite, the great families that cultivated literary studies and sought service in the Han government. This was the second major cause of the Confucian canon's increasing domination of the intellectual field in Han China. The formation of this elite had four basic causes: (1) the increasing importance of the Grand Academy as the route to office, (2) the need to convert office-holding into more permanent forms of wealth, (3) the insecurity due to partible inheritance of land tenure, and (4) the discrimination against mercantile wealth in Han taxation and law.

The importance of the Grand Academy as a means for gaining office was noted in the first section of this chapter. To assure skill in handling the increasingly artificial language in which documents were drafted, Emperor Wu used the disciples of the Academy as the primary pool for recruitment to official posts. Subsequent emperors expanded the number of masters and disciples, while continuing to recruit from those trained at the Academy. By the first century B.C. canonical studies, whether genuine or feigned, had become the standard avenue to office and the wealth gained through office-holding.

However, office could not be indefinitely guaranteed, and those who attained it sought to secure more permanent sources of income through purchasing land or engaging in money lending. Yu Yingshi showed that records of officials converting their temporary wealth into more permanent form through the large-scale purchase of lands appear in the reign of Emperor Wu. This greatly increased the number of scholars possessing wealth and of wealthy families pursuing scholarship.[63] While land was the primary investment, many newly wealthy scholars also engaged in trade or usury.

The third major feature was partible inheritance, in which property was divided among male heirs. The Warring State polity had encouraged division of property to increase the number of households paying taxes and providing services, and to reduce the number of powerful families who could defy local officials. As noted above, Emperor Wu extended the practice to the Han nobility, leaving the emperorship as the only inheritance that was not divided. This meant that over the course of two or three generations even the largest estate would be reduced to numerous small farms. Without income from another source that enabled the purchase of new land, or for one sibling to buy up land from his brothers, landed wealth could not be long preserved. Thus wealthy families needed income from manufacture, commerce, or the holding of office.

Manufacture and commerce formed the final link in the chain. The Qin and Han empires registered traders as a separate legal category and legally discriminated against them in many ways.[64] However, laws were not always strictly enforced, and early Han writers noted that wealthy merchants were wealthier than princes, and their serving girls more finely dressed than empresses.[65] Far more significant was the threat to mercantile wealth posed by the taxation policies of Emperor Wu. Among the taxes employed to fund his foreign wars and elaborate rituals was a property tax based on declaration of worth, with arrest and confiscation of all property as the penalty for under reporting. This tax was levied at twice the rate on merchant capital as on farming property, and it was made efficacious by granting a percentage of the confiscated property to informers. Many of the cruel clerks noted above specialized in the destruction of powerful families, and these tax policies were a major weapon in their armament.

This assault on merchant wealth, combined with the abundance of land that ruined peasants had to sell at low prices, encouraged the transfer of capital into the purchase of property, and the transformation of merchants into landed proprietors. Since officials were also purchasing land and forming estates, and newly landed merchants educating their sons in order to seek office, the same families acted as landlords, merchants, and scholar-officials. It was the opposition of such powerful families that toppled Wang Mang's short-lived Xin dynasty and established Liu Xiu, himself a great landowner, as the first emperor of the Eastern Han. These families dominated the economic and political life of the Eastern Han, as indicated by the government's abandonment of efforts to restrict private land ownership. The great families' combination of agricultural, mercantile, scholarly, and ritual activities is documented in Cui Shi's *Monthly Ordinances of the Four Classes of People (si min yue ling* 四民月令).[66]

Not only did these families challenge the economic and political authority of the imperial court, which was largely dominated by imperial affines or eunuchs in the last century of Han rule, but they also acted as rivals in the realms of textual authority. While the official versions of the classics established in the Western Han remained the curriculum of the Grand Academy in the Eastern Han, study of the old-script texts gained greater prestige among scholars. More importantly, the Grand Academy was in many ways eclipsed or supplanted by private schools founded by leading scholars, and lesser schools that developed throughout the provinces. The ties established between masters and disciples in these schools, or among disciples, helped to forge ever larger networks between powerful local families and their clients.

Moreover, scholars used commentaries on the classics to challenge the power of the central court, and they usurped such imperial prerogatives as the compilation of collective biographies that passed judgment on eminent figures from different regions. The devotion to textual studies was thus crucial to the formation of an extended elite, its achievement of self-consciousness, and the resistance that it was able to offer to the court when many leading figures were banned from holding office between 166 and 184 A.D.[67]

What had begun as a body of texts sanctioned by the state for the training of potential officials in the intricacies of the written language had over the course of three centuries become first the model for the imperial state and then the means by which the Han elite constituted themselves as a group, asserted their privileged status, and claimed a moral basis for their opposition to the court. The crucial role of this textual inheritance in the self-definition and status of the leading families preserved the canon-based imperial ideal through the collapse of the regime that had created it. Firmly rooted in the structures of late Han society, the textual heritage of the pre-imperial era became the permanent foundation for an imperial order that transcended the rise and fall of individual dynasties.

CONCLUSION

As shown in chapter 2, the philosophical traditions of pre-imperial China had claimed a political role, but they maintained themselves as independent associations by rejecting the political practice of their day. They perpetuated themselves over time by obtaining patronage from people not immediately tied to the Warring States polities. Villages, smaller states surviving in the interstices of the great powers, and nobles or high ministers all provided social niches in which the skills or services based on textual mastery were of use. As the great powers themselves became patrons, and even appointed a few of the highest officials from among the philosophically trained, they also attracted ambitious scholars. Nevertheless, the lesser centers continued to offer bases where philosophical activities survived outside the ambit of the royal courts.

The creation of a unified state by Qin reduced the number of such bases, but leading officials and holders of fiefs still acted as patrons, just as Lü Buwei had done in the decades preceding the final conquests, and local society provided positions for teachers and masters of ritual. The creation of fiefs in the early Han reproduced the late Warring States world with kings competing to assemble learned men at their courts. The situation was again reversed, however, by Emperor Wu's policies of establishing a Grand Academy with a state-sanctioned canon, breaking up the feudatories, and attacking powerful local families through confiscation, execution, or resettlement in the capital region. The result of these policies was to have been the realization of Qin's dream of state control of the dissemination of textual knowledge, and the consequent achievement of the identity of official and teacher—the reduced form of the identity of king and sage.

However, Emperor Wu's use of the Academy as a pool for recruiting officials, along with taxation policies that ruined the peasantry and pushed wealthy people to invest in land, led to the formation of a new elite that acted as both scholars and patrons. Among the great families, where wealth could be transmitted across generations only through the combination of land ownership and access to office, the identity of official and teacher meant that scholarship became the appanage of wealth and influence. The Han imperium had created a new type of elite that was tied to the state through its economic dependence on salary and an intellectual commitment—more or less sincere—to the literary culture sanctioned by the court. However, the insecurity of office which the state used to assure the obedience of officials meant that they were obliged to protect their futures, and those of their children, by finding resources outside the state sphere. Having obtained these resources, they ceased to be creatures of the state and became semi-independent local powers in the image of the great clans destroyed by Emperor Wu.

This became the classic form of the imperial Chinese elite, able to maintain itself only by balancing service to the state with the development of local bases. This type of elite was crucial to the functioning of the state, which could never collect tax income sufficient to maintain a bureaucracy that was able to control

the entire population. Instead the state maintained a bureaucracy that could preserve a degree of public order and secure a sufficient income, and then relied on
local powers to keep the peace where the state lacked the manpower to police. The
loyalty of these powers, in turn, was secured through the possibility of gaining
crucial supplementary income through holding office or providing other services
to the state.

In this system, where the polity was created through the combination of
paid agents and local allies, the texts of the imperial canon served as the central
cord binding the state proper to the powerful families on whom it relied. Most
families of the Eastern Han elite had enriched themselves through office gained by
study, or taken up study to secure wealth already gained. The canonical texts thus
provided a major route by which families entered into or remained in state service.
As the texts came to dominate the intellectual sphere, and serve as the *lingua franca*
of citations in which public debate was conducted, they also defined an intellectual
frame in which state and families united in a common vision of society. The canonical texts, instituted as a means of recruiting and controlling officials, thus became
the core of a political system in which officials and dynasties were equally bound,
and on which both depended.

While the imperial court depended upon the great families' commitment to
the scholarly enterprise in order to transmit its writ to all levels of society, this
dependence meant that the state monopoly of text and truth was once again dispersed in multiple centers of patronage. Alternative bases of scholarship allowed
the formation of private schools that outshone the Grand Academy, networks of
teachers and disciples who formed large associations outside the state sphere, and
teachings or doctrines that rejected those propounded by the court, or even condemned the court and called for its overthrow. Earlier chapters have shown how
philosophical works, verse, and history all provided grounds for the rejection of
political practices, and once the canon was disseminated throughout the powerful
families it could serve the same role. When the state defined itself through a group
of texts, and justified itself through their teachings, then these writings could be
invoked to criticize specific policies, or ultimately to condemn the state itself.

These texts, however, also provided the means by which the imperial order
could survive the demise of each of its incarnations. To the extent that this order
was implanted in the values and aspirations of the powerful families, and that it
was crucial both to their economic survival and their claims to superiority over
rivals with no traditions of imperial service, the dream of empire would be carried
forward and a new dynasty established in the rubble of the old. Thus writing was
not only crucial to the administrative functioning of the state, but more important
it served as the seed which, planted in the soil of local society, produced a new state
each time the old one fell. The imaginary state of the *Zhou li* came to define the
imperial order, and the textual realm fashioned in the coded judgments of the
Gongyang endured, while the substantial realities of actual administration all turned
to dust. In this way the Chinese empire became a realm built of texts.

CONCLUSION

When discussing the relation of writing to reality, one always comes to Borges. In "Tlön, Uqbar, Orbis Tertius" he tells of an alternative world invented in writing. The narrator first comes across the imaginary land of Uqbar in an anomalous encyclopedia entry. This relates that the literature of Uqbar dealt only with the imaginary realms of Mlenjas and Tlön, and some years later he stumbles on the eleventh volume of an encyclopedia describing the aforementioned Tlön. The balance of the story describes a world inhabited by beings who perceive and act in line with the precepts of philosophical idealism. In a "Postscript" the author recounts the discovery that the encyclopedia of Tlön is the culmination of a project begun in the late seventeenth century by a group of men committed to the philosophy of idealism who set out to create an imaginary realm. Perpetuated by master-disciple transmission, this society in 1824 received the support of a millionaire who made his patronage conditional on expanding the project to become the writing of a comprehensive encyclopedia of this imaginary world. At the close of the story, the author reveals that material objects from Tlön have suddenly begun to appear in the world. Moreover, the beauty of an orderly world devised entirely by the mind of man has swept aside all earlier human visions, both political ideologies and sciences. In the final paragraph the author announces that the "world will be Tlön."

The evolving role of writing in the Warring States and early empires anticipated this story of a world swallowed up by a parallel planet put together in textual form by a "scattered dynasty of solitary men." Writing created a literary double of the actual world, and this invented world became the highest reality. This process was facilitated by the fact that early state administration drew many of its forms and practices, above all its uses of writing, from the religious sphere, and that political innovations were read back into the spirit world. Thus from its origins the Chinese bureaucratic state was tied to a parallel, imaginary world generated in texts. Textual production in the Warring States period also created groups separate from the state who nevertheless claimed for themselves the authority of monarchs or ministers. Over the centuries they created philosophical texts that articulated their claims to power in the guise of sages, histories of a past that served both as a ground for criticisms of government and a realm in which writing became judicial authority or even kingship, and new types of poetry that created authoritative voices not tied to political office. In all these ways texts created a vision of kingship and nobility that paralleled or negated existing state forms.

These groups fashioned an imaginary world located in a past where sagehood and kingship had been united, and there had been no division between textual and political authority. They imagined the world of their own day as the culmination of a process in which these two realms had been torn apart. In these historical accounts writing originated with kings and kingship with writing, shifted to ministers who doubled the kings, and culminated in the figure of Confucius who without any attribute of kingship acted as a ruler in the parallel realm of writing. The sequence of sages led from a kingship consisting of nothing but the mastery of signs to a purely textual kingship set in opposition to brute political power, but it prophesied the ultimate return of the lost unity. The sages in this process were linked together through their roles as successive creators of the three levels of the *Yi jing*, the trigrams, the line judgments, and the commentarial chapters. The *Yi* in turn was transformed from a divination manual into a potent text that generated the cosmos from the mathematical play of binary opposition, and at the same time created a philosophy of visual signs that paralleled the generative process. As such it served as a statement and demonstration of the parallel interplay between writing and reality.

Toward the end of the Warring States these developments led to the creation of encompassing works that depicted the entire world in writing. Some of these were constructed from the literary remains of the Zhou, transformed by the addition of commentaries into timeless classics that spoke a new truth to each age. Others claimed to depict the principles of cosmic origins that still underlay processes in nature and society. Still others were collective endeavors in which leading political figures gathered scholars from diverse traditions to create syntheses, patterned on natural process, of competing doctrines. In this way the diverse and competing projects of scattered, solitary men took on ever vaster proportions even as philosophical works began to appear in the state sphere.

Texts moved decisively into the world of government with the beginnings of imperial literary policy under the Qin dynasty. The process resumed with the establishment of the primary *ru* texts as a state canon under Emperor Wu of the Han, and the textual world fashioned in the schools moved more deeply into the political realm as the Grand Academy became a major route to political office. This process made literary education an important attribute of powerful families that aspired to office, so the textual culture defined by writing and the literary language gradually formed the mental universe of the Han elite. Basing themselves on a textual heritage now held to define the state, some scholars in the late Han even began to assert the right of opposition to the court that had originally defined the canon, but now was dominated by women and eunuchs. With the fall of the Han and the temporary disappearance of the unitary state, the empire survived only as a dream and a vision, and thus was swallowed up by its textual double. In this form it was to survive and develop till the end of imperial China.

The texts that constituted imperial Chinese culture were not fixed, and the empire's history was closely tied to the development of new modes of writing. New genres of literature emerged, as well as the canons of organized religions. The *ru* canon itself was expanded and read in new ways. Moreover, the canonical culture remained the preserve of a small literate elite. Most of the Chinese population, including much of its political elite, participated in a related but distinct culture that Glen Dudbridge has described as "vernacular," using distinctions in language and fundamental texts to mark the key division in imperial culture.[1] This division played itself out above all in tensions or struggles over the correct forms of cultic practice and interpretations of religious phenomena, struggles that were crucial to the state because it depended as much on control of the imagination as on administration to project its authority. Through all these changes and tensions, texts preserving an artificial, literary language in a nonphonetic script continued to define a distinct "canonical" culture. This culture was committed to the dream of a pan-imperial realm that, like the literary language itself, transcended local variations and temporal modifications. Only in the late empire did this develop into an empirewide "popular" culture that defined China through the dissemination of a shared body of story and lore in theatrical performances, popular novels, and religious rites.[2]

Having begun with Borges, we finish with Genet. In "The Balcony" a group of men take refuge from life in a bordello where they dress up in the costumes of judge, general, and police chief to enact a theater of power. At the conclusion of the play the old regime is swept away, and the costumed figures are led from the brothel to assume their theatrical roles on the stage of life. This pattern was repeated at each Chinese dynastic transition, where men who had learned the roles and assumed the costumes of power in their text-based fantasies were suddenly called on to be judges and executioners. Indeed the Genet play is even closer to the Chinese case in that by the late imperial period the theater had become one of the most important modes for the dissemination in local society of ethics, political principles, and history. People learned how to be Chinese by watching performers dressed in the costumes of fallen dynasties, and even today Chinese religious rites often involve putting on the uniforms of the roles that had defined the imperial state.[3] Invented as an ideal by small bands of scholars, expanded into a detailed program in encyclopedic texts and commentaries, the Chinese empire survived 2,000 years of dynastic rise and fall as a dream preserved first in a body of texts and ultimately in theatrical performances. Now only the texts and the theater remain.

NOTES

Introduction

1. Jack Goody, *The Logic of Writing and the Organization of Society* (Cambridge: Cambridge University, 1986), ch. 3, "The state, the bureau, and the file"; ch. 4, "The letter of the law"; Rosamond McKitterick, *The Carolingians and the Written Word* (Cambridge: Cambridge University, 1989), chs. 2–3; M. T. Clanchy, *From Memory to Written Record* (Cambridge: Harvard University, 1979), chs. 2–3; C. M. Kelly, "Later Roman Bureaucracy: Going Through the Files," in *Literacy and Power in the Ancient World*, ed. Alan K. Bowman and Greg Woolf (Cambridge: Cambridge University, 1994), pp. 161–76; M. Lambert, "La naissance de la bureaucratie," *Revue historique* (1960), pp. 1–26; Marcel Detienne, ed., *Les savoirs de l'écriture en Grèce ancienne* (Lille: Presses Universitaires de Lille, 1988) section II, "Du tribunal aux archives"; Nicole Loraux, "Solon et la voix de l'écrit," in *Les savoirs de l'écriture*, pp. 95–129; Giorgio Camassa, "Aux origines de la codification écrite des lois en Grèce," in *Les savoirs de l'écriture*, pp. 130–55.

2. Benedict Anderson, *Imagined Communities* (rev. ed., London: Verso, 1991), chs. 3–5. Ch. 10, "Census, map, and museum," traces the use of written administrative forms in the creation of nations. Ernest Gellner, *Nations and Nationalism* (Ithaca: Cornell University, 1983), ch. 3, esp. pp. 35–38. Anthony D. Smith, *The Ethnic Origins of Nations* (Oxford: Blackwell, 1986), ch. 8, "Legends and Landscapes," discusses the role of a common mythology in the creation and preservation of a nation, and this mythology is preserved and spread in a range of written forms.

3. Marcel Detienne, "L'espace de la publicité: ses opérateurs intellectuels dans la cité," in *Les savoirs de l'écriture*, pp. 29–81; Françoise Ruzé, "Aux débuts de l'écriture politique: le pouvoir de l'écrit dans la cité," in *Les savoirs de l'écriture*, pp. 82–94.

4. On early inscriptions that gave voices to statues of dead men or gods, see Jesper Svenbro, *Phrasikleia: An Anthropology of Reading in Ancient Greece*, tr. Janet Lloyd (Ithaca: Cornell University, 1993); Svenbro, "J'écris, donc je m'efface: l'énonciation dans les premières inscriptions grecques," in *Les savoirs de l'écriture*, pp. 459–79; Pietro Pucci, "Inscriptions archaïques sur les statues des dieux," in *Les savoirs de l'écriture*, pp. 480–97. On Orphic texts in tombs and their relation to myths of immortality and writing, see Marcel Detienne, *L'écriture d'Orphée* (Paris: Gallimard, 1989), pp. 109–32.

5. Marcel Detienne, *Les maîtres de vérité dans la Grèce archaïque* (Paris: François

Maspero, 1981), esp. pp. 110–11; Walter J. Ong, *Orality and Literacy: the Technologizing of the Word* (London: Methuen, 1982), pp. 96–101. In certain societies, however, written records received less credence than oral testimony, or required a considerable period of time to establish their authority. See Clanchy, *From Memory to Written Record*, ch. 9, "Trusting Writing."

6. Deborah Tarn Steiner, *The Tyrant's Writ: Myths and Images of Writing in Ancient Greece* (Princeton: Princeton University, 1994), pp. 149–54.

7. On the role of writing as a "floating medium" used in exchanges that transcend spoken tongues, see Anne-Marie Christin, *L'image écrite ou la déraison graphique* (Paris: Flammarion, 1995), pp. 32–39.

8. Pierre Lévêque and Pierre Vidal-Naquet, *Clisthène l'Athénien: essai sur la représentation de l'espace et du temps dans la pensée politique grecque de la fin du VIe siècle à la mort de Platon* (Paris: Macula, 1964); François Hartog, *Le miroir d'Hérodote: essai sur la représentation de l'autre* (Paris: Gallimard, 1980), part I, "Les Scythes imaginaires: espace, pouvoir et nomadisme"; Christian Jacob, "Inscrire la terre habitée sur une tablette: réflexions sur la fonction de la carte géographique en Grèce ancienne," in *Les savoirs de l'écriture*, pp. 273–304; Claude Nicolet, *L'inventaire du monde: géographie et politique aux origines de l'empire romain* (Paris: Arthème Fayard, 1988); Anthony Aveni, *Empires of Time: Calendars, Clocks, and Cultures* (London: I. B. Tauris, 1990); L. Schele and M. Miller, *The Blood of Kings: Dynasty and Ritual in Maya Art* (Fort Worth: Kimbell Museum, 1986); Alfred Gell, *The Anthropology of Time: Cultural Construction of Temporal Maps and Images* (Oxford: Berg, 1992), pp. 294–313; Barbara Adam, *Time and Social Theory* (Cambridge: Polity, 1990), ch. 5, "Industrial Time and Power."

9. Different forms of this procedure, with emphasis on the role of writing, are sketched in Claude Calame, *The Craft of Poetic Speech in Ancient Greece*, tr. Janice Orion (Ithaca: Cornell University, 1995), part I.

10. Paul A. Vander Waerdt, ed., *The Socratic Movement* (Ithaca: Cornell University, 1994).

11. Giuseppe Cambiano, "La démonstration géométrique," in *Les savoirs de l'écriture*, pp. 251–72; Roy Harris, *The Origin of Writing* (LaSalle, Illinois: Open Court, 1986), pp. 146–52.

12. Claude Lévi-Strauss, *Tristes tropiques* (Paris: Plon, 1955), pp. 312–19. Lévi-Strauss concludes that the primary function of writing has always been to facilitate enslavement, including in this denunciation both the bureaucratic administration of the "oriental" empires and the links in the modern world between compulsory education and the extension of state control. A criticism of this reading of the anecdote appears in Jacques Derrida, *Of Grammatology*, tr. Gayatri Spivak (Baltimore: Johns Hopkins University, 1974), Part II, ch. 1, "The Violence of the Letter: From Lévi-Strauss to Rousseau." These texts are cited by Deborah Tarn Steiner in her discussion of the dual nature of writing in Greek political thought, where it is invoked both as the public laws that guarantee the equality of citizens, and the decrees and secret dispatches employed by tyrants or conspirators. See Steiner, *The Tyrant's Writ*, pp. 125–42, 149–54, 159–74, 193–251.

13. Christin, *L'image écrite*, pp. 97–108. Writing as a form of secrecy or concealment closely linked to divine omens also figures prominently in Greek tragedy. See Charles Segal, "Greek Tragedy: Writing, Truth, and Representation of the Self," in *Interpreting Greek Tragedy* (Ithaca, N.Y.: Cornell University, 1986), pp. 75–109; Segal, *La musique du sphinx: structure, mythe, langage dans la tragédie grecque* (Paris: La Découverte, 1987); Segal, "Vérité, tragédie et écriture," in *Savoirs de l'écriture*, pp. 330–58.

14. Gerald L. Bruns, *Inventions: Writing, Textuality, and Understanding in Literary History* (New Haven: Yale University, 1982), ch. 1, "Secrecy and Understanding"; Frank Kermode, *The Genesis of Secrecy* (Cambridge: Harvard University, 1979), esp. ch. 6, "The Unfollowable Word." Bruns also argues that in a manuscript culture where texts are constantly reworked "the text is not reducible to the letter; that is, a text always contains more than it says, or more than its letters contain, which is why we are privileged to read between the lines, and not to read between them only but to write between them as well . . . " See Bruns, "Originality of Text in a Manuscript Culture," in *Inventions*, pp. 44–59, esp. p. 55.

Chapter One. Writing the State

1. On this pattern as definitive of the origins of the Warring State polity, see Mark Edward Lewis, *Sanctioned Violence in Early China* (Albany: State University of New York, 1990), chs. 1–2.

2. On pottery marks, see Cheung Kwong-yue, "Recent Archaeological Evidence Relating to the Origin of Chinese Characters," in *The Origins of Chinese Civilization*, ed. David Keightley (Berkeley: University of California, 1983), pp. 323–91; K. C. Chang, *Art, Myth, and Ritual: The Path to Political Authority in Ancient China* (Cambridge: Harvard University, 1983), pp. 81–86. On the oracle bones, see David Keightley, *Sources of Shang History: the Oracle Bone Inscriptions of Bronze Age China* (Berkeley: University of California, 1978).

3. David Keightley states that the inscriptions were "at least partly historical and bureaucratic." See *Sources*, p. 45. Léon Vandermeersch and Sarah Allan argue that recording the "charges" was essential to the efficacy of the rite. See Vandermeersch, *Wang dao ou la voie royale*, vol. 2, *Structures politiques, les rites* (Paris: Ecole Française d'Extrême-Orient, 1980), pp. 163–64; Sarah Allan, *The Shape of the Turtle: Myth, Art, and Cosmos in Early China* (Albany: SUNY, 1991), ch. 5, esp. pp. 121–22. The latter position is more plausible for three reasons. First, recording the inscriptions on bone or shell was very laborious, and the irregular shapes of these objects made them inefficient for storage purposes. If the inscriptions were intended as archives, it would have been easier and more efficient to make them on clay, a substance that had long been used for writing insignia and which the Shang employed in making clay cores for inscribed bronzes. Second, the keeping of archives is attributed to "bureaucratic" needs, although the evidence of the oracle inscriptions suggests that the Shang had no bureaucracy. On this point, see David

Keightley, "The Late Shang State: When, Where, and What?" in *The Origins of Chinese Civilization*, pp. 523–64. Finally, the nonbureaucratic explanation suggested for such an archive is its use to legitimate royal power, but in fact notes verifying the correctness of the king appear in only a small percentage of the inscriptions. It is a weak argument to explain the entire procedure by appeal to an uncommon feature. On the other hand, if the inscription was somehow necessary to the successful completion of the ritual, perhaps by "translating" the gods' response into a human form and thereby binding them to keep their word, then it is not surprising that the "translation" was carved on the same numinous surface in which the reply of the gods had appeared.

4. See Akatsuka Kiyoshi 赤塚忠, *Chūgoku kodai no shūkyō to bunka—In ōchō no saishi* 中國古代の宗教と文化——殷王朝の祭祀 (Tokyo: Kadokawa, 1977); Keightley, "Akatsuka Kiyoshi and the Culture of Early China: A Study in Historical Method," *Harvard Journal of Asiatic Studies* 42.1 (1982): 267–320.

5. On the idea that Shang writing must have developed as a transcription of natural language in daily activities, see, for example, Guo Moruo 郭沫若, "Gudai wenzi zhi bianzheng fazhan 古代文字之辯證發展," *Kaogu* (1972:3), p. 4. On the intimate links between Shang divination practices and the form of the early script, see Vandermeersch, *Wang dao*, vol. II, pp. 289–90, 479–83.

6. Dong Zuobin 董作賓, *Yin li pu* 殷曆譜 (Lizhuang: Institute of History and Philology, Academia Sinica, 1945); Vandermeersch, *Wang dao*, ch. 20.

7. Lothar von Falkenhausen, "Issues in Western Zhou Studies: A Review Article," *Early China* 18 (1993): 145–71. Also of use are the books discussed in this "review," Edward L. Shaughnessy, *Sources of Western Zhou History: Inscribed Bronze Vessels* (Berkeley: University of California, 1991); Jessica Rawson, *Western Zhou Ritual Bronzes from the Arthur M. Sackler Collections. Ancient Chinese Bronzes from the Arthur M. Sackler Collections*, vol. II, parts A and B (Washington, D.C.: Arthur M. Sackler Gallery of Art and Cambridge: Arthur M. Sackler Museum; distributed by Harvard University Press, 1990).

8. Xu Zhongshu 徐中舒, "Jinwen guci shili 金文嘏辭釋例," *Zhongyang Yanjiuyuan Lishi Yuyan Yanjiusuo Jikan* 6.1 (1936): 1–44; Hayashi Minao, "Concerning the Inscription 'May Sons and Grandsons Eternally Use This [Vessel]'," *Artibus Asiae* 53: 1–2 (1993): 51–58.

9. Jean Levi, *Les fonctionnaires divins* (Paris: Seuil, 1989), pp. 204–07.

10. Shirakawa Shizuka 白川靜, "Shaku Shi 釋史," and "Sai sho kankei jisetsu 載書關系字說," in *Kōkotsu kinbungaku ronshū* 甲骨金文學論集 (Kyoto: Hōyū Shoten, 1974): 1–68, 307–64; Donald Harper, "A Chinese Demonography of the Third Century B.C.," *Harvard Journal of Asiatic Studies* 45.2 (1985): 472–74; Vandermeersch, *Wang dao*, vol. II, pp. 473–75.

11. Lewis, *Sanctioned Violence*, pp. 43–50, 67–80; Susan Roosevelt Weld, "Covenant in Jin's Walled Cities: The Discoveries at Houma and Wenxian" (Ph.D. diss., Harvard University, 1990).

12. Shanxisheng Wenwu Gongzuo Weiyuanhui 山西省文物工作委員會, *Houma mengshu* 侯馬盟書 (Shanghai: Wenwu, 1976), texts 1.9, 67.6, 156.20.

13. Gosei Tadako 吾井互弘, "Shunjū jidai no Shin no daifu Ki shi, Yōzetsu shi no ōzato ni tsuite 春秋時代の晉の大夫祇氏, 羊舌氏の邑について," *Chūgoku kodaishi kenkyū* 中國古代史研究 3 (Tokyo: Chūgoku Kodaishi Kenkyū Kai, 1968), pp. 183–209.

14. Guo Moruo 郭沫若, "Houma mengshu shitan 侯馬盟書試探," *Wenwu* (1966:2): 5. See also Yoshimoto Michio 吉本道雄, "Shunjū saisho ron 春秋載書論," *Tōyōshi kenkyū* 43:4 (1985): 1–33.

15. Nishijima Sadao 西島定生, *Chūgoku kodai teikoku no keisei to kōzō—nijū tō shakusei no kenkyū* 中國古代帝國の形成と構造——二十等爵制の研究 (Tokyo: Tōkyō Daigaku, 1961).

16. Shiga Shūzō 滋賀秀三, "Chūgoku jōdai no keibatsu ni tsuite no ichi kōsatsu—sei to mei o tegakari to shite 中國上代の刑罰についての一考察——誓と盟を手か" かりとして," in Shiga Shūzō, ed., *Ishii Ryōsuke sensei kanreki shukuga: Hōseishi ronsō* 石井良助先生還歷祝賀: 法制史論叢 (Tokyo: Sōbunsha, 1977), pp. 5–36.

17. The most systematic study of Zhou inscriptions pertaining to legal disputes is Lutz Schunk, *Dokumente zur Rechtsgeschichte des alten China: Übersetzung und historisch-philologische Kommentierung juristischer Bronzeinschriften der West-Zhou-Zeit (1045– 771 v. Chr.)* (Doktorgrad Diss., Westfälischen Wilhelms-Universität zu Munster, 1994). See also Du Zhengsheng 杜正勝, *Bian hu qi min: chuantong zhengzhi shehui jiegou zhi xingcheng* 編戶齊民: 傳統政治社會結構之形成 (Taipei: Lianjing, 1989), pp. 229–44. The inscription is on p. 239.

18. Yang Bojun 楊伯峻, *Chun qiu Zuo zhuan zhu* 春秋左傳注 (Beijing: Zhonghua, 1981), Lord Zhao year 6, pp. 1274–76; Lord Zhao year 29, p. 1504.

19. Lewis, *Sanctioned Violence*, pp. 69–73.

20. The following account is based on *Shuihudi Qin mu zhu jian* 睡虎地秦墓竹簡 (Beijing: Wenwu, 1978). A translation is available in A. F. P. Hulsewé, *Remnants of Ch'in Law* (Leiden: E. J. Brill, 1985).

21. *Shuihudi*, pp. 281–93.

22. *Shuihudi*, pp. 26–27, 181, 182, 183, 261–62, 263.

23. Donald Harper, "Iatromancy, Prognosis, and Diagnosis in Early Chinese Medicine" (Paper delivered at the Lu Gwei-Djen Memorial Workshop 'Innovation in Chinese Medicine,' Needham Research Institute, Cambridge, England, March 8–11, 1995), pp. 5–11. Similar arguments will appear in Professor Harper's forthcoming chapter in *The Cambridge History of Ancient China*.

24. Harper, "A Chinese Demonography," pp. 470–98.

25. Shirakawa, *Kōkotsu*, pp. 328–29; Harper, "Demonography," pp. 471–79; Katrina McLeod and Robin Yates, "Forms of Ch'in Law," *Harvard Journal of Asiatic Studies* 41:1 (1981), note 57, where they discuss the use of legal terms in a religious context in the story of Bozong in the *Zuo zhuan*. See *Zuo zhuan zhu* Cheng 5,

pp. 822–23. See also *Guo yu* 國語 (Shanghai: Guji, 1978) "Jin yu 晉語 5," pp. 405–06.

26. *Yunmeng Shuihudi Qin mu* 雲夢睡虎地秦墓 (Beijing: Wenwu, 1981) strips 827 verso–814 verso; 886–895. See Kudō Moto'o 江藤元男, "Suikochi Shin bo chikkan 'nissho' ni tsuite 睡虎地秦墓竹簡日書について," *Shiteki* 史滴 (Tokyo: Waseda Daigaku, 1986), pp. 36ff; A. F. P. Hulsewé, "The Wide Scope of Tao 盜 'Theft' in Ch'in-Han Law," *Early China* 13 (1988): 182–83; Robin Yates, "Some Notes on Ch'in Law," *Early China* 11–12 (1985–1987): 245.

27. *Shuihudi*, pp. 92, 93–94, 101–02, 102–03, 103, 136–47; Du, *Bian hu qi min*, pp. 317–72; Lewis, *Sanctioned Violence*, pp. 61–64.

28. *Shuihudi*, pp. 97, 113–14, 114–15, 115–16, 116–17, 117–18, 120, 121, 121–122, 122, 123, 123–24, 125, 125–26, 127–29, 130–31, 131–32, 132–33, 133–35, 136, 136–37, 137, 138, 138–39, 140–41, 142, 148; Hulsewé, *Remnants*, p. 18.

29. *Shuihudi*, pp. 122, 139, 143–44, 144–45, 145–46.

30. Hulsewé, *Remnants*, pp. 14–18; Liu Hainian 刘海年, "Qin lü xingfa kaoxi 秦律刑罚考析," in *Yunmeng Qin jian yanjiu* 云梦秦简研究 (Beijing: Zhonghua, 1981), pp. 171–206.

31. Hulsewé, *Remnants*, pp. 14–18.

32. Although he does not not discuss the Qin laws, Jean Levi makes a similar argument regarding the organization of the bureaucracy in the *Zhou li*. See Levi, *Les fonctionnaires divins*, pp. 229–34.

33. Du, *Bian hu qi min*, pp. 318–32.

34. *Guo yu*, "Zhou yu xia 周語下," pp. 103–04; *Zuo zhuan zhu*, Yin 8, pp. 60–62; Vandermeersch, *Wang dao*, vol. 1, ch. 4; Akatsuka, *Chūgoku kodai no shūkyō to bunka*; Li Xueqin 李学勤, "Kaogu faxian yu gudai xing shi zhidu 考古发现与古代姓氏制度," *Kaogu* (1987:3):253–57, 241; Ma Yong 馬雍, "Zhongguo xing shi zhidu de yange 中国姓氏制度的沿革," *Zhongguo wenhua yanjiu jikan*, vol. 2 (Shanghai: Fudan University, 1985), p. 166; Allen J. Chun, "Conceptions of Kinship and Kingship in Classical Chou China," *T'oung Pao* 76 (1990): 16–48.

35. Du, *Bian hu qi min*, pp. 22–33.

36. Sun Jingming 孙敬明, Li Jian 李剑, and Zhang Longhai 张龙海, "Linzi Qi gucheng nei wai xin faxian de taowen 临淄齐古城内外新发现的陶文," *Kaogu* (1988:2): 83–87; Luo Fuyi 罗福颐, ed., *Guxi huibian* 古玺汇编 (Beijing: Wenwu, 1981).

37. *Shuihudi*, pp. 247–49. Most of the examples in this section of the Qin laws also indicate the need to record name and rank. *Baoshan chu jian*, pp. 17–39.

38. *Zhan guo ce* 戰國策 (Shanghai: Guji, 1978) "Qin 1," p. 115; "Qi 2," pp. 350, 351; "Yan 3," pp. 1134, 1138; *Xunzi jijie* 荀子集解, annotated by Wang Xianqian 王先謙, in *Xin bian zhuzi jicheng* 新編諸子集成, vol. 2 (Taipei: Shijie, 1974) 4 "Rong ru 榮辱," p. 37 ; 8 "Ru xiao 儒效," pp. 73 (2), 74; 9 "Wang zhi 王制," p. 111; 18 "Zheng lun 正論," p. 215; *Shi ji* 史記 (Beijing: Zhonghua, 1959) 53, p. 2014; *Han Feizi jishi* 韓非子集釋, annotated by Chen Qiyou 陳奇猷 (Shanghai: Renmin, 1974) 49 "Wu du 五蠹," p. 1067.

39. *Shi ji* 86, pp. 2532, 2534.

40. *Zuo zhuan zhu*, Xiang 25, pp. 1106–07; *Guanzi jiaozheng* 管子郊正, annotated by Dai Wang 戴望 in *Xinbian zhuzi jicheng* 新編諸子集成, vol. 5 (Taipei: Shijie, 1974), 17 (53 "Jin cang 禁藏"), p. 292; *Lü shi chun qiu jiaoshi* 呂氏春秋校釋, annotated by Chen Qiyou (Shanghai: Xuelin, 1984), "Ji dong 季冬," p. 616; *Shi ji*, p. 289; Sichuan Sheng Bowuguan 四川省博物馆 and Qingchuan Xian Wenhuaguan 青川县文化馆, "Qingchuan Xian chutu Qin geng xiu tian lü mudu 青川县出土秦更修田律木牍," *Wenwu* (1982:1): 11. The text is transcribed and discussed in Yu Haoliang 于豪亮, "Shi Qingchuan xian Qin mu mudu 释青川县秦墓木牍," *Wenwu* (1982:1): 22–24. It is discussed in Steven F. Sage, *Ancient Sichuan and the Unification of China* (Albany: SUNY, 1992), pp. 131–33; Hulsewé, *Remnants of Ch'in Law*, pp. 211–15. Laws on land are also mentioned as a category on one of the wooden "tables of contents" found in the early Han tomb at Yinqueshan in Shandong, although the relevant strips have yet to be reassembled. See Wu Jiulong 吴九龙, ed., *Yinqueshan Han jian shi wen* 银雀山汉简释文 (Beijing: Wenwu, 1985), p. 231.

41. Li Xueqin 李学勤, "Fangmatan jian zhong de zhiguai gushi 放马滩简中的志怪故事," *Wenwu* (1990:4): 43–47; Donald Harper, "Resurrection in Warring States Popular Religion," *Taoist Resources* 5:2 (December, 1994):13–28.

42. On the stories from the *Mozi* and the *Guo yu*, see Jeffery K. Riegel, "Koumang and Ju-shou," *Cahiers d'Extrême-Asie: Special Issue, Taoist Studies II* 5 (1989–90): 57–66; *Huainanzi* 淮南子, in *Xinbian zhuzi jicheng*, vol. 7 (Taipei: Shijie, 1974), p. 119. On the Chu silk manuscript, see Noel Barnard, *The Ch'u Silk Manuscript* (Canberra: Australian National University, 1973), pp. 207–10.

43. *Shuihudi*, pp. 246–47.

44. Hubei Sheng Jingsha Tielu Kaogu Dui 湖北省荆沙铁路考古队, *Baoshan Chu jian* 包山楚简 (Beijing: Wenwu, 1991). Pages 9–12 give a summary of the contents of the strips related to legal matters.

45. *Zuo zhuan zhu*, Xiang 10, pp. 983–84. This case is used in Jia Gongyan's commentary to the *Zhou li* to demonstrate the use of written accusations. See *Zhou li zhushu* 周禮注疏 (Shisan jing zhushu edition) 34 "Da si kou 大司寇," p. 15b.

46. *Zuo zhuan zhu*, Xiang 29, p. 1155; *Shi ji*, pp. 227, 2412, 2416, 2428; *Zhan guo ce* "Qin 3," p. 220, "Zhao 3," p. 699, "Hann 2," p. 972; *Han Feizi jishi*, "Shuo lin shang 說林上," p. 419, "Wai chu shuo zuo xia 外儲說左下," pp. 694, 709; *Lü shi chun qiu jiaoshi* "Zhi yi 執一," p. 1133. For archeological evidence of seals, see Li Xueqin, *Eastern Zhou and Qin Civilizations*, trans. K. C. Chang (New Haven: Yale University), pp. 399–417.

47. *Shi ji*, pp. 227, 2380–81; Wang Guowei 王國維, *Guan tang ji lin* 觀堂集林, 2nd ed. rev. (Beijing: Zhonghua, 1959), 18 "Qin Xinqi hu fu ba," p. 11a; Li, *Eastern Zhou and Qin Civilizations*, pp. 235–37. The best known "tallies" (*jie* 節) pertaining to crossing border passes are the famous *E jun qi jie* 鄂君啓節. These contained long inscriptions inlaid in gold that permitted the holder to pass specified frontier posts without paying transit tax, and also gave details of communication

routes on land and water. See Guo Moruo, "Guanyu E jun qi jie de yanjiu 关於鄂君启节的研究," *Wenwu* (1958:4): 3–6; Yin Difei 殷涤非 and Luo Zhangming 罗长铭, "Shouxian chutu de E jun qi jie 寿县出土的鄂君启节," *Wenwu* (1958:4): 8–11; Li Xueqin, *Eastern Zhou and Qin Civilizations*, pp. 167, note 42, 168. On "matching tallies" with spirits, see *Shi ji*, p. 6. On tallies in Taoism, see *Zhuangzi jishi* 莊子集釋, annotated by Guo Qingfan 郭慶藩, in *Xin bian zhuzi jicheng*, vol. 3, "De chong fu 德充符," pp. 85–100; *Laozi dao de jing zhu* 老子道德經注, annotated by Wang Bi 王弼, in *Xin bian zhuzi jicheng*, vol. 3, 79, p. 46.

48. Lewis, *Sanctioned Violence*, pp. 23, 126.

49. On annual reports and contractual "tallies" see *Xunzi jijie*, 11 "Wang ba 王霸," p. 146; 12 "Jun dao 君道," p. 151; *Shang jun shu zhuyi* 商君書注譯, annotated by Gao Heng 高亨 (Beijing: Zhonghua, 1974), "Quqiang 去强," pp. 109, 113–14; "Jin shi 禁使," p. 497; *Guanzi jiaozheng*, 8 "Xiao kuang 小匡," p. 124; *Zhou li zhushu*, 2 "Da zai 大宰," pp. 24a–b; 3 "Xiao zai 小宰," p. 10a; 7 "Si shu 司書," p. 2a; *Mozi jiangu* 墨子間詁, annotated by Sun Yirang 孫詒讓, in *Xin bian zhuzi jicheng*, vol. 6, 70 "Hao ling 號令," p. 363; *Han Feizi jishi* 14 "Wai chu shuo shang 外儲說上," p. 284; 15 "Nan er 難二," p. 835; *Jing fa* 經法 (Beijing: Wenwu, 1976) "Xing shou 行守," p. 80. Such "contract tallies" may also have been used in legal documents, see *Zhou li zhushu* 35 "Chao shi 朝士," p. 22b; 14 "Si shi 司市." On tallies in contracts, see Zhang Chuanxi 张传玺, *Qin Han wenti yanjiu* 秦汉问题研究 (Beijing: Beijing Daxue, 1985), pp. 140–50, 167–208; Lao Kan, "The Early Use of the Tally in China," in *Ancient China: Studies in Early Civilization*, ed. David Roy and Tsuen-hsuin Tsien (Hong Kong: Chinese University, 1978), pp. 91–98.

50. *Zuo zhuan zhu*, Xiang 10, pp. 983–84; *Zhou li zhushu* 43, "Da si kou," pp. 15a–b.

51. *Shuihudi Qin mu zhu jian*, pp. 55–57.

52. On the links of coinage and law, and the ties of the former and of seals to royal or tyrannical authority, see Richard Seaford, *Reciprocity and Ritual: Homer and Tragedy in the Developing City-State* (Oxford: Clarendon Press, 1994), pp. 199–206; Steiner, *The Tyrant's Writ*, pp. 159–66. On the insistence on numerical calculation as the basis of punishments, see *Xunzi jijie*, "Jie bi 解蔽," p. 262; *Han Feizi jishi*, "You du 有度," p. 87, "Jian jie shi chen 姦劫弒臣," pp. 246, 250, 251, "Shi xie 飾邪," p. 308, "Wen tian 問田," pp. 903, 904; *Shang Jun shu zhuyi*, "Cuo fa 錯法," pp. 231, 234, "Shang xing 賞刑," p. 351, "Jin shi," pp. 490, 491; *Guanzi jiaozheng* "Qi chen qi zhu 七臣七主," p. 285.

53. On ranking officials through salaries measured in grain, see *Lun yu zhengyi* 論語正義, annotated by Liu Baonan 劉寶楠 and Liu Gongmian 劉恭冕, in *Xin bian zhu zi jicheng*, vol. 1, "Yong ye 雍也," p. 115; *Mengzi zhengyi* 孟子正義, annotated by Jiao Xun 焦循, in *Xin bian zhuzi jicheng*, vol. 1, "Gongsun Chou xia 公孫丑下," p. 175; *Mozi jiangu* "Gui yi 貴義," pp. 269–70; *Shi ji*, pp. 231, 1840, 1919; *Zhan guo ce* "Qi 4," p. 420, "Yan 1," p. 1059; *Han Feizi jishi* "Wai chu shuo you xia 外儲說右下," p. 776, "Ding fa 定法," p. 907; *Zhuangzi jishi*, 27 "Yu yan 寓言," p.

410; 28 "Rang wang 讓王," p. 419. On gifts in metal and coin, see *Shi ji*, p. 1797; *Zhan guo ce* "Wei 1," p. 784. For an introduction to types of Warring States period coins, see Li Xueqin, *Eastern Zhou and Qin Civilizations*, pp. 371–98.

54. Hou Ching-lang, *Monnaies d'offrandes et la notion de trésorerie dans la religion chinoise* (Paris: Collège de France Institut des Hautes Etudes Chinoises, 1975), pp. 3–5; Anna Seidel, "Buying One's Way to Heaven: The Celestial Treasury in Chinese Religions," *History of Religions* 17:3–4 (Feb.–May 1978): 419–31.

55. For a recent survey of surviving examples of such "money trees" and textual passages related to their significance, see Susan N. Erickson, "Money Trees of the Eastern Han Dynasty," *Bulletin of the Museum of Far Eastern Antiquities* 66 (1994): 1–116.

56. See *Extrême-Orient—Extrême-Occident* 15: *Le juste nom* (1993); John Makeham, *Name and Actuality in Early Chinese Thought* (Albany: SUNY, 1994), chs. 2–4.

57. *Lun yu zhengyi*, "Zi Lu 子路," pp. 280–83, "Yan Yuan 顏淵," p. 271, "Yong ye," p. 129; "Ji Shi 季氏," p. 364; "Zi Lu," p. 291.

58. *Lü shi chun qiu jiao shi*, "Li Wei 離謂," pp. 1177, 1178, "Yin ci 淫辭," p. 1187, "Bu qu 不屈," pp. 1196–98, "Ying yan 應言," p. 1210; *Zuo zhuan zhu*, Ding 9, pp. 1571–72; *Han shu* 漢書 (Beijing: Zhonghua, 1962), p. 1736; *Zhuangzi jishi*, "Tian dao 天道," pp. 209, 210, 211. For a study of the fragments attributed to Deng Xi, see Helmut Wilhelm, "Schriften und Fragmente zur Entwicklung der staatsrechtlichen Theorie in der Chou-Zeit," *Monumenta Serica* 12:5 (1947): 41–96.

59. *Zhan guo ce*, "Zhao er," p. 646. An earlier use of the term, of uncertain relation to its later political usage, appears in the *Sunzi bing fa*. See *Shiyi jia zhu Sunzi* 十一家注孫子 (Shanghai: Guji, 1978), p. 97. Robin Yates has argued that the political use derives from the military, but the connection is not obvious. See Yates, "New Light on Ancient Chinese Military Texts: Notes on Their Nature and Evolution, and the Development of Military Specialization in Warring States China," *T'oung Pao* 74 (1988): 220–22.

60. Hsiao-po Wang and Leo S. Chang, *The Philosophical Foundations of Han Fei's Political Theory*, Monograph no. 7 of the Society for Asian and Comparative Philosophy (Honolulu: University of Hawaii, 1986), pp. 59–60; Vandermeersch, *Wang dao*, vol. II, pp. 451–52. The character 刑 is used in the sense of "punishment," in *Xunzi jijie*, "Zheng ming 正名," p. 274; *Shi ji*, pp. 261 (the stone inscription of the First Emperor at Kuaiji), 2227. On this inscription, see Kanaya Osamu 金谷治, *Shin Kan shisō shi kenkyū* 秦漢思想史研究, 2nd ed. rev. (Kyoto: Heirakuji, 1981), p. 34. Makeham rejects any anterior sense of "punishment," despite the above passages and the fact that the *Han Feizi* links *xing ming* to correct punishments. See Makeham, *Name and Actuality*, pp. 70, 218 note 23. On the links of punishment and *xing ming* in the *Han Feizi*, see *Han Feizi jishi*, "Zhu dao 主道," p. 68, "Gui shi 詭使," p. 940. Indeed Makeham's assertion does not account for the data he actually presents. He acknowledges that the term existed prior to the *Han Feizi* in intellectual circles that used it in a different manner (Makeham, pp. 69–70), that there was an existing discourse on the relation of names to actuality

which employed the pair *ming shi* 名實 (Makeham, chs. 3–4), and that there are other words (*shi* 事, *gong* 功) in Chinese that would be more commonly used in the role played by 形 in his explanation of the term (Makeham, pp. 74–75, especially the chart on p. 75). This clearly indicates that the term emerged earlier—in writings of the "School of Names" or military treatises—with a distinct meaning, was adopted in the *Han Feizi* for the prestige of the term, and that it was adapted to the "name-actuality" context to provide a "legalist" alternative in one of the most widely discussed questions of philosophy.

61. *Han Feizi jishi*, "Wai chu shuo zuo shang," p. 629.

62. *Han Feizi jishi*, "Nei chu shuo shang 內儲說上," p. 568.

63. Jean Levi, "Quelques aspects de la rectification des noms dans la pensée et la pratique politique de la Chine ancienne," *Extrême-Orient—Extrême-Occident* 15 (1993): 42–43, 23–25.

64. Makeham, *Name and Actuality*, pp. 73–74. Warring States writers used *ming* "name" in the sense of "word." See A. C. Graham, *Disputers of the Tao* (LaSalle: Open Court, 1989), pp. 150–55 and *passim*.

65. *Han Feizi jishi*, "Zhu dao," p. 68, "Ba jing 八經," p. 1029, *Lü shi chun qiu*, "Shen ying 審應," p. 1141; *Shenzi* 申子, quoted in *Qun shu zhi yao* 群書治要 (SPTK), 36 "Da ti 大體," p. 26a.

66. *Han Feizi jishi*, "Zhu dao," pp. 67–69, "Er bing 二柄," pp. 111–12, "Yang quan 揚權," pp. 121–24; "An wei 安危," p. 484; "Wai chu shuo zuo shang," p. 663, "Nan er," pp. 830–31, "Gui shi," pp. 934–36, 940. This last uses *xing* in the sense of "punishments."

67. *Lun yu zhengyi*, 17 "Yang huo," p. 374.

68. *Guo yu*, "Lu yu xia 魯語下," pp. 201, 213. The early Han *Han shi wai zhuan* also has an account of the ability of the "Great *Ru*" to categorize and name all phenomena.

> As for marvelous creatures and strange transformations, things which he has never heard of or seen, when one suddenly arises somewhere he then takes up a controlling category [*tong lei* 統類] in order to respond to it without doubt or embarrassment. He takes up a model and measures it, exactly like matching the two parts of a tally.

Xu Weiyu 許維遹, ed., *Han shi wai zhuan ji shi* 韓詩外傳集釋 (Beijing: Zhonghua, 1980), pp. 172–73. See also Su Yu 蘇輿, ed., *Chun qiu fan lu yi zheng* 春秋繁露義證 (Taipei: Heluo, 1975) 5 "Zhong zheng 重政," pp. 11a–b.

69. *Zuo zhuan zhu*, Zhao 7, pp. 1289–90. See also Zhao 1, pp. 1217–21.

70. *Zuo zhuan zhu*, Xuan 3, pp. 669–70.

71. *Shan hai jing jiaozhu* 山海經校注, annotated by Yuan Ke 袁珂 (Shanghai: Guji, 1980), pp. 179–80, 472.

72. Donald Harper, "Wang Yen-shou's Nightmare Poem," *Harvard Journal of Asiatic Studies* 47:1 (1987): 240–41, 254–82.

73. *Han Feizi jishi*, p. 67. Versions of the phrase about names "being defined

of themselves" and affairs "settled of themselves" appear not only elsewhere in the *Han Feizi*, but also in other texts of the period. See *Han Feizi jishi*, "Yang quan," p. 121; *Jing fa*, "Dao fa 道法," p. 3, "Lun 論," pp. 29–30, "Untitled," p. 88; *Shenzi*, quoted in *Qun shu zhi yao*, 36 "Da ti," p. 26b; *Shizi* 尸子, quoted in *Qun shu zhi yao*, 36 "Fen 分," p. 15a; *Guanzi jiaozheng*, "Bai xin 白心," p. 24; *Huainanzi*, "Miu cheng 繆稱," pp. 153, 158; *Shi ji*, pp. 1637, 3292; *Jiazi xin shu jiaoshi* 賈子新書校釋, annotated by Qi Yuzhang 祁玉章 (Taipei: Qi Yuzhang, 1974) 8 "Dao shu 道術," p. 921.

74. *Jing fa*, pp. 1–2.

75. *Jing fa*, p. 39.

76. *Jing fa*, "Si du 四度," pp. 23, 24, "Lun," pp. 28–29, "Ming li 名理," pp. 41–42, "Li ming 立命," p. 45, "Guan 觀," pp. 48, 49–50; "Guo tong 果童," p. 57, "Zheng luan 正亂," pp. 60, 62, "Cheng fa 正法," p. 73, "Qian dao 前道," p. 80, "Xing shou 行守," p. 83, "Untitled," p. 88.

77. *Jing fa*, "Dao yuan 道原," pp. 101–02. A Daoist-inspired theory of ruling through names also figures prominently in the *He Guanzi*. See Carine Defoort, *The Pheasant Cap Master: A Rhetorical Reading* (Albany: SUNY, 1997), ch. 8–9.

78. Harold D. Roth, "Psychology and Self-Cultivation in Early Taoistic Thought," *Harvard Journal of Asiatic Studies* 51:2 (1991): 649.

79. *Guo yu*, "Chu yu xia 楚語下," pp. 559–60; *Han shu*, p. 1189.

80. *Guanzi jiaozheng*, "Nei ye," p. 268.

81. *Guanzi jiaozheng*, p. 270.

82. *Guanzi jiaozheng*, pp. 270–71.

83. Harold D. Roth, "Redaction Criticism and the Early History of Taoism," *Early China* 19 (1994): 1–46. On the development of the *Zhuangzi*, see pp. 5–7.

84. Graham, *Disputers*, pp. 186–92; *Zhuangzi jishi* 莊子集釋 2 "Qi wu lun 齊物論," pp. 21–22; 7 "Ying di wang 應帝王," p. 138.

85. *Xunzi jijie*, 21 "Jie bi," pp. 263–71. The *Shang jun shu* also discusses the model of the ruler who remains tranquil and spontaneously responds, only to reject it. See *Shang jun shu zhuyi* "Jin shi," p. 497.

86. *Xunzi jijie*, 1 "Quan xue 勸學," p. 4; 8 "Ru xiao 儒效," p. 91; 9 "Wang zhi 王制," p. 105; 15 "Yi bing 議兵," p. 184; 16 "Qiang guo 彊國," p. 194; 21 "Jie bi," p. 265; 23 "Xing e 性惡," p. 296.

87. Eske J. Møllgard, "Confucian Enlightenment," *Early China* 19 (1994): 153–58; Heiner Roetz, *Confucian Ethics of the Axial Age* (Albany: SUNY, 1993), ch. 12; David L. Hall and Roger T. Ames, *Thinking Through Confucius* (Albany: SUNY, 1987), pp. 165–67, 172, 190, 230–31, 248, 271–72.

88. Mark Edward Lewis, "The Sage as Master of Change" (Paper delivered at the Annual Meeting of the Association for Asian Studies, Washington, D.C., April 6–9, 1995).

89. *Shang jun shu zhuyi*, "Geng fa 更法," p. 10; *Han Feizi jishi*, "Wu du 五蠹," p. 1040; *Lü shi chun qiu jiaoshi*, "Cha jin 察今," p. 936. See also *Xunzi jijie* 25 "Cheng xiang 成相," p. 313, stanza 56.

90. Mark Edward Lewis, "Les rites comme trame de l'histoire," in *Notions et perceptions du changement en Chine*, ed., Viviane Alleton and Alexei Volkov (Paris: Collège de France, Institut des Hautes Etudes Chinoises, 1994), pp. 29–39.

91. Isabelle Robinet, "Des changements et de l'invariable," in *Mythe et philosophie à l'aube de la Chine impériale: études sur le Huainan zi*, ed., Charles Le Blanc and Rémi Mathieu (Montreal: Université de Montréal, 1992), pp. 3–13.

92. The major calendars of ritual and legal metamorphosis are the opening sections of the first twelve chapters of the *Lü shi chun qiu*, the "Yue ling" chapter of the *Li ji* (probably assembled from the *Lü shi chun qiu* during the Han), and chapter 5 of the *Huainanzi*. See also *Guanzi jiaozheng*, "Si shi 四時," pp. 238–41, "Wu xing 五行," pp. 242–44. For a sampling of the calendrical passages in the *Huangdi si jing*, see Lewis, *Sanctioned Violence*, pp. 316–17, note 140.

93. The texts of some of the inscriptions are transcribed in *Shi ji* 6, pp. 242–52, 260–62.

94. Keightley, "The Late Shang State," pp. 548–58.

95. Ogura Yoshihiko 小倉芳彥, *Chūgoku kodai seiji shisō kenkyū* 中國古代政治思想研究 (Tokyo: Aoki, 1970), pp. 62–73.

96. *Shi ji* 6, pp. 241–52, 256, 260–64; 28, pp. 1366–69.

97. On the sacred role of mountains, the sacrifices at Mount Tai, and the role of written communication in the ceremonies, see Mark Edward Lewis, "The *Feng* and *Shan* Sacrifices of Emperor Wu of the Han," in *Imperial Ritual in East Asia*, ed. Joseph McDermott (Cambridge: Cambridge University, in press).

98. The religious background of this theme is discussed in David Hawkes, "The Quest of the Goddess," in *Studies in Chinese Literary Genres*, ed. Cyril Birch (Berkeley: University of California, 1974), pp. 42–68.

99. *Shi ji* 117, pp. 3056–62; "Yuan you 遠游," in *Chu ci buzhu* 楚辭補注, annotated by Hong Xingzu 洪興祖 (SPTK ed.), 5. The two poems are closely related, although the nature of the relationship is disputed.

100. *Han Feizi jishi*, "Shi guo 十過," pp. 171–72.

101. Lewis, *Sanctioned Violence*, pp. 182, 187–94.

102. For a brief account of the text and current theories on its date of composition, see the discussion by William Boltz in Michael Loewe, ed., *Early Chinese Texts: a Bibliographic Guide* (Berkeley: Society for the Study of Early China and the Institute of East Asian Studies, 1993), pp. 25–29, 31–32. In addition to the works cited therein, see also Xu Fuguan 徐復觀, *Zhou guan chengli zhi shidai ji qi sixiang xingge* 周官成立之時代及其思想性格 (Taipei: Xuesheng, 1980). Xu defends, unconvincingly, the thesis that the work was forged by Liu Xiang, but he provides a useful discussion of its ideas and organization.

103. Notable exceptions are brief studies of the text by French scholars, who find in it invaluable testimony on the *mentalités et structures* of the period. See Vandermeersch, *Wang dao*, vol. II, chapter 24; Levi, *Les fonctionnaires divins*, pp. 229–34.

104. In his critique of the authenticity of the *Zhou guan*, Charles de Harlez emphasized the implausibility of many of the offices described in the text. Thus he

questions the probability of having officers specializing in the interpretation of dreams; the names, flora, and fauna of mountains and of streams; the expulsion of worms through oral curses; the destruction of nests of inauspicious birds; the purgation of ring worm, and so on. He also emphasizes the sheer number of offices in contrast to those of other sources. See Harlez, "Le Tcheou-li et le Shan-hai-king, leur origine et leur valeur historique," *T'oung Pao* 5 (1894): pp. 15–32. For rebuttals of this last point, see Sven Broman, "Studies on the *Chou li*," *Bulletin of the Museum of Far Eastern Antiquities* 33 (1961): 1–89; Vandermeersch, *Wang dao*, vol. II, pp. 426–31.

105. On subsuming ritual under law, see the phrase *li fa* 禮法 in *Zhou li zhushu*, 3 "Xiao zai," p. 14b; 26 "Xiao shi 小史," p. 17b. On the chief minister controlling officials through law, see *Zhou li zhushu* 2 "Da zai," pp. 3a, 16a, 19a, 19b; 3 "Xiao zai," pp. 1a, 8a—this last stipulates that all sacrifices, court assemblies, and receptions of foreign dignitaries are controlled by law—26 "Da shi 大史," p. 11a. On public display of written laws for each department, see *Zhou li zhushu* 2 "Da zai," p. 16a; 10 "Da si tu 大司徒," p. 21b; 26 "Da shi," p. 12b; 29 "Da si ma 大司馬," p. 5a. Another account of the display of laws at the beginning of the year, in this case only to officials, appears in *Guanzi jiaozheng* 1 "Li zheng 立政," p. 11. On laws for land use, see 10 "Da si tu," pp. 3b, 8a, 9a, 10a, 17b; 13 "Zai shi 載師," p. 7a. On laws controlling funerals, see 26 "Da shi," p. 15b. On law for identifying demons, see 25 "Shi jin 視祲," pp. 4a–b. On divination, see *Zhou li zhushu* 24 "Da bu 大卜," p. 10a. The entire department under the "Da si kou" is devoted to legal administration, written codes, archives of covenants, and "bonds." It includes accounts of prisons, the making of legal accusations, and their adjudication—34 "Da si kou," pp. 14a–15a, 15a–b, 17b; 35 "Xiao si kou," pp. 2a, 5a; 35, all the different levels of 士, pp. 12a–b, 14a–b, 16a–b, 17a, 22a. Ch. 36 lists the varieties of punishments, the levels of prisons, and the uses of oaths. Punishments also appear in 10 "Da si tu," pp. 26a, 27a, 30a.

106. On the fundamental role of punishments, see *Zhou li zhushu* 2 "Xiao zai," p. 10b; 10 "Da si tu," p. 30a; 11 "Xiao si tu," pp. 5b, 12b; 14 "Si jiu 司救," pp. 9b–10a; "Si shi 司市," p. 18a; 26 "Da shi 大史," pp. 11a–12b; 34 "Da si kou," pp. 13a–15a; 35 "Xiao si kou," p. 7a; 36 "Si xing 司刑," p. 1a. On labor service and redemption for title holders, see 36 "Si li 司厲," pp. 9a–b. On awards of titles, see 3 "Xiao zai," p. 9a. The incorporation of "education" within "law" is marked by the repeated use of the phrase *jiao fa* 敎法. See 10 "Xiao si tu," p. 1a; 12 "Xiang dafu," p. 7a. On squads of five and ten with collective responsibility, see *Zhou li zhushu*, 10 "Da si tu," p. 22b; 11 "Xiao si tu," pp. 2b–3a; 12 "Zu shi 族師," pp. 13a–b; "Bi zhang 比長," p. 15a; 15 "Lin zhang 鄰長," p. 26a. Similar models of nested hierarchies of population appear in *Guanzi jiaozheng* 1 "Li zheng," p. 10; "Sheng ma 乘馬," p. 15; 8 "Xiao kuang," pp. 123–25.

107. On the grid of the fields and labor services see *Zhou li zhushu* 11 "Xiao si tu," pp. 5a–6a. On military service and rewards see 29, "Da si ma," pp. 7a–14a; 30 "Xing si ma 行司馬," pp. 1b–3b. The close relation between the institutions of

the *Zhou guan*, both administrative and cultic, and those of Qin led Tanaka Toshiaki 田中利明 to argue that the text was composed around the time of Qin's unification of China. See "Shūrai no seiritsu ni tsuite no ichi kōsatsu 周禮の成立について の一考察," *Tōhōgaku* 42 (August 1971): 15–31. For different reasons a similar conclusion was reached in Guo Moruo, "Zhou guan zhi yi 周官質疑," in *Jin wen congkao* 金文叢考, rev. ed. (Beijing: Renmin, 1954), pp. 49a–81b.

108. See Hayashi Taisuke 林泰輔, "Shūkan ni mietaru jinrin no kankei 周官に見えたる人倫の關系," in *Shina jōdai no kenkyū* 支那上代の研究 (Tokyo: Kōfūkan, 1927), pp. 335–45.

109. *Zhou li zhushu* 3 "Xiao zai 小宰," p. 5b; 7 "Si shu 司書," p. 1a; "Zhi nei 職內," p. 2b; "Nei zai 內宰," p. 11b; 10 "Da si tu," p. 1a; 11 "Xiao si tu," pp. 1b–2a; "Xiang shi 鄉師," pp. 13b–14a; 12 "Xiang dafu 鄉大夫," p. 1b; "Lü xu 閭胥," p. 14a; 13 "Lü shi 閭師," p. 16b; "Xian shi 縣師," p. 19a; 14 "Mei shi 媒氏," p. 13b—these registers were supposedly used to arrange marriages—22 "Zhong ren 冢人," p. 1a; "Mu ren 墓人," p. 4a; 30 "Si shi 司士," pp. 1a, 1b; "Si xian 司險," p. 12b; 33 "Shan shi 山師" and "Chuan shi 川師," pp. 22a–b; 35 "Da si kou," p. 6b; "Xiang shi 鄉士," pp. 12a–b; "Sui shi 遂士," pp. 14a–b; "Xian shi 縣士," pp. 16a–b; "Fang shi 方士," p. 17a.

110. *Zhou li zhushu* 10 "Xiao si tu," p. 30a; 11 "Xiang shi," p. 18b; 12 "Xiang dafu," p. 2b; "Zhou zhang 州長," pp. 8a, 11b; 13 "Xian shi," p. 19a; 14 "Jun ren 均人," p. 2a; 31 "Si shi," p. 6b.

111. The annual public display of laws by each department was cited earlier. In addition see *Zhou li zhushu* 12 "Xiang dafu," p. 5b; "Zhou zhang," pp. 6b, 7b; "Dang zheng 黨正," pp. 8b, 11a; 14 "Si jian 司諫," p. 8b; 26 "Da shi," p. 12b; 30 "Liang ren 量人," p. 6a; 35 "Xiao si kou," p. 2a; "Shi shi 士師," p. 7a; "Ya shi 訝士," p. 19b; 36 "Si yue 司約," pp. 3b–5a; "Si meng 司盟," pp. 5b–7a.

112. On the *Zhou guan* as a symbolic reproduction of the universe, and as a terrestrial administration doubling as a religious body, see Levi, *Les fonctionnaires divins*, pp. 229, 230. On the use of bureaucratic administration as a model of the world, see David L. Hall and Roger T. Ames, *Anticipating China* (Albany: SUNY, 1995), pp. 270–71.

113. *Zhou li zhushu* 2 "Zhong zai," p. 20a; 6 "Zhang ci 掌次," p. 10b; 10 "Da si tu," p. 28a; 13 "Chong ren 充人," p. 5b; 19 "Xiao zong bo 小宗佰," p. 1b; 34 "Da si kou," p. 18b; "Xiao si kou," p. 6a; 35 "Shi shi," p. 10b. On the five *di* as major gods in Qin, see *Lü shi chun qiu jiaoshi* 1 "Meng chun 孟春," p. 1; 4 "Meng xia 孟下," p. 185; 6 "Ji xia 季下," p. 311; 7 "Meng qiu 孟秋," p. 375; "Meng dong 孟冬," p. 515. Colors and directions associated with the five *di* are identical in both texts. Compare *Zhou li zhushu* 18 "Da zong bo," p. 24b.

114. *Zhou li zhushu* 2 "Da zai," pp. 1a–24b; 3 "Xiao zai," pp. 1a–11a.

115. *Zhou li zhushu* 4 "Shan fu 膳夫," pp. 1a, 4a, 4b; "Pao ren 庖人," pp. 6b, 7b, 8a; "Nei yong 內饔," pp. 10b, 12a–b; "Wai yong 外饔," pp. 13a–b, 14a; "Dian shi 甸師," pp. 14b–15a, 15b, 16a.

116. *Zhou li zhushu* 5 "Ling ren 凌人," pp. 19a, 20a; 6 "Mu ren 墓人," pp. 8b–9a; 7 "Si qiu 司裘," pp. 5b–11a.

117. *Zhou li zhushu* 12 "Zhou zhang," pp. 6b–7a. At both these ritual events the district chief was to read the laws to the people. On the use of the archery contest to select officiants for the suburban altar sacrifice, see *Li ji zhushu* 禮記注疏 (Shisan jing zhushu ed., vol. 5) 62 "She yi 射義," p. 12a.

118. *Zhou li zhushu* 12 "Feng ren 封人," pp. 16a–18b; "Gu ren 鼓人," pp. 19a–22b. On the use of the drum in the army to communicate orders and provide rhythm for collective action, see Lewis, *Sanctioned Violence*, pp. 105, 110, 112–14, 121, 145, 184, 226–28.

119. *Zhou li zhushu* 29 "Da si ma," pp. 8b, 12a, 13b, 15b, 20a–b, 23a–b.

120. *Zhou li zhushu* 30 "Liang ren," pp. 5b–7a; "Xiao zi 小子," pp. 7b–8b; "Fu bu shi 服不氏," p. 22b; "She niao shi 射鳥氏," p. 23a; "Luo shi 羅氏," pp. 23b–24a; "Zhang xu 掌畜," pp. 24a–b; 31 "Zhu zi 諸子," pp. 7a–8b; "Fang xiang shi," pp. 12a–b.

121. Although this chapter is the most questionable of those attributed to the reign of King Cheng, it is still probably earlier than any other list of titles that has survived. See the article "Shang shu," in Loewe, ed., *Early Chinese Texts*, p. 379. For lists of officials see *Shang shu zhengyi* 尚書正義, annotated by Kong Yingda 孔穎達 et al. (Shisan jing zhushu ed.), vol. 1, 17, pp. 15a, 16a–b, 20a–b, 26a. For tentative identifications of the offices listed, and a discussion of the idea that the Duke of Zhou created the Zhou government, see Gu Jiegang 顾颉刚, "'Zhou gong zhi li' de chuanshuo he 'Zhou guan' yi shu de chuxian 周公制礼的传说和周官一书的出现," *Wen shi* 6 (June, 1979): 1–4. The "Zhou guan" chapter also lists officers of Zhou, but this chapter is part of the "old script" forgery and hence lies outside our period.

122. For the dating of this text and a list of the fragments, see Gu, "Zhou gong zhi li," p. 7.

123. *Mengzi zhengyi* 10 "Wan zhang xia 萬章下," pp. 398–99.

124. *Xunzi jijie*, 9 "Wang zhi," pp. 106–09. "On the Precedence of Offices *xu guan* 序官," appears to have been a separate essay that was inserted near the end of the chapter by some editor. See John Knoblock, tr., *Xunzi: a Translation and Study of the Complete Works*, vol. 2 (Stanford: Stanford University, 1990), p. 93. There is also a passing reference to royal and feudal offices in 18 "Zheng lun 正論," p. 215.

125. *Li ji zhushu* 11 "Wang zhi," p. 1a. For a passage quoted directly from the *Mencius*, see p. 3a.

126. Graham, *Disputers*, pp. 315–70; A. C. Graham, *Yin-Yang and the Nature of Correlative Thinking* (Singapore: Institute of East Asian Philosophies, 1986).

127. *Zuo zhuan zhu*, Zhao 17, pp. 1386–88.

128. The most detailed account of this story is *Guo yu* "Chu yu xia 楚語下," pp. 559–64. See also *Shi ji*, p. 3295; *Han shu*, p. 1189.

129. Vandermeersch, *Wang dao*, vol. 1, pp. 221ff., 231ff., vol. II, pp. 435–36.

On the links of clouds to the myths of the Yellow Emperor, see Lewis, *Sanctioned Violence*, pp. 180–82.

130. *Guanzi jiaozheng* 41 "Wu xing," pp. 242–44.

131. Closely related to these, although later, is a passage in the "Qu li 曲禮" chapter of the *Li ji*. See *Li ji zhushu* 4 "Qu li xia," pp. 22b–23a. This contains lists of government offices, in multiples of "six" and "five."

132. Nemoto Makoto 跟本誠, *Jōdai Shina hōsei no kenkyū* 上代支那法制の 研究 (Tokyo: Yūhikaku, 1941), pp. 180–206. On numerology in the structure of the *Zhou guan*, see also Vandermeersch, *Wang dao*, vol. II, pp. 427–28, 431–32.

133. *Zhou li zhushu* 1 "Tian guan 天官," pp. 1b–4b; 2 "Da zai," p. 1a; 9 "Di guan 地官," p. 1a; 10 "Da si tu," p. 1a; 17 "Chun guan 春官," p. 1a; 18 "Da zong bo," p. 1a; 26 "Xia guan 夏官," p. 1a; 29 "Da si ma," p. 1a; 34 "Qiu guan 秋官," p. 1a; 35 "Da si kou," p. 1a.

134. Lothar von Falkenhausen, "Sources of Taoism: Reflections on Archaeological Indicators of Religious Change in Eastern Zhou China," *Taoist Resources* 5:2 (December, 1994): 4.

135. Levi, *Fonctionnaires divins*, pp. 257–63.

136. Hubei Sheng Wenwu Kaogu Yanjiusuo 湖北省文物考古研究所, ed., *Jiangling Jiudian Dong Zhou mu* 江陵九店東周墓 (Beijing: Kexueshe, 1995), p. 508; *Chu ci buzhu*, 2 "Guo shang 國殤," pp. 22b–24a.

137. *Zuo zhuan zhu*, Zhao 29, pp. 1502–04; Jean Levi, *Fonctionnaires divins*, pp. 228–29; Riegel, "Kou-mang and Ju-shou," pp. 73–76. This idea of divinity as an office carried forward into Han debates on ritual. See Fujikawa Masakazu 藤川 正數, *Kandai ni okeru reigaku no kenkyū* 漢代における禮學の研究 (Tokyo: Fūkan Shobō, 1968), pp. 62–74.

138. *Shi ji* 130, p. 3295; *Guo yu* "Chu yu xia 楚語下," pp. 559–64; *Zhuangzi jishi* 6 "Da zong shi 大宗師," pp. 112–13.

Chapter Two. Writing the Masters

1. Lewis, *Sanctioned Violence*, pp. 80, 88, 89–90; Masubuchi Tatsuo 增淵龍 夫, *Chūgoku kodai no shakai to kokka* 中國古代の社會と國家 (Tokyo: Kōbundō, 1962), pp. 49–136; Miyazaki Ichisada 宮崎定生, "Yūkyo ni tsuite 游俠について," in *Ajia shi kenkyū* アジア史研究, vol. 1 (Kyoto: Dōshōsha, 1957), pp. 131– 50; James J. Y. Liu, *The Chinese Knight Errant* (London: Routledge & Kegan Paul, 1967); T'ung-tsu Ch'ü, *Han Social Structure* (Seattle: University of Washington, 1972), pp. 161, 188–98, 232, 245–47; Lao Gan 勞榦, "Lun Han dai de youxia 論漢代 的游俠," in *Lao Gan xueshu lunwen ji* 勞榦學術論文集, vol. 2 (Taipei: Yiwen, 1976), pp. 1021–36; Tao Xisheng 陶希聖, *Bianshi yu youxia* 辨士與游俠 (Shanghai: Shangwu, 1933); Chen Shan 陈山, *Zhongguo wuxia shi* 中国武侠史 (Shanghai: Sanlian, 1992), Ch. 1.

2. *Han Feizi jishi* 19 "Wu du 五蠹," pp. 1057, 1058; "Xian xue 顯學," pp. 1091, 1095 (2). See also *Shi ji*, pp. 3181, 3184.

3. An account of the difficulties presented by a pile of loose strips appears in Wu Jiulong, *Yinqueshan Han jian shiwen*.

4. Chen Guying 陳鼓應, "Lun *Laozi* wan chu shuo zai kaozheng fangfa shang chang jian de miuwu 論老子晚出說在考證方法上常見的謬誤," *Daojia wenhua yanjiu*, vol. 4 (Shanghai: Guji, 1994), p. 417, citing Yu Jiaxi 余嘉錫, *Gu shu tong li* 古書通例.

5. Erik W. Maeder, "Some Observations on the Composition of the 'Core Chapters' of the *Mozi*," *Early China* 17 (1992): 27–28.

6. *Mengzi zhengyi* "Teng Wen gong xia 滕文公下," pp. 269 (3), 270; "Jin xin shang 盡心上," pp. 539–40; "Jin xin xia," p. 586.

7. The section on the schools in Liu Xin's catalog of the imperial collection calls each school a *jia* 家, but at the end he refers to them as *zhu zi* 諸子. It employs the phrase *zhu zi shi jia* 諸子十家. See *Han shu*, pp. 1724–46. Earlier texts use the character *bai* 百 "hundred" rather than 諸.

8. *Xunzi jijie* 1 "Quan xue 勸學," pp. 7, 8–9, 10; 14 "Zhi shi 致士," p. 175. A few anecdotes present evidence of reading silently or alone. See *Zhuangzi jishi*, 13 "Tian dao 天道," pp. 217–18; *Zhan guo ce* "Qin 1," p. 85; *Shi ji* 69, pp. 2241–42. The practice, however, appears exceptional.

9. Scholars have recognized for centuries that the *Lun yu* was produced by accretion over a long period of time, and attempts have been made to separate strata. Important modern studies include Kimura Eiichi 木村英一, *Kōshi to rongo* 孔子と論語 (Tokyo: Sōbunsha, 1971); Takeuchi Yoshio 武內義雄, *Rongo no kenkyū* 論語の研究 (Tokyo: Iwanami, 1940); Tsuda Sōkichi 津田左右, *Rongo to Kōshi no shisō* 論語と孔子の思想 (Tokyo: Iwanami, 1946). For a presentation of the scholarly consensus, see Steven Van Zoeren, *Poetry and Personality: Reading, Exegesis, and Hermeneutics in Traditional China* (Stanford: Stanford University, 1991), pp. 19–28, 34–44. In a recent article E. Bruce Brooks attempted to assign years of composition to some chapters, but the evidence offered was insufficient. See Brooks, "The State of the Field in Pre-Han Text Studies," *Sino-Platonic Papers*, 46 (July, 1994), pp. 31–40.

10. For a discussion of the disciples as a group and as individuals, see H. G. Creel, *Confucius and the Chinese Way* (New York: Harper & Row, 1960), pp. 29–36; D. C. Lau, tr., *Confucius: The Analects* (Harmondsworth: Penguin, 1979), Appendix 2, pp. 196–219.

11. On sacrifices to Confucius, see *Lun yu zhengyi* 7 "Shu er 述而," p. 152; 9 "Zi han 子罕," p. 184. On three-year mourning, see *Mengzi zhengyi* "Teng Wen gong shang," p. 231. For passages indicating the closeness and long-lasting nature of the emotional ties, see Robert Eno, *The Confucian Creation of Heaven* (Albany: SUNY, 1990), pp. 46, 54–55. Given the emphasis on family relations in the Confucian school, this assimilation of the teacher-disciple relation to that of father and son is not surprising.

12. Brooks, "The State of the Field," p. 38.

13. On the term and its relation to the "Confucian" school, see Graham, *Disputers*, pp. 31–33; Creel, *Confucius*, pp. 171–72, 173. More detailed discussions

appear in Feng Youlan 馮友蘭, *Zhongguo zhexue shi bu* 中國哲學史補 (Shanghai: Shangwu, 1936), pp. 1–61; Hu Shi 胡適, "Shuo ru 說儒," in *Hu Shi lun xue jin zhu*, vol. 1 (Shanghai: Shangwu, 1935), pp. 3–81. Eno in his *Confucian Creation of Heaven* presents a distinctive interpretation of the term.

14. *Zhuangzi jishi* 33 "Tian xia 天下," p. 462. This passage likewise refers to the "Hundred Schools," but describes them individually as "masters."

15. On "enunciation" as the process whereby language is produced, "utterance of enunciation" as the language situation implied by the structure of the narrative—indications of quotation, pronouns, deixis, and so on—and the "communication situation" as the "real," lived scene in which the language was produced, see Emile Benveniste, *Problèmes de linguistique générale* (Paris: Gallimard, 1966), pp. 251f., 258f.; Benveniste *Problèmes de linguistique générale*, vol. 2 (Paris: Gallimard, 1974), pp. 68f., 72f., 81f.; A. J. Greimas and J. Courtès, *Sémiotique: Dictionnaire raisonné de la théorie du langage* (Paris: Hachette, 1979), pp. 94, 125f.; Tzvetan Todorov, "Problèmes de l'énonciation," *Langages* 17 (1970): 4. An interesting attempt to apply these concepts to the narrative scene in early Greek poetry appears in Claude Calame, *Le récit en Grèce ancienne* (Paris: Méridiens Klincksieck, 1986).

16. One might argue that the master in life derived his authority from the power of his visions or arguments, and that the disciples preserved the master in the text as a permanent ground of the teaching. However, the need to have a master as a ground or origin suggests that doctrine or vision was not thought to be detachable from embodiment in a master as proclaimed by disciples.

17. Van Zoeren, *Poetry and Personality*, pp. 32–35.

18. *Han Feizi jishi* 50 "Xian xue," p. 1080.

19. See the entry on the *Lun yu* in Loewe, ed., *Early Chinese Texts*, pp. 315–16.

20. *Lun yu zhengyi* 18 "Weizi," pp. 390–95; *Zhuangzi jishi* 4 "Ren jian shi 人間世," pp. 83–85; 12 "Tian di 天地," pp. 193–96.

21. Wu Yujiang 吳毓江, *Mozi jiaozhu* 墨子校注, reprinted in *Mozi jicheng* 墨子集成, ed. Yan Lingfeng 嚴靈峰 (Taipei: Chengwen, 1975), vol. 43–44, appendix; Alfred Forke, *Me Ti des Sozialethikers und seiner Schuler philosophische Werke* (Berlin: 1922), pp. 5–15; Stephen W. Durrant, "An Examination of Textual and Grammatical Problems in Mo-tzu," (Ph.D. diss., University of Washington, 1975), pp. 45–90; A. C. Graham, *Later Mohist Logic, Ethics and Science* (London: SOAS and Hong Kong: Chinese University, 1978); Robin Yates, "The City Under Siege: Technology and Organization as Seen in the Reconstructed Text of the Military Chapters of Mo-tzu," (Ph.D. diss., Harvard University, 1980); Yates, "The Mohists on Warfare: Technology, Techniques, and Justification," *Journal of the American Academy of Religion* Thematic Studies Supplement 47:3 (1980): 549–603.

22. Durrant, "An Examination of Textual and Grammatical Problems," pp. 317–18.

23. A. C. Graham, *Divisions in Early Mohism Reflected in the Core Chapters of Mo-tzu* (Singapore: Institute of East Asian Philosophies, 1985); Graham, *Disputers*, pp. 51–53.

24. Maeder, "'Core Chapters' of the *Mozi*," pp. 27–82. On the distinction of *pian* and *ce*, see Tsien Tsuen-hsuin, *Written on Bamboo and Silk: The Beginnings of Chinese Books and Inscriptions* (Chicago: University of Chicago, 1962), p. 109.

25. Maeder, "Core Chapters of the *Mozi*," pp. 54, 58, 63, 68, 74–75, 81–82. David Keegan has shown a similar process of constructing chapters of the *Huangdi nei jing* from a common body of smaller, coherent texts. See David Joseph Keegan, "The 'Huang-ti nei-ching': The Structure of the Compilation; The Significance of the Structure" (Ph.D. diss., University of California, Berkeley, 1988).

26. *Han Feizi jishi* 50, "Xian xue," p. 1080; *Lü shi chun qiu jiaoshi* 2 "Dang ran 當染," p. 96; 4 "Zun shi 尊師," p. 205.

27. Guan Feng 關鋒, *Zhuangzi neipian yijie he pipan*莊子內篇譯解和批判 (Beijing: Zhonghua, 1961); Guan, "Zhuangzi wai za pian chutan 莊子外雜篇初探," in *Zhuangzi zhexue taolun ji* 莊子哲學討論集 (Beijing: Zhonghua, 1962); A. C. Graham, "How Much of *Chuang Tzu* did Chuang Tzu Write?" in *Studies in Chinese Philosophy and Philosophical Literature* (Singapore: Institute of East Asian Philosophies, 1986), pp. 283–321; Liu Xiaogan 劉笑敢, *Zhuangzi zhexue ji qi yanbian* 莊子哲學及其演變 (Beijing: Zhongguo Shehui Kexue, 1988). The parts of this book that analyze the development of the text have been translated by William Savage. See Liu Xiaogan, *Classifying the Zhuangzi Chapters* (Ann Arbor: Center for Chinese Studies, University of Michigan, 1994).

28. For the argument that the text was compiled at the court of Liu An, by scholars in the tradition that Han authors called "Huang-Lao," see Harold Roth, "Who Compiled the *Chuang Tzu*?" in *Chinese Texts and Philosophical Contexts: Essays Dedicated to Angus C. Graham*, ed. Henry Rosemont, Jr. (LaSalle, Illinois: Open Court, 1991), pp. 79–128. It is interesting that Roth argues that those elements of the text that Graham describes as "Syncretist" in fact represent what Han writers called Huang-Lao. The same argument is made in the book by Liu Xiaogan noted above, which Roth does not cite.

29. Liu, *Classifying the Zhuangzi Chapters*, ch. 2. See also pp. 161–66, where as part of an "Afterword" added to the English edition, he criticizes Graham's scheme of dating, which was not available to him at the time of writing the original Chinese version.

30. Graham, *Chuang Tzu: The Inner Chapters*, p. 116—he postulates a "school" of Zhuangzi as a rubric for the Outer Chapters most closely related to the Inner Chapters; Donald J. Munro, "Foreword," in *Classifying the Zhuangzi Chapters*," p. x. Munro notes that Liu implies a Zhuangzi "school" when he divides the Outer Chapters into the products of "legitimate" and "illegitimate" branches, but no evidence is offered to substantiate such a division. See Liu, *Classifying the Zhuangzi Chapters*, pp. xvii, 137. In fact, even one story in the Outer Chapters notes the lack of disciples. See *Zhuangzi jishi* 21 "Tian Zifang 田子方," p. 313.

31. Liu, *Classifying the Zhuangzi Chapters*, p. 170; Munro, "Foreword," p. xix; Graham, *Chuang Tzu: The Inner Chapters*, p. 94. As Liu Xiaogan has noted, these stories all appear at the ends of their chapters, while stories of Zhuang Zhou in

later chapters appear at the beginning or in the middle. Thus the stories in the Inner Chapters are almost certainly later additions. See Liu, pp. 18–21.

32. For summaries of the Western consensus, see the entry on *Laozi* in Loewe, ed., *Early Chinese Texts*, pp. 269–71; Michael LaFargue, *Tao and Method: A Reasoned Approach to the Tao Te Ching* (Albany: SUNY, 1994), Chapter Twelve, note #1, pp. 589–91. The traditional date has been defended in essays published in the series *Daojia wenhua yanjiu*. The most notable essays are Chen Guying 陳鼓應, "Lun *Laozi* wan chu shuo zai kaozheng fangfa shang chang jian de miuwu—jian lun *Liezi* fei wei shu 論老子晚出說在考證方法上常見的謬誤——兼論列子非 偽書," *Daojia wenhua yanjiu* 4 (Shanghai: Guji, 1994), pp. 411–18; Liu Xiaogan 劉 笑敢, "*Laozi* zao chu shuo xin zheng 老子早出說新證," *Daojia wenhua yanjiu* 4, pp. 419–37; Li Xueqin 李學勤, "Shen lun *Laozi* de niandai 申論老子的年代," *Daojia wenhua yanjiu* 6, pp. 71–79. Chen's article attacks a middle or late Warring States date on three grounds: (1) he cites the account of Laozi's relation to Confucius in the *Shi ji* and the many references to such meetings in later Warring States texts, (2) he denies the conventional belief that "private" books produced in the schools began only at the end of the Spring and Autumn period, and (3) he insists that the whole range of late Warring States terms and ideas identified by earlier critics actually existed in the Spring and Autumn period. The first point has already been refuted by A. C. Graham in "The Origins of the Legend of Lao Tan," *Studies in Chinese Philosophy and Philosophical Literature*, pp. 111–24. The second is based on the implausible belief that the texts attributed to certain late Spring and Autumn political figures, texts now vanished, were actually written by them. The third point is asserted with no evidence. Liu's article is based on the demonstration that the rhythms and rhyme styles of the *Laozi* follow those of the *Shi jing*, rather than those of the *Chu ci*. A summary appears in the "Afterword" of *Classifying the Zhuangzi Chapters*, pp. 173– 84. This argument assumes that the appearance of poems in the "southern" style entailed the disappearance of the earlier *shi* forms. However, as Martin Kern has demonstrated, the temple hymns composed at the beginning of the Han dynasty used *Shi jing* style images, rhythms, and rhymes. Consequently, Liu's argument is based on incorrect assumptions. See Martin Kern, "In praise of political legiti- macy: the *miao* 廟 and *jiao* 郊 hymns of the Western Han" (Paper delivered at the Conference on State and Ritual in East Asia, Collège de France, Paris, June 28– July 1, 1995), pp. 7–19. Li's argument has two points. First, he insists that the *Huangdi si jing* develops themes in the *Laozi*, and hence must be later, and he accepts Tang Lan's assertion that the former text must have taken shape no later than 350 B.C. The first point is unproven but likely, but since many of the aphorisms in the *Laozi* existed before the text was put together, it proves nothing about dating. Tang Lan's dating of the *Huangdi si jing* is unproven. The second part of Li's argument is to try to demonstrate that certain passages in the *Lun yu* respond to points in the *Laozi*. The connections are not clear, the aphorisms existed prior to the text, and the passages cited come from later chapters of the *Lun yu*, which are almost certainly

no earlier than the fourth century. Thus the dating to the mid-fourth century or slightly later remains the most plausible.

33. LaFargue, *Tao and Method*, chs. 3–5, 7–12. See especially pp. 153–56 for discussions of evidence of school practices within the text. Apparently a similar model was developed in Victor H. Mair, tr., *Tao Te Ching* (New York: Bantam Books, 1990), but I have been unable to obtain a copy of this volume.

34. Some scholars have assigned a recently discovered chapter of the *Sunzi* featuring a dialogue between Sun Wu and the king of Wu to the late fifth century B.C. on the basis of an incorrect prophecy found in the text. For the relevant chapter, see *Shi yi jia zhu Sunzi* 十一家注孫子 (Shanghai: Guji, 1978), pp. 494–95. For an early date on the basis of the prophecy, see Yates, "New Light on Ancient Military Texts," pp. 217–18; Tay Lien-soo (Zheng Liangshu) 鄭良樹, "Lun *Sunzi* de zuo-cheng shidai 論孫子的作成時代, in *Zhujian boshu yanjiu* 竹簡帛書研究 (Beijing: Zhonghua, 1982), pp. 68–71; Wu Shuping 吳樹平, "Cong Linyi Han mu zhujian 'Wu wen' kan Sun Wu de fajia sixiang 从临沂汉墓竹简吴问看孙武的法家思想," *Wenwu* (1975:4): 6–7. Li Ling, however, has made a persuasive argument that the prophecy suggests a date of composition in the early third century B.C., and that the text as a whole was produced in the middle of the Warring states period. See Li Ling 李零, "Guanyu Yinqueshan jianben *Sunzi* yanjiu de shangque—*Sunzi* zhuzuo shidai he zuozhe de chongyi 關於銀雀山簡本孫子研究的商榷——孫子著作時代和作者的重議," *Wen shi* 7 (December, 1979): 23–24, reprinted in Li Ling, *Sunzi gu ben yanjiu* 孫子古本研究 (Beijing: Beijing Daxue, 1995), pp. 207–23, esp. p. 213. Consequently it is still likely that the examples in the *Mencius* are the earliest surviving dialogues between a scholar and ruler used as a mode of instruction.

35. Yates, "New Light on Ancient Military Texts," p. 230.

36. Graham, *Disputers of the Tao*, pp. 75–95, 137–70, 176–86, 261–67.

37. On the ideal of the "encyclopedia," with its twin virtues of infinite fruitfulness and closure, see Terence Cave, *The Cornucopian Text: Problems of Writing in the French Renaissance* (Oxford: Clarendon Press, 1979), ch. II.I, "Cornucopia."

38. Robert Eno, *The Confucian Creation of Heaven: Philosophy and the Defense of Ritual Mastery* (Albany: SUNY, 1990).

39. On not worrying about recognition, see *Lun yu zhengyi* 1 "Xue er 學而," pp. 3, 19; 4 "Li ren 里仁," pp. 78, 80; 7 "Shu er," p. 140; 13 "Zi Lu," p. 287; 14 "Xian wen 憲問," p. 320; 15 "Wei Ling Gong 衛靈公," p. 342. On Confucius repeatedly eschewing office, see 2 "Wei zheng 爲政," p. 36; 7 "Shu er," p. 142; 9 "Zi han," pp. 184–85; 18 "Wei zi 微子," p. 389 (2); *Mengzi zhengyi* "Wan Zhang xia 萬章下," pp. 396, 415–16; "Gao zi xia 告子下," p. 492.

40. *Lun yu zhengyi* 2 "Wei zheng," p. 36; 4 "Li ren," p. 76; 5 "Gongye Chang 公冶長," pp. 90, 92–93, 103–04; 6 "Yong ye," pp. 118–19; 8 "Tai bo 泰伯," pp. 154, 157, 162, 163; 11 "Xian jin 先進," pp. 250–51, 251; 14 "Xian wen," p. 300; 15 "Wei Ling Gong," pp. 335, 348; 17 "Yang Huo 陽貨," p. 377; 18 "Wei zi," pp. 386, 388, 395–97.

41. *Lun yu zhengyi* 8 "Tai Bo," pp. 155–56; 12 "Yan Yuan," pp. 268, 273, 274 (2), 275; 13 "Zi Lu," pp. 286, 291; 15 "Wei Ling Gong," p. 331.

42. *Lun yu zhengyi* 2 "Wei zheng," p. 34; 15 "Wei Ling Gong," p. 346; 17 "Yang Huo," pp. 366, 369–70, 371–72; 18 "Wei zi," p. 395. In a critical review of Eno's book, Henry Rosemont, Jr., takes the author to task for arguing that the *ru* had no real philosophy and were not interested in state service. The article is devoted almost entirely to the first point. To refute the latter he cites a single passage: "The Master said, 'If states are governable by ritual and deference, no more need be said about it. But if states cannot be so governed, of what use is ritual?'" This is not a call to serve the state, but to replace it with a totally different polity. In terms of Warring States government practice, it constitutes a rejection. See Rosemont, "The Dancing *Ru/Li* Masters," *Early China* 17 (1992), pp. 187–94. There are also passages that simply mention government service without criticism or endorsement. Finally 19 "Zi Zhang 子張," p. 405 argues that a student who can handle all his studies should take office; p. 407 Master Zeng tells a man appointed to be judge that since the government has long been corrupt, he must pity the people and take no joy in the proper execution of his role.

43. For "benevolence" as the single solution to all problems, see *Mengzi zhengyi* "Liang Hui Wang shang 梁惠王上," pp. 22, 32–35, 40–41 (this passage argues that if he will reduce taxes and lighten punishments, the ruler of a tiny state, whose army consists of peasants armed with staves, will be able to defeat the greatest powers of the age); "Liang Hui Wang xia," pp. 79, 84 (defence of nobility); "Gongsun Chou shang 公孫丑上," pp. 110, 130, 131, 134–36 (the abolition of taxes, with peasant labor on state lands providing all the state's income); "Gongsun Chou xia," pp. 152–53 (Mencius alone speaks to the king about benevolence); "Teng Wen Gong shang," pp. 196 (against punishments), 205, 211, 213 (the well-field system and collective labor); "Teng Wen Gong xia," pp. 253–56 (small states with benevolent kings will defeat great military powers); "Li Lou shang 離婁上," pp. 284, 289–90, 290 (in support of hereditary nobility), 292, 302 (quotes a story from the *Lun yu* in which Confucius denounces a disciple who increases tax revenue for his lord), 309; "Li Lou xia," p. 324; "Gaozi shang," p. 472; "Jin xin xia," pp. 579, 587.

In a passage perhaps aimed at the *Mencius*, the *Zhuangzi* has Confucius argue that it is useless to speak of Yao and Shun to the ruler of Qi. See *Zhuangzi jishi* 18 "Zhi le 至樂," pp. 273–74.

44. *Mengzi zhengyi* "Liang Hui Wang shang," pp. 40–41; "Gongsun Chou xia," pp. 148–50; "Li Lou shang," p. 293; "Jin xin xia," p. 566.

45. *Mengzi zhengyi* "Liang Hui Wang shang," pp. 44, 46; "Gongsun Chou shang," pp. 102–03; "Teng Wen Gong," pp. 244–46.

46. *Mengzi zhengyi* "Liang Hui Wang xia," pp. 95–96.

47. *Mengzi zhengyi* "Gongsun Chou shang," pp. 127–28, 144–45; "Teng Wen Gong xia," p. 251, 259–62; "Li Lou shang," p. 287, 312; "Li Lou xia," pp. 324, 357–58; "Wan Zhang xia," pp. 417–18, 430; "Gaozi shang," pp. 469–70; "Gaozi

xia," pp. 509–510; "Jin xin shang," pp. 533, 533–34, 543, 546, 548–49; "Jin xin xia," pp. 596–98 (this claims that all Mencius' actions are based on ancient institutions).

48. *Mengzi zhengyi* "Gongsun Chou xia," pp. 154, 183–84; "Wan Zhang xia," pp. 408–10, 424–26; "Jin xin shang," pp. 523–24. Michael LaFargue discusses several of these passages dealing with the high status of the scholar and his relation to the ruler as examples of what he calls the development of the "*shih*-idealist." See LaFargue, *Tao and Method*, pp. 74–90. However, since Mencius supported a large retinue from the gifts of precious metal and grain that he received from rulers, the extent of his "idealism" might be questioned. See *Mengzi zhengyi* "Gongsun Chou xia," pp. 155–56 (refers to three separate gifts), 162, 175 (here the ruler offers him a house and grain for Mencius' followers), 181–82; "Teng Wen Gong xia," pp. 251–52 (this refers to several hundred followers who live off princely generosity).

49. Benjamin I. Schwartz, *The World of Thought in Ancient China* (Cambridge: Harvard University, 1985), pp. 283–86.

50. For comparisons of kings, hegemons, and current rulers see *Xunzi jijie* 7 "Zhong Ni 仲尼," p. 68; 9 "Wang zhi," pp. 97–98, 99–100; 11 "Wang ba 王霸," pp. 133–34; 15 "Yi bing 議兵," pp. 181, 183. On refusal to serve or speak to a lesser ruler, and the virtue of opposition see 8 "Ru xiao," pp. 81, 93; 13 "Chen dao 臣道," pp. 166, 168. For condemnations of contemporary government, officials, and leading ministers, see 6 "Fei shier zi 非十二子," p. 63; 7 "Zhong Ni," p. 68; 9 "Wang zhi," pp. 98–99; 10 "Fu guo," p. 118; 13 "Chen dao," p. 165. On great *ru* as greater than kings, see 6 "Zhong Ni," pp. 60–91; 8 "Ru xiao," p. 87. On "Mencian" fiscal policy, see 9 "Wang zhi," p. 102; 11 "Wang ba," p. 149. On separation of rulers and scholars, see 11 "Wang ba," p. 142.

51. *Han Feizi jishi* 6 "You du 有度," p. 87 (refusal to take office); 13 "He Shi 和氏," p. 239; 43 "Ding fa," p. 906; 44 "Shuo yi 說疑," pp. 914, 918 (passage quoted); 45 "Gui shi 詭使," p. 935 (refusal to take office); 47 "Ba shuo 八說," pp. 972 (refusal to take office), 974 (damaging law); 49 "Wu du," pp. 1040–42, 1057–58; 1067, 1078; 50 "Xian xue 顯學," pp. 1080, 1090; 51 "Zhong xiao 忠孝," pp. 1107–09; *Shang Jun shu zhuyi* 3 "Nong zhan 農戰," pp. 57, 62, 67, 73; 4 "Qu qiang 去強," pp. 98–99; 6 "Suan di 算地," pp. 162–63; 7 "Kai sai 開塞," p. 195; 13 "Jin ling 靳令," p. 281; 14 "Xiu quan 修權," pp. 296–97; 15 "Lai min 來民," pp. 333–34; 23 "Jun chen 君臣," pp. 476–77, 481; 25 "Shen fa 慎法," p. 517; 26 "Ding fen 定分," p. 542.

52. On geographic patterns of authority in Warring States China, see Mark Edward Lewis, "Warring States Political History," in Edward Shaughnessy and Michael Loewe, ed., *Cambridge History of Ancient China* (Cambridge: Cambridge University, in press).

53. *Lun yu zhengyi* 3 "Ba yi 八佾," p. 72; 5 "Gongye Chang," p. 106; 7 "Shu er," p. 141; 9 "Zi han," pp. 176, 186; 11 "Xian jin," pp. 237, 250; 13 "Zi lu," p. 287; 14 "Xian wen," pp. 300 (this describes mobility as a moral obligation), 325; 18 "Weizi," pp. 391–92, 393–94; *Zuo zhuan zhu* Ding 10, pp. 1577–79; *Mengzi*

zhengyi "Wan Zhang shang," p. 388. Mencius' travels are indicated in several of the chapter titles.

54. Graham, *Disputers*, pp. 33–45.

55. *Mozi jiangu*, 50 "Gongshu 公輸," pp. 293–95.

56. *Mozi jiangu* 46 "Geng zhu 耕柱," pp. 257–58; 49 "Lu wen 魯問," pp. 286 (the son killed in battle), 287, 288 (2), 289 (2). On defending cities see pp. 297–374. Another passage equates students who leave the Mohist school with soldiers who desert from the army. See "Geng zhu," p. 261.

57. *Lü shi chun qiu jiaoshi* 19 "Shang de 上德," pp. 1257–58. This story is also mentioned in *Huainanzi* 20 "Tai zu 泰族," p. 357. On the Mohist-Confucian opposition, see *Xin yu jiao zhu* 新語校注, annotated by Wang Liqi 王利器 (Beijing: Zhonghua, 1986), 12 "Si wu 思務," p. 173.

58. Liang Qichao 梁啓超, *Mozi xue an* 墨子學案 (1921; reprint ed., Shanghai: Shangwu, 1935), p. 78; Masubuchi, *Kodai no shakai to kokka*, pp. 119–132.

59. *Lü shi chun qiu jiaoshi* 1 "Qu si 去私," pp. 55–56. The "Mohist law" cited resembles the "bond of the three regulations" that became the basis of Han law. See *Shi ji*, p. 322; *Han shu*, p. 1096; Wang Fu 王符, *Qian fu lun jian* 潛夫論箋 (Beijing: Zhonghua, 1979), p. 224.

60. On the hypothesis of the emergence of Daoism from these traditions, see Roth, "Redaction Criticism and the Early History of Taoism," pp. 3–11, 34–37.

61. *Huainanzi* 13 "Fan lun 氾論," p. 218; Graham, *Disputers*, pp. 53–64.

62. *Lü shi chun qiu jiaoshi* 2 "Gui sheng 貴生," pp. 74–76. Similar stories are collected in *Zhuangzi jishi* 28 "Rang wang 讓王," pp. 414–26. *Mengzi zhengyi* 13 "Jin xin shang 盡心上," p. 539.

63. *Zhuangzi jishi* 1 "Xiao yao you 逍遙遊," pp. 8–9, 12–13, 14–17; 4 "Ren jian shi 人間事"; 7 "Ying di wang 應帝王."

64. *Zhuangzi jishi* 8–11; 12 "Tian di 天地," pp. 198–99; 14 "Tian yun 天運," pp. 232–34, 234–35; 16 "Shan xing 繕性"; 17 "Qiu shui 秋水," pp. 266–67, 267; 19 "Da sheng 達生, p. 285; 20 "Shan mu 山木," pp. 301–02; 24 "Xu Wugui 徐無鬼," pp. 370–72; 25 "Ze Yang 則陽," pp. 386–87; 26 "Wai wu 外物," pp. 402, 407; 28 "Rang wang 讓王"; 32 "Lie Yukou 列禦寇," pp. 454, 457, 459, 460.

65. On the theme of inversion and paradox in the *Dao de jing*, see LaFargue, *Tao and Method*, pp. 153–56.

66. Lewis, *Sanctioned Violence*, pp. 34–35, 70, 121–32, 203–04.

67. *Han Feizi jishi* 49 "Wu du," pp. 1066–67.

68. See, for example, *Han Feizi jishi* 44 "Shuo yi," p. 904; 45 "Gui shi," p. 936; 47 "Ba shuo," p. 974; *Shang Jun shu zhuyi* 17 "Shang xing 賞刑," pp. 362–63; 26 "Ding fen," pp. 542, 548 (2). The *Xunzi* argues that one should use the regulations of the king as the model for study, but it specifies the regulations of the sage king. See *Xunzi jijie* 21 "Jie bi," p. 271; 25 "Cheng xiang," pp. 311–12 (stanza 49), 313 (stanza 55).

69. *Shi ji*, 87, p. 2546.

70. *Zuo zhuan zhu* Zhao 1, pp. 1217–21, 1221–23; Zhao 7, pp. 1289–90; *Guo*

yu, 3 "Zhou yu xia 周語下," p. 141; 5 "Lu yu xia," pp. 201, 213; Kidder Smith, "*Zhou yi* Interpretation from Accounts in the *Zuozhuan*," *Harvard Journal of Asiatic Studies* 49 (1989): 424–41. The bibliographic monograph of the *Han shu* lists the "yin/yang school" among the philosophers, clearly reflecting the dominant position of correlative cosmology in the Han. It also features a yin/yang section among the military treatises. An entire division—*shu shu* 數術—is devoted to natural philosophy and the occult. It includes texts on astrology, calendars and almanacs, Five Phases, divination by tortoise shell and milfoil, miscellaneous divination techniques, and a section on geomancy and physiognomy. Another section—*fang ji* 方技—lists the medical literature. See *Han shu* 30, pp. 1733–35, 1759–60, 1763–75, 1776–80.

71. For a survey of these finds, see Donald Harper, "Warring States, Qin, and Han Manuscripts Related to Natural Philosophy and the Occult," in Edward L. Shaughnessy, ed., *New Sources of Early Chinese History: An Introduction to Reading Inscriptions and Manuscripts* (Berkeley: Society for the Study of Early China and the Institute of East Asian Studies, 1997); Li Ling 李零, *Zhongguo fangshu kao* 中國方術考(Beijing: Renmin Zhongguo, 1993).

72. *Mengzi zhengyi* 3b "Teng Wen Gong xia," pp. 266–67.

73. Yates, "New Light on Ancient Chinese Military Texts"; Robin Yates, "The Yin-Yang Texts from Yinqueshan: An Introduction and Partial Reconstruction, with Notes on their Significance in Relation to Huang-Lao Daoism," *Early China* 19 (1994): 75–144.

74. *Han shu* 30, pp. 1756–62 for military texts as a separate category; p. 1701 on the use of specialists to prepare the catalogs on these topics. This bibliography will be discussed further in chapter 7.

75. Hsu Cho-yun, *Ancient China in Transition: An Analysis of Social Mobility, 722–222 B.C.* (Stanford: Stanford University, 1965), pp. 100–03. For an example of using this discussion as an authority for interpreting Warring States history, see LaFargue, *Tao and Method*, pp. 54–57.

76. On forms of appointment, see Mark Edward Lewis, "Warring States Political History," note 30; Yang Kuan 杨宽, *Zhanguo shi* 战国史, rev. ed. (Shanghai: Renmin, 1980), pp. 202–03.

77. *Shuihudi Qin mu zhujian*, p. 6. On becoming an official through military service, see *Han Feizi jishi* 50 "Xian xue," p. 1093.

78. *Han Feizi jishi* 47 "Ba shuo," p. 973.

79. The following was inspired by Pierre Bourdieu's study of the social bases of the emergence of a theory of "autonomous" art in nineteenth century France. See Bourdieu, *Les règles de l'art: genèse et structure du champ littéraire* (Paris: Seuil, 1992).

80. *Lun yu zhengyi* 7 "Shu er," p. 138.

81. *Xunzi jijie* 14 "Zhi shi 致士," p. 175; *Han Feizi jishi* 49 "Wu du," p. 1058—as an alternative it suggests practicing virtuous deeds, becoming trusted, and thereby receiving missions, that is, to become a "wandering bravo"; *Zhuangzi jishi* 28 "Rang wang 讓王," p. 420.

82. *Mengzi zhengyi* 1A "Liang Hui wang shang," pp. 35, 57; 3A "Teng Wen gong shang," p. 202.

83. Mawangdui Han mu boshu zhengli xiaozu 馬王堆漢墓帛書整理小組, *Mawangdui Han mu boshu* 馬王堆漢墓帛書, vol. 4 (Beijing: Wenwu, 1985), pp. 150–51. Wen Zhi also appears in *Lü shi chun qiu jiaoshi* 11 "Zhi zhong 至忠," p. 578. On the "Shi wen" see Zhou Yimou 周一謀, "Cong zhu jian 'Shi wen' deng kan daojia yu yangsheng 從竹簡十問等看道家與養生," in *Daojia wenhua yanjiu* 道家文化研究, vol. 5 (Shanghai: Guji, 1994), pp. 239–46.

84. *Shi ji* 105. The Bian Que story appears on pp. 2785–94. For the analysis of the "myth" of Bian Que, see Yamada Keiji 山田慶兒, "Hen Shaku densetsu 扁鵲傳說," *Tōhōgakuhō* 60 (1988): 73–158. Another medical technique denounced by the philosophical schools was the attempt to extend life through breathing exercises. This tradition, exemplified by the exercise chart from Mawangdui and the *Yin shu* from Zhangjiashan, is attacked twice in the *Zhuangzi*. See *Zhuangzi jishi* 1 "Xiao yao you 逍遙遊," p. 7; 15 "Ke yi 刻意," pp. 237–38.

85. *Baoshan chu jian*, transcription on pp. 32–37. See also Li Ling, *Zhongguo fangshu kao*, pp. 255–78; Li Ling, "Formulaic Structure of Chu Divinatory Bamboo Strips," *Early China* 15 (1990): 71–86.

86. Chen Songchang 陳松長 and Liao Mingchun 廖名春, "Bo shu 'Er san zi wen,' 'Yi zhi yi,' 'Yao' shiwen 帛書二三子問易之義要釋文," *Daojia wenhua yanjiu*, vol. 3 (Shanghai: Guji, 1993), p. 435; Liao Mingchun, "Bo shu 'Yao' jian shuo 帛書要簡說," *Daojia wenhua yanjiu*, vol. 3, pp. 202–06; Wang Bo 王博, "'Yao' pian lüe lun 要篇略論," *Daojia wenhua yanjiu*, vol. 6 (Shanghai: Guji, 1995), pp. 320–28; Xing Wen 邢文, "'Heguanzi' yu bo shu 'Yao' 鶡冠子與帛書要," *Daojia wenhua yanjiu*, vol. 6, pp. 336–49; Wang Baoxian 王葆玹, "Bo shu 'Yao' yu 'Yi zhi yi' de zhuanzuo shidai ji qi yu 'Xi ci' de guanxi 帛書要與易之義的撰作時代及其與繫辭的關系," *Daojia wenhua yanjiu*, vol. 6, pp. 350–66; Ikeda Tomohisa 池田知久, "Maōtai Kan bo hakusho Shūeki Yō hen no kenkyū 馬王堆漢墓帛書周易要篇の研究," *Tōyōbunka Kenkyūsho Kiyō* 123 (194): 111–207; Ikeda, "Maōtai Kan bo hakusho Shūeki Yō hen no shisō 馬王堆漢墓帛書周易要篇の思想," *Tōyōbunka Kenkyūsho Kiyō* 126 (1995), pp. 1–105.

87. *Mozi jiangu* 12 "Gui yi 貴義," pp. 270–71.

88. *Xunzi jijie* 8 "Ru xiao," p. 88. See also 1 "Quan xue 勸學," pp. 9–10; 6 "Fei shi er zi 非十二子," p. 66; *Mozi jiangu* "Fei ru xia 非儒下," pp. 180–81. See also *Mengzi zhengyi* 7B "Jin xin xia," pp. 604–05.

89. Lewis, "Les rites comme trame de l'histoire," pp. 33–36.

90. *Shi ji* 28, pp. 1358–77.

91. The historicity of the adoption of water has been questioned by some scholars. For a reasonable assessment of the argument that ultimately accepts Sima Qian's account, see Derk Bodde, "The State and Empire of Ch'in," in *The Cambridge History of China, Vol. 1, The Ch'in and Han Empires, 221 B.C.–A.D. 220*, ed. Michael Loewe (Cambridge: Cambridge University, 1986), pp. 96–97.

92. Kanaya Osamu 金谷治, *Shin Kan shisō shi kenkyū* 秦漢思想史研究, rev. ed. (Kyoto: Heirakuji, 1981), pp. 230–57.

93. *Shi ji* 8, pp. 385–86; 97, pp. 2692, 2699; 99, pp. 2721–24. Shusun Tong dismissed the critics as "rustic *ru* (*bi ru* 鄙儒), who do not recognize the changing of the times." This is a close paraphrase of the *Xunzi*'s "vulgar *ru* (*su ru* 俗儒)" who cling blindly to the ways of the Former Kings.

94. *Mengzi zhengyi* "Gongsun Chou xia," pp. 155–56 (this passage refers to three occasions on which rulers gave him large quantities of gold), 162, 175 (here the ruler offers him a house and grain for his followers), 181–82; "Teng Wen Gong xia," pp. 251–52 (this refers to the several hundred followers).

95. Shi Shen's presence in Wei ca. 330 B.C. is demonstrated by observations of the planet Venus in quotes attributed to him in the Tang dynasty *Kaiyuan zhan jing* 開元占經. See Michel Teboul, "Les premiers développements de l'astronomie des Royaumes Combattants au début de l'ère chrétienne," *Bulletin de l'Ecole Française d'Extrême-Orient* 71 (1982), pp. 152–55.

96. Lewis, "Warring States Political History."

97. Lewis, *Sanctioned Violence*, pp. 76–78.

98. *Shi ji* 75, pp. 2353, 2355, 2360.

99. *Shi ji* 74, p. 2348; 78, p. 2395.

100. The biographies of the Four Princes occupy ch. 75–78 of the *Shi ji*. These chapters are full of stories, several of which also appear in the *Zhanguo ce*, that demonstrate the princes' devotion to attracting retainers. On Huang Xie's scholarly background, see *Shi ji* 78, p. 2387. On the gathering of retainers, often assassins and thieves, see *Shi ji* 75, pp. 2353–54, 2355 (massacre of a whole village by retainers because people mock the Prince of Mengchang for being short), 2359–61, 2363; 76, pp. 2365–66, 2369; 77, pp. 2377–82; 78, p. 2395. On the Four Princes as symbols in the Han dynasty of the ethic of the bravoes, see Lewis, *Sanctioned Violence*, pp. 74, 77, 80, 89.

101. *Shi ji* 85, p. 2510.

102. The *Zhuangzi* divides scholars into six categories: teachers, courtiers, technical experts (in this case devotees of breathing exercises), and two types of hermits. These are then followed by the "complete" scholar who represents the ideal of the proto-Daoist textual tradition. These categories do not coincide exactly with the ones I have suggested, but there is considerable overlap. See *Zhuangzi jishi* 15 "Ke yi," pp. 237–38.

103. Prior to the passages from the *Xunzi* cited earlier, the "petty" *ru* are already denounced in the *Lun yu*. See *Lun yu zhengyi* 10 "Yong ye," p. 122.

104. *Mengzi zhengyi* "Li Lou xia," p. 346; "Gongsun Chou shang," pp. 114–16, 118–19.

105. The phrase "Five Phases" (*wu xing* 五行) in its full-blown theoretical form is attributed to Zou Yan and a "school" of *yin/yang* thought that derives from the mantic or technical traditions. However, it is used in a sense close to that of

Zou Yan in the *Sunzi* and the *Mozi*. Both employ the phrase, "The Five Phases have no constant victor (*wu xing wu chang sheng* 五行無常勝)." See *Mozi jiangu* 41 "Jing xia," p. 195; *Shiyi jia zhu Sunzi*, pp. 101, 154. The *Mencius* borrows the phrase *wu xing*, but explains it as five forms of moral conduct and thereby adapts a technical usage into a sociopolitical theory. The *Xunzi* mentioned this usage in its attack on Mencius. The usage was carried forward in the *Wu xing pian* discovered at Mawangdui. See *Xunzi jijie* 6 "Fei shi er zi," p. 59; 20 "Yue lun," p. 256; Pang Pu 庞朴, *Bo shu wu xing pian yanjiu*, 帛书五行篇研究 (Ji'nan: Qi Lu, 1980); Ikeda Tomohisa 池田知久, *Maōtai Kan bo hakusho gogyōhen kenkyū* 馬王堆漢墓帛書五行篇研究 (Tokyo: Kyūko Shoin, 1993).

For the argument that the image of the body as a bellows was adapted from its use in breathing techniques as found in the medical writings from Mawangdui and Zhangjiashan, see Donald Harper, "The Bellows Analogy in *Laozi* V and Warring States Macrobiotic Hygiene," *Early China* 20 (1995): 381–91.

106. *Lun yu zhengyi* 6 "Yong ye," p. 126; 7 "Shu er," p. 146; 11 "Xian jin," p. 243; *Zuo zhuan zhu* Huan 6, pp. 111–12; Zhuang 10, pp. 182–83; 14, pp. 196–97; 32, pp. 251–53; Xi 5, pp. 309–10; 15, p. 365; 16, p. 369; 19, pp. 381–82; 21, p. 390; 28, pp. 467–68; Xuan 15, pp. 762–63; *Xunzi jijie* 4 "Ru xiao," p. 85 (against hemerology); 5 "Fei xiang 非相," pp. 46–48 (against physiognomy); 17 "Tian lun 天論," 19 "Li lun 禮論," pp. 250–51; 21 "Jie bi 解蔽," p. 270; 22 "Zheng ming 正名," p. 282 (against incantations); 27 "Da lüe 大略," p. 333 (*Yi* not for divination); *Han Feizi jishi* 15 "Wang zheng 亡徵," p. 267; 19 "Shi xie 飾邪," pp. 307–08; 20 "Jie Lao 解老," pp. 338, 356–57. The Mohists, alone among the philosophers, accept the validity of divination to guide conduct, sacrifice for good fortune, and other practices of the technical and mantic experts. This is probably linked to their interests in military technology and practice.

107. The relation between judgment, technical arts, and government was also central to Greek political thought. See Stanley Rosen, *Plato's Statesman: The Web of Politics* (New Haven: Yale University, 1995).

108. *Lunyu zhengyi* 2 "Wei zheng," p. 30; 5 "Gongye Chang," p. 89; 13 "Zi Lu," p. 297. *Qi* 器 in the sense of "capacity" appears in 3 "Ba yi," pp. 66–67. Those who respond to the remark do not seem to grasp its sense, for they take it to refer not to his capacity, but to the vessels he used in daily life or in sacrificial offerings. In 15 "Wei Ling," p. 337 the character 器 refers to a cutting instrument employed by a craftsman.

109. *Lun yu zhengyi* 9 "Zi han," pp. 172, 177, 178; 13 "Zi Lu," p. 284; 19 "Zi Zhang," pp. 402, 403. Among the late stories in which Confucius and his disciples encounter hermits and madmen, one old recluse observes that Zi Lu (or Confucius himself) has never worked with his four limbs and cannot distinguish one type of grain from another. 18 "Weizi," p. 393.

110. *Mengzi zhengyi* "Teng Wen Gong shang," pp. 216–29.

111. *Xunzi jijie* 1 "Quan xue," p. 11; 4 "Rong ru," p. 44; 8 "Ru xiao," pp. 77–78; 10 "Fu guo," pp. 113–14; 21 "Jie bi," p. 266. In another passage the text

contrasts the sages Yao and Yu with craftsmen and farmers because the sages are "complete" (具 in one phrase, 備 in another). See "Rong ru," pp. 39–40. Another passage, echoing Confucius' mocking question of whether he should study archery or charioteering, contrasts the flexible intelligence of the "gentleman" with the specific skills of the greatest archers and charioteers. See 11 "Wang ba 王霸," p. 140.

112. *Shi ji* 8, pp. 380–81.

113. *Mozi jiangu* "Shang xian shang, zhong, xia 尚賢上中下," esp. pp. 32–33; *Han Feizi jishi* 5 "Zhu dao," pp. 67–68; 6 "You du," p. 87; 7 "Er bing," p. 112; 8 "Yang quan," pp. 121, 123; 13 "He Shi," p. 238.

114. *Zhuangzi jishi* 7 "Ying di wang," p. 133; 12 "Tian di," p. 191.

115. *Mengzi zhengyi* "Li Lou xia," p. 322; *Han Feizi jishi* 6 "You du," p. 87; *Xunzi jijie* 9 "Wang zhi 王制," p. 111; 10 "Fu guo," p. 128; 12 "Jun dao 君道," pp. 157, 161; 17 "Tian lun 天論," p. 206; *Shenzi*, quoted in *Qun shu zhi yao* (SPTK), 36 "Da ti," p. 26a; *Lü shi chun qiu jiaoshi* 14 "Ben mei 本昧," p. 740; *Huainanzi* 9 "Zhu shu 主術," p. 148; *Shizi* 尸子, quoted in *Taiping yu lan* 太平御覽, compiled by Li Fang 李昉 (Taipei: Shangwu, 1935), 79, p. 6a; *Di wang shi ji* 帝王世紀, quoted in *Taiping yu lan*, 79, p. 2a. On the prevalence of the same image in the military context, see Lewis, *Sanctioned Violence*, pp. 104–07.

116. *Shang jun shu zhu yi* 3 "Nong zhan 农战," p. 57.

117. For a study of indirection and suggestion as recurring strategies and themes in various fields of Chinese literature and art, see François Jullien, *Le détour et l'accès: stratégies du sens en Chine, en Grèce* (Paris: Grasset, 1995).

118. Against glibness and clever speech, see *Lun yu zhengyi* 1 "Xue er," p. 5; 5 "Gongye Chang," pp. 89, 108; 14 "Xian wen," p. 320; 15 "Wei Ling Gong," p. 345. On glib men as a danger, see 15 "Wei Ling Gong," pp. 337–39; 17 "Yang Huo," p. 379. On the need for the *Odes* to be put into practice, see 13 "Zi Lu," p. 285. On the need for eloquence as a reflection of the times, see 6 "Yong ye," p. 124. Against the glibness of the disciple who engages in disputation, see 11 "Xian jin," p. 251. On speaking little and to the point, see 1 "Xue er," p. 18; 4 "Li ren 里仁," p. 85 (2); 10 "Xiang dang 鄉黨," pp. 196, 224; 12 "Yan Yuan," p. 263; 14 "Xian wen," pp. 308, 317, 319; 15 "Wei Ling Gong," p. 349. On renouncing speech, see 17 "Yang Huo," p. 379.

119. On maintaining trust in words, see *Lun yu zhengyi* 1 "Xue er," pp. 5, 11; 2 "Wei zheng," p. 37; 5 "Gongye Chang," pp. 96, 109–10; 7 "Shu er," p. 147; 13 "Zi Lu," pp. 284; 15 "Wei Ling Gong," pp. 334, 342; 17 "Yang Huo," p. 371; 19 "Zi Zhang," p. 403. On trust as the basis of the state, see 12 "Yan Yuan," p. 266. 13 "Zi Lu," p. 293 criticizes insistence on *absolute* devotion to one's word. This is an attack on the ethic of the "wandering bravoes." See also 17 "Yang Huo," p. 374. On ruling silently through force of example, see 9 "Zi han," p. 190; 13 "Zi Lu," pp. 279, 286; 17 "Yang Huo," p. 379.

120. On the rejection of learning that consists of repeating what one is told, see *Lun yu zhengyi* 9 "Zi han," p. 192; 17 "Yang Huo," p. 377. On deducing all

from one point given, see 1 "Xue er," p. 19; 5 "Gongye Chang," p. 94; 7 "Shu er," p. 139. This point was developed at length in the "Xue ji 學記" chapter of the *Li ji*. See *Li ji zhushu* 36 "Xue ji," pp. 11b, 12b, 16a. On summarizing the entire *Book of Odes* in a single phrase, see 2 "Wei zheng," p. 21. On the need for students to actively pursue questions, see 7 "Shu er," p. 139; 15 "Wei Ling Gong," pp. 336, 341. On the best student not speaking, see 2 "Wei zheng," p. 28; 9 "Zi han," p. 189; 11 "Xian jin," p. 239. On the master giving hints and students developing them, see 1 "Xue er," pp. 18–19; 3 "Ba yi," p. 48–49. On the master dismissing inappropriate questions in order to offer lessons, see 13 "Zi Lu," p. 283; 17 "Xian wen," pp. 380–82. On the master refusing to explain or add to his initial propositions, see 12 "Yan Yuan," p. 278; 13 "Zi Lu," p. 279. For an example of elaborate deductions in which a disciple learns three points with one question, see 16 "Ji shi 季氏," pp. 363–64. For an account of how this method of teaching was experienced by one disciple, see 9 "Zi han," p. 182.

121. *Lun yu zhengyi* 2 "Wei zheng," pp. 25–28. For a similar series on benevolence, see 12 "Yan Yuan," pp. 262–63, 278; 13 "Zi Lu," p. 292.

122. *Lun yu zhengyi* 12 "Yan Yuan," pp. 266, 271, 274 (2), 275; 13 "Zi Lu," pp. 279, 280–83; 15 "Wei Ling Gong," pp. 337–39.

123. *Lun yu zhengyi* 7 "Shu er," p. 153; 13 "Zi Lu," pp. 296, 297, 298.

124. For example, *Lun yu zhengyi* 7 "Shu er," pp. 144, 146; 9 "Zi han," p. 172.

125. For an example of this principle being enacted and explained within a single anecdote, see *Lun yu zhengyi* 11 "Xian jin," p. 149.

126. *Lun yu zhengyi* 4 "Li ren," pp. 82–83.

127. *Han shu* 30, p. 1701; Liu Xie 刘勰, *Wen xin diao long yizhu* 文心雕龙译注, annotated by Lu Kanru 陆侃如 and Mou Shijin 牟世金 (Ji'nan: Qilu, 1984), 18 "Lun shuo 论说," pp. 228–29. The term is applied both to the *Lun yu* and to the *Chun qiu*.

128. The idea that the master's teachings always escape his listeners appears in several anecdotes. In 9 "Zi han," p. 182 Yan Yuan describes how he exhausts all his abilities to follow the master's teachings, but cannot find the way. In another anecdote—16 "Ji shi," pp. 363–64—the disciples interrogate Confucius' son to see if he has received some special instructions denied to the rest of them. The insistence of the different disciples on asking the same questions, and the attempts of some to pursue the master with further queries, show that they do not accept his answers as full or sufficient. Finally, Confucius specifically denies to his disciples that he keeps anything hidden, and asserts that he shares everything he does with them. The explicit denial proves that many believed the contrary. See 7 "Shu er," p. 147.

129. *Mengzi zhengyi* 4B "Li Lou xia," p. 331; 7A "Jin xin shang," p. 529; 7B "Jin xin xia," pp. 576, 593, 594.

130. *Mengzi zhengyi* 2A "Gongsun Chou shang," pp. 123, 125.

131. *Mengzi zhengyi* 3A "Teng Wen Gong shang," pp. 219–31 (this passage is aimed at the "School of the Tillers," which Mencius describes as a "barbarian"

doctrine); 3B "Teng Wen Gong xia," pp. 263–72 (this passage attacks the Yangists and Mohists, and uses the same words to describe their destructive language and harm to the state as those cited in the preceding note); 4A "Li Lou shang," pp. 284–88 (after celebrating the achievements of the sages, this passage ends with a denunciation of the "chatterers" who talk too much and attack the Way of the ancient kings); 4B "Li Lou xia," pp. 344–46 (this passage contrasts those who glibly hold forth on human nature with Yu's work in taming the flood).

132. On Mencius presenting himself as a potential sage, see 2B "Gongsun Chou xia," pp. 182–83; 7B "Jin xin xia," pp. 608–10. Of course, when explicitly asked if he is a sage, Mencius modestly declines the title, but he does so by citing Confucius' own denial of being a sage. He thus places himself in exalted company. See 2A "Gongsun Chou shang," p. 126.

133. For attempts to justify Mencius' analogies as philosophy, see D. C. Lau, "On Mencius's Use of the Method of Analogy in Argument," *Asia Major*, New Series, 10 (1963), reprinted in D. C. Lao, tr., *Mencius* (Harmondsworth: Penguin, 1970), pp. 235–63; A. C. Graham, "The Background of the Mencian Theory of Human Nature," in *Studies in Chinese Philosophy and Philosophical Literature*, pp. 42–49. These scholars, however, rewrite Mencius' discourse as it would be if it were an argument, which proves that in itself it is not. For the position that these assertions are best understood as something other than attempts at proving general truths, see I. A. Richards, *Mencius on the Mind* (London: Kegan Paul, 1932), p. 43; Chad Hansen, *A Taoist Theory of Chinese Thought: A Philosophical Investigation* (Oxford: Oxford University, 1992), p. 188; Jullien, *Le détour et l'accès*, pp. 306–08, where he cites Wang Fuzhi.

134. *Mengzi zhengyi* 7B "Jin xin xia," p. 586.

135. *Mengzi zhengyi* 7A "Jin xin shang," p. 555. The image of education as a timely rain echoes the parable on not helping the sprouts to grow. See 2A "Gongsun Chou shang," pp. 121–22.

136. *Mengzi zhengyi* 4B "Li Lou xia," p. 340; 7B "Jin xin xia," p. 574.

137. *Mengzi zhengyi* 1A "Liang Hui Wang," p. 46; 6B "Gaozi xia," p. 516. There are several passages in the *Lun yu* where Confucius gives instruction by refusing to teach, such as the aforementioned story of the student who asks to study farming. See also *Lun yu zhengyi* 17 "Yang Huo," p. 380.

138. *Mengzi zhengyi* 4B "Li Lou xia," pp. 317–19.

139. *Mengzi zhengyi* 2A "Gongsun Chou shang," pp. 144–48; 5B "Wan Zhang xia," pp. 395–97; 6B "Gaozi xia," pp. 489, 492. Mencius also justifies his own refusal to serve through citing ancient custom and past exemplars of the "Middle Way." See 2B "Gongsun Chou xia, " pp. 152–55; 3B "Teng Wen Gong xia," pp. 259–52; 7B "Jin xin xia," p. 581.

140. *Mengzi zhengyi* 3B "Teng Wen Gong xia," pp. 269–70; 7A "Jin xin shang," pp. 539–41.

141. *Mengzi zhengyi* 5A "Wan Zhang shang," p. 376–77; 5B "Wan Zhang xia," p. 428.

142. The situation is like that of medieval Europe as described by Mary Carruthers, in which "*auctores* were, first of all, texts, not people." This was a world where "both 'authority' and 'author' were conceived of entirely in textual terms, for an 'auctor' is simply one whose writings are full of 'authorities.'" See Mary Carruthers, *The Book of Memory: A Study of Memory in Medieval Culture* (Cambridge: Cambridge University, 1990), p. 190. See also pp. 212–20.

143. *Zhuangzi jishi* 2 "Qi wu lun," pp. 46–50; 4 "Ren jian shi," pp. 61–70, 70–75, 83–85 (Jieyu); 5 "De chong fu," pp. 85–89, 91–93, 93–98; 6 "Da zong shi," pp. 120–26, 128–29 (learns from disciple); 12 "Tian di," pp. 191–92, 193–96 (dialogue with old farmer); 13 "Tian dao," pp. 212–14; 14 "Tian yun," pp. 225–28, 228–31, 231–34, 234–35; 17 "Qiu shui," pp. 262–63; 18 "Zhi le," pp. 273–75; 19 "Da sheng," pp. 281–82, 282–83, 288–89; 20 "Shan mu," pp. 297–99, 299–300, 302–04; 21 "Tian Zifang," pp. 308–10, 310–13; 22 "Zhi bei you," pp. 323–26, 331–33, 333–34; 24 "Xu Wugui," p. 368; 25 "Ze Yang," pp. 386–87, 391–92; 26 "Wai wu," pp. 400–02, 409–10 (praised by Zhuang Zhou), 410–11; 28 "Rang wang," pp. 421 (learns from disciple), 422–23; 29 "Dao Zhi 盜跖," pp. 426–33; 31 "Yu fu 漁父," pp. 443–48; 32 "Lie Yukou," pp. 455–56, 456–57.

144. The Yellow Emperor appears as a teacher in 14 "Tian yun," pp. 222–25 and 22 "Zhi bei you," pp. 319–20, but he receives instruction from a youth in 24 "Xu Wugui," pp. 359–61. Master Lie teaches in 28 "Rang wang," pp. 418–19, but receives instruction in 18 "Da sheng," pp. 278–81; 21 "Tian Zifang," pp. 316–17; 32 "Lie Yukou," pp. 449–50. Zhuang Zhou's dialogue with the skull appears in 18 "Zhi le," pp. 272–73.

145. *Zhuangzi jishi* 27 "Yu yan," pp. 407–08.

146. *Zhuangzi jishi* 33 "Tian xia," p. 475. In this account the "imputed words" provide breadth, the "repeated words" truth, and the "spillover words" endless changes.

147. *Zhuangzi jishi* 6 "Da zong shi," pp. 127–28; 13 "Tian dao 天道," p. 206. On the passage and its importance, see Graham, *Chuang Tzu: The Inner Chapters*, p. 92. A closely related passage describing an unknown human teacher in terms close to those applied to the Way appears in 21 "Tian Zifang," pp. 306–07.

148. Passages in the *Dao de jing* on teaching are discussed in LaFargue, *Tao and Method*, pp. 430–49.

149. See, for example, *Zhuangzi jishi* 12 "Tian di," p. 195; 14 "Tian yun," pp. 231, 234; 16 "Qiu shui," p. 266; 21 "Tian Zifang," p. 307; 29 "Dao Zhi," p. 433.

150. Graham, *Disputers of the Tao*, pp. 176–83, 199–202 discusses the most important passages.

151. On Hui Shi, see *Zhuangzi jishi* 1 "Xiao yao you," pp. 18–20, 20–21; 5 "De chong fu," pp. 99–101; 17 "Qiu shui," pp. 267–68; 18 "Zhi le," pp. 271–72; 24 "Xu Wugui," pp. 362–64, 364–65 (on Hui Shi's tomb); 26 "Wai wu," p. 403; 27 "Yu yan," p. 409. For remarks against disputants, see 2 "Qi wu lun," pp. 37, 39, 40–41; 8 "Pian mu 駢拇," pp. 141–42; 10 "Qu qie 胠篋," p. 164; 12 "Tian di," pp. 185, 191, 200; 13 "Da sheng," pp. 208, 211; 16 "Shan xing," p. 246; 17 "Qiu shui," pp. 263–66 (this is an anecdote attacking Gongsun Long); 18 "Zhi le," p.

273; 22 "Zhi bei you," p. 324; 23 "Kang Sangchu 康桑楚," pp. 350–51; 24 "Xu Wugui," pp. 361, 369.

152. *Zhuangzi jishi* 8 "Pian mu," p. 142; 10 "Qu qie," pp. 161, 162; 11 "Zai you 在宥," p. 170; 12 "Tian di," p. 203; 14 "Tian yun," p. 233; 24 "Xu Wugui," pp. 363 (2), 369; 26 "Wai wu," p. 400.

153. For lists of the "classics," see *Xunzi jijie* 1 "Quan xue," p. 7; 4 "Rong ru," p. 43; 8 "Ru xiao," pp. 84–85; 27 "Da lüe," pp. 328, 333 (2), 336. For lists of rival schools, see 6 "Fei shier zi"; 8 "Ru xiao," p. 78: 17 "Tian lun," p. 213; 21 "Jie bi," pp. 261–62; 25 "Cheng xiang 成相," p. 306.

154. *Xunzi jijie* 5 "Fei xiang," pp. 52–53. This is anticipated in *Lun yu zhengyi* 3 "Ba yi," pp. 49, 56.

155. *Xunzi jijie* 2 "Xiu shen 修身," pp. 12, 14, 16, 20; 4 "Rong ru," p. 40; 5 "Fei xiang," 6 "Fei shier zi," p. 60–61; 11 "Wang ba," p. 143; 14 "Zhi shi 致士," p. 175; 23 "Xing e 性惡," pp. 289 (3), 290, 299; 27 "Da lüe," pp. 323, 333, 336.

156. *Xunzi jijie* 3 "Bu gou 不苟," pp. 28–29. 8 "Ru xiao," p. 81 also describes the gentleman who cultivates his inner virtue. He is trusted without speaking, awesome without anger, glorious even when in poverty or desperate straits. See also 22 "Zheng ming," p. 283 on the speech of the gentleman.

157. *Xunzi jijie* 24 "Junzi 君子," p. 300.

158. *Xunzi jijie* 23 "Xing e," pp. 297–98. A shorter version appears in 27 "Da lüe," p. 339. The reference to the single "controlling category" that allows the sage to speak appropriately of endlessly changing phenomena is clearly echoed in the later *Han shi wai zhuan*, a text closely linked to the *Xunzi*. See *Han shi wai zhuan ji shi*, pp. 172–73. Other passages in this chapter of the *Xunzi* expressing reservations about speech or royal decrees appear on pp. 332, 334, 337, 338. For another passage in the *Xunzi* indicating exceptions for the sage, see 27, "Da lüe," p. 323.

159. *Xunzi jijie* 18 "Zheng lun," pp. 214, 215, 218, 219, 221, 224, 225. The last three theses are attributed specifically to Master Song, that is, Song Xing. See pp. 227, 228, 229.

160. *Xunzi jijie* 22 "Zheng ming," *passim*, especially pp. 275, 276, 279–80, 281, 283, 285.

161. *Xunzi jijie* 19 "Li lun 禮論," p. 237. For other passages denouncing disputation, see 17 "Tian lun," p. 211; 21 "Jie bi," pp. 271–72; 23 "Xing e," p. 294; 25 "Cheng xiang," pp. 306, 307; 27 "Da lüe," p. 339.

162. *Xunzi jijie* 5 "Fei xiang," p. 50; 19 "Li lun," p. 237—"The sage is the endpoint of the Way, so the student certainly studies to become a sage." 21 "Jie bi," p. 271—"The two [sage and king] are sufficient to be the endpoint for all under Heaven, so the student takes sage and king [or 'sage kings'] as his teachers, and accordingly takes the institutions of the sage kings as his model." 25 "Cheng xiang," p. 307—"When essence and spirit revert to one another, when they are one and not two, he becomes a sage."

163. *Xunzi jijie* 5 "Fei xiang," p. 52; 17 "Tian lun," pp. 212–13; 19 "Li lun," p. 248; 24 "Junzi," p. 302; 25 "Cheng xiang," p. 306.

164. *Xunzi jijie* 18 "Zheng lun," pp. 224, 225; 19 "Li lun," pp. 233 (3), 248; 21 "Jie bi," pp. 271, 273; 22 "Zheng ming," pp. 275–76; 23 "Xing e," p. 293; 25 "Cheng xiang," p. 313.

165. *Xunzi jijie* 21 "Jie bi," p. 271; 22 "Zheng ming," p. 276.

166. Wang and Chang, *Philosophical Foundations of Han Fei's Political Theory*. R. P. Peerenboom rejects Wang and Chang's thesis that the *Han Feizi* seeks to ground its theory of statecraft in Daoist thought. He denies that the *Han Feizi* represents "Huang-Lao" thought, a rubric that he reserves for the Mawangdui manuscripts. As discussed in chapter 8, we know the term Huang-Lao only from the *Shi ji*, where it is never defined and seems to have primarily a political sense. The attempt to give it fixed contours is an intellectual red herring. Peerenboom demonstrates that the *Han Feizi* seeks no metaphysical grounding and has no sense of a "foundational," natural law (something he reserves for the Mawangdui text). It is, as he argues, a pragmatic text concerned with practical results. However, to be pragmatic does not mean that it is a collection of empirically based rules of thumb with no underlying principles. The text does seek such principles, and it finds them largely in the language of Daoism. See R. P. Peerenboom, *Law and Morality in Ancient China: The Silk Manuscripts of Huang-Lao* (Albany: SUNY, 1993), ch. 5.

Chapter Three. Writing the Past

1. For discussions of both these works, see their respective entries in Loewe, ed., *Early Chinese Texts*.

2. On the historical significance of the precombat "oath" ceremony in Spring and Autumn China, see Lewis, *Sanctioned Violence*, pp. 18, 24–25, 67–70.

3. Ronald Egan, "Narratives in *Tso Chuan*," *Harvard Journal of Asiatic Studies* 37.2 (1977): 350–52.

4. For a list of the documents see *Early Chinese Texts*, p. 379.

5. Edward L. Shaughnessy, "The Duke of Zhou's Retirement in the East and the Beginnings of the Ministerial-Monarch Debate in Chinese Political Philosophy," *Early China* 18 (1993): 45.

6. Von Falkenhausen, "Issues in Western Zhou Studies," pp. 156–59, 160–64; Shaughnessy, *Sources of Western Zhou History*, pp. 74–75; Virginia Kane, "Aspects of Western Zhou Appointment Inscriptions," *Early China* 8 (1982–83): 16.

7. On these documents see *Early Chinese Texts*, p. 380. The list on this page includes the documents "Wen Hou zhi ming" 文侯之命 and "Lü xing" 呂刑. The former is closely related to standard late Western Zhou investiture inscriptions, and hence can plausibly be dated to the early Eastern Zhou. The latter, however, may well date from much later, as argued in Matsumoto Masaaki 松本雅明, *Shunjū Sengoku ni okeru Shōsho no tenkai* 春秋戰國における尙書の展開 (Tokyo: Kazama, 1968), pp. 399–404. On the later emergence of "oaths" *shi* 誓 as a second stage in the development of the *Shang shu*, see Matsumoto, pp. 4–5. The "oath"

attributed to King Wu prior to his defeat of the Shang at Mu Ford is now generally regarded as a Han composition, but citations in philosophical texts show that earlier versions of this document existed in the middle of the Warring States period. See Matsumoto, pp. 59–181; Chen Mengjia 陳夢家, *Shang shu tong lun* 尙書通論, 2nd ed. rev. (Beijing: Zhonghua, 1985), pp. 53–68; Zhu Tingxian 朱廷獻, *Shang shu yanjiu* 尙書研究 (Taipei: Shangwu, 1988), pp. 53–62.

8. On the dating of these documents to the Warring States, see Matsumoto, *Shōsho no tenkai*, pp. 240–52, 434–64; Chen Mengjia, *Shang shu tong lun*, pp. 135–46—Chen argues that the "Yao dian" is a Qin composition, but his argument is based on a handful of lines that could be later insertions; Shi Nianhai 史念海, *He shan ji* 河山集 (Beijing: Sanlian, 1981), pp. 391–434; Michael Nylan, *The Shifting Center: The Original "Great Plan" and Later Readings*, Monumenta Serica Monograph Series no. 24 (Nettetal: Steyler Verlag, 1992), pp. 105–46.

9. *Shang shu zhushu* 2, pp. 6b, 7b–8a, 9a–10b; 4, pp. 16b–22a; 6, pp. 1a–32b; 12, pp. 1a–26a.

10. *Shang shu zhushu* 2, pp. 7b–10b. On the mythological origins of this document and its dating, see Sarah Allan, *The Shape of the Turtle: Myth, Art, and Cosmos in Early China* (Albany: SUNY, 1991), ch. 3.

11. John S. Major, "The Five Phases, Magic Squares, and Schematic Cosmography," in Henry Rosemont, Jr., ed., *Explorations in Early Chinese Cosmology* (JAAR Thematic Studies 50/2, Chico, Calif.: Scholar's Press, 1984), pp. 133–66; Schuyler Cammann, "The Evolution of Magic Squares in China," *Journal of the American Oriental Society* 80 (1960): 116–24; Cammann, "The Magic Square of Three in Old Chinese Philosophy and Religion," *History of Religions* 1 (1961): 37–80; Cammann, "Old Chinese Magic Squares," *Sinologica* 7 (1963): 14–53; Marcel Granet, *La pensée chinoise* (1934; rep. ed. Paris: Albin Michel, 1968), pp. 145–74; A. C. Graham, *Yin-Yang and the Nature of Correlative Thinking* (Singapore: The Institute of East Asian Philosophies, 1986), pp. 53–57. Some formations in the military treatises might also have been inspired by the idea of the "magic square."

12. Geoffrey R. Waters, *Three Elegies of Ch'u* (Madison: University of Wisconsin, 1985), pp. 34–37.

13. Michael Nylan, *The Shifting Center*, pp. 23–32.

14. Chen, *Shang shu tong lun*, p. 11; Matsumoto, *Shōsho no tenkai*, pp. 17–20.

15. *Lun yu zhengyi* 3 "Ba yi," pp. 49, 56. See also 2 "Wei zheng," p. 39. This indicates that the ritual heritage of the Xia and Shang could be known, but only through survivals in Zhou practice rather than through documentation.

16. Chen, *Shang shu tong lun*, pp. 12–35; Matsumoto, *Shōsho no tenkai*, pp. 277, 373, 376, 407, 515, 517, 518, 568, 570, 611.

17. Matsumoto, *Shōsho no tenkai*, p. 520.

18. Matsumoto, *Shōsho no tenkai*, pp. 566–70, 611–12; Uchino Kumaichirō 內野態一郎, *Shin dai ni okeru keisho keisetsu no kenkyū: betsu hen, in kyō kō* 秦代における經書經說の研究: 別篇, 引經考 (Tokyo: Tōhō Bunka Gakuin, 1940), pp. 55–74, 201–21.

19. Liu Qiyu 刘起于, *Shang shu xue shi* 尚书学史 (Beijing: Zhonghua, 1989), pp. 62–66.

20. Chen Songzhang and Liao Mingchun, "Bo shu 'Er san zi wen,' 'Yi zhi yi,' 'Yao' shi wen," p. 434.

21. Lewis, "Les rites comme trame de l'histoire," pp. 32–33.

22. *Lun yu zhengyi* 3 "Ba yi," pp. 49, 56, 63–66; 2 "Wei zheng," p. 39; 15 "Wei Ling gong," pp. 337–39, 343. References to the absence of written evidence for the rites of the Xia and Shang appear twice in the *Li ji*. See *Li ji zhushu* 21 "Li yun," p. 8a; 53 "Zhong yong," p. 10a.

23. *Lun yu zhengyi* 3 "Ba yi," pp. 41, 43, 46, 73; 4 "Li ren," p. 85; 7 "Shu er," pp. 134, 141, 146, 149; 1 "Xue er," pp. 16, 26; 2 "Wei zheng," p. 29; 9 "Zi han," p. 186; 14 "Xian wen," pp. 318, 327–28; 15 "Wei Ling gong," p. 339; 16 "Ji shi," pp. 354–56, 356; 17 "Yang Huo," p. 378.

24. *Lun yu zhengyi* 5 "Gongye Chang," p. 107; 6 "Yong ye," p. 133; 7 "Shu er," pp. 137, 142; 1 "Xue er," p. 16; 8 "Tai Bo," pp. 154, 162, 165, 166, 167–68, 169–70; 9 "Zi han," p. 176; 11 "Xian jin," p. 246—in this passage the Duke of Zhou is mentioned only in contrast with the wealth of the Ji lineage, and the version of the passage in the *Mencius* does not mention him. See *Mengzi zhengyi* 4A "Li Lou shang," p. 303; 12 "Yan Yuan," p. 278—in this passage Zi Xia uses Shun and Tang as examples to explain a cryptic response by Confucius; 14 "Xian wen," pp. 301–02, 329; 15 "Wei Ling gong," p. 334; 16 "Ji shi," p. 362; 18 "Weizi," pp. 386—this cites three worthies who opposed the wicked last Shang king, 388, 395–97, 399; 19 "Zi Zhang," pp. 407—this discusses not an exemplary sage but the evil King Zhou of Shang, 408; 20 "Yao yue," pp. 411–14. On the Duke of Zhou as archetype of the worthy minister, see Shaughnessy, "The Duke of Zhou's Retirement in the East," pp. 41–43. Because the linking of Yu with frugality and physical toil is an important theme in Mohist doctrine, several scholars have asserted a Mohist origin for the two passages on Yu in the *Lun yu*. See Takeuchi, *Rongo no kenkyū*, p. 98.

25. *Lun yu zhengyi* 3 "Ba yi," pp. 66–69; 5 "Gongye Chang," pp. 101, 105; 14 "Xian wen," pp. 305, 309, 311, 314–15.

26. *Lun yu zhengyi* 7 "Shu er," p. 144.

27. *Lun yu zhengyi* 1 "Xue er," p. 13; 16 "Ji shi," p. 350.

28. For appeals to the "ancient sages," "sages of the three dynasties," or ancient rulers, often followed by lists of names, or to named sages, see *Mozi jiangu* 1 "Qin shi," pp. 1, 3; "Xiu shen," p. 5; "Suo ran," pp. 13, 16; 2 "Shang xian shang," pp. 25, 27, 28; "Shang xian zhong," pp. 29, 29–30, 30 (2), 34–35, 35–37, 37; "Shang xian xia," pp. 39, 40–41, 42, 43; 3 "Shang tong shang," p. 46; "Shang tong zhong," pp. 50, 52, 53, 54 (3); "Shang tong xia," pp. 59, 60, 61; 4 "Jian ai zhong," pp. 67, 67–69 (on Yu's love for the people as demonstrated in his toil), 69–70 (on King Wen's love for the people); "Jian ai xia," pp. 75–79 (lists both sages and hegemons and demonstrates their universal love); 5 "Fei gong xia," pp. 92–95 (distinguishes sages' use of warfare to punish evil from Warring States practice); 6 "Jie yong shang," pp. 99–100; "Jie yong zhong," pp. 101–03 (narrates the sages'

invention of the tools of civilization in the guise of sumptuary regulations restricting their use); "Jie yong xia," pp. 105, 111–12 (on sages' rules for frugal funerals), pp. 112–14 (on the "actual" funerals of Yao, Shun, and Yu), 115 (2), 117; 7 "Tian zhi shang," pp. 120–21 (2), 125, 127; "Tian zhi xia," p. 132; 8 "Ming gui xia," pp. 138, 145, 146, 147 (2), 150, 154; "Fei yue shang," p. 156 (2); 9 "Fei ming shang," pp. 163–64, 165, 166; "Fei ming zhong," pp. 169–70; "Fei ming xia," pp. 172 (2), 173; 11 "Geng Zhu," pp. 255–57, 258–59 (this passage defends the ancient sage kings from a "proto-Daoist" attack on dead writings, and it asserts that the sages are the source of life.); 12 "Gui yi," pp. 266–67, 267 (this passage argues that anything in accord with the ancient sages should be done), 268, 268–69, 270; "Gong Meng," pp. 275, 282, 286–87. On the "violent" kings as the counterexample, sometimes in association with the "fraudulent" (*wei* 偽) people, see 1 "Suo ran," pp. 7–11, 13, 17; 2 "Shang xian zhong," pp. 32, 35–37; 6 "Jie yong xia," p. 115; 7 "Tian zhi shang," pp. 120–21; "Tian zhi zhong," pp. 127–28; 8 "Ming gui xia," pp. 151–52, 152; 9 "Fei ming shang," p. 167; "Fei ming zhong," pp. 170–71, 171; "Fei ming xia," pp. 172, 173, 173–74; 12 "Gui yi," p. 267; "Gong Meng," pp. 275 (Jie and Zhou first deny existence of spirits), 282.

    29. On criticisms of the present, frequently marked by the character 今 *jin*, or calls for contemporaries to imitate the past, see *Mozi jiangu* 1 "Ci guo," pp. 17–22; "San bian," pp. 22–24; 2 "Shang xian shang," p. 28; "Shang xian zhong," pp. 31, 38; "Shang xian xia," p. 43; 3 "Shang tong zhong," pp. 50–51, 52; "Shang tong xia," pp. 56, 61; 4 "Jian ai zhong," pp. 64, 66; 5 "Fei gong zhong," pp. 88, 89, 91–92; 6 "Jie yong shang," p. 101; "Jie yong xia," pp. 114, 115 (2), 115–16 (here contemporary political practice is identified with "custom" *su* 俗 and linked to cannibalism and the abandonment of widows); 7 "Tian zhi shang," p. 118; "Tian zhi xia," pp. 129, 136; 8 "Ming gui xia," pp. 138, 147; "Fei yue shang," pp. 155, 157, 158; 12 "Gui yi," p. 268. Several passages also state that with the passing of the sages "truth" or "righteousness" (*yi* 義) vanished from the world. See 6 "Jie yong shang," p. 100; "Jie zang xia," pp. 105, 110; 8 "Ming gui xia," p. 138. Another passage argues that the Way of the former kings is the basis of *yi* 義. See 12 "Gui yi," p. 270.

    30. *Mozi jiangu* 9 "Fei ming shang," pp. 163–64; "Fei ming zhong," pp. 169–70; "Fei ming xia," pp. 172–73. In this last chapter the standards are called *fa* 法 and the appeal to the "affairs of the ancient sage kings" is called *kao* 考, meaning "to examine" or "old." An earlier chapter makes no explicit appeal to "standards" of judgment, but begins an appeal to the example of the sages with the statement that what all the world held to be true was the model of the sage kings. See 5 "Fei gong xia," p. 88.

    31. *Mozi jiangu* 5 "Fei gong xia," pp. 91–95; 6 "Jie yong xia," pp. 105–06, 112; 8 "Ming gui xia," pp. 147–48, 154; 9 "Fei ming zhong," pp. 170–71, 173–74; 12 "Gong Meng," pp. 286–87.

    32. *Mozi jiangu* 9 "Fei ming zhong," p. 169. This argument still appeals to shared human perceptions, but it does not name it as one of the "three models."

33. *Mozi jiangu* 8 "Ming gui xia," pp. 145–46; 9 "Fei ming zhong," p. 169.

34. *Mozi jiangu* 9 "Fei ming shang," pp. 167–68; "Fei ming zhong," pp. 170–71; "Fei ming xia," pp. 173–74. This chapter also notes the destructive impact of the belief in fate in its own day. See pp. 175–77.

35. *Mozi jiangu* 2 "Shang xian zhong," pp. 33–35; 3 "Shang tong xia," pp. 55–56, 59; 4 "Jian ai zhong," pp. 67–69; "Jian ai xia," p. 75; 7 "Tian zhi xia," p. 137; 12 "Gui yi," pp. 268–69. (In this last passage Master Mo defends his large personal library by citing the example of the Duke of Zhou, who he claims read one hundred rolls of bamboo strips every morning.)

36. *Mozi jiangu* 2 "Shang xian zhong," pp. 31, 33–34, 36–67, 37–38; "Shang xian xia," pp. 41–42; 3 "Shang tong zhong," pp. 51 (2), 52, 53, 54; "Shang tong xia," p. 59; 4 "Jian ai xia," pp. 76, 77, 78; 6 "Jie Yong shang," p. 100; "Jie yong zhong," pp. 101–04 (This cites models/laws [*fa* 法] of the sages as quotations marked by the character 曰 *yue*, so they are regarded as texts.); "Jie zang xia," pp. 111–12; 7 "Tian zhi zhong," p. 123; "Tian zhi xia," p. 137; 8 "Ming gui xia," pp. 146, 147, 147–50, 154; "Fei yue shang," pp. 160–61; 9 "Fei ming shang," pp. 164–65, 166, 167–68; "Fei ming zhong," pp. 169–71; "Fei ming xia," pp. 174–75; 12 "Gong Meng," p. 275.

37. *Mozi jiangu* 4 "Jian ai xia," p. 75; 7 "Tian zhi shang," pp. 127, 128; 8 "Ming gui xia," p. 147; 9 "Fei ming xia," p. 174; 12 "Gui yi," p. 268.

38. *Mozi jiangu* 9 "Fei ming xia," pp. 173–75; 8 "Ming gui xia," p. 154.

39. *Mozi jiangu* 6 "Jie zang xia," pp. 112–16.

40. *Mozi jiangu* 9 "Fei ming shang," pp. 164–65, 166. See also 8 "Ming gui xia," pp. 145–46, 147; 9 "Fei ming zhong," pp. 169, 171; 12 "Gui yi," pp. 268–69. One passage also speaks of the huge number of books in the world that are totally alien to the teachings of the sages. See 7 "Tian zhi shang," p. 122. The authors of the *Mozi* were impressed by the quantity of texts circulating in the fourth century B.C.

41. *Mozi jiangu* 7 "Tian zhi xia," p. 135; 12 "Gong Meng," p. 284.

42. *Mozi jiangu* 8 "Ming gui xia," pp. 139–45.

43. *Mozi jiangu* 8 "Ming gui xia," pp. 144–45. For further discussion of the significance of this story, see Lewis, *Sanctioned Violence*, pp. 198–99.

44. *Mozi jiangu* 13 "Lu wen," p. 285.

45. *Mengzi zhengyi* 1A "Liang Hui Wang shang," pp. 27–29; 1B "Liang Hui Wang xia," pp. 63–64, 65–66, 67, 69, 71–72, 79–81, 86, 89, 90, 96, 97; 2A "Gongsun Chou shang," pp. 104–05, 109, 144–45; 3A "Teng Wen Gong shang," pp. 186, 197–202; 3B "Teng Wen Gong xia," pp. 254–57; 4A "Li Lou shang," pp. 284, 285, 288–89, 289–90, 292, 295–96, 301, 302; 5A "Wan Zhang shang," pp. 374–79, 379–81, 381–85, 385–88; 5B "Wan Zhang xia," pp. 395–98, 398–407 (description of Zhou institutions); 6B "Gaozi xia," pp. 489–94, 501–02, 506, 507; 7A "Jin xin shang," pp. 537, 543, 545; 7B "Jin xin xia," pp. 566, 574.

For a sketch of the "facts" of ancient history as portrayed in the *Mencius*, see D. C. Lau, tr., *Mencius* (Harmondsworth: Penguin, 1970), Appendix 4: Ancient History as Understood by Mencius.

46. *Mengzi zhengyi* 1A "Liang Hui Wang shang," pp. 44–46; 2A "Gongsun Chou shang," pp. 102–03, 130–31; 3B "Teng Wen Gong xia," pp. 244–45; 4B "Li Lou xia," pp. 320–21; 6B "Gaozi xia," pp. 494–500; 7A "Jin xin shang," pp. 544–45.

47. *Mengzi zhengyi* 1B "Liang Hui Wang xia," pp. 81–83; 2B "Gongsun Chou xia," pp. 154–55, 165, 172–74, 184; 3A "Teng Wen Gong shang," p. 190; 3B "Teng Wen Gong xia," pp. 242, 247, 259; 4A "Li Lou shang," p. 314; 4B "Li Lou xia," pp. 334, 335–36, 351; 5A "Wan Zhang shang," pp. 359–73; 5B "Wan Zhang xia," pp. 409–10; 6B "Gaozi xia," pp. 478–81; 7A "Jin xin shang," pp. 523, 531, 548–49; 7B "Jin xin xia," pp. 568, 595.

48. Not only were the "essay" chapters of the Mohist canon devoted to principles defined by opposition to the *ru*, but the last two essay chapters and several of the later "dialogue" chapters were given over to attacks on *ru* positions. See *Mozi jiangu* 9 "Fei ru shang," "Fei ru xia"; 11 "Geng Zhu," pp. 258, 259–60, 261–62 (2); 12 "Gong Meng"; 13 "Lu wen."

On Confucius as a sage or moral paradigm, and his disciples as morally exemplary individuals, see *Mengzi zhengyi* 2A "Gongsun Chou shang," pp. 126–27, 127–28, 128–29, 142–43; 4A "Li Lou shang," p. 308; 4B "Li Lou xia," pp. 327, 331–32, 351–52, 354–56; 5A "Wan Zhang shang," p. 383; 5B "Wan Zhang xia," pp. 396–98, 411–16, 417–18, 420–24, 425–27; 7B "Jin xin xia," pp. 575, 576.

49. *Mengzi zhengyi* 7B "Jin xin xia," p. 560.

50. On the "School of the Tillers," see A. C. Graham, "The *Nung-chia* 'School of the Tillers' and the Origin of Peasant Utopianism in China," *Bulletin of the School of Oriental and African Studies* 42 (1971): 66–100. Reprinted in *Studies in Chinese Philosophy and Philosophical Literature*, pp. 67–110.

51. *Mengzi zhengyi* 3A "Teng Wen Gong shang," pp. 219–30, 232.

52. *Mengzi zhengyi* 3B "Teng Wen Gong xia," pp. 263–72. On the succession of the sages and Mencius as their potential successor, see also 7B "Jin xin xia," pp. 608–10.

53. *Mengzi zhengyi* 4B "Li Lou xia," p. 337. On the character *ji* 迹 in relation to writing, see chapter 7.

54. *Mengzi zhengyi* 3B "Teng Wen Gong xia," pp. 266–67, 271; 4B "Li Lou xia," pp. 337–38.

55. *Mengzi zhengyi* 7B "Jin xin xia," p. 562.

56. *Chun qiu fan lu yizheng* 2, pp. 3a–b. The author cites the opening of the passage in the *Mencius*, and then notes that the *Spring and Autumn Annals* celebrates war waged for revenge. He tries to reconcile the contradiction by asserting that a few exceptions do not overthrow a general truth.

57. *Mengzi zhengyi* 7B "Jin xin xia," p. 565.

58. *Mengzi zhengyi* 5A "Wan Zhang shang," pp. 376–77.

59. For an introduction to the schema of history in the *Xunzi* and its relation to the philosophy of the text, see Knoblock, *Xunzi: A Translation and Study of the Complete Works*, vol. 2, pp. 3–50.

60. *Xunzi jijie* 1 "Quan xue," pp. 1–2, 7, 8–10. On the Way of the sages residing in texts, see also 4 "Rong ru," p. 43; 8 "Ru xiao," pp. 84–85. On the secondary nature of texts, see 8 "Ru xiao," pp. 88–89.

61. On the sages and evil kings as moral types and the consequences of divergent education, see *Xunzi jijie* 1 "Quan xue," p. 11; 2 "Xiu shen," p. 13; 3 "Bu gou," pp. 25–26; 4 "Rong ru," pp. 39–40, 41–42—the prevalence of evil men like Jie and Zhou and the rarity of sages is a result of people's being "boorish and untutored *lou* 陋"—43; 5 "Fei xiang," p. 50; 8 "Ru xiao," pp. 79–80, 83, 90–91; 9 "Wang zhi," p. 109; 11 "Wang ba," pp. 138, 142; 15 "Yi bing," p. 177; 16 "Qiang guo," pp. 197, 198–99, 204; 17 "Tian lun," pp. 205, 209–10; 19 "Li lun," p. 237; 21 "Jie bi," pp. 270–71; 23 "Xing e," pp. 294, 295, 296; 26 "Fu," p. 314.

On the gentleman knowing the distant past through study of what is near at hand, because the past remains in the present, the nature of the sages is the nature of all men, and the Way of all kings is present in the Later Kings, see *Xunzi jijie* 3 "Bu gou," p. 30—"The essential nature of 1,000 men or 10,000 men is that of a single man. The beginnings of Heaven and Earth are still present today. The way of all kings is in that of the Later Kings."—4 "Fei xiang," pp. 51–52; 8 "Ru xiao," pp. 88–89—here the "great *ru*" are distinguished from the "petty *ru*" by the fact that the former seek the truth through the Later Kings—12 "Jun dao," p. 155; 17 "Tian lun," p. 211; 19 "Li lun," p. 248; 22 "Zheng ming," p. 274; 23 "Xing e," p. 293; 24 "Junzi," p. 302.

62. *Xunzi jijie* 4 "Rong ru," p. 44; 5 "Fei xiang," pp. 46–48, 50–51, 51–52—these discuss the disappearance of pre-Zhou texts—53; 6 "Fei shier zi," pp. 58, 59 (2), 63–64; 7 "Zhong Ni," pp. 66–68; 8 "Ru xiao," pp. 73–74, 85–86; 9 "Wang zhi," pp. 96, 97, 110; 10 "Fu guo," pp. 116, 124; 11 "Wang ba," pp. 133–34, 135, 145; 12 "Jun dao," pp. 153, 158–59, 160–61; 13 "Chen dao," pp. 165, 166, 169, 170–71; 15 "Yi bing," pp. 181, 182–83, 184–85, 185–86, 188–89; 16 "Qiang guo," p. 196, 200–02—this compares the insecurity of Qin in the late Warring States with the stability of the Zhou—18 "Zheng lun," pp. 215, 215–18, 219–21, 221; 19 "Li lun," pp. 231, 239, 247–48, 250; 20 "Yue lun," pp. 252–54; 21 "Jie bi," pp. 267–68; 23 "Xing e," pp. 289 (3), 289–90, 290, 291–92 (4), 293 (2), 299; 24 "Junzi," p. 301. The first section of 25 "Cheng xiang" consists of poems that lament the disastrous state of the present. They refer variously to its "disaster" (*yang* 殃), "calamity" (*zai* 災), "misfortune" (*huo* 禍), and "stupidity" (*yu* 愚). See pp. 304–06. By contrast, poems #23–33 celebrate Yao, Shun, Yu, Hou Ji, and Tang. See pp. 307–09.

63. *Xunxi jijie* 4 "Rong ru," p. 37. This conservatism of the lower officials echoes the attitude attributed to them in the *Lü shi chun qiu*, where they are described as those who blindly "defend the laws to the death." See *Lü shi chun qiu jiaoshi* "Cha jin," p. 936. See also *Xunzi jijie* 25, "Cheng xiang," stanza 56.

64. *Xunzi jijie* 6 "Fei shier zi," pp. 60–61, 61–62. On the pairing of Confucius as the sage without political power and the former kings who actually ruled, see 11 "Wang ba," p. 132. On the suppression of the non-*ru* traditions as the hallmark of the true gentleman, see 8 "Ru xiao," pp. 77–78. On *li yi* 禮義 as the invention of

the sages and the basis of order and knowledge, see the following: 3 "Bu gou," pp. 23–24—禮義 is the standard by which the gentleman rejects the arguments of the sophists, p. 27—禮義 is the difference between chaos and order, p. 30—禮義 is what links all the sages; 4 "Rong ru," pp. 40, 44—sage kings create 禮義 to regulate distribution among people; 5 "Fei xiang," p. 53—following 禮義 is parallel to being in accord with the sages as the standard for all language; 6 "Fei shier zi," p. 63; 8 "Ru xiao," p. 75—once again parallels 禮義 and sages as standards, pp. 77, 88—failure to know 禮義 as hallmark of "petty *ru*" that makes them identical to Mohists, pp. 89, 92—the accumulation of 禮義 creates a gentleman; 9 "Wang zhi," p. 94—禮義 distinguishes officials from commoners, p. 96, and so on throughout the text.

65. *Xunzi jijie* 8 "Ru xiao," pp. 73–74, 75–76, 77–78, 93; 10 "Fu guo," pp. 119–22; 11 "Wang ba," pp. 138–39—this passage describes Mohist teachings as the way of the servitor (*yi fu* 役夫) and contrasts them with the *ru* who defend the Way of the sages; 20 "Yue lun," pp. 252–54—this passage describes the sages' invention of music and denounces the Mohist condemnation of music as a rejection of the sages.

66. *Xunzi jijie* 21 "Jie bi," pp. 258–62, 270–72.

67. *Xunzi jijie* 22 "Zheng ming," pp. 276, 280.

68. *Shang Jun shu zhuyi* 1 "Geng fa 更法," pp. 10, 13.

69. *Shang Jun shu zhuyi* 3 "Nong zhan 農戰," p. 73; 6 "Suan di 算地," pp. 146, 169, 170; 8 "Yi yan 壹言," pp. 206, 209–10; 9 "Cuo fa 錯法," p. 222—here the models are the "enlightened rulers of antiquity" (*gu zhi ming jun* 古之明君), later identified as the "Three Kings" and the "Five Hegemons"; 13 "Jin ling 靳令," p. 288; 14 "Xiu quan 修權," pp. 296–97—this asserts that the "former kings" established the practice of ruling through standardized measures, and it employs Yao as the type of the exemplary ruler; 17 "Shang xing 賞刑," pp. 340, 352, 367–68 (three times); 18 "Hua ce 畫策," pp. 378, 397; 20 "Ruo min 弱民," p. 452; 23 "Jun chen 君臣," pp. 476–77; 24 "Jin shi 禁使," pp. 490, 491, 498 (twice); 26 "Ding fen 定分," p. 543—this argues that writings left by the sages can only be understood when received from a teacher, and that such teachers should be officials—pp. 544, 548 (three times).

70. *Shang Jun shu zhuyi* 6 "Suan di," p. 163; 14 "Xiu quan," p. 300; 17 "Shang xing," pp. 343, 353; 25 "Shen fa 慎法," pp. 508, 517.

71. *Shang Jun shu zhuyi* 6 "Suan di," p. 164; 7 "Kai sai 開塞," pp. 189, 191–92; 8 "Yi yan," p. 215; 15 "Lai min 徠民," pp. 333–34; 18 "Hua ce," pp. 372–73.

72. *Shang Jun shu zhuyi* 6 "Suan di," pp. 146, 152, 162, 175; 7 "Kai sai," p. 201; 8 "Yi ran," pp. 214–15; 14 "Xiu quan," p. 301; 18 "Hua ce," p. 376; 23 "Jun chen," p. 481; 24 "Jin shi," pp. 491, 497–98, 498.

73. *Shang Jun shu zhuyi* 15 "Lai min," pp. 311, 312, 329–30; 20 "Ruo min," p. 453.

74. On the sages as great rulers whose policies responded to the needs of their own time but are no longer appropriate, see *Han Feizi ji shi* 19 "Wu du," pp.

1040–42, 1051, 1078. On the sages as disloyal or rebellious, see 15 "Nan yi 難一," pp. 795–96; 16 "Nan san," p. 853; 19 "Zhong xiao," pp. 1107–09. This last chapter also cites the sages and the "Three Kings" as exemplary figures. See pp. 1109–10, 1110. Another chapter refutes the attack on the sages and says that this argument is espoused by traitorous ministers and disorderly rulers. See 17 "Shuo yi 說疑," pp. 925–26. The chapters that treat the sages as the finest examples of general types place them in lists that also include rulers or ministers from the Eastern Zhou period. These include "Nan yan 難言," pp. 49–50; "Ai chen," p. 60; 4 "Shuo nan 說難," p. 222; "Jian jie shi chen 姦劫弒臣," pp. 250, 251; 5 "Nan mian 南面," p. 298.

75. *Han Feizi ji shi* 11 "Wai chu shuo zuo shang," pp. 649–50; 18 "Liu fan," pp. 952, 953; "Ba shuo 八說," p. 976—this passage speaks of the paucity of writings from the sages and consequent disputes among scholars; 19 "Wu du," p. 1078; "Xian xue," pp. 1080—also on lack of textual evidence leading to scholarly disputes, p. 1090.

76. On the "former kings," the "sages," or named ancient rulers and ministers as exemplary figures to whom are attributed the basic principles of the legalist theory of government, see *Han Feizi ji shi* 2 "You du 有度," pp. 87, 87–88, 88 (twice); "Yang quan," pp. 121–22, 123—the sages described in these passages are proto-Daoist figures, p. 123—on the Yellow Emperor; "Shi guo 十過," pp. 186–87—this passage takes ancient times as the highest model and traces a steady decline from Yao through Shun, Yu, and the Yin; 4 "Jian jie shi chen," pp. 249, 250; 5 "Bei nei 備內," pp. 289–90—in these passages ancient traditions and chronicles are cited to prove an argument; "Shi xie 飾邪," pp. 307, 310 (twice); 6 "Jie Lao 解老," pp. 365, 377; 7 "Yu Lao 喻老," pp. 416, 417; "Shuo lin shang 說林上," pp. 417–18, 431, 439, 441; 8 "Shuo lin xia," pp. 457, 460; "Guan xing 觀行," p. 479; "An wei 安危," p. 483 (twice)—this passage discusses the transmission of authoritative writings by the sages, pp. 484, 484–85; "Shou dao 守道," pp. 491, 492; "Yong ren 用人," pp. 498, 500; "Gong ming 功名," pp. 507–08, 508–09; 11 "Wai chu shuo zuo shang," p. 623—in an explanation of why Master Mo was not eloquent, this passage explains that he was transmitting the "Way of the former kings and the words of the sages," so he sought utility rather than style; 13 "Wai chu shuo you shang," pp. 722–23; 17 "Nan shi 難勢," pp. 886, 887, 888–89; "Shuo yi," pp. 918–19, 924–25, 931–32; "Gui shi 詭使," pp. 934–35—this passage contrasts the excellent government of the ancient sages with present (*jin* 今) practice; 18 "Liu fan 六反," pp. 949—this passage cites "an ancient saying" as authority and presents "the proper rule of the sages" as the model of government, p. 952; 19 "Wu du," pp. 1040, 1057–58; "Xian xue," pp. 1097, 1104; 20 "Xin du 心度," pp. 1134, 1135.

77. *Han Feizi jishi* 5 "Bei nei," p. 290; "Shi xie," p. 307; 8 "Guan xing," p. 479; "Shou dao," p. 491; "Yong ren," pp. 498, 499; "Gong ming," p. 508; "Da ti 大體," p. 512; 17 "Gui shi," pp. 934–35; 18 "Liu fan," p. 949; 19 "Wu du," p.

1058; "Xian xue," pp. 1089 (twice), 1090, 1091, 1092 (twice), 1099, 1102, 1103 (twice); 20 "Ren zhu 人主," pp. 1119 (twice), 1120 (twice).

78. *Han Feizi jishi* 1 "Chu jian 初見," pp. 2–3, 4; 2 "You du," p. 85; "Er bing," pp. 111, 112; 3 "Shi guo," pp. 164–205; 4 "Gu fen 孤憤," p. 208; "Shuo nan," p. 223; "He shi 和氏," pp. 238–39; "Jian jie shi chen," pp. 246, 246–47, 248–49, 251, 251–52; 5 "Bei nei," p. 289; "Shi xie," pp. 307, 308–09, 310–11; 8 "Shuo lin xia," pp. 417–47; "Yong ren," p. 499; 9 "Nei chu shuo shang," pp. 516–59; 15 "Nan yi," pp. 791–95, 800–18; "Nan er," pp. 818–43; 16 "Nan san," pp. 844–52, 860–70; "Nan si," pp. 870–85; 17 "Wen tian 問田," pp. 903–04; "Ding fa," pp. 906–08; "Shuo yi," pp. 914–19; 19 "Xian xue," p. 1104; 20 "Ren zhu," p. 1118.

79. Jullien, *Le détour et l'accès*, ch. 6, "La dissidence impossible (idéologie de l'obliquité)."

80. *Laozi dao de jing zhu* #1, p. 1.

81. *Laozi dao de jing zhu* #14, p. 8; #40, p. 25. On seeking out ancient origins, see also #21, p. 12: "Fathomless! Dark! In its midst there are refined spirits. These refined spirits are very pure, and in their midst there is truth. From ancient times to the present its name has not departed, and thereby we can observe the beginnings of things." For other passages on "returning," see #16, p. 9; #22, p. 12; #25, p. 14; #28, p. 16; #52, p. 32; #64, p. 39.

82. *Laozi dao de jing zhu* #28, p. 16; #64, p. 39. On reversing the process of education and going back to one's origins, see #48, p. 29.

83. *Laozi dao de jing zhu* #42, p. 27; #70, p. 42.

84. *Laozi dao de jing zhu* #4, p. 3; #6, p. 4.

85. *Laozi dao de jing zhu* #25, p, 14; #40, p. 26; #52, p. 32. On the origins of the world from the Way, see also #51, p. 31.

86. *Laozi dao de jing zhu* #38, p. 23; #80, pp. 46–47.

87. Several twentieth-century scholars have analyzed the relation between the two texts. See Shimada Kan 島田翰, *Kobun kyūsho kō* 古文舊書考 (Tokyo, 1905); Eva Kraft, "Zum Huai Nan Tzu: Einführung, Übersetzung (Kapitel I und II) und Interpretation," *Monumenta Serica* 16 (1957): 201–09. The results of these studies are summarized in list form in Barbara Kandel, *Wen Tzu—Ein Beitrag zur Problematik und zum Verständnis eines taoistischen Textes* (Frankfurt am Main: Peter Lang, 1974), pp. 323–332. In the body of the book see also pp. 3, 6–9, 66–85.

88. Kandel, in the pages cited above, argues for this theory.

89. For a transcription of the 277 bamboo strips discovered, and an analysis of their relation to the received text, see "Dingzhou Xi Han Zhongshan Huai Wang mu zhu jian 'Wenzi' Shiwen 定州西漢中山懷王墓竹简文子释文," *Wenwu* (1995:12): 27–34; "Dingzhou Xi Han Zhongshan Huai Wang mu zhu jian 'Wenzi' jiaokan ji 定州西漢中山懷王墓竹简文子校勘记," *Wenwu* (1995:12): 35–37. On the significance of this find for dating the text and establishing its relation to the *Huainanzi*, see "Dingzhou Xi Han Zhongshan Huai Wang mu zhu jian

'Wenzi' de zhengli he yiyi 定州西漢中山懷王墓竹简文子的整理和意义,"
Wenwu (1995:12): 38–40; Li Dingsheng 李定生, "'Wenzi' fei wei shu kao 文子非
偽書考," in *Dao jia wenhua yanjiu* 5 (Shanghai: Guji, 1994), pp. 462–73; Zhang
Dainian 張岱年, "Shi tan 'Wenzi' de niandai yu sixiang 試談文子的年代與思
想," in *Daojia wenhua yanjiu* 5, pp. 133–41.

 90. *Jing fa*, "Dao yuan," pp. 101–02.

 91. *Huainanzi*, 1 "Yuan dao," p. 1; *Wenzi yao quan* 文子要詮, annotated by
Li Dingsheng 李定生 and Xu Huijun 徐慧君 (Shanghai: Fudan Daxue, 1988),
pp. 30–31.

 92. On the "Great Man" and his journey, see *Huainanzi* 1 "Yuan dao," p. 3.
On sages, see pp. 1 (Fu Xi and Nü Wa), 3 (Gun, Yu [twice], Li Zhu, Music Master
Kuang, Shen Nong), 6 (Yu), 7 (Gonggong, Yi of Yue, Shun), 10 (Yu), 13 (Zi Xia),
15 (Xu You, Yao). On alien peoples, see pp. 6 (Xiongnu, Di, Wu, Yue), 8 (San
Miao, Suzhen, the Feathered Men, the Naked Men). On materials derived from
the medical traditions, see pp. 3, 12–13, 14–15, 17–18. The "Great Man" and his
journey, but in a metaphorical form, also appears in the *Wenzi*. See *Wenzi yao quan*
1 "Dao yuan," pp. 32–33.

 93. *Huainanzi* 1 "Yuan dao," p. 10; *Wenzi yao quan* 1 "Dao yuan," p. 43. See
Sarah Allan, *The Way of Water and Sprouts of Virtue* (Albany: SUNY, 1997).

 94. *Huainanzi* 1 "Yuan dao," pp. 3–4, 5, 6–7, 8, 10, 12, 13, 15, 16, 17; *Wenzi
yao quan* 1 "Dao yuan," pp. 33, 34–35, 35–37, 39–40, 42, 43–44, 45, 46. The
chapters on the energetics of the human body are *Huainanzi* 7 "Jing shen 精神"
and *Wenzi yao quan* 2 "Jing cheng 精誠." *Wenzi yao quan* 3 "Jiu shou 九守" also
begins with an account of the primal chaos. See p. 67.

 95. *Huainanzi* 1 "Yuan dao," pp. 5, 6–7, 8.

 96. *Jing fa* "Guan," pp. 48–49; "Guo tong 果童," p. 52; "Xing zheng 姓
爭," p. 65; "Cheng fa 成法," p. 73; "Shun dao 順道," p. 85.

 97. Lewis, *Sanctioned Violence in Early China*, pp. 165–74. This discusses the
accounts of origins only as a collective means of writing about the social and institutional developments of the period, without considering their role in interschool
polemics.

 98. Graham, "The *Nung-chia* 'School of the Tillers.'"

 99. That Yao and Shun were the mythic originators of *ru* practice is marked
in the temporal limits of the *Shang shu*. For explicit statements, see *Shi ji* 1, p. 46;
Han shu 30, p. 1728.

 100. *Mengzi zhengyi* 3A "Teng Wen Gong shang," pp. 219–30; 7B "Teng
Wen Gong xia," pp. 263–72; 7B "Jin xin xia," p. 560.

 101. *Mozi jiangu* 25 "Jie zang xia," p. 105. This dispute between the Mohists
and the *ru* over who was the true heir of Yao, Shun, and Yu is also cited in *Han Feizi
ji shi* 19 "Xian xue," p. 1080.

 102. *Mozi jiangu* 11 "Shang tong shang," pp. 44–45; 12 "Shang tong zhong,"
pp. 47–48.

 103. *Mozi jiangu* 21 "Jie yong zhong," pp. 101–04. On the links between the

technical activities of the sages and their organization of society through laws, see Jean Levi, "Le mythe de l'âge d'or et les théories de l'évolution en Chine ancienne," *L'homme* 17 (1977), p. 82.

104. *Shang Jun shu zhu yi* 7 "Kai sai," pp. 182. Related versions of the sages' creation of civilization through the legal imposition of hierarchies appear in 7 "Kai sai," p. 201; 14 "Xiu quan," pp. 296–97; 23 "Jun chen," pp. 476–77. A similar account appears in *Guanzi jiao zheng* 11 "Jun chen," p. 174.

105. *Han Feizi ji shi* 19 "Wu du," pp. 1040–42. Another account of the evolution of forms of rule in response to rising population appears in 18 "Ba shuo," p. 974. The theme of evolution from primitive simplicity to a higher physical culture also appears in 3 "Shi guo," pp. 186–87; 7 "Yu Lao," p. 400. Both these passages adopt a proto-Daoist attitude in privileging natural simplicity and treating the introduction of "higher" technologies as the first step on the road to disaster.

106. *Mozi jiangu* 8 "Ming gui xia," pp. 141, 143, 144, 145—this refers to the chronicles of Zhou, Yan, Song, and Qi; *Mengzi zhengyi* 4B "Li Lou xia," p. 338—this refers to the chronicles of Jin, Chu, and Lu; *Zuo zhuan zhu* Zhao 2, p. 1226—in this story an emissary from Jin inspects the chronicle of Lu and the *Yi* (*Book of Changes*) in the office of the grand historian of Lu; *Guo yu* 13 "Jin yu 7," p. 445; 17 "Chu yu shang," p. 528—these last two both refer to chronicles as elements in the education of rulers.

107. Lewis, *Sanctioned Violence*, pp. 15–16; Tsuda Sōkichi 津田左友吉, *Saden no shisōshiteki kenkyū* 左傳の思想史的研究 (Tokyo: Tōyō Bunko, 1935), pp. 571–643.

108. Masubuchi, *Shunjū sengoku ni okeru Shōsho no tenkai*, pp. 315–83, esp. 372–77; Kamata Tadashi 鎌田正, *Saden no seiritsu to sono tenkai* 左傳の成立とその展開, 2nd ed. (Tokyo: Taishūkan, 1993), pp. 330–61.

109. *Zuo zhuan zhu* Xiang 25, p. 1099.

110. *Zuo zhuan zhu* Xuan 2, pp. 662–63. The same story is recorded in more detail, and with emphasis on the theme of vengeance, in the *Gongyang Commentary*. See *Gongyang zhuan zhu shu* 15 (Xuan 2), p. 6b; (Xuan 6), pp. 10a–14b.

111. *Shang shu zhengyi* 14 "Kang gao," pp. 1b–3a; 15 "Shao gao," pp. 1b–4a; "Luo gao," 14a–14b.

112. *Shang shu zhengyi* 16 "Duo shi," p. 1b; 17 "Duo fang," p. 5a.

113. *Shang shu zhengyi* 7 "Gan shi 甘誓," p. 1b; 9 "Pan Geng," pp. 2b, 10a, 16a; 10 "Gao Zong rong ri 高宗肜日," pp. 9b–10a; "Xi Bo kan li 西伯戡黎," pp. 12a–b; 11 "Mu shi 牧誓," p. 14b.

114. The current consensus on dating, although not unchallenged, places the composition of the text in the fourth century B.C. This would make it the earliest surviving narrative history in Chinese literature. See Bernhard Karlgren, "On the authenticity and nature of the Tso-chuan," *Götesborgs högskolas arsskrift* 32 (1926); rep. ed. Taipei: Chengwen, 1965; Karlgren, "The early history of Chou li and Tso chuan texts," *Bulletin of the Museum of Far Eastern Antiquities* 3 (1931): 1–59; Kamata Tadashi, *Saden no seiritsu to sono tenkai*. Kamata's book contains not only a

good argument for dating the text on the basis of language, intellectual content, and astronomical evidence, but also a thorough critique of the leading alternative theories. See also the entry on the *Chun qiu* in Loewe, ed., *Early Chinese Texts*.

A second issue is the relation of the *Zuo zhuan* to the *Chun qiu*. Many scholars think that the former was originally an independent work that was adapted as a commentary to the *Chun qiu* because of the increasing prestige of the latter. Whether or not the *Zuo zhuan* was originally a commentary, it was certainly a chronicle of events mixed with speeches attributed to participants in the events narrated. As such its essential nature would not have been changed by being linked to the *Chun qiu*.

115. Although secondary scholarship on the *Zuo zhuan* has been dominated by the question of dating, there are a few works that examine the work itself. The most extensive is Tsuda Sōkichi, *Saden no shisōshiteki kenkyū*. A more recent work is Zhang Duansui 張端穗, *Zuo zhuan sixiang tan wei* 左傳思想探微 (Taipei: Xuehai, 1987).

116. Zheng Xuan (A.D. 127–200) 鄭玄, "Liu yi lun 六藝論," in *Quan shanggu san dai Qin Han Sanguo liu chao wen* 全上古三代秦漢三國六朝文 (reprint ed., Beijing: Zhonghua, 1958), vol. 1, p. 928. For a similar observation made a century later, see *Jin shu* 晉書, compiled by Fang Xuanling 方玄齡 (A.D. 578–648) et al. (Beijing: Zhonghua, 1974) 75, p. 1978. For a discussion in English, see Burton Watson, *Early Chinese Literature* (New York: Columbia University, 1962), pp. 40–66.

117. Li Zongtong 李宗侗, "Shi guan zhidu—fu lun dui chuantong zhi zunzhong 史官制度——附論對傳統之尊重," in *Zhongguo shixue shi lunwen xuan ji* 中國史學史論文選集, ed. Du Weiyun 杜維運 and Huang Jinxing 黃進興 (Taipei: Huashi, 1976), vol. 1, pp. 90–91. For the passages attributed to Confucius omitted by Li, see *Zuo zhuan zhu* Cheng 2, pp. 788–89; Xiang 27, p. 1130.

118. See, for example, *Zuo zhuan zhu* Xi 28, p. 473. In this passage Confucius says that for a minister to summon a ruler cannot be "taken as a model" or "followed" (*xun* 訓), but there is no doubt that this act is condemned as a violation of ritual.

119. Lewis, *Sanctioned Violence*, pp. 22–28, 36, 44.

120. Noteworthy among the secondary studies on rituals depicted or mentioned in the *Zuo zhuan* are Song Dingzong 宋鼎宗, "Chun qiu Zuo zhuan bin li jia li kao 春秋左傳賓禮嘉禮考," *Guoli Taiwan Shifan Daxue Guowen Yanjiusuo Jikan* 16 (1972): 199–366; Li Chongyuan 李崇遠, *Chun qiu san zhuan li yi tong kao* 春秋三傳禮儀通考 (Taipei: Jiaxin Shuini Gongsi Jijinhui, 1969).

121. *Zuo zhuan zhu* Yin 1, pp. 10–15. The story is translated in Burton Watson, tr., *The Tso chuan: Selections from China's Oldest Narrative History* (New York: Columbia University, 1989), pp. 1–4.

122. *Zuo zhuan zhu* Yin 3, pp. 32–33 (translated in Watson, *Tso chuan*, pp. 5–6); Yin 11, p. 72; Zhao 26, pp. 1424–25; Ai 7, pp. 1640–41 (translated in Watson, *Tso chuan*, p. xxii).

123. *Zuo zhuan zhu* Zhao 25, pp. 1457–59. Page 1458 explains that "the duties of Earth" are the models for "ruler and minister, superior and subordinate."

124. *Zuo zhuan zhu* Cheng 13, p. 860. See also Wen 15, pp. 612, 614; Cheng 15, p. 873; Zhao 7, p. 1295.

125. *Zuo zhuan zhu* Yin 11, p. 76; Huan 2, p. 92.

126. *Zuo zhuan zhu* Xi 11, p. 338; Xiang 30, p. 1177. This second passage states that ritual is the trunk of the state, and that no calamity is greater than the loss of ritual.

127. *Zuo zhuan zhu* Zhao 26, p. 1480–81. At the end Yan Ying states that ritual was "received from Heaven and Earth by the former kings," thus linking ritual as state regulation with ritual as cosmic principle.

128. *Zuo zhuan zhu* Zhao 5, p. 1266. A second speech on this theme includes the statement cited earlier, "Ritual is the constant principle of Heaven, the duties of Earth, and the conduct of the people." See Zhao 25, pp. 1457–59. On these passages, see Lewis, "Les rites comme trame de l'histoire," pp. 34–35.

129. *Zuo zhuan zhu* Wen 16, p. 614.

130. *Zuo zhuan zhu* Yin 11, p. 72.

131. *Zuo zhuan zhu* Zhuang 18, p. 207; Huan 3, p. 99.

132. *Zuo zhuan zhu* Wen 2, pp. 524–25. The criticism by the "gentleman" is followed by one from Confucius. See pp. 525–26. This double criticism suggests the tremendous importance that the author attached to this issue. A case dealing with a female version of this error, an attempt to give a wife precedence over a mother, figures in Xiang 2, p. 921.

133. *Zuo zhuan zhu* Xi 13, pp. 999–1000.

134. *Zuo zhuan zhu* Zhao 12, pp. 1331–32 tells a story in which Zi Chan refuses to destroy the ancestral temple of the You clan even though this would facilitate the burial of the recently deceased lord of Zheng. At the end of the story the "gentleman" states, "In this [action] Zi Chan understood ritual. Ritual is not harming others in order to complete one's own ends."

135. *Zuo zhuan zhu* Yin 9–10, pp. 65, 69.

136. This has been noted by many scholars, but no one has done more than cite a few examples and give a rudimentary explanation. See Tsuda, *Saden no shisōshi teki kenkyū*, pp. 396–98; Zhang, *Zuo zhuan sixiang tan wei*, pp. 134–36; Watson, *Tso chuan*, pp. xxi–xxiii; Xu Fuguan 徐復觀, *Zhongguo ren xing lun shi xian Qin pian* 中國人性論史先秦篇 (Taipei: Shangwu, 1976), p. 50.

137. The entry on the campaign itself, although not the numerous entries leading up to it, is translated in Watson, *Tso chuan*, pp. 30–37. This entry does, however, refer back to many of the earlier acts that ultimately led to the battle and gave Qin moral superiority. It also contains several prophecies, both on the basis of yarrow divination and on the assessment of the conduct of the adversaries.

138. *Zuo zhuan zhu* Xi 10, pp. 334–35.

139. *Zuo zhuan zhu* 13, pp. 347–48.

140. *Zuo zhuan zhu* Xi 15, pp. 351–52, 353, 354–57, 365. The use of prophecy in battles as an extension of the logical analysis of the factors that produce victory or defeat figures prominently even in such a master of *realpolitik* as Thucydides.

Before battles the opposing commanders analyze the balance of skills, terrain, and morale, and thereby predict the course and outcome of the battle. See Jacqueline de Romilly *Histoire et raison chez Thucydide* (Paris: Belles Lettres, 1967), ch. 2.

141. Six years before the battle of Chengpu, the king of Chu displays the ears of slain enemies to wives of the lord of Zheng, and then takes two of the latter's concubines as his own. The gentleman denounces the first as a violation of ritual. Shu Dan judges the second act likewise, and predicts his death. See Xi 22, pp. 399, 400. Meanwhile, his rival performs meritorious acts, including escorting the Zhou king back to the capital from which he had been driven, and keeping a promise to his own troops not to keep them in a siege more than three days. See Xi 25, pp. 431–32, 435. In the year immediately preceding the battle, the Chu commander whips and mutilates soldiers who do not perform correctly, so that his own predecessor predicts his defeat. See Xi 27, pp. 444–45. Jin, on the other hand, appoints a new commander who is expert in ritual, music, the *Odes*, and the *Documents*. They conduct a three-stage training that culminates in learning ritual. See Xi 27, pp. 445–46. In the campaign itself, the rudeness of the Chu commander's message to the Jin army leads a Jin officer to denounce his violation of ritual and declare that he will be beaten. The Lord of Jin, on the other hand, is meticulous in observing *li*, and withdraws his army a distance of three days' march in order to pay back favors received in the past. These observances are made despite a prophetic song and a dream that foretell his victory. See Xi 28, pp. 457–58, 458–59, 461. The Jin army is described as "having ritual." The Chu commander, by contrast, ignores a dream in which the god of the Yellow River offers to help him in exchange for some jade horse ornaments. This leads two of his officers to predict defeat. They insist, however, that the defeat will be caused not by the god, but by the fact that the commander did not care enough about his troops to sacrifice some ornaments. See Xi 28, pp. 467–68. The account of the campaign is partially translated in Watson, *Tso chuan*, pp. 50–64.

Prior to the battle of Bi the Jin officers hold a debate on whether to fight. One argues that Chu cannot be attacked because it is virtuous, observes ritual, has proper government, extracts service in its proper seasons, and has a well-organized army. A second officer replies that not to fight would be cowardly and that Jin obtained the hegemony through military force. This appeal to courage and force of arms against virtue and ritual ultimately carries the day. Immediately after, there are prophecies of Jin defeat, based on both yarrow divination and analysis of the moral positions of the two sides. See Xuan 12, pp. 722–28. At a second debate in the Jin camp Luan Bo argues that Chu cannot be beaten, but his argument is rejected. One observer predicts the defeat of Jin, and another the ultimate rise to power of Luan Bo. See Xuan 12, pp. 731–32. In conversation with a Chu officer prior to the battle, the Jin officer who led the argument in favor of war lacks proper decorum in his speech. See Xuan 12, pp. 733–34. The account of the campaign is partially translated in Watson, *Tso chuan*, pp. 84–102.

The battle of Yanling is also preceded by a history of ritual errors and prophecies. Four years prior to the battle Chu gives an overly rich welcome to a Jin emissary, who protests that they have left no richer ceremony by which they might welcome the lord of Jin. A Chu officer replies that they would meet the lord of Jin only in battle. When he returns and reports the scene to Fan Wenzi, the latter denounces this violation of ritual, says that Chu will be made to "eat their words," and foretells an imminent battle. See Cheng 16, pp. 857–58. Three years later Chu violates a covenant, and Zi Fan of Chu argues that profit takes precedence over covenants. On hearing of this Shen Shu Shi says that Zi Fan violates ritual and so cannot escape disaster. See Cheng 15, p. 873. In the year of the campaign there is another prophecy of Jin's victory because of its willingness to honor other states for the sake of alliances. This is followed by a long speech by Shen Shu Shi on the moral and ritual bases of warfare, a speech which ends with a warning of Chu's defeat. This in turn is followed by another prophecy of Chu's defeat based on observing the conduct of their army. See Xuan 16, pp. 880–82. The account of the campaign is partially translated in Watson, *Tso chuan*, pp. 127–38.

142. *Zuo zhuan zhu* Zhao 3, pp. 1234–37.

143. *Zuo zhuan zhu* Zhao 28, p. 1496—Confucius predicts the flourishing of Wei and probably its emergence as an independent state; Zhao 29, pp. 1504–05—Confucius predicts the end of Jin for the loss of proper degree and measure; Ding 9, p. 1573—Confucius predicts chaos in the Zhao lineage; Ai 15, p. 1696—Confucius predicts the outcome of a civil war in Wei.

144. *Zuo zhuan zhu* Cheng 13, p. 860.

145. *Zuo zhuan zhu* Zhao 11, pp. 1325–26. Since *qi* also refers to breath, it is not surprising that a failure to project one's voice is interpreted as a loss of *qi*. A similar story appears in Xiang 31, p. 1183, where Mu Shu predicts the imminent death of Zhao Meng because the latter's words are careless and though he is "less than fifty" he "babbles like an eighty-year old." The following year two other speakers observe the same behavior and make the same prediction. See Zhao 1, pp. 1210–11, 1215. The importance attributed in the translated passage to the knots of belts can be confirmed by depictions of clothing from the Warring States and Han periods. See Angela Sheng, "The Disappearance of Silk Weaves with Weft Effects in Early China," *Chinese Science* 12 (1995): 50–56; Shen Congwen 沈從文, ed., *Zhongguo gudai fushi yanjiu* 中國古代服飾研究 (Hong Kong: Commercial Press, 1992), pp. 37, 39, 42–45, 59.

146. *Zuo zhuan zhu* Xuan 4, p. 756; Zhao 25, p. 1456. In this second passage the *hunpo* is identified as the "refined illumination" *jing shuang* 精爽 of the mind.

147. *Zuo zhuan zhu* Ding 15, p. 1601. The passage goes on to argue that the ritual errors of the two princes indicate that they have lost their minds.

148. Hihara Toshikuni 日原利國, *Shunjū Kuyōden no kenkyū* 春秋公羊傳の研究 (Tokyo: Sōbunsha, 1976), ch.1; Sagawa Osamu 佐川修, *Shunjū gaku ronkō* 春秋學論考 (Tokyo: Tōhō Shoten, 1983), pp. 78–85.

149. On Confucius' identification with the text, in addition to the passages in the *Mencius* cited earlier, see also *Zhuangzi ji shi* 14 "Tian yun," p. 234; *Han Feizi ji shi* 9 "Nei chu shuo shang," p. 540; *Shi ji* 47, pp. 1943–44; 130, pp. 3296, 3297–99; *Huainanzi* 9 "Zhu shu," p. 150. Hihara Toshikuni argues that the attribution of

the *Chun qiu* to Confucius is textually attested only from the early Western Han. See *Shunjū Kuyōden no kenkyū*, pp. 5–19. In order to defend this position, he insists that the references to Confucius' authorship in the *Zhuangzi* and the *Han Feizi* are later interpolations, and that when the *Mencius* says that Confucius *zuo* 作 the *Chun qiu* it simply means that he "elevated" it or "caused it to arise." This reading, however, would not account for the following sentence in which Confucius states that later men will know him and blame him through the *Chun qiu*, nor for the reference to Confucius "completing" (*cheng* 成) the text. Rather than adopting a rereading that creates more problems than it solves, arbitrarily redating texts to fit an argument, it is more plausible to assume that the authorship of Confucius was accepted as a fact in the Warring States period. Moreover, the hermeneutic of the *Gongyang* assumes the moral infallibility of the author, and Confucius is the most likely figure to fill such a role.

150. *Shi ji* 130, p. 3297. The association of the *Chun qiu* with judicial procedure also appears in *Shi ji* 47, p. 1944. This link of the myth of Confucius as judge to Confucius as the author of the *Chun qiu* probably underlies the later Han practice of using the *Chun qiu* as a source for legal judgments. A text recounted supposed legal judgments by Dong Zhongshu based on the *Chun qiu*. See *Han shu* 30, p. 1714. Ying Shao also wrote a book on using the *Chun qiu* for making legal decisions, and several Han officials employed it in this way. See T'ung-tsu Ch'ü, *Law and Society in Traditional China* (Paris: Mouton & Co., 1961), p. 276.

151. On the "Three Epochs," see Kang Woo, *Les trois théories politiques du Tch'ouen Ts'ieou interprétées par Tong Tchong-chou d'après les principes de l'école de Kong-yang* (Paris: Librairie Ernest Leroux, 1932), pp. 88–106; Anne Cheng, *Etude sur le confucianisme Han: l'élaboration d'une tradition exégétique sur les classiques* (Paris: Collège de France, Institut des Hautes Etudes Chinoises, 1985), pp. 208–12; Sagawa, *Shunjū gaku ronkō*, pp. 113–30.

152. Woo, *Les trois théories*, pp. 100, 107; Cheng, *Etude sur le confucianisme Han*, p. 211. The relevant passages in the *Gongyang* are *Gongyang zhuan zhu shu* 3 (Yin 10), pp. 15a–b; 18 (Cheng 15), p. 7b.

153. On the kingdom of Lu, see Woo, *Les trois théories*, pp. 107–35. The earliest known reference to Confucius acting as a "king without attributes" in writing the *Chun qiu* appears in the writings of Dong Zhongshu. See *Han shu* 56, p. 2509; *Chun qiu fan lu yi zheng* 23 "San dai gai zhi 三代改制," pp. 132a–134b. The idea also appears in the contemporaneous *Huainanzi* 9 "Zhu shu," p. 150. This simultaneous reference in two such disparate sources suggests that the idea probably originated somewhat earlier.

154. On Confucius as a "king without attributes" who foretold Han institutions in the writing of the *Chun qiu*, see Wang Chong 王充, *Lun heng* 論衡, in *Xin bian zhuzi jicheng*, vol. 7, "Cheng cai 程材," p. 121; "Chao qi 超奇," p. 136; "Xu song 須頌," p. 199; "Ding xian 定賢," p. 269.

155. For analyses of the role of the king in the *Gongyang*, see Katō Jōken 加藤常賢, "Shunjū gaku: Juka kokka tetsugaku 春秋學: 儒家國家哲學," in *Chūgoku*

kodai bunka no kenkyū 中國古代文化の研究 (Tokyo: Nishō Gakusha Daigaku, 1980), pp. 726–44; Katō, "Shunjū gaku ni okeru ō 春秋學における王," in *Chūgoku kodai bunka no kenkyū*, pp. 771–93; Hihara, *Shunjū Kuyōden no kenkyū*, pp. 257–79.

156. *Gongyang zhuan zhu shu* 1 (Yin 1), pp. 5a–8b.

157. *Gongyang zhuan zhu shu* 2 (Yin 3), p. 7b–8b; 12 (Xi 31), pp. 18b–20a.

158. *Gongyang zhuan zhu shu* 1 (Yin 1), p. 21b; 5 (Huan 8), p. 15a; 12 (Xi 24), p. 3a; (Xi 28), pp. 12b, 14a; 15 (Xuan 1), p. 6a; 17 (Cheng 1), p. 2a; 18 (Cheng 12), p. 2a; 24 (Zhao 23), p. 1a.

159. *Gongyang zhuan zhu shu* 2 (Yin 3), p. 8a; 16 (Xuan 10), p. 2a; 24 (Zhao 31), pp. 20b–21a.

160. *Gongyang zhuan zhu shu* 4 (Huan 1), p. 2a; 5 (Huan 8), p. 14b; 8 (Zhuang 19), p. 2b; 10 (Xi 1), p. 2a; (Xi 2), p. 7a; 11 (Xi 14), p. 9b; 12 (Xi 30), p. 17b; 14 (Wen 14), p. 10a; 16 (Xuan 11), p. 4a; 19 (Xiang 1), p. 2a; (Xiang 2), p. 5a; 20 (Xiang 12), p. 2a; 22 (Zhao 4), p. 8a; 23 (Zhao 13), p. 4b; 25 (Ding 1), p. 4b.

161. *Gongyang zhuan zhu shu* 5 (Huan 15), p. 14b; 13 (Wen 9), pp. 16b–17a.

162. *Gongyang zhuan zhu shu* 12 (Xi 24), pp. 3a–b.

163. *Gongyang zhuan zhu shu* 10 (Xi 4), pp. 14a–b.

164. *Gongyang zhuan zhu shu* 6 (Zhuang 4), p. 12a; 10 (Xi 1), pp. 1b–2b; (Xi 2), p. 7a; 11 (Xi 14), p. 9b; 14 (Wen 14), p. 10a; 16 (Xuan 11), p. 4a; 25 (Ding 1), p. 4b.

165. On the *Gongyang*'s affirmation of the hegemons, see Hihara, *Shunjū Kuyōden no kenkyū*, pp. 280–312.

166. This dichotomy is closely related to that between the "normative" (*zheng* 正) and "extraordinary" (*qi* 奇) in military texts. See Lewis, *Sanctioned Violence in Early China*, pp. 122–27.

167. *Gongyang zhuan zhu shu* 5 (Huan 11), pp. 7b–9a.

168. *Gongyang zhuan zhu shu* 8 (Zhuang 19), p. 2b—a great official outside the boundaries of his state can act on his own initiative to "bring peace to the state altars"; 20 (Xiang 19), pp. 11a–1b—praises a minister who refuses to attack a state in mourning. This argument for the power of the commander in the field to ignore the ruler is identical with arguments in the military treatises also based on appeals to *quan* and *qi* 奇.

169. *Gongyang zhuan zhu shu* 6 (Zhuang 4), pp. 10b–12a. For a translation and discussion of this case see Lewis, *Sanctioned Violence*, pp. 82–84.

170. On this unusual feature of the commentary glossing its own vocabulary, see Hihara, *Shunjū Kuyōden no kenkyū*, pp. 30–33, 42–43.

Chapter Four. Writing the Self

1. W. R. Johnson, *The Idea of Lyric: Lyric Modes in Ancient and Modern Poetry* (Berkeley: University of California, 1982), p. 77.

2. The examples preserved in the *Shi jing* are only a small sample of the songs or verse produced. Most verse not collected in the anthologies has been lost,

although some fragments of "lost" poems are preserved in quotations in philosophical texts, and a body of songs largely about hunting was preserved on the rubbings of the "Stone Drums." See Gilbert Mattos, *The Stone Drums of Ch'in*, Monumenta Serica Monograph Series 19 (Netettal: Steyler Verlag, 1988); Akatsuka Kiyoshi, "A New Study of the *Shi-ku Wen*: the Ancient Letters Carved in Ten Drumtype Stones," *Acta Asiatica* 4 (1963): 80–96.

3. The idea of folk origins dates back to the Warring States theory that kings collected the songs of the peasants as evidence of the moral temper of the times. For the relevant passages from the Chinese and their relatively late origins, see Jean-Pierre Diény, *Aux origines de la poésie classique en Chine: étude de la poésie lyrique à l'époque des Han* (Leiden: E. J. Brill, 1968), ch. 1. In the wake of the May Fourth Movement, the group of revisionist historians gathered around Gu Jiegang elaborated the theory of peasant origins as part of their general attack on Confucianism and its accounts of early history. Their scholarly correspondance on the subject of the odes was reproduced in Gu Jiegang 顧頡剛, ed., *Gu shi bian* 古史辨, vol. 3, rep. ed. (Hong Kong: Taiping, 1962). For other important work from this period, see also Fu Sinian 傅斯年, "*Shi jing* jiang yi kao 詩經講義考," in *Fu Mengzhen xiansheng ji* 傅孟眞先生集, vol. 1 (Tiapei: Lianjing, 1980), pp. 185–330; Wen Yiduo 聞一多, "*Shi jing* xin yi 詩經新義," and "*Shi jing* tong yi 詩經通義," in *Wen Yiduo quan ji*, vol. 2 (1948, rep. ed. Beijing: Sanlian, 1982), pp. 67–101, 105–200. The best-known Western attempt to read the poems as evidence of an early peasant society long hidden beneath moralizing Confucian commentaries is Marcel Granet, *Fêtes et chansons anciennes de la Chine*, 2nd ed. (Paris: Leroux, 1929). For a good critique of Granet's argument, see Haun Saussy, *The Problem of a Chinese Aesthetic* (Stanford: Stanford University, 1993), pp. 109–13. On the poems as products of the court, with possible sources from folk traditions, see C. H. Wang, *The Bell and the Drum: Shi Jing as Formulaic Poetry in an Oral Tradition* (Berkeley: University of California, 1974), summarized in Wang, *From Ritual to Allegory: Seven Essays in Early Chinese Poetry* (Hong Kong: Chinese University, 1988), pp. 1–4; Van Zoeren, *Poetry and Personality*, pp. 7–11; Saussy, *Chinese Aesthetic*, pp. 58–73; Chen Shih-hsiang, "The *Shi-ching*: Its Generic Significance in Chinese Literary History and Poetics," in Cyril A. Birch, ed., *Studies in Chinese Literary Genres* (Berkeley: University of California, 1974), pp. 29–32; Qu Wanli 屈萬里, "Lun 'Guo feng' fei min jian geyao de benlai mianmu 論國風非民間歌謠的本來面目," *Zhongyang Yanjiuyuan Lishi Yuyan Yanjiusuo Jikan* 34:2 (1963): 477–504; Zhu Ziqing 朱自清, "Shi yan zhi bian 詩言志辨," in *Zhu Ziqing gudian wenxue lunwen ji* 朱自清古典文學論文集 (Shanghai: Guji, 1981), pp. 201–202, 214.

4. For an argument on the similar role of the anthology in the development of lyric theory in the West, see Paul Allen Miller, *Lyric Texts and Lyric Consciousness: The Birth of a Genre from Archaic Greece to Augustan Rome* (London: Routledge, 1994).

5. See Saussy, *Chinese Aesthetic*, pp. 108–09.

6. Chow Tse-tsung, "The Early History of the Chinese Word *Shih* (Poetry),"

in *Wen-lin: Studies in the Chinese Humanities* (Madison: University of Wisconsin, 1968), pp. 151–209.

7. Edward L. Shaughnessy, "From Liturgy to Literature: The Ritual Contexts of the Earliest Poems in the *Book of Poetry*," *Hanxue Yanjiu* 13.1 (1994): 133–64; Shaughnessy, "Western Zhou Political and Literary History," in *Cambridge History of Ancient China*, ed. Edward Shaughnessy and Michael Loewe (Cambridge: Cambridge University, in press). At this time rhymed passages in the first-person voice of the sponsor often appeared on bronzes, although largely in formulaic phrases. See Shirakawa Shizuka, *Shikyō: Chūgoku no kodai kayō* 詩經: 中國の古代歌謠 (Tokyo: Heibonsha, 1971), pp. 180–81.

8. Jessica Rawson, "Statesmen or Barbarians? The Western Zhou as seen through their Bronzes," *Proceedings of the British Academy* 75 (1989): 89–91; Rawson, *Western Zhou Ritual Bronzes from the Arthur M. Sackler Collections*, vol. 1 (Cambridge: Harvard University, 1990), pp. 108–110.

9. On the origins of the "wu," see *Yi Zhou shu* 4 "Shi fu 世俘," p. 10b. On its reliability for early Zhou history, see Gu Jiegang, "*Yi zhou shu* 'Shi fu pian' jiaozhu xieding yu pinglun 逸周書世俘篇校注寫定與評論," *Wen shi* 2 (April 1963): 1–42; Edward L. Shaughnessy, "'New' Evidence on the Zhou Conquest," *Early China* 6 (1980–81): 57–79. The latter includes an English translation. For the identification of the Odes "Wu 武 (Mao 285)," "Lai 賚 (Mao 295)," and "Huan 桓 (Mao 294)" with three movements of the Wu ritual, see *Zuo zhuan zhu* Xuan 12, pp. 744–46. For modern studies of the Wu ritual, see Wang Guowei, "Shuo 'Da wu' yue zhang kao 說大武樂章考," in *Guantang jilin*, pp. 104–08; Sun Zuoyun 孫作雲, "Zhou chu da wu yue zhang kaoshi 周初大武樂章考實," in *Shi jing yu Zhou dai shehui yanjiu* 詩經與周代社會研究 (Beijing: Zhonghua, 1966), pp. 239–72. On the links of this dance to the war dance that preceded the Zhou victory at the battle of Mu Ford, see Lewis, *Sanctioned Violence*, p. 226.

10. Fu Sinian, "Shi jing jiang yi gao 詩經講義稿," in *Fu Mengzhen xiansheng ji* 傅孟眞先生集, vol. 2B *Zhong pian yi* 中篇乙 (Taipei: Academia Sinica, 1954), pp. 30–33. The three odes in question are "Min yu xiao zi" 閔予孝子 (Mao 286), "Fang luo" 訪落 (Mao 287), and "Jing zhi" 敬之 (Mao 288).

11. *Mao shi zhengyi* 19.3, pp. 9a–11b. Other odes with similar features include "Wei tian zhi ming" 維天之命 (Mao 267), 19.1, pp. 11a–13a; "Lie wen" 烈文 (Mao 269), 19.1, pp. 16a–19a; "Wo jiang" 我將 (Mao 272), 19.2, pp. 3a–5a. These odes are linked in marking a final prayer with the particle 其, a formula that figures in the final invocations of many Zhou bronze inscriptions.

12. *Mao shi zhengyi* 16.3, pp. 6a–10b; 17.2, pp. 1a–8a; "Fu yi" 鳧鷖 (Mao 248), 17.2, pp. 15a–20b.

13. C. H. Wang argues that certain poems in the "Da ya" section were employed as a combination of "poetic narrative and encyclopedia," like the role assigned to the epic by Eric Havelock. See Wang, *From Ritual to Allegory*, pp. 74–75; Eric Havelock, *Preface to Plato* (Cambridge: Belknap Press of Harvard University,

1963), ch. 4, "The Homeric Encyclopedia." Wang limits his theory to poems dealing with the achievements of the Zhou ancestors, and does not include narratives of rituals in his epic "encyclopedia."

14. On the development of "individualism" within the Zhou odes, see Sun Zuoyun, *Shi jing yu Zhou dai shehui*, pp. 398–402; Suzuki Shūji 鈴木修次, *Chūgoku kodai bungaku ron: Shikyō no bungei sei* 中國古代文學論: 詩經の文芸性 (Tokyo: Kadokawa Shoten, 1977), pp. 185–310.

15. See for example, *Mao shi zhengyi* "Shi shu" 碩鼠 (Mao 113), 5.3, pp. 12a–13b; 9.3, "Cai wei" 采薇 (Mao 167), pp. 10b–16a.

16. *Shi ji* 130, p. 3300; 84, p. 2482. This second passage states that the odes in the "Little Elegantia" (*xiao ya*) are characterized by "resentment and criticism, without rebellious disorder."

17. *Mao shi zhengyi* 11.1, pp. 6a–8a; "Jie nan shan" 節南山 (Mao #191) 12.1, pp. 3b, 5a; "Zheng yue" 正月 (Mao #192) 12.1, pp. 9a, 10a, 13a (this last is the same phrase as in the ode "Mian shui"); "Shi yue zhi jiao" 十月之交 (Mao #193) 12.2, p. 9a; "Yu wu zheng" 雨無正 (Mao #194) 12.2, pp. 13b, 14b; "Xiao min" 小閔 (Mao #195) 12.2, pp. 17a, 17b; "Xiang bo" 巷伯 (Mao #200) 12.3, pp. 20a, 20b, 21b, 22a, 22a–b; "Qing ying" 青蠅 (Mao #219) 14.3, pp. 1a, 1b; "Yi" 抑 (Mao #256) 18.1, pp. 16b, 18a; "Sang rou" 桑柔 (Mao #257) 18.2, pp. 8b, 10a; "Zhan ang" 瞻卬 (Mao #264) 18.5, pp. 9a–9b; See also "Yang zhi shui" 揚之水 (Mao #92) 4.4, p. 8a; "Cai ling" 采苓 (Mao #125) 6.2, pp. 16a–17b (3).

18. *Mao shi zhengyi* 12.3, pp. 10a–12b.

19. *Mao shi zhengyi* "Zheng yue," 12.1, pp. 9a, 10a, 17a, 17b; "Shi yue zhi jiao," 12.2, pp. 9b, 10a; "Xiao bian 小弁," (Mao #197) 12.3, pp. 4b, 6a, 8a, 9a; "Si yue 四月," (Mao #204) 13.1, p. 16b; "Sang rou," 18.2, p. 3b; "Zhan ang," 18.5, p. 13b. The refrain of the first part of "He ren si 何人斯," (Mao #199), which deals with the image of someone who has "broken one's bridge" or other connections, is probably also a reference to the theme of isolation. See 12.3, pp. 14b–16b.

20. *Mao shi zhengyi* "Zheng yue," 12.1, p. 13a; "Shi yue zhi jiao," 12.2, pp. 2a–b, 5a–b; "Yu wu zheng," 12.2, pp. 10b, 11b, 12b, 13b; "Xiao min," 12.2, pp. 16a (2), 17b; "Xiao bian," 12.3, pp. 6a, 8a; "Qiao yan," 12.3, pp. 10b–11a, 12a; "Xiang bo," 12.3, pp. 21b, 22a; "Yi," 18.2, pp. 8b, 10a, 10b; "Sang rou," 18.2, pp. 9b, 10a, 10b, 11a.

21. *Mao shi zhengyi* "Shi yue zhi jiao," 12.2, p. 9a; "Yu wu zheng," 12.2, p. 12b; "He ren si," 12.3, p. 16b; "Xiang bo," 12.3, p. 22a; "Zhan ang," 18.5, pp. 11b–12b; "Zhao min" 召閔 (Mao #265) 18.5, p. 14a.

22. *Mao shi zhengyi* "Jie nan shan," 12.1, pp. 3a–b, 4b, 6–7a, 8b; "Yu wu zheng," 12.2, pp. 10b, 12b; "Xiao min," 12.2, pp. 15b; "Qiao yan," 12.3, pp. 10a, 10b; "Ban" 板 (Mao #254) 17.4, pp. 15b, 17a, 18a; "Dang" 蕩 (Mao #255) 18.1, p. 1b; "Yi," 18.1, pp. 10b, 18a; "Sang rou," 18.2, pp. 1b, 3b, 6b; "Zhan ang," 18.5, p. 7b; "Zhao min," 18.5, p. 14a.

23. *Mao shi zhengyi* 18.2, pp. 12b–22a. On the failure of divination, see "Xiao min," 12.2, p. 16b. "Si yue" 四月 (Mao #204) 13.1, p. 15b refers to the ancestors'

refusal or inability to help. All the odes which refer to a pitiless and unjust Heaven also imply the breakdown of the sacrificial basis of the political order.

24. *Mao shi zhengyi* 18.3, p. 11b. It is significant that at the end of this ode, the poet announces himself to be Yin Jifu 尹吉甫, a high official at the court of King Xuan. See 18.3, pp. 17a–b. The ode is presented as an encomium to another leading official, Zhong Shanfu 仲山甫. The differing attitudes toward Heaven may express the different perspectives of those at the pinnacle of power and those who were less successful.

25. *Mao shi zhengyi* "Xiao min," 12.2, pp. 19a–20b; "Xiao yuan" 小宛 (Mao #196) 12.3, pp. 1a (in this the poet expresses his worries in thinking about Kings Wen and Wu), 4b; "Xiao bian," 12.3, pp. 8b–9a; "Qiao yan," 12.3, p. 12a; "Bin zhi chu yan" 賓之初筵 (Mao #220) 14.3, p. 15b; "Yi," 18.1, pp. 8b, 12a.

26. In addition to the two odes for which he claims authorship, Yin Jifu's military successes are the subject of a song. See *Mao shi zhengyi* "Liu yue" 六月 (Mao #177) 10.2, pp. 1a–8a. He also commissioned the casting of a bronze vessel to commemorate his success and appointment to a high office. See Shaughnessy, *Sources of Western Zhou History*, p. 141.

27. *Mao shi zhengyi* 18.3, pp. 1a–10b; 18.3, pp. 11a–17b. The references to authorship and presentation appear on pp. 10b, 17a–b. Both odes are referred to by the character 訟 (*song*), which either indicates the mode of performance or is used for the homophonous 頌 (*song*) and indicates that they are encomia. They apparently included both words and music, as one ode refers to both the "lyrics" (*shi* 詩) and the "tune" (*feng* 風). Whether Yin Jifu actually wrote the odes, or simply had them composed as a gesture of good will to his colleagues, is unknowable.

28. *Mao shi zhengyi* 12.1, pp. 1a–9a; 12.3, pp. 19a–22b. The claims to authorship and naming of their audience appear on 12.1, pp. 8b–9a; 12.3, p. 22b. The author of the first ode calls himself *jia fu* 家父, which looks more like a status ("household head") than a personal name. No title or rank is indicated. Given the ferocity of the attack and the call on the king to reform, the author may have chosen to remain anonymous.

29. *Mao shi zhengyi* "He ren si," 12.3, pp. 18b–19a; "Si yue," 13.1, pp. 18b–19a; "Sang rou," 18.2, p. 12b.

30. Shirakawa, *Shikyō*, pp. 88–102.

31. Shirakawa, *Shikyō*, pp. 134–37. For examples of odes in the voice of abandoned women, see Shirakawa, pp. 134–41; Suzuki, *Chūgoku kodai bungaku ron*, pp. 145–53.

32. See, for example, Suzuki, *Chūgoku kodai bungaku ron*, p. 206.

33. The injunction on oathbreaking appears in "Xiao bian," 12.3, p. 8b, and also in "Yi," 18.1, p. 13a. The allusions to inauspicious stars (*chen* 辰) appear in "Xiao bian," 12.3, p. 6a, and in "Sang rou," 18.2, p. 3b.

34. A late chapter of the *Lun yu* tells of the dispersal of the Zhou music masters at some unspecified point of dynastic decline. See *Lun yu zhengyi* 18 "Weizi," p. 397.

The most elaborate account of the music masters, although not strictly historical, appears in the *Zhou li.* See *Zhou li zhushu* 23 "Da shi 大師" and "Xiao shi 小師." The former is charged with teaching the odes. See p. 13a. See also *Li ji zhengyi* 19 "Yue ji 樂記," *juan* 38, p. 18a. *Zhou li* and *Guo yu* passages on the music masters are collected in Asano Yūichi 淺野裕一, *Kō rō dō no seiritsu to tenkai* 黃老道の成立と展開 (Tokyo: Sōbunsha, 1992), pp. 136–43.

35. *Zuo zhuan zhu* Xiang 29, pp. 1161–65. This story is translated and discussed in Kenneth DeWoskin, *A Song for One or Two: Music and the Concept of Art in Early China* (Ann Arbor: University of Michigan, Center for Chinese Studies, 1982), ch. 2.

36. DeWoskin, *Song for One or Two,* pp. 25–27, 92–94.

37. *Lun yu zhengyi* 15 "Wei Ling Gong," p. 339; 17 "Yang Huo," p. 379; *Li ji zhengyi* 19 "Yue ji," *juan* 38, p. 19a. The tension between classical music and the deviant sounds of Zheng and Wei became the standard schema for musical analysis by Han scholars. See Diény, *Origines de la poésie classique,* ch. 2.

38. Poetic presentation as an element in noble speech, primarily in interstate relations, has been studied by several scholars. A complete collection and translation of quoted odes is made in Tam Koo-yin, "The Use of Poetry in *Tso chuan*" (Ph.D. diss., University of Washington, 1975). A similar collection, also including cases of "noncanonical" poems is Zeng Qinliang 曾勤良, *Zuo zhuan yin shi fu shi zhi shi jiao yanjiu* 左傳引詩賦詩之詩教研究 (Taipei: Wenjin, 1994). Useful treatments include Zhu Ziqing 朱自清, "Shi yan zhi bian 詩言志辨," in *Zhu Ziqing gudian wenxue lunwen ji* 朱自清古典文學論文集 (Shanghai: Guji, 1981), pp. 193–233; Lao Xiaoyu 勞孝輿, *Chun qiu shi hua* 春秋詩話 (Cong shu ji cheng ed.), pp. 1–10, 25–42; Van Zoeren, *Poetry and Personality,* pp. 39–45, 64–67, 71; Jullien, *Le détour et l'accès,* ch. 4.

39. *Lun yu zhengyi* 13 "Zi lu," p. 285.

40. *Lun yu zhengyi* 16 "Ji shi," p. 363. The word "speak" (*shuo* 說) could also be read *shui* "to persuade." This might be the sense intended in this passage, which would refer to the use of odes in official exchanges.

41. *Zuo zhuan zhu* Xi 23, pp. 410–11. The passage is translated and analyzed in detail in Van Zoeren, pp. 39–42, whom I have closely followed.

42. *Mao shi zhengyi* "Mian shui," 11.1, p. 6b. This assumes, following Wei Zhao, that the character 河 given in the title in the story is an error for 沔. See Tam, p. 165, note 4.

43. *Mao shi zhengyi* "Liu yue," 10.2, pp. 2b–3a.

44. *Zuo zhuan zhu* Xiang 14, pp. 1005–07; Xiang 16, pp. 1028–29; Xiang 19, p. 1051; Xiang 26, pp. 1116–17; Xiang 29, p. 1156.

45. *Zuo zhuan zhu* Xiang 28, pp. 1145–46.

46. Liu Baiji 劉佰驥, *Chun qiu huimeng zhengzhi* 春秋會盟政治 (Taipei: Zhonghua Congshu, 1963); Lewis, *Sanctioned Violence,* pp. 43–50.

47. One example of this is the role of chime-bells, which had been central to Zhou sacred music. As Lothar von Falkenhausen has argued, the nobility of the Eastern Zhou period seem to have actively patterned their bell sets on the metropol-

itan Zhou traditions. Bell types and ritual orchestras were largely the same, even in the distant Chu state which had never acknowledged Zhou suzerainty. The several musical systems revealed in the inscriptions of the tomb of Marquis Yi of Zeng used different nomenclatures and principal pitches, but were otherwise compatible and seem to have derived from a single predecessor. Certain surface differences were "contrived and emphasized for political purposes." See von Falkenhausen, "Chu Ritual Music," in *New Perspectives on Chu Culture During the Eastern Zhou Period*, ed. Thomas Lawton (Washington, D.C.: Arthur M Sackler Gallery, Smithsonian Institution, 1991), pp. 47–106; von Falkenhausen, *Suspended Music: Chime-Bells in the Culture of Bronze Age China* (Berkeley: University of California, 1993), pp. 314–20.

48. For an account of the use of verse in creating cultural areas across political boundaries, and the impact of this practice on notions of authorship, see Gregory Nagy, *Pindar's Homer: The Lyric Possession of an Epic Past* (Baltimore: Johns Hopkins, 1990).

49. Sun Zuoyun, "*Shi jing* lian ge fa wei 詩經戀歌發微," in *Shi jing yu Zhou dai shehui*, pp. 295–320; Granet, *Fêtes et chansons*, pp. 155–221; Wang, *From Ritual to Allegory*, ch. 1–2.

50. Zhou Cezong (Chow Tse-tsung) 周策縱, "Gu wu dui yue wu ji shi ge fazhan de gongxian 古巫對樂舞及詩歌發展的貢獻," *Qinghua xuebao* 清華學報 n.s. 13 (Dec. 1982): 1–25; Zhou, *Gu wu yi yu liu shi kao* 古巫醫與六詩考 (Taipei: Lianjing, 1986).

51. On the transformation of the odes from musical performance to written text, as suggested by distinct treatment in different strata of the *Lun yu*, see Van Zoeren, *Poetry and Personality*, ch. 2. One weakness in this study is the assertion that the *Lun yu*'s description of the ode "Guan ju" as "joyful but not abandoned; sorrowful, but not harmfully so!" refers to the musical accompaniment. In fact, this characterization is closely related to the commentary on the lyrics in the *Wu xing pian* discovered at Mawangdui. See Ikeda, *Maōtai Kan bo hakusho gogyōhen kenkyū*, p. 533, and the commentary on the following pages.

52. *Zuo zhuan zhu* Xiang 16, pp. 1028–29.

53. *Zuo zhuan zhu* Xiang 19, p. 1051—Mu Shu repeats his performance; Xiang 14, pp. 1005–07—a Rong chieftain presents a point-by-point refutation of a Jin official who seeks to prevent his participation in a state assembly, then gains the right to participate through an apt quotation; Xiang 26, pp. 1116–17—the rulers of Qi and Zheng come to Jin to seek the release of the imprisoned ruler of Wei. After an exchange of poems to express praise for Jin's beneficence and their continued loyalty, a personal presentation of the argument for mercy is made to a minister and relayed to the lord of Jin who rejects it. This is followed by two poems indicating the value of merciful government, and the ruler of Jin agrees to release his prisoner; Xiang 29, p. 1156—the Ji clan rebel while the Duke of Lu is out of the state. He asks his followers if he should return. One urges him to do so, giving a reasoned argument based on his princely status. He still does not want to return. Another quotes a poem with a line urging return, and the duke agrees to return.

54. *Zuo zhuan zhu* Wen 14, pp. 598–99.

55. Jullien, *Le détour et l'accès*, pp. 91, 98–100.

56. *Shi ji* 130, p. 3300.

57. *Zuo zhuan zhu* Xiang 27, p. 1127—here his failings include costume and chariot too grand for his station, and lack of table manners. His interlocutor chants part of the ode "Xiang shu 相鼠" (Mao #52), which concludes with the line "A man without manners had best die quickly," but he cannot recognize the remonstrance/prophecy; Xiang 28, p. 1149—here Qing Feng presents an overly ornate carriage to the head of the Ji clan in Lu. He also makes no sacrificial offering prior to dining. Mu Shu, who figured in two anecdotes above for his skill in using odes, has an ode of remonstrance sung by one of his musicians, but Qing Feng does not recognize it. On Qing Feng's career, see Henri Maspero, *China in Antiquity*, tr. Frank A. Kierman, Jr. (Amherst: University of Massachusetts, 1978), p. 234.

58. *Zuo zhuan zhu* Wen 4, pp. 535–36. A similar story is told of the celebrated manipulator of odes, Mu Shu. See Xiang 4, pp. 932–34.

59. As an example of the former, the Ode "Liu yue" is used both to render thanks and to promise aid. See *Zuo zhuan zhu* Xi 23, pp. 410–11; Xiang 19, p. 1047. As an example of the latter, see Cheng 9, p. 843.

60. *Zuo zhuan zhu* Xiang 20, pp. 1054–55. For different interpretations of the passage see Du Yu's commentary, cited in Yang Bojun's edition, and Lao, *Chun qiu shi hua*, p. 5.

61. For a collection and analysis of the relevant passages from pre-Qin and Han literature, see Chow, "Early History of the Chinese Word *Shih* (Poetry)," pp. 152–66. Van Zoeren takes this sentence as the basis for his study of the hermeneutic of the odes. For the section on the pre-Qin and Han, see *Poetry and Personality*, ch. 2–4. I have borrowed much from this analysis.

62. Van Zoeren, *Poetry and Personality*, pp. 56–57. 志 also had the meaning of "[written] record," a sense which blurs into the idea of "written verse." Moreover, it is etymologically related to such diverse characters as 待, 侍, 恃, 持, 畤, and 之, all of which may suggest aspects of its meaning. See Chow, "Early History," pp. 189–208.

63. *Zuo zhuan zhu* Xiang 27, pp. 1134–35. A similar story, including one of the same participants, is recorded twenty years later. See Zhao 16, pp. 1378–79. Van Zoeren, *Poetry and Personality*, pp. 64–66 contains a partial translation and an analysis of the first anecdote. Unfortunately, he uses Waley's translation of the ode, which in this case is at odds with the reading offered by the Chinese commentators and obscures certain points in the passage. Most notably, his reading hides the point that the theme of the ode is licit and illicit matings, a point which is essential to Zhao Meng's response, and which led Granet to posit that the poem could be read as a proposal for an alliance of the speaker and Jin state to depose his lord. See Granet, *La pensée chinoise*, pp. 59–60.

64. *Lun yu zhengyi* 5 "Gongye Chang," pp. 109–10; 11 "Xian jin," pp. 252–

61. The passages are translated and discussed in Van Zoeren, *Poetry and Personality*, pp. 59–63.

65. *Lun yu zhengyi* 8 "Tai Bo," p. 160—here Confucius urges the disciples to be "stimulated" (*xing* 興) by the odes; 13 "Zi Lu," p. 285—the passage cited earlier on using odes in diplomatic missions; 16 "Ji Shi," p. 363—the passage cited earlier on having a means to speak; 17 "Yang Huo," p. 374—the odes can be used to stimulate 興, observe 觀 (*guan*), form groups 群 (*qun*), or express resentment 怨 (*yuan*). They can be used to serve one's father or one's prince. They provide knowledge of the names of birds, beasts, plants, and trees (see chapter 1 on the significance of these names).

66. This phrase is used by Haun Saussy in his discussion of the necessity of commentary within Chinese understandings of the role of poetry, but it applies to the morally decontextualized use of odes in the *Zuo zhuan*. See Saussy, *Problem of a Chinese Aesthetic*, p. 98.

67. *Lun yu zhengyi* 1 "Xue er," p. 19; 2 "Wei zheng," p. 21; 3 "Ba yi," pp. 48–49.

68. *Mengzi zhengyi* 1A "Liang Hui Wang shang," pp. 27–29.

69. *Mengzi zhengyi* 1B "Liang Hui Wang xia," pp. 67–68, 81–83.

70. *Mengzi zhengyi* 3A "Teng Wen Gong shang," pp. 201–02.

71. *Mengzi zhengyi* 1A "Liang Hui Wang shang," p. 52; 1B "Liang Hui Wang xia," p. 66; 2A "Gongsun Chou shang," pp. 130–31, 133; 3A "Teng Wen Gong shang," p. 205; 3B "Teng Wen Gong xia," p. 272; 4A "Li Lou shang," pp. 289, 290, 292; 7B "Jin xin xia," pp. 576–77.

72. *Mengzi zhengyi* 5A "Wan Zhang shang," pp. 376–77.

73. *Mengzi zhengyi* 3A "Teng Wen Gong shang," p. 196.

74. *Mengzi zhengyi* 3A "Teng Wen Gong shang," pp. 230–33.

75. *Mengzi zhengyi* 2A "Gongsun Chou shang," p. 132 (Confucius quoted in support); 3B "Teng Wen Gong xia," p. 143; 4A "Li Lou shang," pp. 285, 293, 297–98; 5B "Wan Zhang xia," p. 427; 6A "Gaozi shang," p. 447 (Confucius quoted in support).

76. *Mengzi zhengyi* 4B "Li Lou xia," p. 337.

77. For a list of the ten cases, see Zeng Qinliang, *Zuo shi yin shi fu shi*, p. 449.

78. *Zuo zhuan zhu*, Min 1, p. 256.

79. *Zuo zhuan zhu* Xi 15, p. 365. For the use of odes to criticize reliance on divination and the reading of signs such as eclipses, see also Ai 2, p. 1613; Zhao 7, pp. 1287–88.

80. *Zuo zhuan zhu*, Xi 5, pp. 303–04. This same ode is used elsewhere to insist on the importance of not alienating kin. See Zhao 6, p. 1278. For another use of a different ode to denounce the walling of cities, see Zhao 23, pp. 1447–48. For another use of an ode in self-justification, see Zhao 4, pp. 1254–55.

81. *Zuo zhuan zhu*, Huan 6, p. 113; Zhuang 22, p. 220; Wen 10, p. 578. The use of odes as a form of politeness also figures in their use for flattery prior to a request. See Xiang 21, pp. 1060–61; Xian 24, pp. 1089–90.

82. *Zuo zhuan zhu*, Wen 1, pp. 516–17.

83. See, for example, *Zuo zhuan zhu*, Xiang 31, p. 1189; Zhao 2, p. 1229; Ai 5, p. 1631.

84. *Zuo zhuan zhu*, Xi 24, pp. 422–24.

85. *Zuo zhuan zhu*, Wen 1, p. 516; Xuan 12, pp. 744–45; Xiang 26, p. 1120.

86. *Zuo zhuan zhu*, Xi 20, p. 387; Xi 33, p. 502; Cheng 8, p. 837; Cheng 9, pp. 845–46; Zhao 24, p. 1452.

87. *Xunzi jijie* 1 "Quan xue," p. 10. The ode in question is "Cai shu" 采菽 (Mao #222). See *Mao shi zhengyi* 15.1, p. 6a. The Mao commentary, which traced itself back to Xun Kuang, gives both the literal sense and the figurative reading.

88. *Xunzi jijie* 3 "Bu gou," p. 24; 4 "Rong ru," pp. 44–45; 13 "Chen dao," p. 171; 8 "Ru xiao," p. 81—this line about the crane is part of an ode on the theme that birds and fish have their places of refuge, and only man has none; 10 "Fu guo," p. 116; 21 "Jie bi," p. 265—the *Xunzi*, followed by the Mao commentary, reads this as a poem on divided thoughts because it begins with the image of a woman picking plants and not filling her basket, a couplet that is immediately followed by the information that she longs for her absent husband. Picking plants is a standard opening image (*xing* 興) in poems of abandoned women and is probably related to elements in marriage ritual or binding sexual magic. See Shirakawa Shizuka, *Shikyō kenkyū* 詩經研究 (Kyoto: Hōyū Shoten, 1981), pp. 505–06; Lewis, *Sanctioned Violence*, p. 73.

89. *Xunzi jijie* 3 "Bu gou," p. 26. I have adjusted the word order of this passage to accord with the commentary.

90. *Xunzi jijie* 5 "Fei xiang," p. 54; 12 "Jun dao," p. 152; 15 "Yi bing," p. 191; 6 "Fei shier zi," p. 63; 7 "Zhong Ni," pp. 69–70; 8 "Ru xiao," p. 82; 9 "Wang zhi," p. 103; 17 "Tian lun," p. 208; 10 "Fu guo," p. 117; 12 "Jun dao," p. 162; 18 "Zheng lun," p. 215; 24 "Junzi," p. 300.

91. *Xunzi jijie* 2 "Xiu shen," p. 13; 8 "Ru xiao," p. 79; 10 "Fu guo," p. 122; 22 "Zheng ming," p. 283; 2 "Xiu shen," p. 20; 8 "Ru xiao," p. 77; 11 "Wang ba," p. 140; 10 "Fu guo," pp. 118, 121–22; 12 "Jun dao," p. 155; 16 "Qiang guo," p. 200; 24 "Junzi," p. 302.

92. A similar use of odes citation to justify historical change and innovation figures in *Zuo zhuan zhu* Zhao 32, p. 1520.

93. *Lun yu zhengyi* 2 "Wei zheng," p. 39; 3 "Ba yi," pp. 49, 56. On the doctrine of the "later kings" in the *Xunzi*, see Knoblock, *Xunzi*, vol. 2, pp. 28–50.

94. Three recent scholarly works include annotated English translations and analyses of the preface. See Van Zoeren, *Poetry and Personality*, ch. 4 (translation on pp. 95–97); Saussy, *Problem of a Chinese Aesthetic*, ch. 3 (translation, including commentaries, on pp. 75–83); Stephen Owen, *Readings in Chinese Literary Thought* (Cambridge: Harvard University, 1992), pp. 37–49.

95. *Han shu* 88, p. 3614; Karlgren, "Early History of the *Chou Li* and *Tso Chuan* Texts," p. 33.

96. Hu Pingsheng 胡平生 and Han Ziqiang 韩自强, "Fuyang Han jian

'Shi jing' jianlun 阜阳汉简诗经简论," *Wenwu* (1984:8): 13–21. The discussion of the relations between the discovered text and the received versions is on pp. 15–17.

97. The text of the *Wu xing pian* is published in *Mawangdui Han mu boshu*, vol. 1 (Beijing: Wenwu, 1980), pp. 17–27. On the numerous citations of the odes and their relation to those found in other texts, see Ikeda, *Maōtai Kan bo hakusho gogyō hen kenkyū*, pp. 83, 85, 122, 133, 173, 179, 187, 188, 190, 191, 192, 211, 215, 216, 217, 229, 350, 352–53, 353–54, 358, 361, 364, 365, 372, 374, 375, 382, 420, 427, 429, 430, 435, 443, 508, 512, 517–18, 534, 543, 546, 548, 550, 552, 555, 561.

98. Hu and Han, "Fuyang Han jian," p. 19, Wang Xianqian 王先谦, *Shi san jia yi jishu* 詩三家義集疏 (Beijing: Zhonghua, 1987), pp. 1–17, esp. p. 16.

99. The "Great" and "Minor" prefaces were traditionally divided into "anterior" and "later" strata, a division that might reflect the history suggested above. See Van Zoeren, *Poetry and Personality*, p. 92.

100. Owen, *Readings*, pp. 41–43; Stephen Owen, *Traditional Chinese Poetry and Poetics: Omen of the World* (Madison: University of Wisconsin, 1985), p. 58.

101. The relevant materials and related passages are assembled in Owen, *Readings*, pp. 49–56. For a discussion of the difficulties involved in transferring a theory of music to a theory of language acts, and the manner in which language ultimately asserts itself, see Saussy, *Chinese Aesthetic*, pp. 86–100.

102. Stephen Owen argues that the "protected" status of the poet is comparable to the license granted to Western *poiesis* on the basis of its fictionality. However, he sees no grounds in the argument for privileging poetic criticism, except its spontaneous and irrepressible nature, and he notes that the claim to privilege was often ignored by rulers. See *Readings*, p. 46. Given the depiction of suasion through verse in the *Zuo zhuan*, and the debates on indirect criticism in the genre of the rhapsody, it is possible that the inoffensiveness of poetic criticism hinged on the idea that the ruler would recognize it as criticism only if he were sufficiently educated and sensitive to understand what was said, in which case he would be moved by the power of the verse. A wicked ruler would not even register the presence of criticism.

103. This link between historians and poetry echoes the *Mencius*'s statement that the *Chun qiu* chronicle arose when the odes ceased. It carries forward the same text's practice of reading verse as a form of history. There is evidence in early texts, notably the *Guo yu*, of an overlap between the roles of historians and musicians. See Asano, *Kō rō dō no seiritsu to tenkai*, pp. 136–39.

104. *Mao shi zhengyi* "Ye you si jun 野有死麕," (Mao #23) 1.5, p. 8a.

105. Saussy, *Chinese Aesthetic*, pp. 95–96, 108. Dealing primarily with the Tang lyric, Stephen Owen notes "a complicity between Chinese classical literature and the imperial system." Even in ostensibly private poetry and prose, he argues, "the values of the unified empire are not less present." This observation indicates that the heritage of the Mao commentary did not vanish in later China. See Owen, *Traditional Chinese Poetry and Poetics*, pp. 27–34, 251–53, 259–60.

106. Lewis, *Sanctioned Violence*, pp. 167–74, 212.

107. The quotation of the odes figured in the practice of other schools, but it was not central. The *Mozi* features a half dozen citations, the *Lü shi chun qiu* twenty, and even the *Han Feizi* three, but such quotations are marginal to the arguments of these texts. On quotations of the odes in late Warring States texts, see Uchino, *Shin dai ni okeru keisho keisetsu no kenkyū*, pp. 2–55, 197–201.

108. *Xunzi jijie* 25 "Cheng xiang," pp. 304–13. For secondary studies see Du Guoxiang 杜国庠, "Lun *Xunzi* de 'Cheng xiang pian' 論荀子的成相篇," in *Du Guoxiang wenji* 文集 (Beijing: Renmin, 1962), pp. 168–75; Jiang Shangxian 姜尚賢, *Xunzi sixiang tixi* 荀子思想體系 (Tainan: Self-published, 1966), pp. 362–67; Nakajima Chiaki 中島千秋, *Fu no seiritsu to sono tenkai* 賦の成立とその展開 (Matsuyama: Kan Yōshiten, 1963), pp. 176–80.

109. Knoblock, *Xunzi*, vol. 3, pp. 168–71; Du, "Cheng xiang pian," pp. 159–62; Jiang, *Xunzi sixiang*, pp. 363–65.

110. *Lü shi chun qiu jiaoshi* 18 "Yin ci," p. 1187.

111. For discussions of "shamanism" and the *Chu ci*, see Arthur Waley, *The Nine Songs: A Study of Shamanism in Ancient China* (London: Allen & Unwin, 1955); David Hawkes, tr., *The Songs of the South: An Anthology of Chinese Poems by Qu Yuan and Other Poets* (Harmondsworth: Penguin, 1985), pp. 42–51; Waters, *Three Elegies of Ch'u*, pp. 16–19. For discussions of the use of verse in ancient Chinese rituals, see Fujino Iwatomo 藤野岩友, *Fukei bungaku ron* 巫系文學論 (rev. and expanded, Tokyo: Daigaku Shobō, 1970), pp. 5–37; Hoshikawa Kiyotaka 星川清孝, *Soji no kenkyū* 楚辭の研究 (Tenri: Yōtoku Sha, 1962), pp. 24–35; Fukino Yasushi 吹野安, *Chūgoku kodai bungaku hassō ron* 中國古代文學發想論 (Tokyo: Ryūkan Shoin, 1987), ch. 2, 5, 6.

112. Barnard, *The Ch'u Silk Manuscript*, ch. 4.

113. Graham, *Disputers of the Tao*, pp. 218, 220; Liu Jie 劉節, "Laozi kao 老子考," in *Gu shi cun kao* 古史存考 (Beijing: Renmin, 1958), pp. 196–202. A useful analysis of the rhymes in the *Dao de jing* is in Zhu Qianzhi 朱謙之, *Laozi jiaoshi* 老子校釋 (Beijing: Zhonghua, 1963). The editor has consulted earlier studies of the topic, and at the end of each of the eighty-one stanzas he lists the rhymes, noting where opinions differ. He also has compiled an appendix comparing the rhymes in the *Dao de jing* with those in other early texts, and listed the types of rhyme found in the text. See pp. 201–12.

114. Graham has typographically distinguished verse passages in those sections of the *Zhuangzi* included in his translation. Although I have not seen it, Chen Guying's edition of the *Huangdi si jing* apparently analyzes the rhyme patterns in the text. See Edmund Ryden, "A Literary Study of the Four Canons of the Yellow Emperor: Together with an Edition of the Manuscript of the Four Canons Preceding the Laozi B Text from Mawangdui" (Ph.D. diss., School of Oriental and African Studies, University of London, 1995), p. 222; Chen Guying 陳鼓應, *Huangdi si jing yizhu* 黃帝四經譯注 (Taipei: Shangwu, 1995).

115. Barnard, *The Ch'u Silk Manuscript*, pp. 211–12.

116. Nakajima, *Fu no seiritsu*, pp. 95–187. The author studies the "prosody" of argumentation in all the major works.

117. Graham, *Disputers of the Tao*, pp. 220–21, 223–25, 229, 230.

118. LaFargue, *Tao and Method*, pp. 153–60, 305, 315, 316, 319–20.

119. *Zhuangzi jishi* 2 "Qi wu lun," pp. 41–42, 47–48; 7 "Ying di wang," pp. 133–34—spoken by Lao Dan; 14 "Tian yun," pp. 222–23, 224–25; 15 "Ke yi 刻意," p. 239; 20 "Shan ben," pp. 293–94; 22 "Zhi bei you," pp. 323, 324, 326—spoken by Lao Dan—329; 25 "Ze Yang," pp. 394, 394–95.

120. *Zhuangzi jishi* 3 "Yang sheng," p. 55; 4 "Ren jian shi," pp. 83–85; 5 "De chong fu," pp. 100–01; 7 "Ying di wang," p. 138; 17 "Qiu shui," pp. 260–61; 22 "Zhi bei you," p. 319; 29 "Dao Zhi," p. 435.

121. *Zhuangzi jishi* 2 "Qi wu lun," pp. 25–26; 4 "Ren jian shi," p. 69; 6 "Da zong shi," pp. 106–07; 7 "Ying di wang," p. 137; 9 "Ma ti," p. 151; 11 "Zai you," pp. 173, 173–74, 174, 178; 12 "Tian di," p. 188; 14 "Tian yun," pp. 222–23, 224–25; 15 "Ke yi," p. 239; 17 "Qiu shui," pp. 258–59, 259–60; 20 "Shan ben," p. 293; 27 "Yu yan," p. 409; 29 "Dao Zhi," p. 429. A similar use of verse to describe the ineffable also figures in several of the composed verse passages in the *Xunzi*. See, for example, *Xunzi jijie* 8 "Ru xiao," pp. 83–84; 17 "Tian lun," pp. 211–12; 19 "Li lun," p. 236; 21 "Jie bi," p. 265.

122. *Zhuangzi jishi* 7 "Ying di wang," p. 127; 12 "Tian di," p. 195; 14 "Tian yun," pp. 231, 234; 16 "Qiu shui," p. 266; 21 "Tian Zifang," p. 307; 29 "Dao Zhi," p. 433. The *Zhuangzi* also developed the use of unusual names that signalled the character as something invented for the anecdote. This evolved into such later figures as "Sir Fantasy" in the rhapsody of Sima Xiangru.

123. Question series in song, verse, and prose also appear in *ru* texts, but they are not common. See *Zuo zhuan* Zhao 12, p. 1338; *Mengzi zhengyi* 1A "Liang Hui Wang shang," p. 53; *Xunzi jijie* 21 "Jie bi," p. 265.

124. *Zhuangzi jishi* 2 "Qi wu lun," pp. 28–30, 32, 33–34, 36–37, 38, 39–40, 43–44, 49. A similar pairing appears in 17 "Qiu shui," p. 259. A discussion of the propriety of answering questions, which concludes that the truly knowing do not answer them, appears in Chapter 22 "Zhi bei you." See pp. 318–19.

125. *Laozi dao de jing zhu* 10, p. 5. For analysis of the rhymes, see Zhu, *Laozi jiaoshi*, pp. 26–27. A similar series, placed in the mouth of Lao Dan, appears in *Zhuangzi jishi* 23 "Keng Sangchu," p. 342.

126. *Zhuangzi jishi* 17 "Qiu shui," pp. 258–59. The poem also includes extensive use of repeated binomes to invoke the Way.

127. *Zhuangzi jishi* 11 "Zai you," pp. 166, 167; 14 "Tian yun," pp. 218–19; 32 "Tian xia," p. 474.

128. *Zhuangzi jijie* 18 "Zhi le," p. 273. In his reply, Zhuang Zhou suggests to the skull that he could appeal to the Arbiter of Life Spans (*si ming* 司命) to be restored to life in the flesh, which is what takes place in the story from the tomb at Fangmatan discussed in chapter 1. An abridged version of the story, featuring

Liezi and also including a question series, appears in the same chapter, p. 275. For the later literary history of the story, see Stephen Owen, *Remembrances: The Experience of the Past in Classical Chinese Literature* (Cambridge: Harvard University, 1986), ch. 2.

129. On the *Zhuangzi* adoption of some of the methods of the dialecticians as part of its "assault on reason," see Graham, *Disputers of the Tao*, pp. 176–83.

130. *Zhuangzi jishi* 22 "Zhi bei you," p. 322.

131. *Lü shi chun qiu jiaoshi* 18 "Zhong yan 重言," p. 1156—the same story appears in *Shi ji* 40, p. 1700; *Li ji zhushu* 7 "Tan gong shang 檀弓上," pp. 12a–b. See also *Xunzi jijie* 21 "Jie bi," p. 268.

132. *Han shu* 30, p. 1753. For studies of riddles in Chinese civilization, see Galit Hasan-Rokem and David Shulman, eds., *Untying the Knot: On Riddles and Other Enigmatic Modes* (Oxford: Oxford University, 1996), Section IV, "Chinese Riddling."

133. *Xunzi jijie* 26 "Fu," pp. 313–18. For studies of these pieces, see Nakajima, *Fu no seiritsu*, pp. 164–69; Jiang Shangxian, *Xunzi sixiang*, pp. 367–73; David Knechtges, *The Han Rhapsody: A Study of the Fu of Yang Hsiung* (Cambridge: Cambridge University, 1976), pp. 18–21.

134. Friedrich A. Bischoff, *Interpreting the Fu: A Study in Chinese Literary Rhetoric* (Wiesbaden: Franz Steiner Verlag, 1976). The quotation from Chen Shen is cited on the first page of the introduction.

135. The translation of the title is itself a matter of debate. The traditional explanation, offered by the Eastern Han commentator Wang Yi, says that the meaning of the title is "posing questions to [or 'about'] Heaven." The putative author of the poem, Qu Yuan, in his travels supposedly witnessed pictures depicting the mysteries of Heaven and Earth and the works of the men of ancient times on the walls of the ancestral temples of the kings of Chu. (Wang Yi here attributed to the past the Eastern Han practice of decorating the walls of ancestral shrines with scenes of ancient worthies and mythical beings. See Wu Hung, *The Wu Liang Shrine* [Stanford: Stanford University, 1989]). He posed questions about what he saw in order to give vent to his resentment. However, since Heaven is supreme and cannot be questioned, the word order was inverted. See *Chu ci buzhu* 3 "Tian Wen," p. 1a. David Hawkes finds this argument strained, insists that the regular word order must be respected, and denies the possibility of such a translation. See Hawkes, *Songs of the South*, p. 123. However, Takeji Sadao shows that inversion of verb and object does take place in the period, and that the contents of the book correspond to the traditional reading of the title. Thus, Wang Yi's reading is not impossible, although the story of the wall illustrations is untenable. See Takeji Sadao 竹治貞 夫, *Soji kenkyū* 楚辭研究 (Tokyo: Fūkan Shobō, 1979), pp. 844–52, p. 859, note 6.

136. On the word "Heaven" in the *Xunzi*, see Edward J. Machle, *Nature and Heaven in the Xunzi: A Study of the Tian Lun* (Albany: SUNY, 1993); Kanaya Osamu 金谷治, "Chūgoku kodai ni okeru kami kannen toshite no ten 中國古代にお け る 神觀念 と し て の 天," in *Kami kannen no hikaku bunka ronteki kenkyū* 神觀念の比 較文化論的研究 (Tokyo: Kodansha, 1981), pp. 589–623; Kodama Rokurō 兒 玉六郎, "Junshi ni okeru tensei no gainen 荀子における天政の概念," *Nihon*

Chūgoku Gakkai Hō 日本中國學會報 24 (1972): 51–62; Kodama, "Junshi no ten ni taisuru ichi kōsatsu 荀子の天に對する一考察," *Shinagaku Kenkyū* 支那學研究 33 (1968): 42–49.

137. Hawkes, *Songs of the South*, p. 125; Fujino, *Fukei bungaku ron*, pp. 68–84.

138. Hawkes, *Songs of the South*, pp. 125–26; Stephen Field, "Cosmos, Cosmograph, and the Inquiring Poet: New Answers to the 'Heaven Questions,'" *Early China* 17 (1992): 83–110; Fujino, *Fukei bungaku ron*, pp. 58–68; You Guoen 游国恩, *Chu ci gai lun* 楚辭概論 (rep. ed. Taipei: Shangwu, 1968), pp. 112–17; You, *Chu ci lunwen ji* 楚辭論文集 (Shanghai: Wenyi Lianhe, 1955), pp. 7–8, 152, 294; Wen Yiduo, "Tian wen shi tian 天問釋天," in *Gu dian xin yi* 古典新義, *Wen Yiduo quan ji*, vol. 2, pp. 313–24; Guo Moruo 郭沫若, *Qu Yuan yanjiu* 屈原研究 (n.p.: Qunyi, 1946), pp. 33, 53, 137–40; Guo, "Zhou Qin yiqian gudai sixiang zhi lice 周秦以前古代思想之蠡測," in *Guo gu luncong* 國故論叢, *Xueyi Huikan* 13 (1926): 41–42; Guo, *Qu Yuan fu jin yi* 屈原賦今譯 (Beijing: Renmin Wenxue, 1953), pp. 5–6, 127; Lu Kanru 陸侃如, *Qu Yuan*, 6th ed. (Shanghai: Yadong Tushuguan, 1933), p. 127; Li Qiao 李翹, "*Chu ci* 'Tian wen' guan jian 楚辭天問管見," *Wenlan Xuebao* 文瀾學報 2:1 (January–March 1936): 4–6 (no continuous pagination). Hoshikawa criticizes the assertion that Qu Yuan is a sceptic, but concludes that the "Tian wen" is a "questioning-critical historical poem." He offers a detailed analysis of the uses of questions in the text, and shows that many of them are intended to express the impossibility of knowing or to offer a moral reproof. See Hoshikawa, *Soji no kenkyū*, pp. 383–404. On the identification of Qu Yuan as an early "nationalist" hero, see Laurence A. Schneider, *A Madman of Ch'u: The Chinese Myth of Loyalty and Dissent* (Berkeley: University of California, 1980), ch. 3, 5.

139. Takeji, *Soji kenkyū*, pp. 824–41.

140. For examples of the questioning of Heaven's justice in the text, see Wen Yiduo, ed., *Tian wen shuzheng* 天問疏證 (Beijing: Sanlian, 1980), pp. 17, 52, 55, 61, 75, 87, 89, 95, 99, 100, 101, 102, 111, 123, 124.

141. Stephen Field argues that the use of images and ideas derived from the *shi pan* and Warring States astronomical thought suggests that the author was an "inquiring poet" and a materialist engaged in a "proto-scientific" inquiry. As he himself notes, however, this hypothesis entails a radical break in the poem after verse 22, and it means that the remainder of the poem is divided between a vision of an objective, material Heaven and men at the mercy of an arbitrary deity. However, these internal ruptures and contradictions disappear as soon as one recognizes that although the poem refers to the latest "scientific" practices, it does not embrace them. The passages based on the cosmograph do not appear as answers to questions or solutions to problems, but rather propositions called into question. The techniques of the scientists in the first part of the poem play the same role as the idea of a just Heaven in the latter part, and the two are treated as aspects of a single intellectual project. Both are attempts by men to discover principles by which they can explain and control the cosmos, and both are challenged by the poet with his endless questioning that insists on the uncanny and the amoral. Since modern

science and enlightenment emerged in the West by denying human purposes to nature—Kant's Copernican revolution—Field assumes that Warring States proto-sciences and the visions of a moral cosmos must also have been at odds. However, for the author of the "Tian wen" they were allies in a common cause, and enemies of higher truths.

142. Several modern scholars, beginning with Hu Shi, have made this argument. They point out that these songs employ in a ritual context many phrases and images that are adapted to figurative, literary uses in the poems of complaint and resentment in the "Li sao" tradition. See, for example, Takeji, *Soji kenkyū*, pp. 804, 820; Hoshikawa, *Soji no kenkyū*, pp. 412, 414–15. Both of these also cite Chinese scholars such as Lu Kanru and Gao Heng. The most persuasive argument for treating the "Nine Songs" as the origins of the *Chu ci* tradition has been made by Galal Walker through an examination of the patterns of internal quotation or echoing across the anthology. See Walker, "Toward a Formal History of the 'Chuci'" (Ph.D. diss., Cornell University, 1982), ch. 3, esp pp. 209–23; pp. 429–34.

143. The classic twentieth-century formulation of this theory is Aoki Masaru 青木正兒, "Soji Kyūka no bukyokuteki kekkō 楚辭九歌の舞曲的結構," *Shinagaku* 7 (1934): 1–23; reprinted in Aoki, *Shina bungaku geijutsu kō* 支那文學藝術考 (Tokyo: Kōbundō, 1942), pp. 147–71. Through analysis of the poems he attempted to identify which parts were solo, which choral, and where the shifts came. See also Wen Yiduo, "'Jiu ge' gu ge wu ju xuan jie 九歌古歌舞劇懸解," in *Wen Yiduo quan ji*, vol. 1, pp. 305–34. Efforts to improve on these analyses have been made in Fujino, *Fukei bungaku ron*, pp. 160–97; Hoshikawa, *Soji no kenkyū*, pp. 419–34; Takeji, *Soji kenkyū*, pp. 796–822. David Hawkes also accepts that the poems were written for dramatic performance, but in the absence of stage directions he declines to attempt any definitive reconstruction. See Hawkes, *Songs of the South*, pp. 95–96.

144. Fujino, pp. 133–59; Takeji, pp. 800–01; Hoshikawa, pp. 412–15. Although Fujino relies largely on Han sources, divination texts on bamboo strips excavated from Chu tombs have confirmed that most of the divinities cited in the songs received offerings in Chu. See Li Ling, "Formulaic Structure of Chu Divinatory Bamboo Slips," *Early China* 15 (1990): 84–85. Mainland historians such as Guo Moruo, You Guoen, Lu Kanru, and Gao Heng also support the theory of the songs as liturgy, but they argue that they are popular religious songs adapted by Qu Yuan or some other editor. See Guo, *Qu Yuan fu jin yi*, p. 37; You Guoen, *Chu ci lun wen ji*, p. 308; Sun Zuoyun 孫作雲, "Jiu ge 'Shan gui' kao 九歌山鬼考," *Qinghua Xuebao* 11:4 (1935): 977–1005; Lu Kanru, Gao Heng 高亨, and Huang Xiaoshu 黃孝紓, eds., *Chu ci xuan* 楚辭選 (Shanghai: Gudian, 1956), p. 4.

145. Wen Yiduo, "Shenma shi 'Jiu ge' 甚嗎是九歌," in *Wen Yiduo quan ji*, vol. 1, pp. 263–78; Hawkes, *Songs of the South*, p. 96.

146. *Chu ci buzhu* 2 "Jiu ge," pp. 3b–24a; Hawkes, *Songs of the South*, pp. 103–17.

147. Geoffrey R. Waters argues that the "Nine Songs" are in fact *political* texts, with criticism of the monarch and despair for the state coded into the accounts

of spirits and flights of the soul. He describes this as the "traditional interpretation of the *Ch'u Tz'u* [*Chu ci*]." See Waters, *Three Elegies of Ch'u*. Certainly all of the early poems in the anthology were interpreted as works in which Qu Yuan criticized his ruler and lamented his fate. Nevertheless, anyone who reads Waters's carefully annotated translation will find that he ignores or contradicts the Chinese commentaries more often than he follows them. His reading of the poems owes more to the practices of Friedrich Bischoff than to anything in the Chinese tradition. Chinese characters are sufficiently polyvalent, and the metaphors that have been put to political uses sufficiently varied, that political meanings can be and are found everywhere. If one substitutes near homophones for original characters, as Waters frequently does, then anything can be proved. The fact remains that of the entire anthology, the "Nine Songs" have the least overtly political content.

148. On the figure of Qu Yuan see Schneider, *A Madman of Ch'u*.

149. *Chu ci buzhu* 6, 7.

150. *Shi ji* 84, pp. 2493–95.

151. For a history of the identification of Qu Yuan as author of the "Li Sao," see Walker, "Toward a Formal History of the 'Chuci'," pp. 27–32. Because of the lateness of the identification, and on the basis of an analysis of its language, Walker argues that the entire *Chuci* anthology is a Han composition, a theory earlier espoused by Hu Shi. See pp. 429–31. In light of the clear citations of the "Li Sao" in Jia Yi's poem on Qu Yuan, a Han date of composition seems highly unlikely. Walker admits that his theory is not proven, and separates it from his conclusions on the relative datings of the poems in the anthology.

152. This argument is presented in a recent Ph.D. thesis completed at Columbia University. Unfortunately, it has not been made available for examination.

153. The first-person pronouns appear after the first couple of verses, and they are so frequent as to require no citations. For the insistence on isolation, see, for example, *Chuci buzhu* 1, pp. 13a, 15a, 15b, 16a, 16b.

154. *Chuci buzhu* 1, pp. 11a (2), 13a, 16a, 20a, 24a, 29a, 32b.

155. *Chuci buzhu* 1, pp. 7a, 12a, 14a, 16a, 29a, 38a. This last appears in the closing lines of the poem, signaling the importance of this point.

156. *Chuci buzhu* 1, pp. 5a–5b, 8a, 10a, 21b–22a, 22b, 24a, 25a, 31b–32a, 32b, 33a, 34a.

157. On the significance of the speaker's ancestry and time of birth, see Jiang Liangfu 姜亮夫, *Chongding Qu Yuan fu jiaozhu* 重订屈原赋校注 (Tianjin: Guji, 1987), pp. 4–7. On the relation of the opening of the "Li sao" to the formula of the *zhu ci* 祝辭, see Fujino, *Fukei bungaku ron*, pp. 84–86. On the *zhu ci* as a model for literary developments, see Fukino, *Chūgoku kodai bungaku hassō ron*, ch. 1.

158. *Chuci buzhu* 1, pp. 6a–b, 7b, 13a, 13b, 16b, 19b, 30b–31b.

159. *Chuci buzhu* 1, p. 17a.

160. The poem does not state that the speaker attempts to enter Heaven in search of a jade maiden as bride, but the link of this passage to the search for a mate on earth, and the fact that the Great Man enters Heaven in Sima Xiangru's

rhapsody to carry off a spirit bride suggests the possibility. See *Chuci buzhu* 1, pp. 55a–57a; *Shi ji* 117, p. 3060; Wen Yiduo, "Li sao jiegu 離騷解詁," in *Wen Yiduo quan ji*, vol. 2, pp. 304–06. On "spirit marriages" in early Chinese religion and literature, see Chūbachi Masakazu 中鉢雅量, *Chūgoku no saishi to bungaku* 中國の祭祀と文學 (Tokyo: Sōbunsha, 1988), ch. 7.

161. See Hoshikawa, *Soji no kenkyū*, pp. 325–27. He cites a passage by Wen Huaisha demonstrating that the name indicates a shamanic or spiritual role, but rejects Wen's suggestion that it was the name of a known shaman. He instead supports Wen Yiduo's argument that the names were created for a fictive character. See Wen, "Qu Yuan wenti 屈原問題," in *Wen Yiduo quan ji*, vol. 1, p. 256.

162. *Chuci buzhu* 1, pp. 11a, 38b. In order to make the conclusion of the poem refer to Qu Yuan's suicide, Chinese commentators invented a Peng Xian who had been a minister of Yin and drowned himself. Other writings of the period clearly indicate that Peng Xian was a powerful spirit, although the identity of his dwelling place is uncertain. He is probably identical with the Wu Xian 巫咸 who appears to Ling Jun in the poem. See pp. 29a–32a. On the evidence regarding Peng Xian, see Hoshikawa, *Soji no kenkyū*, pp. 295–313.

163. *Chuci buzhu* 1, pp. 4a–5a, 8b–9a, 10b–11a, 14a.

164. *Chuci buzhu* 1, pp. 25b, 26b, 27a–b, 27b.

165. *Chuci buzhu* 1, pp. 21a–24a, 34a–38a. The account of the spirit escort appears on pp. 23a–b. Numerous passages in the text emphasize the range across the whole world, both horizontally and vertically. In this they anticipate the programs of interlinked travel and sacrifice of the Qin and Han emperors, and their depiction in the rhapsodies of Sima Xiangru. See pp. 14b, 22a, 26a, 30a, 34a.

166. *Chuci buzhu* 1, pp. 6a–7b.

167. *Chuci buzhu* 1, pp. 28a–32a, 34a.

168. Nakajima, *Fu no seiritsu*, pp. 99–113.

169. *Chuci buzhu* 1, pp. 4a, 7a, 8b, 10a, 11a–b, 13b, 14a, 15a, 15b, 19b–20a, 29a, 30a; *Chuci buzhu* 14, "Ai shi ming," p. 6b.

170. *Zuo zhuan zhu* Xiang 24, p. 1088; *Wen xuan* 文選 (Hong Kong: Shangwu, 1978), p. 1128.

171. *Han shu* 62, pp. 2732–35.

172. *Shi ji* 117, pp. 3002, 3063, 3068. The idea that records of Han glory would form a "seventh classic" also figures in *Lun heng* "Xuan Han 宣漢," p. 191.

173. Hong Gua 洪适, *Li shi* 隸釋 8, p. 2b, in *Shi ke shiliao congshu* 石刻史料叢書, vol. 1 (Taipei: Yiwen, 1966).

Chapter Five. The Political History of Writing

1. Lu Jia 陸賈, *Xin yu* 新語, in *Xin bian zhuzi jicheng*, vol. 2, pp. 1–2; *Han Feizi jishi* 49 "Wu du," p. 1042; *Shang jun shu zhu yi* 7 "Kai se," pp. 182–84; 15 "Lai min," pp. 333–34. This chapter of the *Han Feizi* begins with a tripartite scheme dealing entirely with the past: a high antiquity in which sages separated men from

beasts, a middle antiquity when Gun and Yu tamed the flood, and a recent antiquity when Tang and Wu restored order through military force. The passage also cites a present day in which the methods of earlier sages were no longer appropriate. See p. 1040. However, while the passage implies a quadripartite structure, it explicitly refers to three ages, and it follows a schema similar to that of the passages cited above.

2. François Jullien, *Figures de l'immanence: pour une lecture philosophique du Yi king* (Paris: Grasset, 1993), pp. 22–25; Li Weixiong 李威熊, *Zhongguo jingxue fazhan shi* 中國經學發展史 (Taipei: Wen Shi Zhe, 1989), pp. 47, 54–56, 57–59; Fan Wenlan 范文瀾, *Qun jing gai lun* 群經概論 (Beijing: Pushe, 1934), pp. 29–36; Jiang Boqian 蔣伯潛, *Shisan jing gai lun* 十三經概論 (1945, rep. ed., Shanghai: Guji, 1983), pp. 33–44; Shang Binghe 尚秉和, *Zhou yi Shang shi xue* 周易尚氏學 (Beijing: Zhonghua, 1980), pp. 3–6; Pi Xirui 皮錫瑞, *Jingxue lishi* 經學歷史 (rept. ed., Beijing: Zhonghua, 1959), pp. 19–47. This last work was written in the Qing dynasty at the time of the New Text revival led by Kang Youwei. It thus argues that all the classics derive from Confucius and minimizes the role of the Duke of Zhou or King Wen. Nonetheless, it still acknowledges their contribution to the work.

3. *Lun yu zheng yi* 9 "Zi han," p. 184.

4. *Lun yu zheng yi* 19, p. 410; *Mengzi zheng yi* 2A "Gongsun Chou shang," pp. 110, 129. Here Zai Wo declares that Confucius is greater than Yao or Shun, assimilating his status to that of the sage kings.

5. *Zhou yi zheng yi* 8 ("Xi ci xia" 繫辭下), pp. 5a–8a. The links of the individual hexagrams to the inventions with which they are identified can be explained through pictures evoked by the lines, or through concepts entailed by the "judgments" appended to their constitutive trigrams.

6. For a later account attributing the creation of civilization to Fu Xi, see *Bo hu tong de lun* 1, pp. 9a–b. For an early passage that describes the work of the sages and the *Yi* in terms identical to those applied to Fu Xi, see *Zhou yi zheng yi* 7 ("Xi ci xia"), p. 9a.

7. Jullien, *Figures de l'immanence*, p. 7.

8. *Yi qian kun zao du* 易乾坤鑿度, in *Qi wei* 1, pp. 4b–5b; in *Wei shu ji cheng*, 緯書集成 (Shanghai: Guji, 1994), p. 778.

9. *Shuo wen jie zi zhu* 說文解字注, compiled by Xu Shen 許慎 (d. ca. 120 A.D.), annotated by Duan Yucai 段玉裁 (1735–1815 A.D.) (Taipei: Yiwen, 1974) 15, pp. 1a–b.

10. *Chun qiu yuan ming bao* 春秋元命包, in *Qi wei* 七緯 24, p. 24b; in *Wei shu ji cheng*, p. 924. In this account Cang Jie not only gazes up at the images in Heaven and down at the patterns on earth, but he has four eyes to facilitate this action. On Cang Jie's four eyes, see DeWoskin, *A Song for One or Two*, pp. 170–72. In other versions Cang Jie like the Yellow Emperor does not have four eyes, but four faces. See *Chun qiu yuan ming bao*, in *Qi wei* 24, pp. 26b, 28b; *Wei shu ji cheng*, pp. 923, 924. Cang Jie's invention of writing is also mentioned in *Huainanzi* 8 "Ben jing 本經," p. 116.

11. Xu Zongyuan 徐宗元, ed. *Di wang shi ji ji cun* 帝王世紀輯存 (Beijing: Zhonghua, 1964), pp. 4–5; Wang Jia 王嘉, *Shi yi ji* 拾遺記, annotated by Qi Zhiping 齊治平 (Beijing: Zhonghua, 1981), p. 209.

12. The earliest reference to the River Chart appears in the "Gu ming" chapter of the *Shang shu*, where it seems to have been a jade object placed on display at the funeral of King Cheng. As such it was an element of royal regalia with no suggestion of supernatural origin, and it may have had no relation to later accounts except for providing a name. See *Shang shu zheng yi* 18 "Gu ming 顧命," p. 20a. In a passage from the *Lun yu* the master laments, "The phoenix does not arrive. The river does not put forth its chart. I am done for!" See *Lun yu zheng yi* 9 "Zi han," p. 179. Here the River Chart had become an auspicious omen in the same category as the phoenix, and it is supposed to emerge directly from the Yellow River. The *Mozi* clarifies the significance of this omen in a passage indicating that it emerged from the river immediately prior to King Wu's establishment of the Zhou as the royal line. See *Mozi jian gu* 19 "Fei gong xia," p. 95. In this passage the chart is described as "green," perhaps referring back to its original character as an object made of jade. The passage from the *Huainanzi* cited below also describes the chart as green. The idea that the appearance of the River Chart and Luo Writing indicated the transfer of dynastic power and the imminent rise of a sage also appears in *Lun heng* 19 "Gan xu 感虛," p. 52; 64 "Ji yao 紀妖," p. 219.

13. On the rival scholastic origins of the River Chart and Luo Writing, see Schuyler Cammann, "Some Early Chinese Symbols of Duality," *History of Religions* 24.3 (February 1985): 227–31. For a more general treatment, see Michael Saso, "What is the Ho-t'u?" *History of Religions* 17.3/4 (February–May 1978): 399–416. One of the earliest exclusive references to the Luo Writing appears in the *Zhuangzi*. See *Zhuangzi ji shi* 14 "Tian yun," p. 220. This passage refers to it as the "Nine[-fold] Luo." Another piece of evidence indicating the Daoist provenance of the Luo Writing is the fact that the *Huainanzi* lists it prior to the River Chart, whereas most sources give precedence to the latter. See *Huainanzi* 2 "Chu zhen 俶眞," p. 32.

14. *Zhou yi zheng yi* 7 "Xi ci shang," pp. 28b–30a. In the Eastern Han, Wang Chong argued that the trigrams were identical with the River Chart, and that the Luo Writing was identical with the "Hong fan" chapter of the *Shang shu*. See *Lun heng* 81 "Zheng shuo 正說," pp. 271–72. He also argued that the coming forth of the Chart and the Writing was identical to the invention of writing by Cang Jie. See *Lun heng* 19 "Gan xu," p. 52. One Eastern Han apocryphal text lists the River Chart and Luo Writing as the "signs" provided by the Earth, parallel to the markings on birds and animals, which were the signs provided by Heaven. Fu Xi created the *Yi* by copying these signs. See *Li wei han wen jia* 禮緯含文嘉, in *Gu wei shu* 古緯書 17, pp. 3a–b; in *Wei shu ji cheng*, p. 249.

15. See *Laozi dao de jing* 42, pp. 26–27. The account was also adapted in *Huainanzi* 3 "Tian wen xun 天文訓," p. 46; 7 "Jing shen xun," p. 99.

16. *Lun heng* 81 "Zheng shuo," pp. 271–72; *Li wei han wen jia*, in *Gu wei shu* 17, pp. 3a–b; in *Wei shu ji cheng*, p. 249.

17. *Chun qiu yuan ming bao,* in *Qi wei* 24, p. 24b; in *Wei shu ji cheng,* p. 924; Michèle Pirazzoli-t'Serstevens, *The Han Dynasty,* tr. Janet Seligman (New York: Rizzoli, 1982), p. 188, fig. 147; *Bo hu tong de lun,* in *Han Wei cong shu* (Taipei: Xinxing, 1977) 2 "Feng shan 封禪," p. 1b; *Shang shu zhong hou* 尚書中候, in *Gu wei shu* 4, pp. 1b, 2b–3a, 3b (twice), 14a (three times); in *Wei shu ji cheng,* pp. 163, 164, 169; Zheng Xuan's commentary in *Zhou yi zhengyi* 7 "Xi ci shang," p. 30a. Another version of the passage from the *Li wei han wen jia* cited in notes 14 and 16 refers to the Luo Writing as "Turtle Writing" (*gui shu* 龜書). See *Wei shu ji cheng,* p. 116. A story in the *Shi yi ji* depicts Fu Xi revealing the hexagrams as a River Chart to the sage Yu. See *Shi yi ji,* p. 38. The turtle was not the only animal cited as a natural source for writing, since Fu Xi also examined the patterns (*wen*) of birds and beasts, and texts on "insect graphs" (*chong shu* 蟲書) and "bird graphs" (*niao shu* 鳥書) existed in the Han. See *Han shu* 30, pp. 1721, 1722.

18. *Zuo zhuan zhu* Xi 15, p. 365.

19. Mori Yasutarō 林安太郎, *Kōtei densetsu: kodai Chūgoku shinwa no kenkyū* 黃帝傳說: 古代中國神話の研究 (Kyoto: Kyōto Joshi Daigaku Jinbun Gakkai, 1970), pp. 187–93. Mori also argues that the appearance of the character that refers to the lines of the hexagram (*yao* 爻) within the graphs meaning "to teach" and "to study" refers not to instruction in divination, but rather to that in arithmetic. See pp. 191–92. This would also indicate Fu Xi and the *Yi* were closely tied to the use of numbers.

20. *Zhou bi suan jing* 周髀算經, in *Suan jing shi shu* 算經十書, ed. Qian Bao-zong 錢寶綜 (Beijing: Xinhua, 1963), p. 13; *Jiu zhang suan shu* 九章算書, in *Suan jing shi shu,* p. 91. On the datings of these texts, see Joseph Needham, *Science and Civilization in China,* vol. 3, *Mathematics and the Sciences of the Heavens and the Earth* (Cambridge: Cambridge University, 1970), pp. 19–20, 24–25. See also the article on the *Jiu zhang suan shu* in *Early Chinese Texts.* The link between the origin of numbers and the carpenter's square is also noted in *Huainanzi* 2 "Chu zhen," p. 25.

21. Suzuki Yoshijirō 鈴本由次郎, *Kan eki kenkyū* 漢易研究 (Tokyo: Meitoku, 1963), pp. 247–58.

22. *Zhou yi zheng yi,* 9 "Shuo gua 說卦," pp. 4b–5b.

23. *Da Dai li ji jie gu* 大戴禮記解詁, annotated by Wang Pinzhen 王聘珍 (rep. ed.: Beijing: Zhonghua, 1983) 67 "Ming tang 明堂," p. 150.

24. *Yi qian zao du* 易乾鑿度, in *Qi wei* 2, p. 13b; in *Wei shu ji cheng,* p. 792.

25. Schuyler Cammann, "Some Early Chinese Symbols of Duality," pp. 239–42.

26. See the transcription in Li Ling, *Zhongguo fang shu kao,* pp. 180–81.

27. Detailed discussions of Fu Xi and Nü Wa as a couple appear in English in Andrew H. Plaks, *Archetype and Allegory in the Dream of the Red Chamber* (Princeton: Princeton University, 1976), ch. 2; and in N. J. Girardot, *Myth and Meaning in Early Taoism* (Berkeley: University of California, 1983), pp. 202–07 and *passim* (see index under "Fu-hsi," "Nü-kua," and "Primordial Couple"). See also Hayashi Minao 林巳奈夫, *Kan dai no kamigami* 漢代の神神 (Kyoto: Nozokawa, 1989), pp. 287–

99, 306–08; Mitarai Masaru 御手洗勝, *Kodai Chūgoku no kamigami* 古代中國の神神 (Tokyo: Sōbunsha, 1984), pp. 627–36; Shirakawa Shizuka, *Chūgoku no shinwa* 中國の神話 (Tokyo: Chūō Kōron, 1975), pp. 69–74; Yuan Ke 袁珂, *Zhongguo gudai shenhua* 中國古代神話 (rev. and ex., Shanghai: Shangwu, 1957), pp. 40–60.

28. *Chu ci bu zhu* 3 "Tian wen," p. 16a.

29. *Huainanzi* 17 "Shuo lin 說林," p. 292. Nü Wa's transformations, closely linked to her role as creator, are also mentioned in *Shan hai jing jiao zhu* 16 "Da huang xi jing 大荒西經," p. 389—this passage is followed by a note on Nü Wa; *Shuo wen jie zi zhu* 12b, p. 11a. See also Jing Wang, *The Story of Stone: Intertextuality, Ancient Stone Lore, and the Stone Symbolism of Dream of the Red Chamber, Water Margin, and The Journey to the West* (Durham: Duke University, 1992), pp. 44–57.

30. Ying Shao 應劭, *Fengsu tongyi* 風俗通義, annotated by Wu Shuping 吳樹平 (Tianjin: Renmin, 1980), p. 449.

31. *Huainanzi* 6 "Lan ming 覽冥," p. 95. Nü Wa's chopping off the turtle's feet is also mentioned in a discussion of the trigram *kun*. See *Yi qian kun zao du*, in *Qi wei*, 1, p. 13a, in *Wei shu ji cheng*, p. 782. Plaks asserts that the "five-colored minerals" in this account "must reflect the harmonious ordering of the five elements." See *Archetype and Allegory*, p. 39. Marcel Granet cites evidence from the Han and subsequent periods in which the smelting of five-colored minerals refers to the casting of mirrors or swords. He argues that the "marriage" of Fu Xi and Nü Wa and their role as creators of marriage is a late version of myths pertaining to metal casting which treated the process as a "marriage" of water and fire. See Granet, *Danses et légendes de la Chine ancienne* (1926, rev. and expanded, Paris: Presses Universitaires de France, 1994), pp. 498–503. On accounts of the flood, see Rémi Mathieu, "Yu le Grand et le mythe du déluge dans la Chine ancienne," *T'oung Pao* 78 (1992): 162–90.

32. In the *Huainanzi*, as in the *Zhuangzi*, Fu Xi sometimes represents the ideal state of primitive man, and sometimes the beginning of the work of the sages who destroyed that state. See *Zhuangzi ji shi* 4 "Ren jian shi," p. 69—Fu Xi along with other sages embodies the trance state of one in harmony with the Way; 6 "Da zong shi," p. 112—Fu Xi is one who attained the Way, and thereby joined with the "mother of breath/energy" (*qi mu* 氣母); 10 "Qi qie," p. 162—Fu Xi, once again identified with the knotting of cords, is the penultimate ruler of the "age of supreme virtue," when men lived at peace in perfect simplicity; 16 "Shan xing," pp. 243–44—Fu Xi emerges as ruler because of the decline of primitive virtue; 21 "Tianzi Fang," p. 317—Fu Xi is no match for a "perfected man" (*zhen ren* 眞人); *Huainanzi* 2 "Chu zhen," p. 28—Fu Xi embodies the break with primal virtue; 6 "Lan ming," pp. 95–96, 98—Fu Xi is linked with Nü Wa as embodiments of the primitive paradise, and they are said to rule without laws or measures; 9 "Zhu shu," pp. 129–30—Fu Xi and Shen Nong are exemplary teachers who command without words and have audience without being seen; 13 "Fan lun," p. 215—Fu Xi and Shen Nong rule without rewards or punishments, but the people do no wrong.

33. *Huainanzi* 7 "Jing shen xun," p. 99. On Fu Xi and Nü Wa in Han art, see Mark Edward Lewis, "Fu Xi and Nü Wa in Han Mythology and Art," in Wang Tao, ed., *Religion and Art in China* (London: Eastern Art Publishing, in press).

34. *Shi ben ji bu* 世本輯補, annotated by Qin Jiamo 秦嘉謨, in *Shi ben ba zhong* 世本八種 (Shanghai: Shangwu, 1957) 1 "Di xi 帝繫," p. 15; *Di wang shi ji ji cun*, p. 52; Katō Jōken, "Shina ko seishi no kenkyū—Ka U Shi sei kō 支那古姓氏の研究——夏禹姒姓考," in *Chūgoku kodai bunka no kenkyū*, pp. 454–55.

35. Katō, "Shina ko seishi no kenkyū," pp. 437–49; Edward H. Schafer, *The Divine Woman: Dragon Ladies and Rain Maidens in T'ang Literature* (Berkeley: University of California, 1973), pp. 30–31; Shirakawa, *Chūgoku no shinwa*, pp. 60–69; Mitarai, *Kodai Chūgoku no kamigami*, pp. 117–21, 124–25, 131–32.

36. On the signficance of Fu Xi's name, see Mitarai, *Kodai Chūgoku no kamigami*, pp. 631–36; Katō Jōken, "Futsu ki kō 弗忌考," in *Chūgoku kodai bunka no kenkyū*, pp. 303–22. For examples of the depictions of Fu Xi and Nü Wa in Han tomb art, see Käte Finsterbusch, *Verzeichnis und Motivindex der Han-Darstellungen: Band II Abbildungen und Addenda* (Wiesbaden: Otto Harrassowitz, 1971), illustrations 32a, 45, 101–02, 106, 127, 137, 150, 158, 161, 167, 172, 261j, 274, 282, 347, 507c, 508m, 570, 696, 789, 947; Plaks, *Archetype and Allegory*, pp. 238–39; Hayashi, *Kan dai no kamigami*, pp. 288, 289, 290, 291, 292, 293; Mori, *Kōtei densetsu*, p. 203; Shirakawa, *Chūgoku no shinwa*, p. 71; Wu Hung, *The Wu Liang Shrine: The Ideology of Early Chinese Pictorial Art* (Stanford: Stanford University, 1989), pp. 47, 157. For the statement that Fu Xi had the form of a dragon see, for example, *Chun qiu yuan ming bao*, in *Qi wei* 24, p. 26b, in *Wei shu ji cheng*, p. 923; *Chun qiu he cheng tu* 春秋合誠圖, in *Gu wei shu* 8, p. 7b, in *Wei shu ji cheng*, p. 192. A variety of dragons and snakes accompany Fu Xi in the account of his reign of virtue in the *Huainanzi*. See 6 "Lan Ming," p. 95.

37. See, for example, *Shi ji* 28, p. 1358. In this story Lord Wen of Qin dreams of a yellow serpent which hangs down from Heaven to Earth. At the spot where its mouth reached the ground, Lord Wen established the Fu Altar in order to sacrifice to the White Emperor. For Han depictions of rainbows linking Heaven to earth, with the head of a dragon at either end, see, for example, Zhou Dao 周到 and Li Jinghua 李京华, "Tanghe Zhenzhi chang Han huaxiang shi mu de fajue 唐河针织厂汉画像石墓的发掘," *Wenwu* 1973:6, pp. 31, 35; ceiling of the Left Wu Shrine reproduced in Edouard Chavannes, *Mission archéologique dans la Chine septentrionale* (Paris: Imprimerie Nationale, 1913), figure 132; Schafer, *The Divine Woman*, pp. 13–14.

38. On the sun and moon in these depictions as symbols of *yin* and *yang*, see Hayashi, *Kan dai no kamigami*, pp. 289–90. The carpenter's square is associated with Fu Xi not only in art but also in texts. See, *Yi tong gua yan* 易通卦驗, in *Qi wei* 6, p. 1b; in *Wei shu ji cheng*, p. 820. In this passage the carpenter's square is specifically associated with Fu Xi's ability to make distinctions out of primal chaos, a capacity linked to his creation of the hexagrams.

39. On Fu Xi using the carpenter's square to create the trigrams, see *Yi tong gua yan*, in *Qi wei* 6, p. 1b; in *Wei shu ji cheng*, p. 820. On the trigrams as square and the yarrow as round, see *Zhou yi zheng yi* 7 "Xi ci shang," p. 26b.

40. Perhaps the earliest references to Chui is in the *Shang shu* 3 "Shun dian 舜典," p. 24b. Here Chui is appointed chief of the craftsmen (*gong gong* 共工) by Shun. His title is identical with the name of the rebel who causes the flood and the tipping of the heavens in many versions of the flood myth, but the meaning of this link is unclear. On Chui as the inventor of the carpenter's square and the inked cord used as a straightedge, see *Shi ben ji bu* 9 "Zuo 作," p. 360. On Chui as a figure who represents the dangers or uselessness of crafts, see *Zhuangzi ji shi* 10 "Qu qie," p. 161—this passage links eliminating inked cord, straightedge, and compass with "breaking off" Chui's fingers as preconditions for the restoration of true skill; 19 "Da sheng," p. 290—here by keeping his mind detached Chui embodies the powers of the compass and carpenter's square, and his "fingers transform themselves together with the objects"; *Lü shu chun qiu jiaoshi* 18 "Li wei," p. 1179—in this passage the image of Chui with his fingers bitten off is cast on the Zhou tripods, thus warning people against crafts and "craftiness"; *Huainanzi* 8 "Ben jing," p. 117—this passage is an adaptation of the preceding one, but it follows directly after accounts of the negative impact of the invention of writing and of wells; 12 "Dao ying," p. 208.

41. *Li han wen jia* 禮含文嘉, in *Gu wei shu* 17, pp. 3a–b, in *Wei shu ji cheng*, p. 249.

42. *Yi qian zao du*, in *Qi wei* 2, pp. 1b, 2a, 2b, 5b. This last passage states that because it is divided into upper and lower halves, the entire *Yi* text, like the individual hexagrams of which it is composed, is both the image and the root of *yin* and *yang*. On King Wen establishing the hexagrams to unite Heaven and Earth, see *Yi qian zao du*, in *Qi wei* 2, p. 12a, in *Wei shu ji cheng*, p. 791.

43. One of the earliest accounts of a dragon sire is that of the conception of the Han founder. See *Shi ji* 6, p. 341. For tales of dragons fathering sage kings in the Han apocryphal texts see, *Chun qiu yuan ming bao*, in *Gu wei shu* 6, pp. 6b–7a, in *Wei shu ji cheng*, pp. 179–80; *Chun qiu he cheng tu* 8, pp. 9a–b, in *Wei shu ji cheng*, p. 193. In this second story the dragon presents a chart to Yao's future mother before impregnating her. The same story is mentioned in *Chun qiu yuan ming bao*, in *Qi wei*, 24, p. 7b, in *Wei shu ji cheng*, p. 931. On the principle that sages have spirit fathers, see Xu Shen and Zheng Xuan 鄭玄 (127–200 A.D.), *Bo wu jing yi yi* 駁五經異義, in *Hou zhi bu zu zhai congshu* 後知不足齋叢書 (n.p.: Chang Shubao, 1884) *tao* 1, *ce* 1, pp. 19a–b; Yasui Kōzan 安居香山, *Isho no seiritsu to sono tenkai* 緯書の成立とその展開 (Tokyo: Kokusho Kankō, 1981), pp. 413–44.

44. *Guo yu* 16, p. 519; *Shi ji* 4, p. 147.

45. Wolfram Eberhard, *Typen chinesischer Volksmärchen* (Helsinki: F F Communications No. 120, 1937), pp. 102–04; Eberhard, *The Local Cultures of South and East China*, tr. Alide Eberhard (Leiden: E. J. Brill, 1968), pp. 39–40, 231–33; Schafer, *The Divine Woman*, pp. 22–23.

46. *Shan hai jing jiao zhu* "Hai wai xi jing," p. 219; "Hai wai dong jing," p. 263; "Hai nei xi jing," p. 301; "Da huang nan jing," p. 366. In addition to these accounts linking *wu* to snakes, several passages describe spirits who wield snakes, tread on them, carry them on their heads, or wear them at their ears. See "Zhong shan jing," p. 176 (twice); "Hai wai xi jing," p. 227; "Hai wai bei jing," pp. 240, 248; "Hai wai dong jing," p. 253; "Hai nei xi jing," p. 299; "Da huang dong jing," pp. 350, 355; "Da huang bei jing," pp. 425, 426, 427; "Da huang nan jing," p. 370; "Da huang xi jing," p. 401.

47. Wu Rongzeng 吴荣曾, "Zhanguo, Han dai de 'cao she shen guai' ji you guan shenhua mixin de bianyi 战国汉代的操蛇神怪及有关神话迷信的变异," *Wenwu* 10 (1989): 46–52 cites the most important earlier reports. Since the accounts in the *Shan hai jing* may have been based on artistic depictions, the relation between the archeological finds and the textual accounts are probably quite close.

48. Chow Tse-tsung, "The childbirth myth and ancient Chinese medicine: a study of aspects of the *wu* tradition," in *Ancient China: Studies in Early Civilization*, ed. David T. Roy and Tsuen-hsuin Tsien (Hong Kong: Chinese University, 1978), pp. 43–89.

49. *Shuo wen jie zi zhu* 14B, pp. 23b–24a. As the apocryphal *Yi qian zao du* explains, *yang* begins with *hai*. Since *ren* is the ultimate *yin*, it marks the birth of *yang*. Thus it marks the shift from *hai* to *zi*, and by extension the birth of a child.

50. *Shuo wen jie zi zhu* 5A, p. 25a; 8A, p. 9b. It is interesting in terms of the mythology of Fu Xi to find the carpenter's square in this complex of characters pertaining to *wu* and fertility. The gloss on the character *wu* also insists on the fact that it is synonymous with *gong* "skill, artisan." See 5A, p. 26b.

51. *Yi qian kun zao du*, in *Qi wei* 1, p. 6b–7a; *Yi qian zao du*, in *Qi wei* 2, pp. 2b, 5b–6a, 12a–b, 13a, 14a; in *Wei shu ji cheng*, pp. 779, 788, 792. On the intellectual background of these texts linking the trigrams with the emergence of the cosmos, see Yasui Kōzan 安居香山 and Nakamura Shōhachi 中村璋八, *Isho no kisoteki kenkyū* 緯書の基礎的研究 (Kyoto: Kokusho Kankō, 1978), pp. 171–200.

52. *Yi qian kun zao du*, in *Qi wei* 1, p. 8a; *Yi qian zao du*, in *Qi wei* 2, pp. 2a, 3b, 6a; in *Wei shu ji cheng*, pp. 780, 786, 787, 788.

53. *Yi qian kun zao du*, in *Qi wei* 1, p. 16b; in *Wei shu ji cheng*, p. 784.

54. *Yi qian kun zao du: kun zao du*, in *Qi wei* 1, pp. 9a–b; in *Wei shu ji cheng*, p. 780. This text quotes the *Wan xing jing* 萬形經 and the *Xuanyuan ben jing* 軒轅本經 for the two versions of the links between dragons and yarrow. On the age of turtles as crucial to their role in divination, see *Bo hu tong de lun* 2, pp. 14b, 15a. It also refers to the longevity of the yarrow, without mentioning a specific number of years.

55. *Shi ben ji bu* 9 "Zuo," p. 355.

56. *Bo hu tong de lun* 1, p. 9a; *Di wang shi ji ji cun*, p. 3.

57. Luo Bi 羅泌 (d. ca. 1176 A.D.), *Lu shi* 路史, *Hou ji* 後紀 (Si bu bei yao ed.) 2, p. 2a.

58. Wen Yiduo, "Gao Tang shen nü chuanshuo zhi fenxi 高唐神女傳說之
分析," in *Wen Yiduo quan ji*, vol. 1, pp. 97–107; Chen Mengjia 陳夢家, "Gao mei
jiao she zu miao tong kao 高媒校社祖廟通考," *Qinghua Xuebao* 12.3 (1937):
445–72; Chow Tse-tsung, "The childbirth myth and ancient Chinese medicine,
pp. 56, 65; Ikeda Suetoshi 池田末利, *Chūgoku kodai shūkyō shi kenkyū* 中國古代宗
教史研究 (Tokyo: Tōkai Daigaku, 1983), pp. 602–22; Derk Bodde, *Festivals in
Classical China: New Year and Other Annual Observances During the Han Dynasty* (Princeton:
Princeton University, 1975), pp. 243–61. Recently Liu Dunyuan and Zheng Yan
have interpreted depictions of embracing couples in two second-century A.D. tombs
as evidence of the continued practice of this rite. See Liu Dunyuan 劉敦願, "Han
huaxiangshi shang yin shi nan nü—Pingyin Mengzhuang Han mu shizhu jisi gewu
tuxiang fenxi 漢畫像石上飲食男女——平陰孟莊漢墓石柱祭祀歌舞圖像
分析," *Gu Gong Wenwu Yuekan* 古宮文物月刊 141(December 1994), pp. 122–35;
Zheng Yan 鄭岩, "Anqiu Dongjiazhuang Han mu li zhu diaoke tuxiang kao 安丘
董家庄汉墓立柱雕刻图像考," *Jinian Shangdong Daxue kaogu zhuanye chuangjian
ershi zhounian wenji* 纪念山东大学考古专业创建二十周年文集 (Ji'nan: Shandong Daxue, 1992), pp. 397–413.

59. *Fengsu tongyi jiao shi*, p. 449.

60. Wen Yiduo, "Fu Xi kao 伏羲考," in *Wen Yiduo quan ji*, vol. 1, pp. 3–68.
Gourd myths in ancient China are the subject of Girardot, *Myth and Meaning in
Early Taoism*.

61. Henri Maspero, "Légendes mythologiques dans le Chou King," *Journal
Asiatique* 214 (1924), pp. 74–75; Yuan Ke, *Zhongguo gudai shenhua*, p. 46, note 15;
Edward H. Schafer, *The Vermilion Bird: T'ang Images of the South* (Berkeley: University
of California, 1967), p. 13; Mitarai Masaru, *Kodai Chūgoku no kamigami*, pp. 627–
30.

62. *Shi ben ji bu* 9 "Zuo," pp. 358–59; *Li ji zhu shu* 31 "Ming tang wei 明堂
位," p. 16b; *Shuo wen jie zi zhu* 5A, pp. 17a–b; *Fengsu tongyi jiao shi*, p. 246.

63. Liu Xi 劉熙, *Shi ming shu zheng bu* 釋名疏證補, annotated by Wang
Xianqian 王先謙 (rep. ed.: Shanghai: Guji, 1984) 7 "Shi yue qi 釋樂器," pp. 7a–
b. See also *Shuo wen jie zi zhu* 5A, pp. 17a–b.

64. Ma Gao 馬縞, *Zhonghua gu jin zhu* 中華古今注 (rep. ed.: Shanghai: Shangwu, 1956).

65. *Shi ben ji bu* 9 "Zuo," p. 355; *Fengsu tongyi*, pp. 230–31.

66. On Fu Xi and the *qin*, see DeWoskin, *A Song for One or Two*, pp. 53, 57,
59, 60, 111, 112, 146. On the instrument, its symbolism, and its music, see
DeWoskin, ch. 7–8; Robert van Gulik, *The Lore of the Chinese Lute: An Essay in Ch'in
Ideology*, Monumenta Nipponica, no. 3 (Tokyo: Sophia University, 1940).

67. Wu Hung, *The Wu Liang Shrine*, p. 156. The apocryphal literature states
that the *Yi* or the trigrams serve to "make clear the Way of kings" (*ming wang dao* 明
王道) or "fix the royal enterprise" (*ding wang ye* 定王業) and that through them
"the royal transformations [of the people] are completed" (*wang hua quan* 王化全).
They also serve to cause the "royal teachings to arise" (*wang jiao xing* 王教興). See

Zhou yi qian zao du, in *Qi wei* 2, 2a (twice), 10a (twice), 11b; in *Wei shu ji cheng*, pp. 798, 790, 791.

68. *Di wang shi ji ji cun*, p. 3.

69. On the trigrams as the basis of political order, see *Yi tong gua yan*, in *Qi wei* 6, p. 7b; in *Wei shu ji cheng*, p. 823; *Bo hu tong de lun* 1, p. 9b. On the dragons and trigrams, see *Yi qian zao du*, in *Qi wei* 2, p. 18a; in *Wei shu ji cheng*, p. 794.

70. *Yi tong gua yan*, in *Qi wei* 6, pp. 4a–b; in *Wei shu ji cheng*, p. 821; a passage from the same work on p. 3a, *Wei shu ji cheng* p. 820 also links the *Yi* to the *feng* and *shan* sacrifices.

71. On the *feng* and *shan* sacrifices and their linking of dynastic transitions with writing, see Mark Edward Lewis, "The *Feng* and *Shan* Sacrifices of Emperor Wu of the Han," in *Imperial Ritual in China*, ed. Joseph P. McDermott (Cambridge: Cambridge University, in press). On the evolution of script in the inscriptions on Mount Tai, see *Shuo wen jie zi zhu* 15, p. 3a. For an account of the ritual in the Eastern Han, see Stephen Bokenkamp, "Record of the Feng and Shan Sacrifices," in *Religions of China in Practice*, ed. Donald S. Lopez, Jr. (Princeton: Princeton University, 1996), pp. 251–60.

72. *Zuo zhuan zhu* Xi 15, p. 365.

73. *Shuo wen jie zi zhu* 15A pp. 2a–3a. For the gloss on *zi*, see 14B, p. 25a. A similar gloss appears in *Shi ming shu zheng bu* 4 "Shi yan yu 釋言語," p. 2a. The apocryphal literature links the relation of *wen* to *zi* with that of the hexagrams to primal energy. "In high antiquity they transformed patterns into characters, changed energy into the *Yi*, and drew the hexagrams into images (*xiang* 象)." See *Yi qian kun zao du*, in *Qi wei* 1, p. 4b; in *Wei shu ji cheng*, p. 778.

74. Wang Fengyang 王奉养, *Hanzi xue* 汉字学 (Jilin: Jilin Wenxue, 1989), p. 540.

75. *Di wang shi ji ji cun*, pp. 8–9.

76. See, for example, *Yi qian zao du*, in *Qi wei* 2, p. 2b; in *Wei shu ji cheng*, p. 786. Later in the same text, however, King Wen is described as "establishing the hexagrams and uniting Heaven and Earth." See *Qi wei* 2, p. 12a; in *Wei shu ji cheng*, p. 791.

77. *Lun yu zheng yi* 9 "Zi han," p. 176. For a discussion of the meaning of the term *wen* in the ancestral cult, see Lothar von Falkenhausen, "The Concept of *Wen* in the Ancient Chinese Ancestral Cult," *Chinese Literature: Essays, Articles, Reviews*, 18 (December 1996): 1–22.

78. *Zhou yi zheng yi* 8 "Xi ci xia," p. 21b. The same idea, without referring explicitly to King Wen, appears on p. 17a. One hexagram judgment also cites King Wen as a model of remaining cultivated (*wen*) and illumined on the inside, even when beset by great adversity. See *Zhou yi zheng yi* 4, pp. 13b–14a, hexagram #36 "Ming yi 明夷."

79. The theme of the Duke of Zhou as the emblem of claims to ministerial authority is discussed in Edward L. Shaughnessy, "The Duke of Zhou's Retirement in the East and the Beginnings of the Minister-Monarch Debate in Chinese

Political Philosophy," *Early China* 18 (1993): 41–72. On the theme of yielding the throne as it appears in the various philosophical traditions, see Graham, *Disputers of the Tao*, pp. 292–99. The theme is discussed from the perspective of the mythology of Yao, Shun, and Yu in Sarah Allan, *The Heir and the Sage: Dynastic Legend in Early China* (San Francisco: Chinese Materials Center, 1981).

80. For discussions of the Duke of Zhou, his place in early Zhou history, and the reasons for his rise to increased prominence, see Shaughnessy, "The Duke of Zhou's Retirement in the East," esp. pp. 41–44; Shaughnessy, "The Role of Grand Protector Shi in the Consolidation of the Zhou Conquest," *Ars Orientalis* 19 (1989): 51–77. The relevant bronze inscriptions are cited in the articles.

81. *Shang shu zheng yi* 14 "Kang gao," pp. 3a, 4b—imitate not only wise Yin kings but their wise men, 9a; "Jiu gao," pp. 16a—importance of all those who hold office and serve, 17a, 17b—refers to officials who "possess the government" or "govern affairs," 18a—addresses officials who are "sons of the officials who assisted King Wen," 19a–b—Yin's early prosperity based on the king's revering ministers, and employing good officials; 15 "Luo gao," pp. 17b—priority in the sacrifices for the most meritorious ministers, reliance on Zhou officers (twice), 24b— Duke of Zhou and officers consolidate all affairs; 16 "Duo shi," pp. 6a—king only employs the worthy, 7b; "Wu yi," pp. 10a–13a—model of kings as humble men who toil, 15a–b—ancient kings admonished and instructed by their ministers.

82. Shaughnessy, "The Duke of Zhou's Retirement in the East."

83. *Shang shu zheng yi* 21 "Li zheng," pp. 15a–26a.

84. Shaughnessy argues that since these chapters clearly pre-date the rise of the hagiographical tradition that developed from the time of Confucius, they must reflect the "historiographical concerns of the Western Zhou period." However, there is no reason to think that the historiographical concerns of the late Western Zhou necessarily reflected the historical realities of the early decades. The differences in the debate traced by Shaughnessy would then reflect not realities of the Duke of Zhou's career or thought, but rather a reading into the time of dynastic foundations of a dispute that emerged only in the wake of the decline of royal power in the middle of the dynasty.

85. The Duke of Zhou is depicted divining in *Shang shu zheng yi* 12 "Jin teng," pp. 8b, 9b—refers to three divinations; 13 "Da gao," pp. 16a–18b, 20b—refers to multiple divinations; 15 "Luo gao," p. 15a—divines three times and sends a depiction of the results to the king in a chart.

86. *Shang shu zheng yi* 14 "Kang gao," pp. 7b, 8a, 9a–b, 11a, 14a; 15 "Luo gao," p. 17b (twice).

87. *Shang shu zheng yi* 16 "Duo shi," p. 6a.

88. *Shang shu zheng yi* 15 "Luo gao," p. 27b.

89. *Shang shu zheng yi* 13 "Jin teng," pp. 6a–13a.

90. Fukino Yasushi, *Chūgoku kodai bungaku hassō ron*, pp. 3–29; Ikeda Suetoshi, *Chūgoku kodai shūkyō shi kenkyū*, pp. 822–94; Fujino Iwatomo, *Fūkei bungaku ron*, pp. 84–89; Kano Naoki 狩野直喜, *Shinagaku bunsō* 支那學文藪 (Tokyo: Sōbundō,

1936), pp. 71–77; Qiu Xigui, "An Examination of Whether the Charges in Shang Oracle-Bone Inscriptions are Questions," *Early China* 14 (1989): 113–14, and the response by David Nivison, pp. 154–55.

91. On Tang's self-sacrifice, see Sarah Allan, "Drought, Human Sacrifice and the Mandate of Heaven in a Lost Text from the *Shang shu*," *Bulletin of the School of Oriental and African Studies* 47 (1984): 523–29. The Duke of Zhou's action of substitution is discussed on pp. 523–24. For different versions of King Tang's speech, see *Lü shi chun qiu jiao shi* 9 "Shun min 順民," p. 479; *Xunzi ji jie* 27 "Da lüe," pp. 331–32; *Shuo yuan*, in *Han Wei cong shu*, 1 "Jun dao 君道," p. 12a.

92. For the poem, see *Mao shi zheng yi* 8.2, Mao #155 "Chi xiao 鴟鴞," pp. 1b–10a. For a discussion of the use of the poem within the story, a discussion that reflects on the relations of history and poetry as well as different modes of poetry, see Saussy, *The Problem of a Chinese Aesthetic*, pp. 139–47.

93. The equation of these two incidents is strengthened by the fact that they are placed in parallel "slots" in the two halves, both directly preceding a closing speech by the major actor of that section. Other parallels bind the two halves together. Thus the other two "great dukes" appear only twice. The first immediately follows the opening statement that King Wu had fallen ill, while the second immediately precedes the closing statement that the harvest was abundant. This framing suggests that the successful harvest with which it ends is to be understood as an answer to the threat posed by the king's illness with which it begins.

94. *Lun yu zheng yi* 7 "Shu er," p. 137; 8 "Tai Bo," p. 162. The significance of "seeing" or "having audience with" (*jian* 見) deserves further study and reflection. This seeing would probably indicate a visit by the shade of the deceased duke, which would place him in the role of Confucius' guiding spirit, something like Socrates' *daemon*. This intrusion of the duke is less than possession, but considerably more than an intellectual affinity.

The later chapters of the *Lun yu* contain two further references to the Duke of Zhou. See 11 "Xian jin," p. 246; 18 "Weizi," p. 399. In the former Confucius notes that the Ji clan is "richer than the Duke of Zhou." Since the Duke of Zhou was the founding ancestor of the ruling line of Lu, this image is to be understood in terms of the Ji clan's usurpation of the prerogatives of the ruler. The latter claims to quote the Duke of Zhou addressing his son. It asserts that rulers should not cause resentment in their great ministers by not following their advice, should not remove ministers from established families without serious cause, and should not demand complete excellence from any single official. This passage is based on the identification noted above of the Duke of Zhou as patron and sponsor of ministerial power. Here he is specifically associated with the hereditary houses of feudal lords and ministers.

95. *Mengzi zheng yi* 3A "Teng Wen Gong shang," p. 189. He is also paired with King Wu as metonyms for the conquest. See *Mengzi zheng yi* 2A "Gongsun Chou shang," p. 104; 3B "Teng Wen Gong xia," p. 265. The topos of King Wen as a "teacher" (*shi* 師) recurs in *Mengzi zheng yi* 4A "Li Lou shang," pp. 292, 302.

96. *Mengzi zheng yi* 3A "Teng Wen Gong shang," pp. 230–31; 3B "Teng Wen Gong xia," p. 271; 5A "Wang Zhang shang," p. 383.

97. *Mengzi zheng yi* 4B "Li Lou xia," pp. 335–36. As was noted in chapter 2, this trait of combining the good points of each dynasty figured in several passages in the *Lun yu*. Thus this passage likewise treats the Duke of Zhou as the predecessor and guide of Confucius.

98. *Mozi jian gu* 46 "Geng Zhu," p. 261.

99. *Mozi jian gu* 47 "Gui yi," pp. 368–69.

100. For passages that refer to or are based on the Duke of Zhou being the first lord of Lu, see *Zuo zhuan zhu* Xi 24, p. 423—this also lists other states whose rulers descend from him; Wen 12, pp. 588–89; Cheng 16, p. 893; Xiang 12, p. 996; Zhao 7, pp. 1286–87—this refers to a later duke dreaming of the Duke of Zhou; Zhao 10, p. 1318; Zhao 13, p. 1357; Zhao 25, p. 1465; Ding 4, p. 1536; Ai 11, p. 1668; Ai 15, p. 1693.

101. *Zuo zhuan zhu* Xiang 21, pp. 1060–61; Zhao 1, p. 1213.

102. *Zuo zhuan zhu* Yin 8, p. 58; Huan 1, p. 82; Xi 31, p. 489. In addition to these questionable sacrifices from outside Lu, a steward of one of the Lu ministerial houses who gained control of the government offered human sacrifice to the Duke of Zhou, but the practice did not last.

103. *Zuo zhuan zhu* Ding 1, pp. 1519–20. This same theory of a political hierarchy in which the subordinate is the double of his immediate superior is also attributed to the famous musician Shi Kuang. See Xiang 14, pp. 1016–17. The same idea also appears in Huan 2, p. 94, where it describes the relation of collateral lines to the central ones in the *zongfa* system.

104. *Zuo zhuan zhu* Xiang 23, p. 1076; Zhao 20, p. 1411; Zhao 30, p. 1506—on funerals; Ai 16, p. 1699.

105. For sons as doubles of the self (*shen* 身), see *Zuo zhuan zhu* Wen 16, p. 621; *Gu Liang zhuan zhu shu* 穀梁傳注疏, in *Shi san jing zhu shu*, vol. 7, 7 "Xi 5," p. 13a. For a discussion of *er* in the sense of rebellion, its most common use, see Ogura Yoshihiko, *Chūgoku kodai seiji shisō kenkyū*, pp. 252–81.

106. *Xiao jing zhu shu* 孝經注疏, in *Shi san jing zhu shu*, vol. 8, 5 "Sheng zhi 聖治," p. 1a. The theme of *pei* draws in yet another dimension of the theme of "doubling" in the ritual and political realms, but in this context it is Hou Ji and King Wen who serve as the doubles of the high cosmic powers, while the Duke of Zhou plays the role of filial son. See Ikeda Suetoshi, *Chūgoku kodai shūkyō shi kenkyū*, pp. 585–601.

107. *Zuo zhuan zhu* Xi 24, p. 420.

108. *Zuo zhuan zhu* Xi 26, p. 440.

109. *Zuo zhuan zhu* Wen 18, pp. 633–34.

110. *Zuo zhuan zhu* Zhao 2, pp. 1226–27. Another passage linking current ritual, the Zhou foundation, and the Duke of Zhou's virtue appears in Ding 4, p. 1536. This states that as chief minister the Duke of Zhou controlled all under Heaven, lists the honors bestowed on Lu when the fief was founded, states that

they follow the laws of the Duke of Zhou, and concludes that this "makes clear the Duke of Zhou's virtue."

The most detailed modern study of the traditions of the Duke of Zhou as author and compiler is Hayashi Taisuke 林泰輔, *Shū Kō to sono jidai* 周公とその時代 (Tokyo: Okura Shoten, 1915), Part III "Shū Kō to Shū kan Girai Shū Eki to no kankei 周公と周官儀禮周易との關係," pp. 208–783.

111. *Zuo zhuan zhu* Zhao 13, p. 1367. The crediting of a worthy minister, in this case Guan Zhong, with the survival of civilization also figures in the *Lun yu*. See *Lun yu zheng yi* 14 "Xian wen," p. 314. The *Mencius* makes a similar assertion, but it identifies civilization with the "Way of the Duke of Zhou and Confucius." See *Mengzi zheng yi* 3A "Teng Wen Gong shang," pp. 230–32.

112. *Zuo zhuan zhu* Ai 11, p. 1668.

113. *Zuo zhuan zhu* Xiang 29, pp. 1161–65. On the Duke of Zhou, Duke Tai, and King Wen revealed in the odes, see pp. 1162, 1164.

114. Stephen W. Durrant, *The Cloudy Mirror: Tension and Conflict in the Writings of Sima Qian* (Albany: SUNY, 1995). The importance of Confucius to Durrant's understanding of Sima Qian's career is suggested by the fact that the first half of the book revolves around the figure of the sage. Earlier criticisms of the *Shi ji* chapter on Confucius are presented on pp. 29–32.

115. Durrant proposes a similar four-part division: early and brilliant service, departure, trial and wandering, and return. See pp. 35–36. He tries to assimilate these divisions to Joseph Campbell's Jungian schema of the "hero's" career. This is not helpful for several reasons. First, Jungian analysis, like fortune cookies and newspaper horoscopes, operates on the principle of being sufficiently vague to cover anything. Nevertheless, even such a capacious schema cannot fit the tale of Confucius, who does not secure anything on his travels and returns not to triumph but to retire and to toil in hope of future recognition. More important, it occludes the close ties of each stage of Confucius' career to Warring States and early imperial ideas about the nature of the sage, and the relations of these ideas to contemporary practice. More is to be gained by situating the elements of the narrative in the world that produced it then by seeking a least common denominator with radically different narratives dealing with distinct forms of "heroism."

116. *Shi ji* 47, p. 1905–06. For an alternative analysis of this birth legend, see Lionel M. Jensen, "Wise Man of the Wilds: Fatherlessness, Fertility and the Mythic Exemplar, Kongzi," *Early China* 20 (1995): 407–37.

117. The earliest accounts of women being impregnated by spirits in the wilds appear in *Shi jing* versions of the Shang and Zhou origin myths. *Mao shi zheng yi* 17.1, Mao #245 "Sheng min 生民," pp. 1b–6b; 20.3, Mao #303 "Xuan niao 玄鳥," p. 14b; 20.4, Mao #304 "Chang fa 長發," p. 2b. The first contains the story of the ancestress of the Zhou, who makes altar sacrifices to obtain a child. The other two cite the story of the Shang ancestress. They do not mention sacrifices, but Zheng Xuan posits sacrifices to the High Intermediary in order to explain the divine impregnation. The mother of the Han founder also has her sexual encounter

with a dragon in the wild, in this case by the side of a swamp. See *Shi ji* 8, p. 341. Most accounts of the spirit paternity of the early sage kings place their mothers in the wild at the time of impregnation, and several involve offerings. See *Chun qiu yuan ming bao*, in *Gu wei shu* 6, p. 6b–7a—Shen Nong's mother is impregnated by a dragon while on an excursion; 7b—an elaborated version of the Zhou ancestral myth, involving both being in the wild and a temple visit; *Chun qiu yan Kong tu* 春秋 演孔圖, in *Gu wei shu* 8, pp. 6a—Mencius' mother is impregnated by a spirit from Mt. Tai that descends upon her in a dream while she is in the wild; *Chun qiu he cheng tu* 春秋合誠圖, in *Gu wei shu* 8, pp. 9a–b—Yao's mother is herself miraculously born in the wilds, and then in turn conceives Yao through copulating with a dragon in the same spot; *Shi han shen wu* 詩含神霧, in *Gu wei shu* 23, p. 11b—Fu Xi's mother is impregnated through stepping in the print of a dragon by the side of a swamp. See *Wei shu ji cheng*, pp. 179–80, 180, 192, 193, 293.

118. It was a standard feature of Chinese accounts of gifted individuals that their later character would be manifest in early childhood. For examples of this emphasis on the prodigy, see Kenneth D. DeWoskin, "Famous Chinese Child-hoods," in *Chinese Views of Childhood*, ed. Anne Behnke Kinney (Honolulu: University of Hawai'i, 1995), pp. 67–71; Wu Hung, "Private Love and Public Duty: Images of Children in Early Chinese Art," in *Chinese Views*, pp. 101–05; Richard B. Mather, "Filial Paragons and Spoiled Brats: A Glimpse of Medieval Chinese Children in the *Shishuo xinyu*," in *Chinese Views*, pp. 118–22; Audrey Spiro, *Contemplating the Ancients: Aesthetic and Social Issues in Early Chinese Portraiture* (Berkeley: University of California, 1990), pp. 31–32.

119. *Shi ji* 47, pp. 1907–08; *Zuo zhuan zhu* Zhao 7, pp. 1294–96.

120. *Chun qiu yuan ming bao*, in *Gu wei shu* 8, p. 3b; in *Wei shu ji cheng*, p. 190. This describes both an excursion at the side of a tomb mound and a prayer for a child, the same elements as in the *Shi ji* account. The father is identified as the Black Emperor, indicating through Five Phases color symbolism that the story had converged with the theory that Confucius was the earthly emperor who came between the Zhou and the Han dynasties. See Yasui Kōzan and Nakamura Shō-hachi, *Yisho no kisoteki kenkyū*, pp. 160, 165–66. See also *Chun qiu yan Kong tu*, in *Qi wei* 23, p. 1a; in *Wei shu ji cheng*, p. 902; *Lun yu zhuan kao* 論語譔考, in *Gu wei shu* 25, p. 13a; in *Wei shu ji cheng*, p. 309. On the links of spirit conception and physical appearance, see Yasui and Nakamura, *Yisho*, pp. 164–67.

121. *Shi ji* 47, p. 1909. On the idea that the sage kings' influence includes the animals, see Lewis, *Sanctioned Violence*, pp. 151–53, 159–60, 200–01.

122. *Shi ji* 47, pp. 1912–13, 1922. The first two anecdotes were cited in chapter 1, in the discussion of the power of naming. For the third, see *Guo yu* 5 "Lu yu xia," pp. 214–15.

123. All versions of the story are translated and analyzed in Granet, *Danses et légendes*, pp. 171–216.

124. *Shi ji* 47, pp. 1915–16.

125. *Zuo zhuan zhu* Ding 10, pp. 1577–79; *Gongyang zhuan zhu shu* 26 "Ding 10," p. 8a; *Guliang zhuan zhu shu* 19 "Ding 10," pp. 12b–13b; *Xin yu* 5 "Bian huo 辯惑," in *Xin bian zhuzi ji cheng*, vol. 2, p. 9; *Shi ji* 32, p. 1505; 33, p. 1544. The story also figures in the post-Han *Kongzi jia yu*.

126. *Shi ji* 86, p. 2515.

127. *Shi ji* 76, pp. 2366–68; 81, pp. 2440–41. Mao Sui persuaded the king of Chu to join a "vertical" alliance against Qin through the menace of his sword. Lin Xiangru secured the He jade for Zhao and preserved territory demanded by Qin through threatening to destroy the jade. A less closely related story involves the banquet at Hongmen, where Xiang Yu tried to use a banquet to have Liu Bang assassinated during a sword dance. See *Shi ji* 7, pp. 312–15.

128. On Yan Ying's thwarting Confucius, see *Shi ji* 47, p. 1911. On Yan Ying's short stature, see *Yanzi chun qiu ji shi* 晏子春秋集釋, annotated by Wu Zeyu 吳則虞 (Beijing: Zhonghua, 1962) 6, p. 389. On Confucius' great height, see *Shi ji* 47, p. 1909.

129. *Shi ji* 109, p. 2870; 112, p. 2950; 120, pp. 3105, 3108 (2), 3109, 3110; 122, pp. 3136, 3138 (2), 3139 (3), 3140, 3150, 3152; 124, p. 3183.

130. *Shang Jun shu zhu yi* 14 "Xiu quan," p. 292; *Shi ji* 119, p. 3099; *Guanzi jiao zheng* 21 "Ban fa jie 版法解," p. 339.

131. Granet, following Chavannes, argues that part of the commentary was originally in the *Gongyang*, in which case this text did refer to Jiagu and dancing dwarves. If this commentary were transferred, however, it would be at odds with the explanation of the return of the territory given in the text as it stands.

132. *Gongyang zhuan zhu shu* 26, "Ding 10," p. 8a; Huan Kuan 桓寬, *Yan tie lun* 鹽鐵論, in *Xin bian zhuzi jicheng*, vol. 2, 38 "Bei hu 備胡," pp. 41–42; *Huainanzi* 20 "Tai zu 泰族," p. 350.

133. *Shi ji* 122, p. 3147. The same terms also describe the rule of the Yellow Emperor. See *Huainanzi* 6 "Lan ming," p. 94.

134. *Shi ji* 47, p. 1917.

135. *Xunzi ji jie* 28 "You zuo 宥坐," pp. 341–42; *Huainanzi* 13 "Fan lun," p. 229; *Xin yu* 3 "Fu zheng 輔政," p. 6; *Shuo yuan* 15 "Zhi wu 指武," pp. 11a–b; *Bo hu tong* 1 "Zhu fa 誅伐," p. 47b; *Lun heng* 50 "Jiang rui 講瑞," p. 164.

136. In the first century A.D. Wang Chong cites Deputy Mao in a parable on the inability of ordinary men to recognize a sage. In this version Confucius' disciples all desert the master in order to follow Mao, who is clearly a rival philosopher. This account suggests that the execution of Mao was a means of eliminating competition. See *Lun heng* 50 "Jiang rui," p. 164.

137. *Xunzi ji jie* 5 "Fei xiang," p. 56. The opening of the chapter "Wang zhi" also distinguishes between the "primally evil" (*yuan e* 元惡) who should be executed without even attempting to teach them, and the ordinary people who can be morally transformed. See *Xunzi ji jie* 9 "Wang zhi," p. 94. It is worth noting that throughout the *Xunzi* the character *jian* 姦 is frequently applied to rival philosophers.

138. *Xunzi ji jie* 28 "You zuo," pp. 342–43.

139. This distinction also figures in the *Mengzi*, but this text places bandits among the irredeemable. See *Mengzi zheng yi* 5B "Wan Zhang xia," pp. 412–13.

140. I have found only two references in Han sources, and both of them radically simplify the argument on the priority of education. See *Han shi wai zhuan* 3, pp. 11b–12a; *Shuo yuan* 7 "Zheng li 政理," p. 5a.

141. The tradition of Confucius' achievements as administrator appears in several texts from the late Warring States and early imperial periods. See, for example, *Xunzi ji jie* 5 "Ru xiao," pp. 75–76; *Lü shi chun qiu jiao shi* 16 "Le cheng 樂成," p. 989; *Han Feizi ji shi* 10 "Nei chu shuo xia," p. 603; *Huainanzi* 20 "Tai zu," p. 350. The one achievement that does not appear in these accounts is the repulsion of foreigners (*si fang zhi ke* 四方之客). This feat recalls Confucius' actions at the Jiagu meeting, where he repulsed performers of the "music from the edges of the earth" (*si fang zhi yue* 四方之樂).

142. *Shi ji* 47, pp. 1916–17.

143. *Gongyang zhuan zhu shu* 26 "Ding 12," pp. 10b–12b. For records of other expeditions by the Three Huan, see 23 "Zhao 13," p. 1a; 26 "Ding 6," p. 1a; 26 "Ding 10," p. 9b (twice). Surprisingly the *Gongyang* does not condemn Confucius' service of a ministerial house that it elsewhere condemns for usurpation. This is probably due to the fact that the text insists on the need for absolute royal power, and thus condemns the dukes who usurp the king's privileges as much as the ministerial houses who usurp those of the dukes. Indeed, it condemns the former more strongly, because they initiated the process, and the ministers simply followed their model. See *Gongyang zhuan zhu shu* 24 "Zhao 25," pp. 6b–8a.

144. On Confucius serving the Jisun, in addition to the *Gongyang*, see *Lun yu zheng yi* 18 "Weizi," p. 389; *Mengzi zheng yi* 5b "Wan Zhang xia," p. 416; *Xunzi ji jie* 28 "You zuo," p. 342; *Mozi jian gu* 39 "Fei ru xia," p. 186; *Lü shi chun qiu jiao shi* 19 "Ju nan 舉難," p. 1310; *Han Feizi ji shi* 12 "Wai chu shuo zuo xia," p. 689; *Huainanzi* 16 "Shuo shan 說山," p. 281.

Other accounts say Confucius served Duke Ai. See *Xunzi ji jie* 29 "Zi dao 子道," pp. 247–48; 31 "Ai Gong 哀公," pp. 353–59; *Lü shi chun qiu jiao shi* 16 "Le cheng," p. 989; *Zhuangzi ji shi* 5 "De chong fu," pp. 93–98; *Han Feizi ji shi* 9 "Nei chu shuo shang," pp. 528—here he is depicted condemning the Jisun, 540—here he insists on the necessity of executions, 545—here he argues for the use of punishment and rewards; 10 "Nei chu shuo xia," p. 603; 11 "Wai chu shuo xia," pp. 686, 689–90; 16 "Nan san," p. 852—here Confucius argues for employing the talented and being economical; 19 "Wu du," p. 1051. The most frequent references to Confucius and Duke Ai thus occur in the *Han Feizi*, where Confucius is employed as a mouthpiece for "legalist" theories. These passages may underpin Sima Qian's account of Confucius as a centralizing administrator ruling through law and punishments.

145. For references in the encyclopedic texts to the necessary pairing of *wen* and *wu*, see *Lü shi chun qiu jiao shi* 13 "Bu guang 不廣," p. 722; 15 "Yu da 諭大," p. 918; 20 "Zhao lei 召類," p. 1360; *Huainanzi* 9 "Zhu shu," p. 148; 13 "Fan lun,"

pp. 219, 226—the second passage notes that it is difficult for one man to be both *wen* and *wu*; 15 "Bing lüe," pp. 257, 265; 16 "Shuo shan," p. 277; 17 "Shuo lin 說林," p. 299; 18 "Ren jian 人間," p. 324; *Guanzi jiao zheng* 3 "You guan tu 幼官圖," p. 43; 9 "Ba yan 霸言," p. 145; 15 "Ren fa 任法," p. 257; *Han Feizi ji shi* 6 "Jie lao," p. 377.

146. *Han shu* 43, p. 2113; 23, p. 1090. This last passage celebrates the Han founder in a phrase borrowed from the *Yi*. See *Zhou yi zheng yi* 7 "Xi ci shang," p. 27b. Several of the passages cited in the discussion of *wen* and *wu* as aspects of law also insist on combining the two. *Shuo yuan* 1 "Jun dao," p. 1b; 9 "Zheng jian 正諫," pp. 7b–8a; 15 "Zhi wu 指武," pp. 1b, 7a, 10b; 18 "Bian wu 辨物," p. 9a.

147. *Shi ji* 112, p. 2952; 20, p. 1027.

148. *Shi ji* 47, p. 1918.

149. *Lun yu zheng yi* 18 "Weizi," p. 389; *Han Feizi ji shi* 10 "Nei chu shuo xia," p. 603. The *Han Feizi* has another account of Confucius' departure. In this story Zi Lu prepares to feed the workers who have been mobilized to build a channel. Confucius upbraids him for exceeding the bounds of his office and showing concern for the workers. Officials should show concern only for their own people, so in feeding the workers he encroaches on the privileges of his superiors. As if in confirmation, a messenger from the Jisun clan arrives and announces the suspicion that Confucius is using his disciple to steal their subjects. This leads Confucius to flee. See 13 "Wai chu shuo you shang," p. 721.

150. The story appears in two distinct versions in *Lü shi chun qiu jiao shi* 23 "Yong se 壅塞," pp. 1568–69; 24 "Bu gou 不苟," p. 1584; *Han Feizi ji shi* 3 "Shi guo 十過," p. 187; *Shi ji* 5, pp. 192–93, 194.

151. Sending women to supplant an adviser also figures in *Zhan guo ce* 3 "Qin 1," p. 125.

152. In the Han, Zhonghang Yue elaborated this idea of using women and fine cuisine to deal with barbarians. See *Han shu* 94, p. 3759.

153. On the tension between officials and women, see Lewis, *Sanctioned Violence*, pp. 72–75.

154. In the concluding passage of the story, Music Master Ji relays Confucius' words to Ji Huanzi, and the latter remarks that Confucius blames [*zui* 罪] him on account of the women.

155. This pairing of external and internal enemies to block Confucius' work as an official is central to Sima Qian's account of the composition of the *Chun qiu*. "When the Way of Zhou declined and was abandoned, Confucius became the Chief Judge of Lu. The feudal lords [of other states] harmed him, and the hereditary nobles [of his own state] blocked him." See *Shi ji* 130, p. 3297.

156. This theme of blame is reiterated later in the chapter. See *Shi ji* 47, p. 1927.

157. *Shi ji* 33, p. 1544.

158. On sacrifice as a masculine realm menaced by women, see Lewis, *Sanctioned Violence*, pp. 32–33.

159. *Mengzi zheng yi* 6B "Gaozi xia," p. 492. The original Chinese does not have any word corresponding to "pretext," but it is implied by the contrast between 以 *yi* "to take or use [as the reason]" and 爲 *wei* "on account of, because of."

160. The clearest evidence of this tradition is the hermeneutic of the *Chun qiu* commentaries, which insists that Confucius condemns even the most serious of crimes, such as incest, only indirectly through a choice of words that veils the explicit sense. The fact of criticism is revealed only in commentary. There is also the following anecdote in the *Lun yu*.

> Chen Sibai asked if Duke Zhao had understood ritual. Confucius said, "He understood ritual." When Confucius departed, [Chen] saluted Wu Maqi and presented [the case] to him saying, "I have heard that the gentleman does not engage in favoritism [*dang* 黨, literally "form cliques"], but the gentleman [Confucius] indeed protects his favorites. The prince [Zhao] married a woman from Wu of the same surname, so they called her Wu Mengzi [to hide the fault]. If the prince understands ritual, then who does not?" Wu Maqi told this to Confucius. He said, "I am fortunate. If I commit an error, others will certainly know of it."

See *Lun yu zheng yi* 7 "Shu er," p. 150. Although Confucius acknowledges his error, he clearly avoided speaking ill of the ruler. The final remark could also be read as a veiled reproof of Chen Sibai, who did not challenge Confucius' assertion but only spoke of it to "others," mocking the master behind his back. Suggesting the discourtesy and cowardice of this conduct, he hints at the motives for his own.

Finally, the *Xunzi* states that ritual stipulates that one should not speak ill of the nobles or officials in the town where one dwells. See *Xunzi ji jie* 29 "Zi dao," p. 349. On the problem of explicit criticism, see Jullien, *Le détour et l'accès*, ch. 6, "La dissidence impossible (idéologie de l'obliquité)."

161. Cited in Durrant, *The Cloudy Mirror*, p. 38.

162. *Mengzi zheng yi* 5B "Wan Zhang xia," pp. 395–97, 415–16; 6B "Gaozi xia," pp. 488–92—in this passage Mencius explains his ideas about when to stay in a state and when to depart by citing the examples of Bo Yi, Yi Yin, Liu Xiahui, and Confucius; 7B "Jin xin xia," p. 575.

163. *Shi ji* 47, pp. 1919, 1921, 1923, 1930.

164. *Lun yu zheng yi* 7 "Shu er," p. 147; 9 "Zi han," p. 176.

165. On Marshal Huan, see *Mengzi zheng yi* 5A "Wan Zhang shang," pp. 389–90. He is also mentioned in the *Li ji*, where Confucius criticizes him for gross waste in the preparations for his own funeral. This might explain the otherwise unmotivated assault. See *Li ji zhu shu* 8 "Tan gong shang," p. 7a. On the threat of death in Kuang, see *Lun yu zheng yi* 11 "Xian jin," p. 250.

The link of the two accounts is reinforced by Han traditions that Kuang was a town in the state of Song. See *Han shi wai zhuan* 6, pp. 11b–12a; *Shuo yuan* 17 "Za yan 雜言," pp. 10b–11a. The identity of the town Kuang remains a matter of debate. According to Katō Jōken, the character originally had the meaning of "big" or "full" and could be applied to any large settlement. See Katō, *Shina kodai kazoku seido kenkyū* 支那古代家族制度研究 (Tokyo: Iwanami, 1941), pp. 284–86. The same character with the heart radical (*kuang* 恇) is glossed in the *Shuo wen* as "afraid." See *Shuo wen jie zi zhu* 10b, p. 49a. This might be significant because the standard verb in the passages in the *Lun yu* and the later *Shi ji—wei* 畏—also means "fear" or "afraid," and Duan Yucai uses the latter character to gloss the former. Thus the story of Kuang would be derivative from that of Song, using a generic word for "town" that also phonetically revealed the theme of the story. The character *wei* 畏 is also employed in the version of the story in *Lü shi chun qiu jiao shi* 4 "Quan xue 勸學," p. 196.

166. *Zhuangzi ji shi* 14 "Tian yun," p. 226; 20 "Shan mu," p. 229; 28, "Rang wang," p. 422; 31 "Yu fu," p. 446. In these passages the attack consists of having a "tree cut down" on top of him. The same list appears in *Lü shi chun qiu jiao shi* 14 "Shen ren 慎人," p. 803.

167. *Zhuangzi ji shi* 19 "Qiu shui," pp. 262–63; *Xunzi ji jie* 26 "Fu," p. 319; 32 "Yao wen 堯問," p. 364—these two passages deal with the theme of "the world turned upside down" and the unjust suffering of the sages; *Han Feizi ji shi* 1 "Nan yan 難言," p. 49; *Huainanzi* 9 "Zhu shu," p. 150.

168. Although the quote does not appear elsewhere attributed to Confucius, a version of it is pronounced in the *Zuo zhuan* by two nobles of Zheng. See *Zuo zhuan zhu* Xiang 9, p. 971.

169. *Lü shi chun qiu jiao shi* 14 "Shen ren," p. 803; 17 "Ren shu 任數," p. 1066; *Mozi jian gu* 39 "Fei ru," p. 187; *Zhuangzi ji shi* 28 "Rang wang," p. 422; *Xunzi ji jie* 28 "You zuo," pp. 345–46; *Han shi wai zhuan* 7, p. 3b. The event is also mentioned in *Huainanzi* 16 "Shuo lin," p. 287, but this gives no details.

170. *Lun yu zheng yi* 15 "Wei Ling Gong," p. 331. This passage is incorporated in the *Shi ji* account.

171. This could be supported by another passage, which is admittedly obscure. *Lun yu* 11 "Xian jin," p. 237: "The Master said, 'Of those who followed me at Chen and Cai, none were able to reach the gates/great families [*men* 門].'" Zheng Xuan's Eastern Han commentary reads *men* as "gates to political service." The *Mencius* states that when Confucius was in trouble between Chen and Cai, he "had no contact with those above or below." See *Mengzi zheng yi* 7B "Jin xin xia," p. 575. The *Shi ji* version of the story indicates that Confucius finally extricated himself from trouble in Kuang by sending disciples to serve as ministers in Wei. See *Shi ji* 47, p. 1917. The *Li ji* also indicates that he secured passage from state to state by sending disciples to establish links. See *Li ji zhu shu* 8 "Tan gong shang," p. 7b. This cumulatively suggests that the hunger suffered between Chen and Cai was linked to the refusal to accomodate with local powers. The Han dynasty *Yan tie lun* likewise states that this incident was due to the fact that Confucius "could be square but not round," that is, would not compromise his integrity. See *Yan tie lun* 11 "Lun ru 論儒," p. 13.

172. *Mengzi zheng yi* 5B "Wan Zhang xia," p. 416.

173. *Mengzi zheng yi* 6b "Gaozi xia," p. 510.

174. See Aat Vervoorn, *The Men of the Cliffs and Caves: The Development of the Chinese Eremetic Tradition to the End of the Han Dynasty* (Hong Kong: Chinese University, 1990).

175. References to the "pigweed stew" occur in all the versions cited in note #169.

176. *Da Dai li ji jie gu* 56 "Zengzi zhi yan xia 曾子制言下," p. 96; *Mozi jian gu* 49 "Lu wen," p. 289; *Huainanzi* 7 "Jing shen," p. 106—describing Yao's humble fare and attire; 16 "Shuo shan," p. 276; 17 "Shuo lin," p. 293; 18 "Ren jian," p. 318; *Shi ji* 130, p. 3290—Sima Tan's discussion of the "Six Schools," where "pigweed stew" is used to suggest the humble fare consumed by Mohists in their desire to economize.

177. *Mozi jian gu* 39 "Fei ru xia," pp. 187–88.

178. *Lü shi chun qiu jiao shi* 17 "Ren shu," p. 1066.

179. *Lü shi chun qiu jiao shi* 14 "Shen ren," pp. 803–04.

180. *Xunzi ji jie* 28 "You zuo," pp. 345–46.

181. Thus the Qing dynasty scholar Cui Shu suggests that Confucius and his disciples had simply run out of supplies in a region notorious for its poor transport. See Cui Shu 崔述 (1740–1816 A.D.), *Kao xin lu* 考信錄 (rep. ed.: Taipei: Shijie, 1968) 3, pp. 16–18.

182. *Zhuangzi ji shi* 14 "Tian yun," p. 226; 20, "Shan mu," pp. 297, 299, 302; 28 "Rang wang," p. 422 (twice)—these references show Confucius as a Daoist sage, and emphasize his playing music; 29 "Dao Zhi," p. 430; 31 "Yu fu," p. 446.

183. Durrant, *The Cloudy Mirror*, pp. 41–44.

184. *Shi ji* 124, p. 3182; 74, p. 2345; 130, p. 3300.

185. The story of Confucius continuing to play music while "under siege" is echoed in the *Shi ji*'s account of the *ru* in Lu state who continued to devote themselves to music and ritual even while besieged by the Han founder. Their conduct is attributed to the "lingering influence of the sage's transformative power" (*sheng ren zhi yi hua* 聖人之遺化). See *Shi ji* 121, p. 3117.

186. Durrant, *The Cloudy Mirror*, ch. 3. According to the *Shi ji* Confucius departed Lu at the age of 56, spent 14 years in his travels, and died at the age of 73. Thus the literary activities described at the end of the chapter were supposedly carried out in three years. Confucius studied and taught from an early age—see pp. 1908, 1914—but the activities of collecting, editing, and composing texts are presented as a last resort when all hope of action in the world had disappeared.

187. *Han Feizi ji shi* 9 "Nei chu shuo shang," p. 540—this passage depicts Duke Ai of Lu treating Confucius as the author of the *Chun qiu*, and Confucius uses the text to justify the use of punishments; 13 "Wai chu shuo you shang," p. 717— this passage depicts Zi Xia expounding the text. A *Zhuangzi* fragment preserved in *Yi wen lei ju* narrates a conversation between Confucius and Laozi that touches on the composition of the *Chun qiu*. See *Yi wen lei ju* 藝文類聚 (Taipei: Wenguang, 1974) 80, p. 1374.

188. *Jiazi xin shu jiao shi* 賈子新書校釋, attributed to Jia Yi 賈誼 (201–169 B.C.), annotated by Qi Yuzhang 祁玉章 (Taipei: Qi Yuzhang, 1974) 8 "Liu shu 六術," pp. 946–47; *Xin yu* 1 "Dao ji 道基," p. 2; *Huainanzi* 9 "Zhu shu," p. 144; 16 "Shuo shan," p. 287; 20 "Tai zu," pp. 352, 353, 363; *Li ji zhu shu* 50 "Jing jie 經解," pp. 1a–b; *Han shi wai zhuan* 5, pp. 1a, 8a; *Yan tie lun* 6 "Fu gu 復古," p. 7; 10 "Ci fu 刺復," p. 11. Several of the chapters discovered at Mawangdui also list the *Yi* together with the other texts.

189. *Shi ji* 47, pp. 1935–37.

190. One exception is the *Shuo yuan*, in which Confucius writes the text first, and the *qilin* appears in response to his accuracy of judgment and sincerity of intent. See *Shuo yuan* 14 "Zhi gong 至公," p. 6a.

191. *Shi ji* 47, p. 1942; *Gongyang zhuan zhu shu* 28, "Ai 14," pp. 7a–11b.

192. *Shi ji* 47, pp. 1943, 1944.

193. *Shi ji* 130, p. 3300.

194. *Huainanzi* 13, "Fan lun," pp. 213–14. "When the kingly Way was lacking, then the *Odes* arose. When the Zhou house was cast aside, and the rites and music ruined, then the *Chun qiu* arose. The *Odes* and the *Chun qiu* are the finest objects of study, but they are all the creations of times of decline. The *ru* follow them in order to guide the generations, but how can they be as good as the heights of the Three Dynasties? They take the *Odes* and the *Chun qiu* to be the ancient Way and honor them, but there was a time when the *Odes* and the *Chun qiu* had not yet been written. The absence of the Way is not as good as the fullness of the Way. Reciting the *Odes* and *Documents* of the former kings is not as good as hearing their words, and hearing their words is not as good as gaining that which enabled them to speak. Those who gain that which enabled them to speak say what cannot be said."

195. *Shi ji* 47, p. 1944; *Huainanzi* 9 "Zhu shu," p. 150.

196. *Huainanzi* 13 "Fan lun," p. 216.

197. *Shi ji* 130, p. 3299.

198. *Shi ji* 47, p. 1943.

199. *Shi ji* 47, pp. 1945, 1947.

Chapter Six. The Natural Philosophy of Writing

1. *Shi ji* 130, p. 3297; *Han shu* 30, pp. 1703–04. The *Yi* also heads the *Shi ji*'s list of the historical development of the canon. See 130, p. 3299. Putting the *Yi* in the first position became standard in "old texts" canonical studies and was carried forward into later Chinese bibliographic practice. See Zhou Yutong 周予同, *Jing jin gu wen xue* 經今古文學 (1926, rep. ed., Taipei: Shangwu, 1985), pp. 5–12.

2. On the origin of the theories of *yin/yang* and *wu xing* in nonphilosophical, mantic traditions, see Graham, *Disputers of the Tao*, pp. 313–70; Graham, *Yin-Yang and the Nature of Correlative Thinking*.

3. Gao Heng 高亨, "*Zuo zhuan, Guo yu* de *Zhou yi* shuo tong jie 左传国语的周易说通解," in *Zhou yi za lun*, 周易杂论 (Ji'nan: Qi Lu, 1979), pp. 70–110;

Gao Heng, "*Zhou yi* shi fa xin kao 周易筮法新考," in *Zhou yi gu jing tong shuo* 周易古经通说(Beijing: Zhonghua, 1983), pp. 112–30; Li Jingchi 李鏡池, "*Zuo zhuan* zhong *Yi* shi zhi yanjiu 左傳中易筮之研究," in *Zhou yi tanyuan* 周易探源 (Beijing: Zhonghua, 1978), pp. 407–21; Qu Wanli 屈萬里, *Xian Qin Han Wei Yi li shuping* 先秦漢魏易例述評 (Taipei: Xuesheng, 1975), pp. 60–66; Song Zuoyin 宋祚胤, *Zhou yi xin lun* 周易新论 (Changsha: Hunan Jiaoyu, 1982), pp. 54–67; Tsuda, *Saden no shisōshi teki kenkyū*, pp. 424–57; Honda Wataru 本田済, *Ekigaku: seiritsu to tenkai* 易学: 成立と展開 (Kyoto: Heirakuji, 1960), pp. 52–71; Imai Usaburō 今井宇三郎, "*Saden, Kokugo* zeisen kō 左傳國語筮占考," *Kokubungaku Kanbungaku Ronsō* 14 (1969): 51–97; Toda Toyasaburō 戸田豐三郎, "*Sa, Koku* no *Eki* zei kiji kanken 左國の易筮記事管見," *Shinagaku Kenkyū* 16 (1957): 1–11; Edward L. Shaughnessy, "The Composition of the 'Zhouyi,'" (Ph.D. diss., Stanford University, 1983), pp. 36, 60–64, 72–75, 78–101; Kidder Smith, Jr., "*Zhouyi* Interpretation from Accounts in the *Zuozhuan*," *Harvard Journal of Asiatic Studies* 49 (1989): 424–63.

4. Both Shaughnessy and Smith, in the works cited in the previous note, observed changes over time. Such patterns are unlikely to have been invented by a fourth-century B.C. author, nor by Liu Xiang at the end of the Western Han. Working such invisible patterns into the text would have been difficult, and the results would not have been noticed. Moreover, they served no ideological purpose for such authors.

5. Smith, "*Zhouyi* Interpretation," pp. 447–48, 462–63. In the last ten cases recorded, only one involves an astrologer and none features a crack-maker.

6. On the hereditary nature of work as a crack-maker, see *Zuo zhuan zhu* Min 2, p. 263; Wen 18, p. 629; Zhao 5, p. 1263. The classic example of the hereditary transmission of the role of astrologer is the lineage of Sima Qian, which traced its service as astrologers/diviners back to the Zhou, and mythically to the time of Yu. See *Shi ji* 130, pp. 3285–86, 3295.

7. *Zuo zhuan zhu* Min 2, p. 264; Xi 15, p. 353; Cheng 16, p. 885. All three cases of improvisation are performed by a crack-maker or astrologer. Gu Yanwu (1613–1682 A.D.) argued that the lines recited came from divination texts of the Xia and the Shang. However, there is no evidence that such texts existed, except as late forgeries, and modern scholars have pointed to other examples of verse improvisation in related contexts. See Shaughnessy, "Composition," pp. 97–101; Smith, "*Zhouyi* Interpretation," pp. 426–29; Honda, *Ekigaku*, pp. 57–60; Yang Bojun's commentary in the *Zuo zhuan zhu*. An example of a spontaneous rhymed recital with prophetic powers, in this case a "children's ditty," appears in Xi 5, pp. 310–11.

8. Smith, "*Zhouyi* Interpretation," p. 448.

9. *Guo yu* 3 "Zhou yu xia," pp. 90–91.

10. *Guo yu* 3 "Zhou yu xia," p. 98.

11. *Zuo zhuan zhu* Xi 15, p. 365.

12. The same passage is cited in *Zuo zhuan zhu* Zhao 7, p. 1298 to justify combining dream divination with stalk casting. The combination of dreams with

divination, or the use of divination to clarify dreams, also figures in Ai 17, pp. 1709–10. This dream is interesting because the wronged spirit justifies itself in verse, just like a diviner reciting a prognostication.

13. *Zuo zhuan zhu* Xiang 9, pp. 965–66.

14. Another story that features a conflict of interpretations between astrologers and a noble official appears in *Guo yu* 10 "Jin yu 4," p. 362. Once again it is the non-specialist literatus who proves to be a superior reader of divinations. *Zuo zhuan zhu* Ai 9, pp. 1652–54 also contrasts astrologers with a literatus official. This is not a contrast in interpretation, however, for they agree on the reading, but in techniques. The astrologers use tortoise shells, while the official has recourse to yarrow stalks.

15. *Zuo zhuan zhu* Ai 16, p. 1705; Ai 17, pp. 1709–10.

16. One example of a worthy ruler personally divining appears in *Guo yu* 10 "Jin yu 4," p. 362. The final interpretation, however, is established only after a discussion with the astrologers and an official.

17. Smith, "*Zhouyi* Interpretation," p. 436, note 39. For examples of lists of terms with definitions, see *Zuo zhuan zhu* Xuan 12, pp. 722–23; Cheng 9, p. 845.

18. For theories of the original sense of the four characters, see Shaughnessy, "Composition," pp. 124–33; Gao Heng, *Zhou yi gu jing tong shuo*, pp. 87–100. On the innovation of the character-by-character reading, see Song Zuoyin, *Zhou yi xin lun*, p. 63.

19. Thus interpreting one divination depends on deciding whether the character *yuan* 元 refers to the status of the older son or the name of the younger. See *Zuo zhuan zhu* Zhao 7, p. 1298. The story of Nankuai—see note 20—involves several uses of word play to make the argument work. See also *Zuo zhuan zhu* Zhao 5, pp. 1264–65; *Guo yu* 10 "Jin yu 4," p. 362.

20. *Zuo zhuan zhu* Zhao 12, pp. 1337–38.

21. This grounding of divination in natural principle is also reflected in the links between the casting of stalks and astral divination. See *Guo yu* 3 "Zhou yu xia," p. 138; 10 "Jin yu 4," p. 365. *Zuo zhuan zhu* Xiang 28, pp. 1142–44 also links the *Yi* with astral divination, but the former is not used for divination. Instead it is cited as a textual authority for a moral principle that underpins a prediction based on observation of conduct.

22. See, for example, *Zuo zhuan zhu* Xiang 23, p. 1077—here he foretells the death of Cui Wuzi; Xiang 24, pp. 1090–91—here he predicts an invasion of Qi; Xiang 28, p. 1146.

23. *Zuo zhuan zhu* Xiang 25, p. 1096. Another story involving a wicked person who cannot be saved by an accurate divination appears in Ai 17, pp. 1709–10. In this story the ghost of a man unjustly executed appears to the Marquis of Wei in a dream and proclaims his innocence in verse. The marquis divines, and his astrologer informs him that there will be no harm. However, when the ruler rewards the diviner with a town, the latter flees. On making inquiries, the marquis discovers that the prognostication verse actually predicted his doom, but the diviner

suppressed it to avoid punishment. Here the ruler does not actually refuse the result of the divination, but his history of ignoring remonstrance leads to his not receiving its benefit. In fact, the preceding year a diviner used a divination about another dream to maneuver the marquis into exiling a loyal official who refused to bribe the diviner. See Ai 16, p. 1705.

24. The idea that morality and knowledge of human conduct were essential to divination also figures in the *Shi ji*. "The cracks respond to good faith and sincerity within, men of the present day clearly perceive them on the outside. Can this not be called the two [morality and divination] coinciding? The gentleman says, 'To treat divination with contempt and deny the existence of spirits is perverse, but if you turn your back on the Way of man and place your faith in auspicious signs, the spirits will not be correct.' Therefore the *Shu* sets up five strategies for resolving doubts, and divination is the second. To divine five times and follow the most frequent result, this proves that the Way [of divination] exists but is not exclusive." See *Shi ji* 128, p. 3225.

25. *Zuo zhuan zhu* Zhao 29, pp. 1500–03.

26. *Zuo zhuan zhu* Zhao 32, pp. 1519–20. The earlier story appears in Min 2, pp. 263–64.

27. *Zuo zhuan zhu* Xuan 6, pp. 689–90—this passage does not actually quote the line-text, but simply refers to it and assumes that the reader will recognize the reference; Xuan 12, pp. 726–27; Xiang 28, pp. 1142–44.

28. This reading glosses *fei* 飛 as *fei* 蜚. In later Chinese the two were identical when the latter was read in the first tone. When it was read in the third tone, it meant an insect pest that devoured grain. It already appears with the second meaning in the *Zuo zhuan*. See *Zuo zhuan zhu* Yin 1, p. 17.

29. *Zuo zhuan zhu* Zhao 1, pp. 1221–23.

30. *Zuo zhuan zhu* Huan 11, p. 131; Ai 23, p. 1721. On the rejection of divination in the military treatises, see Lewis, *Sanctioned Violence*, p. 287, note 26. Interestingly, Sima Qian insists on the importance of divination precisely in the field of military affairs, and he notes the importance that Emperor Wu attributed to such activities. See *Shi ji* 128, p. 3224. The idea that one does not divine on matters that are not in doubt also underlies the doctrine espoused in the *Gongyang zhuan* that one does not divine prior to regular sacrifices. See *Gongyang zhuan zhu shu* 12 "Xi 31," p. 19a.

31. *Zuo zhuan zhu* Xi 15, p. 365. As noted earlier, the question about being "reached by 'number'" is a pun suggesting that the ruler's crimes were "numberless."

32. *Zuo zhuan zhu* Ai 18, p. 1713. To divine only after resolving one's will contradicts the earlier advice to divine only when in doubt. However, they agree that human will is primary and divination secondary.

33. *Xunzi ji jie* 27 "Da lüe," p. 333, #81. A similar idea, expressed less dogmatically, appears in the *Shi ji*. Sima Qian notes, "Some say that whenever the sage kings confronted an issue they were fixed and knew how to resolve doubts.

These people think that establishing a way to question the spirits was due to the decline of later ages, when the stupid no longer took the wise as their teachers, each man was content with his own opinion, the transforming [Way] was divided into a hundred schools [*shi* 室 'chambers, compartments'], scattered, and without definition. Therefore they traced things back to the most minute [beginnings], seeking to match tallies with the spirits. Others think that crawling things [turtles] have talents that the sages cannot match. In assigning good or ill fortune, or distinguishing the 'so' from the 'not so,' they are correct more often than men." See *Shi ji* 128, p. 3224.

While refusing to divine was a permissable stance, to divine and then reject the results usually led to disaster. See, for example, *Zuo zhuan zhu* Xi 4, pp. 295–96; Zhao 13, p. 1350. In this case King Chu divines on whether he will obtain mastery of the world, and when the results are negative he casts away the tortoise shell, curses Heaven, and declares that he will take the world through his own efforts.

34. *Shi ji* 127. A discrepancy between the description of the chapter in the postface and its actual contents has led many scholars to question its authorship. See *Shi ji* 130, p. 3318. It is unclear whether the chapter is a fragment written by Sima Qian, who was unable to finish it for lack of time or materials, or whether it was filled in later. The fact that it contains a second section added by Chu Xiaosun suggests that the first part probably dates from the Western Han.

35. The work is quoted by Sima Tan under the name of "Great Tradition." See *Shi ji* 130, p. 3288. It was known as "Xi ci zhuan" from the Eastern Han. On the relative datings of the "Ten Wings," see Yamashita Shizuo 山下靜雄, *Shū eki jū yoku no seiritsu to tenkai* 周易十翼の成立と展開 (Tokyo: Kazama, 1977). Iulian K. Schutskii, *Researches on the I Ching*, tr. William L. MacDonald and Tsuyoshi Hasegawa, ed. Hellmut Wilhelm (Princeton: Princeton University, 1979), pp. 181–85, contains a brief discussion in English. See also Zhu Bokun 朱伯崑, *Yixue zhexue shi* 易学哲学史, vol. 1 (Beijing: Beijing Daxue, 1986), pp. 45–49; Taguchi Fukujirō 田口福次郎, *Shū eki no kigen* 周易の起源 (Tokyo: Meiji Shoin, 1961), pp. 106–37; Li Xueqin 李学勤, *Zhou yi jing zhuan su yuan* 周易经传溯源 (Changchun: Changchun Chubanshe, 1992), pp. 231–37. This last deals with the Mawangdui version of the "Great Tradition."

The so-called "Ten Wings" actually consists of seven texts, three of which are divided into two parts. The first two wings, the "Tradition of the Judgments" (*tuan zhuan* 彖傳) is a commentary on the "judgments" or "hexagram statements" of the sixty-four hexagrams, often formulated in terms of the opposition "hard and soft" (*gang ruo* 剛柔). The third and fourth wings are the "Tradition of the Greater Images" (*da xiang zhuan* 大象傳) and the "Tradition of the Smaller Images" (*xiao xiang zhuan* 小象傳). The former describes the images of the two trigrams that make up each hexagram, lists their correlations, suggests how their interaction indicates the name or theme of the hexagram, and offers a moral message. The latter offers a line-by-line commentary on the 384 lines that make up the sixty-four hexagrams. The first four wings are broken up and appended to each hexagram. The fifth and sixth wings are the "Great Tradition," which forms a separate unit. The seventh wing is the "Tradition on the Words of the Text" (*wen yan zhuan* 文言傳), a commentary appended to the first two hexagrams only. The eighth is the "Explanation of the Trigrams" (*shuo gua* 說卦). It is composed of ten sections. The first two are similar in theme and style to the "Great Tradition," and in the *Yi* texts found at Mawangdui they are included in the second part of the "Great Tradition." The rest consists of glosses on the eight trigrams and their correlations. The ninth is the "Sequence of the Hexagrams" (*xu gua* 序卦). It glosses the names of the hexagrams and explains the relation of each hexagram to the one that precedes it and the one that follows. The tenth is the "Mixed [or 'Irregular'] Hexagrams" (*za gua* 雜卦), which provides further glosses on names. These last three, like the "Great Tradition" are appended as separate, distinct texts. Thus the bulk of the "Ten Wings" consists of commentaries on parts of the texts or glosses on the trigrams, the hexagrams, and their correlations. The "Great Tradition" and the opening section of the "Explanation of the Trigrams" are the sole systematic discussion of the entire text that dates to the Warring States period. It is examined in Willard J. Petersen, "Making Connections: 'Commentary on the Attached Verbalizations' of the *Book of Change*," *Harvard Journal of Asiatic Studies* 42 (1982): 67–116.

36. *Zhou yi zheng yi* 7 "Xi ci shang," p. 5a; 8 "Xi ci xia," p. 4b; 9 "Shuo gua 說卦," pp. 1b, 3b.

37. *Zhou yi zheng yi* 7 "Xi ci shang," pp. 32a–b. The same passage, with a different final sentence, appears on pp. 16a–b.

38. *Zhou zheng yi* 7 "Xi ci shang," pp. 15b, 25b, 26b.

39. The character *bian* 變 has the general sense of change, but in some passages in the "Great Commentary" it has the specific sense of "alternation" between correlates. Thus p. 28a, "To close a door is *kun* [all *yin* lines]. To open a door is *qian* [all *yang* lines]. Now closed and now open is called *bian*. To inexhaustibly go and come is called 'to move throughout' [*tong* 通]." Here *bian* means specifically to shift between correlates, metaphorically "open" and "closed," as symbolized by *qian* and *kun*. This is distinct from change or movement through a process or cycle, identified by the character *tong*. The two characters are combined in the text as a more general term for change.

Other passages that indicate the sense of *bian* as "alternate" are 8 "Xi ci xia," p. 1b—"When the hard and soft displace [*tui* 推] each other, *bian* is within." 8 "Xi ci xia," p. 19a—"Hard and soft mutually exchange and cannot form a standard rule. They accord only with *bian*." See Gerald Swanson, "The Concept of Change in the *Great Treatise*," in *Explorations in Early Chinese Cosmology*, ed. Henry Rosemont, Jr. (Chico, Calif.: Scholars Press, 1984), pp. 67–93; Nathan Sivin, "Change and Continuity in Early Cosmology: *The Great Commentary to the Book of Changes*," in *Chūgoku kodai kagaku shi ron zoku hen* 中國古代科學史論續篇, ed. Yamada Keiji 山田慶兒 (Kyoto: Jinbun Kagaku Kenkyūsho, 1991), pp. 3–43.

40. *Zhou yi zheng yi* 7 "Xi ci shang," p. 23b. 8 "Xi ci xia," p. 3b states that the true nature of the sage is revealed in the "phrases" (*ci* 辭) of the *Yi*. Similarly, the "treasure" of the sage lies in "position" (*wei* 位). See 8 "Xi ci xia," p. 4a. *Wei* refers either to rank in the world or one of the six "slots" in which the lines of the hexagrams appear. The latter lies within the *Yi*, while the former is derived from the hexagrams at the beginning of the "Great Tradition." On the basis of the "positions" established by Heaven and Earth out of the hexagrams, the sage "completes the capacities" of things. See 8 "Xi ci xia," pp. 23a–24a.

41. *Zhou yi zheng yi* 7 "Xi ci shang," pp. 29a–b. A similar matching of the sages with Heaven and Earth as physical extensions of the *Yi* also figures in 7 "Xi ci shang," pp. 9a–10a.

42. *Zhou yi zheng yi* 7 "Xi ci shang," p. 29b.

43. *Zhou yi zheng yi* 8 "Xi ci xia," pp. 15b, 17a, 22b.

44. *Zhou yi zheng yi* 7 "Xi ci shang," pp. 30b–31a. The rejection of spoken language in the name of visual signs also appears on pp. 32b–33a.

45. *Zhou yi zheng yi* 7 "Xi ci shang," p. 7a.

46. *Zhou yi zheng yi* 7 "Xi ci shang," pp. 12a, 13a—this refers to the power of the *Yi* in achieving the "Great Enterprise" (*da ye* 大業), which often meant a dynastic foundation, 17b, 24a, 32b–33a; 8 "Xi ci xia," p. 19b.

47. *Zhou yi zheng yi* 7 "Xi ci shang," p. 1b.

48. *Zhou yi zheng yi* 7 "Xi ci shang," p. 9a. See also pp. 3a, 4b, 5a–6a, 10a, 15a—here the vastness of *qian* and *kun* pairs with (*pei* 配) that of Heaven and Earth, while their changes pair with those of the four seasons. The use of *pei* in this passage might echo its significance in sacrificial cult. In sacrifices known ancestors were "paired" (*pei*) with forces such as Heaven, the Five *Di*, and so on. This allowed the sacrificer to emotionally and intellectually grasp things otherwise beyond his ken. In the same way, the hexagrams may have acted as visible, intelligible intermediaries between men and the cosmos. *Zhou yi zheng yi* 8 "Xi ci xia," pp. 3a–b, 8b. These state that the lines and images imitate (*xiao* 效) or represent (*xiang* 像) natural objects and processes. They are based on plays on words. The assertions that the images represent the world in a way that language cannot, and that the sages invented the material foundations of civilization through study of the hexagrams, both also entail a direct correspondence of the *Yi* text to the cosmos and its contents.

49. *Zhou yi zheng yi* 7 "Xi ci shang," pp. 31a–32b. This passage is the only section of the received "Great Tradition" not found at Mawangdui, so it may be a later insertion. Nevertheless, it fits with ideas articulated in the rest of the text, and different versions of the same text existed in the Warring States and early imperial periods. Moreover, as Li Xueqin has pointed out, the frequency of intercalary months indicated in the model would no longer have occurred in the calendars of the Warring States period. Li Xueqin, *Zhou yi jing zhuan su yuan*, pp. 234–35. Consequently, an early date for the procedure is possible.

50. *Zhou yi zheng yi* 8 "Xi ci xia," p. 22a. See also 7 "Xi ci shang," p. 9a.

51. *Zhou yi zheng yi* 7 "Xi ci shang," pp. 9a, 10a–b—this phrase uses the adverb *qu* 曲 "twistingly," in the sense of following every turn, 14b, 24b (twice), 25b (twice); 26b (four times), 29b, 32b; 8 "Xi ci xia," p. 4b, 15b, 16a, 22a, 22b–23a—here it states that "no object is omitted"; 9 "Shuo gua," p. 3b (twice).

52. This is the aim of the "Xu gua 序卦, Ordering the Hexagrams." See *Zhou yi zheng yi* 9, pp. 10b–14b.

53. *Zhou yi zheng yi* 8 "Xi ci xia," pp. 18b–19b. See also 7 "Xi ci shang," pp. 2b, 7a, 7b, 15a, 23b—this links "change" to "movement" *dong* 動, 29a, 29b, 30b, 31b–32a, 32b; 8 "Xi ci xia," pp. 2a, 3b, 6a—"if you alternate, then you go through time, and if you go through time then you are long lasting," 24b.

54. *Zhou yi zheng yi* 8 "Xi ci xia," pp. 1a–2a. The final phrase translated as "follow the time" (*qu shi* 趨時) is still used in modern Chinese to mean "follow the fashions, accord with trends."

55. *Zhou yi zheng yi* 9 "Shuo gua," pp. 4a–b—this lists the images in the *xian tian* order; 4b–5b—this presents the images in the *hou tian* order, explains their mutual derivation, and correlates them with the directions (and by extension the winds and the annual cycle).

56. See Lewis, *Sanctioned Violence*, pp. 214–15, 235.

57. *Zhou yi zheng yi* 1 "Qian," pp. 6a, 18b. See also 7 "Xi ci shang," p. 9a—"The phrases each indicate their destination [*suo zhi* 所之]."

58. *Zhou yi zheng yi* 7 "Xi ci shang," pp. 15a, 29a; 8 "Xi ci xia," p. 20a.

59. *Zhou yi zheng yi* 7 "Xi ci shang," pp. 27b, 28a; 8 "Xi ci xia," pp. 10a, 16a, 20a—"The *Yi*'s nature as writing is to trace back to beginnings and to summarize [or 'control' *yao* 要] ends." *Zhou yi zheng yi* 7 "Xi ci shang," p. 24a; 8 "Xi ci xia," p. 23b refer simply to prognosticating the future.

60. *Zhou yi zheng yi* 9 "Shuo gua," p. 4a.

61. *Zhou yi zheng yi* 7 "Xi ci shang," pp. 4b—"[*Qian* and *kun*] being easy [*yi* 易] and simple, the principles of Heaven and Earth are obtained. The principles of Heaven and Earth being obtained, they complete the positions between them," 7b—"The judgments refer to the images, and the line statements refer to the alternations. . . . Therefore the sequence of noble and base exists in their positions," 21b—"Heaven's numbers are five [the five odd numbers between one and ten], and the Earth's numbers are five [the even ones]. The five positions are obtained, and each has a match"; 8 "Xi ci xia," pp. 1a, 4a, 21b, 22a—"The six lines have their ranks [*deng* 等]," 24a.

62. *Zhou yi zheng yi* 7 "Xi ci shang," pp. 15b, 31b. A related passage appears in *Zhuangzi* 13 "Tian dao," pp. 209–10—"Honor and lowliness, preceding or following, these are the actions of Heaven. Therefore the sage takes his images from them. Heaven is lofty and Earth lowly. These are the positions [*wei* 位] of the illumined spirits [*shen ming* 神明]. Spring and summer come first, while autumn and winter follow. This is the order of the four seasons. The myriad objects transform and arise. . . . Heaven and Earth are the most divine, yet they have an order of loftiness and lowliness, preceding and following. How much more the Way of

man?" Many themes of the "Great Tradition" and even certain phrases appear here. Although there is no explicit reference to the *Yi*, it is hinted at in the reference to the "images" that the sage draws from nature.

63. In addition to the account of Fu Xi, the reference to "looking up" and "looking down" also appears in a discussion of the *Yi* as a paradigm of Heaven and Earth. See 7 "Xi ci shang," p. 9a. The passage also refers to "tracing back to the beginning and reverting to the end," thus linking movement through time with that through space.

64. Thus in hexagram #61 the *yin* line in the third position is judged "not appropriate," while the *yang* line in position five is "correct and appropriate." See *Zhou yi zheng yi* 6 "Zhong fu 中孚," pp. 16b, 17a.

65. *Zhou yi zheng yi* 7 "Xi ci shang," p. 21b.

66. See, for example, *Zhou yi zheng yi* 2 "Xu 需," p. 1a.

67. *Zhou yi zheng yi* 8 "Xi ci xia," p. 9a.

68. *Zhou yi zheng yi* 7 "Xi ci shang," p. 3a.

69. *Zhou yi zheng yi* 7 "Xi ci shang," pp. 7a, 12b—"[The *Yi*] impels the myriad objects," 14b–15a, 16b (twice), 23b, 32b (twice); 8 "Xi ci xia," pp. 1b, 2a—"'Auspicious,' 'inauspicious,' 'remorse,' and 'humiliation' [divinatory formulae] are born from movement," 3b—"The lines and images move on the inside, and good or bad fortune are manifest on the outside," 8b—"The lines imitate the movements of Heaven and Earth."

70. *Zhou yi zheng yi* 7 "Xi ci shang," pp. 13a–b. This aspect of the text was discussed in Edward Shaughnessy, "The Generative Power of Change as Seen in the *Xici*," Conference on the *Xici zhuan*, Chicago, University of Chicago, May 30–June 1, 1997.

71. *Zhou yi zheng yi* 7 "Xi ci shang," pp. 14b–15a—"*Qian*'s stillness is concentrated and its movement is direct. Therefore it greatly produces. *Kun*'s stillness is gathered in and its movement opens up. Therefore it broadly produces," 15b—"Heaven and Earth establish their positions and the changes move between them. They allow the fulfillment of [things's] natures and preserve what exists"; 8 "Xi ci xia," pp. 3b, 20a—"The six lines are mixed together and each is an object with its proper time. That the first is difficult to understand and the last easy to comprehend is because [the former] is the root [hence hidden] while [the latter] is the branch [hence fully visible]," 24b (twice); 9 "Shuo gua," pp. 1b—"In ancient times when the sage created the *Yi*, he was mysteriously assisted by the spirits and it gave birth to the yarrow," 3a—"[The sage] observed the alternations of *yin* and *yang* and established the trigrams. They opened and displayed the hard and soft and gave birth to the lines."

72. *Zhou yi zheng yi* 7 "Xi ci shang," pp. 9a–b.

73. *Zhou yi zheng yi* 7 "Xi ci shang," pp. 28b–29a. The passage follows closely on that of *Dao de jing* 42, pp. 26–27—"The Way gives birth to the one. The one gives birth to the two. The two gives birth to the three. The three gives birth to the myriad objects."

74. *Zhou yi zheng yi* 8 "Xi ci xia," pp. 18a, 20a, 22a.

75. *Zhou yi zheng yi* 7 "Xi ci shang," p. 2a—here they form a series with method/process and objects, 5a—here they are first an aspect of the world revealed by the text and then an image within the text that serves to reveal aspects of the world, 7b—here they are part of a list of diviner's formulae, 8a—here they are an aspect of the world that "exists within the phrases [of the *Yi*]," 16b—an aspect of the world revealed by the phrases, 27b—"shares good and bad fortune with the people," 29b—"the world's good and bad fortune," 30a—part of the text in a series with the images and phrases, 32b.

76. Li Jingqi refers to these as "image–prognostication phrases" (*xiang zhan zhi ci* 象占之辭). See *Zhou yi tan yuan*, p. 108. Richard Kunst call them "omens," and argues that they derive from the practice of looking for signs in natural phenomena. See Kunst, "The Original 'Yijing': A Text, Phonetic Transcription, Translation, and Indexes, with Sample Glosses" (Ph.D. diss., University of California at Berkeley, 1985), ch. 3. Edward Shaughnessy calls them "topics," and considers them one of the four basic elements out of which all line statements are composed. See Shaughnessy, "Composition of the 'Zhouyi'," pp. 137–49.

77. *Zhou yi zheng yi* 5 "Jian," p. 30a; *Mao shi zheng yi* 8.3, Mao #159 "Jiu yu," p. 7b; 11.1, Mao #181 "Hong yan," p. 1b. The *Yi* line statement also rhymes, except for the final prognostication and verification. A rhymed divination text about a man going out on expedition and not returning also appears in *Zuo zhuan zhu* Xiang 10, p. 928. This story is also of interest because the prognosticatory verse begins with a one-line description of the crack in the tortoise shell.

78. See Kunst, "The Original 'Yijing'," pp. 67–81; Shaughnessy, "Composition of the 'Zhouyi'," pp. 98–101, 140–43, 147, 157–58.

79. Kunst, "The Original 'Yijing'," pp. 69, 75–77.

80. *Zhou yi zheng yi* 2 "Bi," p. 11b.

81. Yamashita, *Shū eki jū yoku no seiritsu to tenkai*, pp. 11–12, 275–95. A later example of the "politicization" of the *Yi* was Xun Shuang's Eastern Han commentary. See Ch'en Ch'i-yun, "A Confucian magnate's idea of political violence: Hsün Shuang's (128–90) interpretation of the *Book of Changes*," *T'oung Pao* 54 (1968): 73–115.

82. *Zhou yi zheng yi* 3 "Li," pp. 27a–28b.

83. Yamashita, *Shū eki jū yoku no seiritsu to tenkai*, pp. 12–15, 296–304.

84. *Zhou yi zheng yi* 7 "Xi ci shang," p. 2b. The idea that it is the images that allow perception of the processes of change also figures on 7, p. 24a—"Closing a door is called *kun*. Opening a door is called *qian*. Opening and closing is called alternation. Coming and going inexhaustibly is called 'going throughout.' When visible it is called 'image.'"

Other passages on the association of images with Heaven include pp. 13b, 29a—"For models and images, nothing is greater than Heaven and Earth"; 29b— "Heaven hangs down its images and reveals good and bad fortune"; 8 "Xi ci xia," p. 4b.

85. *Zhou yi zheng yi* 7 "Xi ci shang," p. 29a.

86. Thus the concluding passage of Sima Qian's monograph on celestial phenomena argues that all rulers since the dawn of humanity have observed the stars and established calendars, and it quotes the *Yi* account of Fu Xi to epitomize this process. See *Shi ji* 27, p. 1342. On *xiang* as a technical term in later Chinese astronomy, see Edward H. Schafer, *Pacing the Void: T'ang Approaches to the Stars* (Berkeley: University of California, 1977), pp. 55–56. *Xiang* also indicated non-astronomical phenomena in the sky, that is, meteorological events. Thus the divination text discovered at Mawangdui combines astronomical and meteorological divination. See Guojia Wenwuju Gu Wenxian Yanjiushi 国家文物局古文献研究室, "Xi Han boshu *Tian wen qi xiang za zhan* shi wen 西汉帛书天文气象杂占释文," *Zhongguo Wenwu* 1 (1979): 26–29. A reproduction of the manuscript appears on pp. 1–4. See also Yamada Keiji 山田慶兒, *Shin hakken Chūgoku kagaku shi shiryō no kenkyū* 新發現中國科學史史料の研究 (Kyoto: Kyōto Daigaku Jinbun Kagaku Kenkyūsho, 1985), vol. 1, pp. 45–86. The illustrations of comets are discussed in Michael Loewe, "The Han View of Comets," *Bulletin of the Museum of Far Eastern Antiquities* 52 (1980): 1–31.

87. *Zhou yi zheng yi* 7 "Xi ci shang," pp. 23b, 28a–b; 8 "Xi ci xia," p. 23b.

88. *Zhou yi zheng yi* 7 "Xi ci shang," p. 29b.

89. *Zhou yi zheng yi* 7 "Xi ci shang," pp. 29b–30a.

90. *Zhou yi zheng yi* 7 "Xi ci shang," p. 7b; 8 "Xi ci xia," pp. 1a, 3b, 24a.

91. *Zhou yi zheng yi* 7 "Xi ci shang," pp. 5a–6a.

92. *Zhou yi zheng yi* 8 "Xi ci xia," p. 8b.

93. *Zuo zhuan zhu* Xuan 3, pp. 699–71. The tripods of Yu are also referred to in the *Mozi*, without reference to the images cast on them. See *Mozi jian gu* 11 "Geng zhu," pp. 255–57. See also *Shi ji* 40, p. 1700. On the tripods as a symbol of the transfer of the mandate in Han art and literature, see Wu Hung, *The Wu Liang Shrine*, pp. 59, 92–96, 236.

94. Chang Kwang-chih, *Art, Myth, and Ritual: The Path to Political Authority in Ancient China* (Cambridge: Harvard University, 1983), pp. 95–100; Lewis, *Sanctioned Violence*, pp. 19, 31, 175, 259 note 68. This note lists articles on evidence from tombs for the marking of status through numbers of tripods.

95. *Lü shi chun qiu jiao shi* 16 "Xian shi 先識," p. 947; 17 "Shen shi 慎勢," p. 1110; 18 "Li wei," p. 1179—this passage is quoted in *Huainanzi* 8 "Ben jing," p. 117—18 "Shi wei 適威," p. 1282; 20 "Da yu 達鬱," p. 1374. Because all the other passages refer to specific objects, Yu Xingwu and Chen Qiyou argue that the *xiang* in the first passage refers not to "images" but to "elephants," a specific object depicted by the same graph. Depictions of elephants on Shang bronze decor, and even a bronze in the shape of an elephant have been discovered. The argument may be correct, but it is unclear how "elephants" would evoke the image of comprehensive knowledge of principles. The totality of images, however, as indicated in the *Zuo zhuan* account, would present a complete grasp of the world.

96. Another passage where the images on the tripods are adapted to contemporary concerns occurs in the *Li ji*. Describing the public order attained by a

ruler who understands rituals, Confucius states, "The measures and tripods [or 'tripods of measures'] attain their images [i.e., match the appropriate model]." Here the mythic representations of all objects in the world reappear as the standardized weights and measures of Qin and Han times. See *Li ji zhu shu* 50 "Zhongni yan ju 仲尼燕居," pp. 17a–b.

97. The other hexagram named for an artificial object is #48 "Well" (*jing* 井), which is only partly artificial. It is also significant that it was the rubric for the idealized land-holding system in the *Mencius*, which was itself derived from or provided the pattern for the mythic division of the world into nine provinces by Yu. In this way it is linked to the Nine Tripods, which stand for the nine provinces.

Another hexagram probably named for an implement is #30 (*li* 離), which could mean "net." *Li* 離, however, has numerous meanings. The Wilhelm/Baynes version translates it as "clinging" and Richard Lynn as "cohesion." See Richard Wilhelm and Cary F. Baynes, tr., *The I Ching, or Book of Changes* (Princeton: Princeton University, 1950), p. 535; Richard John Lynn, tr., *The Classic of Changes: A New Translation of the I Ching as Interpreted by Wang Bi* (New York: Columbia University, 1994), p. 323. However, the Chinese authors of the "Great Tradition" suggest that it inspired Fu Xi's invention of the net. See *Zhou yi zheng yi* 8 "Xi ci xia," p. 4b. Moreover, in the Mawangdui manuscript version the hexagram is named *luo* 羅, which also means "net." See Edward L. Shaughnessy, "A First Reading of the Mawangdui *Yijing* Manuscript," *Early China* 19 (1994): 52; Gao Heng 高亨, *Zhou yi da zhuan jin zhu* 周易大传今注 (Shandong: Qi Lu, 1979), p. 9. On the other hand, the author of the "Xu gua" tradition glosses the name as *li* 麗 "to adhere to" or "to cling," thus supporting the translations of Wilhelm and Lynn.

98. Shaughnessy, "Composition of the 'Zhouyi'," pp. 112–16.

99. *Xunzi ji jie* 18 "Zheng lun," p. 218. A version is quoted in *Han shu* 23, pp. 1110–11.

100. *Shuo yuan* 19 "Xiu wen 修文," pp. 7a–b; *Bo hu tong de lun* 2, p. 16b; Yang Xiong 楊雄, *Fa yan* 法言, in *Han Wei cong shu*, vol. 2, 6 "Xian zhi 先知," pp. 5a–5b—explicitly contrasting "punishments by images" with "mutilating punishments"; *Zhou li zhu shu* 36 "Si huan 司圜," p. 11b, the commentary cites the Han apocryphal text *Xiao jing wei* 孝經緯. Ban Gu approvingly quotes the *Xunzi*'s denial of the existence of "punishment through images" and points out that the abolition of mutilating punishments had led to a substantial increase in the use of the death penalty. He concludes that the phrase *xiang xing*—which occurs in the *Shang shu*—simply meant "punishments that imitated Heaven." See *Han shu* 23, pp. 1110–12.

On the use of this myth in Western Han legal debates, see Homer H. Dubs, tr., *The History of the Former Han Dynasty by Pan Ku*, vol. 2 (Baltimore: Waverly Press, 1944), pp. 123–25.

101. *Shang shu zheng yi* 5 "Yi ji 益稷," pp. 4b–5a, 14a. Some translators punctuate the text differently. They break the sentence with the first list of images after the verb "to depict," and then include the vessels of the ancestral temple as objects embroidered on the robes. I find this peculiar.

102. Early in the Western Han Jia Yi decried the fact that wealthy merchants dressed their concubines with patterns of embroidery that were supposed to be the privilege of empresses. See *Han shu* 48, pp. 2242–43.

103. *Hou Han shu*, p. 4266. On the formation and significance of this monograph, see B. J. Mansvelt Beck, *The Treatises of the Later Han: Their Author, Sources, Contents and Place in Chinese Historiography* (Leiden: E. J. Brill, 1990), ch. 11.

104. *Han Feizi ji shi* 6 "Jie lao," p. 368. This opposition between image and "formed object" also figures in *Dao de jing zhu* 21, p. 12; 41, p. 26.

105. On Pierce's definition and use of "icon" as a type of symbol, and the problems with the term, see John Lyons, *Semantics*, vol. 1 (paperback ed., Cambridge: Cambridge University, 1977), pp. 102–05.

106. It is of interest that "bone" would later serve as a critical term in theories of calligraphy and poetry. Moreover, "bone" came to be symbolically associated with the father, semen, black, ink, and writing; in opposition to flowers, flesh, blood, red, the womb, and oral traditions. See Brigitte Berthier, *La Dame-du-bord-de-l'eau* (Nanterre: Société d'Ethnologie, 1988), pp. 8–10, 161–81. This association of writing with the masculine and oral stories with the feminine is also a commonplace in the West. It was already prominent in Plato's critique of myths as tales transmitted by wet nurses, and later led to the invention of such figures as "Mother Goose" and such phrases as "old wives' tale."

107. *Zhou li zhu shu* 14 "Bao shi 保氏," p. 6b; *Han shu* 30, pp. 1720–21; *Shuo wen jie zi zhu* 15a, pp. 3b–7a.

108. The *Zhou li* links the "six types of graph" with the "six arts" (*liu yi* 六藝), "six [types of] music" (*liu yue* 六樂), and the "six [types of] ceremonial" (*liu yi* 六儀). Liu Xiang's bibliographic treatise also gives pride of place to the "six arts," and although the work is divided into seven sections, it actually has six bibliographic categories, with one section devoted to a general survey.

109. *Shuo wen jie zi zhu* 15a, pp. 1a–3a.

110. On the sages as mythic prototypes of the craftsmen, see *Zhou li zhu shu* 39 "Kao gong ji 考工記," p. 5a—"The wise created objects, and the skilled transmitted and preserved them. The world calls these people 'craftsmen.' The affairs of all the craftsmen arose from the sages."

111. The term "pictograph" derives from the Western myth in which writing develops from primitive pictures to advanced alphabets. On the centrality of this myth, see Harris, *The Origin of Writing*, ch. 4. The term is inappropriate to Chinese theory. As noted above, the term *xiang* is not defined by mimetic representation, but the visual "imaging" of structure or process. As will be noted below, Liu Xiang posited categories of characters that imaged function, idea, or sound, as well as shape. Physical resemblance was one possible way of imaging something, but it was not definitive or exemplary of the process.

112. While the category is clear from the examples and name, Xu Shen's definition is cryptic. Translated literally, it reads, "'Form and sound': taking the affair/task [*shi* 事] to be the name, selecting an analogy to complete it." In the

standard commentary Duan Yucai takes the first phrase to refer to the "semantic" element and the second to the phonetic. However, the character "name" (*ming* 名) would generally refer to something spoken (hence its links to *ming* 命 "to charge, to name"; and *ming* 鳴 "birdsong"), and was routinely contrasted with "content" (*shi* 實), which would correspond to the "semantic" element. Likewise the common process for the creation of such characters was that a single graph representing several words with identical or similar pronunciations was divided into multiple graphs through the addition of semantic elements. Thus Duan's gloss assumes that Xu Shen was employing words in a sense directly opposite to their conventional usage, and positing a historical process which was the inverse of what had taken place. It is more likely that the first phrase refers to the "phonetic" element, and that the "analogy" that completes it is the semantic. Such an argument entails that the "phonetic" was not purely a matter of sound, but also thought to relate to the sense of the character, as indicated by the reference to the *shi* 事. This idea was prevalent in the Han.

113. See Paul L. M. Serruys, "A Study of the *chuan chu* in *Shuo wen*," *Lishi Yuyan Yanjiusuo Jikan* 29 (1957): 131–95.

114. Gong Yingde has collected more than 500 cases in which Xu Shen notes that the "phonetic" is also a "semantic" element. See Gong Yingde 弓英德, *Liu shu bian zheng* 六書辯正 (Taipei: Shangwu, 1966), appendix, pp. 1–33. William Boltz also notes the frequency of this pattern, but finds the reasons for it "not entirely clear." See *Early Chinese Texts*, pp. 433–34. Léon Vandermeersch discusses the difficulty in treating the "phonetic" elements in these characters purely as indications of sound. See Vandermeersch, "La langue graphique chinoise," in *Etudes sinologiques* (Paris: Presses Universitaires de France, 1994), pp. 241–47. Consequently many scholars have noted that "form and sound" and "combined meaning" tend to collapse into a single category.

115. Vandermeersch states that Xu Shen's definition posits "the transfer of the linguistic function of reference to an object outside of language, and in no way a simple notation of a word by a graphic sign." See "La langue graphique," p. 248. He also makes the point that one must distinguish actual loan characters, which involve extending the meaning of a graph to represent a homophonous word and are very rare, from scribal substitutions of one graph for a homophone, which are quite common. The latter do not represent developments of the lexicon, but simply scribal convenience or errors.

116. Thus the Vandermeersch article cited in the preceding notes argues that the Chinese script constitutes an independent "graphic language," rather than the written transcription of any spoken tongue. For a critique of this position, not aimed specifically at Vandermeersch, see Jean Levi, *La Chine romanesque: fictions d'orient et d'occident* (Paris: Seuil, 1995), ch. 2, "La voix et l'encre: langue, écriture et tradition romanesque en Chine." The philosophical possibility of an "ideographic" language not reduced to speech is defended in Chad Hansen, "Chinese Ideographs and Western Ideas," *Journal of Asian Studies* 52:2 (May 1993): 373–99.

117. Michael Puett has argued that the latter position was a response to the former. Through their theory of signs the "Great Tradition" and related texts defended text-based authority from the challenge of claims to a direct, intuitive mastery of the cosmos not mediated through writing. See Puett, "The Notion of *Shen* in the *Xici*," Conference on the *Xici zhuan*, Chicago, University of Chicago, May 30–June 1, 1997.

118. *Zhuangzi ji shi* 14 "Tian yun," pp. 234–35. A related anecdote tells of Duke Huan and wheelwright Pian. See *Zhuangzi ji shi* 13 "Tian dao," pp. 217–18.

> Duke Huan was reading documents [*shu* 書] in the raised part of the hall. The wheelwright Pian was chiseling a wheel below. He set down the mallet and chisel, walked up, and asked Duke Huan, "May I dare to ask what words you are reading?" The duke replied, "The words of the sages." Pian asked, "Are the sages still alive?" The duke replied, "They are already dead." Pian said, "Then what you are reading is nothing but the chaff and dregs of ancient men." Duke Huan said, "How can a wheelwright assess what I read? If you can explain yourself, well and good. Otherwise you will die." Wheelwright Pian said, "I will consider it from the point of view of my own work. In chiseling a wheel, if you strike too slowly the chisel will slide and not hold fast. If too quick, then it sticks and doesn't go in. Neither too slow nor too fast, you get [the feel for] it in your hands and it responds in your mind. You can't express it in words, but there is a technique there. I can't teach it to my sons, and they can't receive it from me. So at the age of seventy I am still chiseling wheels. The ancient men died together with that which they could not transmit, so what you are reading is only their dregs and chaff."

119. The introductory section of the chapter epitomizes the stories as follows: "The words of the former kings had trivial elements which the thought of the present generation treats as important, and important elements which the thought of the present day treats as trivial. It is not the case that one certainly recognizes this. The explanation is in the story of the man of Song explaining the *Documents* and the man of Liang reading the records. Therefore the former kings had writings like that from Ying, which later generations largely explain in the manner of the [king of] Yan. To not devote oneself to the service of the state and to make plans for the Former Kings, are all cases of returning home to fetch the measure [of one's own foot]." See *Han Feizi ji shi* 11 "Wai chu shuo zuo shang," p. 614.

120. *Han Feizi ji shi* 11 "Wai chu shuo zuo shang," pp. 649–52. Another anecdote that dismisses writing as the vestiges of words and actions figures in the *Han Feizi*'s commentary on the *Dao de jing*. See *Han Feizi ji shi* 7 "Yu Lao," p. 405.

121. *Han Feizi ji shi* 19 "Xian xue," p. 1080.

122. Other passages that refer to writings as "traces" or "footprints," although not invariably in a negative sense, include *Mengzi zheng yi* 3B "Li Lou xia," p. 337; *Xunzi jijie* 6 "Fei shier zi," p. 61; *Bo hu tong de lun* 2, p. 1a—this refers to inscriptions at the *feng* and *shan* sacrifices; *Mu Tianzi zhuan* 穆天子傳 (Cong shu jicheng ed.),

pp. 9, 16; *Han Feizi ji shi* "Wai chu shuo zhuo shang," pp. 643–44. This last is a parody of the practice of carving inscriptions on mountains, and it describes some-one who actually carves large footprints into the mountain before inscribing his presence in words.

On the epistemological status of physical "traces" and their relation to the writing of history, see Paul Ricoeur, *Temps et récit*, vol. III, *Le temps raconté* (Paris: Seuil, 1985), pp. 175–83, 205, 226–27, 268, 292, 331, 368.

123. Granet, *La pensée chinoise*, pp. 127–28. The discussion of numbers con-tinues until p. 248.

124. Redouane Djamouri, "L'emploi des signes numérique dans les inscrip-tions Shang," *Extrême-Orient, Extrême-Occident* 16 (1994): 13.

125. Karine Chemla, "Nombre et opération, chaîne et trame du réel mathé-matique: essai sur le commentaire du Liu Hui sur *Les neuf chapitres sur les procédures mathématiques*," *Extrême-Orient, Extrême-Occident* 16 (1994): 59.

126. G. E. R. Lloyd, "Learning by numbers," *Extrême-Orient, Extrême-Occident* 16 (1994): 155.

127. For a general discussion of this process of absorbing cosmology or natural science into philosophy, I would again refer the reader to A. C. Graham, *Disputers of the Tao*, pp. 313–70.

128. These formulations relate to Chad Hansen's "mass-noun hypothesis" in the diminished form of A. C. Graham's proposition that "the tendency of Chinese thought is to divide down rather than to add up, to think in terms of whole/part rather than class/member." See Hansen, *Language and Logic in Ancient China* (Ann Arbor: University of Michigan, 1983); Christoph Harbsmeier, "The Mass Noun Hypothesis and the Part-Whole Analysis of the White Horse Dialogue," in *Chinese Texts and Philosophical Contexts*, ed. Henry Rosemont, Jr. (LaSalle, Illinois: Open Court, 1991), pp. 49–66; Graham, *Disputers of the Tao*, pp. 401–02.

129. *Zhou yi zheng yi* 7 "Xi ci shang," p. 11a.

130. In a similar mode, a speech on harmony attributed to Yan Ying in the *Zuo zhuan* traces the nine elements of music from the one, primal *qi* to the "nine songs," with each element matching an integer between one and nine. See *Zuo zhuan zhu* Zhao 20, p. 1420.

In his commentary on the Han mathematical work, the *Jiu zhang suan shu*, Liu Hui pointed out that through changing the denominator of a fraction, one could give a finer or grosser analysis of a number without ever altering the actual sum to which it referred. See *Jiu zhang suan shu*, pp. 95–96. Karine Chemla points out that Liu Hui regards the addition of fractions, based on creating common denominators through ever finer divisions that do not change the actual quantity, as central to all calculation. The central passage in his argument is a quotation from the "Great Tradition" of the *Yi*. See "Nombre et opération," pp. 49–57. The procedures placed at the core of calculation by Liu Hui were also central to the numerological systems of the Warring States and early imperial periods.

131. *Zhuangzi ji shi* 17 "Qiu shui," p. 250; 25 "Ze Yang," pp. 393–94. In the following passage the world is named by two parallel, numerical phrases: "within the four directions" [*si fang zhi nei* 四方之內] and "inside the three dimensions" [*liu he zhi li* 六合之裏]. Elsewhere the "three dimensions" (*liu he* 六合) function in interchangeable parallel with the "Nine Provinces" (*jiu zhou* 九州). See 11 "Zai you," p. 178.

132. *Zhuangzi ji shi* 1, "Xiao yao you," p. 16; 2 "Qi wu lun," p. 39—"The 10,000 things and I are one"; 5 "De chong fu," pp 86–87—"Looked at from their differences, then there is liver and gall, Chu and Yue. Looked at from their similarities, then the 10,000 things are all one"; 12 "Tian di," pp. 181, 182—"Observing comprehensively by means of the Way, the responses of the 10,000 things are complete"; 182—"The *Record* says, 'Thoroughly master the One, and the 10,000 will be brought to completion'"; 184—"The 10,000 things are a single storehouse, and life and death an identical body"; 13 "Tian dao," p. 216—"The Way halts at nothing huge and omits nothing small, so the 10,000 things are complete"; 22 "Zhi bei you," p. 320— "The 10,000 things are one. . . . Thus I say, 'Thoroughly comprehend the single *qi* that is the world.' The sage honors the one."

133. *Zhuangzi ji shi* 25 "Ze Yang," p. 394.

134. *Xunzi ji jie* 22 "Zheng ming," p. 278. Later the author touches on the problem of numbering in relation to making divisions.

> There are things which have the same appearance and different places and hence can be divided. If they have the same appearance and different places, although they can be brought together, we call them two things. There are things with different appearances that exist in the same place [e.g., a sapling and a full-grown tree]. We call this change. There is change but no division, so we call it one thing.

See p. 279.

135. Zhang Zhenglang 张政烺, "Shi shi Zhou chu qingtongqi mingwen zhong de *Yi* gua 试释周初青铜器铭文中的易卦," *Kaogu Xuebao* (1980:4): 403–15 [translated by H. Huber and R. Yates as "An Interpretation of the Divinatory Inscriptions on Early Chou Bronzes," *Early China* 6 (1980–81): 80–96]; Zhang Zhenglang, "Bo shu liushisi gua ba 帛书六十四卦跋," *Wenwu* (1984:3): 9–14; Zhang Yachu 张亚初 and Liu Yu 刘雨, "Cong Shang Zhou ba gua shuzi fuhao tan shifa de jige wenti 从商周八卦数子符号谈筮法的几个问题," *Kaogu* (1981:2): 155–63, 154; Shaughnessy, "Composition of the 'Zhouyi'," pp. 28–30, 46, 59, 108, 118–19; Vandermeersch, *Wangdao*, vol. 2, pp. 300–04. For examples of numeric hexagrams in Warring States manuscripts, see *Bao shan chu jian*, p. 36; Hubei Sheng Jingzhou Diqu Bowuguan 湖北省荆州地区博物馆, "Jiangling Wangjiatai 15 hao Qin mu 江陵王家台15号秦墓," *Wenwu* (1995:1): 40–41; Li Ling, *Zhongguo fangshu kao*, pp. 242–44.

136. The Fuyang bamboo strip version of the *Yi* names the lines as "nine" or "six," but writes them with the old graphs for "one"—an unbroken line—or

"six"—an inverted "v." This appears to be a transitional stage between writing the hexagrams as numbers and writing them as lines.

137. *Zhou yi zheng yi* 7 "Xi ci shang," p. 7a.

138. *Zhou yi zheng yi* 7 "Xi ci shang," pp. 13b—"To trace the numbers to their limit and know the future is called 'prognostication'"; 8 "Xi ci xia," pp. 8b–9a—"*Yang* trigrams are mostly *yin* lines; *yin* trigrams are mostly *yang* lines. Why? Because *yang* trigrams are odd numbered and *yin* trigrams even numbered. What is their virtuous conduct like? *Yang* is one ruler and two subjects. This is the Way of the gentleman. *Yin* is two rulers and one subject. This is the Way of the petty man"; 22a—"The *Yi*'s nature as writing is vast and complete. The Way of Heaven is in it; the Way of man is in it; the Way of Earth is in it. It combines these Three Powers and doubles them [through *yin* and *yang*]. Therefore there are six lines. 'Six' is nothing other than the Way of the Three Powers"; 22b–23a—"[The *Yi*'s] Way is vast. None of the hundred objects is omitted"; 9 "Shuo gua," p. 1b—"In ancient times when the sage made the *Yi*, he was secretly assisted by illumined spirits and gave birth to the yarrow stalks. He established the numbers, making Heaven three [odd, *yang*] and Earth two [even, *yin*]"; 3b—"It combines the Three Powers and doubles them. Therefore the *Yi* draws six lines to complete a hexagram. They divide them into *yin* and *yang*, employing the soft and hard in alternation. Therefore the *Yi* uses six positions to complete the pattern." The passage on the manipulation of yarrow stalks is 7 "Xi ci shang," pp. 20a–22b, with a misplaced fragment on p. 26b.

139. *Zhou yi zheng yi* 7 "Xi ci shang," pp. 24a–b.

140. *Shiyi jia zhu Sunzi*, pp. 28–30. On this practice and its relation to other ideas in the text, see Li Ling, "Du *Sunzi* zha ji 讀孫子劄記," in *Gu ben Sunzi yanjiu*, pp. 302–04. On the use of counting rods in calculations, see Alexeï Volkov, "Large numbers and counting rods," *Extrême-Orient, Extrême-Occident* 16 (1994): 80–82.

141. Two "Liu bo" sets with six rods were found in the Qin tomb at Shuihudi. See *Yunmeng Shuihudi* (Beijing: Wenwu, 1981), pp. 55–56. The early Western Han set found at Fenghuangshan contained both six rods and an eighteen-sided die. See *Wenwu* 1974 (6): 50–51. For depictions of the rods laid out like a trigram, see Finsterbusch, *Verzeichnis und Motivindex, Band II*, illustrations #49 (?), 118, 143, 148, 260 (?), 1001. This link of games of chance with myths of the origins of writing and divination also appears in Greek mythology. See Detienne, "Une écriture inventive, la voix d'Orphée, les jeux de Palamède," in *L'écriture d'Orphée*, pp. 101–15.

142. *Han shu* 21a, p. 973.

143. *Han shu* 21a, pp. 979–83; *Jin shu* 11, p. 498. For discussions of these calendars, see Michel Teboul, *Les premières théories planétaires chinoises* (Paris: Institut des Hautes Etudes Chinoises, 1983); Nathan Sivin, "Cosmos and Computation in Early Chinese Mathematical Astronomy," *T'oung Pao* 55 (1969): 1–73, esp. 8–9. On the role of the "Great Tradition," particularly its reference to the "Great Expansion" (*da yan* 大衍), to later discussions of calendar reform and the problem of infinite numbers, see Volkov, "Large numbers and counting rods," pp. 74–79.

144. Hans Ulrich Vogel, "Aspects of Metrosophy and Metrology during the Han Period," *Extrême-Orient, Extrême-Occident* 16 (1994): 136. On references to the "Great Tradition" in this monograph, see Nōda Chūryō 能田忠亮 and Yabuuchi Kiyoshi 藪內清, *Kan sho ritsureki no kenkyū* 漢書律曆の研究 (Tōyō Bunka Kenkyū-sho Kenkyū Hōkoku, Kyoto: Zenkoku Shobō, 1947), pp. 187, 192, 193, 201, 224.

145. *Han shu* 21a, p. 970; *Huainanzi* 5 "Shi ze," pp. 86–87—translated in Joseph Needham, *Science and Civilization in China*, vol. 4:1, *Physics* (Cambridge: Cambridge University, 1962), pp. 15–17; John S. Major, *Heaven and Earth in Early Han Thought: Chapters Three, Four, and Five of the Huainanzi* (Albany: SUNY, 1993), pp. 264–66. Major shows the relation of the passage to the myth of Fu Xi and Nü Wa.

146. *Shi ji* 6, pp. 237–38 states that Qin adopted water as its patron phase and hence took the number six as its standard of measure. Thus officials' tassels, chariots, and teams of horses were measured in units of six, and six "feet" (*chi* 尺) constituted a "pace" (*bu* 步). *Shi ji* 6, p. 239 records that the empire was divided into 36 commanderies and that 12 statues were cast from the weapons confiscated from the conquered states. This insistence on the importance of the number six is followed by the account of the unification of measures of weight, volume, and distance; the length of chariot axles; and the written script. There is, however, no explicit reference to numerology in these measures.

147. *Shuo wen jie zi zhu* 15a, pp. 19a–21b.

Chapter Seven. The Encyclopedic Epoch

1. The chapter "Rectifying Assessments" (*zheng lun* 正論) also criticizes doctrines, sometimes naming the master who propounded them, but it focuses on refuting particular points rather than attacking the phenomenon of intellectual disputation. Nevertheless, certain arguments presuppose the polarity of universality versus partiality. Thus one of the denunciations of Song Xing suggests that he is wrong because he pits his solitary opinion, based on "a morning's reflection" against univerally approved customs that have been unchanged for "myriad generations." To do so is like using "balls of mud to block up rivers and oceans." See *Xunzi ji jie* 18 "Zheng lun," p. 229. The final metaphor also evokes the image of the reprobate Gun, who sought to end the flood by blocking flowing water with dams of earth.

The concluding passage of the "Assessment of Heaven" (*tian lun* 天論) also contains a list of rival philosophers criticized for their partiality. See *Xunzi ji jie* 17 "Tian lun," p. 213.

2. *Xunzi ji jie* 6 "Fei shi er zi," pp. 57–60—describes the six errors and lists the twelve masters, 60–61—describes the all-encompassing reach of the sages. Wang Niansun points out that the verb *cai* 財=裁 is often linked with or glossed by *cheng* 成 and thus suggests "completion" or "perfection."

3. The ultimate consequence of the disappearance of the fractious doctrines is that the "footprints/traces" (*ji* 跡) of the sage kings become clearly visible. As shown in chapter 6, this idea of "traces" is closely associated with writing. Indeed,

the only other use of the phrase "traces of the sage kings" in the *Xunzi* appears in an argument that one should take the "later kings," that is, the Zhou, as models because they have writings and hence their "traces" are "bright" (*can ran* 粲然). See *Xunzi ji jie* 5 "Fei xiang," pp. 50–51.

4. *Xunzi ji jie* 21 "Jie bi," p. 258.

5. *Xunzi ji jie* 21 "Jie bi," pp. 261–62.

6. *Xunzi ji jie* 21 "Jie bi," p. 271.

7. *Zhuangzi ji shi* 33 "Tian xia," pp. 462–64. The ideal identity of sage and king is also asserted in the *He Guanzi*. See Defoort, *The Pheasant Cap Master*, pp. 120–27.

8. *Zhuangzi ji shi* 33 "Tian xia," pp. 476–81; *Xunzi ji jie* 21 "Jie bi," pp. 272–73.

9. The privileging of totality over partiality figured in earlier chapters in the *Zhuangzi*. One provides the *locus classicus* for the most famous image of a limited vision, the frog who knows only his own little well and cannot imagine the vastness of the Eastern Sea. See *Zhuangzi ji shi* 17 "Qiu shui," pp. 264–65. The contrast between the giant, world-traversing *peng* bird and the little quails makes a similar point, as does the assault on how each person distinguishes between "this or that" and "right or wrong" from his own particularist standpoint. See *Zhuangzi ji shi* 1 "Xiao yao you," pp. 2–7; 2 "Qi wu lun," pp. 30–32.

10. On the sage ruler as defined by constant adaptation, see *Han Feizi ji shi* 19 "Wu du," pp. 1040–42. For criticisms of the *ru* for clinging to outmoded practices and private interests, see 19 "Wu du," pp. 1051, 1057–58, 1078; 19 "Xian xue," pp. 1090–91, 1100, 1102. For the criticism of Yang Zhu, see 19 "Xian xue," p. 1090. For criticisms of the schools for their mutually contradictory positions, internal divisions, and inability to know even the doctrines of their own founders, see 19 "Xian xue," pp. 1080, 1085, 1089, 1091. For criticisms of rhetoricians and elaborate language, see 19 "Wu du," pp. 1058, 1055, 1067, 1078; 19 "Xian xue," pp. 1090–91, 1092–93. For criticisms of the exponents of alliances, see 19 "Wu du," pp. 1067–69. For criticisms of theorists of administration and warfare, see 19 "Wu du," pp. 1066–67. For criticisms of allowing literary studies and teaching to be a road to private wealth, see 19 "Wu du," pp. 1057–58, 1066, 1075, 1078; 19 "Xian xue," pp. 1091, 1095, 1099–2000. On no texts except the law and teachers except the officials, see 19 "Wu du," p. 1067.

11. *Shi ji* 87, pp. 2546–47.

12. *Shi ji* 130, pp. 3288–89.

13. *Huainanzi* 21, "Yao lüe 要略," pp. 375–77.

14. *Shuo wen jie zi zhu* 13a, pp. 2b–3a.

15. Zhang Binglin 張炳麟, "Wen xue zong lüe 文學總略," in *Guo gu lun heng* 國故論衡 (Tokyo: Kokugaku Kōshūkai, 1910), pp. 73–74. This etymology was adopted by "materialist" authors in the early decades of this century. See, for example, Gu Jiegang, "Zi xu 自序," in *Gu shi bian*, vol. 1, pp. 26–28. Gu denounces *Guo gu lun heng*, but makes an exception of the etymological analysis of the characters *jing* 經 and *zhuan* 傳. See also Fan Wenlan, *Qun jing gai lun*, p. 1.

16. *Shuo wen jie zi zhu* 11b, p. 3b. The same character with the water radical 涇 also figures as the name of a river. See *Shuo wen jie zi zhu* 11a, p. 11b.

17. Bernhard Karlgren, *Grammata Serica Recensa* (rep. ed., Stockholm: Museum of Far Eastern Antiquities, 1957), p. 219.

18. *Shi ming shu zheng bu* 6 "Shi dian yi" 釋典藝," p. 12a.

19. *Shuo wen jie zi zhu* 1b, p. 33a; 4b, p. 26a; 7b, p. 33a; 9a, p. 4a—the *Shuo wen* glosses *jing* 頸 "neck" as the "stalk/trunk of the head" *tou jing* 頭莖—13b, p. 52a. The character *jing* 頸 "neck" is converted into *jing* 剄 "to cut the neck/throat" by the substitution of the "knife" radical for the "head." The character *jing* 勁 is glossed with the character *qiang* 彊 "strong," but also interchangeably with *jiang* 僵 "stiff, unmoving." This identity is suggested by the fact that the paralyzing contraction or stiffening of the muscles *jing* 痙 is glossed as *qiang ji* 彊急. For a discussion of this cluster of characters and their shared meanings, see Tōdō Akiyasu 藤堂明 安, *Kanji gogen jiten* 漢字語源辞典 (Tokyo: Gakutōsha, 1965), pp. 498–99.

20. Seven inscriptions in which the character appears are listed in Hiraoka Takeo 平岡武夫, *Keisho no seiritsu* 經書の成立 (Tokyo: Sōbunsha, 1983), pp. 12–13.

21. *Mengzi zheng yi* 3A "Teng Wen Gong shang," pp. 205–06.

22. *Zuo zhuan zhu* Xiang 4, p. 938.

23. *Zhou li zhu shu* 14 "Si shi," p. 18a. In the next two sentences the verbs that parallel *jing* 經 are *ping* 平 "to make level, to control" and *jun* 均 "to make even, to equitably distribute."

24. *Zhou li zhu shu* 41 "Jiang ren," p. 24b.

25. *Huainanzi* 4 "Di xing xun" 地形訓, p. 59. An identical passage appears in *Da Dai li ji jie gu* 13 "Yi ben ming" 易本命, p. 285.

26. *Zuo zhuan zhu* Yin 11, p. 76.

27. *Guo yu* 10 "Chu yu shang," p. 557. On the etymology of *ying* 營, see Katō Jōken, *Kanji no kigen* 漢字の起源 (Tokyo: Kadokawa, 1972), p. 82; Tōdō Akiyasu, *Kanji gogen jiten*, p. 513. The latter also discusses its association with *jing* 經 in the sense of placing fields in order, citing a passage from the "Li sao." They are also linked as verbs in the *Ode* cited by Mencius that describes King Wen's building of the "Numinous Tower" in his hunting park. See *Meng zi zheng yi* 1A "Liang Hui Wang shang," p. 27.

28. On the sense of *ying* as "setting up a military camp," see *Wei Liaozi zhijie*, pp. 65b–66a. On *jing* meaning "to rule" see *Lü shi chun qiu jiao shi* 22 "Qiu ren" 求 人, p. 1515; *Xunzi ji jie* 6 "Fei shi er zi," p. 59. Even in this second example, however, the phrase *jing guo* 經國 is immediately linked with *ding fen* 定分 "to establish divisions."

29. *Mengzi zheng yi* 7B "Jin xin xia," p. 608; *Xunzi ji jie* 21 "Jie bi," p. 258.

30. *Zuo zhuan zhu* Yin 11, p. 77—"the constant norm of ritual," with *jing* 經 parallel to *ze* 則 "standard, norm"; Xi 24, p. 425—"the constant norm of virtue and duty" (*de yi zhi jing* 德義之經); Xuan 12, p. 722—"the constant norm of government" (*zheng* 政), p. 725—"the constant norm of martiality" (*wu* 武); Xiang

21, p. 1063—"the constant norm of ritual"; Zhao 25, p. 1457 (twice)—"the constant norm of Heaven" and "the constant norm of Heaven and Earth"; Zhao 26, p. 1478—"the constant norm of the Former Kings," here parallel to their "mandate/commands" (*ming* 命); Ai 5, p. 1630—"the constant norm of duty"; *Xunzi ji jie* 1 "Quan xue," p. 8—"the constant norm of study." Commentators suggest that in this passage *jing* 經 is used for *jing* 徑 "the direct route" or "the Way"; 8 "Ru xiao," p. 75—"the constant norm of controlling all things and nourishing the common people" (*cai wan wu yang bai xing zhi jing ji* 財 = 裁萬物養百姓之經紀); 20 "Yue lun," p. 255—"the constant norm of ritual"; 22 "Zheng ming," p. 281— "the constant norm/principle [*jing li* 經理] of public order"; 25 "Cheng xiang," p. 307—"the constant norm of public order"; p. 312—"the constant norm of adjudication"; *Lü shi chun qiu jiao shi* 13 "You shi" 有始, p. 657—"the great constant norm of life"; 20 "Jiao zi" 驕恣, p. 1404—"the constant norm of the ruler of men."

31. *Lü shi chun qiu jiao shi* 20, "Zhi fen" 知分, p. 1346—"the *jing* 經 of benefit and harm," parallel to "the division [*fen* 分] of life and death"; 22 "Cha zhuan" 察傳, p. 1527—"the *jing* 經 of right and wrong must be distinguished [*fen* 分]"; *Zuo zhuan zhu* Zhao 25, p. 1458—ritual "creates man and wife, the outer and inner, in order to *jing* 經 the two objects [*yin* and *yang*]"; p. 1459—ritual as the "warp and weft" (*jing wei* 經緯) of Heaven and Earth. For "warp and weft" as a general term for all proper conduct, again determined by ritual, see also *Xunzi ji jie* 1 "Quan xue," p. 9. For "warp and weft" as a verb meaning "to structure, to give order" see *Xunzi ji jie* 21 "Jie bi," p. 265.

32. *Xunzi ji jie* 9 "Wang zhi," p. 96.

33. *Zhuangzi ji shi* 33 "Tian xia," p. 467.

34. Graham, *Later Mohist Logic, Ethics, and Science,* pp. 22–24, 243–44.

35. *Guanzi jiao zheng,* pp. 1–47. For examples of the formula "number + *jing* 經," see pp. 29, 32.

36. *Han Feizi ji shi* 18 "Ba jing," pp. 996–1039.

37. *Han shu* 30, pp. 1776–77.

38. *Han Feizi ji shi* 9–14 "Nei chu shuo shang," "Nei chu shuo xia," "Wai chu shuo zuo shang," "Wai chu shuo zuo xia," "Wai chu shuo you shang," "Wai chu shuo you xia." For the formulaic principles as *jing* 經, see pp. 526, 576, 621, 676, 715, 761. The *Han Feizi* also has two chapters which expound the political applications of many of the aphorisms from the *Dao de jing,* although these do not use the terms *jing* 經 and *shuo* 說. Each exposition concludes with the quotation of the original aphorism. Hence these chapters work exactly like the "Collected Explanation" chapters, except that the explanation precedes the "canonical" sentence. See *Han Feizi ji shi* 6 "Jie Lao" 解老; 7 "Yu Lao" 喻老.

39. *Han shu* 30, pp. 1705, 1707, 1709, 1716, 1718, 1729, 1744.

40. *Shuo wen jie zi zhu* 8a, p. 25a; *Shi ming shu zheng bu* 5 "Shi gong shi" 釋宮室, p. 13b; 6 "Shi shu qie" 釋書契, p. 7b—this second definition identifies *zhuan* 傳 with a document presented when passing a frontier or customs station; "Shi dian yi," p. 13a.

41. *Zhou li zhu shu* 38 "Xing fu" 行夫, p. 13b—he "is in charge of the petty task of the state's relaying and delivering" (*zhuan ju zhi xiao shi* 傳遞之小事); *Li ji zhu shu* 30 "Yu zao" 玉藻, pp. 25b–26a.

42. *Lun heng* 82 "Shu jie" 書解, p. 276.

43. *Zhuangzi ji shi* 14 "Tian yun," p. 234; *Xunzi ji jie* 1 "Quan xue," p. 7.

44. *Xin yu* 1 "Dao ji," p. 2—"The later sage [Confucius] then fixed the Five Canons to make clear the Six Arts"; *Jiazi xin shu jiao shi* 8 "Liu shu," pp. 946–47; *Huainanzi* 20 "Tai zu," pp. 352–53, 363; *Shi ji* 130, p. 3290; *Chun qiu fan lu yi zheng* 1 "Yu bei" 玉杯, pp. 24a–b. This last passage refers to the "six [fields of] study" (*liu xue* 六學) as well as the "Six Arts." The term *liu xue* 六學 also appears in *Han shu* 88, p. 3592. For a discussion of the significance of the "Six Arts" and their role in Han theories of writing and education, see Durrant, *The Cloudy Mirror*, ch. 3.

45. How the commentaries on the five "core" chapters of the *Shang shu* turned speeches regarding particular problems and events into a philosophical program of kingship and a theory of the role of Heaven in the world is discussed in Hiraoka, *Keisho no seiritsu*, part 3.

46. The relation of commentary and opacity is noted in the *Han shu* bibliographic monograph. The last section on the "texts of the Six Arts" (*liu yi zhi wen* 六藝之文) notes the particular virtue of each category of writing. "The *Ritual* serves to illuminate the body/essential part (*ti* 體). What is illuminated is clearly seen, so there are no glosses." See *Han shu* 30, p. 1723. The same chapter also explains the creation of commentaries for the *Chun qiu* as a means of preventing differences of interpretation. See p. 1715.

47. The *Guanzi* could be considered another example of this type of text. However, the two cited texts were integrally composed over relatively brief spans of time—one or two decades—under known historical circumstances, while the *Guanzi* is a collection of essays whose dates of composition may well span several centuries, and the historical setting of its compilation remains a mystery. Consequently it does not share many of the basic features of the other texts.

48. *Shi ji* 85, p. 2510; *Han shu* 44, p. 2145; *Huainanzi*, 1.

49. For the argument for individual authorship see, for example, Charles LeBlanc, "Historical and Textual Studies," in *Huai-nan Tzu: Philosophical Synthesis in Early Han Thought* (Hong Kong: Hong Kong University, 1985), pp. 26–27. For the case for multiple authorship, based on an examination of the historical accounts and the diversity of style and contents in the work, see Harold D. Roth, *The Textual History of the Huai-nan Tzu* (Ann Arbor: AAS Monograph Series, 1992), pp. 18–23. For arguments within the text on the superiority of mobilizing the collective wisdom of many people from diverse backgrounds over relying on the intelligence of even the wisest individual, see *Huainanzi* 9 "Zhu shu," pp. 131, 139–40. These arguments, under the rubric "utilizing the people" (*yong zhong* 用眾), are discussed in Roger Ames, *The Art of Rulership: A Study in Ancient Chinese Political Thought* (Hawaii: University of Hawaii, 1983), ch. 5.

50. *Lü shi chun qiu jiao shi* "Xu yi" 序意, p. 648.

51. *Lü shi chun qiu jiao shi* 17 "Bu er" 不二, pp. 1123–24.

52. *Han shu* 30, pp. 1741–42. This states, "The current of 'mixing' the schools derives from those officials who debated policy. They brought together the *ru* and the Mohist, joined the school of names and the legalists. They knew that the essential elements of a state included these. They perceived that there was nothing that the royal order did not penetrate. This was their strength."

53. On the *Lü shi chun qiu* see Xu Fuguan 徐復觀, *Liang Han sixiang shi* 兩漢思想史, vol. 2 (Taipei: Xuesheng, 1976), pp. 1–83; John M. Louton, "The *Lüshi chunqiu:* An Ancient Chinese Political Cosmology" (Ph.D. diss., University of Washington, 1981), chs. 2, 3; James Darryl Sellman, "Timeliness and sociopolitical order in the 'Lü-shih ch'un-ch'iu'" (Ph.D. diss., University of Hawaii, 1990), chs. 2, 3. On the *Huainanzi*, see Kanaya Osamu, *Shin Kan shisō shi kenkyū*, ch. 5; Ames, *The Art of Rulership*, chs. 1–6; Anne Cheng, "Taoïsme, confucianisme et légisme," in *Mythe et philosophie à l'aube de la Chine impériale: études sur le Huainan Zi*, ed. Charles LeBlanc and Rémi Mathieu (Montreal: L'Université de Montréal, 1992), pp. 127–42; Nathalie Pham, "Quand les extrêmes se rencontrent," in *Mythe et philosophie à l'aube de la Chine impériale*, pp. 143–58.

54. *Lü shi chun qiu jiao shi* "Xu yi," p. 648.

55. Zhang Xuecheng 章學誠 (1738–1801), *Wen shi tong yi* 文史通義 (Hong Kong: Taiping, 1964), p. 22; Xu Fuguan, *Liang Han sixiang shi*, vol. 2, pp. 3–5; Louton, "The *Lüshi chunqiu*," Appendix 1.

Some scholars have tried to explain the position of the postface by arguing that it appears after the "Registers" not because these were the first written and originally an independent work, but because they had appeared *after* the other sections. As supporting evidence, they note that Sima Qian twice lists the contents of the works as *lan* 覽, *lun* 論, and *ji* 紀 and once refers to the work as the *Lü lan* 呂覽. See *Shi ji* 14, p. 510; 85, p. 2510; 130, p. 3300. The exponents of this argument are discussed in Louton's "Appendix" cited above. The central problem with this position is that the "postface" clearly identifies the work in question as the "Twelve Registers," with no reference to the "Eight Overviews" and "Six Assessments." Since nothing in the passages in the *Shi ji* indicates that Sima Qian is citing the sections in their order of presentation or composition, it is far more plausible to treat the "Registers" as the earliest section and the core of the work. As Louton notes, Sima Qian's identification of the text as the *Lü lan* occurs in a passage arguing that men produce great writings in response to frustration or failure, a passage wherein the *Han Feizi* is identified by a reference to two chapters dealing with Han Fei's problems making his way in the world. It is possible that Sima Qian focuses on the *lan* precisely because they were *later* products, reflecting Lü Buwei's declining fortunes, and because they dealt more frequently with the issue of misunderstood virtue and good men unappreciated by rulers. On this theme see *Lü shi chun qiu jiao shi* 14 "Chang gong" 長攻, pp. 790–91; "Shen ren" 慎人, pp. 802–03; "Yu he" 遇合, pp. 815–16; "Bi ji" 必己, p. 830; 15 "Bu guang," p. 917.

56. The text is also related to other calendars from the period, including the "Lesser Annuary of the Xia" *xia xiao zheng* 夏小正, the first three sections from the sixth *juan* of the *Yi Zhou shu* ("Zhou yue jie" 周月解, "Shi ze jie" 時則解, and "Yue ling jie" 月令解), several essays in the *Guanzi*, and the Chu silk manuscript. For a list of the relevant texts, references to translations and studies of them, and a sketch of the organization of the "Yue ling," see Major, *Heaven and Earth in Early Han Thought*, pp. 217–24.

57. Sellman, "Timeliness and Sociopolitical Order," ch. 2.

58. *Huainanzi* 21 "Yao lüe," p. 369. A similar characterization of the text immediately precedes the brief history cited earlier of the emergence of texts out of rulers' and scholars' responses to crises. It discusses the same tension between the need to preserve both the one Way and its infinite manifestations, to use both elaborate language for wide-ranging details and simplicity for the essentials. It concludes that the twenty chapters "comprehensively penetrate" (*tong* 通) the world, "go throughout" (*jing* 徑) the universe, go beyond Heaven and Earth, cover the mountains and rivers, and guide and shape the myriad objects. See p. 374.

59. These are based on the doctrine of the Five Phases, conventionally attributed to Zou Yan. His work seems to have exemplified the dream of a text-based wisdom encompassing all things, but all that survives is a brief epitome in the *Shi ji* and a few quotations preserved in later works.

60. John Louton, "Concepts of Comprehensiveness and Historical Change in the *Lü-shih ch'un-ch'iu*," *Journal of the American Academy of Religious Studies Thematic Studies* 50/2: *Explorations in Early Chinese Cosmology* (Chico, Calif.: Scholars Press, 1984), pp. 105–17; Jeffrey A. Howard, "Concepts of Comprehensiveness and Historical Change in the *Huai-nan-tzu*," *JAAR Thematic Studies* 50/2, pp. 119–31.

61. *Lü shi chun qiu jiao shi* 7 "Dang bing" 蕩兵, p. 383; "Zhen luan" 振亂, pp. 393–94; 13 "Ying tong" 應同, p. 678; "Jin ting" 謹聽, p. 705; 16 "Guan shi" 觀世, p. 958; 20 "Shi jun" 恃君, pp. 1321–22.

62. *Lü shi chun qiu jiao shi* 17 "Bu ren," pp. 1123–24; "Zhi yi" 執一, p. 1132.

63. See, for example, *Huainanzi* 6 "Lan ming," pp. 96–97; 8 "Ben jing," pp. 114–15, 118–19; 9 "Zhu shu," pp. 138, 141; 11 "Qi su," p. 185; 15 "Bing lüe," p. 252; 19 "Xiu wu," p. 332.

64. *Han shu* 62, p. 2735. The three final phrases have been the subject of much scholarly discussion. See Bai Shouyi 白壽彝, "Jiu tian ren zhi ji 究天人之际, tong gu jin zhi bian 通古今之变, cheng yi jia zhi yan 成一家之言," in *Shi ji xin lun* 史记新论 (Beijing: Qiushi, 1981), pp. 20–71; Ruan Zhisheng 阮芝生, "Shi lun Sima Qian suo shuo de 'tong gu jin zhi bian' 試論司馬遷所說的通古今之變," in *Zhongguo shixue shi lun wen xuan ji* 中國史學史論文選集, ed. Du Weiyun 杜維運 and Huang Jinxing 黃進興 (Taipei: Huashi, 1980), vol. 3; Zhang Dake 张大可, *Shi ji yanjiu* 史记研究 (Lanzhou: Gansu Renmin, 1985), pp. 22–35, 338–60; Shi Ding 施定, "Lun Sima Qian de tong gu jin zhi bian 论司马迁的通古今之变," in *Sima Qian yanjiu xin lun* 司馬遷研究新論 (Beijing: Henan

Renmin, 1982), pp. 17–47; Lai Changyang 赖长扬, "Lun Sima Qian de lishi zhe-xue 论司马迁的历史哲学," in *Sima Qian yanjiu xin lun*, pp. 59–84; Wen Chongyi 文崇一, "Lun Sima Qian de sixiang 論司馬遷的思想," in *Shi ji lunwen xuan ji* 史記論文選集, ed. Huang Peirong 黃沛榮 (Taipei: Changan, 1982); Xu Fuguan, "Lun Shi ji 論史記," in *Liang Han sixiang shi*, vol. 3 (Taipei: Xuesheng, 1979), pp. 323–33; Durrant, *The Cloudy Mirror*, pp. 124–29. On "comprehensiveness" (*tong* 通) as an ideal in the *Shi ji*, see Yang Yanqi 杨燕起, "Sima Qian de lishi sixiang 司马迁的历史思想," in *Sima Qian he Shi ji* 司马迁和史记, ed. Liu Naihe 刘乃和 (Beijing: Beijing Daxue, 1987), pp. 41–48.

In a different approach to Sima Qian's understanding of the historian's voice, Li Wai-yee cites the above list of literary exemplars, along with other passages, to argue that he grounded his claims to truth in personal experience, empathy, and the power of writing to derive meaning from the interplay of capricious fate and personal endeavour. See Li Wai-yee, "The Idea of Authority in the *Shi ji* (*Records of the Historian*)," *Harvard Journal of Asiatic Studies* 54:2 (1994): 345–405.

65. Sima Tan stated that the abundance of *ru* texts meant that their teach-ings could not be "completely mastered" (*tong* 通) nor their rituals "exhausted" (*jiu* 究). These are the verbs that Sima Qian applied to the aims of his own work.

66. Bai Shouyi, "Shuo 'cheng yi jia zhi yan' 说成一家之言," in *Sima Qian he Shi ji*, pp. 31–40; Zhang Dake, "Shi lun Sima Qian de yi jia zhi yan 试论司马迁 的一家之言," in *Shi ji yanjiu*, pp. 338–60; Zhang Dake, *Shi ji yanjiu*, p. 30; Durrant, *The Cloudy Mirror*, p. 125.

67. The phrase I have translated "establish a thread" is *ke tiao* 科條, which appears in Warring States texts as a noun phrase meaning "laws and regulations." In this sentence it is clearly a verb, and I think that the character *tiao* 條, which originally meant "branch, thread, line" here functions as a synonym gloss that explains the character *ji* 紀. These chapters provide the temporal "thread" or "cord" around which the work is structured. In this way, as will be discussed below, they are like the *jing* 經 section of the *Chun qiu*.

68. *Shi ji* 130, p. 3319.

69. Lewis, "Les rites comme trame de l'histoire."

70. The explanation of the inclusion of this chapter in the postface notes that Confucius "pursued and cultivated the arts of the canons [*jing shu* 經術] in order to attain the kingly Way," that he established "models/statutes of decorum [*yi fa* 儀法] for the whole world," and that he "handed down the unifying/guiding cord [*tong ji* 統紀] of the 'Six Arts' to later generations." This stipulates his kingly status, his role as "legislator," and his ability to establish a descent. The other anomalous "Hereditary House," that of Chen She, is justified by asserting a paral-lel between Chen She's role in overthrowing Qin and Confucius' composition of the *Chun qiu*, which "overthrew" the Zhou. See *Shi ji* 130, p. 3310.

71. On the category of *lie zhuan* in relation to such collective rubrics as *lie su* 宿, *lie xing* 星, *lie guo* 國, and *lie hou* 侯, see Li Shaoyong 李少雍, *Sima Qian zhuan ji*

wenxue lun gao 司马迁传记文学论稿 (Chongqing: Chongqing Chuban she, 1987), pp. 63–78.

72. For reconstructed pronunciations and definitions, see Karlgren, *Grammata serica recensa*, pp. 219 (#831c–d), 251 (#953i). For an example of *jing* and *ji* as a synonym compound, see note 30 of this chapter.

73. *Shi ji* 14, pp. 509–10. In addition to Sima Qian's statement that Zuo Qiuming had written the work from Confucius' own words to avoid misinterpretations by disciples, modern scholars have traced Sima Qian's reliance on the *Zuo zhuan* as a source. See, for example, Gu Lisan 顧立三, *Sima Qian chuan xie Shi ji caiyong Zuo zhuan de yanjiu* 司馬遷傳寫史記採用左傳的研究 (Taipei: Zhongzheng, 1981); Grant Hardy, "The Interpretive Function of *Shi chi* 14, 'The Table of Years of the Twelve Feudal Lords,'" *Journal of the American Oriental Society* 113.1 (1993): 14–24.

74. *Shi ji* 130, p. 3296. Sima Qian also discusses the relation of the set of canonical texts to his work on pp. 3297, 3299.

75. Stephen Durrant, "Ssu-ma Ch'ien's Portrayal of the First Ch'in Emperor," in *Imperial Rulership and Cultural Change in Traditional China*, ed. Frederick P. Brandauer and Chun-chieh Huang (Seattle: University of Washington, 1994), pp. 35–46.

76. *Shi ji zheng yi*, printed in the additional material at the end of *Shi ji* vol. 10, p. 13. This was expanded from a briefer version by Sima Zhen. For a discussion of the numeric structuring of the *Shi ji*, see Zhang Dake, "Shi ji ti zhi yi li jian lun," 史记体制义例简论, in *Shi ji yanjiu*, pp. 203–20. On the use of seventy or seventy-two as a magic number in Han texts, see Wen Yiduo, "Qi shi er 七十二," in *Shenhua yu shi* 神話與詩, in *Wen Yiduo quan ji*, vol. 1, pp. 207–20.

77. *Shi ji* 130, p. 3285; *Guo yu*, pp. 559–64; *Han shu* 25a, pp. 1189–91; Derk Bodde, "Myths of Ancient China," in *Mythologies of the Ancient World*, ed. Samuel Noah Kramer (New York: Doubleday, 1961), pp. 389–94; Anne Birrell, *Chinese Mythology: An Introduction* (Baltimore: Johns Hopkins University, 1993), pp. 91–95.

78. Jean Levi, *La Chine romanesque*, pp. 149–55; *Zuo zhuan zhu* Zhao 29, pp. 1500–02.

79. The following discussion of the sacrifices and Sima Qian's use of them is adapted from Mark Edward Lewis, "The Feng and Shan Sacrifices of Emperor Wu of the Han."

80. *Shi ji* 130, p. 3320. For the application of the phrase *ming shan* 名山 to the *feng* and *shan* sacrifices, see *Shi ji* 28, p. 1404.

81. *Shi ji* 130, p. 3295.

82. *Shi ji* 130, pp. 3297–3300.

83. *Shi ji* 28, p. 1355.

84. The *Shi ji's* use of accounts of Qin Shihuang to indirectly criticize Emperor Wu is discussed in detail in Michael Nylan, "Ying Shao's *Feng su t'ung yi:* An Exploration of Problems in Han Dynasty Political, Philosophical, and Social Unity" (Ph.D. diss., Princeton University, 1982), pp. 126–40.

85. The idea that criticism of Emperor Wu was central to the *Shi ji* dates back to Han times. After Wang Yun had killed the rebel general Dong Zhuo at the end of the dynasty, he condemned to death the scholar, calligrapher, and composer of funerary inscriptions, Cai Yong. The latter argued that he should be allowed to live in order to complete his history of the Han. Wang Yun replied that Emperor Wu had failed to execute Sima Qian and thereby allowed him to complete his "slanderous writings" (*bang shu* 謗書) and hand them down to later ages. See *Hou Han shu* 60b, p. 2006. For modern compilations of Sima Qian's criticisms of Emperor Wu, see Su Chengjian 苏诚鉴, "'Shi ji' shi dui Han Wudi de pipan shu 史记是对汉武帝的批判书," in *Sima Qian he Shi ji*, pp. 75–100; Shi Ding 施丁, "Sima Qian xie 'jin shang (Han Wudi)' 司马迁写今上 (汉武帝)," in *Sima Qian yanjiu xin lun*, pp. 137–62. For Levi's arguments, see *La Chine romanesque*, "Les Mémoires Historiques de Sima Qian: l'histoire rattrapée par le roman," pp. 140–72, esp. pp. 149–50; Levi, *Le fils du ciel et son annaliste* (Paris: Gallimard, 1992).

86. This doubling of the world by the text and the replacement of the former by the latter is described by Jean Levi. "The annals of the Grand Historian of the Han claim to substitute themselves for reality. When the events have taken place long ago, when the actors have been dead for centuries or even millennia, when the documents are all dispersed, lost, or destroyed, so that nothing remains but a single witness, then this witness has every chance to identify himself with the facts that he has preserved from nothingness. Existing only in and for this witness, the history ends by coinciding with the text that relates it. The event is swallowed by its trace, the real by its reflection. . . . Breaking the chain that attached it to reality, the history of Sima Qian attains the infinity and solitude of the work of art—alone and infinite in that it founds, like the work of art, its own world, a world where words and things fuse to engender an autonomous body, folded in on itself, withdrawn from all contact with the exterior." See *La Chine romanesque*, pp. 147–48.

87. *Shi ji* 117. The best study of Sima Xiangru's work is Yves Hervouet, *Un poète de cour sous les Han: Sseu-ma Siang-jou* (Paris: Presses Universitaires de France, 1964). Chapter Three of Hervouet's work discusses the evolution of verse between the examples discussed in chapter 3 and the writings of Sima Xiangru. Similar treatments in English are Watson, *Early Chinese Literature*, pp. 254–85; Knechtges, *The Han Rhapsody*, ch. 2, "The Rhapsody before Yang Hsiung."

88. Hervouet devotes chapters to both nouns and descriptive binomes in the poetic works. See *Sseu-ma Siang-jou*, ch. 6, "Noms propres et vocabulaire concret," ch. 7 "Le vocabulaire descriptif."

89. *Shi ji* 117 p. 3015

90. *Shi ji* 117, p. 3036.

91. *Shi ji* 117, pp. 3041–42.

92. Vendler, *The Odes of John Keats* (Cambridge: The Belknap Press of Harvard University, 1983), pp. 266–67.

93. *Shi ji* 117, p. 3016.

94. *Shi ji* 117, pp. 3044 (twice), 3051, 3067. Similar arguments appear in the

writings of the Eastern Han author Wang Chong, who demonstrated the superiority of the Han to even the idealized Zhou because the former received tribute from the states of Central Asia, which the latter had never obtained. See *Lun heng* 57 "Xuan Han" 宣漢, p. 191. Related passages in Sima Xiangru's prose pieces also note the spread of the emperor's rule to all creatures, a theme also suggested by the inclusive lists of plants and animals in the rhapsody. See *Shi ji* 117, pp. 3049, 3051, 3065 (twice), 3067, 3070.

95. The conflation of these two forms of "tribute" is shown in the first version of the temple hymns from the reign of Emperor Wu that commemorate obtaining new breeds of horses from Central Asia. The first hymn describes the arrival of a "spirit horse" (*shen ma* 神馬) from Wuwa as tribute (*gong* 貢) from the Grand Unity. This horse is also called a celestial horse (*tian ma* 天馬), as were the "blood-sweating" horses of Ferghana in a song written a few years later. In this second poem the arrival of the horses is identified with the submission of the Western peoples, and attributed to the emperor's awesome, spiritual power. Thus the same events are interpreted as both magic signs from Heaven and tribute from alien peoples. See *Shi ji* 24, p. 1178. Revised versions of the poems appear in *Han shu* 22, pp. 1060–61. On the history of the obtaining of the horses, see Dubs, *History of the Former Han Dynasty*, vol. 2, pp. 132–135, "The Blood-Sweating Horses of Ferghana." The writings of Wang Chong also link animals received as tribute with the appearance of magical animals. See the chapter cited in the preceding note, pp. 190–91.

96. For a list of the major positions and assessment of their relative merits, see Hervouet, *Sseu-ma Siang-jou*, pp. 288–302; Paul W. Kroll, "On 'Far Roaming'," *Journal of the American Oriental Society* 116.4 (October–December 1996): 653–55.

97. *Shi ji* 117, pp. 3063–65.

98. That the ruler's benevolence should reach to the lowest creatures had become a standard rhetorical trope by the late Warring States period. See *Lü shi chun qiu jiao shi* 8 "Jian xuan," p. 441; *Shi ji* 6, pp. 245, 252—these quote the stone inscriptions erected by Qin Shihuang; *Shizi* 2, p. 12a; *Wen xuan* 3, pp. 29a, 30a, 32a; Jia Yi, quoted in *Han shu* 48, p. 2253; *Shang shu da zhuan ji jiao* 1, pp. 11a–b.

99. Sima Xiangru also describes the *feng* and *shan* sacrifices as the culmination of Han power in his address to the people of Ba and Shu. See *Shi ji* 117, p. 3052.

100. *Han shu* 30, p. 1720. The work is entitled *Fan jiang* 凡將, a phrase which has no meaning and appears to be simply the first two characters of the work. This practice also provides the title of the work that immediately follows it in the catalog, the *Ji jiu* 急就. For a brief discussion of these works, see Hervouet, *Sseu-ma Siang-jou*, pp. 335–36.

101. After first reading the "Rhapsody on the Great Man," Emperor Wu had the feeling of floating on the clouds, as though he were wandering between earth and Heaven. See *Shi ji* 117, p. 3063.

102. *Shi ji* 117, pp. 3067–68. A call for turning records of the Han dynasty's glory into a "seventh classic" also appears in Wang Chong, *Lun heng*, "Xuan Han," p. 191.

103. *Shiji* 117, p. 3072.

104. *Shiji* 117, pp. 3002, 3053. Stories of discovery through writing and stuttering also figure in the *Shiji* biography of Han Fei, and the account of stuttering uses identical words. One account is patterned on the other. See *Shiji* 63, pp. 2146, 2155. I think it more likely that stories about his recent contemporary were read back into the past than vice versa, but this cannot be proven.

105. *Shiji* 117, p. 3063.

106. *Shiji* 117, pp. 3044, 3038. In both cases Sima Xiangru is charged by the emperor to let the people understand or know his idea/intention (*yi* 意).

107. Sima Qian states that after Sima Xiangru had presented the rhapsody, the emperor "had the energy/spirit [*qi* 氣] of one loftily soaring on the clouds, and evinced the untrammeled thoughts of one wandering between Heaven and Earth." See *Shiji* 117, p. 3063. The poem attains that of which the emperor can only dream.

108. Rudolf Pfeiffer, *History of Classical Scholarship*, vol. 1, *From the Beginnings to the End of the Hellenistic Age* (Oxford: Clarendon Press, 1968), Part I, ch. 3 "The Masters of Philosophy in Athens: Socrates, Plato, and Aristotle"; Part II, ch. 1, "The Rise of Scholarship in Alexandria." See also Miller, *Lyric Texts and Lyric Consciousness*, pp. 120–23.

109. See, for example, *Han shu* 36, p. 1970. Here Liu Xin argues that the "old text" versions of canonical texts demonstrated that many readings of these texts and the resultant philosophical positions elaborated in the early Han were based on mutilated copies that had lost their original sense. As a result, the established textual authorities sought to suppress the newly recovered versions. In his defense, Liu Xin stated:

> In the past, scholars who pieced works together did not think of the lacunae produced by discarded passages or abandoned traditions. They sloppily followed received stupidities and accepted blank spaces, breaking up characters and analyzing individual words, verbosely talking in petty, overdetailed phrases. Scholars grew old without being able to reach the end of a single canon. They put faith in orally transmitted explanations and ignored written records, treating as correct teachers of recent times and denouncing antiquity. It got so bad that when the state was going to have a major ritual, such as ceremonies for establishing the *biyong* [辟雍, the building for the Grand Academy], the *feng* and *shan* sacrifices, or imperial processions, then all was silence and darkness and no one knew their origins. They still clung to their tatters and fragments [of documents], clutching fearfully to private opinions that had been demolished, with no public-minded spirit that followed the good and submitted to the right. Some harbored petty jealousies, did not examine the facts, imitated one another in every detail, according with received reputations in deciding right and wrong. They suppressed these three [fields of] study, arguing that the [orally transmitted] *Shang shu* was complete and that Master Zuo [Qiuming] had not transmitted [or "made a commentary on"] the *Spring and Autumn Annals*. Is this not pitiful?

110. Alvin Kernan, *Printing Technology, Letters & Samuel Johnson* (Princeton: Princeton University, 1987), pp. 245–46. For a study of libraries in early China, see Jean-Pierre Drège, *Les bibliotèques en Chine au temps des manuscrits* (Paris: Ecole Française d'Extrême-Orient, 1991).

111. *Han shu* 30, p. 1701. The "collective epitome" (*ji lüe* 輯略) which preceded that on the Six Arts presumably characterized the entire collection. As the most comprehensive discussion it was put in the first position. However, it was removed between the time of Liu Xin and Ban Gu, or perhaps by Ban Gu himself.

112. Elsewhere Liu Xiang traces a sagely line from the Yellow Emperor through Yao, Shun, Yu, Tang, King Wen, King Wu, and the Duke of Zhou, and ending with Confucius. See *Han shu* 36, p. 1956.

113. The monograph does not state that the canons were produced by kings, but this doctrine is enunciated elsewhere in the *Han shu*. Thus the beginning of the collective chapter on *ru* states, "The 'Six Arts' are the guiding documents of royal teaching, the means by which the former sages illumined the Way of Heaven, corrected human relations, and achieved a complete model for supreme order." See *Han shu* 88, p. 3589. Moreover, the individual "arts" are virtually all attributed to sages in the catalog. See *Han shu* 30, pp. 1704—the *Yi* "as for people it passed through the three sages [Fu Xi, Duke of Zhou, Confucius], and as for ages it passed through the Three Antiquities"; 1706—the *Documents* originated in the sages copying of the "River chart" and the "Luo Document"; 1708—the *Odes* were "the means by which the kings observed the customs"; 1710—the *Rites* originated in the "alternation of simplicity and ornament of the Thearchs and kings, each age having what it subtracted or added"; 1711—music was created by the former kings, from the Yellow Emperor down to the Three Dynasties"; 1715—the *Annals* originated from "the astrologers/historians of the ancient kings" who recorded the kings' words and actions. Each of the canons is also identified with the sages through having been edited or transmitted by Confucius. That the *Annals* alone is associated with an office rather than the king may reflect the fact that it is the one canonical text supposedly written, rather than merely edited, by Confucius, and hence is not the work of actual kings, but only a "king without attributes" in the realm of literature. The importance of Confucius is emphasized by the inclusion of the *Lun yu* and the *Xiao jing* under the rubric of canonical "arts," even though they were not officially canonical texts. On the ambiguous status of these two works in the Han, see Tsai Yen-zen, "Ching and Chuan: Towards Defining the Confucian Scriptures in Han China" (Ph.D. diss., Harvard University, 1993), pp. 206–79.

114. The writings of the *ru* tradition are said "to move among the six canons." See p. 1728. The justification of the Daoists mentions the *Yi*—p. 1732. The "school of names" is said to derive from the *Rites*, and the justification cites Confucius on the rectification of names—p. 1737. Mohist doctrines are traced back to ritual teachings on funerals and related matters—p. 1738. The "school of alliances" is justified by reference to Confucius' insistence on the use of the *Odes* on diplomatic missions—p. 1740. The justification of the "agrarian school" cites the "Hong fan"

chapter of *Shang shu* and Confucius—p. 1743. The category of "petty talk" (*xiao shuo* 小說) is justified by a quote from Confucius—p. 1745. The general discussion of the category of the masters cites the *Yi* and Confucius, and argues that all the masters are "branches" and "currents" of the six canons—p. 1746. The discussion of lyric verse and rhapsody justifies these writings as derivatives from the canonical *Odes*—pp. 1755–56. The military texts are all explained as derivations from the "Hong fan," the *Yi*, and the writings of Confucius. The *Sima fa*, classed as a ritual text, is the sole military treatise identified as the legacy of the sages. The Warring States period treatises, by contrast, represent a corruption of military thought—p. 1762. The subcategories of "numbers and divination" are justified with reference to the *Yi* or the *Shu*—pp. 1765, 1769, 1771, 1773, 1775. The category of "formulae and techniques" alone cites no canonical roots, although it clearly states that these were likewise the charge of the king's officials, and that the major medical thinkers "assessed illnesses in order to reach to [knowledge] of the state, and began with diagnosis in order to know about government"—p. 1780.

115. *Han shu* 30, p. 1746.

116. *Han shu* 30, p. 1756.

117. This treatment of the rhapsody as an inferior derivative of the ode was embraced by Ban Gu in his "Rhapsodies on the Two Capitals," both in the preface and his decision to close the piece with a set of odes. See *Wen xuan*, pp. 1, 22–24.

118. *Han shu* 30, p. 1723.

119. *Han shu* 30, pp. 1704—the account of Fu Xi's invention of the hexagrams from the patterns of Heaven and Earth introduces the monograph proper and the discussion of the *Yi*, 1706, 1708—the justification of the *Shi* cites the *Shu*'s statement about "the articulation of aspirations," but since the *Shu* was justified by a quotation from the *Yi*, the latter provides the ultimate grounding, 1710.

120. *Han shu* 30, pp. 1728, 1732, 1734, 1736, 1737, 1738, 1740, 1742, 1743, 1745, 1755, 1762, 1775, 1780.

121. On the definition by Liu Xiang of the canon as what is constant (*chang* 常) and runs through all things (*tong* 通), see *Han shu* 36, p. 1941.

122. *Han shu* 30, pp. 1704, 1706, 1708, 1710, 1715, 1717, 1719. This faulty transmission of the canonical texts is summarized in the discussion of the *ru* tradition.

> The splendors of Yao and Shun, the flourishing of the Shang and Zhou, the work of Confucius, these were already tested and proved efficacious. But the deluded lost their refined subtleties, and the biased followed the changing fashions of the times. They turned against and departed from the foundations of the Way. They acted heedlessly in order to delude the masses and seek favor. Those who came later followed them, so that the Five Canons were distorted and fragmented, and *ru* studies gradually waned. This was the calamity of biased *ru*.

See p. 1728.

123. *Han shu* 30, pp. 1728, 1732, 1734–35, 1736, 1737, 1738, 1740, 1742, 1743, 1745.

124. *Han shu* 30 pp. 1756, 1762–63, 1765, 1767, 1769, 1771, 1773, 1776, 1778, 1779, 1780.

125. One possible exception is the inclusion of writings on agriculture under the rubric of the "masters." This probably reflects the fact that most agricultural writing was actually about government, for example, the teachings in the tradition of Shen Nong, and that no technical specialist on agriculture was at the court.

126. On the links of the rhapsody genre to word magic and the casting of spells, see Harper, "Wang Yen-shou's Nightmare Poem," pp. 240–41, 254–82.

Chapter Eight. The Empire of Writing

1. Most Asian scholars, such as Kanaya Osamu, Uchino Kumaichirō, and Xu Fuguan, do not even broach the question. Benjamin Schwartz suggests how the "classics" were distinguished from other texts, but says nothing on their establishment as a state canon. See Schwartz, *The World of Thought*, ch. 10, esp. pp. 400–06. Michael Loewe traces the establishment and development of the canon, without suggesting any explanation for the process. See Loewe, *Chinese Ideas of Life and Death: Faith, Myth and Reason in the Han period* (London: Allen & Unwin), ch. 16. Robert Kramers argues that the official canon was established because Emperor Wu was interested in rituals, administration, and the recruitment of officials. However, none of these were exclusive *ru* preserves, and in terms of the second and third points the *ru* were inferior to their rivals. See Kramers, "The Development of the Confucian Schools," *Cambridge History of China: Volume 1, The Ch'in and Han Empires* (Cambridge: Cambridge University, 1986), pp. 755–56. Homer Dubs suggests four reasons: (1) Confucianism was suited to be a philosophy of imperial government because Confucius had held office and many of his pupils had done likewise, (2) *ru* who did not serve the state became teachers, hence those who wanted to study the major texts had recourse to the *ru*, and even rulers were trained by *ru*, (3) a proto-examination system based on literary ability was graded by *ru* and hence they controlled access to office, and (4) the advantage of intellectually unifying the country under one system of thought was recognized. See Dubs, tr., *History*, vol. 2, pp. 341–53, esp. pp. 351–53. The first reason is wrong, both because of *ru* attitudes to service discussed in chapter 2 and the fact that the "historical" Confucius had little to do with the activities of Han *ru*. The third is fantasy. Candidates were submitted by those eminent in their communities and their essays were read by the emperor or his advisers. After the establishment of the Imperial Academy, annual examinations in the *ru* canon led to office, but this was effect and not cause. The fourth explains the desire for a state canon, but not the choice made. The second explanation was a significant factor, but it was only one among several, and not the most important.

2. The significance of making inscriptions in stone, their derivation from the earlier use of bronzes, and their links to later funerary practice are discussed in K. E. Brashier, "Evoking the Ancestor: the Stele Hymn of the Eastern Han Dynasty" (Ph.D. diss., Cambridge University, 1997).

3. *Shi ji* 121, p. 3117.

4. *Shi ji* 57, pp. 2071–72; 84, p. 2492; 97, p. 2700.

5. Qian Mu 錢穆, "Liang Han boshi jia fa kao 兩漢博士家法考," in *Liang Han jingxue jin gu wen pingyi* 兩漢經學今古文平議 (Taipei: Dadong, 1978), pp. 174–75.

6. All prior discussions of the question were largely jettisoned in the wake of the discovery of the silk manuscripts at Mawangdui, but these have resolved nothing. Peerenboom in his *Law and Morality* defines "Huang-Lao" exclusively through the Mawangdui manuscripts. Roth in his articles cited earlier defines it through the Mawangdui manuscripts, the four chapters of the *Guanzi* discussed in chapter 1, the "syncretic" chapters of the *Zhuangzi*, the *Huainanzi*, and Sima Tan's account of Daoism in the postface of the *Shi ji*. John Major, in his translation of chapters from the *Huainanzi*, takes this text as definitive of Huang-Lao. The only philosophers to whom Sima Qian attributes the term, Han Fei and Shen Buhai, are universally rejected as cases of reading Han categories back into earlier periods. Since the only person to use the term in writing when the philosophy supposedly existed is rejected as a source for defining it, "Huang-Lao" is doomed to serve only as a convenient shorthand for modern scholars formulating their own analyses of the intellectual currents in the early Han period.

7. Although written before the Mawangdui finds became available, Kanaya Osamu's study of "Huang-Lao" remains in many ways the most valuable, because he follows the *Shi ji* in treating it as primarily a phenomenon among political figures, with its scholastic antecedents remaining secondary and diffuse. See Kanaya, *Shin Kan shisō shi kenkyū*, pp. 113–89. In addition to being espoused by followers of the Han founder whose military successes had led to high office, men such as Cao Shen, Chen Ping, and Zhang Liang, the intellectual transmission of Huang-Lao traced by Sima Qian enters history when transmitted for several generations by members of the Le family. This was a family of hereditary military commanders, and the first masters of Huang-Lao were the immediate descendants of Le Yi, a famous general. See *Shi ji* 80, p. 2436.

One Western scholar who has argued that the term Huang-Lao defined a fundamentally political stance is Hans van Ess. See his "The Meaning of Huang-Lao in *Shi ji* and *Han shu*," *Etudes chinoises* 12:2 (1993): 161–77; "Die geheimen Worte des Ssu-ma Ch'ien," *Oriens Extremus* 36:1 (1993): 5–28.

8. The Yellow Emperor was the mythic inventor of warfare and punishments. He embodied rule through force in mythic opposition to such figures as the Divine Husbandman. The Mawangdui manuscript is full of discussions of the necessity and proper conduct of warfare. See Lewis, *Sanctioned Violence*, ch. 5. As for the *Dao de jing*, its language of reversal—both natural process as reversal and the

overturning of conventional expectations—played a prominent role in the writings of the military treatises. The *Shiji* attributes Zhang Liang's military brilliance to a text received from an incarnation of Laozi. See Lewis, *Sanctioned Violence*, pp. 100–01; Christopher Rand, "The Role of Military Thought in Early Chinese Intellectual History" (Ph.D. diss., Harvard University, 1977), p. 91, note 7, pp. 93–94, note 18.

9. *Shiji* 57, p. 2074; 120, p. 3107.

10. *Shiji* 55, p. 2048; 56, pp. 2062–63. Several of the leading political actors associated with Huang-Lao or proto-Daoism were prone to repeated illness. Whether this was a result of unusual diets, or a cause of their interest in longevity is not clear. See *Shiji* 55, p. 2040; 120, pp. 3105, 3107.

11. *Shiji* 54, pp. 2028–30. The Master Gai from whom Cao Shen learns the arts of Huang-Lao is listed in Sima Qian's account of the tradition as having studied under Le Chengong, thus having received the doctrine directly from the family with whom it seems to have originated. See *Shiji* 80, p. 2346. The association with Qi state might also be significant, for the Yellow Emperor was prominent in that region. On Chen Ping, see *Shiji* 56, pp. 2052, 2060–62.

12. *Shiji* 84, p. 2492; 101, pp. 2746, 2747; 104, pp. 2824–25; *Han shu* 48, pp. 2230, 2233–34, 2237–43.

13. *Shiji* 49, p. 1975; 121, pp. 3117, 3122. The Dowager Empress's two brothers had tutors provided by Zhou Bo and Guan Fu, the leaders of the "military" faction. See *Shiji* 49, p. 1974.

14. *Shiji* 121, p. 3122; 130, p. 3288.

15. *Shiji* 121 p. 3123.

16. *Shiji* 120, pp. 3105, 3106.

17. On Zhang Tang's use of laws to destroy locally powerful families and his introduction of the Confucian classics into the field of law, see *Shiji* 122, pp. 3137–47. See especially p. 3139, which describes Zhang Tang's use of the *Documents* and *Chun qiu* to decide cases, and the way he "manipulated texts to skillfully condemn" (*wu wen qiao di* 舞文巧詆).

18. *Shiji* 120, pp. 3107–08. The linking of Zhang Tang—leading advocate of rule through elaborate legal codes—and Gongsun Hong—leading advocate of rule through ritual and canonical texts—throughout the biography of Ji An is echoed in the career of Ni Kuan, a second-generation disciple of Fu Sheng's transmission of the *Shang shu*. Having mastered this *ru* classic, he was recommended to the court where he studied with Kong Anguo. At court he attracted the attention of Zhang Tang, whose assistant he became. He later rose to the highest posts at court, where he was noted for skillful compliance with the emperor's desires, and never seeking to remonstrate or correct. See *Shiji* 121, p. 3125.

19. *Shiji* 109, p. 2876. The year after Li Guang's death, a cousin of his also committed suicide to avoid the clerks. The clerks' "eraser-knives" are also linked with the taking of lives in *Shiji* 120, p. 3143.

20. *Shiji* 130, pp. 3289, 3290.

21. On the philosophical and institutional origins of this principle in the Warring States, see Lewis, *Sanctioned Violence*, pp. 121–33. On its still being practiced in the early Han, see *Shi ji* 57, p. 2074; *Han shu* 67, p. 2910.

22. *Shi ji* 111, pp. 2927–28, 2929. Wei Qing's biography is shared with Emperor Wu's other favorite general, He Qubing, who also gained office as a relative of the emperor by marriage.

23. *Shi ji* 120, p. 3107 refers to Emperor Wu receiving Wei Qing while the emperor is in the toilet.

24. Yu Yingshi 余英時, "Gudai zhishi jieceng de xingqi yu fazhan古代知識階層的興起與發展," in *Zhongguo zhishi jieceng shi lun* 中國知識階層史論 (Taipei: Lianjing, 1980), pp. 85–86.

25. For accounts of the means by which feudatory princes attracted scholars, see *Shi ji* 58, p. 2083; 59, p. 2093; 118, p. 3077. On Sima Xiangru see *Shi ji* 117, p. 2999.

26. Liu An is the subject of biographies in *Shi ji* 118 and *Han shu* 44. Modern studies include Benjamin Wallacker, "Liu An, the Second King of Huai-nan," *Journal of the American Oriental Society* 92 (1972): 36–51; Kanaya Osamu, *Rōso teki sekai: Enanji no shisō* 老莊的世界: 淮南子の思想 (Kyoto: Heirakuji Shoten, 1959), pp. 19–67.

27. *Shi ji* 121, p. 3121. On the duties of the office of Prefect of the Gentlemen-of-the-Palace, later retitled "Superintendent of the Imperial Household," see Hans Bielenstein, *The Bureaucracy of Han Times* (Cambridge: Cambridge University, 1980), pp. 23–31.

28. *Shi ji* 103, pp. 2768–70; 107, p. 2841.

29. *Han shu* 6, pp. 155–56. Because this memorial is not mentioned in the *Shi ji*, Sima Qian dismisses Wei Wan as a man who did "nothing worth mentioning," and Wei Wan was rapidly discharged, Qian Mu argues that the memorial must have come from Dong Zhongshu. He identifies it with Dong Zhongshu's three replies to Emperor Wu's questions in *Han shu* 56, pp. 2495–523. See *Liang Han jingxue jin gu wen*, pp. 175–77. This argument is groundless. The *Han shu* distinguishes the two proposals not only in their contents but also their nature, describing the one as a memorial and the other as a set of replies to questions. While the account in *Han shu* 56 seems to suggest that the replies were made in 140 B.C., that in *Han shu* 6, pp. 160–61 makes it clear that Dong Zhongshu first emerged in the call for appointments made in 134 B.C. There is no evidence of a ban on students of the stipulated philosophers after 140, and Emperor Wu's approval of Wei Wan's proposal should be interpreted as a simple mark of respect for an old teacher who was soon to be removed from his post of influence.

The causes of Wei Wan's dismissal are not clear. One account merely confirms that he was removed in 140 B.C. A second states that he retired on account of ill health. A third says that the new emperor removed him for having failed to help some falsely imprisoned officials in the last years of the reign of Emperor Jing. See

Shi ji 22, p. 1133; 103, p. 2770; 107, p. 2842. In all likelihood the new emperor simply desired to free himself from a man appointed by his father to keep him under control. The removal would have been supported by his grandmother who still was a powerful force in the court.

30. Accounts of this factional struggle are scattered through several chapters. See *Shi ji* 12, p. 452; 28, p.1384; 107, p. 2843; 121, pp. 3121–23. The *Han shu* adds the detail that the dowager empress accused Zhao and Wang of acting like Xinyuan Ping. See *Han shu* 88, p. 3608. This figure had faked portents in order to persuade Emperor Wen to establish sacrifices to the Five Emperors (*wu di* 五帝) and begin preparations for the *feng* and *shan* sacrifices. See *Shi ji* 28, pp. 1382–83. Thus there was some overlap in his ritual reforms and those proposed at the beginning of the reign of Emperor Wu.

31. *Han shu* 6, p. 159 records that erudites for the five classics were established in 136, a year before the empress's death. This event is not mentioned in the *Shi ji*, and it is unlikely to have taken place against the empress's wishes after the debacle of 139 B.C. In all likelihood the single line in the *Han shu* is out of place.

32. On the calls for recommendations of scholars, see *Shi ji* 28, p. 1384; *Han shu* 6, pp. 155–56, 160. *Han shu* 56, the biography of Dong Zhongshu, is based largely on the section on this scholar from *Shi ji* 121, pp. 3127–28, with the addition of the three questions and responses, a couple of anecdotes, and a list of his writings. The narrative in the *Han shu* chapter suggests that all the questions and replies occurred in 140, immediately followed by Dong Zhongshu's appointment as chief minister in the fief of Jiangdu, but the point of insertion in a borrowed narrative is scarcely conclusive. Many scholars have discussed the issue, but there is no real evidence and all the conclusions amount to guesswork. See, for example, Li Weixiong 李威熊, *Dong Zhongshu yu Xi Han xueshu* 董仲舒與西漢學術 (Taipei: Wen Shi Zhe, 1978), pp. 8–10; Dubs, *History of the Former Han Dynasty*, vol. 2, p. 38; Qian Mu, *Qin Han shi* 秦漢史 (Taipei: Sanmin, 1969), pp. 76–77; Sarah Queen, *From Chronicle to Canon: the Hermeneutics of the "Spring and Autumn" According to Tung Chung-shu* (Cambridge: Cambridge University, 1996), pp. 21–25.

33. Sima Qian divides the scholarly world of the reign of Emperor Wu into two groups: flatterers and sycophants who flourished, and forthright scholars who did not. Men like Gongsun Hong and Zhang Tang fall into the former group, as do the numerous masters of esoteric arts (*fang shi* 方士) who sought the emperor's favor. Men such as Ji An, Shen Pei, Dong Zhongshu, and Sima Qian himself are in the latter group. This contrast parallels that between simple military men like Li Kuang and Li Ling, on the one hand, and flatterers like Wei Qing on the other. The *Han shu* tries to play up Dong Zhongshu's success by extensive quotation of his responses and one remark that the emperor found his first response "distinctive" or "unusual" (*yi* 異). Nevertheless, the conclusion of the chapter rejects Liu Xiang's suggestion that Dong Zhongshu was a match for such leading ministers as Yi Yin, Tai Gong, Guan Zhong, and Yan Ying, and opts for Liu Xin's milder praise.

Zhongshu encountered the aftereffects of Qin's destruction of scholarship. The Six Classics were scattered, so he "pulled down his curtain" [retired from public life to teach] in anger, and immersed himself in the great task [of restoring the classics]. He gave a unity to later scholars, and became the head/founder of the *ru* group. However, if you examine what flowed from his teachings, he did not reach the level of Zi You or Zi Xia. To say that Guan Zhong or Yan Ying were no match for him, or that he was on a level with Yi Yin or Tai Gong, is exaggerated.

See *Han shu* 56, pp. 2506, 2526. This judgment—that Dong Zhongshu was of significance only as a scholar and teacher, that his primary importance was his influence on later generations, and that even in that field he was not to be placed in the first rank—seems fair.

34. *Shi ji* 121, pp. 3118–20. Sima Qian places Gongsun Hong's appointment and this memorial directly after the statement that as chancellor from 135, Tian Fen had "demoted the words of Huang-Lao, *xing-ming*, and the hundred schools, and invited several hundred *ru* educated in texts." Thus he clearly regards this as the moment in which textual studies were established within the government.

35. On the changing numbers of disciples, erudites, and texts, see Bielenstein, *Bureaucracy*, pp. 138–41.

36. On the Music Bureau and its relation to *ru* theories, see Diény, *Aux origines de la poésie classique en Chine*. On the importance of Emperor Wu as a patron for verse, see David Knechtges, "The Emperor and Literature: Emperor Wu of the Han," in *Imperial Rulership and Cultural Change in Traditional China*, pp. 51–76.

37. The "Fundamental Chronicle" of Emperor Wu's reign begins with the statement that he "particularly reverenced sacrifices to ghosts and spirits" (*you jing gui shen zhi si* 尤敬鬼神之祀), and the chapter is devoted almost entirely to ritual activities. See *Shi ji* 12, p. 451. It is based largely on *Shi ji* 28, the "Monograph on the *Feng* and *Shan* Sacrifices," which concentrates on rituals performed by Emperor Wu.

38. The classic treatment of this development is Lao Gan 勞榦, "Lun Han dai de nei chao yu wai chao 論漢代的內朝與外朝," *Lishi Yuyan Yanjiusuo Jikan* 13 (1948): 227–67. In English, see Wang Yü-ch'üan, "An Outline of the Central Government of the Former Han Dynasty," *Harvard Journal of Asiatic Studies* 12 (1949): 166–73; T'ung-tsu Ch'ü, *Han Social Structure*, ed. Jack L. Dull (Seattle: University of Washington, 1972), pp. 170–71, 216–17; 234–35. The closer control of generals, culminating in the absorption of the highest military command in the "inner court," was part of the same phenomenon.

39. Michael Loewe, "The Campaigns of Han Wu-ti," in *Chinese Ways in Warfare*, ed. Frank A. Kierman, Jr. (Cambridge: Harvard University, 1974), pp. 67–122; Ying-shih Yü, *Trade and Expansion in Han China: A Study in the Structure of Sino-Barbarian Economic Relations* (Berkeley: University of California, 1967).

40. The classic account remains Katō Shigeru 加藤繁, *Shina keizaishi kōshō* 支那經濟史考證 (Tokyo: Tōyō Bunko, 1952–53), vol. 1, pp. 41ff, 60ff. In English,

see Nancy Lee Swann, *Food and Money in Ancient China* (Princeton: Princeton University, 1950), pp. 62ff, 278ff, 366ff. See also Li Jiannong 李劍農, *Xian Qin liang Han jingji shi gao* 先秦兩漢經濟史稿 (Beijing: Sanlian, 1957), pp. 249ff.

41. *Shi ji* 122, pp. 3133–34—this first case actually occurs in the reign of Emperor Jing, and the official is executed at the demand of Empress Dou; 3135, 3139—this passage notes that the most severe clerks were literary scholars, apparently *ru*, for they or their superior are praised by Gongsun Hong; 3140—this passage links the introduction of the imperial monopolies and coinage reform with the law-based assaults on powerful families; 3145, 3145–46, 3146, 3148, 3150.

42. *Shi ji* 17, p. 802; 21, p. 1071; 112, p. 2961; *Han shu* 6, p. 170; 14, p. 395; 15, p. 427; 53, p. 2425; 64a, p. 2802.

43. *Han shu* 9, p. 277. "When he [the heir-apparent] had grown up, he was soft and benevolent, and loved the *ru*. He saw that Emperor Xuan employed many clerks versed in written law, who used *xing ming* as a standard for the people. . . . Once while attending on [Emperor Xuan] at a banquet, he urged, 'Your majesty wields punishments too greatly, you ought to employ the *ru* scholars.' Emperor Xuan scowled and said, 'The Han house has its own institutions, based on the mixing of the Way of kings and that of hegemons. How can we simply rely on transformation through virtue, and use Zhou policies? Moreover, the vulgar *ru* do not understand what is suitable to the times. They love to affirm antiquity to criticize the present, thereby causing people to be confused about names and realities. Not knowing what must be protected, how could they merit being employed?' He then sighed, 'The one who will bring chaos to our house is the heir-apparent!'"

44. Cho-yun Hsu, "The Changing Relationship between Local Society and the Central Political Power in Former Han: 206 B.C.–8 A.D.," *Comparative Studies in Society and History* 7 (July 1965): 358–70; Li Weitai 李偉泰, *Han chu xueshu ji Wang Chong "Lun heng" shu lun gao* 漢初學術及王充論衡述論稿 (Taipei: Changan, 1986), ch. 1.

45. Sun Yutang 孫毓堂, "Xi Han de bing zhi 西漢的兵制," in *Zhongguo shehui jingji shi congkan* 中國社會經濟史叢刊 5 (Shanghai: Shangwu, 1937), pp. 1–74; Sun Yutang, "Dong Han bing zhi de yanbian 東漢兵制的演變," in *Zhongguo shehui jingji shi congkan* 6 (Shanghai: Shangwu, 1939), pp. 1–34; Lao Gan, "Han dai bing zhi ji Han jian zhong de bing zhi 漢代兵制及漢簡中的兵制," *Lishi Yuyan Yanjiusuo Jikan* 10 (1948): 23–55; He Changqun 賀昌群, "Dong Han geng yi shu yi zhidu de feizhi 東漢更役戍役制度的廢止," *Lishi Yanjiu* 5 (1962): 96–115; Hamaguchi Shigekuni 濱口重國, *Shin Kan Zui Tō shi no kenkyū* 秦漢隋唐史の研究, vol. 1 (Tokyo: Tōkyō Daigaku, 1966), pp. 291–325; Mark Edward Lewis, "The Han Abolition of Universal Military Service," in *Military Thought and Practice in China*. ed. Hans van de Ven (Cambridge: Cambridge University, in press).

46. The decline of the free, small-scale yeomanry and rise of landlordism, as well as state responses to these developments, have been traced in several studies. See Nishijima Sadao, "The economic and social history of Former Han," and Patricia Ebrey, "The economic and social history of Later Han," in *Cambridge History*

of China, Vol. 1, the Ch'in and Han Empires, pp. 551–648; Nishijima, *Chūgoku kodai no shakai to keizai* 中國古代の社會と經濟 (Tokyo: Tōkyō Daigaku, 1981), ch. 3; Cho-yun Hsu, *Han Agriculture: the Formation of the Early Chinese Agrarian Economy* (Seattle: University of Washington, 1980), ch. 1–2.

47. *Lun yu zhengyi* 16 "Ji shi," pp. 354–56. See also 3 "Ba yi," pp. 41, 43, 46, 56; 8 "Tai Bo," p. 163; 16 "Ji shi," p. 356; 17 "Yang Huo," p. 378; 19 "Zi Zhang," pp. 407, 408.

48. The *Xunzi* is not so negative as the *Mencius,* in that like the *Lun yu* it accepts some actions of the hegemons as appropriate to their times, and some later chapters take a positive interest in the reforms of Qin. Nevertheless, in advocating the Zhou "later kings" as the highest political model and condemning its own age (the late Warring States), the *Xunzi*'s model of history is closely linked to that of the *Mencius.*

49. Lewis, *Sanctioned Violence,* pp. 44–45.

50. The association of the decline of the Zhou with the murder of rulers and fathers first appears in the *Mencius,* which links these phenomena with the appearance of rival philosophical schools in its account of Confucius' composition of the *Chun qiu.* See *Mengzi zhengyi* 6 "Teng Wen Gong xia," pp. 266–67. The *Xunzi* describes its own age in similar terms, including the murder of princes and superiors in a list of crimes committed by the people due to the introduction of currency, as well as taxes on agriculture and commerce. See *Xunzi ji jie* 10 "Fu guo," p. 118. By the Han it had become a convention to cite the *Chun qiu* as a work that recorded the assassinations of princes, the murders of fathers, and the destruction of states. See, for example, *Huainanzi* 9 "Zhu shu," p. 150; *Shuo yuan* 3 "Jian ben" 建本, p. 8a; 19 "Xiu wen," p. 19a—this last refers to the murder of rulers and fathers together with the recurrent formula used in the *Gongyang* to describe the age of Confucius, in which there is no Son of Heaven and no hegemons of the four quarters. The idea that the *Chun qiu* pays great attention to such murders is confirmed by an examination of the *Harvard-Yenching Institute Sinological Index Series, No. 11, Combined Concordances to Ch'un-Ch'iu, Kung-yang, Ku-liang and Tso-chuan,* which has over three pages of references to such events. See pp. 2290–93.

51. *Shi ji* 130, pp. 3297, 3299.

52. This last position resembles the philosophy that Sima Qian called "Huang-Lao," but descriptions of the participants, and their frequent references to the *ru* canon and an idealized Zhou, show that this was not the case. They represent the position of provincial *ru* who had no place in the court and objected to its intrusion in local affairs. They were the descendants of the "petty *ru*" denounced by the *Xunzi.*

53. For an account of the *Yan tie lun,* see Loewe, ed., *Early Chinese Texts,* pp. 477–82. For an English translation in two parts, see Esson M. Gale, *Discourses on Salt and Iron* (Leiden: E. J. Brill, 1931); Gale, with Peter A. Boodberg and T. C. Lin, "Discourses on Salt and Iron (*Yen T'ieh Lun*: Chaps: XX–XXVIII)," *Journal of the*

North China Branch of the Royal Asiatic Society 65 (1934): 73–110. These were reissued in a single volume as *Discourses on Salt and Iron* (Taipei: Chengwen, 1967). An English summary of the arguments appears in Michael Loewe, *Crisis and Conflict in Han China* (London: George Allen & Unwin, 1974), ch. 3. The most useful study is Xu Fuguan 徐復觀, "*Yan tie lun* zhong de zhengzhi shehui wenhua wenti 鹽鐵論中的政治社會文化問題," *Xinya Xuebao* 11 (September 1975): 337–418; reprinted in Xu Fuguan, *Liang Han sixiang shi* 兩漢思想史, vol. 3 (Taipei: Xuesheng, 1980), pp. 117–216.

54. See note #43.

55. For the passage, which deals with the rise of the Yellow Emperor, see *Lü shi chun qiu jiao shi* 13 "Ying tong 應同," p. 677. Another version of the story appears in *Shi ji* 28, p. 1366. On Qin's adoption of the patron phase "water" and associated policies, see *Shi ji* 6, pp. 237–38.

56. Gu Jiegang, *Gu shi bian* 古史辯 (rep. ed., Shanghai: Guji, 1982), vol. 5, pp. 430–49, 492–99; Loewe, *Chinese Ideas of Life and Death*, pp. 153–54; Wu Hung, *The Wu Liang Shrine*, pp. 88–91.

57. On the pre-imperial use of the term *shi* 士 and the evolving nature of political service, see Lewis, *Sanctioned Violence*, pp. 30–33, 75–78.

58. These doctrines are discussed in Hihara, *Shunjū Kuyōden no kenkyū*, ch. 5.

59. *Han shu* 48, pp. 2254–58; *Jiazi xin shu jiao shi* 2 "Jie ji 階級," pp. 241–82. On the debates in commentaries on ritual texts, see Yang Bojun's commentary to the *Zuo zhuan* in *Zuo zhuan zhu* Ai 16, p. 1699; *Wei shu* 108.4, p. 2794.

60. *Han shu* 56, pp. 2512, 2520–21.

61. *Yan tie lun* 1 "Ben yi 本議," pp. 1, 2 (twice); 4 "Cuo bi 錯幣," p. 5; 9 "Ci quan 刺權," p. 11; 10 "Ci fu 刺復," p. 12; 13 "Yuan chi 園池," p. 15; 17 "Pin fu 貧富," pp. 19, 20; 18 "Hui xue 毀學," p. 21; *Shuo yuan* 7 "Zheng li 政理," pp. 1b–2a—this passage argues for the use of rewards and punishments in ranking people, with rewards and salary to distinguish those of merit and punishment to keep the people in line; 14 "Zhi gong 至公," p. 1b—"The public-spiritedness of an official lies in not engaging in family business while administering official duties, and not speaking of goods and profit while in the public buildings"; 14 "Fu en 復恩," p. 1a—"The ruler and minister draw together through the Way of the market. The ruler bestows a generous salary, and the minister exhausts his strength to pay it back."

62. This ideal figured in the Han myths of Confucius, particularly the accounts of his starvation between Chen and Kuang. The *Xin xu* gathers stories on this theme in chapters 7 "Jie shi 節士" and 8 "Yi yong 義勇." The *Shuo yuan* collects them in chapters 4 "Li jie 立節" and 6 "Fu en 復恩." For stories in the *Han shi wai zhuan* on "scholars' integrity" in relation to the economic position of scholars and ties to the ruler, see Xu Fuguan, *Liang Han sixiang shi*, vol. 3, pp. 34–42. On the theme of the exchange of devotion for recognition as the organizing principle supporting the emergence of a "bureaucratic" mode of government, see Lewis, *Sanctioned Violence*, pp. 75–78.

63. Yu Yingshi 余英時, "Dong Han zhengquan zhi jianli yu shi zu da xing zhi guanxi 東漢政權之建立與士族大姓之關系," *Xinya Xuebao* 1:2 (February 1956): 209–16.

64. For surveys of the status of merchants in the Han, see the pages listed in the index entry on "Merchants" in Ch'ü, *Han Social Structure*; Nishijima, "The economic and social history of Former Han," pp. 574–85.

65. See, for example, the remarks of Jia Yi in *Han shu* 48, pp. 2242–45; *Jiazi xin shu jiao shi* 3 "Shi bian 時變," pp. 306–22; "Nie chan zi 孽產子," pp. 335–46.

66. The emergence of the great families and their shifting relations with the court are traced in He Changqun 賀昌群, *Lun liang Han tudi zhanyou xingtai de fazhan* 論兩漢土地佔有形態的發展 (Shanghai: Renmin, 1956). Chapter 6 of this book epitomizes the situation of the great families as *san wei yi ti* 三位一體 "three positions for a single body," that is, one group of families that held the largest estates, engaged in trade, and dominated office holding. On the role of these families in the overthrow of Wang Mang and the establishment of the Eastern Han, see Yu Yingshi, "Dong Han zhengquan zhi jianli," pp. 216–63. The *Si min yue ling* is translated in Hsu, *Han Agriculture*, pp. 215–228, and discussed on pp. 58–61. For more general examinations of the Eastern Han great families, see Ebrey, "The economic and social history of Later Han," and Yang Lien-sheng 楊聯陞, "Dong Han de haozu 東漢的豪族," *Qinghua xuebao* 11:4 (1936): 1007–63, translated as Yang Lien-sheng, "Great Families of the Eastern Han," in *Chinese Social History*, ed. E-tu Zen Sun and John De Francis (Washington, D.C.: American Council of Learned Societies, 1956), pp. 103–34.

67. The role of education and scholarship in the formation of the Eastern Han elite as a self-conscious group organized in webs of interpersonal ties is described in Ebrey, "The economic and social history of Later Han," pp. 626–46. On the use of commentary on canonical texts to assert great family resistance to the court, see Chi-yun Chen, "A Confucian Magnate's Idea of Political Violence: Hsün Shuang's (A.D. 128–90) Interpretation of the *Book of Changes*," *T'oung Pao* 54.1–3 (1968): 73–115.

Conclusion

1. The distinction between "vernacular" culture and the "canonical/official" one is traced in Glen Dudbridge, *Religious Experience and Lay Society in T'ang China* (Cambridge: Cambridge University, 1995).

2. On this development see, for example, David Johnson, Andrew J. Nathan, and Evelyn S. Rawski, eds., *Popular Culture in Late Imperial China* (Berkeley: University of California, 1985); David Johnson, ed., *Ritual Opera and Operatic Ritual* (Berkeley: Chinese Popular Culture Project, 1989); David Johnson, ed., *Ritual and Scripture in Chinese Popular Religion: Five Studies* (Berkeley: Chinese Popular Culture Project, 1995).

3. On the links of empire and popular religion, see Stephan Feuchtwang, *The Imperial Metaphor: Popular Religion in China* (London: Routledge, 1992).

WORKS CITED

Primary Sources

Baoshan Chu jian 包山楚簡. Edited by Hubei sheng Jingsha tielu kaogu dui 湖北省荆沙铁路考古队. Beijing: Wenwu, 1991.

Bo hu tong de lun 白虎通德論. In *Han Wei cong shu* 漢魏叢書. Vol. 1. Taipei: Xinxing, 1977.

Bo wu jing yi yi 駁五經異義. By Xu Shen 許慎 and Zheng Xuan 鄭玄. In *Hou zhi bu zu zhai congshu* 後知不足齋叢書. n.p.: Chang Shubao, 1884.

Chu ci buzhu 楚辭補注. Annotated by Hong Xingzu 洪興祖. Si bu cong kan 四部叢刊 edition.

Chun qiu fan lu yi zheng 春秋繁露義證. Annotated by Su Yu 蘇輿. Taipei: Heluo, 1975.

Chun qiu Gongyang zhuan zhu shu 春秋公羊傳注疏. In *Shisan jing zhu shu* 十三經注疏. Vol. 7. Taipei: Yiwen, 1976.

Chun qiu Guliang zhuan zhu shu 春秋穀梁傳注疏. In *Shisan jing zhu shu*. Vol. 7. Taipei: Yiwen, 1976.

Chun qiu he cheng tu 春秋合誠圖. In *Gu wei shu* 古緯書. In *Wei shu ji cheng* 緯書集成. Shanghai: Guji, 1994.

Chun qiu yan Kong tu 春秋演孔圖. In *Gu wei shu*. In *Wei shu ji cheng*.

Chun qiu yuan ming bao 春秋元命包. In *Qi wei* 七緯. In *Wei shu ji cheng*.

Chun qiu Zuo zhuan zhu 春秋左傳注. Annotated by Yang Bojun 楊伯峻. Beijing: Zhonghua, 1981.

Da Dai li ji jie gu 大戴禮記解詁. Annotated by Wang Pinzhen 王聘珍. Rep. ed. Beijing: Zhonghua, 1983.

Di wang shi ji jicun 帝王世紀輯存. Compiled by Xu Zongyuan 徐宗元. Beijing: Zhonghua, 1964.

Fa yan 法言. By Yang Xiong 楊雄. In *Han Wei cong shu*. Vol. 2. Taipei: Xinxing, 1977.

Fengsu tongyi 風俗通義. By Ying Shao 應劭. Annotated by Wu Shuping 吳樹平. Tian jin: Renmin, 1980.

Guanzi jiaozheng 管子郊正. Annotated by Dai Wang 戴望. In *Xin bian zhuzi jicheng* 新編諸子集成. Vol. 5. Taipei: Shijie, 1974.

Guo yu 國語. Shanghai: Guji, 1978.

Han Feizi jishi 韓非子集釋. Annotated by Chen Qiyou 陳奇猷. Shanghai: Renmin, 1974.

Han shi wai zhuan ji shi 韓詩外傳集釋. Annotated by Xu Weiyu 許維遹. Beijing: Zhonghua, 1980.

Han shu 漢書. Beijing: Zhonghua, 1962.

Houma mengshu 侯馬盟書. Edited by Shanxi sheng wenwu gongzuo weiyuanhui 山西省文物工作委員會. Shanghai: Wenwu, 1976.

Huainanzi 淮南子. Annotated by Gao You 高誘. In *Xin bian zhuzi jicheng*. Vol. 7. Taipei: Shijie, 1974.

Jiangling Jiudian Dong Zhou mu 江陵九店東周墓. Edited by Hubei sheng wenwu kaogu yanjiusuo 湖北省文物考古研究所. Beijing: Kexueshe, 1995.

Jiazi xin shu jiaoshi 賈子新書校釋. Annotated by Qi Yuzhang 祁玉章. Taipei: Qi Yuzhang, 1974.

Jin shu 晉書. Beijing: Zhonghua, 1974.

Jing fa 經法. Beijing: Wenwu, 1976.

Jiu zhang suan shu 九章算書. In *Suan jing shi shu* 算經十書. Edited by Qian Baozong 錢寶綜. Beijing: Xinhua, 1963.

Laozi dao de jing zhu 老子道德經注. Annotated by Wang Bi 王弼. In *Xin bian zhuzi jicheng*. Vol. 3. Taipei: Shijie, 1974.

Li ji zhu shu 禮記注疏. In Shisan jing zhushu. Vol. 5. Taipei: Yiwen, 1976.

Li shi 隸釋. Compiled by Hong Gua 洪适. In *Shi ke shiliao congshu* 石刻史料叢書. Vol. 1–3. Taipei: Yiwen, 1966.

Li wei han wen jia 禮緯含文嘉. In *Gu wei shu* 古緯書. In *Wei shu ji cheng*.

"Liu yi lun 六藝論." By Zheng Xuan 鄭玄. In *Quan shanggu san dai Qin Han Sanguo liu chao wen* 全上古三代秦漢三國六朝文. Vol. 1. Reprint ed. Beijing: Zhonghua, 1958.

Lu shi 路史. By Luo Bi 羅泌. Si bu bei yao 四部備要 edition.

Lü shi chun qiu jiao shi 呂氏春秋校釋. Annotated by Chen Qiyou. Shanghai: Xuelin, 1984.

Lun heng 論衡. By Wang Chong 王充. In *Xin bian zhuzi ji cheng*. Vol. 7. Taipei: Shijie, 1974.

Lun yu zhuan kao 論語譔考. In *Gu wei shu*. In *Wei shu ji cheng*.

Lun yu zhengyi 論語正義. Annotated by Liu Baonan 劉寶楠 and Liu Gongmian 劉恭冕. In *Xin bian zhuzi jicheng*. Vol. 1. Taipei: Shijie, 1974.

Mao shi zhengyi 毛詩正義. In *Shi san jing zhu shu*. Vol. 2. Taipei: Yiwen, 1976.

Mawangdui Han mu boshu 馬王堆漢墓帛書. Edited by Mawangdui Han mu boshu zhengli xiaozu 馬王堆漢墓帛書整理小組. Vol. 4. Beijing: Wenwu, 1985.

Mengzi zhengyi 孟子正義. Annotated by Jiao Xun 焦循. In *Xin bian zhu zi jicheng*. Vol. 1. Taipei: Shijie, 1974.

Mozi jiangu 墨子間詁. Annotated by Sun Yirang 孫詒讓. In *Xin bian zhuzi jicheng*. Vol. 6. Taipei: Shijie, 1974.

Mu Tianzi zhuan 穆天子傳. Cong shu ji cheng 叢書集成 edition.

Qian fu lun jian 潛夫論箋. By Wang Fu 王符. Beijing: Zhonghua, 1979.

Shan hai jing jiaozhu 山海經校注. Annotated by Yuan Ke 袁珂. Shanghai: Guji, 1980.

Shang jun shu zhuyi 商君書注譯. Annotated by Gao Heng 高享. Beijing: Zhonghua, 1974.

Shang shu da zhuan ji jiao 尙書大傳輯校. Annotated by Chen Shouqi 陳壽祺. In *Huang Qing jing jie xubian* 皇清經解續編. n.p.: Nanqing Shuyuan, 1888.

Shang shu zhengyi 尙書正義. In Shisan jing zhushu. Vol. 1. Taipei: Yiwen, 1976.

Shang shu zhong hou 尙書中候. In *Gu wei shu*. In *Wei shu ji cheng*.

Shenzi 申子. Quoted in *Qun shu zhi yao* 群書治要. Si bu cong kan edition.

Shi ben ji bu 世本輯補. Annotated by Qin Jiamo 秦嘉謨. In *Shi ben ba zhong* 世本八種. Shanghai: Shangwu, 1957.

Shi han shen wu 詩含神霧. In *Gu wei shu*. In *Wei shu ji cheng*.

Shi ji 史記. Beijing: Zhonghua, 1959.

Shi ming shu zheng bu 釋名疏證補. By Liu Xi 劉熙. Annotated by Wang Xianqian 王先謙. Rep. ed. Shanghai: Guji, 1984.

Shi san jia yi jishu 詩三家義集疏. Annotated by Wang Xianqian 王先谦. Beijing: Zhonghua, 1987.

Shi yi ji 拾遺記. By Wang Jia 王嘉. Annotated by Qi Zhiping 齊治平. Beijing: Zhonghua, 1981.

Shiyi jia zhu Sunzi 十一家注孫子. Shanghai: Guji, 1978.

Shizi 尸子. Quoted in *Qun shu zhi yao*.

Shuihudi Qin mu zhu jian 睡虎地秦墓竹簡. Beijing: Wenwu, 1978.

Shuo wen jie zi zhu 說文解字注. Compiled by Xu Shen 許慎. Annotated by Duan Yucai 段玉裁. Taipei: Yiwen, 1974.

Shuo yuan 說苑. Collected by Liu Xiang 劉向. In *Han Wei cong shu*. Vol. 1. Taipei: Xinxing, 1977.

Tian wen shuzheng 天問疏證. Annotated by Wen Yiduo 聞一多. Beijing: Sanlian, 1980.

Wen xin diao long yizhu 文心雕龍译注. By Liu Xie 刘勰. Annotated by Lu Kanru 陆侃如 and Mou Shijin 牟世金. Ji'nan: Qilu, 1984.

Wen xuan 文選. Hong Kong: Shangwu, 1978.

Wenzi yao quan 文子要詮. Annotated by Li Dingsheng 李定生 and Xu Huijun 徐慧君. Shanghai: Fudan Daxue, 1988.

Xiao jing zhu shu 孝經注疏. In *Shi san jing zhu shu*. Vol. 8.

Xin yu 新語. By Lu Jia 陸賈. In *Xin bian zhuzi jicheng*. Vol. 2. Taipei: Shijie, 1974.

Xin yu jiao zhu 新語校注. Annotated by Wang Liqi 王利器. Beijing: Zhonghua, 1986.

Xunzi jijie 荀子集解. Annotated by Wang Xianqian 王先謙. In *Xin bian zhuzi jicheng*. Vol. 2. Taipei: Shijie, 1974.

Yan tie lun 鹽鐵論. By Huan Kuan 桓寬. In *Xin bian zhuzi ji cheng*. Vol. 2. Taipei: Shijie, 1974.

Yanzi chun qiu ji shi 晏子春秋集釋. Annotated by Wu Zeyu 吳則虞. Beijing: Zhonghua, 1962.

Yi qian kun zao du 易乾坤鑿度. In *Qi wei*. In *Wei shu ji cheng*.

Yi qian zao du 易乾鑿度. In *Qi wei*. In *Wei shu ji cheng*.

Yi tong gua yan 易通卦驗. In *Qi wei*. In *Wei shu ji cheng*.

Yi wen lei ju 藝文類聚. Taipei: Wenguang, 1974.

Yi Zhou shu 逸周書. In *Han Wei cong shu*. Vol. 1. Taipei: Xinxing, 1977.

Yinqueshan Han jian shi wen 银雀山汉简释文. Edited by Wu Jiulong 吴九龙. Beijing: Wenwu, 1985.

Yunmeng Shuihudi Qin mu 雲夢睡虎地秦墓. Beijing: Wenwu, 1981.

Zhan guo ce 戰國策. Shanghai: Guji, 1978.

Zhonghua gu jin zhu 中華古今注. By Ma Gao 馬縞. Rep. ed. Shanghai: Shangwu, 1956.

Zhou bi suan jing 周髀算經. In *Suan jing shi shu*.

Zhou li zheng yi 周禮正義. Annotated by Sun Yirang. Shanghai: Zhonghua, 1934.

Zhou li zhushu 周禮注疏. In *Shisan jing zhushu*. Vol. 3. Taipei: Yiwen, 1976.

Zhou yi zhengyi 周易正義. In *Shisan jing zhushu*. Vol. 1. Taipei: Yiwen, 1976.

Zhuangzi jishi 莊子集釋. Annotated by Guo Qingfan 郭慶藩. In *Xin bian zhuzi jicheng*. Vol. 3. Taipei: Shijie, 1974.

Secondary Works in Chinese and Japanese

Akatsuka, Kiyoshi 赤塚忠. *Chūgoku kodai no shūkyō to bunka—In ōchō no saishi* 中國古代の宗教と文化──殷王朝の祭祀. Tokyo: Kadokawa, 1977.

Aoki, Masaru 青木正兒. "Soji Kyūka no bukyokuteki kekkō 楚辭九歌の舞曲的結構." *Shinagaku* 7 (1934): 1–23. Reprinted in Aoki, *Shina bungaku geijutsu kō* 支那文學藝術考. Tokyo: Kōbundō, 1942.

Asano, Yūichi 淺野裕一. *Kō rō dō no seiritsu to tenkai* 黃老道の成立と展開. Tokyo: Sōbunsha, 1992.

Bai, Shouyi 白寿彝. "Jiu tian ren zhi ji 究天人之际, tong gu jin zhi bian 通古今之变, cheng yi jia zhi yan 成一家之言," In *Shi ji xin lun* 史记新论. Beijing: Qiushi, 1981.

Chen, Guying 陳鼓應. *Huangdi si jing yizhu* 黃帝四經譯注. Taipei: Shangwu, 1995.

———. "Lun *Laozi* wan chu shuo zai kaozheng fangfa shang chang jian de miuwu 論老子晚出說在考證方法上常見的謬誤." In *Daojia wenhua yanjiu* 道家文化研究. Vol. 4. Shanghai: Guji, 1994.

Chen, Mengjia 陳夢家. "Gao mei jiao she zu miao tong kao 高媒校社祖廟通考." *Qinghua Xuebao* 12.3 (1937): 445–72.

———. *Shang shu tong lun* 尚書通論. 2nd ed. rev. Beijing: Zhonghua, 1985.

Chen, Shan 陈山. *Zhongguo wuxia shi* 中国武侠史. Shanghai: Sanlian, 1992.

Chen, Songchang 陳松長 and Liao, Mingchun 廖名春. "Bo shu 'Er san zi wen,' 'Yi zhi yi,' 'Yao' shiwen 帛書二三子問易之義要釋文." *Daojia wenhua yanjiu*. Vol. 3. Shanghai: Guji, 1993.

Chūbachi, Masakazu 中鉢雅量. *Chūgoku no saishi to bungaku* 中國の祭祀と文學. Tokyo: Sōbunsha, 1988.

Cui, Shu 崔述. *Kao xin lu* 考信錄. Rep. ed. Taipei: Shijie, 1968.

"Dingzhou Xi Han Zhongshan Huai Wang mu zhu jian 'Wenzi' de zhengli he yiyi 定州西漢中山懷王墓竹簡文子的整理和意义." *Wenwu* (1995:12): 38–40.

"Dingzhou Xi Han Zhongshan Huai Wang mu zhu jian 'Wenzi' jiaokan ji 定州西漢中山懷王墓竹簡文子校勘记." *Wenwu* (1995:12): 35–37.

"Dingzhou Xi Han Zhongshan Huai Wang mu zhu jian 'Wenzi' Shiwen 定州西漢中山懷王墓竹簡文子释文." *Wenwu* (1995:12): 27–34.

Dong, Zuobin 董作賓. *Yin li pu* 殷曆譜. Lizhuang: Institute of History and Philology, Academia Sinica, 1945.

Du, Guoxiang 杜国庠. "Lun *Xunzi* de 'Cheng xiang pian' 論荀子的成相篇." In *Du Guoxiang wenji* 文集. Beijing: Renmin, 1962.

Du, Zhengsheng 杜正勝. *Bian hu qi min : chuantong zhengzhi shehui jiegou zhi xingcheng* 編戶齊民: 傳統政治社會結構之形成. Taipei: Lianjing, 1989.

Fan, Wenlan 范文瀾. *Qun jing gai lun* 群經概論. Beijing: Pushe, 1934.

Feng, Youlan 馮友蘭. *Zhongguo zhexue shi bu* 中國哲學史補. Shanghai: Shangwu, 1936.

Fu, Sinian 傅斯年. "Shi jing jiang yi gao 詩經講義稿." In *Fu Mengzhen xiansheng ji* 傅孟眞先生集. Vol. 2B 中篇乙. Taipei: Academia Sinica, 1954.

———. "*Shi jing* jiang yi kao 詩經講義考." In *Fu Mengzhen xiansheng ji* 傅孟眞先生集. Vol. 1. Taipei: Lianjing, 1980.

Fujikawa, Masakazu 藤川正數. *Kandai ni okeru reigaku no kenkyū* 漢代における礼学の研究. Tokyo: Fūkan Shobō, 1968.

Fujino, Iwatomo 藤野岩友. *Fukei bungaku ron* 巫系文學論. Rev. ed. Tokyo: Daigaku Shobō, 1970.

Fukino, Yasushi 吹野安. *Chūgoku kodai bungaku hassō ron* 中國古代文學發想論. Tokyo: Ryūkan Shoin, 1987.

Gao, Heng 高亨. *Zhou yi da zhuan jin zhu* 周易大传今注. Ji'nan: Qi Lu, 1979.

———. "*Zhou yi* shi fa xin kao 周易筮法新考." In *Zhou yi gu jing tong shuo* 周易古经通说. Beijing: Zhonghua, 1983.

———. "*Zuo zhuan, Guo yu* de *Zhou yi* shuo tong jie 左传国语的周易说通解." In *Zhou yi za lun* 周易杂论. Ji'nan: Qi Lu, 1979.

Gong, Yingde 弓英德. *Liu shu bian zheng* 六書辯正. Taipei: Shangwu, 1966.

Gosei, Tadako 吾井互弘. "Shunjū jidai no Shin no daifu Ki shi, Yōzetsu shi no ōzato ni tsuite 春秋時代の晉の大夫祇氏,羊舌氏の邑について." *Chūgoku kodaishi kenkyū* 中國古代史研究 3. Tokyo: Chūgoku Kodaishi Kenkyū Kai, 1968, pp. 183–209.

Gu, Jiegang 顧頡剛, ed. *Gu shi bian* 古史辨. Vols. 3, 5. Rep. ed. Hong Kong: Taiping, 1962.

———. "*Yi zhou shu* 'Shi fu pian' jiaozhu xieding yu pinglun 逸周書世俘篇校注寫定與評論." *Wen shi* 2 (April 1963): 1–42.

———. "'Zhou gong zhi li' de chuanshuo he 'Zhou guan' yi shu de chuxian 周公制礼的传说和周官一书的出现." *Wen shi* 6 (June 1979): 1–4.

———. "Zi xu 自序." In *Gu shi bian*. Vol. 1.

Gu, Lisan 顧立三. *Sima Qian chuan xie Shi ji caiyong Zuo zhuan de yanjiu* 司馬遷傳寫史記採用左傳的研究. Taipei: Zhongzheng, 1981.

Guan, Feng 關鋒. "Zhuangzi wai za pian chutan 莊子外雜篇初探." In *Zhuangzi zhexue taolun ji* 莊子哲學討論集. Beijing: Zhonghua, 1962.

———. *Zhuangzi neipian yijie he pipan* 莊子內篇譯解和批判. Beijing: Zhonghua, 1961.

Guo, Moruo 郭沫若. "Guanyu E jun qi jie de yanjiu 关於鄂君启节的研究." *Wenwu* (1958:4): 3–6.

———. "Gudai wenzi zhi bianzheng fazhan 古代文字之辯證發展." *Kaogu* (1972:3): 2–13.

———. "Houma mengshu shitan 侯馬盟書試探." *Wenwu* (1966:2): 4–6.

———. *Qu Yuan fu jin yi* 屈原賦今譯. Beijing: Renmin Wenxue, 1953.

———. *Qu Yuan yanjiu* 屈原研究. n.p.: Qunyi, 1946.

———. "Zhou guan zhi yi 周官質疑." In *Jin wen congkao* 金文叢考. Rev. ed. Beijing: Renmin, 1954.

———. "Zhou Qin yiqian gudai sixiang zhi li ce 周秦以前古代思想之蠡測." In *Guo gu luncong* 國故論叢. *Xueyi Huikan* 13 (1926): 21–43.

Guojia Wenwuju Gu Wenxian Yanjiushi 国家文物局古文献研究室. "Xi Han boshu *Tian wen qi xiang za zhan* shi wen 西汉帛书天文气象杂占释文." *Zhongguo Wenwu* 1 (1979): 1–4, 26–29.

Hamaguchi, Shigekuni 濱口重國. *Shin Kan Zui Tō shi no kenkyū* 秦漢隋唐史の研究. Vol. 1. Tokyo: Tōkyō Daigaku, 1966.

Hayashi, Minao 林巳奈夫. *Kan dai no kamigami* 漢代の神神. Kyoto: Nozokawa, 1989.

Hayashi, Taisuke 林泰輔. *Shū Kō to sono jidai* 周公とその時代. Tokyo: Okura Shoten, 1915.

———. "Shūkan ni mietaru jinrin no kankei 周官に見えたる人倫の關系." In *Shina jōdai no kenkyū* 支那上代の研究. Tokyo: Kōfūkan, 1927.

He, Changqun 賀昌群. "Dong Han geng yi shu yi zhidu de feizhi 東漢更役戍役制度的廢止." *Lishi Yanjiu* (1962:5): 96–115.

———. *Lun liang Han tudi zhanyou xingtai de fazhan* 論兩漢土地佔有形態的發展. Shanghai: Renmin, 1956.

Hihara, Toshikuni 日原利國. *Shunjū Kuyōden no kenkyū* 春秋公羊傳の研究. Tokyo: Sōbunsha, 1976.

Hiraoka, Takeo 平岡武夫. *Keisho no seiritsu* 經書の成立. Reprint ed. Tokyo: Sōbunsha, 1983.

Honda, Wataru 本田済. *Ekigaku: seiritsu to tenkai* 易学: 成立と展開. Kyoto: Heirakuji, 1960.

Hoshikawa, Kiyotaka 星川清孝. *Soji no kenkyū* 楚辭の研究. Tenri: Yōtoku Sha, 1962.

Hu, Pingsheng 胡平生 and Han, Ziqiang 韩自强. "Fuyang Han jian 'Shi jing' jianlun 阜阳汉简诗经简论." *Wenwu* (1984:8): 13–21.

Hu, Shi 胡適. "Shuo ru 說儒." In *Hu Shi lun xue jin zhu*. Vol. 1. Shanghai: Shangwu, 1935.

Hubei Sheng Jingzhou Diqu Bowuguan 湖北省荆州地区博物馆. "Jiangling Wangjiatai 15 hao Qin mu 江陵王家台 15 号秦墓." *Wenwu* (1995:1): 37–43.

Ikeda, Suetoshi 池田末利. *Chūgoku kodai shūkyō shi kenkyū* 中國古代宗敎史研究. Tokyo: Tōkai Daigaku, 1983.

Ikeda, Tomohisa 池田知久. "Maōtai Kan bo hakusho Shūeki Yō hen no kenkyū 馬王堆漢墓帛書周易要篇の研究." *Tōyōbunka Kenkyūsho Kiyō* 123 (194): 111–207.

———. "Maōtai Kan bo hakusho Shūeki Yō hen no shisō 馬王堆漢墓帛書周易要篇の思想." *Tōyōbunka Kenkyūsho Kiyō* 126 (1995): 1–105.

———. *Maōtai Kan bo hakusho gogyōhen kenkyū* 馬王堆漢墓帛書五行篇研究. Tokyo: Kyūko Shoin, 1993.

Imai, Usaburō 今井宇三郎. "*Saden, Kokugo* zeisen kō 左傳國語筮占考." *Kokubungaku Kanbungaku Ronsō* 14 (1969): 51–97.

Jiang, Boqian 蔣伯潛. *Shisan jing gai lun* 十三經概論. 1945. Rep. ed. Shanghai: Guji, 1983.

Jiang, Liangfu 姜亮夫. *Chongding Qu Yuan fu jiaozhu* 重订屈原赋校注. Tianjin: Guji, 1987.

Jiang, Shangxian 姜尙賢. *Xunzi sixiang tixi* 荀子思想體系. Tainan: Self-published, 1966.

Kamata, Tadashi 鎌田正. *Saden no seiritsu to sono tenkai* 左傳の成立とその展開. 2nd ed. Tokyo: Taishūkan, 1993.

Kanaya, Osamu 金谷治. "Chūgoku kodai ni okeru kami kannen toshite no ten 中國古代における神觀念としての天." In *Kami kannen no hikaku bunka ronteki kenkyū* 神觀念の比較文化論的研究. Tokyo: Kodansha, 1981.

———. *Rōso teki sekai: Enanji no shisō* 老莊的世界: 淮南子の思想. Kyoto: Heirakuji, 1959.

———. *Shin Kan shisō shi kenkyū* 秦漢思想史研究. 2nd ed. rev. Kyoto: Heirakuji, 1981.

Kano, Naoki 狩野直喜. *Shinagaku bunsō* 支那學文藪. Tokyo: Sōbundō, 1936.

Katō, Jōken 加藤常賢. "Futsu ki kō 弗忌考," in *Chūgoku kodai bunka no kenkyū* 中國古代文化の研究. Tokyo: Nishō Gakusha Daigaku, 1980.

———. *Kanji no kigen* 漢字の起源. Tokyo: Kadokawa, 1972.

———. *Shina kodai kazoku seido kenkyū* 支那古代家族制度研究. Tokyo: Iwanami, 1941.

———. "Shina ko seishi no kenkyū—Ka U Shi sei kō 支那古姓氏の研究——夏禹姒姓考." In *Chūgoku kodai bunka no kenkyū*.

———. "Shunjū gaku: Juka kokka tetsugaku 春秋學: 儒家國家哲學." In *Chūgoku kodai bunka no kenkyū*.

———. "Shunjū gaku ni okeru ō 春秋學における王," in *Chūgoku kodai bunka no kenkyū*.

Katō, Shigeru 加藤繁. *Shina keizaishi kōshō* 支那經濟史考證. Vol. 1. Tokyo: Tōyō Bunko, 1952–53.

Kimura, Eiichi 木村英一. *Kōshi to rongo* 孔子と論語. Tokyo: Sōbunsha, 1971.

Kodama, Rokurō 兒玉六郎. "Junshi ni okeru tensei no gainen 荀子における天政の概念," *Nihon Chūgoku Gakkai Hō* 日本中國學會報 24 (1972): 51–62.

———. "Junshi no ten ni taisuru ichi kōsatsu 荀子の天に對する一考察." *Shinagaku Kenkyū* 33 (1968): 42–49.

Kudō, Moto'o 江藤元男. "Suikochi Shin bo chikkan 'nissho' ni tsuite 睡虎地秦墓竹簡日書について." In *Shiteki* 史滴. Tokyo: Waseda Daigaku, 1986.

Lai, Changyang 赖长扬. "Lun Sima Qian de lishi zhexue 论司马迁的历史哲学." In *Sima Qian yanjiu xin lun*. Beijing: Henan Renmin, 1982.

Lao, Gan 勞榦. "Han dai bing zhi ji Han jian zhong de bing zhi 漢代兵制及漢簡中的兵制." *Lishi Yuyan Yanjiusuo Jikan* 10 (1948): 23–55.

———. "Lun Han dai de nei chao yu wai chao 論漢代的內朝與外朝." *Lishi Yuyan Yanjiusuo Jikan* 13 (1948): 227–67.

———. "Lun Han dai de youxia 論漢代的游俠." In *Lao Gan xueshu lunwen ji* 勞榦學術論文集. Vol. 2. Taipei: Yiwen, 1976.

Lao, Xiaoyu 勞孝輿. *Chun qiu shi hua* 春秋詩話. Cong shu ji cheng edition.

Li, Chongyuan 李崇遠. *Chun qiu san zhuan li yi tong kao* 春秋三傳禮儀通考. Jiaxin Shuini Gongsi Jijinhui, 1969.

Li, Dingsheng 李定生. "'Wenzi' fei wei shu kao 文子非僞書考." In *Daojia wenhua yanjiu*. Vol. 5. Shanghai: Guji, 1994.

Li, Jiannong 李劍農. *Xian Qin liang Han jingji shi gao* 先秦兩漢經濟史稿. Beijing: Sanlian, 1957.

Li, Jingchi 李鏡池. "*Zuo zhuan* zhong *Yi* shi zhi yanjiu 左傳中易筮之研究." In *Zhou yi tanyuan* 周易探源. Beijing: Zhonghua, 1978.

Li, Ling 李零. *Sunzi gu ben yanjiu* 孫子古本研究. Beijing: Beijing Daxue, 1995.

———. *Zhongguo fangshu kao* 中國方術考. Beijing: Renmin Zhongguo, 1993.

Li, Qiao 李翹. "*Chu ci* 'Tian wen' guan jian 楚辭天問管見." *Wenlan Xuebao* 文瀾學報 2:1 (January–March 1936): 689–98.

Li, Shaoyong 李少雍. *Sima Qian zhuan ji wenxue lun gao* 司马迁传记文学论稿. Chongqing: Chongqing Chuban she, 1987.

Li, Weitai 李偉泰. *Han chu xueshu ji Wang Chong "Lun heng" shu lun gao* 漢初學術及王充論衡述論稿. Taipei: Changan, 1986.

Li, Weixiong 李威熊. *Dong Zhongshu yu Xi Han xueshu* 董仲舒與西漢學術. Taipei: Wen Shi Zhe, 1978.

———. *Zhongguo jingxue fazhan shi* 中國經學發展史. Taipei: Wen Shi Zhe, 1989.

Li, Xueqin 李学勤. "Fangmatan jian zhong de zhiguai gushi 放马滩简中的志怪故事." *Wenwu* (1990:4): 43–47.

———. "Kaogu faxian yu gudai xing shi zhidu 考古发现与古代姓氏制度." *Kaogu* (1987:3): 253–57, 241.

———. "Shen lun *Laozi* de niandai 申論老子的年代." In *Daojia wenhua yanjiu*. Vol. 6. Shanghai: Guji, 1995.

———. *Zhou yi jing zhuan su yuan* 周易经传溯源. Changchun: Changchun Chu-banshe, 1992.

Li, Zongtong 李宗侗. "Shi guan zhidu—fu lun dui chuantong zhi zunzhong 史官制度——附論對傳統之尊重." In *Zhongguo shixue shi lunwen xuan ji* 中國史學史論文選集. Edited by Du Weiyun 杜維運 and Huang Jinxing 黃進興. Vol. 1. Taipei: Huashi, 1976.

Liang, Qichao 梁啓超. *Mozi xue an* 墨子學案. 1921. Reprint ed. Shanghai: Shangwu, 1935.

Liao, Mingchun 廖名春. "Bo shu 'Yao' jian shuo 帛書要簡說." In *Daojia wenhua yanjiu*. Vol. 3. Shanghai: Guji, 1993.

Liu, Baiji 劉佰驥. *Chun qiu huimeng zhengzhi* 春秋會盟政治. Taipei: Zhonghua Congshu, 1963.

Liu, Dunyuan 劉敦願. "Han huaxiangshi shang yin shi nan nü—Pingyin Meng-zhuang Han mu shizhu jisi gewu tuxiang fenxi 漢畫像石上飲食男女——平陰孟莊漢墓石柱祭祀歌舞圖像分析." *Gu Gong Wenwu Yuekan* 古宮文物月刊 141(December 1994): 122–35.

Liu, Hainian 刘海年. "Qin lü xingfa kaoxi 秦律刑罚考析." In *Yunmeng Qin jian yanjiu* 云梦秦简研究. Beijing: Zhonghua, 1981.

Liu, Jie 劉節. "Laozi kao 老子考." In *Gu shi cun kao* 古史存考. Beijing: Renmin, 1958.

Liu, Qiyu 刘起于. *Shang shu xue shi* 尚书学史. Beijing: Zhonghua, 1989.

Liu, Xiaogan 劉笑敢. "*Laozi* zao chu shuo xin zheng 老子早出說新證." *Daojia wenhua yanjiu*. Vol 4. Shanghai: Guji, 1994.

———. *Zhuangzi zhexue ji qi yanbian* 莊子哲學及其演變. Beijing: Zhongguo She-hui Kexue, 1988.

Lu, Kanru 陸侃如. *Qu Yuan* 屈原. 6th ed. Shanghai: Yadong Tushuguan, 1933.

Lu, Kanru, Gao, Heng 高亨, and Huang, Xiaoshu 黃孝紓, eds. *Chu ci xuan* 楚辭選. Shanghai: Gudian, 1956.

Luo, Fuyi 罗福颐, ed. *Guxi huibian* 古玺汇编. Beijing: Wenwu, 1981.

Ma, Yong 马雍. "Zhongguo xing shi zhidu de yange 中国性氏制度的沿革." In *Zhongguo wenhua yanjiu jikan*. Vol. 2. Shanghai: Fudan Daxue, 1985.

Masubuchi, Tatsuo 增淵龍夫. *Chūgoku kodai no shakai to kokka* 中國古代の社會と國家. Tokyo: Kōbundō, 1962.

Matsumoto, Masaaki 松本雅明. *Shunjū Sengoku ni okeru Shōsho no tenkai* 春秋戰國における尚書の展開. Tokyo: Kazama, 1968.

Mitarai, Masaru 御手洗勝. *Kodai Chūgoku no kamigami* 古代中國の神神. Tokyo: Sōbunsha, 1984.

Miyazaki, Ichisada 宮崎定生. "Yūkyo ni tsuite 游俠について." In *Ajia shi ken-kyū* アジア史研究. Vol. 1. Kyoto: Dōshōsha, 1957.

Mori, Yasutarō 林安太郎. *Kōtei densetsu: kodai Chūgoku shinwa no kenkyū* 黃帝傳說: 古代中國神話の研究. Kyoto: Kyōto Joshi Daigaku Jinbun Gakkai, 1970.

Nakajima, Chiaki 中島千秋. *Fu no seiritsu to sono tenkai* 賦の成立とその展開. Matsuyama: Kan Yōshiten, 1963.

Nemoto, Makoto 跟本誠. *Jōdai Shina hōsei no kenkyū* 上代支那法制の研究. Tokyo: Yūhikaku, 1941.

Nishijima, Sadao 西島定生. *Chūgoku kodai no shakai to keizai* 中國古代の社會と經濟. Tokyo: Tōkyō Daigaku, 1981.

———. *Chūgoku kodai teikoku no keisei to kōzō—nijū tō shakusei no kenkyū* 中國古代帝國の形成と構造——二十等爵制の研究. Tokyo: Tōkyō Daigaku, 1961.

Nōda, Chūryō 能田忠亮 and Yabuuchi, Kiyoshi 藪內清. *Kan sho ritsureki no kenkyū* 漢書律曆の研究. Tōyō Bunka Kenkyūsho Kenkyū Hōkoku. Kyoto: Zenkoku Shobō, 1947.

Ogura, Yoshihiko 小倉芳彥. *Chūgoku kodai seiji shisō kenkyū* 中國古代政治思想研究. Tokyo: Aoki, 1970.

Pang, Pu 庞朴. *Bo shu wu xing pian yanjiu* 帛书五行篇研究. Ji'nan: Qi Lu, 1980.

Pi, Xirui 皮錫瑞. *Jingxue lishi* 經學歷史. Rept. ed. Beijing: Zhonghua, 1959.

Qian, Mu 錢穆. "Liang Han boshi jia fa kao 兩漢博士家法考." In *Liang Han jingxue jin gu wen pingyi* 兩漢經學今古文平議. Taipei: Dadong, 1978.

———. *Qin Han shi* 秦漢史. Taipei: Sanmin, 1969.

Qu, Wanli 屈萬里. "Lun 'Guo feng' fei min jian geyao de benlai mianmu 論國風非民間歌謠的本來面目." *Zhongyang Yanjiuyuan Lishi Yuyan Yanjiusuo Jikan* 34:2 (1963): 477–504.

———. *Xian Qin Han Wei Yi li shuping* 先秦漢魏易例述評. Taipei: Xuesheng, 1975.

Ruan, Zhisheng 阮芝生. "Shi lun Sima Qian suo shuo de 'tong gu jin zhi bian' 試論司馬遷所說的通古今之變." In *Zhongguo shixue shi lun wen xuan ji* 中國史學史論文選集. Edited by Du Weiyun and Huang Jinxing. Vol. 3. Taipei: Huashi, 1980.

Sagawa, Osamu 佐川修. *Shunjū gaku ronkō* 春秋學論考. Tokyo: Tōhō Shoten, 1983.

Shang, Binghe 尙秉和. *Zhou yi Shang shi xue* 周易尙氏學. Beijing: Zhonghua, 1980.

Shen, Congwen 沈從文, ed. *Zhongguo gudai fushi yanjiu* 中國古代服飾研究. Hong Kong: Commercial Press, 1992.

Shi, Ding 施定. "Lun Sima Qian de tong gu jin zhi bian 论司马迁的通古今之变." In *Sima Qian yanjiu xin lun* 司馬遷研究新論. Beijing: Henan Renmin, 1982.

———. "Sima Qian xie 'jin shang (Han Wudi)' 司马迁写今上 (汉武帝)." In *Sima Qian yanjiu xin lun*.

Shi, Nianhai 史念海. *He shan ji* 河山集. Beijing: Sanlian, 1981.

Shiga, Shūzō 滋賀秀三. "Chūgoku jōdai no keibatsu ni tsuite no ichi kōsatsu—sei to mei o tegakari to shite 中國上代の刑罰についての一考察——誓と盟を手がかりとして." In *Ishii Ryōsuke sensei kanreki shukuga: Hōseishi ronsō* 石井良助先生還歷祝賀: 法制史論叢. Edited by Shiga Shūzō. Tokyo: Sōbunsha, 1977.

Shimada, Kan 島田翰. *Kobun kyūsho kō* 古文舊書考. Tokyo, 1905.

Shirakawa, Shizuka 白川靜. *Chūgoku no shinwa* 中國の神話. Tokyo: Chūō Kōron, 1975.

———. *Kōkotsu kinbungaku ronshū* 甲骨金文學論集. Kyoto: Hōyū Shoten, 1974.

———. *Shikyō: Chūgoku no kodai kayō* 詩經: 中國の古代歌謠. Tokyo: Heibonsha, 1971.

———. *Shikyō kenkyū* 詩經研究. Kyoto: Hōyū Shoten, 1981.

Sichuan Sheng Bowuguan 四川省博物馆 and Qingchuan Xian Wenhuaguan 青川县文化馆. "Qingchuan xian chutu Qin geng xiu tian lü mudu 青川县出土秦更修田律木牍." *Wenwu* (1982:1): 1–14.

Song, Dingzong 宋鼎宗. "Chun qiu Zuo zhuan bin li jia li kao 春秋左傳賓禮嘉禮考." *Guoli Taiwan Shifan Daxue Guowen Yanjiusuo Jikan* 16 (1972): 199–366.

Song, Zuoyin 宋祚胤. *Zhou yi xin lun* 周易新论. Changsha: Hunan Jiaoyu, 1982.

Su, Chengjian 苏诚鉴. "'Shi ji' shi dui Han Wudi de pipan shu 史记是对汉武帝的批判书." In *Sima Qian he Shi ji* 司马迁和史记. Edited by Liu Naihe 刘乃和. Beijing: Beijing Daxue, 1987.

Sun, Jingming 孙敬明, Li, Jian 李剑, and Zhang, Longhai 张龙海. "Linzi Qi gucheng nei wai xin faxian de taowen 临淄齐古城内外新发现的陶文." *Kaogu* (1988:2): 83–87.

Sun, Yutang 孫毓堂. "Dong Han bing zhi de yanbian 東漢兵制的演變." In *Zhongguo Shehui Jingji Shi Congkan* 中國社會經濟史叢刊 6. Shanghai: Shangwu, 1939.

———. "Xi Han de bing zhi 西漢的兵制." In *Zhongguo Shehui Jingji Shi Congkan* 5. Shanghai: Shangwu, 1937.

Sun, Zuoyun 孫作雲, "Jiu ge 'Shan gui' kao 九歌山鬼考." *Qinghua Xuebao* 11:4 (1935): 977–1005.

———. *Shi jing yu Zhou dai shehui yanjiu.* 詩經與周代社會研究. Beijing: Zhonghua, 1966.

Suzuki, Shūji 鈴木修次. *Chūgoku kodai bungaku ron: Shikyō no bungei sei* 中國古代文學論: 詩經の文芸性. Tokyo: Kadokawa Shoten, 1977.

Suzuki, Yoshijirō 鈴木由修次. *Kan eki kenkyū* 漢易研究. Tokyo: Meitoku, 1963.

Taguchi, Fukujirō 田口福次郎. *Shū eki no kigen* 周易の起源. Tokyo: Meiji Shoin, 1961.

Takeji, Sadao 竹治貞夫. *Soji kenkyū* 楚辭研究. Tokyo: Fūkan Shobō, 1979.

Takeuchi, Yoshio 武內義雄. *Rongo no kenkyū* 論語の研究. Tokyo: Iwanami, 1940.

Tanaka, Toshiaki 田中利明. "Shūrai no seiritsu ni tsuite no ichi kōsatsu 周禮の成立についての一考察." *Tōhōgaku* 42 (August 1971): 15–31.

Tao, Xisheng 陶希聖. *Bianshi yu youxia* 辨士與游俠. Shanghai: Shangwu, 1933.

Tay, Lien-soo (Zheng, Liangshu) 鄭良樹. "Lun *Sunzi* de zuocheng shidai 論孫子的作成時代." In *Zhujian boshu yanjiu* 竹簡帛書研究. Beijing: Zhonghua, 1982.

Toda, Toyasaburō 戶田豐三郎. "*Sa, Koku no Eki* zei kiji kanken 左國の易筮記事管見." *Shinagaku Kenkyū* 16 (1957): 1–11.

Tōdō, Akiyasu 藤堂明安. *Kanji gogen jiten* 漢字語源辞典. Tokyo: Gakutōsha, 1965.

Tsuda, Sōkichi 津田左右. *Rongo to Kōshi no shisō* 論語と孔子の思想. Tokyo: Iwanami, 1946.

———. *Saden no shisōshiteki kenkyū* 左傳の思想史的研究. Tokyo: Tōyō Bunko, 1935.

Uchino, Kumaichirō 內野態一郎. *Shin dai ni okeru keisho keisetsu no kenkyū: betsu hen, in kyō kō* 秦代における經書經說の研究: 別篇, 引經考. Tokyo: Tōhō Bunka Gakuin, 1940.

Wang, Baoxian 王葆玹. "Bo shu 'Yao' yu 'Yi zhi yi' de zhuanzuo shidai ji qi yu 'Xi ci' de guanxi 帛書要與易之義的撰作時代及其與繫辭的關系." In *Daojia wenhua yanjiu*. Vol. 6. Shanghai: Guji, 1995.

Wang, Bo 王博. "'Yao' pian lüe lun 要篇略論." In *Daojia wenhua yanjiu*. Vol. 6. Shanghai: Guji, 1995.

Wang, Fengyang 王奉养. *Hanzi xue* 汉字学. Jilin: Jilin Wenxue, 1989.

Wang, Guowei 王國維. *Guan tang ji lin* 觀堂集林. 2nd ed. rev. Beijing: Zhonghua, 1959.

Wen, Chongyi 文崇一. "Lun Sima Qian de sixiang 論司馬遷的思想." In *Shi ji lunwen xuan ji* 史記論文選集. Edited by Huang Peirong 黃沛榮. Taipei: Changan, 1982.

Wen, Yiduo 聞一多. "Fu Xi kao 伏羲考." In *Wen Yiduo quan ji*. Vol. 1. 1948. Rep. ed. Beijing: Sanlian, 1982.

———. "Gao Tang shen nü chuanshuo zhi fenxi 高唐神女傳說之分析." In *Wen Yiduo quan ji*. Vol. 1.

———. "'Jiu ge' gu ge wu ju xuan jie 九歌古歌舞劇懸解." In *Wen Yiduo quan ji*. Vol. 1.

———. "Li sao jiegu 離騷解詁." In *Wen Yiduo quan ji*. Vol. 2.

———. "Qi shi er 七十二." In *Shenhua yu shi* 神話與詩. In *Wen Yiduo quan ji*. Vol. 1.

———. "Qu Yuan wenti 屈原問題." In *Wen Yiduo quan ji*. Vol. 1.

———. "Shenma shi 'Jiu ge' 甚嗎是九歌." In *Wen Yiduo quan ji*. Vol. 1.

———. "*Shi jing* tong yi 詩經通義." In *Wen Yiduo quan ji*. Vol. 2.

———. "*Shi jing* xin yi 詩經新義." In *Wen Yiduo quan ji*. Vol. 2.

———. "Tian wen shi tian 天問釋天." In *Gu dian xin yi* 古典新義. In *Wen Yiduo quan ji*. Vol. 2.

Wu, Rongzeng 吴荣曾. "Zhanguo, Han dai de 'cao she shen guai' ji you guan shenhua mixin de bianyi 战国汉代的操蛇神怪及有关神话迷信的变异." *Wenwu* (1989:10): 46–52.

Wu, Shuping 吳樹平. "Cong Linyi Han mu zhujian 'Wu wen' kan Sun Wu de fajia sixiang 从临沂汉墓竹简吴问看孙武的法家思想." *Wenwu* (1975:4): 6–13.

Wu, Yujiang 吳毓江. *Mozi jiaozhu* 墨子校注. Reprinted in *Mozi jicheng* 墨子集成. Edited by Yan Lingfeng 嚴靈峰. Vol. 43–44, appendix. Taipei: Chengwen, 1975.

Xing, Wen 邢文. "'Heguanzi' yu bo shu 'Yao' 鶡冠子與帛書要." In *Daojia wenhua yanjiu*. Vol. 6. Shanghai: Guji, 1995.

Xu, Fuguan 徐復觀. *Liang Han sixiang shi* 兩漢思想史. 3 Vols. Taipei: Xuesheng, 1972–79.

———. "*Yan tie lun* zhong de zhengzhi shehui wenhua wenti 鹽鐵論中的政治社會文化問題." *Xinya Xuebao* 11 (September 1975): 337–418.

———. *Zhongguo ren xing lun shi xian Qin pian* 中國人性論史先秦篇. Taipei: Shangwu, 1976.

———. *Zhou guan chengli zhi shidai ji qi sixiang xingge* 周官成立之時代及其思想性格. Taipei: Xuesheng, 1980.

Xu, Zhongshu 徐中舒. "Jinwen guci shili 金文嘏辭釋例." *Zhongyang Yanjiuyuan Lishi Yuyan Yanjiusuo Jikan* 6.1 (1936): 1–44.

Yamada, Keiji 山田慶兒. "Hen Shaku densetsu 扁鵲傳說." *Tōhōgakuhō* 60 (1988): 73–158.

———. *Shin hakken Chūgoku kagaku shi shiryō no kenkyū* 新發現中國科學史史料の研究. Vol. 1. Kyoto: Kyōto Daigaku Jinbun Kagaku Kenkyūsho, 1985.

Yamashita, Shizuo 山下靜雄. *Shū eki jū yoku no seiritsu to tenkai* 周易十翼の成立と展開. Tokyo: Kazama, 1977.

Yang, Kuan 楊寛. *Zhanguo shi* 战国史. 2nd ed. rev. Shanghai: Renmin, 1980.

Yang, Liansheng [Yang, Lien-sheng] 楊聯陞. "Dong Han de haozu 東漢的豪族." *Qinghua Xuebao* 11:4 (1936): 1007–63.

Yang, Yanqi 杨燕起. "Sima Qian de lishi sixiang 司马迁的历史思想." In *Sima Qian he Shi ji* 司马迁和史记. Edited by Liu Naihe 刘乃和. Beijing: Beijing Daxue, 1987.

Yasui, Kōzan 安居香山. *Isho no seiritsu to sono tenkai* 緯書の成立とその展開. Tokyo: Kokusho Kankō, 1981.

———. and Nakamura, Shōhachi 中村璋八. *Isho no kisoteki kenkyū* 緯書の基礎的研究. Kyoto: Kokusho Kankō, 1978.

Yin, Difei 殷滌非 and Luo, Zhangming 罗长铭. "Shouxian chutu de E jun qi jie 寿县出土的鄂君启节." *Wenwu* (1958:4): 8–11.

Yoshimoto, Michio 吉本道雄. "Shunjū saisho ron 春秋載書論." *Tōyōshi Kenkyū* 43:4 (1985): 1–33.

You, Guoen 游国恩. *Chu ci gai lun* 楚辭概論. Rep. ed. Taipei: Shangwu, 1968.

———. *Chu ci lunwen ji* 楚辭論文集. Shanghai: Wenyi Lianhe, 1955.

Yu, Haoliang 于豪亮. "Shi Qingchuan xian Qin mu mudu 释青川县秦墓木牍." *Wenwu* (1982:1): 22–24.

Yu, Yingshi 余英時. "Dong Han zhengquan zhi jianli yu shi zu da xing zhi guanxi 東漢政權之建立與士族大姓之關系." *Xinya Xuebao* 1:2 (February 1956): 209–80.

———. "Gudai zhishi jieceng de xingqi yu fazhan 古代知識階層的興起與發展." In *Zhongguo zhishi jieceng shi lun* 中國知識階層史論. Taipei: Lianjing, 1980.

Yuan, Ke 袁珂. *Zhongguo gudai shenhua* 中國古代神話. Rev. ed. Shanghai: Shang-wu, 1957.

Zeng, Qinliang 曾勤良. *Zuo zhuan yin shi fu shi zhi shi jiao yanjiu* 左傳引詩賦詩之詩教研究. Taipei: Wenjin, 1994.

Zhang, Binglin 張炳麟. "Wen xue zong lüe 文學總略." In *Guo gu lun heng* 國故論衡. Tokyo: Kokugaku Kōshūkai, 1910.

Zhang, Chuanxi 張传玺. *Qin Han wenti yanjiu* 秦汉问题研究. Beijing: Beijing Daxue, 1985.

Zhang, Dainian 張岱年. "Shi tan 'Wenzi' de niandai yu sixiang 試談文子的年代與思想." In *Daojia wenhua yanjiu.* Vol. 5. Shanghai: Guji, 1994.

Zhang, Dake 张大可. *Shi ji yanjiu* 史记研究. Lanzhou: Gansu Renmin, 1985.

Zhang, Duansui 張端穗. *Zuo zhuan sixiang tan wei* 左傳思想探微. Taipei: Xue-hai, 1987.

Zhang, Xuecheng 章學誠. *Wen shi tong yi* 文史通義. Rep. ed. Hong Kong: Taiping, 1964.

Zhang, Yachu 张亚初 and Liu, Yu 刘雨. "Cong Shang Zhou ba gua shuzi fuhao tan shifa de jige wenti 从商周八卦数子符号谈筮法的几个问题." *Kaogu* (1981:2): 155–63, 154.

Zhang, Zhenglang 张政烺. "Bo shu liushisi gua ba 帛书六十四卦跋." *Wenwu* (1984:3): 9–14.

———. "Shi shi Zhou chu qingtongqi mingwen zhong de *Yi* gua 試釋周初青銅器銘文中的易卦." *Kaogu Xuebao* (1980:4): 403–15.

Zheng, Yan 郑岩. "Anqiu Dongjiazhuang Han mu li zhu diaoke tuxiang kao 安丘董家庄汉墓立柱雕刻图像考." In *Jinian Shandong Daxue kaogu zhuanye chuangjian ershi zhounian wenji* 纪念山东大学考古专业创建二十周年文集. Ji'nan: Shandong Daxue, 1992.

Zhou, Cezong (Chow Tse-tsung) 周策縱. "Gu wu dui yue wu ji shi ge fazhan de gongxian 古巫對樂舞及詩歌發展的貢獻." *Qinghua Xuebao* 清華學報 n.s. 13 (Dec. 1982): 1–25.

———. *Gu wu yi yu liu shi kao* 古巫醫與六詩考. Taipei: Lianjing, 1986.

Zhou, Dao 周到 and Li, Jinghua 李京华. "Tanghe Zhenzhi chang Han huaxiang shi mu de fajue 唐河针织厂汉画像石墓的发掘." *Wenwu* (1973:6): 26–32.

Zhou, Yimou 周一谋. "Cong zhu jian 'Shi wen' deng kan daojia yu yangsheng 從竹簡十問等看道家與養生." In *Daojia wenhua yanjiu.* Vol. 5. Shanghai: Guji, 1994.

Zhou, Yutong 周予同. *Jing jin gu wen xue* 經今古文學. 1926. Rep. ed. Taipei: Shangwu, 1985.

Zhu, Bokun 朱伯崑. *Yixue zhexue shi* 易学哲学史. Vol. 1. Beijing: Beijing Daxue, 1986.

Zhu, Qianzhi 朱謙之. *Laozi jiaoshi* 老子校釋. Beijing: Zhonghua, 1963.

Zhu, Tingxian 朱廷獻. *Shang shu yanjiu* 尙書研究. Taipei: Shangwu, 1988.

Zhu, Ziqing 朱自清. "Shi yan zhi bian 詩言志辨." In *Zhu Ziqing gudian wenxue lunwen ji* 朱自清古典文學論文集. Shanghai: Guji, 1981.

Secondary Works in Western Languages

Adam, Barbara. *Time and Social Theory*. Cambridge: Polity, 1990.

Akatsuka, Kiyoshi. "A New Study of the *Shi-ku Wen*: the Ancient Letters Carved in Ten Drum-type Stones." *Acta Asiatica* 4 (1963): 80–96.

Allan, Sarah. "Drought, Human Sacrifice and the Mandate of Heaven in a Lost Text from the *Shang shu*." *Bulletin of the School of Oriental and African Studies* 47 (1984): 523–39.

———. *The Heir and the Sage: Dynastic Legend in Early China*. San Francisco: Chinese Materials Center, 1981.

———. *The Shape of the Turtle: Myth, Art, and Cosmos in Early China*. Albany: SUNY, 1991.

———. *The Way of Water and Sprouts of Virtue*. Albany: SUNY, 1997.

Ames, Roger. *The Art of Rulership: A Study in Ancient Chinese Political Thought*. Honolulu: University of Hawaii, 1983.

Anderson, Benedict. *Imagined Communities*. 2d ed. rev. London: Verso, 1991.

Aveni, Anthony. *Empires of Time: Calendars, Clocks, and Cultures*. London: I. B. Tauris, 1990.

Barnard, Noel. *The Ch'u Silk Manuscript*. Canberra: Australian National University, 1973.

Benveniste, Emile. *Problèmes de linguistique générale*. 2 vols. Paris: Gallimard, 1966–1974.

Berthier, Brigitte. *La Dame-du-bord-de-l'eau*. Nanterre: Société d'Ethnologie, 1988.

Bielenstein, Hans. *The Bureaucracy of Han Times*. Cambridge: Cambridge University, 1980.

Birrell, Anne. *Chinese Mythology: An Introduction*. Baltimore: Johns Hopkins University, 1993.

Bischoff, Friedrich A. *Interpreting the Fu: A Study in Chinese Literary Rhetoric*. Wiesbaden: Franz Steiner Verlag, 1976.

Bodde, Derk. *Festivals in Classical China: New Year and Other Annual Observances During the Han Dynasty*. Princeton: Princeton University, 1975.

———. "Myths of Ancient China." In *Mythologies of the Ancient World*. Edited by Samuel Noah Kramer. New York: Doubleday, 1961.

———. "The State and Empire of Ch'in." In *The Cambridge History of China, Vol. 1, The Ch'in and Han Empires, 221 B.C.–A.D. 220*. Edited by Michael Loewe. Cambridge: Cambridge University, 1986.

Bokenkamp, Stephen. "Record of the Feng and Shan Sacrifices." In *Religions of China in Practice*. Edited by Donald S. Lopez, Jr. Princeton: Princeton University, 1996.

Bourdieu, Pierre. *Les règles de l'art: genèse et structure du champ littéraire*. Paris: Seuil, 1992.

Brashier, K. E. "Evoking the Ancestor: the Stele Hymn of the Eastern Han Dynasty." Ph.D. dissertation. Cambridge University, 1997.

Broman, Sven. "Studies on the *Chou li*." *Bulletin of the Museum of Far Eastern Antiquities* 33 (1961): 1–89.

Brooks, E. Bruce. "The State of the Field in Pre-Han Text Studies." *Sino-Platonic Papers* 46 (July 1994): 1–66.

Bruns, Gerald L. *Inventions: Writing, Textuality, and Understanding in Literary History.* New Haven: Yale University, 1982.

Calame, Claude. *The Craft of Poetic Speech in Ancient Greece.* Translated by Janice Orion. Ithaca: Cornell University, 1995.

Camassa, Giorgio. "Aux origines de la codification écrite des lois en Grèce." In Detienne, ed. *Les savoirs de l'écriture.*

Cambiano, Giuseppe. "La démonstration géométrique." In Detienne, ed. *Les savoirs de l'écriture.*

Cammann, Schuyler. "The Evolution of Magic Squares in China." *Journal of the American Oriental Society* 80 (1960): 116–24.

———. "The Magic Square of Three in Old Chinese Philosophy and Religion." *History of Religions* 1 (1961): 37–80.

———. "Old Chinese Magic Squares." *Sinologica* 7 (1963): 14–53.

———. "Some Early Chinese Symbols of Duality." *History of Religions* 24.3 (February 1985): 215–54.

Carruthers, Mary. *The Book of Memory: A Study of Memory in Medieval Culture.* Cambridge: Cambridge University, 1990.

Cave, Terence. *The Cornucopian Text: Problems of Writing in the French Renaissance.* Oxford: Clarendon Press, 1979.

Chang, K. C. *Art, Myth, and Ritual: The Path to Political Authority in Ancient China.* Cambridge: Harvard University, 1983.

Chavannes, Edouard. *Mission archéologique dans la Chine septentrionale.* Paris: Imprimerie Nationale, 1913.

Chemla, Karine. "Nombre et opération, chaîne et trame du réel mathématique: essai sur le commentaire du Liu Hui sur *Les neuf chapitres sur les procédures mathématiques*." *Extrême-Orient, Extrême-Occident* 16 (1994): 43–70.

Chen, Chi-yun. "A Confucian magnate's idea of political violence: Hsün Shuang's (128–190) interpretation of the *Book of Changes*." *T'oung Pao* 54 (1968): 73–115.

Chen, Shih-hsiang. "The *Shi-ching*: Its Generic Significance in Chinese Literary History and Poetics." In *Studies in Chinese Literary Genres.* Edited by Cyril A. Birch. Berkeley: University of California, 1974.

Cheng, Anne. *Etude sur le confucianisme Han: l'élaboration d'une tradition exégétique sur les classiques.* Paris: Collège de France Institut des Hautes Etudes Chinoises, 1985.

———. "Taoïsme, confucianisme et légisme." In Charles LeBlanc and Rémi Mathieu, ed. *Mythe et philosophie à l'aube de la Chine impériale: études sur le Huainan Zi.*

Cheung, Kwong-yue. "Recent Archaeological Evidence Relating to the Origin of Chinese Characters." In Keightley, ed. *The Origins of Chinese Civilization.*

Chow, Tse-tsung, "The childbirth myth and ancient Chinese medicine: A study of aspects of the *wu* tradition." In *Ancient China: Studies in Early Civilization*. Edited by David T. Roy and Tsuen-hsuin Tsien. Hong Kong: Chinese University, 1978.

———. "The Early History of the Chinese Word *Shih* (Poetry)." In *Wen-lin: Studies in the Chinese Humanities*. Madison: University of Wisconsin, 1968.

Christin, Anne-Marie. *L'image écrite ou la déraison graphique*. Paris: Flammarion, 1995.

Ch'ü, T'ung-tsu. *Han Social Structure*. Seattle: University of Washington, 1972.

———. *Law and Society in Traditional China*. Paris: Mouton, 1961.

Chun, Allen J. "Conceptions of Kinship and Kingship in Classical Chou China." *T'oung Pao* 76 (1990): 16–48.

Clanchy, M. T. *From Memory to Written Record*. Cambridge: Harvard University, 1979.

Creel, H. G. *Confucius and the Chinese Way*. New York: Harper & Row, 1960.

Defoort, Carine. *The Pheasant Cap Master: A Rhetorical Reading*. Albany: SUNY, 1997.

Derrida, Jacques. *Of Grammatology*. Translated by Gayatri Spivak. Baltimore: Johns Hopkins University, 1974.

Detienne, Marcel. *L'écriture d'Orphée*. Paris: Gallimard, 1989.

———. "L'espace de la publicité: ses opérateurs intellectuels dans la cité." In Detienne, ed. *Les savoirs de l'écriture*.

———. *Les maîtres de vérité dans la Grèce archaïque*. Paris: François Maspero, 1981.

———, ed. *Les savoirs de l'écriture en Grèce ancienne*. Lille: Presses Universitaires de Lille, 1988.

DeWoskin, Kenneth D. "Famous Chinese Childhoods." In Kinney, ed. *Chinese Views of Childhood*.

———. *A Song for One or Two: Music and the Concept of Art in Early China*. Ann Arbor: University of Michigan, Center for Chinese Studies, 1982.

Diény, Jean-Pierre. *Aux origines de la poésie classique en Chine: étude de la poésie lyrique à l'époque des Han*. Leiden: E. J. Brill, 1968.

Djamouri, Redouane. "L'emploi des signes numérique dans les inscriptions Shang." *Extrême-Orient, Extrême-Occident* 16 (1994): 13–42.

Drège, Jean-Pierre. *Les bibliotèques en Chine au temps des manuscrits*. Paris: Ecole Française d'Extrême-Orient, 1991.

Dubs, Homer, tr. *The History of the Former Han Dynasty*. 3 vols. Baltimore: Waverly, 1938–1955.

Dudbridge, Glen. *Religious Experience and Lay Society in T'ang China*. Cambridge: Cambridge University, 1995.

Durrant, Stephen W. *The Cloudy Mirror: Tension and Conflict in the Writings of Sima Qian*. Albany: SUNY, 1995.

———. "An Examination of Textual and Grammatical Problems in Mo-tzu." Ph.D. dissertation. University of Washington, 1975.

———. "Ssu-ma Ch'ien's Portrayal of the First Ch'in Emperor." In *Imperial Rulership and Cultural Change in Traditional China*. Edited by Frederick P. Brandauer and Chun-chieh Huang. Seattle: University of Washington, 1994.

Eberhard, Wolfram. *The Local Cultures of South and East China*. Translated by Alide Eberhard. Leiden: E. J. Brill, 1968.

———. *Typen chinesischer Volksmärchen*. Helsinki: F. F. Communications No. 120, 1937.

Ebrey, Patricia. "The Economic and Social History of Later Han." In *Cambridge History of China, Vol. 1, the Ch'in and Han Empires*. Edited by Michael Loewe. Cambridge: Cambridge University, 1986.

Egan, Ronald. "Narratives in *Tso Chuan*." *Harvard Journal of Asiatic Studies* 37.2 (1977): 323–52.

Eno, Robert. *The Confucian Creation of Heaven*. Albany: SUNY, 1990.

Erickson, Susan N. "Money Trees of the Eastern Han Dynasty." *Bulletin of the Museum of Far Eastern Antiquities* 66 (1994): 1–116.

van Ess, Hans. "Die geheimen Worte des Ssu-ma Ch'ien." *Oriens Extremus* 36:1 (1993): 5–28.

———. "The Meaning of Huang-Lao in *Shi ji* and *Han shu*." *Etudes chinoises* 12:2 (1993): 161–77.

von Falkenhausen, Lothar. "Chu Ritual Music." In *New Perspectives on Chu Culture During the Eastern Zhou Period*. Edited by Thomas Lawton. Washington, D.C.: Arthur M. Sackler Gallery, Smithsonian Institution, 1991.

———. "The Concept of *Wen* in the Ancient Chinese Ancestral Cult." *Chinese Literature: Essays, Articles, Reviews* 18 (December 1996): 1–22.

———. "Issues in Western Zhou Studies: A Review Article." *Early China* 18 (1993): 145–71.

———. "Sources of Taoism: Reflections on Archaeological Indicators of Religious Change in Eastern Zhou China." *Taoist Resources* 5:2 (December 1994): 1–12.

———. *Suspended Music: Chime-Bells in the Culture of Bronze Age China*. Berkeley: University of California, 1993.

Feuchtwang, Stephan. *The Imperial Metaphor: Popular Religion in China*. London: Routledge, 1992.

Field, Stephen. "Cosmos, Cosmograph, and the Inquiring Poet: New Answers to the 'Heaven Questions'." *Early China* 17 (1992): 83–110.

Finsterbusch, Käte. *Verzeichnis und Motivindex der Han-Darstellungen: Band II Abbildungen und Addenda*. Wiesbaden: Otto Harrassowitz, 1971.

Forke, Alfred. *Me Ti des Sozialethikers und seiner Schuler philosophische Werke*. Berlin: Kommissionsverlag der Vereinigung wissenschaftlicher Verleger, 1922.

Gell, Alfred. *The Anthropology of Time: Cultural Construction of Temporal Maps and Images*. Oxford: Berg, 1992.

Gellner, Ernest. *Nations and Nationalism*. Ithaca: Cornell University, 1983.

Girardot, N. J. *Myth and Meaning in Early Taoism*. Berkeley: University of California, 1983.

Goody, Jack. *The Logic of Writing and the Organization of Society*. Cambridge: Cambridge University, 1986.

Graham, A. C. "The Background of the Mencian Theory of Human Nature." In *Studies in Chinese Philosophy and Philosophical Literature*. Singapore: Institute of East Asian Philosophies, 1986.

———. *Disputers of the Tao*. LaSalle: Open Court, 1989.

———. *Divisions in Early Mohism Reflected in the Core Chapters of Mo-tzu*. Singapore: Institute of East Asian Philosophies, 1985.

———. "How Much of *Chuang Tzu* did Chuang Tzu Write?" In *Studies in Chinese Philosophy and Philosophical Literature*.

———. *Later Mohist Logic, Ethics and Science*. London: SOAS and Hong Kong: Chinese University, 1978.

———. "A Neglected Pre-Han Philosophical Text: *Ho Kuan-tzu*." *Bulletin of the School of Oriental and African Studies* 52.3 (1989): 497–532.

———. "The *Nung-chia* 'School of the Tillers' and the Origin of Peasant Utopianism in China." *Bulletin of the School of Oriental and African Studies* 42 (1971): 66–100. Reprinted in *Studies in Chinese Philosophy and Philosophical Literature*.

———. "The Origins of the Legend of Lao Tan." In *Studies in Chinese Philosophy and Philosophical Literature*.

———. *Yin-Yang and the Nature of Correlative Thinking*. Singapore: Institute of East Asian Philosophies, 1986.

Granet, Marcel. *Danses et légendes de la Chine ancienne*. 1926. Rev. ed. Paris: Presses Universitaires de France, 1994.

———. *Fêtes et chansons anciennes de la Chine*. 2nd ed. Paris: Leroux, 1929.

———. *La pensée chinoise*. 1934. Rep. ed. Paris: Albin Michel, 1968.

Greimas, A. J. and Courtés, J. *Sémiotique: dictionnaire raisonné de la théorie du langage*. Paris: Hachette, 1979.

van Gulik, Robert. *The Lore of the Chinese Lute: An Essay in Ch'in Ideology*. Monumenta Nipponica, no. 3. Tokyo: Sophia University, 1940.

Hall, David L. and Ames, Roger T. *Anticipating China*. Albany: SUNY, 1995.

———. *Thinking Through Confucius*. Albany: SUNY, 1987.

Hansen, Chad. "Chinese Ideographs and Western Ideas." *Journal of Asian Studies* 52:2 (May 1993): 373–99.

———. *Language and Logic in Ancient China*. Ann Arbor: University of Michigan, 1983.

———. *A Taoist Theory of Chinese Thought: A Philosophical Investigation*. Oxford: Oxford University, 1992.

Harbsmeier, Christoph. "The Mass Noun Hypothesis and the Part-Whole Analysis of the White Horse Dialogue." In *Chinese Texts and Philosophical Contexts*. Edited by Henry Rosemont, Jr. LaSalle, Illinois: Open Court, 1991.

Hardy, Grant. "The Interpretive Function of *Shih chi* 14, 'The Table of Years of the Twelve Feudal Lords'." *Journal of the American Oriental Society* 113.1 (1993): 14–24.

Harlez, Charles. "Le Tcheou-li et le Shan-hai-king, leur origine et leur valeur historique." *T'oung Pao* 5 (1894): 11–42, 107–22.

Harper, Donald. "The Bellows Analogy in *Laozi* V and Warring States Macrobiotic Hygiene." *Early China* 20 (1995): 381–91.

———. "A Chinese Demonography of the Third Century B.C." *Harvard Journal of Asiatic Studies* 45.2 (1985): 459–98.

———. "Iatromancy, Prognosis, and Diagnosis in Early Chinese Medicine." Paper delivered at the Lu Gwei-Djen Memorial Workshop 'Innovation in Chinese Medicine,' Needham Research Institute, Cambridge, England, March 8–11, 1995.

———. "Resurrection in Warring States Popular Religion." *Taoist Resources* 5:2 (December 1994):13–28.

———. "Wang Yen-shou's Nightmare Poem." *Harvard Journal of Asiatic Studies* 47:1 (1987): 239–83.

———. "Warring States Natural Philosophy and Occult Thought." In *Cambridge History of Ancient China*. Edited by Edward Shaughnessy and Michael Loewe. Cambridge: Cambridge University, in press.

———. "Warring States, Qin, and Han Manuscripts Related to Natural Philosophy and the Occult." In *New Sources of Early Chinese History: An Introduction to Reading Inscriptions and Manuscripts*. Edited by Edward L. Shaughnessy. Berkeley: Society for the Study of Early China and the Institute of East Asian Studies, 1997.

Harris, Roy. *The Origin of Writing*. LaSalle, Illinois: Open Court, 1986.

Hartog, François. *Le miroir d'Hérodote: essai sur la représentation de l'autre*. Paris: Gallimard, 1980.

Hasan-Rokem, Galit and Shulman, David, eds. *Untying the Knot: On Riddles and Other Enigmatic Modes*. Oxford: Oxford University, 1996.

Havelock, Eric. *Preface to Plato*. Cambridge: Belknap Press of Harvard University, 1963.

Hawkes, David. "The Quest of the Goddess." In *Studies in Chinese Literary Genres*. Edited by Cyril Birch. Berkeley: University of California, 1974.

———, tr. *The Songs of the South: An Anthology of Chinese Poems by Qu Yuan and Other Poets*. Harmondsworth: Penguin, 1985.

Hayashi, Minao. "Concerning the Inscription 'May Sons and Grandsons Eternally Use This [Vessel]'." *Artibus Asiae* 53: 1–2 (1993): 51–58.

Hervouet, Yves. *Un poète de cour sous les Han: Sseu-ma Siang-jou*. Paris: Presses Universitaires de France, 1964.

Hou, Ching-lang. *Monnaies d'offrandes et la notion de trésorerie dans la religion chinoise*. Paris: Collège de France, Institut des Hautes Etudes Chinoises, 1975.

Howard, Jeffrey A. "Concepts of Comprehensiveness and Historical Change in the *Huai-nan-tzu*." *Journal of the American Academy of Religious Studies Thematic Studies* 50/2: *Explorations in Early Chinese Cosmology*. Chico, Calif.: Scholars Press, 1984.

Hsu, Cho-yun. *Ancient China in Transition: An Analysis of Social Mobility, 722–222 B.C.* Stanford: Stanford University, 1965.

———. *Han Agriculture: The Formation of the Early Chinese Agrarian Economy.* Seattle: University of Washington, 1980.

———. "The Changing Relationship between Local Society and the Central Political Power in Former Han: 206 B.C.–8 A.D." *Comparative Studies in Society and History* 7 (July 1965): 358–70.

Hulsewé, A. F. P. *Remnants of Ch'in Law.* Leiden: E. J. Brill, 1985.

———. "The Wide Scope of Tao 盜 'Theft' in Ch'in-Han Law." *Early China* 13 (1988): 166–200.

Jacob, Christian. "Inscrire la terre habitée sur une tablette: réflexions sur la fonction de la carte géographique en Grèce ancienne." In Detienne, ed. *Les savoirs de l'écriture.*

Jensen, Lionel M. "Wise Man of the Wilds: Fatherlessness, Fertility and the Mythic Exemplar, Kongzi." *Early China* 20 (1995): 407–37.

Johnson, David, Nathan, Andrew J., and Rawski, Evelyn S., eds. *Popular Culture in Late Imperial China.* Berkeley: University of California, 1985.

———, ed. *Ritual Opera and Operatic Ritual.* Berkeley: Chinese Popular Culture Project, 1989.

———, ed. *Ritual and Scripture in Chinese Popular Religion: Five Studies.* Berkeley: Chinese Popular Culture Project, 1995.

Johnson, W. R. *The Idea of Lyric: Lyric Modes in Ancient and Modern Poetry.* Berkeley: University of California, 1982.

Jullien, François. *Le détour et l'accès: stratégies du sens en Chine, en Grèce.* Paris: Grasset, 1995.

———. *Figures de l'immanence: pour une lecture philosophique du Yi king.* Paris: Grasset, 1993.

Kandel, Barbara. *Wen Tzu—Ein Beitrag zur Problematik und zum Verständnis eines taoistischen Textes.* Frankfurt am Main: Peter Lang, 1974.

Kane, Virginia. "Aspects of Western Zhou Appointment Inscriptions." *Early China* 8 (1982–83): 14–28.

Kang, Woo. *Les trois théories politiques du Tch'ouen Ts'ieou interprétées par Tong Tchong-chou d'après les principes de l'école de Kong-yang.* Paris: Librairie Ernest Leroux, 1932.

Karlgren, Bernhard. "The early history of Chou li and Tso chuan texts." *Bulletin of the Museum of Far Eastern Antiquities* 3 (1931): 1–59.

———. *Grammata Serica Recensa.* Rep. ed. Stockholm: Museum of Far Eastern Antiquities, 1957.

———. "On the authenticity and nature of the Tso-chuan." *Götesborgs högskolas arsskrift* 32 (1926). Rep. ed. Taipei: Chengwen, 1965.

Keegan, David Joseph. "The 'Huang-ti nei-ching': The Structure of the Compilation; The Significance of the Structure." Ph.D. dissertation. University of California at Berkeley, 1988.

Keightley, David. "Akatsuka Kiyoshi and the Culture of Early China: A Study in Historical Method." *Harvard Journal of Asiatic Studies* 42.1 (1982): 267–320.

———. "The Late Shang State: When, Where, and What?" In Keightley, ed. *The Origins of Chinese Civilization.*

———, ed. *The Origins of Chinese Civilization.* Berkeley: University of California, 1983.

———. *Sources of Shang History: the Oracle Bone Inscriptions of Bronze Age China.* Berkeley: University of California, 1978.

Kelly, C. M. "Later Roman Bureaucracy: Going Through the Files." In *Literacy and Power in the Ancient World.* Edited by Alan K. Bowman and Greg Woolf. Cambridge: Cambridge University, 1994.

Kermode, Frank. *The Genesis of Secrecy.* Cambridge: Harvard University, 1979.

Kern, Martin. "In praise of political legitimacy: the *miao* 廟 and *jiao* 郊 hymns of the Western Han." Paper delivered at the Conference on State and Ritual in East Asia, Collège de France, Paris, June 28–July 1, 1995.

Kernan, Alvin. *Printing Technology, Letters and Samuel Johnson.* Princeton: Princeton University, 1987.

Kinney, Anne Behnke, ed. *Chinese Views of Childhood.* Honolulu: University of Hawai'i, 1995.

Knechtges, David. "The Emperor and Literature: Emperor Wu of the Han." In *Imperial Rulership and Cultural Change in Traditional China.* Edited by Frederick P. Brandauer and Chun-chieh Huang. Seattle: University of Washington, 1994.

———. *The Han Rhapsody: A Study of the Fu of Yang Hsiung.* Cambridge: Cambridge University, 1976.

Knoblock, John. *Xunzi: A Translation and Study of the Complete Works.* 3 vols. Stanford: Stanford University, 1988–1994.

Kraft, Eva. "Zum Huai Nan Tzu: Einführung, Übersetzung (Kapitel I und II) und Interpretation." *Monumenta Serica* 16 (1957): 191–286; 17 (1958): 128–207.

Kramers, Robert. "The Development of the Confucian Schools." *Cambridge History of China, Vol. 1, The Ch'in and Han Empires.* Edited by Michael Loewe. Cambridge: Cambridge University, 1986.

Kroll, Paul W. "On 'Far Roaming.'" *Journal of the American Oriental Society* 116.4 (October–December 1996): 653–69.

Kunst, Richard. "The Original 'Yijing': A Text, Phonetic Transcription, Translation, and Indexes, with Sample Glosses." Ph.D. dissertation. University of California at Berkeley, 1985.

LaFargue, Michael. *Tao and Method: A Reasoned Approach to the Tao Te Ching.* Albany: SUNY, 1994.

Lambert, M. "La naissance de la bureaucratie." *Revue historique* (1960): 1–26.

Lao, Kan. "The Early Use of the Tally in China." In *Ancient China: Studies in Early Civilization.* Edited by David Roy and Tsuen-hsuin Tsien. Hong Kong: Chinese University, 1978.

Lau, D. C. "The Disciples as They Appear in the *Analects.*" In *The Analects.* Translated by D. C. Lau. Harmondsworth: Penguin, 1979.

————. "On Mencius's Use of the Method of Analogy in Argument." *Asia Major*, New Series, 10 (1963). Reprinted in D. C. Lao, tr., *Mencius*. Harmondsworth: Penguin, 1970.

LeBlanc, Charles. "Historical and Textual Studies." In *Huai-nan Tzu: Philosophical Synthesis in Early Han Thought*. Hong Kong: Hong Kong University, 1985.

———— and Mathieu, Rémi, eds. *Mythe et philosophie à l'aube de la Chine impériale: études sur le Huainan zi*. Montreal: Université de Montréal, 1992.

Lévêque, Pierre and Vidal-Naquet, Pierre. *Clisthène l'Athénien: essai sur la représentation de l'espace et du temps dans la pensée politique grecque de la fin du VIe siècle à la mort de Platon*. Paris: Macula, 1964.

Levi, Jean. *La Chine romanesque: fictions d'orient et d'occident*. Paris: Seuil, 1995.

————. *Le fils du ciel et son annaliste*. Paris: Gallimard, 1992.

————. *Les fonctionnaires divins*. Paris: Seuil, 1989.

————. "Le Mythe de l'âge d'or et les théories de l'évolution en Chine ancienne." *L'homme* 17 (1977): 73–103.

————. "Quelques aspects de la rectification des noms dans la pensée et la pratique politique de la Chine ancienne." *Extrême-Orient, Extrême-Occident* 15 (1993): 23–53.

Lévi-Strauss, Claude. *Tristes tropiques*. Paris: Plon, 1955.

Lewis, Mark Edward. "The *Feng* and *Shan* Sacrifices of Emperor Wu of the Han." In *Imperial Ritual in East Asia*. Edited by Joseph McDermott. Cambridge: Cambridge University, in press.

————. "Fu Xi and Nü Wa in Han Mythology and Art." In *Religion and Art in China*. Edited by Wang Tao. London: Eastern Art Publishing, in press.

————. "The Han Abolition of Universal Military Service." In *Military Thought and Practice in China*. Edited by Hans van de Ven. Cambridge: Cambridge University, in press.

————. "Les rites comme trame de l'histoire." In *Notions et perceptions du changement en Chine*. Edited by Viviane Alleton and Alexei Volkov. Paris: Collège de France, Institut des Hautes Etudes Chinoises, 1994.

————. *Sanctioned Violence in Early China*. Albany: SUNY, 1990.

————. "Warring States Political History." In *Cambridge History of Ancient China*. Edited by Edward Shaughnessy and Michael Loewe. Cambridge: Cambridge University, in press.

Li, Ling. "Formulaic Structure of Chu Divinatory Bamboo Strips." *Early China* 15 (1990): 71–86.

Li, Wai-yee. "The Idea of Authority in the *Shi ji* (*Records of the Historian*)." *Harvard Journal of Asiatic Studies* 54:2 (1994): 345–405.

Li, Xueqin. *Eastern Zhou and Qin Civilizations*. Translated by K. C. Chang. New Haven: Yale University, 1985.

Liu, James J. Y. *The Chinese Knight Errant*. London: Routledge & Kegan Paul, 1967.

Liu, Xiaogan. *Classifying the Zhuangzi Chapters*. Translated by William Savage. Ann Arbor: Center for Chinese Studies, University of Michigan, 1994.

Lloyd, G. E. R. "Learning by numbers." *Extrême-Orient, Extrême-Occident* 16 (1994): 153–67.

Loewe, Michael. "The Campaigns of Han Wu-ti." In *Chinese Ways in Warfare*. Edited by Frank A. Kierman, Jr. Cambridge: Harvard University, 1974.

———. *Chinese Ideas of Life and Death: Faith, Myth and Reason in the Han period.* London: Allen & Unwin, 1982.

———. *Crisis and Conflict in Han China.* London: Allen & Unwin, 1974.

———, ed. *Early Chinese Texts: A Bibliographic Guide.* Berkeley: Society for the Study of Early China and the Institute of East Asian Studies, 1993.

———. "The Han View of Comets." *Bulletin of the Museum of Far Eastern Antiquities* 52 (1980): 1–31.

Loraux, Nicole. "Solon et la voix de l'écrit." In Detienne, ed. *Les savoirs de l'écriture.*

Louton, John. "Concepts of Comprehensiveness and Historical Change in the *Lü-shih ch'un-ch'iu.*" *Journal of the American Academy of Religious Studies Thematic Studies* 50/2: *Explorations in Early Chinese Cosmology.* Chico, Calif.: Scholars Press, 1984.

———. The *Lüshi chunqiu:* An Ancient Chinese Political Cosmology." Ph.D. dissertation. University of Washington, 1981.

Lyons, John. *Semantics.* Vol. 1. Paperback ed. Cambridge: Cambridge University, 1977.

McLeod, Katrina and Yates, Robin. "Forms of Ch'in Law." *Harvard Journal of Asiatic Studies* 41:1 (1981): 111–63.

McKitterick, Rosamond. *The Carolingians and the Written Word.* Cambridge: Cambridge University, 1989.

Machle, Edward J. *Nature and Heaven in the Xunzi: A Study of the Tian Lun.* Albany: SUNY, 1993.

Maeder, Erik W. "Some Observations on the Composition of the 'Core Chapters' of the *Mozi.*" *Early China* 17 (1992): 27–82.

Major, John S. "The Five Phases, Magic Squares, and Schematic Cosmography." In *Explorations in Early Chinese Cosmology.* Edited by Henry Rosemont, Jr. JAAR Thematic Studies 50/2. Chico, Calif.: Scholar's Press, 1984.

———. *Heaven and Earth in Early Han Thought: Chapters Three, Four, and Five of the Huainanzi.* Albany: SUNY, 1993.

Makeham, John. *Name and Actuality in Early Chinese Thought.* Albany: SUNY, 1994.

Mansvelt Beck, B. J. *The Treatises of the Later Han: Their Author, Sources, Contents and Place in Chinese Historiography.* Leiden: E. J. Brill, 1990.

Maspero, Henri. *China in Antiquity.* Translated by Frank A. Kierman, Jr. Amherst: University of Massachusetts, 1978.

———. "Légendes mythologiques dans le Chou King," *Journal Asiatique* 214 (1924): 1–100.

Mather, Richard B. "Filial Paragons and Spoiled Brats: A Glimpse of Medieval Chinese Children in the *Shishuo xinyu.*" In Kinney, ed. *Chinese Views of Childhood.*

Mathieu, Rémi. "Yu le Grand et le mythe du déluge dans la Chine ancienne." *T'oung Pao* 78 (1992): 162–90.

Mattos, Gilbert. *The Stone Drums of Ch'in*. Monumenta Serica Monograph Series 19. Nettetal: Steyler Verlag, 1988.

Miller, Paul Allen. *Lyric Texts and Lyric Consciousness: The Birth of a Genre from Archaic Greece to Augustan Rome*. London: Routledge, 1994.

Møllgard, Eske J. "Confucian Enlightenment." *Early China* 19 (1994): 145–60.

Nagy, Gregory. *Pindar's Homer: The Lyric Possession of an Epic Past*. Baltimore: Johns Hopkins University, 1990.

Needham, Joseph. *Science and Civilization in China, Vol. 3, Mathematics and the Sciences of the Heavens and the Earth*. Cambridge: Cambridge University, 1970.

———. *Science and Civilization in China, Vol. 4:1, Physics*. Cambridge: Cambridge University, 1962.

Nicolet, Claude. *L'Inventaire du monde: géographie et politique aux origines de l'empire romain*. Paris: Arthème Fayard, 1988.

Nishijima, Sadao. "The Economic and Social History of Former Han." In *Cambridge History of China, Vol. 1, the Ch'in and Han Empires*. Edited by Michael Loewe. Cambridge: Cambridge University, 1986.

Nylan, Michael. *The Shifting Center: The Original "Great Plan" and Later Readings*. Monumenta Serica Monograph Series no. 24. Nettetal: Steyler Verlag, 1992.

———. "Ying Shao's *Feng su t'ung yi*: An Exploration of Problems in Han Dynasty Political, Philosophical, and Social Unity." Ph.D. dissertation. Princeton University, 1982.

Ong, Walter J. *Orality and literacy: the technologizing of the word*. London: Methuen, 1982.

Owen, Stephen. *Readings in Chinese Literary Thought*. Cambridge: Harvard University, 1992.

———. *Remembrances: The Experience of the Past in Classical Chinese Literature*. Cambridge: Harvard University, 1986.

———. *Traditional Chinese Poetry and Poetics: Omen of the World*. Madison: University of Wisconsin, 1985.

Peerenboom, R. P. *Law and Morality in Ancient China: The Silk Manuscripts of Huang-Lao*. Albany: SUNY, 1993.

Petersen, Willard J. "Making Connections: 'Commentary on the Attached Verbalizations' of the *Book of Change*." *Harvard Journal of Asiatic Studies* 42 (1982): 67–116.

Pfeiffer, Rudolf. *History of Classical Scholarship, Vol. 1, From the Beginnings to the End of the Hellenistic Age*. Oxford: Clarendon Press, 1968.

Pham, Nathalie. "Quand les extrêmes se rencontrent." In Charles LeBlanc and Rémi Mathieu, ed. *Mythe et philosophie à l'aube de la Chine impériale: études sur le Huainan zi*.

Pirazzoli-t'Serstevens, Michèle. *The Han Dynasty*. Translated by Janet Seligman. New York: Rizzoli, 1982.

Plaks, Andrew H. *Archetype and Allegory in the Dream of the Red Chamber*. Princeton: Princeton University, 1976.

Pucci, Pietro. "Inscriptions archaïques sur les statues des dieux." In Detienne, ed. *Les savoirs de l'écriture.*

Puett, Michael. "The Notion of *Shen* in the *Xici.*" Conference on the *Xici zhuan.* Chicago, University of Chicago, May 30–June 1, 1997.

Queen, Sarah. *From Chronicle to Canon: the Hermeneutics of the "Spring and Autumn" According to Tung Chung-shu.* Cambridge: Cambridge University, 1996.

Qiu, Xigui. "An Examination of Whether the Charges in Shang Oracle-Bone Inscriptions are Questions." *Early China* 14 (1989): 77–114.

Rand, Christopher. "The Role of Military Thought in Early Chinese Intellectual History." Ph.D. dissertation. Harvard University, 1977.

Rawson, Jessica. "Statesmen or Barbarians? The Western Zhou as seen through their Bronzes." *Proceedings of the British Academy* 75 (1989): 71–95.

————. *Western Zhou Ritual Bronzes from the Arthur M. Sackler Collections. Ancient Chinese Bronzes from the Arthur M. Sackler Collections.* Vol. 2. Washington, D.C.: Arthur M. Sackler Gallery of Art and Cambridge: Arthur M. Sackler Museum; distributed by Harvard University Press, 1990.

Richards, I. A. *Mencius on the Mind.* London: Kegan Paul, 1932.

Ricoeur, Paul. *Temps et récit, Vol. 3, Le temps raconté.* Paris: Seuil, 1985.

Riegel, Jeffery K. "Kou-mang and Ju-shou." *Cahiers d'Extrême-Asie: Special Issue, Taoist Studies II* 5 (1989–90): 55–83.

Robinet, Isabelle "Des changements et de l'invariable." In Charles LeBlanc and Rémi Mathieu, ed. *Mythe et philosophie à l'aube de la Chine impériale: études sur le Huainan zi.*

Roetz, Heiner. *Confucian Ethics of the Axial Age.* Albany: SUNY, 1993.

de Romilly, Jacqueline. *Histoire et raison chez Thucydide.* Paris: Belles Lettres, 1967.

Rosemont, Henry. "The Dancing *Ru/Li* Masters." *Early China* 17 (1992): 187–194.

Rosen, Stanley. *Plato's Statesman: The Web of Politics.* New Haven: Yale University, 1995.

Roth, Harold D. "Psychology and Self-Cultivation in Early Taoistic Thought." *Harvard Journal of Asiatic Studies* 51:2 (1991): 599–650.

————. "Redaction Criticism and the Early History of Taoism." *Early China* 19 (1994): 1–46.

————. *The Textual History of the Huai-nan Tzu.* Ann Arbor: AAS Monograph Series, 1992.

————. "Who Compiled the *Chuang Tzu?*" In *Chinese Texts and Philosophical Contexts: Essays Dedicated to Angus C. Graham.* Edited by Henry Rosemont, Jr. LaSalle, Illinois: Open Court, 1991.

Ruzé, Françoise. "Aux débuts de l'écriture politique: le pouvoir de l'écrit dans la cité." In Detienne, ed. *Les savoirs de l'écriture.*

Ryden, Edmund. "A Literary Study of the Four Canons of the Yellow Emperor together with an edition of the manuscript of the four canons preceding the Laozi B text from Mawangdui." Ph.D. dissertation. School of Oriental and African Studies, University of London, 1995.

Sage, Steven F. *Ancient Sichuan and the Unification of China.* Albany: SUNY, 1992.

Saso, Michael. "What is the Ho-t'u?" *History of Religions* 17:3–4 (February–May 1978): 399–416.

Saussy, Haun. *The Problem of a Chinese Aesthetic.* Stanford: Stanford University, 1993.

Schafer, Edward H. *The Divine Woman: Dragon Ladies and Rain Maidens in T'ang Literature.* Berkeley: University of California, 1973.

———. *Pacing the Void: T'ang Approaches to the Stars.* Berkeley: University of California, 1977.

———. *The Vermilion Bird: T'ang Images of the South.* Berkeley: University of California, 1967.

Schutskii, Iulian K. *Researches on the I Ching.* Translated by William L. MacDonald and Tsuyoshi Hasegawa. Edited by Hellmut Wilhelm. Princeton: Princeton University, 1979.

Schwartz, Benjamin I. *The World of Thought in Ancient China.* Cambridge: Harvard University, 1985.

Schele, L. and Miller, M. *The Blood of Kings: Dynasty and Ritual in Maya Art.* Fort Worth: Kimbell Museum, 1986.

Schneider, Laurence A. *A Madman of Ch'u: The Chinese Myth of Loyalty and Dissent.* Berkeley: University of California, 1980.

Schunk, Lutz. *Dokumente zur Rechtsgeschichte des alten China: Übersetzung und historisch-philologische Kommentierung juristischer Bronzeinschriften der West-Zhou-Zeit, 1045–771 v. Chr.* Doktorgrad dissertation. Westfälischen Wilhelms-Universität zu Munster, 1994.

Seaford, Richard. *Reciprocity and Ritual: Homer and Tragedy in the Developing City-State.* Oxford: Clarendon Press, 1994.

Segal, Charles. "Greek Tragedy: Writing, Truth, and Representation of the Self." In *Interpreting Greek Tragedy.* Ithaca, N.Y.: Cornell University, 1986.

———. *La musique du sphinx: structure, mythe, langage dans la tragédie grecque.* Paris: La Découverte, 1987.

———. "Vérité, tragédie et écriture." In Detienne, ed. *Savoirs de l'écriture.*

Seidel, Anna. "Buying One's Way to Heaven: The Celestial Treasury in Chinese Religions." *History of Religions* 17:3–4 (Feb.–May 1978): 419–31.

Sellman, James Darryl. "Timeliness and Sociopolitical Order in the 'Lü-shih ch'un-ch'iu.'" Ph.D. dissertation. University of Hawaii, 1990.

Serruys, Paul L. M. "A Study of the *Chuan Chu* in *Shuo wen.*" *Lishi Yuyan Yanjiusuo Jikan* 29 (1957): 131–95.

Shaughnessy, Edward L. "The Composition of the 'Zhouyi'." Ph.D. dissertation. Stanford University, 1983.

———. "The Duke of Zhou's Retirement in the East and the Beginnings of the Ministerial-Monarch Debate in Chinese Political Philosophy." *Early China* 18 (1993): 41–72.

———. "A First Reading of the Mawangdui *Yijing* Manuscript." *Early China* 19 (1994): 47–73.

————. "From Liturgy to Literature: The Ritual Contexts of the Earliest Poems in the *Book of Poetry*." *Hanxue Yanjiu* 13.1 (1994): 133–64.

————. "The Generative Power of Change as Seen in the *Xici*." Conference on the *Xici zhuan*. Chicago, University of Chicago, May 30–June 1, 1997.

————. "'New' Evidence on the Zhou Conquest." *Early China* 6 (1980–81): 57–79.

————. "The Role of Grand Protector Shi in the Consolidation of the Zhou Conquest." *Ars Orientalis* 19 (1989): 51–77.

————. *Sources of Western Zhou History: Inscribed Bronze Vessels*. Berkeley: University of California, 1991.

————. "Western Zhou Political and Literary History." In *Cambridge History of Ancient China*. Edited by Edward Shaughnessy and Michael Loewe. Cambridge: Cambridge University, in press.

Sheng, Angela. "The Disappearance of Silk Weaves with Weft Effects in Early China." *Chinese Science* 12 (1995): 50–56.

Sivin, Nathan. "Change and Continuity in Early Cosmology: *The Great Commentary to the Book of Changes*." In *Chūgoku kodai kagaku shi ron zoku hen* 中國古代科學史論續篇. Edited by Yamada Keiji 山田慶兒. Kyoto: Jinbun Kagaku Kenkyūsho, 1991.

————. "Cosmos and Computation in Early Chinese Mathematical Astronomy." *T'oung Pao* 55 (1969): 1–73.

Steiner, Deborah Tarn. *The Tyrant's Writ: Myths and Images of Writing in Ancient Greece*. Princeton: Princeton University, 1994.

Smith, Anthony D. *The Ethnic Origins of Nations*. Oxford: Blackwell, 1986.

Smith, Kidder. "*Zhou yi* Interpretation from Accounts in the *Zuozhuan*." *Harvard Journal of Asiatic Studies* 49 (1989): 424–63.

Spiro, Audrey. *Contemplating the Ancients: Aesthetic and Social Issues in Early Chinese Portraiture*. Berkeley: University of California, 1990.

Svenbro, Jesper. "J'écris, donc je m'efface: l'énonciation dans les premières inscriptions grecques." In Detienne, ed. *Les savoirs de l'écriture*.

————. *Phrasikleia: An Anthropology of Reading in Ancient Greece*. Translated by Janet Lloyd. Ithaca: Cornell University, 1993.

Swann, Nancy Lee. *Food and Money in Ancient China*. Princeton: Princeton University, 1950.

Swanson, Gerald. "The Concept of Change in the *Great Treatise*." In *Explorations in Early Chinese Cosmology*. Edited by Henry Rosemont, Jr. Chico, Calif.: Scholars Press, 1984.

Tam, Koo-yin. "The Use of Poetry in *Tso chuan*." Ph.D. dissertation. University of Washington, 1975.

Teboul, Michel. *Les premières théories planétaires chinoises*. Paris: Institut des Hautes Etudes Chinoises, 1983.

————. "Les premiers développements de l'astronomie des Royaumes Combattants au début de l'ère chrétienne." *Bulletin de l'Ecole Française d'Extrême-Orient* 71 (1982): 147–67.

Todorov, Tzvetan. "Problèmes de l'énonciation." *Langages* 17 (1970).

Tsai, Yen-zen. "Ching and Chuan: Towards Defining the Confucian Scriptures in Han China." Ph.D. dissertation. Harvard University, 1993.

Tsien, Tsuen-hsuin. *Written on Bamboo and Silk: The Beginnings of Chinese Books and Inscriptions*. Chicago: University of Chicago, 1962.

Van Zoeren, Steven. *Poetry and Personality: Reading, Exegesis, and Hermeneutics in Traditional China*. Stanford: Stanford University, 1991.

Vander Waerdt, Paul A., ed. *The Socratic Movement*. Ithaca: Cornell University, 1994.

Vandermeersch, Léon. "La langue graphique chinoise." In *Etudes sinologiques*. Paris: Presses Universitaires de France, 1994.

———. *Wang dao ou la voie royale*. 2 vols. Paris: Ecole Française d'Extrême-Orient, 1977–1980.

Vendler, Helen. *The Odes of John Keats*. Cambridge: The Belknap Press of Harvard University, 1983.

Vervoorn, Aat. *The Men of the Cliffs and Caves: The Development of the Chinese Eremetic Tradition to the End of the Han Dynasty*. Hong Kong: Chinese University, 1990.

Vogel, Hans Ulrich. "Aspects of Metrosophy and Metrology during the Han Period." *Extrême-Orient, Extrême-Occident* 16 (1994): 135–52.

Volkov, Alexeï. "Large numbers and counting rods." *Extrême-Orient, Extrême-Occident* 16 (1994): 71–92.

Waley, Arthur. *The Nine Songs: A Study of Shamanism in Ancient China*. London: Allen & Unwin, 1955.

Walker, Galal. "Toward a Formal History of the 'Chuci'." Ph.D. dissertation. Cornell University, 1982.

Wallacker, Benjamin. "Liu An, the Second King of Huai-nan." *Journal of the American Oriental Society* 92 (1972): 36–51.

Wang, C. H. *The Bell and the Drum: Shi Jing as Formulaic Poetry in an Oral Tradition*. Berkeley: University of California, 1974.

———. *From Ritual to Allegory: Seven Essays in Early Chinese Poetry*. Hong Kong: Chinese University, 1988.

Wang, Hsiao-po and Chang, Leo S. *The Philosophical Foundations of Han Fei's Political Theory*. Monograph no. 7 of the Society for Asian and Comparative Philosophy. Honolulu: University of Hawaii, 1986.

Wang, Yü-ch'üan. "An Outline of the Central Government of the Former Han Dynasty." *Harvard Journal of Asiatic Studies* 12 (1949): 134–87.

Waters, Geoffrey R. *Three Elegies of Ch'u*. Madison: University of Wisconsin, 1985.

Watson, Burton. *Early Chinese Literature*. New York: Columbia University Press, 1962.

Weld, Susan Roosevelt. "Covenant in Jin's Walled Cities: The Discoveries at Houma and Wenxian." Ph.D. dissertation. Harvard University, 1990.

Wilhelm, Helmut. "Schriften und Fragmente zur Entwicklung der staatsrechtlichen Theorie in der Chou-Zeit." *Monumenta Serica* 12:5 (1947): 41–96.

Wu, Hung. "Private Love and Public Duty: Images of Children in Early Chinese Art." In Kinney, ed. *Chinese Views of Childhood*.

————. *The Wu Liang Shrine: The Ideology of Early Chinese Pictorial Art.* Stanford: Stanford University, 1989.

Yang, Lien-sheng. "Great Families of the Eastern Han." In *Chinese Social History.* Edited by E-tu Zen Sun and John De Francis. Washington, D.C.: American Council of Learned Societies, 1956.

Yates, Robin. "The City Under Siege: Technology and Organization as Seen in the Reconstructed Text of the Military Chapters of Mo-tzu." Ph.D. dissertation. Harvard University, 1980.

————. "The Mohists on Warfare: Technology, Techniques, and Justification." *Journal of the American Academy of Religion* Thematic Studies Supplement 47:3 (1980): 549–603.

————. "New Light on Ancient Chinese Military Texts: Notes on Their Nature and Evolution, and the Development of Military Specialization in Warring States China." *T'oung Pao* 74 (1988): 212–48.

————. "Some Notes on Ch'in Law." *Early China* 11–12 (1985–1987): 243–75.

————. "The Yin-Yang Texts from Yinqueshan: An Introduction and Partial Reconstruction, with Notes on their Significance in Relation to Huang-Lao Daoism." *Early China* 19 (1994): 75–144.

Yü, Ying-shih. *Trade and Expansion in Han China: A Study in the Structure of Sino-Barbarian Economic Relations.* Berkeley: University of California, 1967.

INDEX